THE SOCIOLOGICAL OUTLOOK: A TEXT WITH READINGS

D1508364

THE SOCIOLOGICAL OUTLOOK: A TEXT WITH READINGS

THIRD EDITION

Reid Luhman

Collegiate Press

Collegiate Press
San Diego, California

Executive editor: Christopher Stanford
Senior editor: Steven Barta
Senior developmental editor: Arlyne Lazerson
Design: John Odam Design Associates
Cover art: Paul Slick
Typography: Execustaff

Copyright: 1992 by Collegiate Press

All rights reserved under International and Pan-American copyright conventions. No part of this book may be reproduced in any form or by any means, electronic or mechanical, including photocopying, without permission in writing from the publisher. All inquiries should be addressed to Collegiate Press, 8840 Avalon Street, Alta Loma, CA 91701. Telephone (619) 697-4182.

Library of Congress Card Number: 91-78103

ISBN: 0-939693-25-9

Printed in the United States of America

10 9 8 7 6 5 4 3 2 1

To the Foot sisters (Betty and Clare)—
the two writers of the family who did
much to pave the way for what follows.

Photo Credits

1—Jackie Estrada; 2—Larry Mangino/Image Works; 6—Reid Luhman; 7—Peter Vandermark/Stock, Boston; 20—Bruce Roberts/Photo Researchers; 24—Peter Menzel/Stock, Boston; 32—The Bettmann Archive; 46—James Andanson/Sygma; 48—George Holton/ Photo Researchers; 54—Reid Luhman; 55—Paul Winther; 56—Eric Roth/The Picture Cube; 57—Owen Franken/Stock, Boston; 64—Chris Kleine; 66—Reid Luhman; 85—Melanie Carr/Zephyr Pictures; 88—Allen Green/Photo Researchers; 93—Reid Luhman; 95—reproduced from the Collections of the Library of Congress; 105—Stephen Dunn; 112—Bettina Cirone/Photo Researchers; 128—Ellis Herwig/Stock, Boston; 130—G. Marche/FPG; 140—Glen Kleine; 146—UPI/Bettmann; 153—Michael Weisbrot/Stock, Boston; 155—AP/Wide World; 172—Dorothea Lange, reproduced from the Collections of the Library of Congress; 174—Alon Reininger/Woodfin Camp; 179—Stephen Dunn; 183—David S. Strickler/ Monkmeyer; 186—Stephen Dunn; 189—Frank Biteman/Picture Cube; 194—Spencer Grant/Photo Researchers; 212—Leo Gradinger/Zephyr Pictures; 215—The Bettmann Archive; 216—Historical Picture Services, Inc.; 224—Charles Gatewood/Image Works; 223—Kirk Schlea/Zephyr Pictures; 236—Bob Adelman/Magnum Photos; 237—David Hurn/Magnum Photos, Inc.; 256—Ellis Herwig/Stock, Boston; 263—David E. Kennedy/ TexaStock; 266—Marc PoKempner/TSW; 271—Glen Kleine; 280—Dorothea Lange; courtesy of the National Archives Trust Fund Board; 282—Chicago Historical Society; 285—Barbara Rios/Photo Researchers; 300—Reid Luhman; 302—Stock/Boston; 305—photo courtesy of Franziska Heberle; 311—Stephen Dunne; 313—Reid Luhman; 329—Tony Howarth/Woodfin Camp; 331—Ellis Herwig/Picture Cube; 332—James R. Holland/Stock, Boston; 346—courtesy Susan Holtz; 348—Laima Druskis/ Photo Researchers; 352—Michael D. Sullivan/ TexaStock; 353—J. D. Sloan/Picture Cube; 355—Cary Wolinsky/Stock, Boston; 378—Russ Gilbert/The San Diego Union; 383—UPI/Bettmann; 391—Bettman Archive; 393—UPI/Bettmann; 394—AP/Wide World; 395—Stacy Pick/Stock, Boston; 405—Glen Kleine; 410—AP/Wide World; 411—J. L. Atlan/ Sygma; 442—P. Robert/Sygma; 444—Patrick Ward/ Stock, Boston; 454—Rene Burri/Magnum Photos, Inc.; 461—Stephen Dunn; 466—Perry Alan Werner/Image Works; 467—Stephen Dunn; 478—Bossu/Sygma; 481—Daemmrich/Image Works; 484—Alain Nogues/Sygma; 491—John Filo/*Valley Daily News*, Tarentum, PA; 498—Mary Lou Foy/The Miami Herald; 501—Culver Pictures.

Contents

Part Three Social Inequality 172

Preface

This Third Edition of *The Sociological Outlook* incorporates a number of changes. Statistics have been updated, of course, as has research, though change for the sake of change has not been the guiding rule. I chose to include new research that offered a new perspective or that reversed old findings; the quality "classics" of sociology remain. A number of topics and issues appear in this edition for the first time and in a new order of presentation. The most significant change from the second edition is the expansion of the institutions chapter to three chapters, offering much more complete coverage. In addition, a major new section on sociological theory was added to Chapter 2, introducing the dominant theoretical traditions in sociology. Finally, themes of gender and inequality have been woven throughout the Third Edition. Inequality was a major theme in the Second Edition and still receives the attention of an entire chapter. Gender issues play a major role in the new institutions chapters while receiving additional attention in other chapters and through new readings.

The readings, which follow each chapter, retain the best selections from the first two editions. In addition, some outstanding new articles appear for the first time. As with the earlier editions, I selected all readings with regard to intrinsic interest to students and readability as well as sociological content; all are designed to add color and life to material presented before them in each chapter. Four readings written specifically for the first two editions (those by Denton, Gilham, Murai, and Winther) have been retained because students responded to them with great interest and enthusiasm. Of the new readings, several were written specifically for the third edition; these include John Curra's look at serial murder (and serial murderer Ted Bundy in particular) and Aaron Thompson's autobiographical view of the interplay between education and the black family. I have also chosen a number of new articles that were originally published elsewhere and that struck me as illuminating and interesting (see Contents listing). Because both students and instructors responded so favorably to the readings in the previous two editions, this Third Edition contains an expanded number of readings covering a wider variety of topics.

A large number of people have contributed their time and skill to this book. In particular, many important suggestions and criticisms were offered by Vance Wisenbaker concerning Chapters 1, 2, 4, and 12; by John Curra concerning Chapters 5 and 6; by John Denton concerning Chapter 6; by Marc Goldstein concerning Chapter 5; and by Alan Banks concerning Chapters 7 and 9. Much additional help was provided by my colleagues Paul Winther, Steve Savage, Gunseli Tamkoc, Dick Futrell, Doug Burnham, Aaron Thompson, and Amiya Mohanty. All these people, along with my other colleagues, have also provided less tangible assistance through the working environment they have created and I have enjoyed over the years; they are a singularly intelligent and decent group of people. Valuable secretarial assistance was provided by Cathy Newsome, Carol Lane, Shannon Brian, and Toni Garlick.

This book would not have been possible without considerable work at the publishing end. Arlyne Lazerson oversaw the editorial process calmly and efficiently. Jill Malena, of John Odam

Associates, came up with a pleasing and clear graphic design. Paul Slick exercised his considerable creative talents in producing the cover illustration and design. Execustaff did a fine job of typesetting and composition.

Valuable suggestions and criticisms of first and second editions of this book were contributed by sociologists at several institutions around the country. They were Richard S. Bobys, Morningside College; Marion Dearman, California State University, Los Angeles; Jeanne G. Gobalet, San Jose City College; Laura Gordon, Montclair State College; William Kenkel, University of Kentucky; Arnold J. Kuhn, Wilbur Wright College; Carol Lewis, Jefferson Community College; Reece McGee, Purdue University; Don Metz, Marquette University; John S. Miller, University of Arkansas at Little Rock; Rita Phyllis Sakitt, Suffolk County Community College; and Richard Voorhees, Inver Hills Community College.

After it was printed, the Second Edition of this book received extensive and extremely useful reviews from both teachers and students who worked with it. The effort put forth on this process by those involved proved to be of invaluable help in making the third edition better meet the needs of the people in classrooms where it is used. The list of those comprising the Editorial Board for *The Sociological Outlook,* Third Edition, appears right after this Preface.

Finally, no one lived more closely with this project than the members of my immediate family. My wife, Susan, not only showed great patience with the process of writing but also offered very valuable help through reading the manuscript and letting me know when my writing style was getting either boring or confusing (and often both). Her constant encouragement plays a major role in all that I do. My children, Chad and Sara, have grown up with the different editions of this book, changing from having objections to my overly occupied time on the first edition to becoming interested in what I've been writing all this time.

EDITORIAL ADVISORY BOARD

Professor Charles H. Ainsworth
Department of Sociology
Tougaloo College
Tougaloo, MS 39174

Professor Eugene B. Antley
Department of Sociology and Anthropology
Edinboro University
Edinboro, PA 16444

Professor Michele Aronica
Department of Social Science
Saint Josephs College
North Windham, ME 04062

Professor Grace Auyang
Department of Behavioral Science
University of Cincinnati, Raymond Walters College
Cincinnati, OH 45236

Professor Diane Balduzy
Department of Sociology and Anthropology
North Adams State College
Church Street
North Adams, MA 01247

Professor Jerome Barber
Department of Social Science
Erie Community College South
4140 Southwestern Boulevard
Orchard Park, NY 14127

Professor Sharon Barnartt
Department of Sociology
Gallaudet University
7th and Florida Avenue East
Washington, DC 20002

Professor David Bartlett
Department of Social and Behavioral Sciences
South Suburban College
South Holland, IL 64073

Professor Carol Barton
Department of Social Science
Bacone College
Muskogee, OK 74401

Professor Mary Ellen Batiuk
Department of Continuing Education
Wilmington College
Wilmington, OH 45177

Professor Richard Behnke
Department of Liberal Arts
Pensacola Junior College-Warrington
5555 West Highway 98
Pensacola, FL 32507

Professor Melvin Bender
Department of General Education
Central Baptist College
Conway, AR 72032

Professor Rodney Berthelsen
Department of Liberal Arts
Lamar University-Port Arthur
Port Arthur, TX 77640

Professor Rudee Devon Boan
Department of Social Science
Gardner Webb College
Boiling Springs, NC 28017

Professor Walter Boland
Department of Sociology
University of North Carolina
One University Heights
Asheville, NC 28814

Professor Raymond Bosse
Department of Human Development
Hellenic College
50 Goddard Avenue
Brookline, MA 02146

Professor Jennifer Braaten
Department of Humanities
College of Boca Raton
Boca Raton, FL 33431

Professor Ron Brockmeyer
Department of Social Studies
Iowa Lakes Community College
300 South 18th Street
Estherville, IA 51334

Professor R. Allen Brown
Department of Social and Behavioral Science
Calument College Saint Joseph
2400 New York Avenue
Whiting, IN 46394

Professor Norman Budow
Department of Social Science
Truman College
1145 West Wilson Avenue
Chicago, IL 60640

Professor Richard Dello Buono
Department of Sociology
Rosary College
7900 West Division
River Forest, IL 60305

Professor Jerry Burton
Department of Social Science
Methodist College
Methodist College Post Office
Fayetteville, NC 28301

Professor Rudolph Cain
Unit Coordinator & Mentor
Empire State College/Bedford-Stuyvesant
20 New York Avenue
Brooklyn, NY 11216

Professor Marvin Camfield
Department of Social and Behavioral Science
Walters State Community College
500 South Davy Crockett
Morristown, TN 37813

Professor Nicole Cauvin
Department of Sociology
Sacred Heart University
Bridgeport, CT 06606

Professor Foster Chason
Department of Public Service
Chattanooga State Technical Community College
4501 Amnicola Highway
Chattanooga, TN 37406

Professor Ollie Christian
Department of Sociology and Anthropology
Xavier University of Louisiana
Palmetto and Pine Streets
New Orleans, LA 70125

Professor Alfred Clarke
Department of Human Studies
61 Bellwood Road
Springfield, MA 01119

Professor Rosalie Cohen
Department of Sociology
Temple University
Philadelphia, PA 19122

Professor Steve Cornish
Department of Sociology and Anthropology
University of Redlands
Redlands, CA 92373

Professor Reed Coughlan
Empire State College
The State University of New York
207 Genesee Street
Utica, NY 13204

Professor Jeffrey L. Crane
Department of Social Science
University of Hawaii at Hilo
Hilo, HI 96720

Professor P. Crawford
Department of Sociology
Indiana University Purdue University
Indianapolis, IN 46202

Professor Irene J. Dabrowski
Department of Social Science
Saint Johns University
300 Howard Avenue
Staten Island, NY 10301

Professor Peter Roche De Coppens
Department of Sociology and Anthropology
East Stroudsburg University
East Stroudsburg, PA 18301

Professor Warren Deutsch
Department of Sociology
Georgian Court College
Lakewood, NJ 08701

Professor Mary K. Diaz
Department of Sociology and Anthropology
Knapp Hall Room 22
S U N Y College of Technology
Farmingdale, NY 11735

Professor Samuel Dogbe
Department of Sociology
Hampton University
Hampton, VA 23668

Professor Norman Dolch
Department of Social Science
Louisiana State University
8515 Youree Drive
Shreveport, LA 71115

Professor Marjorie E. Donovan
Department of Social Science
Pittsburg State University
Pittsburg, KS 66762

Professor Ramona L. Dunckel
Department of Social Science
Bob Jones University
Greenville, SC 29614

Professor David A. Edwards
Department of Sociology
San Antonio College
1300 San Pedro Avenue
San Antonio, TX 78284

Professor Pamela Elkind
Department of Sociology
Eastern Washington University
Cheney, WA 99004

Professor E. Douglas Farley
Department of Social Science
Niagara County Community College
3111 Saunders Settlement Road
Sanborn, NY 14132

Professor Kathryn M. Feltey
Department of Sociology
University of Akron
Akron, OH 44325

Professor James Finn
Department of Business and Social Science
Westmoreland County Community College
College Station Armbrust
Youngwood, PA 15697

Professor James E. Floyd
Department of Social Science
Macon College
College Station Drive
Macon, GA 31297

Professor Jamia Fox
Department of Sociology
University of Central Arkansas
Conway, AR 72032

Professor Michael Francisconi
Department of Social Science
Navajo Community College
Tsaile, AZ 86556

Professor Marvin D. Free
Department of Sociology
University of Wisconsin-Marathon
518 South 7th Avenue
Wausau, WI 54401

Professor Albeno P. Garbin
Department of Sociology
University of Georgia
Athens, GA 30602

Professor Mary Glover
Department of Sociology
Thomas More College
Crestview Hills, KY 41017

Professor Glenn Goodwin
Department of Sociology
Pitzer College
Claremont, CA 91711

Professor Joseph G. Green
Department of Sociology
Assumption College
500 Salisbury Street
Worcester, MA 01609

Professor Eddie M. Griggs
Department of Social Science
Abraham Baldwin Agricultural College
Tifton, GA 31793

Professor Sue Hammons
Department of Social Science
Abraham Baldwin Agricultural College
Tifton, GA 31793

Professor Clyde Harvey
Department of Sociology and Social Work
Fort Valley State College
Fort Valley, GA 31030

Professor Joan M. Hill
Department of Sociology and Philosophy
Chicago State University
95th Street at King Drive
Chicago, IL 60628

Professor Birgie Houston
Department of Humanities
Michigan Christian College
800 West Avon Road
Rochester, MI 48063

Professor Jo Ann Howard
Department of Social Science
Langston University
Langston, OK 73050

Professor Herschel Hudson
Department of Political Science
Citadel Military College of South Carolina
Charleston, SC 29409

Professor Gary Jaworski
Department of Social Sciences
Fairleigh Dickinson
Madison Campus
Madison, NJ 07940

Professor Thomas H. Jenkins
Department of Sociology
University of Cincinnati
McMicken College
Cincinnati, OH 45221

Professor Ronald Jewett
Department of Behavioral Sciences
North Central Bible College
910 Elliott Avenue
Minneapolis, MN 55404

Professor Clifton R. Jones
Department of Sociology and Anthropology
Howard University
2400 Sixth Street Northwest
Washington, DC 20059

Professor Effie Jones
Department of General Education
Crichton College
2485 Union Avenue
Memphis, TN 38182

Professor Dennis Kalob
Department of Sociology
Loyola University
6363 Saint Charles Avenue
New Orleans, LA 70118

Professor Geoffrey Kapenzi
Department of Liberal Arts
Babson College
Babson Park
Wellesley, MA 02157

Professor John Karlin
Department of Social and Behavioral Sciences
Phillips University
University Station
Enid, OK 73701

Professor Peter J. Kivisto
Department of Sociology
Augustana College
639 38th Street
Rock Island, IL 61201

Professor Edward Knisley
Department of Social Science (CAS-371)
University of Alaska Anchorage Campus
3211 Providence Avenue
Anchorage, AK 99508

Professor Shirley Kolack
Department of Sociology
University of Lowell
Lowell, MA 01854

Professor Merle Kruschke
Department of Social Science
Northland Community College
Highway 1 East
Thief River Falls, MN 56701

Professor Raj Kurapati
Department of Social Science
Community College Micronisa
P. O. Box 159 Kolonia
Ponape Island, TT 96941

Professor Louis La Bombard
Department of Social Science and Education
Navajo Community College
Tsaile, AZ 86556

Professor Philip Lampe
Department of Science
Incarnate Word College
4301 Broadway
San Antonio, TX 78209

Professor Richard Lance
Department of General Education
Haywood Community College
Freedlander Drive
Clyde, NC 28721

Professor P. Dwight Landua
Department of Sociology
Southeastern Oklahoma State University
Durant, OK 74701

Professor Phylis Lan Lin
Department of Behavioral Science
University of Indianapolis
1400 East Hanna Avenue
Indianapolis, IN 46227

Professor Joseph Larry
Department of Social Science
Fairmont State College
Fairmont, WV 26554

Professor Paul L. Leslie
Department of Social Science
Greensboro College
Greensboro, NC 27401

Professor Beverly Le Van
Department of Humanities and Social Sciences
San Juan College
4601 College Boulevard
Farmington, NM 87401

Professor James McLeod
Department of Social Science
Ohio State University Mansfield Campus
Mansfield, OH 44906

Professor David McMahon
Department of Behavioral Science
Saint Francis College
Loretto, PA 15940

Professor Marshall Maddox
Department of Social and Behavioral Science
Central Piedmont Community College
Elizabeth at North Kings
Charlotte, NC 28235

Professor Ali-Akbar Mahdi
Department of Anthropology and Sociology
Adrian College
Adrian, MI 49221

Professor Jerry Malone
Department of Social Science
Central College
McPherson, KS 67460

Professor Geraldine A. Manning
Department of Sociology
Suffolk University
Beacon Hill
Boston, MA 02108

Professor F. Martens
Department of General Education
Pennsylvania State University
Allentown Campus
Fogelsville, PA 18051

Professor Duane Matcha
Department of Social Science
Findlay College
1000 North Main Street
Findlay, OH 45840

Professor Raymond C. Matura
Department of Liberal Arts
University of Rio Grande
Rio Grande, OH 45674

Professor Elaine Mayer
Department of Sociology and Anthropology
Salve Regina College
Ochre Point Avenue
Newport, RI 02840

Professor Merle Miles-Adams
Department of Social Science
Huston Tillotson College
1820 East 18th Street
Austin, TX 78702

Professor Margaret A. Miller
Department of Liberal Arts
Christian Brothers College
650 East Parkway South
Memphis, TN 38104

Professor Randy K. Mills
Department of Arts and Sciences
Oakland City College
Oakland City, IN 47660

Professor Neville Morgan
Department of Behavioral Science
Kentucky State University
Frankfort, KY 40601

Professor George Mucherson
Department of Cluster A
Los Angeles Mission College
1212 San Fernando Road
San Fernando, CA 91340

Professor Sharon Murphy
Department of Arts and Sciences
College of Saint Joseph
Clement Road
Rutland, VT 05701

Professor Jack E. Niemonen
Department of Sociology and Anthropology
University of South Dakota
Vermillion, SD 57069

Professor Alton M. Okinaka
Department of Social Science
University of Hawaii at Hilo
Hilo, HI 96720

Professor Barry E. Packard
Department of General Education
Lancaster Bible College
Lancaster, PA 17601

Professor Bruce Pamperin
Department of Social Science
University of Wisconsin, Stout
322 Harvey Hall
Menomonie, WI 54751

Professor Keith D. Parker
Department of Sociology
University of Nebraska
7220 Father Hall
Lincoln, NE 68588

Professor Robert E. Parker
Department of Sociology
University of Nevada
4505 Maryland Parkway
Las Vegas, NV 89154

Professor Florence Parkinson
Department of Sociology and Psychology
College of Staten Island
Staten Island, NY 10301

Professor Travis Patton
Department of Sociology and Anthropology
University of Nebraska at Omaha
Omaha, NE 68182

Professor Jane Penney
Department of Social Science
Eastfield College
3737 Motley Drive
Mesquite, TX 75150

Professor Helen E. Plotkin
Department of Social and Behavioral Science
Holy Family College
Philadelphia, PA 19114

Professor Zoraida Porrata
Department of Social Science
University of Puerto Rico
Cayey University College
Cayey, PR 00633

Professor Ved Prakash
Department of Behavioral Science
Fayetteville State University
Fayetteville, NC 28301

Professor Bonnie B. Price
Department of Behavioral Science
Reading Area Community College
Reading, PA 19603

Professor Neil P. Ramsey
Department of Social Science
Virginia Wesleyan College
Wesleyan Drive
Norfolk, VA 23502

Professor Bruce Ravelli
Department of Anthropology and Sociology
Okanagan College
1000 K.L.O. Road
Kelowna, BC V1Y 4X8 CANADA

Professor Edward Raymaker
Department of Humanities and English
Eastern Maine Voc Tech
354 Hogan Road
Bangor, ME 04401

Professor Gabino Rendon
Department of Behavioral Sciences
New Mexico Highlands University
Las Vegas, NM 87701

Professor Terry Reuther
Department of Social Science
Anoka Ramsey Community College
11200 Mississippi Boulevard
Coon Rapids, MN 55433

Professor Phillip Robinette
Department of Social Science
Southern California College
55 Fair Drive
Costa Mesa, CA 92626

Professor Robert D. Ruth
Department of Anthropology and Sociology
Davidson College
Davidson, NC 28036

Professor Jai P. Ryu
Department of Sociology
Loyola College
4501 North Charles Street
Baltimore, MD 21210

Professor Carl Saalbach
Department of Social Science
Warner Southern College
U.S. Highway 27 South
Lake Wales, FL 33853

Professor Raymond W. Sagedy
Department of Sociology
Salem State College
Salem, MA 01970

Professor Maggie Schultz
Department of Health Occupations
D'Youville College
320 Porter Avenue
Buffalo, NY 14201

Professor Anna Wall Scott
Department of Social Science
Parkland College
2400 West Bradley Avenue
Champaign, IL 61821

Professor Richard A. Shankar
Department of Sociology
Stonehill College
North Easton, MA 02357

Professor Stephanie L. Shanks-Meile
Department of Sociology and Anthropology
Indiana University-Northwest
3400 Broadway
Gary, IN 46408

Professor Carol Slone
Department of Behavioral Science
John C. Calhoun State Community College
Decatur, AL 35602

Professor Harold Sorknes
Department of General Education
Sisseton-Wahpeton Community College
Sisseton, SD 57262

Professor Stella N. Spiewak
Department of General Education
Jefferson Technical College
4000 Sunset Boulevard
Steubenville, OH 43952

Professor Larry L. Stearley
Department of Social Science
Mott Community College
1401 East Court Street
Flint, MI 48502

Professor Kenneth L. Stewart
Department of Sociology and Psychology
Angelo State University
San Angelo, TX 76909

Professor Tim Sullivan
Department of Business and Social Science
Cedar Valley College
3030 North Dallas Avenue
Lancaster, TX 75134

Professor Bruce Sydow
Department of Social Science
Skagit Valley College
2405 College Way
Mount Vernon, WA 98273

Professor Kenneth N. Taylor
Department of Behavioral Science
Grace College and Seminary
200 Seminary Drive
Winona Lake, IN 46590

Professor Rance Thomas
Department of Liberal Arts
Lewis and Clark Community College
Godfrey, IL 62035

Professor Ivan L. Torres
Department of Behavioral Science
Reading Area Community College
Reading, PA 19603

Professor Marshall K. Tribble
Department of Sociology
Anderson College
316 Boulevard
Anderson, SC 29621

Professor Rufus Turner
Department of Sociology and Psychology
Campbell University
Buies Creek, NC 27506

Professor Cynthia Tweedel
Department of Social Science
Springfield College in Illinois
1500 North Fifth Street
Springfield, IL 62702

Professor Elaine Vincent
Department of Related Studies
Orangeburg Calhoun Technical College
3250 Saint Matthews Road
Orangeburg, SC 29115

Professor J. Thomas Walker
Department of Sociology and Anthropology
Susquehanna University
Selinsgrove, PA 17870

Professor John W. Wallace
Dean, Director of Continuing Education
Taylor University
Upland, IN 46989

Professor Leigh Walter
Department of Sociology and Philosophy
Francis Marion College
Florence, SC 29501

Professor Frances Watson
Department of Sociology
Benedictine College
Atchison, KS 66002

Professor Michael G. Weinstein
Department of Sociology
University of Hawaii at Manoa
2424 Maile Way
Honolulu, HI 96822

Professor David West
Department of Social Science
College of San Mateo
1700 West Hillsdale Boulevard
San Mateo, CA 94402

Professor Stewart B. Whitney
Department of Sociology and Social Work
Niagara University
Niagara, NY 14109

Professor John M. Wilkes
Department of Social Science
Worcester Poly Institute
Worcester, MA 01609

Professor Sharon Wyatt
Department of Arts and Sciences
Shenandoah College and Conservatory
Winchester, VA 22601

Professor George Yelagotes
Department of Sociology and Anthropology
Millersville University
Millersville, PA 17551

Professor M. Yesulaites
Department of Social Science
Mohegan Community College
Mahan Drive
Norwich, CT 06360

Professor T. Zawistowski
Department of Sociology
Pennsylvania State University
Worthington Scranton Campus
Dunmore, PA 18512

Professor Marty Zusman
Department of Sociology and Anthropology
Indiana University-Northwest
3400 Broadway
Gary, IN 46408

PART One
INTRODUCTION

CHAPTER 1 THE SOCIOLOGICAL OUTLOOK: THE INDIVIDUAL AND SOCIETY

We humans seem endlessly fascinated by the other members of the animal kingdom with which we share a planet. We keep them as pets, visit them in zoos, and even name them in our wills. In particular our fascination focuses on the ways different species of animals "earn their living." Spiders spin webs and wrap up their catches for midnight snacks, cheetahs hunt their food by running faster than any other animal, termites attack our houses in organized groups, and honeybees organize small factories to manufacture their food and provide their housing. All of these creatures go about their business on a planet that we dominate, at least temporarily.

What talents do we humans possess that have allowed us to dominate the earth? We are not very strong for our body mass, nor very swift afoot. Our senses of smell and hearing are well below par for mammals, although we do have fairly good stereoscopic vision. Our body hair is minimal, which would leave us quite cold in winter without our clothes. Our claws are neither strong nor sharp, and our fangs are nonexistent. There are, of course, some points to be made on the other side. We have thumbs, for example. Specifically, we have *opposable* thumbs—which means that we can do very fine handwork by opposing the thumb to each of the other digits, one at a time. A great variety of human products and skills would be impossible without the thumb. But thumbs are not usually the first things we think of when the secret of human dominance is in question. The first thought is usually of the human brain.

Humans don't have the largest brains in the animal kingdom; whales, for example, have much larger ones. But whales also have large bodies for their brains to operate, so their brains are busy directing muscles and supervising bodily processes, with little leisure time for solving equations. In terms of having a relatively large brain for body size, humans are right up at the top of the animal world along with dolphins—and dolphins don't have thumbs. A large brain coupled with a relatively small body mass has given humans a facility in thinking that sets them apart from other animals. But how have we used that facility in thinking to dominate the planet? At first glance it would seem that our tools—from the stone axe to the nuclear reactor—form the secret of our dominance. However, I would like to call your attention to a much more basic and more important product of our intelligence: Before we became great toolmakers, we used our intelligence to organize ourselves into coordinated groups.

Humans are not the only animal to hit upon this secret of survival. Many other species of mammal live in coordinated groups, and, of course, the most striking examples come from the insect world. Whatever the species, the benefits are more or less the same. Baboons, wolves, bees, ants, and humans all have less difficulty surviving because they live in groups. The one distinctive feature about human groups, however, is that, whereas other animals make their societies by instinct, we *consciously create* the kind of coordination our groups will have and then *consciously teach* that way of life to our children each generation. Although we get attached to a way of life over time and may not want to change, the fact that we organize ourselves and teach each other consciously means that at least we have the potential to change the way we live, as we change or as conditions change. Bees have never been known to retool their industry when pollen becomes scarce.

The manner in which humans organize themselves into coordinated groups inspires the outlook of sociology. Sociology, like some other perspectives, tries to explain *why* people think and act in the ways that they do. The unique feature of the sociological outlook is that it looks for answers to that question by examining the *social groups* within which people do their thinking and acting. Humans are born into social groups and are dependent upon them for everything from the outset. Older individuals in those social groups then teach the younger members about the particular way they live. As those younger members become older, they come to look and act remarkably like the members who initially taught them. The sociological outlook suggests that an examination of social groups and the pattern of coordination within them gives us a fuller understanding of why people behave as they do.

In this chapter we will focus on the ways humans coordinate a variety of activities in their attempts to earn their living on this planet, and how that overall coordination develops over time into larger human societies. As we look at the social groups that humans have created, we will also look at how those groups, in effect, create humans. It is as impossible to imagine a human being without a human society as it is to imagine a honeybee without the hive. This chapter will provide an overview of the rest of the book. We will introduce some of the basic terms used by sociologists in order to emphasize the connections among these terms; all the terms will be developed in greater detail in later chapters. We will also look at some examples of sociologists at work, showing how sociological research applies the sociological outlook to help understand everyday life.

SOCIETY AS A HUMAN CREATION

When sociologists talk about societies, they are thinking not so much about people as about the ways particular groups of people live. The difference is that the ways of living change much more slowly than the people who learn to live by them. Specifically, a **society** is a relatively large, self-sufficient collection of people that (1) shares and transmits a common heritage from one generation to another, (2) contains patterns of behavior that govern interaction, and (3) occupies a given territory.

When you notice that large numbers of people in any society tend to be doing very similar things on any given day, and that those same people tend to keep doing those same things from one day to the next, you are observing patterns of behavior. If you are reading this paragraph for a sociology class, for example, you can be assured that many other people are reading similar paragraphs today in similar books for more or less the same reasons that you are. Furthermore, students behaved that way in the last generation and more than likely will continue to behave that way in the next. As we grow up in a society, we learn about the standard patterns of interaction that others already follow, and ultimately we follow them ourselves.

The sociologist is interested primarily in the ongoing patterns of behavior that people follow. These patterns of behavior in a society are far more than just random forms of interaction; they are highly coordinated so that while one kind of need is being taken care of through one set of patterns, other kinds of needs are being tended to through other patterns. It is the *coordination* of behavior patterns that makes a society a useful means of survival.

Coordination as a Mode of Adaptation

Coordinated patterns of behavior in a society permit a variety of needs to be taken care of simultaneously. When different activities form in a society and different people come to specialize in those activities, sociologists refer to it as a **division of labor**. We could imagine an early society in which certain people might specialize in caring for children, others might specialize in gathering food from the environment, and still others might specialize in hunting and group protection. Thus, a variety of needs are taken care of simultaneously, and each need might be taken care of quite well since the individuals entrusted with it would have ample opportunity to perfect their skills through repetition.

Once a division of labor occurs, there is no limit to the number of divisions that can arise. Looking just at hunters, for example, we could imagine a group of twenty or so individuals out to capture a large animal—a task none could accomplish alone. One subgroup might be in charge of fashioning a trap, another might specialize in driving the animal toward the trap, and still another might have perfected the art of slaughtering the animal, once trapped. The image of humans as toolmakers is striking in this example, but even more striking is the complex coordination of activities without which the tools would be useless. Primitive tools cannot fell an elephant, for example, unless they are used by coordinated groups in some kind of systematic fashion. Modern tools (such as an elephant gun) can accomplish the same end with only one hunter, but the complicated nature of modern tools requires coordination in the manufacturing process. Tools may be our secret of success, but coordinated groups are the secret behind the secret.

Coordination and Communication How would it be possible for groups of people to work together if they were unable to communicate? Indeed, how would it be possible for *any* coordinated group to function without communication? A beehive requires communication. If the hive is attacked, the "guards" will sound an alert. If a worker bee finds a pollen source, it is able to communicate both the direction and the distance of the source upon returning to the hive so that the other workers can retrieve the pollen (Dadant and Sons, 1975). Human groups take this process one step further: Humans are conscious of their communication as they communicate (see Premack, 1986).

The importance of being conscious of communication becomes apparent when you look more closely at communication itself. In its most fundamental sense, *communication* means that an idea or thought or experience of mine can become known to you through your experience of my behavior. My experience of pain, for example, can be communicated to you through your experience of watching me writhe in agony and hearing me scream. But this communication is not conscious on my part; in such pain, I would probably not care about communicating effectively. Nevertheless, my experience is communicated. As far as we know, this is the kind of communication that goes on in beehives.

At another level of communication I can communicate consciously with you through the use of symbols. A **symbol** can be anything that you and I both agree will stand for (or communicate) something else. A colored piece of cloth can stand for a nation-state, a hand gesture can communicate respect or disrespect, a sound produced by the vocal cords can stand for an object or an idea, and these black marks on white paper that you are looking at right now stand for the ideas I was thinking as I entered them by means of my keyboard. Symbols are both limitless and flexible. They are limitless in that any new thing or idea can be communicated through a symbol designed for that purpose. They are flexible in that you and I can alter the

Coordination allows social animals to function as groups. The worker bees surrounding the queen illustrate the kinds of coordination found in all societies, whether human or nonhuman. The main difference between the two (as far as we know) is that humans are conscious of the forms of coordination by which they live.

meaning that we want a particular symbol to communicate. Symbols are tied to the things they communicate only in the specific ways and for the length of time that people in groups choose to have them serve that purpose.

The ultimate human symbol use is in the symbol system of language. A **language** is essentially a code (like Morse code or a spy's secret code) in which meaning is encoded into (or changed into) particular symbols according to the rules of the code, which are referred to as *grammar.* It is then possible for anyone who knows the rule system of the code to decode (or change back into meaning) the symbols used in communication. To communicate through language, two people have to agree on which words will stand for which ideas and, in addition, on the rules by which the words will be strung together. In English, for example, "John hit Mary" communicates a very different meaning from "Mary hit John," even though the three words are identical in both cases. If all this makes language sound complicated, it is. Symbolic communication is truly one of the great and complex human creations.

Coordination and Human Values As human behavior becomes coordinated in social groups, it is organized into ongoing patterns that are accepted as proper within the group. Language use, for example, depends on people following a particular symbol system from one day to the next so that they can understand each other. Such patterns endlessly fascinate the

sociologist; the people in the social group who follow them are aware of them also, though they don't have the same kind of awareness that the sociologist has as an outside observer. A fish probably has less understanding of swimming than we do since the fish is not aware of alternatives. But the fish has a greater attachment to swimming. A similar situation is found within human social groups: People get attached to their patterns.

Any habits—which are patterns of behavior—are hard to break. When habits are not just individual but are followed by everyone in a group, the force of others' expectations is added to the force of habit in general. Such patterns of behavior may begin because they are useful in dealing with some problem the social group has; over time they become important in their own right simply because they are there. They may continue when they are no longer useful or perhaps are even destructive to the social group, but habits are hard to change. In short, habits, or patterns of behavior, can become values in a social group.

A **value** is an ideal agreed upon by a social group as to what is good or desirable. Americans, for example, value freedom, technology, motherhood, apple pie, and money—not necessarily in that order. Within the general range of values, the everyday patterns of behavior come to be valued by the people who follow them. Thus, wearing clothes in public is not only a pattern of American behavior, it is also valued as a desirable behavior. We come to believe strongly in our habits. And all of this results from the conscious manner in which humans coordinate themselves into social groups. Whatever patterns develop, those who follow them will notice them and think all manner of thoughts about them. Sociologists sum up this phenomenon by saying that humans develop cultures.

BOX 1.1

PRIMATE COMMUNICATION: THE LEARNING OF LANGUAGE

Humans are not the only animals that have learned to communicate. Presumably, however, humans are the only animals that have developed a true symbol system—a language—and that are capable of learning a language. Until recently the assumption was that the same kind of mental ability was required for creating and for understanding language. This assumption faced its first major challenge in 1966 when Project Washoe began.

In 1966 Washoe was a very young female chimpanzee living with her owners, Alan and Beatrice Gardner. In their home environment the Gardners began teaching Washoe to communicate through the American Sign Language for the Deaf, in which particular gestures stand for particular words. After twenty-two months of training, Washoe had mastered over thirty such signs (she consistently used them correctly) and was still learning more (Gardner and Gardner, 1969). But was Washoe an unusually intelligent chimpanzee?

Roger Fouts (1973) continued work on teaching sign language to chimpanzees and discovered that Washoe was far from unique. Some chimpanzees were more receptive than others, but all could learn. It was also discovered that the chimps were doing a great deal of fairly sophisticated thinking about the signs they were learning. One in particular, Lucy, had acquired a vocabulary of seventy-five signs when the following observation occurred:

> When presented with a radish, Lucy signed "fruit food" or "drink" for the first 3 days. On the fourth day she bit into the radish, spit it out, and signed "cry hurt food." From that point on she used either "cry" or "hurt" to describe the radish. In describing a watermelon, Lucy signed "candy drink" or "drink fruit" even though the experimenter used the signs "water" and "melon." These novel combinations not only demonstrated Lucy's ability to form new combinations from the signs in her vocabulary, but also revealed Lucy's ability to express her concepts of items in her environment. (Fouts and Couch, 1976: 153)

The Development of Culture: Reason and Rules for Coordination

Culture is the most general concept used by a sociologist. It refers to all the objects, skills, ideas, beliefs, and patterns of behavior that are developed and shared by members of a social group. In short, *anything* that is created and shared by given groups of humans is part of culture. The patterns of everyday behavior in social groups that have held our attention up until now form the core of culture and develop only as culture develops. All the elements of culture, from tools to religious beliefs, develop simultaneously and in an interconnected manner; changes in one element of culture result in changes in the other elements of culture. The development of the automobile for the mass market in the United States, for example, affected patterns of living, traveling, eating, praying, romancing, and consuming, to name just a few. Conversely, the automobile could not have been developed had not other elements of American culture provided large-scale industry, cities filled with wage workers, assorted technological advances necessary to the production of the automobile, and so on.

As patterns of behavior become habitual over time for a group of people, their consciousness of those patterns is reflected in their culture. The members of the group come to agree that certain things should be done by certain people in certain ways at certain times and in certain places. Such agreements come to be expressed as the norms of a culture. **Norms** are the shared rules that govern the wide variety of patterned behavior within the culture. Norms cannot be seen or touched, but their existence can be unmistakably felt through the negative responses of others when we violate the agreed-upon rules of behavior.

Norms only provide the what, where, how, and when of patterned behavior; it is left to values to provide the why. **Values** back up norms by providing the reasons for following them. Values may hold individuals to the norms when the force of habit fails and the utility of following the norm is called into question. Values may also keep individuals following norms when no one is watching to see that the norm is adhered to. People give their lives in the defense of values they believe in strongly, so it is small wonder that values play a major role in maintaining conformity to cultural norms. Unlike bees, which follow their patterns without question, humans develop elaborate systems of justification in their cultures so that individuals following current norms will not consciously search for alternatives. They would undoubtedly find some if they looked.

As culture develops, it organizes patterned behavior into **roles**, the expected behavior patterns that develop for specific activities or positions in a society. Because roles respond to the expectations of others, they may also be described as norm-governed behavior. To play a role is to follow a set of norms; conversely, to *not* play a role is to break a set of norms. Roles are often conveniently labeled in a culture. In American society, for example, one individual might simultaneously be a daughter, sister, cousin, aunt, mother, wife, student, church member, best friend, shopper, political activist, union member, PTA member, and professional sociologist, just to scratch the surface of possibilities. Each of these roles demands different kinds of behavior, and there is generally a pattern within each role so that one individual behaves more or less like other individuals playing the same role. Most individuals take to this variety as a duck takes to water, finding little difficulty in keeping track of the variety of expectations within each role and the different expectations from one role to the next.

In a manner of speaking, being born into a human society and its culture is like entering into an ongoing game. Whether field games like baseball or board games like Monopoly, games provide positions or roles for the players, rules that govern the play, artifacts with which to play, and ready-made values in the player's desire to win. Also, as with our cultures, we tend to get caught up in the playing of a game, perhaps feeling hate for our best friends while going bankrupt at Monopoly. Just as the game places a context around the patterned behavior that makes up the game, so culture provides a context for the patterned behavior that allows humans to survive in their societies. It provides them with technology, skills, knowledge, norms, values, and roles.

Since culture develops far more slowly than the individuals who learn about it and keep it thriving each generation, it is easy to forget that culture is a human creation. Even though culture was begun by humans and is added to or changed by each generation of humans, it in turn creates the humans of each generation who will live within it. Parents who are caught up in the playing of their cultural "games" pass on that culture to their children, who generally accept it simply because it is there. This observation brings us to one of the central problems for the sociologist. Societies and cultures are simultaneously the *creations* and the *creators* of human beings. We make up the games ourselves but often forget that fact in the excitement of play.

HUMANS AS A SOCIAL CREATION

Few other creatures in the animal kingdom are dependent for as many years after birth as humans. Long after puppies and kittens are out on their own, human infants are just learning to crawl. Part of the reason for this is physiological; human bodies have slow maturation built into their design. But another reason brings us back to human societies: Humans do not inherit their forms of coordination, as bees do; they must learn them from other humans. This process takes time and requires that young individuals remain around older individuals. A growing physical maturity then comes to be accompanied by a growing social maturity. Both are necessary to function as a human being in society.

How much of what people do is learned, and how much are they born with? Do murderers, for example, learn their behavior from others, are they born with murderous instincts, or both? This basic question—usually called the *heredity versus environment* question—is far from being solved. Humans begin learning from the moment of birth, if not before, so it is almost impossible to sort out the learning from the genes twenty or so years later. One thing we do know, however, is that there are few limits to the things humans can learn from their cultures.

There is remarkable cultural variation around the world. There are some things that every human group must do, such as take care of dependent children, but the ways they do these things vary considerably. Families can be large or small, male dominated or female dominated, run democratically or with an iron hand. They can be geared toward religious concerns, economic concerns, warfare concerns, or all three. However families are organized, the children born into them find little difficulty learning how they work and learning to believe in them. Unlike bees, humans have a wide variety of means for organizing the hive. A child born to parents in one culture can be adopted at birth by parents from another culture and have no problems with adjustment (unless members of the new culture reject the child). The hearts and minds of humans are both highly moldable and highly flexible. In the terminology of sociology this process is called socialization.

Socialization: The Internalization of Culture

Socialization is the ongoing process by which humans come to learn about and believe in their cultures. It is a process that begins at birth and continues until death. The process is different, of course, at different stages of life. Infants are starting from scratch and require the broad brush strokes of the basics from the culture they are born into, whereas older people generally face a continuing series of "finishing touches" of socialization from their associates. Whatever the case, socialization never stops.

The persistence of socialization in social groups can be attributed to the group members themselves. Group members never tire of watching the behavior of others and of noting when that behavior is out of line according to the shared norms of the group. That "noting" can take the form of comments, snickers, ridicule, withholding of affection, exile, or violence, depending on how strongly the group members feel about the norm that has been broken. Any of these responses serves to communicate to the offending members (a) the fact that a norm has been broken, (b) a definition of the norm so that it can be followed in the future, and (c) the seriousness of the norm. Along with this information comes enforcement; ridicule, for example, not only communicates the group's displeasure but is, in itself, an unpleasant experience that most of us seek to avoid. We can use the information so communicated to help us avoid such penalties in the future. Any enforcement of group norms (by any means whatever) is called **social control** by sociologists. The reading by Peter Berger following this chapter explores some of the ways that group norms are enforced.

Just as group members never tire of socializing us, we generally never tire of helping them do so. Human beings are irretrievably social creatures. The social isolation of an adult is one of the most extreme punishments that can be inflicted; the social isolation of an infant leads to either death or mental disorder. This emotional need for others can be seen even in infant monkeys, as described in Box 1.2. Our need for each other makes each of us a willing participant in the process of socialization. In many cases we will seek out the norms of our social groups at the same time that other group members are virtually shining spotlights on them to help us find them. This situation of avid learners coupled with determined teachers gives a tremendous strength and vitality to the process of socialization.

The study of socialization is not as simple as its theoretical description. In actuality American society is filled with disagreements and violence as "learners" rebel at the best efforts of the "teachers." Socialization is often less than smooth, and social control is not always effective. The reason stems in large part from the cultural diversity in American society. Within our overall society many smaller groups live and think very differently from each other. The average American adult comes into daily contact with a variety of groups and social situations that are incompatible with one another in terms of norms and values. A professional criminal can be a dedicated church member; a ruthless businessman can be a loving father and husband; a college student can be a model son or daughter and good student yet have one foot in the drug culture. The problem in the study of socialization is not that social groups don't have great power over their members but that there are so many different groups doing the socializing. The more influence one such group has, the less open will be individuals of that group to the socialization and social control of other groups. The enthusiasm with which many members of the People's Temple apparently followed their leader into mass suicide in Jonestown in 1978 illustrates both the failure of socialization of more normal American culture and the power of socialization within a closed group.

Socialization leads to a curious development in the thinking of the individuals it affects. As infants, we see ourselves as pretty much the center of the universe. As socialization continues, we become more aware of how others view us; our emotional needs are changing, and we will want to ensure the continued affection of those most important to us. As we focus on the views others have of us and our behavior, we come to look at ourselves more and more as others do. If others treat us as an unpleasant nuisance, we will come to see ourselves as an unpleasant nuisance. Once we get used to seeing ourselves this way, we will not even need others physically around to respond to us; we will be able to imagine their responses based on our knowledge of their past responses.

As we come to see ourselves in terms of our social group, we are internalizing the culture of the social group. **Internalization** is the process by which we come to know the norms of a culture and, more importantly, come to hold the values of a culture as our own. When you accept someone else's view of who you are, you will also be accepting many other aspects of that person's values. If, for example, your social group believes that women should be homemakers and mothers and it communicates to you that you are a good little girl for playing with dolls, you will tend to internalize the general value for women at the same time that you internalize the view of yourself as a "good little girl." All members of society seek positive views of themselves from others whose views are important to them; more general values tend to sneak in the back door at the same

BOX 1.2

THE INFANT'S ATTACHMENT TO ITS MOTHER: THE HARLOW STUDY OF RHESUS MONKEYS

The power of socialization begins at birth for all mammals. The source of that power stems from the dependency of the infant on the mother for its basic needs. In his now-famous study of rhesus monkey infants, Harry Harlow (1958) examined the nature of that dependency.

The infant's need of the mother's milk had been suggested by some to be the source of the infant's attachment to the mother. Harlow decided to study the emotional components of that attachment. He placed rhesus monkey infants in a cage with two artificial mothers. One artificial mother was made of wire but dispensed milk to the infant. The other artificial mother dispensed no milk but was warm and furry. Invariably, the infant monkeys preferred the warm and furry mother to the wire milk factory, turning to the latter only to satisfy their hunger. Presumably, the monkeys had an inborn need for contact with other members of their species, and the furry artificial mother was the closest the infants could come to satisfying that need. When Harlow and Zimmermann (1959) tried adding a rocking motion to the warm and furry artificial mother, it attracted the infants even more.

Humans are not the same as rhesus monkeys, yet the outcome of Harlow's studies seems basic enough to tell us something about human infants. Unlike insects or fish that hatch impersonally from a deserted egg, human infants are born with a need for sociability along with the more basic need for food. Beyond a mere openness to others, this *need* for the sociability of others is the powerful first step on the road to socialization.

time. This all happens more or less unconsciously, so that one day you wake up and the values are your own. Once they are established, they may be almost immovable, even if you become aware of them, don't like them, and desire to change them. The example of women's roles illustrates this, but consider a simpler and more graphic example: We are taught in American society to value cow flesh as a food but not grasshopper flesh, even though both are good sources of protein. Try to eat grasshopper for dinner tonight, and you will experience an internalized value.

Internalization involves more than accepting the values of our society. We also internalize the knowledge of our culture. Some parts of that knowledge are obvious—for example, the skills and general information that we learn. Learning how to read, how to fry chicken, how to drive a car, how to vote, and how to play baseball are all parts of knowledge that we are conscious of, both when we teach them and when we learn them. We internalize them in the sense that they become added to the repertoire of things we can do. But our cultural knowledge also provides us with a world view or general perception of the world. A cultural world view is seldom either taught or learned consciously but develops along with the skills and information that are. For example, most Americans believe that individuals are all different and should have some personal liberty, that private property is fundamental to social life, that dreams don't really happen and aren't overly important, and that the earth is here for humans to live on rather than live with. We don't have to look too hard to find cultures that differ from our own on each of these elements. Sociologists are interested in the internalization of a cultural world view because it colors (or, from another point of view, limits) what people see. As the United States deals with the growth of Islamic fundamentalism in the Middle East and the different values and perspectives that drive its adherents, the limitations in outlook caused by culture appear to be an increasingly important obstacle to peace in that area.

The overall picture of socialization painted by sociologists is that every part of the individual's personality is in some way affected by membership in a social group. The fact that we are conscious of much of this socialization gives us a false belief that we are aware of *all* of it. Our very desire to be members of and accepted by at least one social group overrides our ability to stand back and understand what the social group does to us in return. Such an understanding is a fundamental part of the sociological outlook. But in calling attention to the ways in which we are unconsciously manipulated by our social groups, the sociological outlook brings up questions of freedom and conformity in society that are not necessarily comforting.

Freedom versus Conformity in Society

Sociology paints a coercive picture of social groups. Members of social groups demand conformity from each other and employ ruthless tactics of social control when they don't get it. At the same time, group members facing social control seem desperate to learn the group's norms so that they might conform voluntarily. In spite of this overall orientation, however, only a few sociologists would relegate humans to the status of behavioral robots. The variety of social groups that most people associate with lessens the influence of each, as we have seen; ridicule from one group will not be quite as devastating if we get respect from some other group. Moreover, socialization may not be the sledgehammer that sociologists describe; people are very likely more than just a blank sheet of paper waiting for the writing of society. But, for all of this, we still come back to the basic observation that many people are more than happy to turn over their freedom of choice to the social group.

Looking at the ways social groups provide basic patterns of behavior for their members offers a new perspective on the question of freedom. If we fit ourselves into the ongoing patterns that our social groups provide, we give up our freedom to decide what to do, but we are also saved from the responsibility of having to decide. A soldier who fires at the enemy in wartime has been given an order, and if he is a good soldier (if he has internalized the role), he will not feel guilty. It was the decision of the officer who gave the order that made the enemy soldier die, not the action of the private who pulled the trigger. When our roles carry with them directives of this sort, we can always blame the role for what we do and hold it, rather than ourselves, responsible.

On the other side of the coin, people are far from being role robots; indeed, social experiences often place us in too many conflicting situations for roles to be followed with unquestioned obedience. Soldiers who take orders share uniforms with other soldiers who ignore orders. New roles can develop within such situations, as, for example, the "fragging" of officers by enlisted personnel in Vietnam who quietly killed their commanding officers when they disapproved of the orders given. Orders can also become confusing, as during the short-lived Soviet Union coup of 1991 when soldiers at various levels had to decide which orders were appropriate; their subsequent siding with Boris Yeltsin and their refusal to fire on demonstrators did much to determine the outcome of both the coup and the Soviet Union itself.

The basic question of freedom versus conformity is one for which sociology has no answer; it simply provides better ways to ask it. Too much personal freedom is highly disruptive and can be dangerous to personal welfare; we don't want to give others the right to murder on the pretext of not limiting their liberty. On the other hand, some of the great horrors of history—

the Spanish Inquisition, Hitler's Third Reich, and the mass suicide of People's Temple followers at Jonestown—all happened in the name of conformity. People didn't have the power or weren't psychologically able to say no; they fit into the patterns provided for them and passed the responsibility for their own actions on to others. All these cases of individual submersion in the group raise interesting questions about human behavior.

The social groups we create turn around and seduce us into being loyal members. By focusing on the processes of socialization, sociology brings that seduction more into the light. Individuals can thus use the sociological outlook to watch the process of manipulation in action. That does not mean that we will be immune from those processes, as everyone needs some kind of social group to survive, but at least we will have some protection provided by the understanding.

On a more general level, the sociological outlook focuses on the sources of social groups themselves. It is easy to forget that society and culture are the creations of humans and, as such, are open to change by humans. Living in a social group, playing its roles according to its norms, and accepting its values take on the characteristics of a game played for so long that the participants forget they're playing it. Just as people become caught up in the playing of a game, so people become caught up in their social groups. Being rich and powerful in American society can make you feel good and important, just as owning the major properties in a Monopoly game can make you feel good for an afternoon. By bringing society itself into question, sociology places all the rules and values we live by into a sharper perspective. We become aware of where they come from, how we came to accept them, and how they make us feel. This understanding gives them a little less control over our freedom.

SUMMARY

This chapter has been both an introduction to and an overview of sociology. Society is considered as the coordination of activities, this coordination being a source of strength and an aid to survival. Unlike other animals, humans consciously build societies. Thus they have the flexibility of being able to change their societies should circumstances require it and of having a changeable system of communication. In spite of the conscious nature of their societies, however, humans become attached to their particular forms of coordination and include within their cultures a system of values supporting their lifestyle.

The conscious and flexible nature of human societies requires that each generation become socialized into the culture. Socialization results in the internalization of culture as the individual comes to hold cultural values as his or her own. As social creatures, humans desire the company and acceptance of others; they are capable of freedom, yet they often desire conformity to the ways of their cultures.

These general observations about human societies can be applied more specifically toward understanding everyday life. Even the most trivial social situations are norm-governed, and other participants will expect us to follow those norms. If we are not familiar with the norms, the other participants will generally attempt to socialize us into behavior that follows the norms and perhaps into an acceptance of the values behind those norms. If a newcomer to the social group internalizes these values, the newcomer comes to see himself or herself in a new light.

GLOSSARY

Culture The configuration of humanly created objects, skills, ideas, beliefs, and patterns of behavior that are learned and transmitted by members of a society in a shared fashion.

Division of labor The separation of activities within a society, coupled with specialization in these activities by different societal members.

Internalization The process by which individuals come to see themselves in terms of the roles they play and come to share in the values of the social group, making those values their own.

Language A symbol system that functions as a code into which meaning is encoded and from which meaning is decoded according to particular rules.

Norms The shared rules that govern the wide variety of patterned behavior within a given culture, forming the expectations for behavior in particular social situations.

Roles The expected behavior patterns that develop for specific activities or as typical for specific positions within a society.

Social control The enforcement of group norms by any agency through the imposition of sanctions in response to behavior.

Socialization The ongoing process by which humans come to learn about and believe in their cultures, from learning the roles to sharing the values. Through socialization the individual becomes a member of the social group and develops a sense of self.

Society A relatively large, self-sufficient collection of people that (1) shares and transmits a common heritage from one generation to another, (2) contains patterns of behavior that govern interaction, and (3) occupies a given territory.

Symbol A word, gesture, object, or image of any sort that, by the agreement of two or more people, stands for another idea or object.

Value An ideal agreed upon by a social group as to what is good or desirable.

SUPPLEMENTARY READINGS

Berger, Peter *Invitation to Sociology: A Humanistic Perspective.* Garden City, N.Y.: Anchor, 1963.
A short and clearly written introduction to the sociological perspective, with many examples drawn from everyday life. Along with introducing basic concepts Berger discusses the implications of sociology for human action.

Denton, John A. *Society and the Official World: A Reintroduction to Sociology.* Dix Hills, N.Y.: General Hall, Inc., 1990.
Denton offers a different kind of sociological introduction, focusing on an "unofficial" and often unnoticed social world that commonly escapes the attention of sociologists.

Giddens, Anthony *Sociology: A Brief but Critical Introduction.* New York: Harcourt Brace Jovanovich, 1983.
A brief (as advertised) introduction to the major schools of thought that compete for the attention of sociologists. This is a useful book, particularly for the beginning sociology major.

Giglioli, Pier Paolo (ed.) *Language and Social Context.* Baltimore, Md.: Penguin, 1972.
A collection of essays on the role of language and knowledge in social groups, focusing on the importance of language use for other social processes.

Goffman, Erving *The Presentation of Self in Everyday Life.* Garden City, N.Y.: Anchor, 1959.
A sociological classic. Goffman's book focuses on people as social actors, playing the roles available to them and manipulating social situations in their interactions.

Mills, C. Wright *The Sociological Imagination.* New York: Oxford University Press, 1959.
A general introduction to the sociological perspective from a major American sociologist. Mills points out how sociology transforms an individual's perspective on society by illuminating the social processes behind the individual's experience.

Riesman, David, with Nathan Glazer and Reuel Denney *The Lonely Crowd.* New Haven, Conn.: Yale University Press, 1950.
A wide-ranging discussion of American society and the American character as seen through the sociological perspective. Riesman focuses on changes in basic American personality types as reflections of other social changes in the society.

READING

Invitation to Sociology

PETER BERGER

Peter Berger's short book *Invitation to Sociology* appears in the Supplementary Readings section of this chapter, just in case the following excerpt motivates you to become better acquainted with this sociologist. Berger has explored a variety of areas within the discipline throughout the course of his career, but this particular book is particularly well suited for the beginning sociologist (for whom it is intended)—and for this chapter, since it explores the sociological perspective on human freedom. Since most of us are brought up to believe ourselves to be individuals who make our own decisions and chart our own courses in life, the sociological perspective presents us with a challenge by emphasizing how our thoughts and behaviors are affected by outside influences. In the following section from his book, Berger explores the influences (termed "social control" by sociologists) that tend to keep us in line, with or without our consent.

Social control is one of the most generally used concepts in sociology. It refers to the various means used by a society to bring its recalcitrant members back into line. No society can exist without social control. Even a small group of people meeting but occasionally will have to develop their mechanisms of control if the group is not to dissolve in a very short time. It goes without saying that the instrumentalities of social control vary greatly from one social situation to another. Opposition to the line in a business organization may mean what personnel directors call a terminal interview, and in a criminal syndicate a terminal automobile ride. Methods of control vary with the purpose and character of the group in question. In either case, control mechanisms function to eliminate undesirable personnel and (as it was put classically by King Christophe of Haiti when he had every tenth man in his forced-labor battalion executed) "to encourage the others."

The ultimate and, no doubt, the oldest means of social control is physical violence. In the savage society of children it is still the major one. But even in the politely operated societies of modern democracies the ultimate argument is violence. No state can exist without a police force or its equivalent in armed might. This ultimate violence may not be used frequently. There may be innumerable steps before its application, in the way of warnings and reprimands. But if all the warnings are disregarded, even in so slight a matter as paying a traffic ticket, the last thing that will happen is that a couple of cops show up at the door with handcuffs and a Black Maria. Even the moderately courteous cop who hands out the initial traffic ticket is likely to wear a gun—just in case. And even in England, where he does not in the normal course of events, he will be issued one if the need arises.

In Western democracies, with their ideological emphasis on voluntary compliance with popularly legislated rules, this constant presence of official violence is underemphasized. It is all the more important to be aware of it. Violence is the ultimate foundation of any political order. The commonsense view of society senses this, and this may have something to do with the widespread popular reluctance to eliminate capital punishment from the criminal law

From *An Invitation to Sociology* by Peter Berger. Copyright © 1963 by Peter L. Berger. Used by permission of Doubleday, a division of Bantam Doubleday Dell Publishing Group, Inc.

(though this reluctance is probably based in equal measure on stupidity, superstition and the congenital bestiality that jurists share with the bulk of their fellow citizens). However, the statement that political order rests ultimately on violence is just as true in states that have abolished capital punishment. Under certain circumstances the use of their weapons is permitted to state troopers in Connecticut, where (much to their freely expressed gratification) an electric chair graces the central penal establishment, but the same possibility exists for their colleagues in Rhode Island, where police and prison authorities have to get along without this facility. It goes without saying that in countries with less of a democratic and humanitarian ideology the instruments of violence are much less gingerly displayed—and employed.

Since the constant use of violence would be impractical and also ineffective, the official organs of social control rely mostly on the restraining influence of the generally known availability of the means of violence. For various reasons this reliance is usually justified in any society that is not on the brink of catastrophic dissolution (as, say, in situations of revolution, military defeat or natural disaster). The most important reason for this is the fact that, even in dictatorial and terroristic states, a regime tends to gain acceptance and even acceptability by the simple passage of time. This is not the place to go into the sociopsychological dynamics of this fact. In democractic societies there is at least the tendency for most people to share the values on behalf of which the means of violence are employed (this does not mean that these values have to be fine—the majority of the white people in some Southern communities may be, for instance, in favor of using violence, as administered by the police agencies, in order to uphold segregation—but it does mean that the employment of the means of violence is approved by the bulk of the populace). In any functioning society violence is used economically and as a last resort, with the mere threat of this ultimate violence sufficing for the day-to-day exercise of social control. For our purposes in this argument, the most important matter to underline is that nearly all men live in social situations in which, if all other means of coercion fail, violence may be officially and legally used against them.

If the role of violence in social control is thus understood, it becomes clear that the, so to speak, penultimate means of coercion are more important for more people most of the time. While there is a certain uninspired sameness about the methods of intimidation thought up by jurists and policemen, the less-than-violent instrumentalities of social control show great variety and sometimes imagination. Next in line after the political and legal controls one should probably place economic pressure. Few means of coercion are as effective as those that threaten one's livelihood or profit. Both management and labor effectively use this threat as an instrumentality of control in our society. But economic means of control are just as effective outside the institutions properly called the economy. Universities or churches use economic sanctions just as effectively in restraining their personnel from engaging in deviant behavior deemed by the respective authorities to go beyond the limits of the acceptable. It may not be actually illegal for a minister to seduce his organist, but the threat of being barred forever from the exercise of his profession will be a much more effective control over this temptation than the possible threat of going to jail. It is undoubtedly not illegal for a minister to speak his mind on issues that the ecclesiastical bureaucracy would rather have buried in silence, but the chance of spending the rest of his life in minimally paid rural parishes is a very powerful argument indeed. Naturally such arguments are employed more openly in economic institutions proper, but the administration of economic sanctions in churches or universities is not very different in its end results from that used in the business world.

Where human beings live or work in compact groups, in which they are personally known and to which they are tied by feelings of personal loyalty (the kind that sociologists call primary groups), very potent and simultaneously very subtle mechanisms of control are constantly brought to bear upon the actual or potential

deviant. These are the mechanisms of persuasion, ridicule, gossip and opprobrium. It has been discovered that in group discussions going on over a period of time individuals modify their originally held opinions to conform to the group norm, which corresponds to a kind of arithmetic mean of all the opinions represented in the group. Where this norm lies obviously depends on the constituency of the group. For example, if you have a group of twenty cannibals arguing over cannibalism with one noncannibal, the chances are that in the end he will come to see their point and, with just a few face-saving reservations (concerning, say, the consumption of close relatives), will go over completely to the majority's point of view. But if you have a group discussion between ten cannibals who regard human flesh aged over sixty years as too tough for a cultivated palate and ten other cannibals who fastidiously draw the line at fifty, the chances are that the group will eventually agree on fifty-five as the age that divides the *déjeuner* from the *débris* when it comes to sorting out prisoners. Such are the wonders of group dynamics. What lies at the bottom of this apparently inevitable pressure towards consensus is probably a profound human desire to be accepted, presumably by whatever group is around to do the accepting. This desire can be manipulated most effectively, as is well known by group therapists, demagogues and other specialists in the field of consensus engineering.

Ridicule and gossip are potent instruments of social control in primary groups of all sorts. Many societies use ridicule as one of the main controls over children—the child conforms not for fear of punishment but in order not to be laughed at. Within our own larger culture, "kidding" in this way has been an important disciplinary measure among Southern Negroes. But most men have experienced the freezing fear of making oneself ridiculous in some social situation. Gossip, as hardly needs elaboration, is especially effective in small communities, where most people live their lives in a high degree of social visibility and inspectability by their neighbors. In such communities gossip is one of the principal channels of communication, essential for the maintenance of the social fabric. Both ridicule and gossip can be manipulated deliberately by any intelligent person with access to their lines of transmission.

Finally, one of the most devastating means of punishment at the disposal of a human community is to subject one of its members to systematic opprobrium and ostracism. It is somewhat ironic to reflect that this is a favorite control mechanism with groups opposed on principle to the use of violence. An example of this would be "shunning" among the Amish Mennonites. An individual who breaks one of the principal tabus of the group (for example, by getting sexually involved with an outsider) is "shunned." This means that, while permitted to continue to work and live in the community, not a single person will speak to him ever. It is hard to imagine a more cruel punishment. But such are the wonders of pacifism.

It is possible, then, to perceive oneself as standing at the center (that is, at the point of maximum pressure) of a set of concentric circles, each representing a system of social control. The outer ring might well represent the legal and political system under which one is obligated to live. This is the system that, quite against one's will, will tax one, draft one into the military, make one obey its innumerable rules and regulations, if need be put one in prison, and in the last resort will kill one. One does not have to be a right-wing Republican to be perturbed by the ever-increasing expansion of this system's power into every conceivable aspect of one's life. A salutary exercise would be to note down for the span of a single week all the occasions, including fiscal ones, in which one came up against the demands of the politico-legal system. The exercise can be concluded by adding up the sum total of fines and/or terms of imprisonment that disobedience to the system might lead to. The consolation, incidentally, with which one might recover from this exercise would consist of the recollection that law-enforcement agencies are normally corrupt and of only limited efficiency.

Another system of social control that exerts its pressures towards the solitary figure in the center is that of morality, custom and manners.

Only the most urgent-seeming (to the authorities, that is) aspects of this system are endowed with legal sanctions. This does not mean, however, that one can safely be immoral, eccentric or unmannered. At this point all the other instrumentalities of social control go into action. Immorality is punished by loss of one's job, eccentricity by the loss of one's chances of finding a new one, bad manners by remaining uninvited and uninvitable in the groups that respect what they consider good manners. Unemployment and loneliness may be minor penalties compared to being dragged away by the cops, but they may not actually appear so to the individuals thus punished. Extreme defiance against the *mores* of our particular society, which is quite sophisticated in its control apparatus, may lead to yet another consequence—that of being defined, by common consent, as "sick."

Discussion Questions

1. Berger says that violence is the basis of societal social control but that it is also generally impractical. What does he mean by this? Why isn't violence practical?
2. Ostracism or "shunning" is singled out by Berger as being one of the most devastating and effective means of social control. Why should a *lack* of response from others be more effective than either a violent or non-violent direct response from other group members? If Berger is right, what does that say about importance of social group membership to most individuals?

CHAPTER 2 SOCIOLOGY AS A SOCIAL SCIENCE

Sociology is an outlook, a way of looking at people in hopes of understanding why they do the things they do. Of course, in order to explain why people act as they do, sociology must also pay some attention to the what, where, how, and when of human actions, but the ultimate aim of sociology is always to explain why. In the search for explanations of human action the sociological outlook is only one perspective among many. It differs, for example, from religious explanations of human action and, to a lesser extent, from psychological explanations of human action. Different perspectives provide different kinds of explanations since they begin with different assumptions about how the world works. Specifically, **sociology** is a social science that seeks the causes of human behavior in the workings of the social groups and institutions within which people live. This book invites you to add the sociological perspective to your arsenal of outlooks, giving you access to an additional kind of explanation for the people and situations you encounter.

This chapter will look more closely at sociology in practice. After comparing sociological explanations with psychological explanations of human action in the first section, we will view sociology in a more formal manner, introducing it as a social science.

SOCIOLOGY VERSUS PSYCHOLOGY: DIFFERENT KINDS OF EXPLANATIONS

In order to compare two kinds of explanation, we first need something to explain. For that purpose, consider the following fictional account:

> Johnny Smith had spent the last half of his twelve years in and out of trouble. He had been a polished shoplifter at the age of six. Older boys on the block would create some kind of distraction in the corner grocery to cover the theft they had assigned to Johnny. Needless to say, Johnny finally got caught—which enhanced his reputation in the neighborhood as well as providing an additional frustration for his mother.
>
> Johnny's mother worked as a shipping clerk in a nearby factory and tried to apply her small paycheck and limited free time to the raising of her three children. Johnny was her oldest and had been only four when his father deserted the family. With his father absent and mother working, Johnny had a lot of free time on his hands without the restrictions of parental supervision.
>
> Johnny's experience in the first grade was less than adequate, and it went downhill from there. He never learned to read and fell farther and farther behind the expectations of the grades into which he was constantly promoted. As the years went by, Johnny began to associate almost exclusively with other boys having the same frustrating school experience as he was. Johnny became the leader of a group of seven boys, which, as a group, began to specialize in petty theft and minor extortion. By the time he was eleven, Johnny was well known to the police and apparently beyond the control of his mother.
>
> By the time he turned twelve, Johnny was well established as the leader of his gang (which now had a name, a secret handshake, and an official meeting place in an abandoned building). After an unpleasant run-in with school authorities and a subsequent suspension, Johnny organized his gang into an evening's activity of vandalizing their school. When Johnny was arrested for this action, he told the authorities that he was very sorry for what he had done and hadn't meant to. From time to time, Johnny said, he simply lost control of his actions.

This brief description of Johnny gives us some factual information on the hows, wheres, and whens of Johnny's childhood but leaves open the question of why. Why did Johnny spend much of his time in trouble with the police and why did he finally vandalize his school? Of the many answers that could be given, consider the following explanations:

1. Johnny is the victim of a basic personality disorder (or is "mentally ill"). He has consistently had trouble with personal relationships in his family and at school, reacting violently to the best efforts of his mother and teachers to help him. His constant aggressive behavior toward others and his final senseless aggression toward the school building itself indicate his inability to cope. His own admission that he often feels not in control of his actions supports this explanation.
2. Most of the experiences Johnny has faced in his life have attacked his self-esteem. First, his father deserted the family, leaving Johnny without a significant male role model and giving him the feeling that perhaps something he did made his father leave. Later, his failure at school made him feel unworthy and led him to look for social experiences in which he could be successful. He found these experiences as the leader of a young gang in which other boys looked up to him and respected his decisions. As his gang increased in importance in his life, his family and school experiences decreased in importance and lost influence over his behavior. By ignoring his family and attacking his school, he was attacking the situations that he felt had attacked him.
3. Public education in the United States today does little to help the poor to advance; poor children tend to fail in the classroom while the children of high-income families tend to succeed. The institution of education also serves to cluster together children of the same age and to draw their attention to their peer group. When schools introduce children to each other and then give poor children the experience of failure in the classroom, those children have much in common. One of the things they have in common is opposition to the school that does not serve them well. In this manner the institution of education as it operates in the United States today helps to create youth gangs among the poor and stimulates those gangs to commit acts of violence against the school.

Explanation 1 could be characterized as a psychological explanation. As a perspective, psychology focuses on individuals, emphasizing their attitudes, emotions, and abilities to cope with other individuals. In a manner of speaking, psychology finds the "causes" of human behavior to be inherent in (or inside) human beings themselves. Thus, Johnny's actions are seen as reflections of other occurrences (frustration, anger, and so on) that are going on inside Johnny.

Explanation 3, at the other extreme, could be characterized as a sociological explanation. Sociology finds the causes of human behavior somewhere in the workings of the social groups and institutions within which humans live. It is even possible (as suggested by explanation 3) to provide a sociological explanation of an individual's behavior without ever looking inside the head of the individual whose behavior is being explained.

Explanation 2 includes a little of both psychology and sociology; it could best be characterized as social psychology. It finds the "causes" of Johnny's behavior in the groups and institutions within which Johnny lives, but it also suggests that Johnny's personal response to those social situations plays a major role in explaining his behavior.

The three explanations are perhaps as fictional as the story of Johnny they were designed to explain. Explanations 1 and 3, in particular, are extreme (or ideal types of) psychological and sociological explanations; it would be rare today to find a psychologist who completely ignored the social environment of an individual or a sociologist who completely ignored an individual's response to his or her social experiences. Psychology and sociology differ from each other primarily in the emphasis they place on different factors in their explanations. Social psychology, which sees the importance of both factors, is a recognized subdiscipline of both sociology and psychology.

Before we leave this comparison of different outlooks, it might be interesting to note a few more possible explanations outside the realms of both sociology and psychology. It could be argued that Johnny behaved as he did because:

4. He was possessed by the devil.
5. He was under the influence of an alien being from another planet.
6. His astrological sign periodically led him into conflict with the astrological signs of his mother and teachers.
7. He inherited a group of genes from his parents that gave him a body chemistry prone to violence and aggression.
8. He normally consumed an unbalanced diet with large quantities of sugar (or some other behavior-altering substance) that increased his aggressive tendencies.

This short list of explanations by no means exhausts the possibilities.

The important point to remember is the connection between different outlooks and the explanations they provide. A religious outlook might lead to explanation 4, while biochemistry might suggest explanation 7. We might think explanation 5 is limited to the realm of science fiction, but remember that traveling in rockets to the moon used to be limited to it, too. It is important to consider also how different explanations for problems lead to different "remedies": A psychological explanation leads us to change Johnny, whereas a sociological explanation leads us to change social factors, such as the school environment. A biochemical explanation would lead us to treat Johnny with drugs. Accepting a sociological outlook and its explanation does not replace other outlooks and explanations; it can be added to them and applied when it seems most useful. One of the clearest statements on the sociological perspective has been offered by American sociologist C. Wright Mills (see the reading at the end of this chapter). As he puts it, the sociological imagination turns your private troubles into public issues by the way you come to think about them.

SOCIOLOGY AS A SCIENCE

Unlike a religious outlook, a sociological outlook is scientific. Unlike biochemistry (which is also a scientific outlook), sociology is a *social* scientific outlook. Understanding the sociological outlook requires an understanding of social science. Sociology does not always live up to its scientific ideals, but an understanding of those ideals should bring the nature of sociological research into clearer focus. Knowing what sociologists are trying to achieve in their research should help you understand why they go about it in the ways they do.

Some organizations prefer that offices have a uniform look. Decorative items must be approved before being put up. Such rules obviously do not apply in this environment. Sociologists can study such differences and come up with conclusions about the different characters of the organizations involved. They can also study the decorations and come up with hypotheses about the roles and attitudes of the individual who chose them.

Science, whether social, natural, or physical, is a way or a method for understanding. To the scientist *understanding* generally means explaining why something under study acts or behaves the way it does. The explanation is the product of the scientist's thought and involves constructing concepts and specifying how those concepts relate to one another. Thus, for example, a scientific explanation of how you catch a cold would involve concepts such as *virus* and *antibody.* It would then proceed to explain how viruses enter the human body and how the body attacks them. A logically organized scientific explanation is called a **theory**. A scientific orientation does not stop at that point, however. The theory must be tested according to scientific methods. If the theory predicts that certain kinds of behavior (of viruses, people, or whatever) will occur under certain kinds of circumstances for certain kinds of reasons, it is up to the scientist to check that prediction. If the behavior does in fact occur under the specified circumstances, there is a good chance the reasons offered for that prediction (in other words, the theory) are correct. We will discuss theories further in the next section.

Ideally, science proceeds in the same manner regardless of the object under study. Social scientists should differ from other scientists only in their concern with human behavior as opposed to the behavior of viruses or electrons; a **social science** is a scientific discipline that studies human behavior through a perspective on the social context of that behavior. The actual situation, however, is much more complicated. Viruses and electrons rarely object to being studied, nor do they offer suggestions directly to the scientist while under investigation. Perhaps even more importantly, the physical or natural scientist has no direct vested interest in the behavior of the objects under study; the scientist will not have a brother or sister married to a virus. The social scientist, on the other hand, faces all of the above complications plus many more. The biologist can create and destroy viruses during experiments, but the social scientist *cannot* (or certainly *should* not) experiment on people that way. In other words, the human subject matter affects the research methods of the social scientist as well as presenting a unique object of study.

In this section we will look at the methods of science as practiced by the social science of sociology. For purposes of clarity this examination will be separated into two sections: We will look first at ways sociologists create and use concepts and theories, and second at the methodologies they employ to test those theories. Remember, however, that this logical separation is not generally a practical separation; the collection and testing of scientific data are part of the process of building concepts and theories (and vice versa).

Concepts and Theories in Sociology

The concept is the building block of science, but the use of concepts is not limited to scientists. Concepts are the building blocks of all human thinking; scientists are just more systematic and self-conscious about the way they use them. A brief look at the way we use concepts in everyday life might therefore aid us in understanding scientific concepts.

Concepts A **concept** directs our perceptions of the world around us by specifying what we should notice and what we should ignore; it calls our attention to certain similarities among objects or ideas and at the same time directs us to ignore all differences. A *chair,* for example, is a concept that directs our attention to objects that provide a place to sit and include some kind of backrest. Chairs can be large or small and can be constructed of a variety of materials, but the concept directs us to ignore all those differences and to focus on two basic similarities. The concept *chair* is useful because people like to sit and they want to be able to recognize places to sit, even in an otherwise strange environment. Concepts therefore reflect the interests of the people who created them.

All concepts are human creations. Chairs are not inherently similar to each other; they are similar only because we want to think of them that way. Similarly, hamburgers and apples are both *food* because we think of them as things to eat. Grasshoppers, on the other hand, are not normally included within the concept *food* in our culture—not because we cannot eat them, but because we don't want to eat them. People create and use concepts to deal with an otherwise impossibly complex situation. We live in a world in which no two things or events are ever exactly the same; to cope with that complexity, we must simplify the variation. Concepts are the tools we use to do that.

As concepts direct our attention, they simultaneously limit us. By calling attention to some basic similarities among objects or ideas, they discourage us from looking for other similarities unspecified by the concept. We get used to our concepts just as we get used to our other habits. If we look at the world in one way long enough, we might not want a new concept that will give us a different perspective. Because we see most of the world through our concepts, those parts of the world not highlighted by our concepts must necessarily pass us by until we develop concepts to corner them.

This discussion of concepts is of crucial importance to scientists because they attempt to use concepts in a systematic and self-conscious manner. Scientists must always be aware of how their thoughts and observations are subject to conceptual limitations. If the wrong concepts are employed, a scientific problem can be stared at forever and never understood. In medicine, for example, the concepts *bacteria, virus,* and *protozoan* made it possible to understand disease and respond to it effectively. Until that conceptual breakthrough, disease was a vast puzzle; it was known only to be contagious. Malaria, for example, was narrowed down to swampy areas in the summertime, especially where large numbers of people slept outside at night. If you're not looking at a problem with useful concepts, staring at it won't solve it, even if the malaria-carrying mosquito lights on your nose.

We can illustrate the effects of concepts on observations with some of the sociological concepts introduced in Chapter 1. Consider the concept *role,* for example. A nonsociologist would probably attempt to understand a particular individual's behavior by thinking about the similarity of the behavior in question to other behaviors of that individual. The concept *individual* directs your attention to those similarities, and it is certainly a useful concept. But *role* sheds a different kind of light on the problem. The concept *role* redirects your attention to the behavior of other individuals in the same situation. The norms that govern roles in that particular situation may explain the behavior in question. If you currently occupy the role of student, is your behavior totally predictable from knowledge about you in other situations, or would it help to know something about the expectations of teachers and other students with whom you interact as a student? The noisy extravert at a party is sometimes a quiet, passive student in the classroom.

Theories Concepts are important to science, but the real goal of scientific inquiry is theory construction. A **theory** specifies relations among concepts, predicting the degree to which they affect each other, and why. The concept *virus,* for example, is not very useful in preventing disease without a theory that explains how viruses enter bodies, their impact on life processes within bodies, and the means by which bodies counteract that impact. In fact, this *germ theory* of disease made possible the development of vaccinations, which make the individual immune to specific viruses in the future.

How scientists create theories is one of the great mysteries; although scientists are generally imagined to be very down-to-earth and methodical, there is something truly creative and artistic in theory creation. Many aspects of Albert Einstein's famous theory of relativity could not be tested until the development of space flight many decades later. How could he have formed such a theory without the ability to test his preliminary ideas against the world?

A theory states that one concept causes changes in another concept and specifies the degree of those changes. The germ theory of disease specifies the changes in the body caused by disease-causing microorganisms. It also specifies the degree of those changes, which has enabled researchers to develop the correct dosage of vaccine.

Sociology has a vast array of concepts to offer, but exact predictions of how they cause each other to change are few and far between. We know, for example, that group pressure can cause an individual to change his or her attitudes. But how much can those attitudes be changed, and why are some individuals more vulnerable to group pressure than others? Sociology can demonstrate relationships among concepts, but exacting predictions seem to be overcome by the complexity of human beings and their societies.

At least part of the problem in the development of sociological theory stems from problems inherent in sociological research. A scientist can manipulate viruses in the laboratory, but there are limits to the kinds of experiments humans can be used in. The question of human experimentation is, in fact, a major concern of sociologists today, as some experiments have stepped close to or over the line of ethical research. But even if sociologists were not limited in their laboratory research, how do we know that an individual's reaction in a laboratory situation would be anything like his or her reactions in real social situations? We already know that people play different roles in different situations; laboratory experiments may tell us a lot about laboratory roles and not much else. The problems of theory building are closely tied to the methods of scientific inquiry, but before turning to those methods, we will examine some of the major theoretical traditions that have developed in sociology.

Major Theoretical Perspectives in Sociology

Structural-functionalism: The Order Theorists **Structural-functionalism** is a perspective that views the different parts (or structures) of society in terms of the functions they fulfill for the overall society. Just as your heart fulfills the function of pumping blood so that the rest of your organs receive the oxygen they need to operate, so the different "organs" in the social body do their bit to keep the society healthy. Religion, for example, could be viewed as having the positive function of maintaining social values by effectively teaching those values to members of the society—socializing them. One such religious value might be that people should work hard, so those who believe in that value will go out and work hard at jobs that fulfill other functions for the society. To the structural-functionalists, society is a finely tuned machine (or a complex organism like the human body) in which all the parts are interdependent and operate for the good of the whole.

This concern about the interdependence of parts of society and the roles played by each to further the harmony of the whole developed during the nineteenth century, when European societies were going through massive changes due to industrialization. Economies and governments were changing rapidly, and individual lives were caught up in those changes as people found their current jobs and locations (usually farming in rural areas) to be no longer viable. Cities grew rapidly as workers flocked to new industrial employment. This general upheaval in people's lives affected their feelings about family, religion, and many other aspects of life that had previously been taken for granted. Thus, the cohesion of society was called into question for the first time. It was during this period, and largely because of it, that the discipline of sociology entered its infancy.

Nineteenth-century French sociologists such as August Comte, who gave sociology its name (1798-1857), and Emile Durkheim (1858-1917) helped to develop the functionalist perspective by raising an interesting first question. Instead of asking, "Why is society changing so much?" they asked, "What normally holds society together?" The cohesion of society, formerly taken for granted, was now a topic of investigation. The search for this "social glue" helped produce many basic tenets of functionalism as sociologists searched for the forces that bound people together. In short, these early sociologists wondered what caused social consensus.

Given the other scientific advances of the time, it is not unusual that comparisons between social structures and the parts of organisms were made. In addition, the idea of biological evolution, which viewed biological change as responsive to environmental changes over time, seemed an appealing model for early sociological theorizing. Perhaps the ultimate example of this point of view came from English sociologist Herbert Spencer (1820-1903), who viewed societies as becoming increasingly complex in structure over time (just as humans had become more complex than single-celled animals), with each part of that structure responsible for helping maintain the overall functioning of the system. Just as animals evolve so as to better adapt to their environment, a society must change through a natural and gradual process. An implication of this perspective is that no part of a society should be altered unless all of the society's functions are clearly known; otherwise, the meddling social surgeon might remove an essential kidney rather than an expendable appendix. Spencer became progressively more conservative over the years, arguing that *any* attempt to meddle in the natural state of society would, by definition, counter the laws of nature and produce social problems.

Later thinkers such as American sociologists Talcott Parsons (1902-1979) and Robert Merton (1910-   ) developed and refined functionalism without altering its basic nature. These two promoted the functionalist perspective to a point of dominance in American sociology during the 1950s. Merton observed that functions could be divided into manifest and latent functions. **Manifest functions** are the obvious functions provided by social structures. For example, educational systems serve to pass on cultural knowledge to each generation. **Latent functions** are the unintentional or hidden functions provided by social structures, which may not be known or understood until the structure is altered. For example, educational systems tend to keep wealth in the hands of the wealthy across generations because the children of the wealthy have access to better schools and do better in school, and people with more education get better jobs and earn more money. (We will examine both of these points in much more detail in Chapter 10).

Are all social structures functional by definition? Is every aspect of society necessary by the fact of its existence? Herbert Spencer seemed to think so (although even he had a moment or two of doubt), but other sociologists in this tradition have considered the possibility of nonfunctional social structures. Early American sociologist William Graham Sumner (1906) believed that some of the most basic elements of culture occasionally outlive their usefulness and end up either serving no function or creating problems by their continued existence. Robert Merton coined the term **disfunction** to refer to social structures that seem to produce negative consequences for society.

The structural-functionalists are sometimes called *order* theorists by critics who suggest that it focuses attention on maintaining social order and the status quo at the expense of understanding social change. These critics say that structural-functionalists look at social change as if it were a sickness in society rather than a common process. Defenders of the perspective point out that the functional perspective offers a unique and clear picture of social cohesion in society by unearthing the forces that build consensus among its members.

Conflict Theory The sociological perspective known as conflict theory is generally traced to the pioneering work of Karl Marx (1818-1883), in particular, his study of the social inequality characteristic of capitalist economies in industrial societies. Marx and later sociologists with this perspective observed that human inequality is not just a result of some individuals being stronger or smarter than others; rather, a structural inequality is built into the very fabric of society. Over time, for example, certain kinds of positions in society (such as a lord in feudalism) come to exercise power and hold wealth. Individuals come and go from the positions, but it is expected that someone will occupy such positions at all times. In this sense, we can say that inequality is structured into society because the inequality is part of the social structure itself. Even the strongest and most intelligent individuals will not hold power and wealth if their social position prohibits them access.

Conflict theorists assume that built-in differences in power and wealth will produce conflict in society between those who have them and those who don't. The favored few will fear those less favored while the have-nots will feel envy. The favored will work to maintain the status quo (as it clearly benefits them), while the remainder of society will be encouraged to compete for greater power and wealth. In short, **conflict theory** focuses on the structured inequality of society, which produces conflict as individuals and groups with different interests compete with one another.

If all these assumptions are correct, why are most social relations apparently so peaceful? The conflict theorists answer by pointing to efforts by the powerful to maintain the status quo. Power and wealth give the haves greater access to weapons, for example, with which they might dominate others. But weapons are not a very efficient means of control if they have to be used on more than a small minority of a society's members (see the reading by Berger following Chapter 1). Power also provides access to less obvious means of control, however. Power and wealth mean that you can publish the books (and determine their content), structure the school curriculum, purchase the politicians (or buy an office yourself), make the movies, influence the major religions, and, in general, have a major impact on the kinds of ideas and beliefs that most members of your society are likely to have. Many of these ideas are part of a set of coordinated ideas, termed **ideology**; conflict theorists say that the set of ideas promulgated by the ruling members of society always support their own interests. Most Americans, for example, believe firmly that private property is a fundamental right of all Americans. We are taught this in school and read it in our newspapers. Does such a belief benefit the average American as much as it does the Rockefellers or the DuPonts? Conflict theorists would point to this idea as an example of attempts by the more privileged to control the less privileged. Of course, the result is a fairly high level of agreement among members of a society. Note, however, how structural-functionalists and conflict theorists look at exactly the same thing—this high level of agreement—but provide very different explanations for its existence. Instead of looking for value consensus, conflict theorists roam the corridors of power relations, asking questions about how power develops, how it is used, and what its results are. Unlike structural-functionalism, conflict theory provides a definite insight into social change, showing how internal contradictions in societies can lead to change over time.

We will return to the debate between structural-functionalism and conflict theory in Chapter 7, when we examine the social stratification system—the system through which inequality is structured.

The differences and strengths of the two approaches stand out most clearly when applied to that topic. In the meantime, the sociological research you will encounter in this book is more easily understood if you look for the underlying theoretical perspective each researcher takes.

The Interactionist Perspective Both structural-functionalism and conflict theory can be described as *macro* theoretical perspectives in that they take the wide view, starting their explanations of human behavior by examining some of the most basic aspects of society. Individual behavior sometimes gets lost in such approaches, appearing only as the actions of robots responding automatically to social forces. While it is in the nature of the science of sociology to focus on group processes, sociology is not blind to the thoughts and feelings of individuals. As we saw at the opening of this chapter, the realm between sociology and psychology often provides fruitful insights into individuals' thoughts and feelings. If we enter that realm from the sociological point of view, we come prepared with the interactionist perspective.

The **interactionist perspective** (sometimes called the *symbolic* interactionist perspective) maintains that human behavior is a meaningful response to an agreed-upon social reality shared by members of society; in order to understand a response, we need to understand that social reality. But what exactly is "social reality" to the interactionists? *Why* does it need to be "agreed upon"? And *how* does it come to be agreed upon? The answers to these questions make up the central focus of this perspective.

To the interactionists, the reality of society exists only in the imaginations of society's members. Why do you wear clothes when you leave your home in the morning? Because in American society, covering the body in certain specified ways is considered to be appropriate in public. I feel that way, you feel that way, and so does your neighbor. More to the point, your neighbor would act out his or her sense of inappropriateness if he or she were to see you walking to the bus stop unclothed; even unclothed, you would understand that feeling because you are able to interpret your neighbor's negative reactions, guessing the meaning that lies behind them. As your neighbor and other observers react similarly and you interpret their behavior, you come to understand their shared sense of social reality: they agree that public nudity is inappropriate and act upon that belief. Each person's action reinforces the belief in others who had already shared the belief but have come to hold it more strongly upon confronting so many allies. In short, public nudity is inappropriate in American society because Americans believe that to be the case and maintain the shared nature of that belief by reminding one another as they interact. The belief lives in their shared imaginations and nowhere else. In this sense, the social world is a collective imagination and survives only so long as we agree to continue imagining it. If new imaginations arise and come to be shared, society changes.

The interactionist idea of social reality as a shared imagination places the individual social actor on center stage. But a person does not have total freedom to act because he or she is constrained by the actions of others, who act out their imaginations. Individuals also tend to be constrained by their own imaginations because we humans can only imagine actions we have experienced or have learned. Nevertheless, this perspective presents a view of social reality on the level of individual interaction and the possibility of changing that reality as an outcome of that interaction.

The interactionist perspective arose from many sources within sociology. German sociologist Max Weber (1864-1920), who took sociology in many different directions, is often credited with nudging the interactionist perspective into existence through his emphasis on the importance of meaning in social action. To Weber, we can only understand, explain, and predict an individual's action if we first know what that action means to the individual. Individuals, argued Weber, act only after interpreting the actions of others in some way that is meaningful to them. Sociologists must gain an understanding of this meaning (Weber termed this attempt at sociological understanding **Verstehen**).

American sociologists George Herbert Mead (1863-1931) and Charles Cooley (1864-1929) continued this tradition in sociology and are generally credited with laying the foundation of the interactionist perspective. Mead, in particular, outlined an approach to human behavior in his lectures at the University of Chicago. The human mind, said Mead, is the product of social interaction. As we think about ourselves, we do so in terms of how others react to us. Over time, the mind comes to reflect the general attitudes and perspectives of an individual's social community. Cooley used the term "looking glass self" to refer to this process. Our interactions with others result in our carrying society around inside our heads, as the attitudes of the social groups to which we belong become our own personal attitudes.

We return to the interactionist perspective in Chapter 4 (when we look more closely at the process of socialization); its focus on individuals' responses to their social environment gives it particular value in helping us understand the force of socialization in shaping individuals. Beyond that, however, look for aspects of the interactionist perspective in other sociological theories and studies that you come across in this book; as one example, the interactionist perspective helps structural-functionalists picture the growth and maintenance of consensus in society.

In general, understanding the theoretical perspective of a scientist will help you not only understand what that scientist *does* see but will also alert you to what that scientist *does not* see. When you shine a light in one direction, it makes the darkness seem all the denser in other directions.

The Methods of Sociological Research

A fundamental part of the scientific orientation is the testing of theories through research. The relationship between theory and research runs both ways: The theory must be transformable into hypotheses, the elements of which can be measured and tested repeatedly. A **hypothesis** states a prediction, which follows from the theory ("*If* this happens, *then* that will happen."). Research proceeds by finding a way to measure the elements of the hypothesis and then to test the relationship between the measurements. It should be possible for anyone to repeat the research under the conditions specified in the theory and to achieve the same results.

Continuing our example of viruses and disease, the germ theory of disease would lead to a hypothesis such as, "If I inject this virus into these laboratory animals, then I should be able to detect specific changes in the animals as the virus multiplies." This hypothesis (which would actually be stated in more specific terms) can be tested in the laboratory. If some or many of the injected animals do not respond as predicted, the scientist must either reexamine the experiment or reexamine the theory that led to the experiment. As is common in all scientific inquiry, the theory is likely to need either change or development. The new theory that results from this process will then lead to further hypotheses, which, when tested, will lead to further changes in theory. Although greatly oversimplified, this is one way science changes.

When testing hypotheses, it becomes necessary to measure the predicted changes. We often think of **measurement** as the assignment of numbers to some characteristic according to some specified rule. We turn length, for example, into feet or meters so that we can speak of it in an exact sense. For sociologists, measurement often has this traditional meaning. We might measure an attitude, for example, by asking individuals a series of questions relating to the attitude and then ranking their responses along some kind of numbered scale as to how strongly they responded to the questions. We might measure an individual's personal ties to a social group by asking other group members whether they think of the individual as a friend and then counting the number who responded affirmatively. However, measurement takes on an additional problem for the sociologist. The concept of *length* is pretty clearly the distance from here to there. But what, exactly, is an attitude?

Sociological concepts such as attitude, group cohesion, social role, and so on are not easily turned into any kind of systematic measurement (numbers being the most systematic). If it were possible for observers to watch groups and determine their degree of cohesion with a method of observation that others could copy, we could say that the concept was measured. But what looks like cohesion to one observer may seem to be disunity to the next. One solution is the **operational definition**, or definition of a concept in terms of the way it is measured. Thus, intelligence could be defined as a score on an intelligence (IQ) test. The nature of sociological concepts makes measurement an ever-present problem. Sociologists often have the feeling that the concept they have imagined in their theory is not quite being tapped through

French sociologist Emile Durkheim (1858-1917). Durkheim played an important role in the early growth of sociology through his refinement of the theories and methods of sociological inquiry.

BOX 2.1

THE SOCIOLOGICAL STUDY OF SUICIDE: EMILE DURKHEIM

How would you view suicide through the sociological outlook? Very few actions seem as personal and individualistic as suicide, yet, as with most of our behavior, the sociological outlook points out the social and group aspects of even this apparently solitary action. One of the first pieces of sociological research into suicide is also considered by many sociologists to be a research classic—*Suicide,* an 1897 study by French sociologist Emile Durkheim.

Durkheim theorized that suicide resulted from certain specific ways people might be connected to their social groups. For example, individuals very tightly connected to their social groups might see themselves as insignificant and think nothing of terminating their life for the benefit of the group. Durkheim termed this *altruistic suicide* and pointed to the behavior of soldiers during warfare as an example. Overly loose connections between the individual and the group can also lead to suicide. Individuals not closely connected to others in their social groups and to group goals might be likely to take their own lives in what Durkheim called *egoistic suicide.* Finally, Durkheim proposed a third type of suicide based on the amount of control the social group has on the individual. Our social groups give us our goals, convincing us to strive for certain ends while ignoring others. In this sense, our social groups also make us happy or unhappy; if we are taught to want things we are capable of getting, we will be happier than if we are taught to want the unobtainable or if our desires are not limited in some way. Durkheim identified the situation of unlimited desire, which he termed *anomie,* as a cause of suicide.

How would you test Durkheim's theory of suicide? Durkheim set out in search of social situations that would foster altruism, egoism, and anomie. According to his theory, each of these situations should produce higher rates of suicide than situations lacking those theoretical elements. But where would you find the social situations in question?

Durkheim looked to the military for his example of altruism. He found that soldiers were more likely than civilians to commit suicide. Carrying his measure of group cohesion one step further, he also found that officers had a higher rate of suicide than enlisted men; officers are presumably more highly committed to the military group than enlisted men, and this finding concerning suicide among officers supported Durkheim's theory.

How would you find social situations of varying degrees of egoism for which you could compare suicide rates? One piece of information Durkheim had was the religion of individuals who committed suicide. Of Protestants, Catholics, and Jews, Protestants seemed the most egoistic, with their emphasis on individualism, while Catholicism placed more emphasis on the group. Judaism emphasized the individual, yet the persecution Jews faced created a strong group cohesion. As Durkheim predicted, Protestants had higher suicide rates than Catholics, and Catholics had slightly higher rates than Jews.

Finally, Durkheim looked for anomie in various social situations. The lack of societal regulation of our desires that characterizes anomie occurs during economic depressions as individuals are forced to reevaluate their goals. But it would seem that economic depressions could also cause suicide by increasing poverty and thereby adding to human unhappiness. Durkheim solved this

BOX 2.1 (continued)

dilemma by pointing out that rapid economic growth as well as economic depression creates anomie. If anomie is a cause of suicide, rates of suicide should increase with rapid changes in the economy, *regardless of the direction of those changes.* By comparing suicide rates with economic statistics, Durkheim discovered just such a double connection, finding support for his theory.

Durkheim's theory is not perfect, nor were his research methods beyond criticism (although both were amazingly sophisticated for 1897). His study of suicide does, however, illustrate one of the ways that sociologists go about the business of building a theory and testing the predictions that come from that theory. *Suicide* remains one of the true classics in sociology.

whatever measurement techniques they have developed. And if measurement is not precise, the outcome of research will carry the same imprecision.

The Formal Experiment Hypothesis testing is best carried out through the formal experiment, whether the hypothesis relates to physics or sociology. The **formal experiment** consists of randomly assigning people (or laboratory rats, chemical compounds, and so forth) to two groups—the *control group* and the *experimental group.* It is important that the assigning be random so that any differences among the individuals will be found equally in each group. The control group is left alone, while the experimental group is subjected to whatever experimental treatment is prescribed by the hypothesis. The experimental treatment consists of some variable you think important in causing other things (attitudes, behavior, and so on) to happen. Scientists refer to this treatment as the *independent variable.* (A **variable** is a trait or characteristic subject to changes from case to case.) The changes that are caused by this variable are thought of as changes in a *dependent variable.* In other words, the dependent variable is the thing you want to explain, while the independent variable is what you believe to be its cause. At the end of your experiment any differences between the groups ($D_2 - D_1$ in Figure 2.1) are assumed to be the result of whatever you did to the experimental group, since the two groups were the same (or contained the same variety of difference) when the experiment began. This process is depicted in Figure 2.1, but perhaps an example would make the process clearer.

Consider the following hypothesis: If individuals experience frustration, then their attitudes of prejudice toward others will be increased. To test this hypothesis, you first need to develop some kind of method for measuring attitudes of prejudice, presumably some kind of written questionnaire or structured interview. Second, you will need to think of some kind of frustrating experience to which you can subject people without getting arrested. Finally, you will need some people. The people are then randomly assigned to control and experimental groups, at which point their respective levels of prejudice are measured. This is called the pretest (see Figure 2.1). If by chance, the experimental group members are more prejudiced than the control group members, the pretest will measure this. The individuals assigned to the experimental group face the frustration you have devised for them (the independent variable), and then the individuals in both groups face your prejudice-measuring technique again (the posttest). If the experimental group members exhibit significant changes in attitudes of prejudice (the

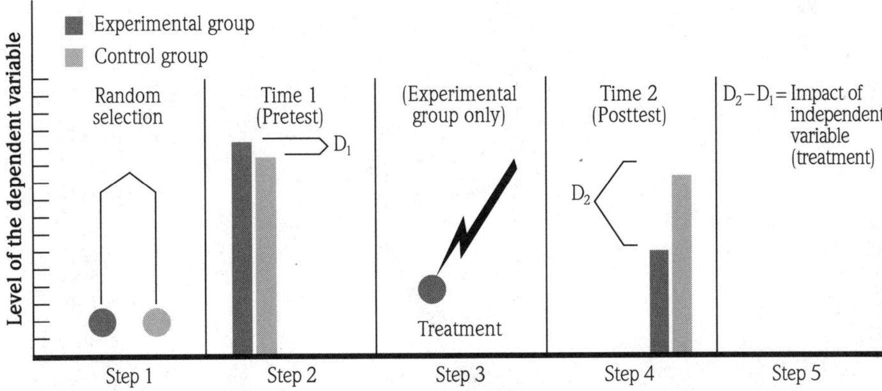

Figure 2.1 Experimental design. (Based on a drawing by Vance Wisenbaker.)

dependent variable) when compared with control group individuals, you will have support for your hypothesis.

The formal experiment is certainly a powerful research method, but the reactions of individuals in a laboratory situation may be very different from their reactions in everyday life. Though it is not often feasible, it is possible to conduct an experiment in a natural setting. The main problem is finding naturally occurring control and experimental groups—two groups that are alike in every way in terms of the range of individuals that make them up. You could then subject one of these groups to your experimental situation and compare the two groups later. Generally speaking, however, two groups of people found in a natural setting would already have differences in membership. Two university classrooms would have different kinds of people in them since, for example, different kinds of people take art classes than take business classes. How about using two business classes? Perhaps different kinds of people prefer each of the two teachers. How about two sections from the same teacher? Perhaps different kinds of people sign up for morning classes than for afternoon classes. The possibilities for built-in differences are endless. If you find differences in the two groups after your experiment, you will never know whether those differences are the result of your experiment or were present when you began.

A more typical but less powerful sociological method is to begin with groups that we pretend to be control and experimental groups. For example, how would you test a hypothesis concerning the effects of religious beliefs on political attitudes? You could find a group of people who adhere to one kind of belief, evaluate their political attitudes, and then compare that evaluation with the attitudes of another group of people who adhere to some other religious belief. But is that an experiment? The problem is that two religious groups (Catholics and Protestants, for example) already differ from each other in so many ways that you will never know whether the difference in political attitudes is caused by differences in religious beliefs or by some other difference. Just for example, as a group Protestants in the United States are wealthier than Catholics. Protestants also vote Republican more often. Do they vote Republican because they are Protestants, because they are wealthier, or for some other reason? In this kind of research, cause and effect

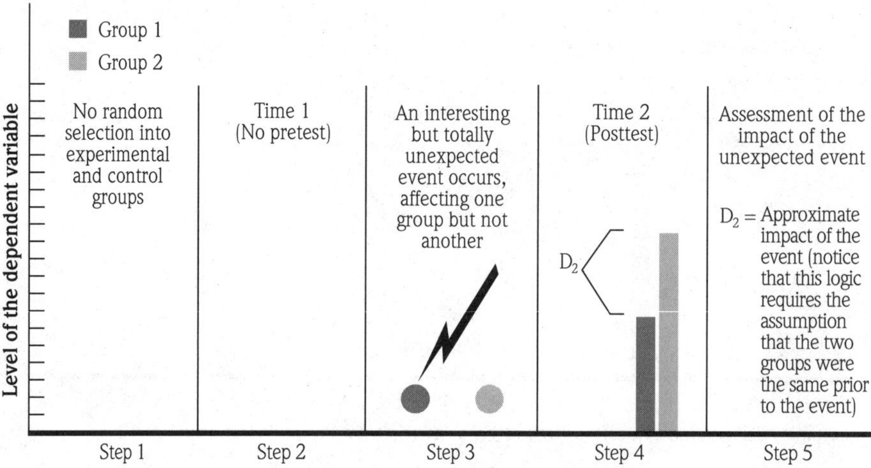

Figure 2.2 Design of nonexperimental research. (Based on a drawing by Vance Wisenbaker.)

is difficult to pin down. Figure 2.2 graphically illustrates the shortcomings of such research when compared to the formal experiment (Figure 2.1).

Participant Observation In **participant observation** the sociologist becomes personally involved in the everyday lives of the people under study—lives with them, talks to them, jokes with them, dines with them, works with them, and worships with them. The sociologist is half an observer of their lives and half a participant in their lives. This style of research gives the sociologist an idea of how the people under study think and feel about themselves and others. The general sociological observer might know where and how they work, but the participant observer knows what they think about their jobs. Following our earlier example about religious beliefs and political attitudes, the participant observer might learn about the political concerns of the people under study and whether or not those people link their political concerns to their religious beliefs.

Participant observation has some disadvantages along with its advantages. The personal nature of this research makes it impractical for any kind of large-scale study. It is also limited directly by the perspective of the sociologist, who may have difficulty separating personal values and beliefs from observations. Furthermore, there is no guarantee that the people under study will tell the truth to the sociologist. They may lie intentionally or, more likely, present a side of themselves that reflects the way they prefer to be perceived rather than how they actually are. Finally, and to some most importantly, participant observation does not lend itself to the scientific *rule of replication.* Because a second sociologist is likely to get different information or have a different perspective from the first, a study is almost impossible to repeat.

Gathering Information In addition to creating their own data (or information) through some of the methods I have described, sociologists frequently gather a wide variety of information on social characteristics and behavior. Probably best known method is the personal interview or questionnaire (the national census proceeds in this manner). Through such means the sociologist can collect both factual information about individuals and less concrete information such as attitudes and beliefs. A questionnaire might ask for your religious affiliation and then ask you to agree or disagree with a series of political statements in order to arrive at a relationship between political and religious beliefs. Sociologists also make use of voting results, economic trends, consumer behavior, and figures on population change or geographical movement; anything people do that can be counted sooner or later finds its way into sociological research. Keep in mind also that social behavior in the past is also fair game for sociological inquiry. Historical data make up an important part of the sociological undertaking in that history allows sociologists to deal with issues of social change. Alan Banks's article at the end of Chapter 9 provides an excellent example of historical data used to answer sociological questions.

Research Ethics Before leaving this brief discussion of sociological methods, a word about research ethics is in order. Sociologists are bound by the same rules of ethics that are followed outside the boundaries of scientific inquiry. For example, it might be useful in a scientific sense for the sociologist to observe behavior after starting a revolution, setting fire to a crowded theater, or generating hatred between two racial groups—but it certainly wouldn't be ethical. The question of ethics in research is complicated; there is often disagreement as to exactly where the line should be drawn. It is impossible to develop a single code of ethics for sociological research without creating objections from some sociologists. In particular, one branch of sociology known as applied sociology seeks to use sociological knowledge to bring about social change. Social change, by definition, invariably ruffles someone's feathers, and that someone would no doubt declare the applied sociologist unethical. By the same token, a sociologist working to prevent social change might be viewed as unethical by the applied sociologist. Beyond following basic rules of human decency, the line of ethics in sociological research is difficult to nail down.

Statistics A stereotypical view of the sociologist is someone who goes out into the world armed with a questionnaire and returns with a mountain of statistics. As with most stereotypes, there is some truth to the image. For the beginning sociologist, statistics seem to make research results more complicated even though the reason for using them is to simplify results. The purpose of statistics is to turn observations into numbers so that (a) they become subject to the rules of mathematics, which makes analysis of the observations more flexible; and (b) it becomes possible to compare large numbers or a wide variety of observations. It is important to remember that statistics are just a means of communication. For some kinds of observation they are not feasible; for others they are useful. You can get your feet wet in data collection procedure by following the instructions in Box 2.2.

The numbers provided by statistics allow the sociologist to describe observations in a simplified manner commonly called **descriptive statistics**. The most simplified form is the basic tally. For example, we tally votes after an election; we can then say that candidate X received so many votes rather than describing each voter's trip to the polls followed by a rundown of Mr. Jones's vote and Ms. Smith's vote.

Now that you can think of numbers as simplifications rather than complications, consider the following observations: The same test is given to students in several different classes with

BOX 2.2

INTERSECTION WITH OBSERVERS

This exercise involves observing traffic patterns and coding your observations into tables. It will provide experience with data collection (observation) as well as experience in setting up and interpreting tables.

Step 1. This exercise should be done in small groups (3 to 5 observers) whenever possible. Select an intersection with one through street and one stop street. Select one easily observable characteristic of drivers such as age, race, or sex. As each eastbound vehicle approaches the intersection, Observer 1 should record the sex (or age) of the driver and then code the driver's response to the stop sign (a system of codes is given below). Observer 2 should record the same information for westbound drivers. Each group of observers should have a preliminary meeting to work out the details of the study and then spend at least 30 minutes observing traffic and recording data. Develop at least one hypothesis about the relationship between your two variables. For example, "Male drivers will be more likely to obey the stop sign than female drivers."

Step 2. Using the data collected in Step 1, construct a table modeled after the example table given below. Compute percentages for inclusion in your table along with the frequencies.

Step 3. Test your hypothesis using the data in the table.

Codes

Code	Description
1	Driver brings vehicle to a complete stop.
2	Driver brings vehicle to a near stop.
3	Driver slows down for the sign.
4	Driver continues through the intersection at a normal speed.

Example table (hypothetical data): Reaction to stop sign by sex of driver.

Driver's sex	Class 1	Class 2	Class 3	Class 4	Total
Female	12 (38%)	9 (29%)	7 (23%)	3 (10%)	31 (100%)
Male	6 (21%)	5 (17%)	10 (34%)	8 (28%)	29 (100%)

different teachers who are supposed to be covering the same material. The purpose of the test is to locate outstanding students. Two students achieve a score of 98 on the test (known as a *raw score*), one student from a morning class and one student from an afternoon class. Are the students equal? They certainly are in terms of knowing the material on the test, but are their achievements in learning that material equal? The rest of the tests in each of those two classes reveal that all of the scores in the morning class are quite high; the average (or mean) score is 81. In the afternoon class, however, the students as a group have done much more poorly on the test; their average (or mean) is only 63. Why the difference?

Since we didn't run a formal experiment with random assignment to classes, the difference could be the result of any number of factors. One possibility we might want to track down is the quality of teaching in the two classes. Assume we discover that the afternoon class teacher has missed over half the classes during the semester and has delivered poorly organized lectures in the other half. Our afternoon student with the 98 has probably had to work much harder for that score than the individual from the morning class. But how much harder?

Descriptive statistics allow us to change the number scores so that we will know exactly how far ahead of the rest of their respective classes each student who scored 98 was. The two students now have newly assigned scores (called *standard scores*) that reflect how far ahead of the pack they are. The two students may be equal in knowledge but unequal in perseverance. The raw score on the test will give us information on the first observation, whereas the standard score will tell us about the second. Descriptive statistics allow us to manipulate numbers so as to provide different kinds of observations or to view the same observations in different lights.

Because scientists are often interested in how measurements of variables relate to one another (which is what theories are all about, after all), they often subject those measurements to correlational analysis. **Correlations** measure the degree to which measurements of variables go up and down together. A high positive correlation means that as one observation goes up, so does the other. If we measured the heights and weights of one hundred people, we would find a high positive correlation, since taller people generally weigh more than shorter people. This is not true in every case, of course, but it is true in general. With this example, however, we know the cause. "Tallness" causes greater weight since it creates a bigger frame upon which to hang extra pounds. Scientists must be careful, however, as correlational statistics don't provide causal information along with the correlational information. Furthermore, they may lead the scientist in a totally wrong direction. For example, there is a correlation between rape and ice cream consumption: When more ice cream is consumed in a community, the incidence of rape goes up, and vice versa. However, ice cream does not *cause* rapists to attack; both rape and ice cream consumption go up in warm weather, and the two have no connection other than that (see Figure 2.3). On the other hand, early correlational research connecting cigarette smoking with health problems has since been shown to be a causal relation. Correlations can be useful, but they can also be hazardous to your scientific inquiry.

A second important use of statistics in sociological research is somewhat more complicated. **Inferential statistics** basically convey information on probabilities. The scientist is always on the lookout for the relations among the objects of study; when relationships pop up, one important question concerns the probability that they might have occurred by chance. Inferential statistics are used to analyze descriptive statistics in order to find how likely they were to turn out that way by happenstance.

Returning to our two classes and the different test scores in each, how likely is it that the average student in the morning class scored 81 while the average student in the afternoon class scored 63 purely by chance? Perhaps the teachers were of the same quality after all. It's also possible to flip a coin ten times and come up with ten heads, but it's unlikely. Inferential statistics tell us just how unlikely.

Use of inferential statistics in sociology ranges from relatively simple applications to very elaborate manipulations of numbers possible only with modern computers. A computer can look at a set of observations in a thousand different ways simultaneously, providing relationships among the observations that the lone scientist could never achieve. However elaborate some of these modern techniques are, we still return to the original assertion with which we

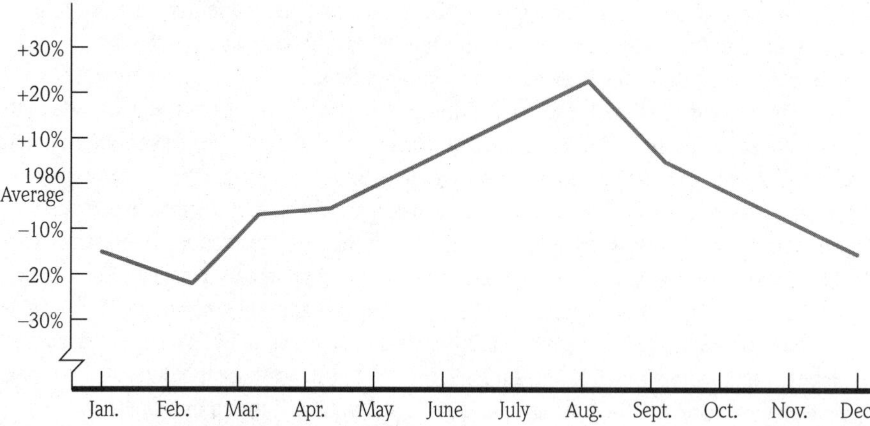

Figure 2.3 Reported forcible rape by month—variation from the annual average. Imagine how closely a graph of ice cream consumption would match this one. (Data from U.S. Department of Justice, 1986.)

began this section: Numbers simplify. Some of the most elaborate techniques take a great many observations and reduce them to just a few numbers.

You have probably noticed that, in this short section on statistics you have not learned to do anything. At this stage of your encounter with sociology, it is more useful just to acquire a general picture. Beginning students of methods and statistics sometimes miss the forest while they spend time inspecting the trees. There is much to be learned in the area of sociological research, but it is very important not to lose sight of what you are doing while you are doing it. Research is a means for testing theory, and statistics are a means for doing research. If you find the sociological outlook worth pursuing, you will have the opportunity to return to the methods of research when you have an important question that needs an answer.

SUMMARY

The sociological outlook is distinctive in the kinds of explanations it provides for human behavior. The sociologist looks for the "causes" of behavior in the coordinations of social groups, viewing individuals as group members and their actions in terms of group norms and values. Sociology differs from the discipline of psychology largely in the emphasis it places on the importance of social groups in individual behavior: Sociology seeks explanations in social groups, whereas psychology seeks explanations within the individual.

Though the sociological outlook is a distinctive perspective on human behavior, sociology as a social science has many similarities with other social sciences in the formation and testing of theories. Theories are the organized and logical explanations produced in any scientific endeavor. Theories are composed of concepts, which provide distinctive ways to view objects under study. Theories also predict the relations among those concepts, suggesting how changes in one concept would produce changes in another and why.

The sociological tradition has produced a wide variety of theories, many of which fall under three major headings. The structural-functionalist tradition focuses on the causes of consensus in society by investigating social structures to see how they help to maintain agreement among members of a society. The conflict tradition focuses on the manner in which social inequality is structured into the basic nature of society; theoretical research in this tradition attempts to explain how the strains caused by social inequality lead to social change or, alternately, how societal members in positions of power attempt to prevent that change from occurring. The interactionist tradition focuses more on the individual in society, emphasizing the manner in which individuals create social reality as their ongoing interactions lead to agreements (as well as changes in those agreements) concerning the basic norms and values of society.

Because sociology is a science, sociologists are under an obligation to test their theories according to the rules of the scientific method. Generally, the most accurate test is the formal experiment, in which the predicted "cause" of change is isolated. An experimental group of individuals is subjected to this isolated cause, while a similar control group is not; if changes occur in the first group after the experiment, this is an indication that the theory is accurate.

Although the formal experiment is a powerful research technique, sociologists are often unable to employ it because of the kinds of questions they are interested in. Moreover, some theories in sociology emphasize the voluntary nature of human action in the natural setting, which leads to less formal means of data collection.

Sociologists commonly transform the data they collect into numbers. This process, known as statistics, consists of two basic parts—description and inference. Descriptive statistics simplify observations by placing many observations into the same frame of reference; this process more fully describes the matter under observation. Inferential statistics, on the other hand, test theories by predicting the probabilities that certain relationships among the phenomena under study might have occurred by chance.

GLOSSARY

Concept An idea or notion created by focusing upon specific similarities among perceptions while ignoring differences.

Conflict theory A school of sociological theory that focuses on the inherent strains and conflicts in social relations and the use of power by members of society to further their interests in the light of that conflict.

Correlation A descriptive statistic (usually varying from -1.0 to $+1.0$) that measures the degree to which two or more observations (or variables) rise and fall together, suggesting a relationship between the two.

Descriptive statistics The transformation of observations into numbers in such a way that the observations are described (how many, to what extent, etc.).

Experiment (formal) A method of hypothesis testing in which the objects to which the hypothesis applies (people, white rats, or whatever) are assigned randomly to two groups, the experimental and the control groups. The experimental group is then subjected to a particular experimental condition (the presumed "cause"), while the control group is not. Resulting differences between the two groups should be due to the experimental condition.

Hypothesis An experimental prediction based on a causal theory. ("If this happens, then that should happen.")

Ideology An idea or set of ideas that represents a particular interest of a particular social group. As defined by Karl Marx, it refers specifically to the set of beliefs that supports the interests of a ruling class in society.

Inferential statistics The analysis of scientific observations that assesses the probability of certain relationships occurring by chance.

Interactionist perspective A school of sociological theory that perceives human behavior as a meaningful response to an agreed-upon social reality shared by and created by members of society.

Latent functions The unintentional or hidden functions provided by social structures that may not be known or understood until the structure is altered.

Manifest functions The obvious (or intended) functions provided by social structures.

Measurement The assignment of numbers to some specific characteristic according to a specified rule.

Operational definition The definition of a concept in terms of the way it is measured.

Participant observation A form of sociological analysis in which the sociologist becomes personally involved in the everyday lives of the people under study, hoping to learn how they see their world and how they feel about it.

Science A form of knowledge that attempts to provide causal explanations of phenomena and tests of those explanations through empirical research.

Social science A scientific discipline that studies human behavior through a perspective on the social context of that behavior. Included are such disciplines as sociology, psychology, anthropology, political science, and geography.

Sociology A social science that seeks the causes of human behavior in the workings of the social groups and institutions within which humans live.

Structural-functionalism A school of sociological theory that focuses on the interrelations among the elements of a society, emphasizing how elements of the social structure function to maintain the society.

Theory A specification of relationships among concepts that predicts the degree to which they affect each other and explains why.

Variable A trait or characteristic subject to changes (or variations) from case to case (such as an individual's height, weight, level of education, or income). *Independent* and *dependent variables* make up a pair of such traits or characteristics in which one (the independent variable) is believed and demonstrated to cause changes in the other (the dependent variable).

Verstehen A method of sociological interpretation in which the sociologist attempts to gain an understanding of what an individual thinks about or means by his or her social behavior.

SUPPLEMENTARY READINGS

Cole, Stephen *The Sociological Method* (2nd ed.). Chicago: Rand McNally, 1976.
Cole introduces the reader to sociological research techniques by focusing on the logic of sociological inquiry and the ability of various techniques to match that logic. He includes many clear examples.

Collins, Randall, and Michael Makowsky *The Discovery of Society* (4th ed.). New York: Random House, 1989.
An introduction to sociological theory, both classic and modern. Collins and Makowsky take a difficult topic and present it with great clarity and with an eye to the implications of the work of each theorist they discuss.

Cuzzort, R. P. *Using Social Thought: The Nuclear Issue and Other Concerns.* Mountain View, CA: Mayfield Publishing Co.
Cuzzart answers a question that some sociology students raise in their first theory class: "What's the point?" Each chapter spins off from a major social thinker and explores the ramifications of that social view for understanding contemporary social problems as well as current philosophical issues.

Dushkin Publishing Group, Inc. *The Encyclopedic Dictionary of Sociology* (3rd ed.). Guilford, CT: Dushkin, 1986.
Half encyclopedia and half dictionary, this volume contains a little of what every sociologist should know about everything sociological. A must for the bookshelf of any sociology major.

Hoover, Kenneth R. *The Elements of Social Scientific Thinking* (2nd ed.). New York: St. Martin's, 1980.
A brief, clear discussion of a complex topic. Hoover views social scientific research as an extension of science in general and social science in particular. He particularly emphasizes the nature of scientific thinking and its implications for the knowledge produced in its name.

Oppenheim, A. N. *Questionnaire Design and Attitude Measurement.* New York: Basic Books, 1966.
An in-depth discussion of questionnaires and their use in providing scales for the measurement of attitudes.

Phillips, Bernard *Sociological Research Methods: An Introduction.* Homewood, Ill.: Dorsey Press, 1985.
An introduction to both research design and statistical data analysis. The writing style is easy to read, and Phillips includes many examples and illustrations that make difficult material easier to follow.

Reynolds, Paul D. *Ethics and Social Science Research.* Englewood Cliffs, N.J.: Prentice-Hall, 1982.
Research ethics are a particular problem for sociology and all the social sciences. Reynolds considers the research problems presented by ethical roadblocks and offers some solutions.

Selltiz, Claire, Lawrence S. Wrightsman, and Stuart W. Cook *Research Methods in Social Relations* (3rd ed.). New York: Holt, Rinehart and Winston, 1976.
A general and comprehensive overview of social research, including discussions of logic, types of research design, problems of measurement, methods of data collection and analysis, and research ethics.

Smith, Gary *Statistical Reasoning* (2nd Ed.). Boston: Allyn & Bacon, 1988.
One of the celarest and most comprehensive introductions to the world of statistical analysis, this volume comes to us from the world of economics, not sociology. Nevertheless, numbers are numbers, and clear writing is always an asset.

Wax, Rosalie *Doing Fieldwork.* Chicago: University of Chicago Press, 1978.
Rosalie Wax is a cultural anthropologist who employs the method of participant observation often used by sociologists. In this somewhat autobiographical book, Wax takes the reader through many of her own experiences with fieldwork.

The Sociological Imagination

C. WRIGHT MILLS

C. Wright Mills became a prominent American sociologist in the 1950s, bringing both enthusiasm and a critical attitude to the discipline. The following excerpt is from his book *The Sociological Imagination,* published in 1959. In it he points out the basic difference between private troubles and public issues. Private troubles are those that occur at the individual level, whereas public issues are those problems that have their root in the workings of society. A fundamental aspect of the sociological imagination, says Mills, is to understand the impact of society on its members.

Perhaps the most fruitful distinction with which the sociological imagination works is between "the personal troubles of milieu" and "the public issues of social structure." This distinction is an essential tool of the sociological imagination and a feature of all classic work in social science.

Troubles occur within the character of the individual and within the range of his immediate relations with others; they have to do with his self and with those limited areas of social life of which he is directly and personally aware. Accordingly, the statement and the resolution of troubles properly lie within the individual as a biographical entity and within the scope of his immediate milieu—the social setting that is directly open to his personal experience and to some extent his willful activity. A trouble is a private matter: values cherished by an individual are felt by him to be threatened.

Issues have to do with matters that transcend these local environments of the individual and the range of his inner life. They have to do with the organization of many such milieux into the institutions of an historical society as a whole, with the ways in which various milieux overlap and interpenetrate to form the larger structure of social and historical life. An issue is a public matter: some value cherished by publics is felt to be threatened. Often there is a debate about what that value really is and about what it is that really threatens it. This debate is often without focus if only because it is the very nature of an issue, unlike even widespread trouble, that it cannot very well be defined in terms of the immediate and everyday environments of ordinary men. An issue, in fact, often involves a crisis in institutional arrangements, and often, too, it involves what Marxists call "contradictions" or "antagonisms."

In these terms, consider unemployment. When, in a city of 100,000, only one man is unemployed, that is his personal trouble, and for its relief we properly look to the character of the man, his skills, and his immediate opportunities. But when in a nation of 50 million employees, 15 million men are unemployed, that is an issue, and we may not hope to find its solution within the range of opportunities open to any one individual. The very structure of opportunities has collapsed. Both the correct statement of the problem and the range of possible solutions require us to consider the economic and political institutions of the society, and not merely the personal situation and character of a scatter of individuals.

Consider war. The personal problem of war, when it occurs, may be how to survive

From *The Sociological Imagination* by C. Wright Mills. Copyright © 1959 by Oxford University Press, Inc.; renewed 1987 by Yaraslava Mills. Reprinted by permission of the publisher.

it or how to die in it with honor; how to make money out of it; how to climb into the higher safety of the military apparatus; or how to contribute to the war's termination. In short, according to one's values, to find a set of milieux and within it to survive the war or to make one's death in it meaningful. But the structural issues of war have to do with its causes; with what types of men it throws up into command; with its effects upon economic and political, family and religious institutions, with the unorganized irresponsibility of a world of nation-states.

Consider marriage. Inside a marriage a man and a woman may experience personal troubles, but when the divorce rate during the first four years of marriage is 250 out of every 1,000 attempts, this is an indication of a structural issue having to do with the institutions of marriage and the family and other institutions that bear upon them.

Or consider the metropolis—the horrible, beautiful, ugly, magnificent sprawl of the great city. For many upper-class people, the personal solution to "the problem of the city" is to have an apartment with private garage under it in the heart of the city, and forty miles out, a house by Henry Hill, garden by Garrett Eckbo, on a hundred acres of private land. In these two controlled environments—with a small staff at each end and a private helicopter connection—most people could solve many of the problems of personal milieux caused by the facts of the city. But all this, however splendid, does not solve the public issues that the structural fact of the city poses. What should be done with this wonderful monstrosity? Break it all up into scattered units, combining residence and work? Refurbish it as it stands? Or, after evaluation, dynamite it and build new cities according to new plans in new places? What should those plans be? And who is to decide and to accomplish whatever choice is made? These are structural issues: to confront them and to solve them requires us to consider political and economic issues that affect innumerable milieux.

Insofar as an economy is so arranged that slumps occur, the problem of unemployment becomes incapable of personal solution. Insofar as war is inherent in the nation-state system and in the uneven industrialization of the world, the ordinary individual in his restricted milieu will be powerless—with or without psychiatric aid—to solve the troubles this system or lack of system imposes upon him. Insofar as the family as an institution turns women into darling little slaves and men into their chief providers and unweaned dependents, the problem of a satisfactory marriage remains incapable of purely private solution. Insofar as the overdeveloped megalopolis and the overdeveloped automobile are built-in features of the overdeveloped society, the issues of urban living will not be solved by personal ingenuity and private wealth.

What we experience in various and specific milieux, I have noted, is often caused by structural changes. Accordingly, to understand the changes of many personal milieux we are required to look beyond them. And the number and variety of such structural changes increase as the institutions within which we live become more embracing and more intricately connected with one another. To be aware of the idea of social structure and to use it with sensibility is to be capable of tracing such linkages among a great variety of milieux. To be able to do that is to possess the sociological imagination.

Discussion Questions

1. What is Mills's distinction between private troubles and public issues? In your own life situation, how might you tell whether a particular difficulty is one or the other?
2. Why is Mills's perspective on public issues specifically a *sociological* perspective?
3. Pick a problem that you currently face in your life. Describe it first as a private trouble (you probably already have) and then list possible kinds of solutions to it. Second, describe that same problem as public issue, placing it more into a sociological perspective as described by Mills. What different kinds of solutions arise now?

Hollywood

PART TWO

SOCIAL PROCESSES AND INTERACTIONS

CHAPTER 3 THE GROWTH OF CULTURE: THE BASIS FOR SOCIETY

As we have seen, humans are the only animals that live in coordinated groups self-consciously, which gives them the possibility of consciously changing the coordinated patterns by which they live. In Chapter 1 we introduced the concept of culture. A **culture** contains all the objects, skills, ideas, beliefs, and patterns of behavior that are developed and shared by members of social groups; anything that is created and shared by groups of humans is part of culture. This chapter returns to the discussion of culture, providing a more detailed look at the elements of culture and how they develop.

CULTURE AND SOCIETY

Culture is commonly divided into two aspects. The physical creations of humans are referred to as **material culture**. This book you are holding and the technology that produced it, for example, are elements of your material culture; the book exists not only as a result of my actions as author but as a result of the actions and inventions of a great many other people, both alive and dead. Also included within material culture are those physical objects that are naturally created but given meaning by humans. Gold, for example, is a very important part of every culture in the industrial world. The way naturally occurring objects can become part of culture suggests an important facet to material culture that will be developed later on: Objects become part of culture not just because people create them but because of the way people think about them.

Nonmaterial culture refers to all human creations that are not physical—ideas, beliefs, skills, language, and so on. Nonmaterial culture is the foundation of culture, for it is ideas that make objects a part of culture. Those ideas also stand behind and give meaning to every human activity. To the sociologist nonmaterial culture represents a vast array of ideas, beliefs, and traditions that are developed over time and passed on to each new generation. A major portion of this chapter will be devoted to an examination of the many elements that make up nonmaterial culture.

In a large and complex society such as the United States it is difficult to speak of a single culture, either material or nonmaterial. Although many things, ideas, and beliefs are common to much of the population, poor people, for example, use different things, think different thoughts, and hold different beliefs than rich people. Black people are different from white people, rural people are different from city people, sociologists are different from used-car salesmen, and punk rockers are unlikely to spend their afternoons mingling with retired couples. The people in each of these pairs live in some degree of physical or social isolation from each other. They all share some elements of American culture, but their isolation makes them different over time. We can use the concept *subculture* to describe these differences. A **subculture** refers to those specific objects, skills, ideas, beliefs, and patterns of behavior that are unique to individual segments of an overall population and that differ from the larger culture. Subcultures develop through isolation, whether that isolation is caused by physical or social separation. Subcultures develop from differences in geography, occupation, age, race, ethnicity, income, education, hobbies, politics, or religion, to name a few of the possibilities.

The concept of *subculture* is particularly useful to the sociologist because it focuses attention on degrees of cultural difference and similarity. For example, you and I both speak English, but I can use terms specific to the discipline of sociology that you may not understand. In return you could use terms specific to your background that I would not understand. If we met, these differences might seem large and important, making us feel very separate from each other. If we were joined by someone from Outer Mongolia, however, our cultural differences from each other would seem less important in contrast to our mutual differences from our foreign guest. In the terms of sociology we share the same culture but occupy different subcultures. In trying to understand us, the sociologist might emphasize either the similarity of culture or the difference in subculture, depending on the question under investigation.

Cultural Variations

Outside the forms of coordination necessary to human survival that it provides, culture can vary tremendously from one social group to another or even within the same social group from one time to another. For example, in the United States, there have been major changes in the family just within the last three generations. People do different things for entertainment, have different standards for behavior, and hold different values. Box 3.1 documents a few of the many changes in sexual behavior that have occurred in Western culture over time, fluctuating between times of sexual openness and sexual repressiveness.

More striking examples of cultural variation can be found in different cultures around the world. The Semai of Malaya live with the utmost cooperation in their daily lives, and they have no system of social stratification. They avoid violence at all costs and have an extremely nonviolent view of themselves. At the other extreme the Yanomamo tribe in South America has turned fighting and aggression into the reason for its existence. Hostile behavior occurs in almost all social situations, and warfare with neighboring tribes is an ongoing state with a beginning no one can remember and with no end in sight.

Everyday practices in cultures around the world often seem strange from our perspective. Among Eskimos traditionally, male visitors to a home might have sexual intercourse with the host's wife as part of the general hospitality shown them. This practice carries much of the symbolic meaning that sharing food and drink has in American culture. Lest you think Eskimos are simply promiscuous, having intercourse with a man's wife without his permission is considered adultery and is a serious offense. The Etero and Marind-anim tribes in New Guinea follow norms that prohibit sexual relations between men and women during most of the months of the year; as a result, both of these tribes are primarily homosexual in their behavior. The Caribs in South America practice the *couvade,* in which women return to their daily routine immediately after having babies, while their husbands take to bed for a lengthy recovery from the ordeal of childbirth. Some Indian tribes in Canada used to practice the *potlatch,* a ritual gift-giving social occasion during which gifts of great value would sometimes be destroyed by the giver as a symbolic gesture aimed at tribal rivals.

Although cultures around the world seem to have infinite variation, they are nonetheless somewhat limited by the necessities of survival. Culture must provide for basic human needs and, in so doing, must take the local environment into account: A culture that effectively satisfies human needs in the jungle will not work well in the desert. Sociologists and anthropologists deal with these limitations through the concepts of cultural universals and cultural adaptation.

BOX 3.1

Sex Through the Ages

No two cultures are alike, but even the same culture can look as different as day and night at two different time periods. Consider Judd Marmor's (1971:165-166) description of the changes in sexual practices in Western culture over the years:

> Even a cursory look at the recorded history of human sexuality makes it abundantly clear that patterns of sexual behavior and morality have taken many diverse forms over the centuries. Far from being "natural" and inevitable, our contemporary sexual codes and mores, seen in historical perspective, would appear no less grotesque to people of other eras than theirs appear to us. Our attitudes concerning nudity, virginity, fidelity, love, marriage, and "proper" sexual behavior are meaningful only within the context of our own cultural and religious mores. Thus, in the first millennium of the Christian era, in many parts of what is now Europe, public nudity was no cause for shame (as is still true in some aboriginal settings), virginity was not prized, marriage was usually a temporary arrangement, and extramarital relations were taken for granted. Frank and open sexuality was the rule, and incest was frequent. Women were open aggressors in inviting sexual intercourse. Bastardy was a mark of distinction because it often implied that some important person had slept with one's mother. In early feudal times new brides were usually deflowered by the feudal lord (*jus primae noctis*). In other early societies all the wedding guests would copulate with the bride. Far from being considered a source of concern to the husband, these practices were considered a way of strengthening the marriage in that the pain of the initial coitus would not be associated with the husband.
>
> It was not until the Medieval Church was able to strengthen and extend its control over the people of Europe that guilt about sexuality began to be a cardinal feature of Western life. Even the early Hebraic laws against adultery had nothing to do with fidelity but were primarily concerned with protecting the property rights of another man (the wife being considered property). Married men were free to maintain concubines or, if they preferred, multiple wives; also, there was no ban in the Old Testament on premarital sex. The Medieval Church, however, exalted celibacy and virginity. In its efforts to make license in sexual intercourse as difficult as possible, it sanctioned it only for procreative purposes and ordained laws against abortion—laws that had not existed among the Greeks, Romans, or Jews. At one time it went so far as to make sexual intercourse between married couples illegal on Sundays, Wednesdays, and Fridays, as well as for forty days before Easter and forty days before Christmas, and also from the time of conception to forty days after parturition. (By contrast, Mohammedan law considered it grounds for divorce if intercourse did not take place at least once a week.)

(continues)

BOX 3.1 (continued)

The ideals of romantic love and marriage for love which are taken for granted today are a relatively late development in Western history and did not make their appearance until the twelfth century A.D. Clearly, there is nothing about our current sexual attitudes and practices that can be assumed to be either sacrosanct or immutable. They have been subject to much change and evolution in the past, and they will undoubtedly be different in the future. (Copyright 1971, American Medical Association. Reprinted by permission.)

Variations in culture over time show us that although any one way of living may seem right to us, it is not the only way to live. This description of changes in sexual practices also reminds us that current lifestyles often convince us to alter our memories of the past. The way we live now seems more valid if we can convince ourselves that "it's always been that way."

Cultural Universals

Cultural universals are those beliefs, behavior patterns, and institutions that are found in all known cultures. This concept is difficult to work with. Since no two cultures could ever be exactly alike, it becomes necessary to decide when similarity can be called "the same." For example, all cultures regulate sexual behavior and specify people between whom sexual relations must never occur; anthropologists call these specifications the rules of incest, or *incest taboos.* In American society the rules of incest prohibit sexual relations between parents and children, between siblings, and usually between first cousins. With only a very few and highly unusual exceptions, every human culture prohibits sexual relations between parents and children and between siblings; many cultures in fact go much further in their incest restrictions. Presumably, therefore, some form of incest can be called a cultural universal.

Could the family be called a cultural universal? This question brings us face to face with the ambiguity of the concept. To the extent that a family is a social organization that creates and cares for babies, yes. A culture that does not get that job done will not be around long enough for an anthropologist to discover it. On the other hand, you will not find the same family organization in any two cultures. All families create and care for babies but they do so in endlessly creative ways.

The concept *cultural universal* calls our attention to many of the basic problems all humans must solve if they are to survive. The more alike different cultures are with regard to a particular element—such as incest rules—the more necessary that element probably is to survival. Presumably, cultures that ignored the regulation of sex ran into difficulties somewhere along the line.

Cultural Adaptation

Cultural adaptation refers to the manner in which people adapt their cultures to the necessities of survival. These necessities may stem from our animal needs or from the physical or social environment. Some sort of family organization, for example, is necessary because of the manner in which humans are born and their long period of helplessness; a culture must adapt to that requirement. In a society that has become industrialized and densely populated, small families would be valued; we can see this in changes over the last fifty years in American culture. A culture adapted to a desert would, of necessity, develop means for coping with sand and conserving water. Whatever the source of the necessity, culture can adapt.

If we look at cultural adaptation together with cultural universals, some interesting questions about human cultures arise. The universality of incest rules, for example, suggests that all cultures must have faced the same necessity to have adapted in the same way. One suggestion is that rules of incest are necessary to keep peace in the family—imagine the jealousies that could develop if mothers left their husbands for their sons. Other observers have suggested that rules of incest are necessary to eliminate confusions in inheritance, since property follows kinship lines in most cultures. Still others suggest that mating within families leads to genetic complications and that cultures have coped with this problem either instinctively or through trial and error with rules of incest. Whichever (if any) explanation is true, the universality of incest rules as a cultural adaptation sheds some light on the problems of survival that human cultures attempt to solve. All cultural adaptations direct our attention to the relation between culture and human survival and the many variations that human beings have developed for dealing with the problems of survival.

MATERIAL CULTURE

As we have seen, the concept of material culture includes all the physical things that humans create for their use and also naturally occurring objects to which humans add meaning. Not only is this general definition practical, it also calls attention to the unbreakable connection between material and nonmaterial culture: An object cannot be part of the material culture unless people think about it in the realm of the nonmaterial culture. Nevertheless, there are important differences between the two realms. In this section we will look first at how material and nonmaterial culture affect each other and then at the ways in which meanings are attached to elements in the material culture.

How Material and Nonmaterial Culture Affect Each Other

One theory about the connections between material and nonmaterial culture is William Ogburn's *theory of cultural lag* (Ogburn, 1964). Ogburn observed that elements of culture seem to change at different rates. In particular, he noted, the things that people think and believe are often more appropriate to the lives they used to live rather than to what they are currently doing. For example, in the United States today one in two marriages ends in divorce, yet ideals of married bliss and "till death do us part" are still very much part of our nonmaterial culture.

Part of the reason for this "lag" is that humans don't always know what will result from their technology; building something new may significantly affect the way people live before they really have a chance to think about it. The automobile, for example, was initially seen as a cute new toy that would never replace the horse. It wasn't until Henry Ford began mass producing cars that their impact on every aspect of American life could be seen. Other reasons for cultural lag stem from the attachments that people come to feel for their cultures. The force

Cultural universals are those elements that are found more or less in the same form in all known cultures. All cultures provide means for acquiring or manufacturing food and distributing it. However, no two cultures are exactly alike, and a great many differences may be noted upon close inspection.

of habit and tradition keep elements of nonmaterial culture thriving even when they appear to be fighting a losing battle against the changing times.

Ogburn's theory of cultural lag doesn't deny the connection between material and nonmaterial culture. Even if nonmaterial culture lags behind developments in technology (and the like), it is nevertheless affected by those developments and changes accordingly. The automobile did come to be an integral part of American nonmaterial culture. We even value cars in their own right, desiring certain models and styles. Some observers suggest that the cars we buy are extensions of our sexual feelings about ourselves, providing us a sense of power and mastery over our environment. A technological development in this case turned into a love affair. Another inescapable part of American life now is television, which shapes our leisure time, our attitudes, our knowledge about the world, and even our behavior.

As the technology of material culture affects the nonmaterial culture, so changes in the nonmaterial culture affect technology in return. The introduction of the automobile led to many changes in American life as values developed related to cars and their use, but those new values in turn affected cars. The speed of cars led us to value speed, which led us to create cars that

could go faster. As cars went faster, it became necessary to improve the technology of road construction so the new cars would have a place to run. As roads were built, it became possible to develop a trucking industry for the transportation of goods. As trucks made waterways and railroad tracks less important, cities grew in different places. Such interrelations between material and nonmaterial culture could be continued indefinitely. As Ogburn pointed out, the elements of culture don't always change at the same rate, but they are all part of the whole and none changes alone.

The Attachment of Meaning to Material Culture

"Things" become part of material culture only when humans think about them and attach meaning to them. A church building, for example, could be just another building, but any member of American culture knows the difference. Americans think about their church buildings differently than they think about banks or supermarkets. Consider, for example, how different your reaction would be to hearing that a local church was vandalized as opposed to hearing the same about the local supermarket. You would probably assume that the vandal also thought and felt differently in each case. Such differences in meaning are not inherent in the objects themselves but are added to them by social groups. As the members of social groups come to think about objects differently over time, so the objects become different objects for all intents and purposes.

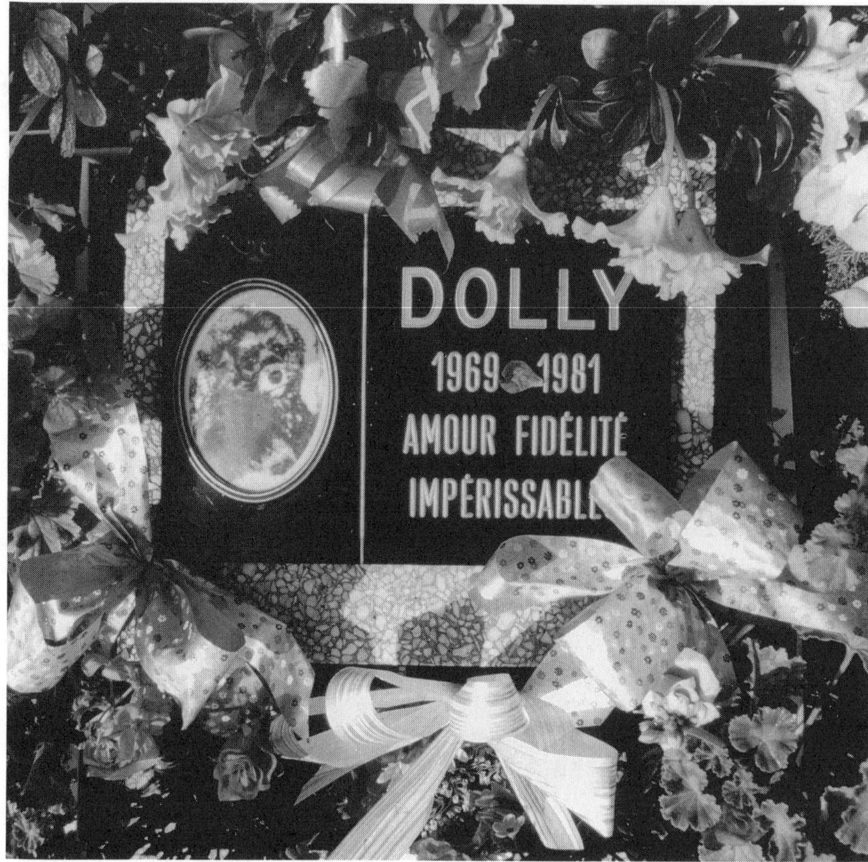

In some cultures dogs are cherished pets. This gravestone commemorating Dolly is in France, where dogs are welcome to accompany their owners into many restaurants. In other cultures, dogs may serve a more utilitarian need, as in this market in China.

The meanings attached to material culture can be seen in all walks of life and at all levels of society. How do you act, for example, when you have guests in your home? You might offer them something to eat, but in offering that part of your material culture you are also offering a symbolic welcome to your home in the nonmaterial culture. Inviting someone to eat with you does far more than satisfy the hunger of the guest; it communicates a facet of your social relationship. Is your guest thirsty? Consider the difference between offering a glass of water, a cup of coffee, or a glass of fine (and expensive) wine. A glass of water contains only a small welcome, while the glass of wine contains a large one. It could be argued that the money invested in each item determines the size of the welcome, but coffee (or tea) has traditionally carried a symbolic welcome whether expensive or inexpensive. Or perhaps it is the labor of the host in making the coffee that carries the meaning. All of these explanations are possible. But a piece of material culture can also contain meaning for no other reason than that the members of a social group agree it should. You may think gold is valuable because it's hard to find, but albino squirrels are also hard to find.

Perhaps an even better example of this process can be seen in the world of art. What makes a painting expensive? Obviously, the demand for the work of a particular artist makes certain paintings expensive, but where does the demand come from? The demand comes from decisions made and agreed to by certain people who are influential in shaping the tastes of the art-buying public. If those influential people decide that Rembrandt does good work, Rembrandt's work becomes important and then valuable. It is common for the paintings of an artist unknown during his or her lifetime (van Gogh, for example) to become very valuable later. Do the paintings change, or is it just that new meanings become attached to them? The material culture doesn't change, but in a sense it becomes transformed as the meanings change. Objects such as paintings come to be looked at more closely or perhaps just in a different light as the nonmaterial culture assigns them new meanings.

These examples of art, gold, and socializing over food and drink all illustrate a fundamental aspect of the relationship between material and nonmaterial culture: The meanings attached by the nonmaterial culture *must be shared* by the members of the social group if they are to be considered part of the culture. You may personally decide that albino squirrels are important and begin collecting them, but unless you can convince others to value them similarly, your personal meanings regarding them will remain personal and will not be cultural. By the same token, welcoming a guest with coffee or wine carries no significance unless your guest recognizes those objects as symbols of welcome (that is, shares the meaning that you attach to those objects in that situation). As we saw earlier, an Eskimo host may offer his wife's sexual favors to a guest as a symbol of welcome, but such an action would conjure up very different ideas within most segments of American culture.

You may wonder why this discussion of material culture has focused largely on nonmaterial culture. The emphasis has been intentional. It points to the central nature of nonmaterial culture in all human affairs. The only complexity in material culture is that introduced by the nonmaterial culture. Of particular interest to sociologists is the fact that nonmaterial culture is the product of *collective* human imaginations and is ultimately shared by the humans that create it. The remainder of this chapter will examine the primary elements that make up the nonmaterial culture in human societies.

NONMATERIAL CULTURE

In turning our attention to the nonphysical realm of human creations in nonmaterial culture, we encounter a wide range of ideas, beliefs, expectations, and meanings. All these facets of the human imagination are learned through socialization, are added to, deleted, or changed over time, and are subsequently passed on to the next generation. As human societies persist, their nonmaterial cultures can grow extremely complex. This complexity can be made a little more manageable by separating nonmaterial culture into two basic categories: modes of social interaction and meanings of social interaction. The *modes of social interaction* include concepts such as norm and role, which call our attention to the patterned behavior that societal members follow and the society's expectations that others should follow these patterns. The *meanings of social interaction* include cultural elements such as values and knowledge that direct our attention to the thoughts that members of a society have about their behaviors and the reasons they develop for following them.

In practice, both modes and meanings of social interaction exist together. For example, a student in modern American society plays the role of student in response to the normative expectations to be found in the institution of education. Playing that role and following those norms involve conforming to a wide variety of patterned behavior. At the college level these patterns include registering, securing living arrangements, developing a major program of study, getting up in the morning to go to classes, finding classrooms, taking a seat, buying books, taking notes and tests, avoiding direct insults to teachers and administrators, and so on. All of these behaviors typical of the student role fall under the heading of modes of social interaction. But why play the role in the first place? American culture values education and the people who get it from acceptable (accredited) sources. You may hope to attain occupational and other rewards in the future for playing that role today. If you have accepted the American value of education, you may enjoy playing the student role in its own right as you move toward a goal of graduation and thinking of yourself as an "educated person." These meanings attached to education give people reasons for playing the roles.

Norms and Roles: Modes of Social Interaction

Social scientists observe that human behavior is both patterned and coordinated. But the repetition of social life is not lost on the social actors themselves. People come to plan on following the patterns of behavior within their cultures and, perhaps more important, come to expect that others will do the same. Such shared expectations are referred to as **norms.**

Norms In referring to norms as shared expectations, sociologists mean that two individuals who share a culture also share expectations as to each other's behavior. If you and I share a culture, this means that the plans I make for what I will do next are more or less in tune with what you expect me to do next. And one of the things I will take into consideration as I plan is my expectation that you will have an expectation that corresponds with my plan. Putting this into words makes it sound confusing, but in everyday life the process itself is not difficult. In making our plans of action, we spend much of our time guessing as to others' expectations. Generally, we become aware of this guessing process only when we guess wrong and others respond to us in ways we had not prepared for. This can happen when behavior is misinterpreted ("No, Mary, that's not what I meant by that") or when others hold norms we are unaware of ("No, Tom, going out to dinner with you does not mean that you're welcome to spend the night").

Norms make up the rules we follow in our social behavior, and they can become as complex as we want to make them. Imagine meeting a good friend on a street corner, starting a conversation, and then being joined in turn by a priest, your employer, the town mayor, a panhandler, and one of your parents. Consider how the social situation would change with each new addition to the group. Each newcomer might make it necessary to change the topic of conversation, alter your word selection, and even change your physical posture. Any such changes would be responses to social norms as you alter your behavior in response to new expectations.

In order to understand norms, you must have an elaborate knowledge of your culture and of all the slight differences among social relationships within it. Our children, who haven't had time yet to learn all this, often embarrass us in public by saying the wrong thing at the wrong time to the wrong person ("No, Jimmy, Daddy's boss doesn't want to hear what Daddy calls him at home"). The irony is that once we learn all the complexity for our particular culture, it seems simple, and we alter our behavior automatically in response to slight changes in norms.

Folkways, Mores, and Laws Cultures vary in the importance that is placed on different norms. In American society, for example, slurping your soup is not looked upon with as much concern as murdering the cook. While norms vary across a gradual range from the trivial to the serious, they are often divided into two general categories identified by early American sociologist William Graham Sumner (1840-1910): folkways and mores. **Folkways** are the less serious norms, which, when broken, bring only mild disapproval from others. Slurping your soup would clearly fall into this category. **Mores**, on the other hand, are the norms that are adhered to more forcefully in a culture. They make up the basic beliefs and patterns of behavior common to a social group that form a foundation for the everyday patterns of life. In American society, the unauthorized taking of a human life falls into this category. The only real way to distinguish folkways from mores is to watch what happens when the norm is broken. An emotional or violent response from others means that you have assaulted one of their mores; snickers, frowns, and mild ridicule indicate a violated folkway.

Mores commonly find their way into the rule of law. A *law* is perhaps the ultimate model of the norm, for it is an expectation for behavior that is written down and backed with the force of the society. But as complicated as law is, it can only scratch the surface of societal norms; as a result, only the more important norms (the mores) usually receive this treatment. Of soup slurping and murder, only the latter has found its way into our law. In the United States, where the norm is to have only one spouse at a time, we have laws against bigamy (having more than one spouse). In cultures where bigamy coincides with the mores, having more than one spouse is not only tolerated but respected. Even though bigamy does not do the damage that murder does, sanctions against it are equally a part of American mores and are represented by law.

Ideal and Real Norms There is often a difference between what we claim to expect from others and what we actually expect from them. In American society, for example, we claim to expect that marriages will last a lifetime and that adultery will not occur; in reality, however, we know that half of all marriages will end in divorce and that adultery is both a common and popular activity. Sociologists refer to these two kinds of expectations as ideal and real norms. **Ideal norms** are the expectations that we value and want to think will be followed. **Real norms** represent the patterns of behavior that people actually follow.

Differences between ideal and real norms exist because norms are always backed up by values. As patterns of behavior (or norms) develop in a society, reasons for following them (**values**) develop simultaneously. As we observed earlier, humans come to consciously value the forms of their sociability. As society changes, however, it may become necessary to develop new patterns of behavior. Because norms change more rapidly than values, we may find ourselves having to do things in opposition to our values. One way we cope with this conflict is to create ideal norms, which represent our values, and real norms, which guide our everyday lives.

The distinction between ideal and real norms allows us to understand some of the inconsistencies in our society, but it also calls attention to a basic problem confronting the sociologist. If a sociologist wants to learn the norms in a social group, asking group members how they act will only bring forth the ideal norms. The real norms may well be hidden from observation and hard to locate. One possible but sometimes impractical and dangerous approach is for the sociologist to break norms intentionally and observe how people react. The sociologist may be told that a norm is very important to a social group but, upon breaking it, discover that it is an ideal norm that many group members do not follow anyway.

Roles Norms and roles are closely connected in any society. Norms represent expectations for behavior, while **roles** represent the patterned behavior itself that follows these expectations. The term *role* comes to us from the theater. Actors step into roles in a play. The actors must be creative about how they portray the role, but much of the work is already done for them. The writer provides all the lines, some background on the character, and stage directions. The actor follows these directions and knows when to move, where to stand, what to say and to whom. Actors come and go, but roles remain for each new generation of actors.

Roles are not as well planned or as restrictive as theatrical roles, but there are many similarities. An employee, for example, must arrive for work on time and accomplish the work that he or she was hired to do. The employee will also soon discover how the boss expects to be treated, how co-workers expect to be treated, and so on. Some of these expectations may be written down as job descriptions; some will simply be "understood" and will be learned on the job. The employee does not, however, have exact lines written down to be said word-for-word in each situation as the actor does. A role consists only of general directives and limitations, within which the role player may be creative. An employee might be a little on the talkative side or more quiet and reserved without stepping beyond the boundaries of the role. A college student can quietly take notes or join in class discussions without stepping outside the role. In any case, roles are very real, with very real boundaries set by social norms. And like theatrical roles, social roles must be learned and practiced to be played properly.

From the individual's point of view, living in a society is the process of learning many roles and playing them according to the norms that govern different social situations. In a fairly complex society such as the United States the average adult will play a great many roles just in the course of one day. You might wake up in the morning and step into a variety of family roles (husband or wife, son or daughter, father or mother, sister or brother). You may switch from one of these roles to another in a matter of seconds, planning the day's activities with your husband in one room and then talking to your child in the next room, for example. As you switch roles, you will be responding to different norms, and your behavior will be quite different. You might stop at a store on your way to work and play the role of consumer in response to some stranger who is playing the role of retail clerk. (That clerk probably kissed his or her family good-bye shortly before, but you encounter the clerk only within the clerk role.) When you arrive at work, you will encounter another variety of roles, perhaps simultaneously playing the roles of employee, co-worker, and boss (if you have people working under you). You might then go to lunch with a co-worker who is also a close friend and, while in the restaurant, play the role of customer to someone else playing the role of waiter. We have only arrived at lunchtime, and already the complexity is evident. The amazing thing is that most of us have no difficulty whatever keeping track of all these roles. We step into and out of them automatically, change our behavior drastically as we do, and rarely become aware of ourselves as actors.

Playing roles takes much of the guesswork out of living. Of the many millions of things we say and do every day only a small number require any conscious planning. The plans come to us ready-made with the role. I can walk into a strange drugstore and buy a strange pack of chewing gum from a strange clerk without giving a thought to the process. I can automatically play the consumer role that I've played in other stores in the confidence that the clerk will behave much the same as many other store clerks I've encountered. Daily life under any circumstances would be difficult without roles, but consider how impossible city life would be without them. Cities are full of people who are strangers to us, but luckily those strange people play familiar roles. Without such patterns of behavior in daily life we would never be able to get through the day.

As we encounter others in their roles, so they encounter us in ours. As a result no single person will ever know the "whole you." Even your best friend may not know the side of you that comes out in the role of son or daughter or perhaps in the role of employee. You may discuss those roles with your best friend, but that friend will never experience you in those roles firsthand; it would be inappropriate to treat your best friend as your mother or your boss. In fact, you probably would not be able to keep a straight face if you tried it. This "compartmentalization" of ourselves into our roles becomes even more evident when we deal with strangers in roles or with less personal roles. The drugstore clerk no doubt has a full life, but your encounters with the clerk will give you the illusion that he or she lives in the store and has no other activities or interests. You will encounter only a very small part of that person, and he or she of you. Similarly, though you may have an everyday ongoing relationship with your employer, it may be limited to formal kinds of conversations relating to your work. Roles allow us to interact with people constantly without ever getting to know them if that is our choice (see Box 3.2).

Role Conflict The picture of role playing presented thus far gives the impression that roles make society a well-oiled and smooth-running machine. Few societies, however, exist without conflict. People may make mistakes in their roles through not having learned them properly, or they may choose not to play their roles according to the expectations of others. Either of these situations would lead to a disruption in the patterns of interaction. But additional problems exist in the realm of the role playing that sociologists term role conflict.

Role conflict occurs when people become confused as to how they should play their roles or even which role is appropriate in a given situation. In the first circumstance (sometimes called *role confusion* or *role strain*) people must play their roles to an "audience" whose members hold varying expectations as to how the role should be played (Goode, 1960). All teachers, for example, face this kind of role conflict. In any classroom there will inevitably be differences of opinion among the students as to whether the teacher should emphasize lectures or discussion. Some students will find certain modes of explanation and examples useful and interesting, while other students will find those same explanations and examples meaningless and boring. The teacher can't please everyone and must make a decision as to which expectations should be followed. In a highly diverse society, such as the United States, this kind of role conflict occurs to some degree in almost any situation where two or more people are responding to a role.

The second circumstance of role conflict is less common but a little more colorful. Usually, we keep our many roles separate from each other since they are specific to social situations that occur in different places at different times. But what do you do when two of those situations overlap? I was teaching an evening sociology class once when my four-year-old son came running into the classroom shouting "Daddy!" Should I continue to play the role of teacher or play the role of daddy? This kind of role conflict generally requires a choice on the part of the role player. The two roles may well be mutually exclusive to the point where no single role could please both audiences.

Values and Knowledge: Meanings of Social Interaction

Our culture gives us meaning for our lives. As we have seen, it tells us how to live, but more important, it tells us why to live. For example, unless you are an orphan, you are or were a son or a daughter. *Son* or *daughter* is a role in American culture, and, while we all play this

BOX 3.2

Experiencing People as Their Roles: The Cabdriver as "Nonperson"

When our interactions with others become standardized into role playing, we often see others not as individual people but only in terms of the role they play when we encounter them. This is particularly true when we encounter another individual in one role only. As one example of this process, Fred Davis offers the cabdriver, an individual with whom our interactions are both impersonal and fleeting. Under these circumstances the cabdriver ceases to be a person with whom the passenger shares an automobile but is responded to mechanically according to the norms of interaction for cabdrivers and fares. This relationship leads to a variety of unusual occurrences in the back seat. Davis tells of

> the chorus girl who made a complete change from street clothing into stage costume as [the cabdriver] drove her to her theater. More prosaic instances include the man and wife who, managing to suppress their anger while on the street, launch into a bitter quarrel the moment they are inside the cab; or the well-groomed young couple who after a few minutes roll over on the back seat and begin petting; or the businessman who loudly discusses details of a questionable business deal. Here the driver is expected to, and usually does, act as if he were merely an extension of the automobile he operates. In actuality, of course, he is acutely aware of what goes on in his cab, and, although his being treated as a nonperson implies a degraded status, it also affords him a splendid vantage point from which to witness a rich variety of human schemes and entanglements. (Davis, 1959: 159-160)

The cabdriver is only an extreme example of the growing number of impersonal role relationships in modern life. In cities we encounter vast numbers of individuals in the course of a day, but we see each only within circumscribed roles. Rather than encountering others in the intricate detail of their personal uniqueness, we see them as interchangeable actors within their roles. In extreme cases such as the cabdriver they almost become robots in our experience.

role a little differently, there are nevertheless definite similarities, especially in comparison to the behaviors for this role in a very different culture. Sons and daughters respond to specific norms regarding how they should behave toward their parents. In American culture that relationship has a highly valued meaning providing us with notions of family importance and leading us to see the family relationship as a central part of our lives. When is the last time you heard a politician attack motherhood? When you are interacting with your parents, a culturally provided voice in your head tells you that you are doing something important and meaningful. If you dislike your parents, that same voice will probably try to make you feel guilty, even if your parents are thoroughly unlikeable people. Without that cultural meaning, interacting with your parents would be on a par with your interaction with the drugstore clerk.

Cultural meaning is communicated through symbols. Symbols are anything that people agree will stand for (or communicate) something else. Through our responses to symbols, we communicate how we feel about the "something else" being symbolized. People at this convention are proudly waving the flag—symbol of America—to show their loyalty and support. Others have burned the flag to demonstrate displeasure with the country.

In a similar manner culture provides meaning for every role we play. I am a teacher, and my culture explains to me the importance of communicating knowledge to others and the importance to our society of having educated people. You are likely a student; American culture values students, for they acquire socially useful skills, learn how to think clearly, and expand their horizons of knowledge. You may or may not think all these beliefs are accurate, but the meanings are present nevertheless. They can't help but influence at least a part of how you think of yourself. Just as important, they influence how others see you. If you lose interest in going to school, perhaps a stern talking to by your cultural values will convince you to give it another try. Cultures don't do their own talking, of course, but the shared nature of cultural values leads individuals to act as stand-ins for those values in convincing you of their worth. If you drop out of school to become a dishwasher, the values will find you.

As we have seen, all of the meanings that culture provides have come about through the thinking that people do about the lives they lead. Much of this thinking, which falls under the general heading of what we call *knowledge,* ultimately finds its way into cultural values. This section will examine that process.

Symbols **Symbols**, as we discussed in Chapter 1, are anything that people agree will stand for (or communicate) something else. The symbol can be a gesture, an object, a mark, a sound—anything that is recognizable will do. The object of communication can be an idea, a thing, or anything else. The ability to create and use symbols is the basis for the way culture assigns meaning to human behavior. Cultural meaning is shared meaning, and before it can be shared it must be communicated. I must be able to communicate to you what I think of your actions before you can know what those actions mean to me. The flexible nature of symbols allows us to be endlessly creative in the way we assign meaning to our actions. Symbols are cultural building blocks.

Social Status One of the clearest illustrations of the way culture assigns meaning and uses symbols is the concept of social status. **Social status** is an individual's social position within the social group, particularly in terms of prestige. Typically, social status is closely tied to roles and the ranking of those roles within a system of social stratification; if your primary occupation is medical doctor, for example, you will have a high social status in the United States. The concept of status ignores what you actually do and focuses on what people think of what you do. For obvious reasons it is pleasant to be well thought of.

Social status is also useful for the acquiring of specifc ends. For instance, when you apply for a job, you will wear your best clothes and try to present yourself to your prospective employer in the best light possible. When you do this, you are trying to create the image of high social status so that you will be seen as a valuable person and a good candidate for the job. When you apply for a loan, you will want to present an image of respectability and responsibility so that you will be seen as a good credit risk. If you are going out on a date with a person for the first time and hope to see him or her again, you will want to be viewed as a valuable person. You may try to drop hints regarding your skills, abilities, accomplishments, and possessions to create this image. Your image of high social status may even lead the drugstore clerk to treat you a little more courteously during your brief encounter. The impression others have of you affects all the details of your everyday life, from the most important to the most trivial.

Social status is conveyed through **status symbols**, anything that communicates your social position to others. An expensive possession communicates that you have the wealth (or the credit) to purchase it; having particular knowledge or skills communicates the kinds of people you associate with and activities you engage in; your style of speech communicates the kinds of people you talk with; and the color of your skin or your last name communicates the ethnic group you come from. Just as others are aware of these symbols, you, too, are aware of them. Putting on your best clothes and manner for a job interview indicates a basic way that status symbols are manipulated to create specific and hoped-for impressions. The most obvious status symbol is the expensive possession. As American culture values wealth, you can be valued if you have it or appear to have it. The car you drive, the neighborhood you live in, and the clothes you wear all communicate this aspect of your status. But note that possessions serve

A status symbol is any symbol that communicates social status. These men are instantly recognizable as college professors through their distinctive dress.

this function only when their value is clear to others. In his classic *Theory of the Leisure Class* (see Box 3.3) Thorstein Veblen discusses one of the most common symbols of wealth—waste.

In any society social status can be acquired through two basic means—ascription and achievement. **Ascribed status** is any status you acquire through birth. In American society both your sex and racial or ethnic status are acquired in this manner and will affect the rest of your life no matter what else you do. Other aspects of status are at least partially acquired through ascription. You are born into the social class of your parents, and at least initially, your society will respond to you in terms of that status. Although it is possible in American society to change your social class, it is far from easy to do so; much of that difficulty stems from the skills and abilities you get or don't get from your family. This topic will be examined in greater detail in Chapter 7.

Achieved status is any status you acquire through your own actions (or achievements). In American society a job gives you an achieved status, since few jobs are assigned at birth (although many are influenced by birth—you might inherit millions and spend your life in the occupation of stock investor). The fact that most social status in American society is based on achievement provides an interesting comparison with other cultures. Industrial societies tend to be based more on achievement, while nonindustrial societies are based more on ascription. In the latter, it is not unheard of for an individual's entire life to be set at birth—including future

BOX 3.3

CONSPICUOUS CONSUMPTION AS A STATUS SYMBOL: THORSTEIN VEBLEN'S THEORY OF THE LEISURE CLASS

Thorstein Veblen was an American sociologist of the late 1800s and early 1900s. He was quite a colorful figure in the quiet academic world of his day. His critical perspective on society, along with his unorthodox lifestyle, led him into a number of controversies. *Theory of the Leisure Class* (1899) is one of the best remembered of Veblen's writings. In that book Veblen trained his critical eye on the people of wealth in the United States—the leisure class. Within this class he found that the primary symbol of high status was the visible waste of time (conspicuous leisure) and goods (conspicuous consumption).

The truly wealthy should not have to work for a living; their work should be done for them by others, such as servants. If they want other people to be aware of their high status, however, they must make their nonwork visible. The presence of servants symbolizes this lack of activity, as do a number of leisure pursuits. Veblen pointed out that wealthy individuals who privately pursue some obscure form of scholarship or who engage in the breeding of race horses or exotic dogs are making visible the fact that they need not concern themselves with their own survival. This "conspicuous leisure" communicates to others that the individual in question has made it into the leisure (and upper) class.

The wealthy not only waste time, they also waste consumable items. By *waste* Veblen referred to consumption that is not directly related to survival. All humans must seek food and drink, for example, but when food becomes a fancy and expensive gourmet dish and drink a rare and expensive wine, conspicuous consumption is at hand. As with conspicuous leisure, the point of conspicuous consumption is to symbolize status. An individual who can visibly and extravagantly consume nonessentials conveys to observers that he or she need not worry about money. Conspicuous consumption thus makes a statement to the community about social position.

One of the more interesting and less obvious modern examples of both conspicuous leisure and conspicuous consumption is the suntan. In times past, a suntan symbolized low status since it meant that the tanned individual engaged in hard and lower-class work, such as agriculture, which occurred mostly outside. In fact, to have absolutely white skin used to be a mark of high status, for it meant you never worked. In the United States today, however, most lower- and middle-class jobs occur indoors during the hours of sunshine. Under such circumstances an individual with a tan communicates that he or she has the leisure to lie in the sun for hours, doing nothing but accumulating progressively darker skin. In the colder climate areas of the United States an early spring tan also communicates that the bearer has the income to travel to sunnier areas and the leisure to lie in the sun while there. Consequently, most of us see a suntan as attractive since it symbolizes attractive social position. Not surprisingly, there is a thriving industry in sun lamps, artificial tanning lotions (that don't require the sun), and tanning salons that give you a quick tan during a January snowstorm in Michigan. As with all status symbols, there is always an interest in acquiring the symbol even if you can't achieve the status.

(continues)

BOX 3.3 (continued)

It is interesting to predict yet further changes in the relation between tanned skin and social status. Throughout the 1980s, Americans have been warned continually about the dangers of skin cancer and its relation to exposure to the ultraviolet rays of the sun. What price are we willing to pay for beauty? Cigarette smoking used to be an integral part of every movie romantic scene as well as symbolic of macho tough guys. Now, with symbols like Humphrey Bogart and John Wayne dead of cancer, cigarettes have come to carry a different cultural meaning. Perhaps the suntan will follow a similar route and, in this case, the situation will return full circle to the positive value placed on a pale complexion.

spouse, occupation, and place in the community. Societies such as the United States must necessarily place more emphasis on achievement to match the demands of their diverse and competitive economic systems.

Values The foregoing discussion of social status should underscore the importance of values in understanding cultural meaning. High or low social status is assigned to roles or individuals according to how that role or individual fits into dominant cultural values. In American society, we value doctors above garbage collectors, for example. Ironically, most doctors would probably agree that more lives are saved through good sanitation than through medical treatment, yet doctors have our respect. Why? That is always a difficult question. Perhaps we want to value people who are trying to save our lives, or perhaps doctors have had good public relations. Whatever the reason, we can see a clear connection between cultural values and the way social status is assigned.

Though their existence indicates nothing more than the fact that we have convinced ourselves which things, people, or activities are good and which are bad, values provide the ultimate basis for the assignment of meaning to life. If you convince yourself (with the help of others) that your activities are good, they become inherently meaningful. You now have a reason to continue. We pay professional ballplayers large sums of money to perform for us, but what is meaningful about being able to hit a small ball with a stick? In some societies it is in fact a meaningless activity, but in American society (where we value competitive sports in general and baseball in particular) it is a highly valued skill. Not being sociologists, however, ballplayers probably do not spend a great deal of time questioning the meaning of their existence, for most people accept their cultural values without question.

Humans tend to accept their cultures along with the air they breathe and the ground they walk on. Cultures are far more powerful than the individual—they are there waiting for us when we are born, and they go on existing after we die. Whatever habits and values we acquire through socialization will come to seem both reasonable and natural to us as adults; other cultures will often seem silly, stupid, or immoral. Sociologists refer to this perspective on other cultures as **ethnocentrism** (Sumner, 1906). The ethnocentric individual (which is all of us, to some extent) values only his or her own cultural ways and is unable to look on other cultures objectively. Ethnocentrism is inherent in cultural values: As you internalize the values of your culture, you become ethnocentric.

Values are part of culture, and through socialization, they become part of us. They are the basis of everything we do since they are the way we "make sense" of what we're doing. Interpreting someone else's actions must begin with an understanding of that individual's values. We must, in short, be able to look at the world from others' perspectives before we will be able to understand how their actions are meaningful to them. Ethnocentrism makes this difficult for both the layman and the sociologist. And just as ethnocentrism makes it difficult to look at other cultures objectively, it also makes it hard to look at our own culture objectively; it's hard to be objective about something you love. (See the reading by Winther following this chapter for a good example of this problem.)

Knowledge and Language At perhaps their most basic level cultures direct how we think and how we express the things we think about. Just as scientists' concepts direct their observations of certain phenomena (leading other phenomena to be ignored), every individual acquires a conceptual orientation from his or her culture that has the same effect. This effect can best be seen by looking at the differences in subcultures within American culture. Artists and architects are much more likely to notice shape, color, and design than the rest of us, as they have been trained to observe them. Botanists will have a different experience walking through the woods than the rest of us who simply see a lot of trees. When they walk into a bank building, carpenters will notice methods of construction, bank robbers will note alarm systems and the presence or absence of rear exits, and sociologists will note the group dynamics before, during, and after a bank robbery. But perhaps the best example comes from children. Being too young to have fully accepted and understood the way their culture looks at the world, children are endlessly creative in their perceptions. Most of us write this off by observing that children have vivid imaginations, but a child's perceptions tell us as much about what we have lost as what we have gained by accepting the knowledge of our culture.

The relationship between knowledge and language is unclear. One argument (called the *Sapir-Whorf hypothesis,* after its originators) states that the form and structure of language limits the way we think (Whorf, 1956). Eskimos, for example, have over twenty different words for types of snow but no single word for snow, as we do. The implication of the Sapir-Whorf hypothesis is that the Eskimos have no concept of snow as we do but will notice all the fine variations in snow texture that Americans are not linguistically directed to notice. Languages differ also in their use of pronouns, verbs, sentence structure, and so on, all of which direct and limit an individual's perceptions. For instance, if you forget to bring something with you, you say, "I forgot it," taking personal responsibility for the forgetting. In Spanish, however, you would say (in rough translation), "It forgot itself on me," seemingly placing all the blame on the object you forgot. Does this mean that Spanish speakers refuse to take responsibility for their actions?

An alternative perspective on the relation between knowledge and language suggests that many language forms are simply convention and don't actually limit our perception. The difference between Spanish and English in expressing forgetting would not necessarily indicate two different ways of thinking but rather two different ways of putting the same thought into language. Considering the Eskimos and their many words for snow, a person holding this perspective would argue that experience with and the importance of snow leads the Eskimos to become more precise in observation and simultaneously develop more precise terms for those observations. This quickly becomes a chicken and egg question: Does the experience lead to the language changes, or do the language changes lead to new experiences? Both are possible. A student, for example, might learn the language of botany along with knowledge of the subject in a classroom and discover that his or her observations are now more precise because of the new labels for acquiring and storing those observations in memory. (It's easier to distinguish oak trees from maples when you can label them accordingly.) On the other hand, a skier would presumably notice a great many things about snow by falling down in it even without the convenience of the Eskimo's labels ("There's that slick, hard-packed snow that always makes me slip").

One linguistic example that lends support to the second perspective comes from the use of pronouns in English as compared with other European languages (Brown and Gilman, 1960). For the second-person pronoun, English has only one choice—you. In French, Spanish, and German, however, there are two choices (*tu* and *vous* in French, *tu* and *usted* in Spanish, and *du* and *Sie* in German). In each of these languages you must first decide on your relationship to the person you are addressing before you can decide which pronoun to use. In French you would use *tu* for close friends and *vous* with strangers. Even more important for our discussion, social class differences are also noted by this means. A French employer might use *tu* to an office boy, but the office boy would have to use *vous* in addressing his employer. Ironically, English used to have this same distinction (thou served the *tu* function), but the term dropped out of use long ago as being antidemocratic. The question, therefore, is whether English speakers are less aware of status differences because those differences don't receive attention in their pronoun choice.

Obviously, we English-speaking Americans are very aware of status differences. Linguistically, we can make the same distinction in other ways—for instance, in the use of titles (*Dr. Jones* as opposed to *Bob* or, under slavery, *Massa Jones* as opposed to *boy*) or in speech styles ("Would you mind closing the door while you're up?" as opposed to "Go close the door") (Brown and Gilman, 1960). This example suggests that parts of important knowledge in a society (in this case status distinctions) will continue regardless of language forms. As with the expulsion of *thou* many years ago, political movements often seek to change thinking by changing speech. Recently, the women's movement has sought to substitute *Ms.* for *Mrs.* and *Miss,* and *chairperson* for *chairman.* A change in language can be an important starting point for getting people to change the way in which they think, but language changes only become truly meaningful when accompanied by changes in the social world to which language refers.

While language may not be a determinant of culture, it is most certainly a reflection of culture. Beyond providing an abstract symbol system designed to communicate meaning, language use is also a social act that, like all other social acts, is governed by the norms of culture. Before we speak, we interpret the social situation confronting us to determine what (if anything) should be said, how it should be said, and to whom it should be said (Hymes, 1974; Fishman, 1971). A social situation can be changed by the addition or subtraction of only one individual. How would your speech change if you were discussing your date last night with a few friends and were suddenly joined by your priest, minister, or rabbi? You would probably alter your choice of words, your sentence structure, your pronunciation, and, most probably, your topic. Knowing such rules regarding language use is just as important as knowing the basic grammar rules of the language.

Not all language is verbal. Basso (1970) shows how silence communicates effectively among the Apache Indians of the United States. In many of their social situations, particularly those marked by ambiguity, Apache will generally remain silent, which, depending on the situation, communicates deference, uneasiness, or other social meanings. Newly courting couples will always remain silent on their first "dates" due to the strangeness of their being together. Edward Hall (1959) has focused attention on **body language**—communication through gestures, expressions, body position, and the like. We can communicate a great deal by making (or breaking) eye contact, looking at our watches while someone speaks, or slumping back in classroom chairs while a professor drones on. Within this general area, the topic of personal space has received considerable research attention. Personal space refers to the distance we maintain between ourselves and others. This preferred distance will vary depending on the social situation in which we find ourselves. Burgoon and Jones (1976) have found that preferences in personal space vary by degrees of friendship and differences in age, race, and social status. Pederson (1973) notes in general that men stand farther apart than women. Hall and Hall (1971) emphasize the cultural aspect of all this by noting variations in such preferences from one culture to another. Germans, for example, prefer a lot of space between them when conversing, whereas Latin Americans and Arabs like to stand quite close. The implications are clear: People from different cultures may never be able to find an appropriate distance at which both individuals are comfortable.

Differences in Language and Knowledge Among Social Groups Groups vary in the kinds of things or experiences they find important and in the ways they add meaning to those things and experiences. As thinking varies, so, too, does talking. Technically, different groups may all speak the same language, but they use different words, different sentence structure, and different pronunciation. Is your carbonated beverage *pop, soda,* or a *soda drink?* When your frying pan is covered with grease, is it greasy with an *ssss* sound or with a *zzzz* sound? And is the pan itself a *frying pan* or a *skillet?* All of these language forms vary according to geographical regions of the United States; language also varies according to occupation, interest group, and, perhaps most important, social class.

William Labov, a reasearcher in sociolinguistics (a discipline combining sociology and linguistics), has done considerable work in relating speech differences to other social differences. For example, he discovered that the *th* sound is pronounced slightly differently by the members of each social class in New York City (Labov, 1970). The upper class uses one pronunciation and the lower class another; the social classes in between vary between the two extremes. It could be possible, therefore, to know a lot about a person's background from his or her pronunciation of one word.

Linguists are trained to notice these differences, but do other people? In spite of many claims to the contrary, the average person is as good a listener as a talker. Most people are not aware of the exact differences in speech from one social class to the next, but they can tell the difference. We are, of course, consciously aware of differences in word choice and grammar among the people we listen to, but we also hear the differences in pronunciation. Dean Ellis (1967) found that a significant number of people could place the social class of speakers on a tape recording when the speakers were counting from one to twenty; the only possible differences from speaker to speaker could be in pronunciation of the various sounds in those twenty words.

When it enables us to tell a person's social group, speech can be described as a **boundary marker** of that social group—it communicates to all who know about it just who is in the group and who is not. And by giving us that information, it allows us to place the boundaries between social groups, separating the people of different classes simply by listening to them. There are a great many such boundary markers in addition to speech. The upper and lower classes generally dress differently, for example, but clothing can be altered much more easily than styles of speaking or the styles of thinking expressed by speech, so dress is not a reliable boundary marker. Any boundary marker can become a basis for discrimination, as we will see in Chapter 5.

Language can also mark the boundaries between social groups by *preventing* communication between them (Gumperz, 1968). This may seem a strange function for language, but the members of social groups often go out of their way to alter their speech so outsiders will not understand them. Criminal groups, for example, may use a lot of slang so as to more easily recognize a police undercover agent through speech errors. A revolutionary group would have a similar motive. A religious cult might create language differences so that its members would feel set apart from the rest of society and therefore be less likely to return to it. Professionals such as doctors, lawyers, government bureaucrats, or sociologists express themselves in speech that only their colleagues can understand. This makes it more difficult for outsiders to evaluate the services they provide. Keeping their activities clouded in mystery keeps these activities under their own control. To put that same thought in sociological jargon, "one latent function of highly differentiated linguistic patterns within the subcultures of occupational categories is to legitimate an ideological orientation which maintains the authority position of the category." If it's my job to understand society, and if you can't understand how I do it, you'll either have to come to me when you want advice or continue reading.

Power and Authority **Power** is the probability that you can control the behavior of others. Holding a club over someone's head, for example, may lead to a high probability that he will do what you want him to. **Authority** is a special kind of power in which the people under your control feel that you have the right to give orders. Under these circumstances you don't need a club most of the time. Power that relies basically on raw force or intimidation exists in both the human and the nonhuman world. Authority is a relationship specific to human society that gains its force in the meaning system of culture.

In all but the most simple societies relationships of authority make possible the coordination on which the society runs. Authority means that people in certain roles or positions within the society typically give certain kinds of orders to certain kinds of people. It is the work of culture to convince all concerned that this is a practical, reasonable, and just arrangement: The leaders must be willing to lead, and the followers must be willing to follow.

When authority becomes established in a culture, most members of the society come to take that authority for granted, just as they accept the rest of their culture. While some argue that this kind of acceptance is changing in American society, Americans generally believe what their doctors tell them about health, their judges tell them about law, their presidents tell them about government, and their teachers tell them about knowledge. Even if we do question authority, it usually requires an effort for us to get out of the habit of acceptance. We believe our president until forced to believe otherwise, for example. The Milgram experiment described in Box 3.4 illustrates how many Americans follow even a presumed authority just because they are so used to taking orders. The existence of authority in any society creates a strange chain of responsibility for actions—individuals used to taking orders are also used to passing on the responsibility for their actions to the authority that gave the orders.

Following World War II the government of the United States called the principle of authority into direct question with the Nuremberg Trials of Nazi war criminals. The now-famous plea of "I was only following orders" became the dominant line of defense for many of the men whose actions were on record. The decision that many of them were guilty of war crimes implied that people who follow orders are responsible for their actions along with the people who give orders. This decision returned to haunt the United States government during the Vietnam War, when draft resisters stated that they were responsible for their own actions and would not kill Vietnamese people. The United States government, not surprisingly, looked on the situation differently. The curious fact of authority in a culture is that no society functions without authority, yet the authority relations in some other cultures seem arbitrary and pointless while our own seem reasonable and essential. Nevertheless, in spite of both the Nazi trials and the Vietnam experience, the sense of responsibility that people feel following the orders of an authority has changed little.

An important early study of authority in society was done by Max Weber (1864-1920), a versatile and creative German sociologist. Weber separated authority into three basic types: traditional, charismatic, and legal/rational. *Traditional authority* refers to those forms of authority that people follow through the sheer weight of time and tradition. Monarchs are clear examples of traditional authority, the king or queen generally being a member of a royal family that has governed for some time. When a society's members get used to taking certain orders from certain people for generations, the tradition itself gives force to the authority and increases the probability that orders will be followed. As we shall see, the force of time affects other forms of authority as well. The presidency of the United States is not an example of traditional authority, yet the 200-year tradition of that office gives modern presidents an authority that George Washington did not have.

The second and, in some ways, the most interesting authority type that Weber presented is charismatic authority. *Charismatic authority* exists when an individual possesses particularly persuasive personality traits (termed *charisma*) that convince others to obey his or her orders. Charismatic individuals sometimes base their authority on a claim of spiritual closeness to a deity, but others are just as effective through the force of their personality and their ability to persuade. Charisma cannot be easily defined or measured, as it is an intangible quality. It can perhaps best be described by naming some leaders in recent history who possessed it: Adolf Hitler, Martin Luther King, Jr., John F. Kennedy, Franklin D. Roosevelt, Charles De Gaulle, and Jim Jones (of the People's Temple) all had charismatic control over people. As is obvious from the list, they were very different people who used their charisma to very different ends—yet they all had the quality in common.

Finally, and to Weber most importantly, we come to legal/rational authority. *Legal/rational authority* is authority specifically and consciously attached to a given office or position in a society for the purpose of producing a certain kind of societal coordination. A classic example

BOX 3.4

OBEDIENCE TO AUTHORITY: THE MILGRAM STUDY

In what has become one of the most famous studies on human behavior, Stanley Milgram (1974) conducted an experiment to determine the degree to which people would take orders. Subjects solicited through advertising were instructed that they would be taking part in a memory experiment designed to test the effectiveness of punishment on learning. The punishment was to consist of electric shocks administered whenever mistakes on the memory test occurred. The experiment was to consist of two individuals—a "teacher," who would administer the shocks upon receiving wrong answers, and a "learner," whose job was to remember meaningless word pairs and receive shocks for memory lapses. In reality, however, experimental subjects who answered the advertisement were always placed in the role of teacher, while the learner was an actor and not actually hooked up to the impressive-looking shock machine. The teacher's instructions were to increase the voltage on the shock machine for each subsequent wrong answer. The shock machine was marked with switches ranging from 15 to 450 volts. The real point of the experiment was to determine how long subjects would continue to administer what they thought were painful electric shocks while the "learner" screamed for the experiment to end and the experimenter calmly insisted that the experiment continue.

Would you have obeyed those orders? Milgram asked a variety of people, including professional psychiatrists, how far they thought most people would go before refusing to continue the experiment. The psychiatrists agreed that most subjects would discontinue the experiment at the first request of the "learner" to terminate it and that only 1 in 1,000 would continue long enough to administer 450 volts. When he conducted the experiment, Milgram discovered that approximately 50 percent of the subjects could be convinced without excessive pressure to continue until the 450-volt level—over the screams of agony and complaints of heart trouble from the actor in the next room.

Are people naturally sadistic? No, says Milgram. They are just accustomed to taking orders in their everyday lives and easily slide into that role in the laboratory. The subjects who continued the experiment to the end were visibly upset and unhappy about what they were doing but became convinced that the researcher, not they, was responsible for their actions.

The sense of responsibility is perhaps the key to understanding both these experimental results and the functioning of authority in society. When we become used to taking orders from an established authority (such as a government), we also become used to holding that authority responsible for the things we ourselves do. A soldier is not supposed to feel responsible for the people he kills in war because he is just "following orders." Industrial societies such as the United States are based on elaborate systems of authority to which their members become accustomed. Many Americans have looked on the ruins of Nazi Germany and proclaimed, "It can't happen here." According to the Milgram study, it can happen anywhere.

of legal/rational authority is the United States Constitution, which created a variety of offices from thin air for the purpose of governing the new United States. In the Constitution we find the presidency, the justices of the Supreme Court, senators, representatives, and so on. The Constitution specifies exactly how these offices are to be filled and exactly what kind of authority each is to have. Once the offices were created, all members of society were subject to their authority, including the individuals who created the offices in the first place.

An important aspect of legal/rational authority is that it is attached to roles or offices and not to individuals. Individuals have authority only while they occupy an office of authority, and they have only the authority that has been specifically given to that office. If they go beyond those bounds, as Richard Nixon did in his presidency, there are usually means by which they may be removed from office. It is very easy for both leaders and followers to forget this source of authority in everyday life; the individual in the office begins to "own" the part and others begin to associate that individual with the authority he or she wields. Nevertheless, legal/rational authority is not a personal possession.

Weber felt that legal/rational authority was clearly the dominant form of authority in any modern or industrialized society and would become increasingly dominant over time. The clearest example is the modern bureaucracy (to be described in Chapter 6), in which a chain of command among offices is delineated, and who gives orders to whom and exactly what those orders may be are specified. A modern military organization is one of the best examples of such a system. With each office backed up by still another office with still more legal/rational authority, the control over behavior becomes awesome. The old expression "You can't fight city hall" indicates something of this force. Nevertheless, as with all forms of authority, legal/rational authority gets its strength from the meaning system of the culture. Societies can and do have revolutions in which an entire structure of authority may be terminated, usually to be replaced by another one. Russia turned into the Soviet Union in 1917 and the Soviet Union turned into the Commonwealth of Independent States in 1991; similarly, the British colonies in the New World turned into the United States a couple of centuries back. Authority is always bestowed by the people who are willing to take orders; if the people remove that acceptance, authority figures are left only with power (such as the military). And power without authority is a cumbersome and generally ineffective way to run a society.

SUMMARY

Culture is the ultimate human creation. It refers to all of the objects, skills, ideas, beliefs, and patterns of behavior that are developed and shared by members of societies. It provides the basis for human societies, creating ongoing coordinated patterns of behavior for survival and giving meaning to human existence. As the problems of survival change or vary from place to place, culture is capable of adapting. Beyond the necessity of providing for the survival of societal members cultures vary considerably around the world.

Culture can be separated into material and nonmaterial realms. Material culture consists of all the physical creations of humans as well as naturally occurring physical objects to which humans attach meaning (such as gold). Nonmaterial culture is the source of that meaning, specifying both patterns of behavior (modes of social interaction) and reasons for following those patterns (meanings of social interaction). From the meanings of social interaction humans acquire knowledge from their culture along with a system of values that directs their desires and encourages them to follow the patterns of their culture.

The concept of culture is the foundation for the basic theme of social coordination that runs throughout this book and sociology in general. In this chapter we've examined the many different facets of culture. Our cultures provide us with ready-made patterns of behavior, and they give us appropriate thoughts and feelings to have about those patterns. Humans are not robots, and they can change those patterns, thoughts, and feelings, but that process of change is also part of culture. More than any other single concept from sociology, culture describes the way we live our everyday lives and provides a realm of meaning within which we experience our lives.

GLOSSARY

Achieved status Social status acquired through an individual's actions or achievements.

Ascribed status Social status acquired by and set at birth.

Authority The probability for control over the behavior of others based on their belief in the right of the authority figure to issue orders.

Body language Nonverbal communication in which body movements such as gestures, expressions, and body placement carry social meaning.

Boundary marker Any symbol that communicates group membership.

Cultural adaptation The manner in which people adapt their cultures to the necessities of survival.

Cultural universals Particular cultural elements (beliefs, behavior patterns, etc.) that are found in all known cultures.

Culture The configuration of humanly created objects, skills, ideas, beliefs, and patterns of behavior that are learned and transmitted by members of a society in a shared fashion.

Ethnocentrism A positive value placed on the cultural elements of one culture by its members, typically coupled with negative evaluations of cultural alternatives.

Folkways Less serious social norms, which, when broken, bring about only mild disapproval from others. As originally defined by William Graham Sumner, folkways are the habitual patterns of behavior common to a social group.

Ideal norms Expectations for behavior within a social group that are based more on group values than on the realities of everyday life.

Material culture Physical creations or objects to which people assign cultural meaning.

Mores Basic beliefs and patterns of behavior common to a social group that form a foundation for the everyday patterns of life. Mores are norms that are adhered to forcefully by members of the social group.

Nonmaterial culture All culturally shared human creations that are not physical, including ideas, beliefs, skills, and language.

Norms The shared rules that govern the wide variety of patterned behavior in a culture, forming the expectations for behaviors in particular social situations.

Power The probability for control over the behavior of others.

Real norms Expectations for behavior within a social group based on past experiences of what individuals are likely to do.

Role The expected behavior patterns that develop for specific activities or as typical for specific positions in a society.

Role conflict Confusion by an individual as to how a given role should be played or which role is appropriate in a given social situation.

Social class Collections of individuals whose activities (or roles) are similar in terms of the rewards they bring to their participants.

Social status An individual's social position within the social group, particularly with respect to his or her prestige.

Social stratification The arrangement of different activities (or roles) into a hierarchy, whereby activities ranked high are highly rewarded and activities ranked low are poorly rewarded. The rewards generally consist of money, prestige, and influence over others.

Status symbol Anything that communicates the social status of an individual to others.

Subculture Specific objects, skills, ideas, beliefs, and patterns of behavior unique to specific groups within a larger culture.

Symbol A word, gesture, object, or image of any sort that stands for another idea or object through the agreement of two or more people.

Value An ideal agreed upon by a social group as to what is good or desirable.

SUPPLEMENTARY READINGS

Benedict, Ruth *Patterns of Culture.* Boston: Houghton Mifflin, 1934.
Truly one of the classics, Ruth Benedict's anthropological work presents the concept *culture* in its diversity through the comparison of three traditional societies.

Ember, Carol R., and Melvin Ember *Cultural Anthropology.* (5th ed.). Englewood Cliffs, N.J.: Prentice-Hall, 1988.
A good general introduction to the field of cultural anthropology and extremely useful to sociologists as well. There is considerable overlap between the two fields, and that which doesn't overlap helps sociology expand its perspectives.

Hall, Edward T. *The Silent Language.* Greenwich, Conn.: Fawcett, 1959.
Any easy-to-read examination of the importance of culture in everyday life, with an emphasis on how our cultures "teach" us to view time and space in particular ways.

Humphreys, Laud *Tearoom Trade.* Chicago: Aldine, 1970.
A controversial sociological study of a homosexual subculture. This book is a good illustration both of a subculture formed around deviant activity and of a particular type of research. Some questions regarding research ethics can be raised.

Kessler, Evelyn *Anthropology: The Humanizing Process.* Boston: Allyn & Bacon, 1974.
An engagingly written introduction to the field of cultural anthropology, which is certainly the best place to acquire the meaning of the concept *culture.*

Mead, Margaret *Sex and Temperament in Three Primitive Societies.* New York: Morrow, 1935.
A classic piece of anthropological interpretation, comparing the differences in sex roles across cultures. In the face of much popular belief in 1935, Mead concluded that the way we think and feel about sex comes from our culture and not from our genes.

Slater, Phillip *The Pursuit of Loneliness.* Boston: Beacon Press, 1976.
A critical analysis of American culture and its impact on the American character.

Wardhaugh, Ronald *An Introduction to Sociolinguistics.* New York: Basil Blackwell, 1986.
Sociolinguistics is an interdisciplinary field that exists in the cross-section of sociology and linguistics. In this easy-to-read introductory text, Wardhaugh shows how social aspects of life affect language use.

READING

The "Killing" of Neni Bai

PAUL WINTHER

Our culture is composed not only of the things we do every day but also of the meanings we give to that everyday life. We cannot, for example, separate the act of going to church from the religious beliefs of individuals who attend; going to church is different from going to a ballgame because of the meanings we attach to these two activities. Understanding culture is difficult for all social scientists, but it is a particular problem for cultural anthropologists, who study cultures around the world and must learn to cope with vastly different kinds of meanings from those they are used to.

In the following article cultural anthropologist Paul Winther describes his research in a small traditional village in India. In particular, he describes an event that was very upsetting to him—the murder of a teenage girl by her own father. He was upset not so much by the "crime" as by the fact that few of the people in the village viewed it as a crime; within their cultural outlook, the act was justified. His task as an anthropologist was to learn to look at the world in such a way that this act could take on the same insignificance for him that it had for the villagers.

Winther's account is separated into two parts. Part One describes his role in the village as an anthropologist and the circumstances surrounding the death of the girl Neni Bai. Part Two explains the cultural outlook of the villagers. Part Two may be more difficult for us to deal with, but as Winther explains, the central ideas and assumptions of one culture cannot be easily transformed into the modes of expression of another culture. If you do have some difficulty in understanding the villagers' point of view, you will learn something about the fundamental differences between the cultures humans create.

Part One

It is not an exaggeration to say that seldom does a visitor to India soon forget the experience. The number, variety, and intensity of feelings can multiply as a tour evolves into months and years. The contrasts between beauty and ugliness, real and disturbing, alternately assault and soothe your sensitivities. That these emotions may persist suggests that you don't so much travel in India as the place begins to occupy you. You don't "see" the country; you "feel" it. It is a phenomenon that can alter your consciousness in ways much more subtle and ultimately more profound than merely recognizing differences in wealth and reacting to deprivation.

For me India was, and continues to be, a surreptitious encounter that changed my attitude to existence. I want to relate to you how this happened to me. I want to tell you about a young girl who died. Or was she killed? Perhaps murdered is a better word for it. Maybe nothing really ever happened to her.

More than twelve years have passed, but the events are still vivid. I was a graduate student in anthropology, doing a participant observation study in north central India. Participant observation simply means learning the rudiments of a society's language prior to arrival, supplemented by intensive study of its history and culture, and then residing in a specific locale for

Essay © 1982 by Paul Winther. Used by permission of the author.

one to two years—in my case, a village of approximately 2,000 people. You attempt to become "part of the furniture," so to speak, being very cautious not to violate any local rules of etiquette or taboos. As you ask questions, you observe, and in the quiet moments of the day you write about what you have seen, heard, and felt in the form of field notes. This is the material from which you abstract ideas for future publications.

During the innumerable walks I took through the village and adjoining land as part of my work, I often met people tending fields. These were landowners, sharecroppers, and hired labor, usually from the community. They would acknowledge my presence with a look or a wave and a smile. And, occasionally, I would stop to have a cup of tea with those I knew particularly well. Boiled in prodigious amounts of buffalo milk and sugar, the beverage was compensated only by the relaxed flow of talk. I learned much about the village and its people from these encounters. It was as if the shade and the privacy in which we sat encouraged people to speak about things they would normally keep to themselves.

One series of meetings was particularly memorable. It involved two brothers, both Brahmans, a caste of high ritual status. The men were very friendly and always asked the same questions concerning me and the United States, to which I replied with the same answers. They responded with the same expressions of amazement or partial comprehension. I believe the inquiries were intentionally repetitious because they thought me to be a bit weird. Their questions, which I came to know by heart, were demonstrations of friendship, discreetly phrased in such a way as not to strain my apparently limited mental capacities. How else to explain and treat a foreigner 12,000 miles away from home, who sits and asks questions about such things as lineages, clans, and the like? Pancham Ram, one of the brothers, was an oddity for me as well. He wore a beard, and a bearded Brahman in the village was a rarity. We joked about this and compared respective lengths.

Pancham Ram was married and had six children, the oldest of whom, a girl, was deceased. Then there was another girl, Neni Bai, followed by four brothers down to the age of one and a half years. Pancham Ram, his wife, and children lived in a small dwelling with his unmarried brother. The family had a high ritual status but modest economic resources. The small amount of land they owned yielded sufficient produce to feed them, although it left little to sell at the market beyond the village.

Pancham Ram's daughter, Neni Bai, was in her early teens. I never talked to her or made inquiries about her until after her disappearance. An unmarried male, and a foreigner at that, does not ask questions about single females of high caste and marriageable age in the community and expect to remain in the village. But I noticed her each time I left my room above my landlord's cow pen and walked down the path to the village platform where the "important" men gathered when I took the shortcut to the highway where I waited for a bus to the nearest city. Often she would be there when I returned. She, like so many residents, became part of the animated scenery, stopping whatever was being done, the old women staring, the younger casting furtive glances beneath veils, the little girls giggling, and the boys shouting "White monkey!" and scampering away in good-natured mock fright. I grew accustomed to these acknowledgments of my presence, and, cut off from everything resembling my previous American existence, they helped make occasional bouts of loneliness less difficult and prolonged.

Neni Bai was in that field the first winter when temperatures were unexpectedly low and I nearly froze; she was there in the incredibly dry heat of May and June, and she was there during the monsoon season, seemingly oblivious to the danger of the water-inundated gully threatening to engulf the village. And she was there the autumn day I left to visit distant New Delhi. It was a cool, clear morning. With the same dull, expressionless look she observed my departure. The only thing that ever seemed to move was her eyes, insufficiently striking to detract from her exceedingly plain face. A beauty Neni Bai was not, even less so because she had a club foot. Others said that she was retarded, and I believed them. It would cost her father much money to find her a husband. She was a human being, however, and I felt sorry for her.

Neni Bai was gone when I came back. But I was so absorbed in data collection that initially I only dimly sensed her absence. The people I met that first day seemed pleased to see me again. I felt good. I remember meeting one man who looked vaguely familiar and hearing him greet me. But I was in a hurry, said hello, and went to an appointment. I met the same man later with his brother in Pancham Ram's field. Then I realized it was Pancham Ram, but without a beard. I kidded him about the hairless jaw, and when I asked him why no beard, he and his brother laughed, Pancham waving his hand in that typical Indian way signifying so many things. I assumed he had become tired of the growth and didn't give my debearded friend's new appearance any more thought.

Only several days later did one of my informants mention the village meeting that had taken place during my absence. It had been called by the village headman (*sarpanch*). Other people's descriptions suggested that it had been a perfunctory occasion, serving to satisfy inquiries initiated by the police. I was sorry that I had not witnessed the events and issues prompting the meeting. I was politely insistent that they tell me more. The *sarpanch,* I was told, had ordered Pancham Ram's beard shaved. Furthermore, no one was to talk to him for three days, and if they did, their crops would fail.* I sensed that Neni Bai's absence, the village meeting, and Pancham Ram's beardless condition were related. In retrospect, maybe I should have left the puzzle unsolved, for what I was to discover was disquieting.

Neni Bai was indeed gone. She had become pregnant by a lower caste male. Her throat had been cut and her body thrown into a dry well on Pancham Ram's land. Pancham did not deny having perpetrated the act. My shock was intensified when I was told that he had strangled another daughter—the one he had mentioned months before—two years before my arrival. The same well had been used as a disposal site. The agitation I experienced during these sessions may have been evident, but my feelings did not appear to be shared by others. It is difficult to describe the villagers' reactions in exact terms, but they gave the impression of a perplexing indifference, a casually nonchalant attitude, and one I thought was merely a disguise affected so as to calm me. However, unobtrusive inquiries during the remainder of my stay generated similar reactions.

In those early days I was convinced that these people had been just as upset as myself. It was, after all, merely human to be ashamed of a fellow villager who had committed such a horrible act. I assumed without question that they felt as I did, and I strove to discover reasons why their reactions were not following these assumptions. I realize now how engrained in my consciousness were my assumptions about the act of killing called into question because of Neni Bai. The villagers' awareness of the girl, of her father, and of the significance of their relationship attained in my eyes seemed to be predicated upon different principles, which hitherto I had had no reason to think differed from my own.

I eventually went to the local police station to find more details about the Neni Bai/Pancham Ram incident. The superintendent, whom I knew fairly well and who did not hail from the area, told me that he was aware of the village meeting and had sent a policeman to investigate. Since the case was closed, he showed me the files. He also perceived my incredulity. He volunteered that the police do not usually pursue these matters in the surrounding villages. It was not a "crime" in the sense that I understood the term. While it was a violation in legal theory, it was nothing very out of the ordinary for these people, he continued. I was becoming decidedly uncomfortable. The community meeting, the beard shaving, and the *sarpanch*'s warning were apparently little more than empty ritual designed to pay lip service to the power of the Indian state, its conception of legality based upon Western, Judeo-Christian-derived principles. The

*Nobody refrained from talking with Pancham Ram during this period, and no crops failed due to the infringement of the *sarpanch*'s admonition.

constable's investigation, the file sheets stamped and placed on record, prevented anyone from protesting insufficient implementation of the law.

So much for justice, I thought. But I was unsatisfied. Being able to comprehend the underlying logic intellectually is different from accepting it emotionally without feeling estranged. I had prided myself on beginning to understand how the villagers viewed the world around them. I was reacting to the contradiction between what I felt to be an exceptional event and my friends' treatment of it as less than exceptional. As I walked back to the village that day, I felt lonely, depressed, and apprehensive. The community appeared unappealingly foreign to me. They had become strangers all over again. The hard part of the research lay ahead, I thought—a realization that my concept of "human being" might not be shared by the people amongst whom I was living.

Part Two

What I ultimately gained from trying to understand Neni Bai's departure and the milieu in which it took place was a heightened awareness of the power of culture to condition an individual's perception of reality. My informants, friends, and acquaintances and I shared perceptions of Neni Bai. For example, she was a female, young, unattractive. This overlapping made the disagreement regarding the significance of her death so disconcerting to me. Given my need and desire to remain in the community and accomplish my goals, I was impelled to examine engrained assumptions and modify basic attitudes typical of our society's world view. I was divesting myself of the cocoonlike security, the complacency such unquestioned assumptions provide, and was assimilating in subtle, albeit commanding, ways aspects of a fundamentally different consciousness. It is a trip I perhaps never fully returned from.

It is impossible to convey the complexity of thought my covillagers were employing in their interpretations of Neni Bai; only an inadequate attempt can be made. What they were articulating were themes found in the classical texts of Hinduism and their idiosyncratic interpretation at the local level. These ideas pertain to their notion of time and the phenomenal world it embraces.

One dominant idea in classical Hinduism is that of transcendental reality underlying and sustaining all of the phenomenal world. While this does not discourage recognition of different objects, "in the end" all entities having status as "facts" and articulated by all languages are not *the* absolute. In the Hindu world view the things perceived may not possess emotive potential identical to that of the Judeo-Christian world. Both Western and Indian cultures have the concept of time, but even a cursory reading of the texts of Hinduism suggests a different kind of sensitivity toward its nature and, by implication, those entities "occupying" time.

For those dominated by such ideas, things populating their world are seen as always in movement. Neni Bai's birth, for example, was not denied. Her actions during the course of her short life were acknowledged, but it was an acknowledgment of different significance from that I accorded her. For me her actions, all those qualities I had perceived as well as those I had not had a chance to observe but accorded her, *were her*. They defined her. Her uniqueness in time was my reality. But the villagers envisaged Neni Bai—as they probably do all human entities—as a surface phenomenon. Reality to them is something other than the outward appearance that I deemed as significant. Neni Bai, myself, them—and you, the reader—are part of a ceaseless flux, the underlying reality of which is left unchanged. Lives are created, lives are stopped, but the substance of things remains unchanged. And what I label dynamics, in motion, is perceived by my Hindu friends as but a manifestation of ultimate "unchange."

Although I could accept, rather than merely say I understood, that time was not a distinct entity and absolute in its independence, I still had difficulty seeing how Neni Bai related to this esoteric intellectual orientation. In other words, I was uncomfortable with their conceptualization of form. Gradually I realized that it is the "ultimate nonreality of any instant" that provides the foundation for their conception of human beings. I held a distinction between living and dead, between existence and nonexistence. These sets of contrasts are, for Westerners, facets of the human condition. We believe there exists a physical life, and the majority of us posit a spiritual existence also. The Western religions vary in how they perceive the latter after cessation of physical life, but the notion that one "lives on" after the other is familiar.

The people attempting to educate me in this south Asian community reflect an absence of this duality. For them existence and nonexistence are not different aspects of a thing residing in time and do not entail physical bodies evolving and culminating in cessation. Rather, existence and nonexistence are the thing itself, different manifestations of the same underlying, unfathomable sameness. Life and death, then, need not have the identical moral implications they do for us. Their indigenous cultural code conditions them to perceive, experience, and react in a manner I did not anticipate. The physical demise of a person can occur, the villagers perceive it, but the range of reactions does not automatically generate synonymous responses. Death taking place in time was not accorded the same status in regard to "reality" as I accorded it. The result was the curious, and for us probably unnerving, realization that Neni Bai's extinction was the dissolution of a "form," but her consequent "nonexistence" was coequal with her "existence." For them what was important was neither the death of Neni Bai as an event-in-itself nor a concern with the injustice I thought had been inflicted upon her.

The notions of the village people, while different from ours, are neither more barbaric nor more civilized. They do have definite perceptions of time and of the "human beings" populating it, but it is a concern with time on a cosmic order. While we attach importance to the passing events of a person's life and to grand historical episodes, they tend to see these events not as indications of change, progress, and evolution, but as revelations of the eternalness of the social order, of the world, and of the universe. On a far less grandiose level each person—Neni Bai, you, myself—is but a transient instance, an inconsequential "form" repeatedly appearing in a limitless "time."

Neni Bai and the milieu in which she lived forced me to become aware of how I had unquestioningly accepted one culture's definition of common sense. It now also enables me to recognize the usually unrecognized contradictions in the Judeo-Christian legacy regarding the creation, appearance, continuance, and cessation of human life. My problem is that I see and feel these contradictions in an environment not conducive to acting upon such realization; your problem may be that you see no contradictions at all. If you are among the latter, it will be difficult for you to accurately comprehend the phenomenon of violence and crime in a comparative perspective. You will engage in assigning labels to people and events that will be dramatically different from the interpretations of the participants themselves.

There is little in our genetic makeup that makes us prone, or not prone, to engage in ending human life. Rather, our responses are situationally defined. And it is our culture, through its numerous institutions, that conditions our consciousness. The irrationality of killing humans is transformed into the rational, the legitimate, and the acceptable, by society. Our institutions define when killing is to be condoned and when the annihilation of others warrants censure because of inappropriate circumstances. Stand aside for only a moment and reflect upon how our society—or any society—constructs the proper setting for extermination of individuals or groups of humans.

There are probably many of you who, with some encouragement, would readily kill "for your country," or for your God. But we seem to be disturbed by merely killing, or by the label used to designate it. We feel better, we are ethical, if the institutional fabric of our society can satisfy our need for the legitimation of its performance. So killing for Christ and the U.S.A. is effectively conveyed to us in the form of protecting ourselves from some amorphous devil. One subtle function of the groups to which we belong is to lift us out of the emotional quagmire of morality. Not only do such institutions provide us with a sense of identity, security, and the satisfaction of human needs, they also alleviate us of the burden of serious reflection. We are free, but free to conform. Our institutions define the situations when we can kill with gusto, without debilitating feelings of guilt, or at least categorize the act(s) as unfortunate but necessary.

I could understand the phenomenon called Neni Bai only with an eventual willingness to recognize, and to shed, the ethnocentric tendencies inculcated since my childhood. And only by engaging in a similar process can you begin to comprehend "crime" in your society and "crime" as it is defined and conceptualized by inhabitants of the many societies around the world. While all peoples may possess an intellectual category called *crime,* the contents of the compartment are shaped in numerous ways by their respective cultures. A heinous act in one culture may be a nonevent in another, or a performance of remarkably different emotional significance for those involved. This status is not due to any barbarism of the practitioners; it is a reflection of culture's ability to condition us and to invest acts with a multitude of equally logical, sensible interpretations. No one explanation is correct or constitutes a more perfect approximation of some ultimate "truth" existing independently of us, residing "out there." There are, according to the wise men in that Indian village, merely many diverse ways by which human beings express their self-deception.

Discussion Questions

1. What is the source of ethnocentrism in any culture? How are social scientists limited in their ability to understand other cultures by their own ethnocentrism?
2. Consider the difficulties that anthropologist Winther had in explaining in the English language the world view of the people he studied. To what degree do you think a person's language limits the thoughts that he or she is capable of having?
3. How is culture differently understood by the people who live it and outsiders who observe it? Is one picture more accurate than the other?

CHAPTER 4 SOCIALIZATION: LEARNING THE GAME AND BECOMING A PLAYER

Socialization—the ongoing process by which humans come to learn about and believe in their cultures, from learning the roles to sharing the values—is one of the most basic concepts social science has to offer; it calls attention to the fact that humans learn about the ways they live rather than inherit them. Both the personalities we develop and the actions we perform in our social groups are highly related to other personalities and actions that have existed before us. There is no one else exactly like you in any way, but there are many other people who are much like you in most ways. That similarity is the result of common patterns of socialization within your social group. Of all the activities coordinated within a society, the preparation for new members is one of the most important and most closely looked after. Both slow learners and uncooperative learners are apt to face some form of social control from other members of their social groups as group norms are enforced. The pressures you face every day (as others attempt to change your behavior) are far from accidental. The discussion in Chapter 5 shows how adults can be very similar even though they grew up in different places. Such similarity is possible because of coordinated socialization.

Because of its central position in the social sciences, the concept of socialization was introduced in Chapter 1. In this chapter socialization will be explored in much greater detail. The first section will cover the agents of socialization, analyzing the many sources in society that provide us with both cultural information and coercive forms of social control. The following two sections will detail the processes of socialization, with a focus on the changes at different stages in the life cycle and in different situations. The fourth section will examine the "self," that ongoing product of socialization, with an eye to better understanding where individual personalities come from and why people view themselves the way they do. The final section will be concerned with resocialization, an extreme form of socialization that produces dramatic changes in adult personalities and behavior.

AGENTS OF SOCIALIZATION

An **agent of socialization** is often a person but it need not be; it is any social source that communicates elements of the culture or requires conformity to them. Your parents, for example, are important agents of socialization because of the amount of time you spend with them and the crucial stage of your life when you spend that time. They communicate information to you about the culture you live in and spend a good deal of energy enforcing their teaching. The television shows you watch, however, are also important agents of socialization. They communicate a great deal of cultural information and, in methods varying in subtlety, "encourage" you to behave in certain ways (people won't like you if you have bad breath, drive an old rusted automobile, or tell the wrong kind of jokes). And, in fact, if other people have been watching the same programming and are influenced by it, they may *not* like you if you exhibit those characteristics. Living in any society means that you will encounter agents of socialization at every turn.

Individuals as Agents of Socialization

In spite of the importance of the more abstract socialization agents such as television (which we'll look at in the next section), nothing replaces people as socializers. Most of us enter families as defenseless infants and spend quite some time at their mercy before we have the skills or the independence to receive socialization elsewhere. The first socialization we receive in life is by far the most important; a 5-year-old is more like an adult than like a newborn infant. Additionally, this first, or primary socialization consists of time spent with a few individuals; the infant is little affected by or interested in strangers, abstractions, television, Acts of Congress, or fluctuations in the economy. Parents may encounter interference from society if they abuse the child physically, but short of that, they have pretty much a free hand. People may need a license to drive a car and formal education to get a job, but anyone can have and raise a child. This overall situation makes parents extremely important agents of socialization; their impact can be seen throughout their child's life.

Other family members can also be important agents of socialization for the child. Although they are less important than parents because they don't satisfy as many needs, brothers and sisters certainly play a major role in early training. Other adult family members, such as aunts, uncles, and grandparents, are socialization agents of steadily declining importance in American society as family living units become smaller and geographically more dispersed. If you grew up in a nuclear family (with only parents and children), consider how different you might be today had you shared your home with a set of grandparents and perhaps an uncle or two. It is not uncommon in other cultures to find the major childrearing role bestowed on someone other than the biological parents. The American mode, in which parents do the raising while grandparents do the spoiling, suggests something of how we delegate our childrearing duties.

As the American family declines in size, it has also been declining in influence over its offspring. Many American children today attend day-care centers or nursery schools, and most attend some kind of formal schooling by the age of 6. Beyond increasing the importance of the school (which we'll look at in the next section), this shift places greater importance on peers as agents of socialization. It is at this stage that the growing child often encounters the first major contradictions in socialization, for the demands of the peer group may be either different from or in opposition to the expectations of the parents. From the child's perspective, increasing interactions within the peer group often make peer expectations more important than the parents' expectations. The domination of certain fads within adolescent peer groups and the rapidity with which they change suggest the importance of conformity to peer demands.

As life goes on, the importance of individuals as agents of socialization may decrease somewhat. This change is due partly to the process of maturation, but much of it results from the increasing numbers of individuals that most of us face as adults; the more individual agents we face, the less significance any one is likely to have. Nevertheless, as adults, most of us live with or around a small group of "significant" individuals who have a major influence over us.

Institutions as Agents of Socialization

Most of the activities we engage in every day are parts of interrelated clusters of activities known as **institutions.** (This concept is presented in detail in Chapters 9-11.) If you are currently a student, for example, you are involved in one of the many activities that make up the American institution of education. While other individuals socialize you every day, the sum total of a great many individuals involved in a great many activities within an institution affects you on a different scale. Television as an agent of socialization falls into this category.

Children growing up in a society torn by violence will be socialized to deal with things never encountered in peaceful societies. These eight- and nine-year-olds are growing up in Beirut, Lebanon, in a refugee camp for Palestinians. Part of their "scout" training includes the use of sophisticated weapons of war.

Television joins radio, magazines, newspapers, and other forms of communication under the general heading of *mass media.* What you see on television, hear on the radio, or read in the paper is not the work of one individual but the result of a great many individuals working in concert. If your experience with the media socializes you by teaching or influencing you, that influence can be explained only through an understanding of the institution it comes from. For example, a child watching cartoons on Saturday morning will learn that candy and sugar-coated cereals are desirable things to eat. This message is conveyed not because the cartoon makers want young Americans' teeth to rot but because they must have sponsors if they wish to appear on commercial television. In this case financing within the institution of the media leads to a certain form of socialization. Lawmakers have considered placing some form of control on advertising for children. Should they do so, the political institution plus its relation to the media will help to determine what children learn on Saturday mornings.

Like television, the institution of education is an important agent of socialization in American society. Children enter this institution around the age of 6 and generally remain under its influence for a minimum of ten years. Like the media, education is the result of many individuals occupying roles that act in concert. If you are interested in understanding why teachers teach the way they do or why they teach what they teach, you will have to understand the overall workings of the institution: Who trains the teachers? Who trains the trainers? Who writes the textbooks? Who buys the textbooks? How are schools funded? How are schools affected by legislators or by the electorate? All of these questions (plus many more) must be answered before you will understand why Johnny and Jeannie have specific experiences in their third-grade classroom. Ask yourself how many decisions, influences, and activities resulted in your holding this book in your hands right now. If you are a college student reading this book for a sociology class, a conscious attempt is being made by the institution of education to socialize you into looking at the world sociologically.

Similar claims could be made about all the institutional arenas in American society. As an adult, you will respond to the world of politics and alter your life in response to changes in the economy. Your experiences on the job, both intended and unintended by your employer, will change you in many ways. If you are drafted and sent to fight a war, you will return a different person. Coming full circle, you may discover that your parents raised you according to a book written by someone within the institution of education and published by a firm with clear economic interests in the book's success.

Institutions are impossible to escape. As agents of socialization, they permeate modern American life and ultimately are responsible for much of the individual socialization we confront. But while individual socialization seems obvious (as when our friends try to change us), socialization from institutions often affects us without our knowledge, unless we're looking for it. The sociological outlook directs you to look for it—to become aware of the many norms that are enforced and values supported through the ongoing activities within societal institutions and the ways you and your friends mirror the institutions that have already socialized you. If you think that wearing Levi's 501 blues, Air Jordans, and a T-shirt with the emblem of your favorite band is an expression of your individuality, think again—you might have been watching too much television.

PRIMARY SOCIALIZATION: THE EARLY YEARS

Primary socialization is the socialization that occurs during the first several years of life, from whatever source. It is distinctive because (1) it is the first socialization encountered in the life cycle, and (2) the infant or young child is biologically immature and responds very differently than older children or adults. Since the biological development of the child will be an important point in our discussion, it might be useful at the outset to address the heredity versus environment dispute with the basic question: How much is a child born with and how much does he or she learn?

Heredity versus Environment

All organisms inherit their biological makeup and then must survive in some sort of environment. As we watch them (or ourselves) behave in that environment, we might wonder where the behavior came from. At one extreme we might assume that they inherited their behavior genetically, which would lead us to label that behavior *instinct*. The natural world is full of many examples of obviously inherited behavior. How do spiders know how to spin webs or bees to make honey? Even birds seem to find their way south without a roadmap or a guide. These sorts of observations give weight to the heredity side of the argument.

At the other extreme we might observe the lessons provided for the organism by the environment—either the physical environment or from other organisms like itself. On the environment side of the argument we note all instances in which organisms "learn" behavior, either through their own trial and error or by watching others. As spiders tend to lend support for the heredity side of the argument, human beings—with the tremendous amount of learning they do after birth—provide a good example for the environment side.

The dispute over heredity and environment has been going on for centuries and is far from concluded, even though the battlefields have changed many times. One hundred or so years ago, the heredity side of the dispute was in command, and even many human behaviors were explained genetically. It was assumed that criminals were genetically predisposed to crime, musicians were all born with great musical talent, the insane inherited mental instability, and different races and ethnic groups inherited specific mental and physical talents or deficiencies. "Everybody knew" that murderers had "bad blood," Latins had "hot blood," and aristocrats had "blue blood."

More recently, the environment side of the dispute has come to practically displace the heredity side, largely as a result of the growing influence of the social sciences. While the social sciences have allowed many animals to have their instincts, they constantly attack assertions that humans have them. Murderers now come from a "bad environment," Latins live in a culture that encourages displays of emotion, and aristocrats rule not because they are superior but because their culture and weapons give them the power.

Still more recently, there have been some stirrings for a return to genetic explanations of human behavior. Some psychologists have argued that there may be racial differences in intelligence. There is also a growing field of scientific inquiry known as **sociobiology**, defined by Edward O. Wilson, one of its founders, as "the systematic study of the biological basis of all social behavior" (Wilson, 1975:595). Sociobiology seeks to determine what genetic basis there may be in animal social behavior, particularly in regard to monkeys, apes, and humans. For example, Wilson notes that there are ongoing social systems in which males dominate females among almost all the primates (in other words, there is a similarity between ape societies and most human cultures) and asks whether it is not possible that male members of the species inherit more aggressive behavior, particularly through the male hormones. However, sociobiology has been criticized for the inability of its adherents to verify their theories according to the scientific method (Kitcher, 1985).

There is no definitive answer to the questions posed by sociobiology or even to Wilson's theory. Our inability to answer these questions stems directly from the nature of human socialization and the inseparable bond between humans and their societies. No other animal depends as much on learning as humans do. Once we begin to socialize our infants, it becomes impossible to separate learned behavior from inherited behavior. The difference between the two could not be tested for practical reasons as well as the obvious ethical ones; as noted in Chapter 1, human infants require sociability in addition to food and shelter if they are to survive, and such a test would require removing that sociability. Locating cross-cultural similarities is also not a complete answer, as similarities in human adaptation (such as male dominance) might have more to do with our planet's environment than our genes.

The best possible position regarding the heredity versus environment dispute at this point is to keep an open mind. You should also be aware of the biases of the individual or discipline that responds to the dispute. Sociology, as a social science, is biased toward the environment side of the dispute, and this book is no exception (a point you should remember while reading the rest of it). Nevertheless, the topic of socialization brings us the closest that sociology comes to the biological position. As we look at the processes of socialization, you will see something of this interplay as the social forces of society encounter a growing and biologically changing child.

Freud's Theory of Psychosexual Stages

Sigmund Freud (1856-1939) is known as the father of psychoanalysis (although many of his ideas have been dropped or modified by modern psychoanalysts). More generally, his insights provided some of the major turning points that shaped the modern social sciences, sociology included. Perhaps his greatest contribution was his idea of the human *unconscious.*

Freud theorized that people are not consciously aware of many of their desires, angers, lusts, fears, and other feelings. In particular, they are unconscious of whatever feelings their society defines as wrong or inappropriate. Through socialization individuals repress these inappropriate feelings; **repression** involves moving such feelings from the conscious mind into the unconscious. After repressing these feelings, an individual can see himself or herself as a "good" person (as defined by society). However, the inappropriate feelings don't disappear, they just go beneath the surface into the unconscious. They may respond to this inhospitable treatment later by giving one ulcers, headaches, bad dreams, fits of depression, or a variety of other ailments. Opening up the unconscious, Freud felt, could bring some of these feelings back into the conscious mind of the individual and stop the damage they were doing. Such tapping of the unconscious was the purpose of Freud's approach to therapy, which he dubbed *psychoanalysis.*

The knot that ties Freud's theory to sociology is repression. Without society and the values that are socialized into us, repression would not be possible. Hating your mother or father, for example, would cause you fewer problems if your society did not place a strong value on loving one's parents. Freud became interested in the processes of socialization in hopes of learning just how the values of society come to be part of an individual; as a result, he developed his theory of the *stages of psychosexual development.*

The newborn infant is in the *oral stage.* At this stage the infant receives sexual satisfaction through biting and sucking; everything encountered goes into the mouth. (This can be a trying stage for a parent.) In approximately the second and third years of life the child is in the *anal stage,* during which time the child's attention shifts from the mouth to the anus. Commonly the period in which toilet training occurs, this stage was of great interest to Freud. The young child has no inborn interest in becoming toilet trained, but the parents are greatly interested. The child must acquire the parents' value of using the toilet (being "clean" as opposed to "dirty") and come to view himself as they do. When the child becomes happy at being toilet trained, the value has been internalized and socialization is progressing.

Freud's third, or *phallic,* stage has received considerable attention. It begins around age three or four and continues until five or six. During this stage the child once again shifts the focus of sexual interest, from the anus to the penis or clitoris. Freud posits that at this time the *Oedipus complex* develops: The young male comes to desire his mother and hate his father (who presumably is first in line for his mother's attentions). The young female, on the other hand, desires her father and fears her mother. By repressing these inappropriate feelings, boys and girls come to *identify* with their same-sex parent.

The fourth, or *latency,* stage begins around age six and continues through the school years until puberty, when the fifth and final stage, the *genital stage,* begins. During these stages the developing child becomes increasingly bound up in his or her social environment and learns to develop a wide variety of "appropriate" feelings. The true power of society can be seen in these stages, as the values of society become increasingly internalized. We will return to this topic at the end of the following section on secondary socialization when the socialization of older children is discussed. The importance of Freud's stages for the discussion now is their emphasis on the maturation of the child. The concerns of the parents change as the child grows older, but so do the concerns of the child. Freud's stages are focused somewhat narrowly on the sexual and emotional concerns of the child. We can broaden our perspective by considering the work of Jean Piaget and his theory of cognitive development.

Piaget's Theory of Cognitive Development

Cognition is the process of perception or knowing; cognitive development refers specifically to the mental development of the child and focuses our attention on changes in the mental capabilities of children as they mature. Just as a 5-year-old is biologically incapable of understanding adult sexual desire or throwing a football very well, so the same child is biologically incapable of understanding calculus. Jean Piaget (1896-1980), a Swiss psychologist, concluded that the best method for understanding the thinking processes of adults is to begin with infants and trace their development. His work in this area has been truly monumental, and as with Freud, there are many lessons in it for the sociologist. (A good overview of Piaget's work is provided by Ginsburg and Opper—see the supplementary readings for this chapter.)

Piaget constructed a general theory of knowledge, part of which must be understood in order to follow his theory of cognitive development. Piaget posits that humans, like all organisms, adapt to their environment. This means that they orient their thinking and their actions to the things and problems in their environment. The human need for food and shelter would lead to very different adaptations in jungles or deserts; desert dwellers, for example, would have to develop special means of adaptation to find and conserve water. The same principle holds true for the infant, who must learn to cope with the strange environment of the home and the other people in it, both of which were not present in the womb. The newborn knows how to suck, grasp, and make noise, and for a while does quite a bit of all three. Previously unencountered objects, such as a mother's breast, can be grasped and sucked. This early adaptation to the new environment is the first step on the road of cognitive development—the child has expanded her horizons by developing an important skill.

Adaptation continues as the child builds from these rudimentary skills. New elements in the environment are dealt with in old ways (a thumb can also be sucked, for instance), and over time old elements can be dealt with in new ways. Piaget calls these growing abilities *psychological structures.* Structures involving physical manipulation are referred to as *schemes.* The infant develops a sucking scheme, for example, and by employing that scheme with other objects in the environment can thereby learn.

A second type of psychological structure is the *operation.* Whereas the scheme is a behavioral adaptation, the operation is an intellectual adaptation. Like schemes, operations develop through maturation as the child becomes increasingly able to think in more complicated ways. As just

BOX 4.1

PIAGET'S STAGES: A TEST YOU CAN DO

The theories of Jean Piaget are far more than abstract ideas that occurred to him in his study. Piaget worked very closely with children in all of his research, constantly testing his ideas against the capabilities of the children. Many of his testing techniques were ingenious, to say the least. Of the variety he created, here is one you might find interesting to try yourself, as it does not require much in the way of materials. You will need:

One early preoperational child (age three to four should do)

Two identical glass tumblers

One glass tumbler that is obviously shorter and wider or taller and thinner than the other two

This experiment measures the child's ability to conserve continuous quantity—or, in short, to understand the idea of volume. Fill each of the two identical tumblers with an equal amount of water; half full should be a good amount. Then ask the child whether the two glasses have the same amount or have different amounts. He or she will tell you they are the same. Then you pour (or have the child pour) the contents from one of the tumblers into the different-shaped tumbler. Ask the child if there is still the same amount of water in the two tumblers. Since the water level will now be very different in the two tumblers, he or she will tell you that there are now different amounts of water, even though no water was lost or added. According to Piaget, this means that

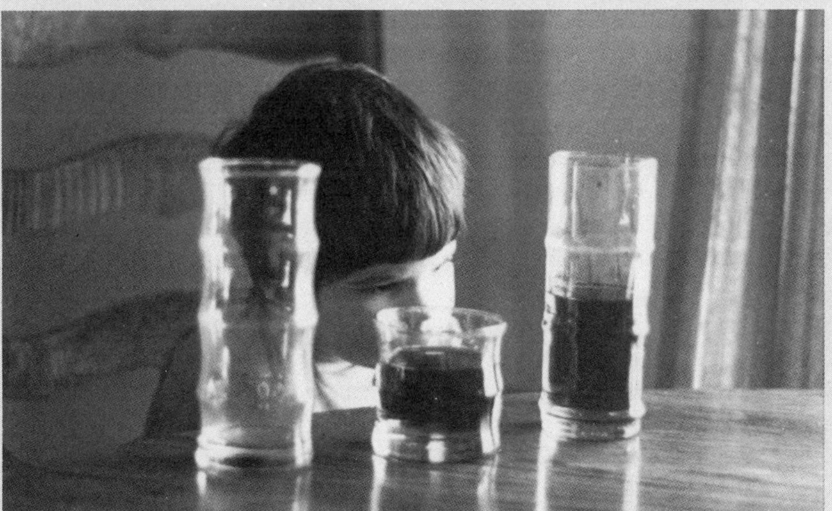

Piaget's test for the conservation of volume. Does the tall, thin glass contain the same amount of liquid as the short, wide one? Children are asked to respond right after they have seen the liquid poured from one to the other.

(continues)

BOX 4.1 (continued)

the child is not able to conserve quantity in his or her mind—an indication that the child is at the preoperational stage of development.

If you want to get a little more elaborate, try this experiment on children of different ages, and after you do it with them once, let them test you. You will discover both how dramatically children change as they develop and how intensely they cling to their current level. Children who can't conserve quantity will adamantly maintain that there are different amounts of water after you pour the water into the different-shaped tumbler. If they give you the test and you answer correctly (from the adult perspective), the children will look at you as if you are crazy. At the other extreme, children who have learned to conserve continuous quantity will have no trouble answering your questions correctly and, furthermore, will think the experiment dumb and boring. When we learn things, we're ready to move on.

one of the many examples from Piaget's research, younger children find it difficult to answer the question, "Are there more girls or more children in the room?" This apparently easy (to an adult) question is difficult for young children because they find it difficult to think of the girls twice—first as girls and second as children. The question involves two levels of generality.

Piaget concluded through his studies of children at different ages that cognitive development occurs in definite stages as children reach new levels of understanding. His first stage of cognitive development is the *sensorimotor* period, which lasts roughly from birth until age two. This is a period dominated by the acquisition of motor skills, hand-eye coordination, and so on. While the young infant may go through great effort to grasp a rattle, the older infant in this period may be experimenting with elaborate patterns of imitation, developing new schemes.

The second stage, which Piaget calls the *preoperational* period, lasts from ages two to seven. The preoperational child is going through considerable mental development, especially in the area of language. Of particular interest to sociologists is the *egocentrism* typical of this period: The preoperational child has difficulty in separating himself from others, or looking at anything from the perspective of someone else. As we will see, this is a fundamental skill to be derived from socialization. Piaget tells us that until a certain age a child is simply not mature enough to learn it.

The third stage, the *concrete operational* period (ages seven to eleven), is followed by the fourth and final stage of *formal operations* (twelve and over). In both of these stages the child is developing increasingly sophisticated mental skills, becoming capable of systematic logic and finally abstract thought. The fundamental difference between the two stages is suggested by the word *concrete*; the child at the concrete operations stage can achieve fairly sophisticated thought provided the objects of that thought are physically present.

The ages given for each stage are far from absolute; individual children might move from one stage to the next before or after the years specified. The important points are that (1) all children go through these stages *in order* (each stage builds upon the one before it as the child adapts); and (2) these stages are part of the child's biological maturation; adult socializers should exercise patience and wait for the child to be ready to acquire certain kinds of information. Box 4.1 presents an experiment that will help you understand the strength with which children cling to their stages of cognitive development.

Taking the Role of the Significant Other: George Herbert Mead

George Herbert Mead (1863-1931) was an American sociologist. Socialization was one of Mead's primary concerns, and he reached many conclusions similar to those of both Freud and Piaget. He was convinced that the "self" is a product of society (through socialization), and he set out to discover how it develops (Mead, 1934).

To Mead the infant's first experience with social interaction comes through her or his understanding of communication. The child may discover, for example, that crying produces mother at the crib or that laughing makes mother laugh. This interaction, referred to by Mead as a conversation of gestures, represents the child's first efforts at communication. Specifically, **gestures** are nonsymbolic forms of communication that begin randomly but come to be associated with elements in the environment. Communication is, of course, the first step on the road to socialization.

Around age two the child begins to develop the ability to use language. Language is the ultimate symbol system of human societies, and, for Mead, this development increases communication greatly and opens many more doors to socialization. As the child's communication skills increase, he or she will simultaneously be learning to take the role of the other. In order to communicate, the child must learn to imagine how he or she looks to others. When someone makes a negative response, the child realizes that his or her behavior is being seen in a negative light and comes to look at himself or herself in the same light.

When two people communicate through language, the words presumably create the same meanings in the minds of both people simultaneously. And since each person can look at the communication from the perspective of the other, each can be assured that the other is receiving

American sociologist George Herbert Mead (1863-1931). Mead was influential in turning the attention of American sociologists toward the importance of socialization and the development of the self.

the meaning intended. The ability of the child to see himself or herself from the perspective of others thus allows the child to fully understand language and all forms of symbolic communication. This process is in many ways the foundation of Mead's theory of socialization; the social self, to Mead, develops only as we come to see ourselves through the responses of other people.

As the child begins to take the role of the other, he or she enters the *play stage* of development. During this stage, the child's imagination leads to actually playing out the many "others" the child has encountered. Probably the clearest example of this stage is the childhood game of dress-up, in which the child puts on Mommy's or Daddy's clothes and, in play, actually becomes Mommy or Daddy. This kind of physical acting out is necessary because taking the perspective of another person is a difficult mental operation for the developing child; using some props and talking out loud like Mommy or Daddy helps to make the understanding more meaningful. I recall an argument I had with my son when he was three. He was sent to his room, and for the next half-hour I heard our argument continuing with my son playing both parts. Not only did he get rid of some of his anger this way, but he also produced in his own mind a clearer image of my expectations (however unreasonable they might have been). He was learning to see himself as I saw him.

Taking the role of the other is fundamental to socialization and to the communication that makes up that socialization. The basic form of the process is present even in young children, though it is difficult for them because of their level of maturation. Recall Piaget's description of children at the preoperational stage: The preoperational child is focused strongly on his or her own desires and has difficulty realizing that others have similar strong desires. Mead's explanation is that the child can take the perspective of others but only one "other" at a time—and even then with some difficulty. Young children clearly can distinguish between different expectations from one person to another. The child may discover that some behavior tolerated by Mommy will result in punishment from Daddy, and vice versa. The expectations of grandparents will likely be something else entirely. It is very interesting watching a child of three or four in the company of both parents and some grandparents—which "other" is in charge? The answer comes through an experience of trial and error, often painful to all concerned.

The overall picture of primary socialization that emerges from the various theories is a composite. Freud, Piaget, and Mead all emphasize the maturation of the child as an important factor in determining the process of socialization. Just as your thinking processes can never return to where they once began, no adult can ever experience primary socialization. Furthermore, as all three theorists emphasize, the child's coming to view himself or herself through the perspectives of others is the true source of the developing end product—the social self. As we turn now to a discussion of secondary socialization, we will get a still clearer picture of this process, as the child becomes biologically more receptive and the agents of socialization become more insistent.

SECONDARY SOCIALIZATION: A LIFELONG PROCESS

Consider all that goes into adult conversation, even at its most basic level. For example:

John: *Hello, Mary. Where are you going?*

Mary: *Hello, John. I'm walking to the library to get a book.*

John: *I just came from there. The library is closed.*

How is it that John and Mary understand each other? This very brief communication is more than enough to make the point. Here is the same conversation as it occurs inside the heads of John and Mary:

John: *(There's my friend Mary. I think I'll give her a friendly greeting along with a polite question about her activities. I speak English, and I know from past experience that Mary does, too, so I'll string some English words into a sentence that will communicate my thoughts to Mary.)*

Mary: *(John has just said, "Hello Mary. Where are you going?" Now what would I have been thinking to myself if I had just met someone like myself and selected those particular words to say? I would probably have simply wanted to convey a friendly greeting coupled with a polite question as to current activities. Assuming that John meant what I would have meant if I had spoken those words, I'll return the friendly greeting along with some information about my current activities. I'll try to create an English sentence that conveys my thinking as nearly as possible.)*

John: *(Mary has just responded to my original remarks by saying, "Hello John. I'm walking to the library to get a book." Before she decided on that reply, she placed herself in my original position and asked herself what she would have meant had she made my original remark. She then made assumptions that I actually meant what she would have meant under similar conditions, responded to that meaning in her own thoughts, and tried to place that response back into English for my benefit. Now if I had been making those assumptions about what I originally meant and had then produced the utterance that she just produced, what would I have meant? I will assume that she actually meant what I would have meant under those conditions and respond as if that is actually what she did mean. If all my assumptions are correct, I think that she might find it useful to hear about my recent experience at the library. I'll try to create an English sentence that will convey that recent experience.)*

It is a wonder of human communication that we can do all that thinking and assuming in a split second with very little conscious effort at all. We must constantly place ourselves in someone else's position all through a conversation if we are to understand each other. We usually become aware of this process only when communication breaks down. People sometimes make faulty assumptions about another's meaning and take offense at a comment that was not meant that way; it can be very difficult to backtrack along a conversation to find exactly where the mistaken assumption occurred.

The process by which we "take the role of the other" tells us as much about socialization in general as it does about human communication. **Secondary socialization** is the socialization that occurs after the first few years of life, when the individual is capable of symbolic communication and developing a social sense of self. It has truly begun when a child can imagine himself or herself in someone's position as automatically as John and Mary do in the above conversation. Such imagining requires considerable mental agility, which a very young child does not possess. The secret of this automatic "role taking," according to Mead, is not just the speed, but the complexity, with which it occurs. There are many times when we must take into account the perspectives of many roles simultaneously; for this we need what Mead calls a generalized other.

The Development of the Generalized Other

A **generalized other** is your imagination of what you believe a large number of people (or people in general) expect of you. For all practical purposes your generalized other will relate not to a group of actual people but to roles. When you walk into a supermarket, you can imagine how other customers and clerks expect you to behave; your imagination need not get more specific than that because the coordination of society creates enough regularity in roles. The expectations held of one role by other roles have already been defined as norms; thus we can simplify the definition of *generalized other* to your understanding of social norms and how they affect you. Everyday social interaction could not occur without generalized others; patterns of social behavior depend on people constantly checking their own behavior against norms.

When the child is mature enough to construct a generalized other, he or she has moved from Mead's play stage to the *game* stage. A child can *play* by himself or herself (even if other children are in the play group), but a *game* requires the child to view a common activity from many perspectives at once. Mead uses the game of baseball as an example.

How do you play first base in the game of baseball? Physically you play only one position, but mentally you play every position. You imagine yourself as the batter and take on that perspective. The batter probably wants to get a hit and make it to first base. Let's assume the batter does hit the ball on the ground to the second-base player. You now have to imagine yourself as the batter and the second-base player simultaneously: The batter will be trying to run to first base, and the second-base player will try to catch the ball and throw it to first base ahead of the runner. Since you are the first-base player, you had better run to first base in anticipation of the throw that you expect from the second-base player. You anticipate all this because you can imagine what you would do in both of the other positions simultaneously. In short, says Mead, you understand how to play a game. But before you can play a game, you must be able to construct a generalized other.

Piaget (1965) noticed the same phenomenon in his study of how children learn to play the game of marbles. The Swiss children he studied seemed to play marbles at very young ages, but upon watching them closely and talking to them, Piaget discovered they didn't understand what they were doing as a "game." They were just shooting marbles at other marbles. They were not competing against the other children, since to compete one must understand how a game is played with winners and losers. The key to any game is its rules. Young children do not understand a rule and are unable to look at the game from the perspective of others simultaneously and then win or lose accordingly. Piaget further discovered that, at a certain point in life, a "light went on" in the minds of the children, and they comprehended the rules of the game. From then on they didn't just play; they played a *game.*

Note the similarity between Piaget's idea of the child's relation to the rule and Mead's idea of the generalized other as an understanding of norms. A norm, after all, is nothing but a rule in a social game; it specifies who should do what and when. A very young child may understand what Mommy expects (the "rule" of an individual) but cannot understand what people in general expect (the norms). To a child every new situation is new because the people are different; to an adult situations that are technically new may in fact be nothing more than an old game played with new players at a new location. A supermarket, after all, is a supermarket, wherever you find it.

If we want to understand how children react to socialization, we must know something about how they come to understand norms. The very young child can deal only with individual others because he or she is biologically limited to that kind of mental perspective. This limitation is one of the reasons the actions of our parents are so important to the way we turn out. We perceive Mommy's expectations as extremely important; they fill the whole world of our imagination. As adults, however, we see the expectations of other individuals as often just representations of more general group norms. We are also more capable as adults of associating with a variety of groups that may have different norms (and we will develop a different generalized other for each group). Having this variety in our experience gives us a different perspective altogether on the importance of norms: We may come to see them as arbitrary rules agreed upon by a social group. The young child, on the other hand, experiences the expectations of an individual other as virtually carved in granite.

But socialization conveys more than just norms; socialization also conveys *values*. The ultimate goal of socialization is not only to teach you the norms but to make you want to follow them. Values provide reasons for following the norms or, more basically, convince you that following your group's norms is important. If values were not part of socialization, we would be spending most of our time policing other members of social groups, seeing to it that they followed the norms. When individuals respond to socialization by coming to believe in the values of their social group, we say those values are **internalized**.

Internalization: The Basis of Morality and Social Constraint

Try the following experiment: Cover your hands with honey, chocolate, or anything you can find that is sticky. Then leave them that way for an hour or two. If you have internalized the American value of cleanliness, it will drive you crazy ("Cleanliness is next to Godliness"). Babies are not born wanting to be clean; if anything, they seem to be inclined the other way. How is it possible to take a nice sticky baby and turn it into an adult who can't stand a little goo? This may not seem an important question, since similar changes happen to all of us, but to a sociologist it's a miraculous transformation.

Piaget understood this function of socialization very well in his study of children and their marble games, titled *The Moral Judgment of the Child* (1965). What's moral about marbles? Not much. But the basis of any kind of group morality is an understanding of how your group looks at its rules. As with the Ten Commandments, there is always an inseparable bond between a group's rules and its values. Morality, therefore, can begin with marbles. The child's first understanding of adhering to a moral code will occur simultaneously with his or her understanding of the rules in a game.

Perhaps the most famous part of Freud's theory is an elaboration on this idea. The human personality, says Freud, contains a facet called the *id*, which consists of our basic drives and desires. Humans are born with a well-developed id; a baby is concerned with its own wants and, as we have seen, is incapable of appreciating the wants of anyone else. The part of the human personality controlled by the id is referred to by Freud as the *primary process*. As socialization occurs, the id is joined by a growing *superego*, that portion of the personality that has internalized the values of the social group. Freud refers to the part of the personality controlled by the superego as the *secondary process*. Repression occurs when the superego comes into conflict with the id and wins, driving the desires of the id into the unconscious. The third, and final, facet of the human personality is the *ego,* which acts as something of a mediator between the id and the superego, striving to satisfy both as much as possible while dealing with the realities of the world.

Freud's concept of the superego is very similar to the common idea of the conscience—that part of you that keeps track of "right" and "wrong" and makes you feel guilty when you do "wrong." Freud's observation was that the conscience is very real, but it must be understood as a social creation. The conscience contains the values of the social group; if it makes you feel guilty, that means that you have internalized those values to the point where they are now part of you.

Mead conceived of value internalization in a manner similar to Freud. According to Mead, there is a part of every human personality, which he termed the "**I**," that is spontaneous and creative; it initiates or encourages action by the individual. Mead also conceived of another part of the personality that he termed the "**Me**." Much like Freud's superego, the "Me" is the part that is socialized by the group and contains the group's values; it sometimes battles the "I" for control over your behavior. The "Me" directs or channels action by the individual into socially approved forms.

Mead's somewhat unusual choice of pronouns as names for his concepts relates to his conception of the reflective manner in which socialization occurs. The pronoun *I* is always used as a subject in a sentence, as in "I saw Mary"; it always refers to something active. The pronoun *me,* on the other hand, is grammatically an object, as in "Mary saw me." While *I* does the doing, something is being done to *me.* Since socialization occurs as we come to look at ourselves as objects viewed by others, it is fitting that the socialized part of the self should be a grammatical "object" rather than a "subject." We are fully socialized when we carry our social group around inside us, constantly evaluating our own behavior according to the group's standards. Though our generalized other informs us what those standards are, we must also have internalized values if we are to care about adhering to those standards. We have a police force to enforce many of these standards, but that force could never be large enough if most of us didn't police our own behavior.

Figure 4.1 graphically sums up the connections among all the concepts in the sociological view of socialization. On one side we find the social group with its norms, values, and roles. The goal of socialization (to the socializer) is to firmly place those norms and values into a potential new group member, in hopes of producing a new role player. The process of socialization itself turns group norms into a generalized other (the individual's knowledge of the group norms), and group values into a "Me" (or a superego). The individual may then choose to play an appropriate role. Along with each role comes appropriate feelings and emotions; we acquire these emotions through socialization and also learn how, when, and where to express them (Kagan, 1984).

An individual will never be a carbon copy of the group; one individual will seldom be aware of all the group's norms, nor will he or she be likely to have internalized *all* the group's values. Unlike the painter who declares the painting finished, members of social groups never tire of putting a few finishing touches of socialization into their interactions.

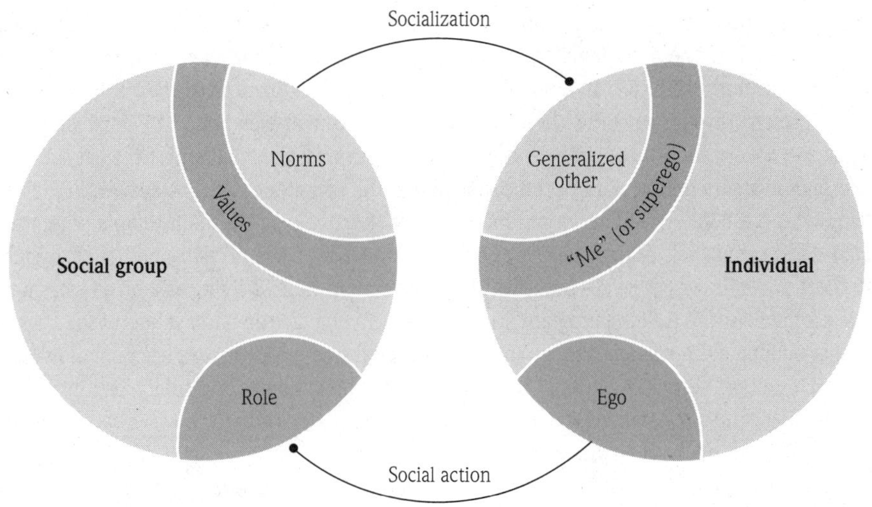

Figure 4.1 The process of socialization.

Learning Norms and Internalizing Values

Whenever you enter a social situation new to you, or begin interacting with members of an unfamiliar social group, you will likely have a limited or confused knowledge of the norms that operate, and as part of the process of learning them, you will make mistakes. No matter how old you are, there is a little of the experience of childhood in learning new norms. The "new kid on the block" has to learn slowly just where and how to fit in.

In a highly mobile society such as the United States, wherever you find social groups and social situations, you will also find newcomers trying to cope with them. Because socialization is a two-way street, the newcomer is often as anxious as older group members for the socialization to be successful. In the case of **anticipatory socialization** the newcomer may even begin socializing himself or herself in an imaginatory sense before real socialization begins; a high school student who wants to be a doctor may start to "feel the part" long before medical school.

An individual who enters an official training program (or college major) will "learn" many things at different levels. Beyond the program content, the individual will face a variety of efforts from teachers and others in the program to change his or her values and perceptions of self. A professional college program (nursing, education, law enforcement, and the like) not only passes on knowledge related to the prospective job but also seeks to make students think of themselves as future practitioners of the job. There may be official courses on the ethics and values of the occupation, but more important are the informal settings (clubs, associations, casual conversations) that slowly but surely make the student identify with others in the occupation and, ultimately, with the occupation itself.

Most occupations require individuals to change their self-view somewhat, but some demand this more than others. One interesting example of this process is provided by Jason Ditton's (1977) study of a training program for bread salesmen in England. The salesmen were required to sell bread door to door. Such a form of selling, with a great many exchanges of money, led to a problem. Mistakes were bound to occur in figuring prices or making change, but customers were much more likely to call attention to mistakes in their own favor than to mistakes in the salesmen's favor. Over time, therefore, the bread salesman was bound to come up short. Since the bakery took these errors out of the salesman's wages, it became necessary for the salesman to assure that he did not come out short at the end of the day. The answer, in English slang, was the fiddle. To fiddle was to intentionally short change those customers who were unlikely to count their change as a way of making up for mistakes in favor of other customers. In short, to fiddle was to steal—but it was the only way to make a living as a bread salesman. The problem for the training program, therefore, was to change the basic values of the trainee so that fiddling did not seem wrong. This was accomplished by saving the teaching of fiddling until the end of the training course and then introducing it slowly and subtly. By the end of the training course the trainee would have become committed to being a bread salesman and would be more open to changing his values.

Another newcomer situation concerns immigrants. America is often labeled the nation of immigrants, and we can look to the history of the many who came (and are still coming) to learn the problems of newcomers. The problems have been much the same for a German immigrant in 1800, an Italian immigrant in 1900, or a Vietnamese immigrant in the 1980s. They encounter differences in language, religion, political processes, occupations, clothing styles, food, childrearing practices, education, sex roles, entertainment forms—the list could go on forever. The newcomer problem for the immigrant is made even more difficult because, unlike some other newcomer situations with avid socializers, the "old-timers" may keep the immigrant away from experiences needed for socialization. Old-timers with particular job skills, for example, may not want an immigrant to learn those skills and become a competitor.

Such complexity makes the socialization of the immigrant take a long time. In general, the individual who immigrates as an adult will always be a newcomer, even after forty or fifty years. A "foreign accent" is only a concrete sign of a great many other elements of the original culture that the immigrant retains. The immigrant's children, however, face a different situation. Even though they may not have access to many sectors of the society because of discrimination against their group, they nevertheless will be native-born members of their parents' adopted society. They have fundamentally different experiences from their parents and, as a result, will think and act differently from them.

THE DEVELOPMENT OF THE SELF: SOCIETY AND PERSONALITY

If we look at people as learners who are "taught" how to be human by other members of their social groups, your **self** and your personality have more to do with your social group than with your own hopes and desires. By the time you are old enough to form definite goals and preferences, your social group has already had sufficient time to affect the kinds of goals and preferences you'll create. When you look to your adult self for a little decision making about your future, many of those decisions will in fact have been made for you by others and hidden in your personality for you to discover later on. You may decide, for example, that you wish to have a job with power over others, that you like art and want to paint, or that you want to get married and have babies. In each case it will be your decision—but, like much in society, it will come with a little help from your friends.

Charles Cooley: The Looking-Glass Self

Charles Cooley (1864-1929) was an American sociologist who helped direct sociological attention to the study of the primary group and its importance to the socialization of the individual. He is best known today for one of the concepts he employed in describing his process—the **looking-glass self**, the process by which we acquire a sense of self from the way others view us. We constantly (1) imagine how others see us, (2) imagine how others judge us, and (3) add those imaginations to our overall view of self, consequently feeling, for example, proud or ashamed (Cooley, 1909). Other people, of course, are interested in socializing us and may go out of their way in helping us be clear about exactly what their views and judgments of us are. If other people think you are physically unattractive, for example, they may tell you that (1) you are ugly, and (2) being ugly is a characteristic that disgusts them. As a result, according to Cooley, you will come to see yourself as (1) an ugly person, and (more important in the long run) (2) a disgusting person.

Cooley's concept of the looking-glass self is consistent with the theories of Freud, Piaget, and Mead. In each case there is an emphasis on the reflective nature of socialization, as we come to view ourselves through the eyes of others, who represent the norms and values of our social groups. Our self develops as a mirror image; we can only see ourselves as a reflection from the responses of other people. To some extent your adult self will be the sum of other people's responses to you throughout your life. Keep in mind, however, that not all other views will affect your self-image equally. Your parents' views will have a much greater impact on you than a neighbor's impression; your best friends will have much more effect on your self-image than casual acquaintances will.

Your view of self is also flexible because of its dynamic nature. For example, you could spend several years in a social situation where everyone responded to you as if you were unintelligent; they might ignore your opinions, ridicule your thoughts, or (if they wished to leave no doubt in the matter) simply call you stupid. Almost certainly you would come out of this situation with the impression that you were not too bright. If you changed social situations, however, you could conceivably encounter others who were greatly impressed with your mental skills and abilities. In this new situation you would slowly but surely acquire a new self-image as an intelligent person. To explain your past, you might also become convinced that your past associates were not too bright themselves and therefore unable to appreciate your true gift of intelligence.

How to Avoid a Self: An Active Approach to Role Playing

Your self-image is a reflection of other people's responses to you *in a specific role.* As an adult, you will discover that you have acquired a variety of self-images specific to certain roles. Your employer may think you're incompetent, while your husband may think you're very capable (or vice versa). This situation would give you a negative self-image in the role of employee and a positive self-image in the role of wife (or, again, vice versa). Most of us are in fact very aware of the roles that give us positive feedback and try to spend as much time in them as possible. A bad situation at work will find us rushing home at the end of the day to a positive family life; a bad situation at home might make us workaholics, dedicated to our jobs. We slip fondly into the roles we find the most comfortable.

Responses to you in your roles can vary by how well others feel you play the role, but they can also vary according to the role itself. The role of prisoner, for example, produces a negative self-image no matter how well other prisoners and guards feel that you play it. The same could be said for the roles of slave, welfare recipient, garbage collector, janitor, or mental patient. In each case the role itself tends to have a negative connotation in American society; identifying yourself as a player of that particular role thus tends to produce a negative self-image. You may know in your heart that being a really good janitor is difficult and that you do your job very well indeed, but the responses of others to "what you do" will always make you feel as if you are in a second-class occupation. You may conclude that you are "not as good" or "not as smart" as other people—a conclusion to avoid.

Since your view of yourself comes from roles, an alternative view of yourself depends upon an alternative role that will provide you with a more positive self-image. Such an alternative role can be achieved through the imagination. John Updike's (1960) novel *Rabbit, Run* tells the story of an ex-high school basketball star (nicknamed Rabbit) for whom nothing has gone well since school. He responds to his current problems by an imaginary reliving of his fame on the court just a few years back. Although still a young man in his twenties, Rabbit turns his back on his dead-end job and nagging wife to "run" his imagination back into his days of glory and a self-image he found satisfying. People can also imagine themselves into the future and avoid identifying with a current unpleasant job, for example, by imagining some position of importance they plan to occupy in the future. College students often put up with extremely unpleasant summer jobs in this way. Ely Chinoy (1952) noted some similar imaginings among full-time automobile workers in the United States. Most of the men he interviewed recognized, when pressed, that they would probably never be doing anything but what they were doing, yet many had alternative activities alive in their imaginations. For example, many of them talked of leaving the factory one day to operate some kind of small business. A light at the end changes a hole into a tunnel.

The human imagination is an amazing phenomenon, but it can't compete with the reality and involvement of everyday life. The habit of role taking that is so necessary for even the most basic forms of communication opens the door to socialization. An employer who thinks poorly of you, for example, will communicate that thought with every interaction between the two of you. And you can't refuse to interact with your employer. Your imagination will remind you that better times are ahead and that your boss is a feeble excuse for a human being (whose opinions should therefore be disregarded), but the everyday experience of negative responses will have a wearing effect. You may come to doubt the reality of both past and present alternative roles as your current situation imperceptibly alters your self-image.

The social self that we develop over the years is in fact a shaky construction that is constantly in need of strengthening and repair work. Most adults will think this assertion contrary to their own experience, for most of us perceive no major changes in our personalities over the years and think of ourselves as "set." Selves are seldom set, however. Most people never find themselves in social situations that drastically attack the social self they have developed; in

Secondary socialization is the socialization we experience as adults. Young women going into occupations that have been largely male dominated often experience heavy doses of it at first.

fact, most of us go out of our way to avoid such situations. We like to remain around familiar places, people, and social situations, where we're comfortable. This kind of constancy hides the effect our social lives have on our selves; we are unaware of how our everyday experiences have become a "fix" to which we become addicted to maintain our personalities. If you receive respect in your everyday life, for example, you will feel happy, content, and strong and you may have the impression that you will be basically that way in any situation. An unpleasant new role could change all that, however.

The most effective way to minimize the impact of a particular role on your self-image is to cultivate another self-image in another, more positive role. A good job can make a bad family situation more bearable, and vice versa. The positive self-image we acquire in one role helps to counteract the negative self-image offered to us in another. We can also add groups of friends, club memberships, and so on to further extend the roles available to us. With such a variety of messages concerning our selves available, we can use the more positive messages as psychological ammunition against the negative messages. A bad day at work makes you even happier than usual to get home; you've probably used up your ammunition that day and need to reload.

We sometimes need to convince others along with ourselves that a particular role does not represent who we think we are. We respond to this need with **role distance**—playing our roles in some creative fashion that communicates to others that "our heart is not in it." Erving Goffman (1961a), who has researched role distance in various settings, observed it among adolescent boys on merry-go-rounds. Feeling that riding the merry-go-round might undermine their growing sense of maleness, those boys would make fun of the merry-go-round and its horses as they rode, hopping from horse to horse, not holding on, or perhaps holding onto a horse's tail. They wanted to make it quite clear both to themselves and to others that they had not taken the childlike role of merry-go-round rider to heart. A similar example of role distance can be found in Box 4.2, which describes the attitudes of jazz musicians who are forced by their employers to play music they consider beneath them.

Role distance can also be maintained through the artful creation of alternative roles to play alongside a distasteful role. When I was a sophomore in college, a good friend dropped out of school and took a job as a janitor in the cafeteria of the student union building. We sometimes coordinated our evening coffee breaks, his from dishwashing and mine from the library. One evening, as we were sitting in the empty cafeteria with two cups of coffee, a middle-aged male janitor came in and asked, "Might I avail myself of a sponge?" *Avail?* Even people who use that word normally would be unlikely to use it in regard to a sponge. The question, as it turned out, had much more to do with us than it had to do with sponges. The janitor told us his life story, which included many advanced university degrees, a prison sentence for refusing the draft during World War II, and a dedication to doing common work with his hands so as not to prostitute his intellect. Nevertheless, it was obviously important to him that we not mistake him for a "common" janitor; if we didn't, neither would he. As he joined our coffee break, moved the topic of discussion to a theological debate (which was over our heads), and invited us to join the evening discussion group he had organized, it became clear that his alternative role was working well for him.

Wherever distasteful roles are found, role distance will be found. It is perhaps a natural response from any individual in a modern, complex society. The vast number of roles that all of us play make us very aware of the differences among them as well as the different kinds of effects they have on us. If a role doesn't fit, try on a new one; if you can't get out of the old one, add one to it. Even though most of us prefer to see ourselves as having one basic personality, the large number of roles we play provide many facets to our personalities. Our multiple roles give us multiple selves.

Multiple Selves: The Modern Individual

As we've seen, the image you see when you look at yourself was put there by others as they responded to you throughout your life. The infant, in spite of being clearly self-centered, really has no view of self since the infant is unable to imagine how he or she appears to others. When individuals develop this ability, they begin building a self-image that becomes quite complex over time. As an adult, you probably make a great many fine points and subdistinctions in your self-image; you may see yourself as skilled to a certain specified degree in certain specified tasks while finding yourself just as specifically lacking elsewhere. You are not just attractive or unattractive—your hair looks good, your mouth is acceptable, and your nose is too big. We make similar fine distinctions in all aspects of our self-images because the responses we get from others come complete with those distinctions. Do all of these elaborate fine points describe just one person or many?

Our cultural knowledge contains the idea that all individuals are different from each other, but nowhere do we hear that each individual has parts that are different from each other. This might even sound to you like a description of some form of mental illness such as the "split

BOX 4.2

Role Distance on the Job: The World of Jazz Musicians

The world of professional music making has become a mass of specialized activities producing specialized music for specialized audiences. About forty years ago, however, the occupational world of music was less complicated. Aside from classical music, music was either "popular" or "jazz." The first category contained most of the tunes that audiences preferred (popular songs, polkas, etc.), while the second category contained what the musicians wanted to play. Since audiences pay musicians to play, this difference of taste often led to problems. Though the world of music has changed over the years, this dispute is still very much with us.

Howard Becker (1963) was one of the first sociologists to study jazz musicians as an occupational group, examining their sense of occupational identity and their relationship to their audience. He discovered that jazz musicians felt they were very different from all other people, especially the "squares" who hired them. If they wanted to eat, however, they played what the squares wanted. Their identity as jazz musicians continued through a variety of forms of role distance achieved by rebelling at the popular musician role and forming alternative roles. This rebellion was usually mild, often taking the form of barricading the band off in a corner to keep the audience away, to "provide protection from the squares." Within the jazz musicians' community alternative roles existed. Most jazz musicians socialized only with other jazz musicians or show people; within this social environment it was possible to maintain self-respect as a jazz musician by constantly criticizing the squares on the outside.

Robert Stebbins (1969) continued the study of jazz musicians and, in particular, their role distance techniques. One of their major problems, he noted, occurred when the jazz band had to play in some social setting where the audience might request music the band did not want to play. Since they were getting paid, they had to be polite, but it was also important for the individual musician to make his disgust known to the rest of the band. For instance, as the request was passed along to the band members, each member could add a tone of disgust to his voice to indicate his distance from the tune in question. Once the music started, other techniques were available. As Stebbins describes it,

personality." But are you the same person all the time? Do you always act the same way, or even with the same style? Are you the same person in a peaceful mood that you are when you lose your temper? When we pause to reflect, we usually justify all this diversity as parts of our one "self." But do you even see the same self when you are in different situations or in different moods?

A modern industrial society is characterized by an extremely high division of labor. This means that a great variety of activities are going on and also that each individual will generally have more roles than in a nonindustrial society. You may have only one work role, but you have plenty of other roles in other areas of life. Roles are highly specialized in a modern industrial society, with each one requiring different skills and providing different activities. And each one provides a different "self."

Besides being specialized, roles in a modern society tend to be highly compartmentalized (or segregated). Particularly in the world of work, people engaged in one activity frequently don't know (or care) much about the activities of others. The ideal of the well-rounded individual is fast being replaced by the competent but limited specialist who knows more and more about less and less. As we keep our roles separate, played in special arenas for special audiences, the possibilities for multiple selves become endless. We come to direct a specific part of our personality toward each role we play, and as a result, a different version of self emerges. A hired contract killer can become president of the PTA and feel little if any contradiction.

RESOCIALIZATION

Resocialization is an extreme form of secondary socialization in which drastic changes are deliberately brought about in the thinking and behavior of an adult. It can occur only when the agent of socialization has almost total influence or control over the individual to be socialized. The process of resocialization requires a systematic breaking down of the already socialized adult individual so that his or her previous patterns of behavior and thought become disorganized. Once the individual's previous "selves" have been displaced, it then becomes possible for the agent of socialization to replace those selves with a previously selected "self," coupled with appropriate patterns of behavior. Resocialization typically occurs in total institutions (such as prisons, mental institutions, and political "reeducation" programs) and in extreme social movements (such as revolutionary political groups or religious cults). As these examples suggest, individuals can be subjected to resocialization against their will, or they may submit to it willingly. In either case the result is an almost complete transformation of the individual.

This section will discuss resocialization techniques in two types of settings. First, the basic techniques of resocialization will be highlighted through an examination of their most common setting—the total institution. Second, we will turn to the world of everyday life and look at how some individuals are lured out of that world into religious cults by techniques of resocialization that do not require either compulsory participation or physical control over the individual.

The Impact of the Total Institution

A **total institution** provides a regimented living and working existence for its members, who are isolated from the rest of society. The most common examples are prisons, mental institutions, and to some extent, the military (see the article on Marine recruit training at the end of this chapter). Some total institutions are organized solely to provide a highly controlled custody for those whom social authorities want isolated. Even when resocialization is not a conscious goal in such situations, it occurs nevertheless through the institution's control over the behavior of inmates. A custodial total institution requires submission to the rules. With no alternative, many individuals come to take on a self-image appropriate to their role of submissive inmate. It is quite common, in fact, for individuals who have spent many years in total institutions to be incapable of living elsewhere. People who have spent many years in prison, for example, have been known to commit very obvious crimes upon their release for the sole purpose of regaining entry to the prison. This process, whereby individuals become completely adjusted to and dependent on the total institution, is known as **institutionalization**.

If the total institution is an effective resocializer even in the absence of conscious effort, its influence is awesome when directed consciously. The first goal of resocialization is to create a break between the individual and his or her previous life. Incoming mental patients, for example, may be stripped of their clothes and have all their personal possessions removed (Goffman, 1961b). Similarly, Westerners who went through "brainwashing" at the hands of the Chinese during the Korean War were cut off from the outside world and confined to cells (see Lifton, 1969, and Schein et al., 1961). Whatever the particulars, the intent is to disorient by separating the individual from all past social realities. It is at this stage of resocialization that the social nature of the self is very evident. Even a piece of clothing can provide a tie to a past life; when removed, it makes that past life (and self) more remote.

Initial separation is followed by introduction of the individual to the new reality of the total institution. In more extreme cases of resocialization various forms of physical abuse may introduce the individual to the rules of the institution. In our modern world of elaborate technological advances in torture, some of the most effective techniques are the most simple. Solitary confinement, sleep deprivation, and hunger will make anyone disoriented and susceptible to suggestion. The agent (or agents) of socialization offer suggestions in the form of attacks on the individual's previous self and behavior, together with instructions for improving both. Americans "brainwashed" during the Korean War were constantly reminded of their past "sins" as capitalists, encouraged to feel guilt for that behavior, and constantly instructed on the advantages of a communist state (Schein et al., 1961).

Similar procedures occur in most total institutions, although they are not always coupled with physical disorientation. Part of "curing" the "mentally ill," for example, consists of convincing patients of their illness in the past; patients who do not see themselves as "sick" will find that attitude taken as a further symptom of illness. People imprisoned for criminal activity must feel guilty about their past behavior if they are to achieve the label *rehabilitated.* The Marine recruit will learn to see his past self as a soft civilian compared to the tough Marine he now is.

Perhaps most important, the total institution places the individual among a select group of associates. The more total the institution, the more clearly this occurs. Those individuals being "reeducated" during the Korean War were placed in carefully selected cells with other successful converts (Schein et al., 1961). As we will see in the next section, this social aspect of resocialization is extremely important among converts to religious cults. If the institution is not total enough, inmates may find a variety of ways around the hoped-for results. Goffman (1961b) describes the variety of relationships mental patients form with staff members or outsiders in attempts to achieve distance from the mental patient role. Prisons are famous for their underground drug rings, gang relationships, and homosexual activities, all of which subvert the presumed goals of rehabilitation.

The basis of resocialization is to be found in the social nature of the self and the day-to-day interactions that maintain it. Control over the individual and those interactions (which the total institution provides) gives the agent of socialization enormous influence over the individual's self-image. Once the individual has been pried from former personalities and well situated into the ongoing roles of the total institution, resocialization is already well on its way. The amazing ease with which this process occurs is illustrated with frightening clarity in the experiment described in Box 4.3. As is apparent, you control your personality only to the extent that you control the social groups with which you interact and the roles you play. As the total institution takes that control from you, it is also essentially free to remove your personality.

The Growth of Religious Cults

Most of the situations described above involved unwilling participants. The realization that you are totally at the mercy of someone else (whose motives and goals you may only partially understand) would place you in a naturally weak position for holding up against resocialization. How is it possible, therefore, for resocialization to occur when individuals are physically free to walk out the door? The growth of religious cults in the United States during the 1970s has shown that it is very possible.

While the 1960s brought us antiwar protests, the civil rights movement, and flower power, the 1970s brought us Scientology, the Unification Church, Krishna Consciousness, Synanon, and the People's Temple. The 1980s witnessed the rise of fundamentalist religious sects as new religious leaders such as Jimmy Swaggert and Jim Bakker came to have large followings. With the exception of the most revolutionary political movements of the 1960s, none of the political organizations resocialized their members; they attracted members only as long as they satisfied members' political interests. The religious cults of the 1970s and 1980s, by contrast, developed a much stronger hold on their members, often resulting in blind obedience to the cult's leaders; the mass suicide of People's Temple followers at the command of leader Jim Jones may be the most sensational illustration, but all of the cults mentioned were able to achieve amazing loyalty. While none of them applied the initial physical coercion of the total institution, their methods were otherwise very similar.

Bridge-Burning Activities: Examples from the Unification Church A prime example of religious cults is the Unification Church founded by Korean Sun Myung Moon. The problems faced by the Unification Church in finding and resocializing converts are common to most of the religious cults. These problems can be summarized under the heading of *bridge-burning activities.* When you burn your bridges behind you, leaving the cult and returning home becomes difficult, if not impossible. With the total institution social bridges are burned automatically when the individual is placed under the physical control of the institution and is prevented from leaving. With religious cults the individual must be convinced to slowly burn one bridge after another before resocialization can occur. John Loflands (1977) study of the Unification Church (*Doomsday Cult*) makes the nature of bridge burning clear.

The most important element in the success or failure of conversion is the human relationships of the potential convert. Lofland found that the most successful converts were "loners" before their meeting with cult members, and they came to develop intense and satisfying social

BOX 4.3

The Pathology of Imprisonment: The Zimbardo Study of Prison Roles

Your sense of self is the continuing product of the socialization you receive from your social groups. It develops in response to the way others treat you in the roles you play, and it is continuous in that it is never finished forming and always open to change, even drastic change, if the social situations you encounter demand it.

In 1972, Philip Zimbardo, a professor of psychology at Stanford University, created such a social situation by forming a mock prison on campus. He advertised for college students to take part in an experiment (paying $15 a day) in which half would be placed in the role of prisoners while the other half would play the role of guards. Those placed in the prisoner roles (through the flip of a coin) were unexpectedly picked up at their homes, run through normal booking procedure at the local police department, and taken blindfolded to the university, where they were stripped, deloused, put in a prison uniform, and placed in a cell. The "guards" were instructed to make up rules for maintaining law, order, and respect. Beyond that, the subjects were on their own.

Zimbardo was forced to cancel the experiment after six days. As he describes the situation,

> In less than a week the experience of imprisonment undid (temporarily) a lifetime of learning; human values were suspended, self-concepts were challenged and the ugliest, most base, pathological side of human nature surfaced. We were horrified because we saw some boys (guards) treat others as if they were despicable animals, taking pleasure in cruelty, while other boys (prisoners) became servile, dehumanized robots who thought only of escape, of their own individual survival and of their mounting hatred for the guards. (Zimbardo, 1972:4)

Some of the prisoners had to be released from the experiment after the first four days because of such behavior as hysterical crying. Others asked for parole (part of the experiment), were turned down, and seemed to forget that they were really college students who could leave at any time by simply giving up their pay. The guards seemed similarly caught up in the experiment, several of them engaging in brutal behavior (such as locking up one of the prisoners in a small closet for refusing to eat). Zimbardo's only conclusion was that the self is more the result of social situations than it is the possession of the individual.

Behavior similar to Zimbardo's experiment can be found in any American prison, both from the guards and the prisoners. These particular roles appear to be directly attached to the conflict inherent in the situation of imprisonment. These same principles, however, can be applied outside this experiment and outside the realm of prisons. All roles affect us, and most of us play or will play roles with built-in stress and conflict. Knowledge of what roles can do may not prevent their effect, but at least you might understand as you watch your personality change.

relationships with cult members. This is very similar to the enforced techniques used during the Korean War, when individuals were placed among those who had already converted to communism. A former loner takes on the new cult role and new cult self in return for sociability.

The power of the Unification Church in resocializing the cult's members is obvious in this photo of a mass wedding ceremony. The brides and grooms did not choose each other but were matched up by the Church.

Individuals who had preexisting social ties outside the cult were unlikely converts if those preexisting relationships were strong enough to withstand the individual's first brief attraction to the cult.

The maintenance of social ties outside the cult is always a direct threat to the conversion process. Thus, part of the bridge-burning activities is convincing the potential convert to break past ties, which may be defined either as "agents of Satan" or just "negative influences," depending on the cult in question. The following quotation from a Unification Church member (a response to her mother's rejection of her conversion) illustrates the style with which cults deal with this issue:

> At first it was the deepest hurt I had ever experienced. But I remember what others in our [Unification Church] family have given up and how they too experienced a similar rejection. But so truly, I can now know a little of the rejection that our beloved Master experienced. I can now begin to understand his deep grief for the Father as he sat peering out of a window singing love songs to Him because he knew that the Father would feel such grief. I can now begin to feel the pain that our Father in heaven felt for 6,000 years. I can now begin to see that to come into the Kingdom of heaven is not as easy as formerly thought. I can now see why many are called but few are chosen. I begin to understand why men will be separated, yes, even from their families. I begin to see the shallowness of human concern for God as a Father and their true blindness. Oh, my heart cries out to Our Father in grateful praise and love for what He has given. (Lofland, 1977:56)

The majority of religious cults provide for communal living for their members, ranging from the almost total isolation of Jonestown (in the South American country of Guyana) for People's Temple members to simply having members share apartments within a city. Whatever the arrangements, communal living decreases the time spent by converts with noncult people while simultaneously increasing the time spent with (usually) veteran cult members, already at a further stage of conversion. As Lofland noted, one of the most effective alterations in changing potential converts to converts was moving them into one of the cult's communal living situations.

Last, but not least, we come to money and other material possessions. Many religious cults, like the Unification Church, encourage or insist that all worldly possessions be turned over to the cult; others, like the Church of Scientology, achieve almost the same end by charging extremely high prices for the essential services they provide for their members. In either case the result is the same: The convert (no longer potential) winds up very poor. Meanwhile, not only does the cult become wealthy (and ultimately powerful), but the individual burns both a practical as well as psychological bridge away from the cult; leaving the cult will require new means of support. On the psychological level, an individual would later find it difficult to justify having turned over wealth should he or she return to a lifestyle that valued it. Ironically, most of us would find it easier to justify time wasted with a cult than money wasted. By the time the Unification Church acquired the wealth of its converts, it could rest assured that it had in fact converted them.

Resocialization: A Final Look If young children are amazingly adaptable to their cultures in primary socialization, it appears that adults can be made equally adaptable under the pressures of resocialization. In primary socialization the child acquires his or her first self; in resocialization the adult replaces an old self with a new one. Remarkably similar principles appear to be at work. Our sense of who we are (our self) comes initially from the social group, and it must continue to come from that group on a day-to-day basis if it is to survive. If your personality appears to you to have remained fairly stable during your life, it is likely that there has been considerable continuity among your roles and social groups. If there is one major point to this section, it is this: Continuity is not guaranteed, and if change comes, you are likely to change with it.

SUMMARY

Socialization is the process by which, through agents of socialization, individuals learn about and come to believe in their culture. These agents may be other individuals (parents, for example), or they may be societal institutions, the experience of which can be an effective socialization force.

Primary socialization is the first socialization faced by the young child. During this period the interests of the socializers collide with the biological development of the child. Freud described this biological development in terms of stages of psychosexual development, as the child slowly internalizes the perspective of society (known as the superego), which often restricts inborn desires (known as the id). Piaget describes the child's intellectual development during this same period as an increasing ability to master abstract thought. One element of this abstract thought is the child's ability to understand rules, which reflects the child's ability to look at himself or herself in terms of general expectations. Mead focused his attention on the emotional identification of the child as the child comes to view himself or herself in terms of significant others and later in terms of the generalized other. When this stage has been reached, secondary socialization has begun.

Secondary socialization begins when the child is biologically mature and capable of understanding the rules of society through the general expectations of others. Internalization occurs when the values of the social group become the values of the group member (or become the superego of the group member).

From the very beginning the child develops a self-image that is a reflection of other people's views. The child develops this image through the responses of others so that ultimately he or she can predict those responses and view himself or herself accordingly. This process is called the looking-glass self. To the extent that everyone has a variety of roles, an individual may acquire a variety of selves, each appropriate to the responses received in specific roles. This variety permits role distance—the ability of an individual to avoid acquiring a self-image from the responses of a specific role.

Although they can never return to primary socialization, adults can be resocialized. Resocialization results in a major personality transformation brought about by rigid socialization techniques. These techniques usually require placing the individual in an isolated and highly controlled environment where, shut off from the past, a new self begins to develop. Resocialization is common to total institutions (such as prisons or mental institutions) and also occurs in organizations such as religious cults.

GLOSSARY

Agent of socialization Any social source (a person, an institution, etc.) that communicates elements of culture or requires conformity to them.

Anticipatory socialization Socialization in anticipation of acquiring a specific role at some time in the future.

Cognition The process of perception or knowing.

Generalized other An individual's imagination of what a large number of people (or people in general) expect in social behavior.

Gestures Nonsymbolic forms of communication that begin randomly but come to be associated with elements in the environment.

"I" As defined by George Herbert Mead, the element of the self that is creative, is spontaneous, and tends to initiate action.

Institution A cluster (or sphere) of interrelated activities within a society coupled with the knowledge, beliefs, and objects that relate to those activities. Institutions are typically stable configurations of social forms that meet social needs in specific areas.

Institutionalization The psychological adaptation of an individual to life in a total institution to the point of dependence on the institution.

Internalization The process by which individuals come to see themselves in terms of the roles they play and come to share in the values of the social group, making those values their personal beliefs.

Looking-glass self As defined by Charles Cooley, the process by which an individual acquires a sense of self through imagining how he or she looks to others.

"Me" As defined by George Herbert Mead, the element of self that has internalized the expectations and values of others in the social group.

Primary socialization Socialization that occurs during the first several years of life, distinctive due to the individual's biological immaturity.

Repression The "placement" of inappropriate feelings and desires in the unconscious mind as opposed to the conscious mind. Part of Freud's psychoanalytic theory, repression occurs as the individual responds to the demands of society.

Resocialization An extreme form of secondary socialization in which major changes are deliberately brought about in the thinking and behavior of an adult.

Role distance An individual's introduction of unusual or creative elements in role playing that communicate to others a distance between the individual and the role being played.

Secondary socialization Socialization that occurs after the first few years of life, when the individual is capable of symbolic communication and developing a social sense of self.

Self The process by which the individual develops a sense of who he or she is based on the responses of others. The emergence of a social self indicates that the individual shares with others in the social group a set of common meanings, including a definition of the individual's place in interactions with others.

Socialization The ongoing process by which humans come to learn about and believe in their cultures, from learning the roles to sharing the values. Through socialization the individual becomes a member of the social group and develops a sense of self.

Sociobiology The systematic study of the biological basis of all social behavior.

Taking the role of the other The ability of an individual to view the self from the perspective of others in the social environment, making the self an object and allowing for the development of common symbols.

Total institution A social group that provides a regimented living and working existence for its members, isolated from the rest of society.

SUPPLEMENTARY READINGS

Barker, Eileen *The Making of a Moonie: Choice or Brainwashing.* New York: Basil Blackwell, 1984.
Barker takes us in for a closer look at the conversion process in the Unification Church. We see resocialization in action.

Brim, Orville G., Jr., and Stanton Wheeler *Socialization After Childhood: Two Essays.* New York: Wiley, 1966.
Two clear discussions on socialization among adults and young adults. Together, the essays present theoretical orientations toward socialization along with the application of their orientations to socialization within particular settings.

Clausen, John A. *The Life Course: A Sociological Perspective.* Englewood Cliffs, N.J.: Prentice-Hall, 1986.
Clausen offers a general introduction to socialization and, as the title suggests, emphasizes that socialization occurs at all stages of the life course.

Ginsburg, Herbert, and Sylvia Opper *Piaget's Theory of Intellectual Development: An Introduction.* Englewood Cliffs, N.J.: Prentice-Hall, 1969.
An excellent, clearly presented introduction to a difficult and extensive subject—the life work of child psychologist Jean Piaget.

Goffman, Erving *Asylums.* Chicago: Aldine, 1961.
One of the classics in the study of socialization, *Asylums* discusses socialization patterns within total institutions, focusing on the social relations within mental institutions.

Hewitt, John P. *Self and Society: A Symbolic Interactionist Social Psychology* (3rd ed.). Boston: Allyn & Bacon, 1983.
Social psychology exists in the gray area that lies between (or in the intersection of) sociology and psychology. This shared territory is, however, dealt with differently by each discipline. Hewitt offers a view of that landscape from the sociologist's side.

Keller, Helen *The Story of My Life.* Garden City, N.Y.: Doubleday, 1954.
Helen Keller was both blind and deaf from infancy, yet she was able to learn through the insistence of a gifted teacher. Many critical aspects of the socialization we all go through are highlighted by her experience.

Skinner, B. F. *Beyond Freedom and Dignity.* New York: Knopf, 1971.
A classic statement of the behaviorist position on socialization from a noted American psychologist.

Stoner, Carroll, and Jo Anne Parke *All God's Children.* New York: Penguin, 1979.
A description of a variety of modern American religious cults such as the "Moonies," Scientology, Krishna Consciousness, and others, from a critical perspective.

READING

The Marines Build Men: Resocialization in Recruit Training

STEVEN A. GILHAM

Before being socialized into his present occupation of sociologist, Steven Gilham was a dedicated U.S. Marine, the successful product of the intensive resocialization program known as recruit training. This article takes you through that experience with him, from the frightened first day to the pride of recruit graduation. The recruit program is typical of many resocialization programs in the techniques it uses to transform the adult individual. Gilham shows how that transformation occurs, both from his experience of the program then and from the sociological perspective he employs now.

Perhaps a warning should be issued to the fainthearted before beginning. The United States Marines have many differences from other social groups in American society, and one of the most notable is their use of language not normally found in polite company. Recruit training in particular is unimaginable without four-letter words. This article is recommended for mature audiences.

Night, about 9:30, San Diego. Chillier than I had expected for southern California in mid-November. Several of us—I do not remember now how many; seven or eight, maybe—standing around outside the airport, waiting: Anticipatory, anxious, excited maybe. When I had asked the recruiter about training and job opportunities, he had glared flatly at me and said in a deep voice, "Look, I can't promise you anything but a hard time. We generally find that the people who make the best Marines just wanna be Marines." That is how he got me. No song and dance, just plain old macho. Well, we would soon see.

Here it came. A long, olive green, double-cab pickup, with an emblem on the front doors and covered in the rear. The driver's door opened, slammed shut; crisp, clicking steps behind the truck. Then he appeared at the rear: stocky, erect, a recruiting poster Marine. Closest to the truck, I reached for the handle of the passenger-side door to the rear seat. I was cut short by a booming, guttural voice. "Get your goddam hand off the truck! Spit out that gum and get your fuckin' hand out of your pocket, you fat piece of shit." Brief, stunned silence all around. "Get in the rear of the truck. Everybody. Hurry, up, hurry up, hurry up!" Scrambling. "Sit with your eyes front and your mouths shut. I don't wanna hear a fuckin' word." "Jeesus" (a low whisper). "Shut up, maggot!" Silence. Was he still outside the truck? No matter. More footsteps approaching; several people, muted voices. "Shut up and get in the truck. Keep your eyes straight ahead. Hurry up, hurry up." Then we were off.

After several turns I had lost my sense of direction. We made a few halting attempts at conversation, but soon we passed through a gate with an MP at a guardhouse. We heard one low wail from somewhere outside, "You'll be sorree!" We had arrived at the Marine Corps Recruit Depot (MCRD). Then we stopped, and seconds later the tailgate was unlatched and dropped. "Get out and form lines on the yellow footprints. On the double! Keep your eyes straight ahead and don't move. *Lines,* asshole, not ranks. You know what a fuckin' line is? When you're called, go one at a time through that hatch on the right,

Essay © 1982 by Steven A. Gilham. Used by permission of the author.

right line first. First three, move!" We waited. "Next . . . Next . . . Next." My turn. Inside, the barbers' chairs on the left. "Here. Sit down, look straight ahead." It took twenty, maybe thirty, seconds; hardly any hair left, only a couple of nicks. "Out to the left. Next!"

Moving past a counter like a coat-check stand, each of us was given our basic issue: a galvanized pail; a wooden scrub brush; a pair of high-top tennis shoes; a pair of olive green socks; heavy, olive green cotton trousers (never again to be called pants under any circumstances); a matching cap (ever after, a cover); a long web belt and brass buckle; underwear (skivvies); a book of coupons (chits) redeemable at a recruit base exchange (BX); red shorts with yellow stripe and Marine Corps emblem; and a bright yellow sweatshirt emblazoned with an equally bright red eagle, globe, and anchor, and the words *U.S. Marine Corps.* Thus supplied, we filed into yet another room and lined up along opposite sides of two very long tables divided into stalls. The guy across from me could not keep his eyes still. They darted, clicked, rolled in a frenzy as he scanned everything, trying, it seemed, even to see behind himself. Mine, too, maybe; but I was watching him. Suddenly a big square face was next to his, booming, "What the fuck you lookin' at maggot-eyes?" "Nothing." "Yer ass! You callin' me nothing, puke?" "No, sir." "Bullshit! Sir! The first fucking word out of your mouth is always *sir.* Do you understand that!" (Not, of course, a question at all.) "Yes, sir!" "Bullshit!" "Sir! Yessir!" "What the fuck you laughin' at you big stringy hunk of shit. . . ."

And so on until we were all in and were once again addressed as a group. "When I give you people the word, you will strip and place everything you brought with you in the bin in front of you. You will then stand with your eyes front and your hands at your sides until further word. You have thirty seconds. Do it! Hurry up, hurry up, goddam it! Stop! If that fat piece of shit at the other end doesn't freeze right now, I'm gonna come down there and take his goddam head off!"

We next boxed up our belongings—everything except watches and wallets, which we could keep but not wear for the next twelve or so weeks—to be sent home. After showers and bedding issue we joined earlier arrivals in a dorm (squadbay) where we slept—interrupted by another group of later arrivals—until 5:30. We were then awakened and led off, shuffling and stumbling, to breakfast. (Chow. All meals are chow, distinguished only by time of day.) Upon return we were settled into a classroom and introduced formally to the United States Marine Corps by the same thick-necked staff sergeant who had met us at the airport. Of course, we would not call him Sergeant or Staff Sergeant anything. He and all uniformed personnel, we learned, would be addressed as *sir,* irrespective of their ranks. Our trainers were drill instructors (DIs), who would always be called *sir,* except when spoken to or about in the third person, when they would be called by their positions—drill instructor or platoon commander—rather than by rank. These were the people to whose care we would be entrusted when enough of us to form a training company (or series) had collected at Receiving Barracks. We were then instructed in forms of address: "Sir, Pvt. (last name) requests permission to speak to the drill instructor." "Sir, Pvt. ________ reporting as ordered." Knock three times. "Sir, Pvt. ________ requests permission to enter the duty office." Each of us was then given a pocket-size, red vinyl, ringbound book with nearly everything we would need to know in it. Finally, we were put to work policing the barracks and its surroundings, picking up cigarette butts, polishing brass fixtures (brightwork), cleaning windows (portholes), sweeping and mopping floors (swabbing decks), and emptying trashcans (shitcans). If we looked about us at all, we could see strategically placed red and yellow signs: "To be a Marine you have to believe in: Yourself . . . Your fellow Marine . . . Your Corps . . . Your Country . . . Your God. Semper Fidelis." Or, quoting Field Marshall Erwin Rommel (Hadn't he been "the enemy" once? I thought): "The more we sweat in peace, the less we bleed in war."

Recruits sometimes wait for days in receiving; we did not. Within forty-eight hours we had been taken by two of our DIs to four corrugated steel quonset huts—two on either side of and opening onto an asphalt strip we would call the platoon street—that would be home for nearly three months. Immediately began the task of preparing us for the actual training routine. For over a week they instructed us in the fundamentals of our new lives—how to make a bed (rack), stand at attention, mark and wear our clothing—and marched us all over to MCRD for additional clothing issue, tests, dental checks and physical examinations, and purchases at the BX. There we all bought the same items—identical brands of razor, shave cream, soap, shoe polishes and brushes, toothbrush, and toothpaste—which we were later taught to arrange, along with issued gear, identically in our footlockers.

After this we settled into the routine that would prevail over the remainder of boot camp, to be interrupted only by two weeks at the rifle range (actually a wholly separate facility at Camp Pendleton, near Oceanside) and a week of mess or maintenance duty. Reveille, exercise, head call (toilet and shave), chow, classes, chow, classes, exercise, chow, review sessions, head call (with shower), free time, taps. "Academic" classes—in military history, weapons, military justice, hygiene and first aid, and so on—were held indoors; "practical" ones—close order drill (COD), bayonet training, calisthenics and distance running—outdoors. We would spend over two hours a day on the drill field (parade deck, grinder) alone. There were breaks between, usually for exercise, and occasional business tasks such as swimming tests (twice), weapons and web gear issue, BX run, measurement and fitting for dress uniforms. Everywhere we went, we went in formation at either a march or a run. And always we carried in the hip pockets of our utility trousers the little red book we were to study anytime we might find ourselves waiting for some scheduled activity.

Throughout the routine we acquired numerous physical skills and some "book" knowledge that few of us had previously possessed. But just as important, perhaps more important, from our trainers' point of view were the lessons we would learn about ourselves. It was not that we would acquire deeper insight into our extant, already formed selves; rather, we would acquire new selves. By the end we would look, walk, and talk remarkably alike. Some of our attitudes and general beliefs, no doubt, would be relatively unmoved—for example, our tastes in music, literature, art, civilian dress, and recreation—but those were inessential to the transformation at hand and were of little interest to the Corps. What was essential was that we learn and adhere to a new code of conduct. That code comprises several stipulations: Obey immediately and unquestioningly. ("When I tell you people to jump, you jump and ask how high on the way up.") Do not quit. Be sharp, mentally and in appearance and demeanor. It will not be particularly helpful to attempt an exhaustive listing of the rules here—some of them will be clear later on anyway—but they conjoin to form the exhortations "Be a man! Be a Marine!"

The transformation from civilian to Marine involves little or none of the exploration, experimentation, and curiosity typical of infants' and children's learning. It is also effected with a rapidity, efficiency, and self-consciousness on the part of the trainers that far exceed the gradual socialization of the young. It is that process to which I now turn. The first stage of the process is a deliberate stripping of all our ties to our old selves—what Erving Goffman has called a *degradation ritual.* The basic recipe goes something like this: Plunge recruits into a situation in which numerous, repetitive failures of all sorts are virtually inevitable, strip them of as many distinguishing characteristics as possible, sever their ties to preexisting networks of association, prevent or restrict as far as possible the formation of new linkages except those to their trainers, and ritualize their relations to the trainers. In short, leave them with as few resources—as little that is useful, valued, or a source of positive evaluation—as possible. All of that can be achieved with great predictability through any or all of the following devices: introducing and requiring the use of a new and unfamiliar "language," holding recruits accountable for violations of rules or standards of performance of which they have not been informed, continually escalating standards of performance some measure beyond actual achievement, and/or applying rules or commands arbitrarily or contradictorily. At each breach the recruits' failures are announced loudly and publicly in a literal bombardment of negative sanctions. One of the favored techniques is the use of games that cannot be won (by recruits).

> "Private Gilham to the duty office! On the double!"
>
> Knock, knock, knock. "Sir! Pvt. Gilham reporting as ordered, sir."
>
> "Well, well, well. Is that a little goddam mouse at my hatch? You better put some balls in that little pussy voice, maggot! I can't hear you!"
>
> "Aye, aye, sir!" THUMP! THUMP! THUMP! "SIR! Pvt. Gilham reporting as ordered, SIR!"
>
> "Get your ass in here, Private."

Next time:

> THUMP! THUMP! THUMP! "SIR! Pvt. Gilham requests permission to speak to the drill instructor, SIR!"
>
> "Jeesus H. Christ, Private! Don't break my fuckin' hatch! What the fuck you screamin' at me for? I'm only ten feet away. Try again, asshole."
>
> "Aye, aye, Sir!" THUMP! THUMP . . .
>
> "Bullshit! Didn't your mother ever teach you how to knock?" He rises and demonstrates a polite knock at the door.

Such experiences help demolish any unified, positive sense of self, create confusion and apprehension, and deliver a message that neither old habits nor present efforts will do. It matters little how well recruits have previously known themselves; for the persons they were are repudiated as "scuzzy civilians," and in any event, all the props that would support their former identities are gone. And their present selves are hardly desirable—confused, clumsy, and (some at least) frightened (frightened enough, for example, that most of us were awake and moving before reveille as soon as the electronic pop of the PA system signaled that it was on in an attempt to avoid the unavoidable harangues about our slothfulness). Add to this disorientation the recruit's appearance, and the degradation is complete (but by no means over). Their haircuts and uniforms are constant reminders of the recruits' new status, but they also make recruits, by both civilian and military standards, ugly, or at least funny-looking. The tremendous contrast between them—shorn, rumpled, sweaty, dusty, and stinking—and the clean, fresh, well-tailored appearance of their overseers (who sometimes change uniforms two or three times a day to maintain that appearance) further reinforces recruits' conceptions of their own worthlessness.

Thus, each of us who had come to the situation with a variety of ideas of ourselves as somehow good or distinctive—smart, tough, good-looking, nice, and so forth—discovered almost instantly that we had been wrong: that we were instead ugly, stupid, soft, and inept and that no initiative on our part was safe. You need only assume that each individual wants or needs to think of him- or herself as basically "okay" to understand how susceptible recruits are made to taking on a new self that will confer on them some measure of respect or dignity. Nearly any praise, and the conduct required to "earn" it, seems acceptable.

That this stripping away of self-esteem takes place as it does illustrates dramatically its reliance on some preestablished conditions that confine recruits to the situation and subordinate them to their trainers' control. First among these are the rules and contingencies that bind recruits to the training regimen. For we have no reason to expect any individuals to voluntarily shed a positive sense of self, to endure a process that strips them of it, or to accept a bombardment of verbal and physical abuse if other, more attractive, options are freely available. In this case they are not; any attempt to leave, or even successful flight, would cost dearly.

Any separation from others to whom we are bound by some agreement—informal or formal, traditional or contractual—has costs that will exceed some of the unpleasantness we might experience within those relationships. Most institutions rely on a concerted effort to escalate these costs as high as possible so that they exceed markedly (for most folks) any nastiness we may experience while "in" the institution. (Some, of course, like many employers, simply benefit from conditions over which they may have little or no direct control, such as a wretched labor market.) But leaving Uncle Sugar (Uncle Sam) is not like leaving a friend, lover, club, college, family, or spouse whose charms have worn thin or become aggravating, with prospects of bluer skies or greener grass ahead. For Uncle Sugar's agreement with his recruits is a contract that only he is legally free to terminate.

Recruits, or any service personnel, who leave or even try to leave will not only forfeit some benefits such as pay or, where possible, rank, they will also face some actual punishments ranging from extra duty through restriction to quarters, brig time, and hard labor to expulsion via a bad conduct (BCD), undesirable, or dishonorable discharge (DD). These are not penalties among which the violator has choices, nor are they mutually exclusive. The lesser penalties may be linked to, and very many on one's record will lead to, the most severe ones. And discharge at any level below an honorable, or at worst a general, discharge means additional post-service costs by way of reduced job opportunities after release. Even a successful escape from recruit training would necessitate years of separation from family or friends if the other penalties are to be avoided, as the ex-recruit would become a fugitive. Add the promise of better days after boot camp to this scheme of punishments, and the recruit's interest in staying and enduring even considerable misery is clear, so long as life "inside" is not on balance worse than the potential consequences of flight.

It is not the DI's principal responsibility to enforce these rules even though his job depends on them. Neither are the punishments outlined above ones a DI is authorized to employ or to decide. Those available to the DI are both less enduring in their consequences and more immediate, requiring no juridical procedures prior to their use. Their potential effectiveness is not ensured merely by recruits' enforced presence; it is necessary that the sanctioning resources be securely under the control of the drill instructors only. That monopoly is ensured by two general types of rules: those that isolate recruits from any other effective source of positive sanctions and those that deprive them of any negative sanctions of their own. Let us take the first.

Not only are symbolic ties severed by returning civilian articles home, but communication with the world outside MCRD is strictly limited: no phone calls in or out, no radios or TV, no liberty (time off-duty, off-base); newspapers and visitors (if a boot is lucky enough to have relatives near enough to visit) only on Sundays, and then only after the seventh week. Outgoing mail is limited practically, if not officially, by the amount of free time allotted recruits: Usually thirty to forty-five minutes per evening and one to two hours on Sundays (after the first two or three weeks) are set aside for rifle cleaning; polishing of boots, shoes, and belt buckles (all mandatory); and, finally, letter writing. Incoming mail is regulated in other ways: no scented letters ("Well, Private, you just tell that little skirt of yours that if she keeps this up, you aren't gonna be getting *any* mail. *I* might read 'em, though."), no money ("Tell those folks back home you got plenty."), and no food.

"You don't need that fruitcake do you, fat boy?"

"Sir, No, Sir!"

"Shitcan it."

"Aye, aye, Sir." PLUNK.

"Now you write those people and tell 'em that was the best fuckin' fruitcake you ever ate, y' hear?"

"Sir! Yes, Sir."

•••

"There aren't enough of those cookies for everybody to have some are there, Private?"

"No, SIR."

"Then I guess you'll just have to eat 'em, won't you?"

Faint, hopeful smile. Pleased. "Yes, Sir!"

"Now."

"Sir?"

"Every goddam one of 'em. Do it."

Indeed mail call itself, and certainly the time to read the letters, might be treated as a privilege that could be suspended, even if for no more than a day or two. And, of course, talk, simple small talk among recruits—"Where you from? What'd ya do before this?"—is never authorized. Speak only when spoken to or, if on a detail, when giving orders. Important as all of those rewards are, they are not the source of livelihood. The latter kind of resources—pay, promotion, and the service records on which all decisions about Marines depend throughout their service—belong only to the Corps from the beginning.

Just as recruits are deprived of effective alternative sources of reward, so are they deprived of means, other than compliance, of influencing their keepers. No hitting back, no name calling, no sneering, no votes, no strikes. Resorting to any of these could constitute punishable offenses under the Uniform Code of Military Justice (UCMJ). The only possible sources of clout, since the DI's pay and career are also controlled from above, are a request for mast (a meeting with the commanding officer) or connection to a political official who might instigate an investigation. Mast might get the DI a mild reprimand, and no investigation of a DI will be undertaken without accusations of extreme malfeasance. In either case any attempt to initiate an investigation, or cooperation in one, would brand a recruit as a trouble maker throughout MCRD.

The most any recruit can do is simply refuse to yield to the Marine role. If he does so, he may retain something like dignity or integrity, though he gains no power; he simply deprives the Corps of its power over him. Neither side can get what it wants from the other—a stalemate in which the costs for the recruit are momentous, for the Corps, trivial.

The last real threat to the Corps's power over its recruits (and its other personnel) is collective action. Both the sanctions at the drill instructors' disposal and their use of those sanctions are calculated to prevent that.

The DI thus becomes the sole effective, legitimate source of rewards and punishments. Your compatriots may *care* when you get nailed, but there is precious little they can *do* to support you. ("From now on, girls, I am your mother, your father, your sister, your brother, and your girlfriend; and you aren't *even* gonna screw me.") Among the negative sanctions DIs use, most are relatively mild. ("Well, no shit, dippy. What the fuck you think you're doin' there?" or "Jeesus Keerist! You are the stupidest piece of shit I ever saw." or "Whoa, mob! Look around. You really fucked that move up good, didn't you? You look like a bunch of dumbfucks.") Some are more serious. A recruit drops his rifle or calls it a gun, offenses almost equal in severity: "You dickhead! You'll sleep with that sonofabitch tonight. Field strip it and sleep on it. I'll be there to be sure you do."

A recruit scratches his nose while in formation. "You like to scratch, maggot? Scratch! Scratch that sonofabitch until I give you the word. And tell all the rest of these turds how much you like to scratch. Say, 'I like to scratch.' " He says repeatedly, "I like to scratch," and scratches until his nose bleeds.

A recruit is caught sleeping, seated on his footlocker with a newspaper on his lap, during Sunday free time. His rack and the footlocker's contents are dumped and strewn over part of the squadbay. "You've got three minutes to square that shit away." His neighbor joins to help, and the DI returns. "So you wanna clean up, too?" He dumps both racks and both footlockers. "Now you two have exactly two minutes to get squared away." He returns. Replay. "Clean up this mess. When I come back you *will* be at attention beside your racks." Moral: A Marine on duty (twenty-four hours a day for recruits) has no friends.

It is possible to go on ad nauseum with similar examples. Rust on a rifle at a weekly inspection. The rifle is buried in sand, two or three buckets of water poured over it, and it lies there for several hours before the recruit is allowed to retrieve and clean it. Or we do poorly at COD and are banished to the platoon street for exercise. We begin push-ups or squat thrusts, say fifty repetitions. We do not count (sound off) loudly enough. We start over after ten or so. We do not count in unison. We start over. Somebody quits. We start over. Or someone leaves the padlock on his footlocker or his rifle (to be locked to the rack) unlocked. We return from classes to find the squadbay a shambles. And so on.

Finally there are the most severe penalties—expulsion to the Special Training Unit (Special Training Platoon, STU, STP, fat farm) or Correctional Custody (CC).

> "Keep draggin' your ass, shitbird, and you'll find yourself breakin' rock with the other discipline problems over in CC."
>
> "Drop out of this run, lardass, and you'll go straight to the fat farm."

It is important to note, however, that, as often as these sanctions are employed, their threat is actually more important than their actual use. It is not that, if they were used constantly, recruits would get used to them; rather, there must be some real difference in consequences between good performance and ready compliance, on the one hand, and poor performance and recalcitrance, on the other hand. Only then does anyone have an interest in compliance unless the things to be learned are intrinsically rewarding to the learner. The boot camp regimen is obviously calculated to create incentives for recruits to do things (at times, to an extent, and in ways) that few if any of them find intrinsically rewarding. The more recruits learn and the more quickly, the more free of penalties their lives become. The threat and the actual administration of punishment are calculated to keep them from backsliding.

There are additional considerations that discourage frequent actual punishment. The DI is not utterly free in his use of sanctions, for he too is evaluated by his peers and superiors. Any DI who constantly resorts to punitive measures is regarded by superiors as one who cannot effectively maintain order and train troops. Such evaluations diminish his chances for promotion and may ultimately lead to relief from duty and a transfer, a blemish on his record with potentially serious long-term consequences. And, finally, time spent in punishment is time not spent in the teaching and practice of skills recruits are to learn, and the DI does have a schedule to meet.

This last point does not imply that punishment teaches nothing; for in fact many sanctions are loaded with information that constitutes (and in turn depends on) a whole world view. In particular, certain evaluative standards have to be established so that invidious comparisons to which recruits are subjected are clearly undesirable in their eyes as well as their trainers'. Some examples are explicit in their ordering of the universe. ("You people are boots. That's lower than whaleshit and that's on the bottom of the ocean.") Some are less clearly so. ("Whatsamatter, girls? Are we tired?" or "My four-year-old daughter could do this shit.")

It soon became clear to me that there was a distinct hierarchical order to the world, at the top of which sat Marines—a goal we had not attained. ("You turds wouldn't make a pimple on a professional Marine's ass.") Beneath that were three general categories in approximately the following order of inferiority: the other services and their members, civilians, and all things not American. Marines' only peers, in this view, are British Marines and, with some reservations, elite units such as Army Green Berets, Navy Seal Teams, and Korean Marines (utterly ruthless, so the mythology went)—all bested, of course, by the Marines' elite Force Reconnaissance units.

Racial and ethnic categories were out for purposes of denigrating recruits because of the recruit population's heterogeneity. They were, however, used—usually jokingly. And they were used often enough to remind us that we were not, after all, entirely alike and to discourage any fellow feeling strong enough to serve as a basis for banding together in opposition to our trainers' interests.

This was all, by the way, a distinctly male world. Another wholly separate hierarchy, paralleling the first but lower at each of its levels, was women. Apart from references to body parts and body functions, the most frequent negative evaluations we heard involved civilians and women; but the two were used in significantly different ways. The former usually referred to appearance or demeanor—hands in pockets, slouching—the latter almost always were used when our performance was to be impugned. Furthermore, the references were not to *women* or *females* but to *girls, weak sisters,* or any of the multitude of genitally based terms by which women could be called. It soon became clear to us that there could be no worse judgments of our performance than those likening it to women's. The message was clear: Women were regarded as weak, not very bright, generally incompetent, sexual objects. The status of women Marines illustrates that neatly. As Marines, they would presumably be regarded as superior to civilians or other servicewomen. They were, indeed, regarded as tougher, but they were also presumed to be largely failures as *women*—not as attractive as civilian women, unable to get men, and simultaneously more sexually accessible and less desirable (because tougher).

This image of women was linked to the only real taboo, homosexuality. Since it was impossible that any of us *were* women (sex change operations notwithstanding), being called a girl or worse always retained a metaphorical character that allowed occasionally (and increasingly frequent as training progressed) joking usages. *Queer*, however, was always a vicious epithet, even though jokes about "them" were permissible and even desirable (keeping in mind that all jokes come from the DIs). We were warned repeatedly that actual homosexuality would bring dishonorable discharge from the Corps, the consequences of which—immensely restricted job opportunities in the outside world (no government agency or government subcontractor could hire a BCD or DD)—were so severe that we should never regard calculated engagement in homosexual activity as a reasonable way of trying to get kicked out. It would be better to go crazy.

The way in which these evaluative standards were used implies a lesson in language. When name calling was used, it was always the disvalue of the referent and/or the traits it implied rather than the crudity of the language itself that carried the greatest weight. Thus, terms like *asshole, shitbird,* or *fucking maggot* were indignities not so much because they were ugly but because they implied that we had no human value. And in *fat/scrawny/weak/stupid piece of shit* it was the *fat/scrawny/weak/stupid* that carried the greatest weight. Similarly, all of the uglier synonyms for women were indistinguishably degrading as against the fact that our performance had been judged feminine or inferior to that. The other terms, in fact, became commonplace. You should have noticed by now that the simple word *fuck* could be adapted to any part of speech—noun, verb, adverb, adjective, interjection, conjunction. Indeed, all of us not only heard jokes about, but lived through, experiences after boot camp in which we would embarrass ourselves by the use of any number of such terms in "polite" civilian company. That language and the special military vocabulary we were taught would further serve to distinguish us from others and to bind us as a brotherhood.

But it is a brotherhood bound together only against the "outside" world; within there is fragmentation sufficient to prevent the group from developing and enforcing norms opposed to the interests of their trainers. Sanctions are administered so as to keep each recruit mindful of his own interests and to encourage him to act on those interests. Action on the basis of collective interests or in the name of some greater good is generally given mere lip service. ("Get down on your knees and pray, girls. Pray for war. 'Cause that's the only way you're gonna get promoted.") This fragmentation is a consequence of the fact that most rewards and punishments are directed at individuals. Should there ever arise, for example, conflict between the DI's order and perceived expectations of a boot's peers, the DI's virtual monopoly of punitive sanctions creates a clear interest in compliance with the order. In addition, the competition for the scarce individual rewards available—personal orderly (mouse) to a DI, platoon secretary, and the positions of platoon guide and squad leaders (which almost automatically carry with them promotion to PFC at graduation from recruit training)—further encourage recruits to look out for themselves.

For purposes of controlling an entire group, however, it would be inefficient and impractical to rely always on individual rewards and punishments. Sending an entire platoon to STU or CC would be horrendously costly, and discharges of large numbers of recruits would deprive the Corps of the troops it demands. One of the DI's problems, therefore, is how to get maximum effectiveness and efficiency out of the sanctions at his disposal. The solution is occasionally to punish or to withhold rewards from an entire platoon for the misdeeds of one or a few of its members.

This device has an interesting result from the point of view of socialization theory. Assume that any recruit has an interest in avoiding punishment and/or obtaining rewards. So long as he can do so by his own compliance, his primary interest is in his own behavior. When he is punished or deprived of some reward for others' errors, however, he acquires a direct interest in their behavior, as does everybody else in his. That is true even in matters where he would otherwise be tolerant or indifferent of their conduct or would himself want to act as he now wants to prevent others from acting. Each recruit, of course, will grant some latitude to others for outright error, just as he expects some tolerance of his own mistakes; but when one recruit (or a few) consistently provides occasions for collective punishment or loss of promised rewards, his peers may move to control him. If a platoon does not spontaneously initiate such controls, the DI will remind it that, while he cannot hit anyone, he cannot prevent someone from slipping in the shower, falling over a footlocker, or otherwise "injuring himself."

The message is not lost on recruits. However, they do not resort first (or even often) to physical force as a means of control. Warning glances, whispers, and mutters usually suffice, but less subtle measures are also available. A miscreant recruit may get his heels kicked during COD or a run, or he may find that Sunday afternoon athletics become contact sports. If he protests aloud, it is he who is out of order and who will suffer the DI's wrath. Finally, he may be the guest at a nighttime blanket party at which his hosts cover his head with a blanket (to protect their anonymity) and pummel him. The entire platoon need not join in; they merely assent by "looking the other way," as will the DI. ("What happened to you Pvt. Dodo? You slip on a bar of soap?" "Sir! No, Sir! They hit me." "Someone hit you? Is that true platoon?" In unison: "Sir! No, Sir!" "You calling all the rest of these recruits liars, Private?")

Alternatively, the DI may use the platoon more directly. I remember one such incident in particular. I do not remember the person's infraction or series of infractions, but I do recall our part in his humiliation. It sickened me then; it chills me in retrospect.

> "You're crazy aren't you, Pvt. Dodo?"
> "Sir! No, Sir!"
> "Oh, yes, you are. Isn't he platoon?"
> A chorus: "Sir! Yes, Sir!"
> "See? The platoon thinks you're crazy. You must be crazy. Aren't you, Private?"
> "Sir! No, Sir!"
> "Bullshit! Tell 'im, platoon. Tell 'im 'You're crazy, Pvt. Dodo!'"

And we did. Until he cried. It is unlikely that we convinced him he was crazy, but his isolation from any peer support could not have been made more clear. He was dropped—to STU—within a week.

The points to be made by all this are, first, that making a whole group liable for the wrongs of one or a few engenders a collective control mechanism that looks much like normative control; and, second, that it would be a mistake to regard the rules thus enforced as norms arising from group interaction. Some general societal norms such as cleanliness, it is true, merely get additional "official" support in boot camp; but most of the rules are ones imposed on one group by another. They differ, in content and in the interests underlying them, from norms that arise out of collective preferences or collective concern for the harms done by some acts. None of that implies that recruits do not develop some norms among themselves. Given their common interests in avoiding negative sanctions or getting positive ones and in minimizing the burdens of an already onerous training schedule, the strongest are "Don't squeal on your peers (let the DI's catch them)," and "Don't give them any ideas for additional things for us to do." Even these, clearly, are formed in response to the organizational structure of the recruit training situation.

Finally, something remains to be said about the nature of the transformation into Marines. There are, as I have implied, some rewards along the way. There are cigarettes. ("The smoking lamp is lighted for o-o-one cigarette!" "Sir! The smoking lamp is lighted for one cigarette! Aye, aye, Sir!" "Light 'em. Burn 'em." "Sir! Aye, aye, Sir!") And there are movies. (We went to two during the twelve weeks; Marines figured heavily in both. *The Sands of Iwo Jima* must play six times a year at every Marine Corps base in the world.) Cigarettes are optional (nonsmokers may write letters for five minutes); movies are not. ("You *will* enjoy this flick, and you will keep your goddam mouths shut or the shit'll hit the fan when we get back here.")

We needed no telling to understand that these were rewards. But some—the symbolic rewards associated with being Marines—required construction of a proper evaluative base, just as some punishments do. To that end we heard lectures, classroom reviews, and countless sea stories ennobling the Corps's history (first to fight), extolling the toughness and courage of its heroes, and recounting the pugilistic and sexual exploits of Marines on liberty. Much of this included no small bit of bragging on the part of the DIs. Marines, it was to be understood, are men like no others and an exclusive fraternity the uninitiated would never truly understand.

On that foundation we were then given periodic indications of our gradual progress toward the exalted goal. First we were allowed to starch and block our covers (so that they held a recognizable shape) and to send one pair of utilities to the base laundry service to be starched. The crisp feel of truly clean clothing and the change in our own appearance wrought by pressed, sharply creased uniforms helped dissolve some of the feeling of slovenliness and ugliness with which we had been burdened; it also clearly distinguished us from newer recruits.

We were then "allowed" to blouse our trousers (turn the trouser leg up inside an elastic blousing garter so that the trouser "blouses" over the boottop). We were thus known on sight as at least fifth-week recruits. Then we began to be accorded the honor of learning songs to sing as we ran. ("One, two, three four; we love the Marine Corps.") Later came fittings for dress uniforms and, still later, inspections during which we wore them. All of these events, of course, also tempered our suffering by providing milestones on the twelve-week road to graduation. Even better were those moments of simple, overt verbal praise. (We march in rhythm with the sing-song cadence. "Hehp, toop, threep . . . keep parallelp, toop, keep parallel. . . . Good. Keep it up, keep it up. One heel. I want to hear the sound of one heel. . . . Outstanding! Co-o-olumn, right! Har! . . . Out-fucking-standing! You people are starting to look like Marines!")

Any of this can be taken away. ("Oh, that's right. Don't march; just mill around. Stop. Unblouse your trousers. You turds think you can come out here and embarrass me in front of my peers? Get off my fucking grinder! Now! Run! Assholes and elbows!") But such occasions become even more rare until, finally, graduation. Even then there is one last show. After the ceremony, complete with the base band, we were granted a four-hour base liberty during which we got our first phone calls, junk food, beer (if we were old enough; most of us were not), and unlimited smokes since twelve weeks before. We returned to the platoon area for our last afternoon and night at MCRD. "Well, girls, I hope you had a good time, 'cause now we're gonna sweat all that shit out. You got five fuckin' minutes to give me a for-fuckin'-mation out here in utilities. Do it!" Then we ran—five or six miles; most of us believed six—singing and clapping our hands to the rhythm of seventy or so pairs of boots stomping double-time in unison.

This time they all ran with us—platoon commander and both DIs. Finally we stopped, and the platoon commander, the "head honcho," asked, "You girls tired?" "Sir! No, Sir!" "Well I sure as shit am." It had never before happened. From this man who had never allowed an imperfection, never wavered in his cold sternness, never shown humility or admitted human frailty, never permitted himself to breathe hard after exercise or shiver in the cold, always made us hate him and then never let us beat him at any games, we heard it. "I'm tired." It is unlikely he was any more tired than we, probably less; but he said it. And the next morning he and both junior DIs spoke to each of us, in formation of course, and found something praiseworthy to say about every recruit in the platoon. The rite of passage was over and the illusion complete. We were now Marines.

The bubble would be burst soon enough as we discovered the secrets from which our isolation had protected us—for example, that there were also tough soldiers, sailors, and aviators—and as we rediscovered that we were really not all that different from others in the world. But in the heady atmosphere of graduation we were hardly encouraged to think about that.

These final days are important for fixing the transformation; for there is an irony in the whole process that graduation resolves. Anyone subjected permanently or indefinitely to the conditions recruits live through would have little reason for pride. More likely they would feel like slaves. But the final ritual dissolves that prospect, even though the remainder of service differs mostly in degree from training and in one's eventual promotion to higher positions. (Many of us expressed plans to try for DI school later.) Having been scum and become cream, we were able to look at our past indignities as tests, as proof of our worth, rather than as humiliations. And we were able to claim that, having survived, we had triumphed (even though that had been planned for us by others) and were in some permanent way different from everyone who had never done what we had done.

This is similar to what people experience emerging from college, police training, mental hospitals, or prisons. What really separates "graduates" from "inmates," however, is what happens to them afterward—the laurels (or stigma) attached to the end of the process, their associations and their work—rather than the process itself. Ultimately, it is life afterward that will account most for the permanence or impermanence of the changes wrought in behavior and self-concept.

In the absence of the recruit training regimen, many of the changes we had undergone showed little permanence. They did not evaporate; they simply no longer "worked" or proved necessary. Maintaining the level of disciplined dress, walk, posture, efficiency, and obedient responsiveness we had learned at MCRD has fairly high costs (in effort, for example, or time taken from other pursuits), which rather soon clearly exceed any benefits to be derived from them. There are those persons, of course, who come to love the discipline itself—perhaps those few for whom their identities as Marines are their best sense of self to date and their best hope for the future. Most, however, eventually slouch again, put their hands back in their pockets, stop spit-shining all their shoes, cease daily exercise except when required, stop walking in step with others when not in formation, and let their hair grow longer (even pushing military regulations). Most also openly complain about the Corps generally ("this fucking Green Machine"), even though they bristle at anyone else's attack on the institution and the implicit attack on themselves. (You are what you belong to?) Whatever happens, the Marine does not remain a boot. He becomes an old salt, who takes liberties with the rules; a former Marine, who revels in past glories; or an ex-Marine, who wonders how he ever allowed himself to be taken in in the first place.

Discussion Questions

1. What techniques are used to separate Marine recruits from their previous "selves"?
2. Resocialization typically relies on breaking down the support for the past "reality" of an individual and replacing that vacuum with supports for a new "reality." How do the Marines do this?
3. Social control operates in diverse ways in most social groups, ranging from formalized sanctions to the informal ways group members pressure each other to conform. What kinds of social control techniques are found in Marine recruit training? Which are the most important and why?
4. Are the Marines a subculture in American society? What kinds of beliefs and behaviors set them apart?

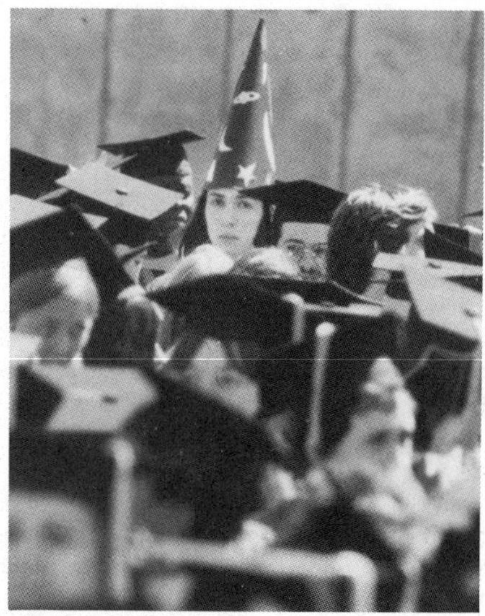

CHAPTER 5 SOCIAL CONTROL AND DEVIANCE

The coordination of society provides us with ready-made roles coupled with norms; "normal" human behavior is behavior that follows those norms. This is the behavior you see every day and take for granted. But what of the other kind? You no doubt frequently encounter people new at a particular role (still learning the norms) who make "mistakes." You also meet people who choose not to follow a particular set of norms for a role you would prefer them to play. Many of the people in this second category are in fact following *other* norms that apply to *other* roles; for example, individuals who dress very differently from you (and who may look strange to you) are very likely conforming to the fashion dictates of their social group at the same time they violate the fashion dictates of your social group. The more complex a society, the more such disagreements there are likely to be concerning which behavior is appropriate when and where. The United States contains a large array of social groups that differ greatly from each other; the disagreements that arise from all these differences make up the sociological study of deviance.

Sociological definitions of deviance vary. One common point, however, is that **deviance** is always behavior that violates the norms *of a social group*. Behavior is not inherently deviant; it is deviant only from the point of view of members of a particular social group in relation to their particular social norms. Behavior that is deviant here may not be deviant there; behavior deviant today may not be tomorrow.

Our basic definition of deviance provides a start but does little in the way of pointing a direction for understanding the phenomenon. Knowing that deviance is behavior that meets disapproval doesn't tell us why it meets that disapproval, the form that disapproval will take (a smirk or a firing squad), or how the disapproval will affect the deviant behavior. Our definition also leaves out one of the most important questions: Why do people engage in deviance? We will consider all of these questions in this chapter as we look at the place of deviance in society, at some theories of why deviance exists, and at group responses to the deviance of others. To understand those topics, however, we first need to examine some of the types of behavior that are generally labeled *deviance* in American society today (keeping in mind that there is not total, or sometimes even general, agreement that these behaviors are deviant). Let's look, then, at the crooks, weirdos, freaks, sluts, maniacs, and perverts that keep the study of deviance from getting boring. As we turn to all these broken norms and the people who break them, don't become immediately convinced that you've encountered a major break in the wall of social coordination. Prostitution, for example, has been considered deviant *and* has been engaged in enthusiastically for hundreds of years. Such consistency both in behavior and in attitudes toward it suggests that much deviant behavior is just one more facet to the social organization with which we live.

TYPES OF DEVIANCE

Deviant behavior produces a wide variety of responses from observers, depending on their attitudes toward the norms that are in the process of being violated. Breaking a casual norm may bring only a stern look one's way, while violating a norm felt to be central (or sometimes sacred) in a culture can result in violent responses. Societies typically systematize such reactions into law, reserving special punishments for behavior that breaks norms encoded in a legal system. Keeping in mind that laws change over time as the importance placed on individual

Young people commit numbers of crimes way out of proportion to their numbers in the population. A separate apparatus of law enforcement and courts exists to deal with this juvenile delinquency.

norms changes, the distinction between illegal (or criminal) deviance and legal (or noncriminal) deviance provides a clear starting point for the study of deviance.

Criminal Behavior

Criminal behavior is behavior that violates the laws of a society. Strictly speaking, that behavior must also occur during the time those laws are in effect. For example, heroin was legal in the United States until 1914, and therefore its use was not criminal behavior until after that time. Behavior becomes criminal behavior when a social norm becomes a law. A law is nothing but a formalized social norm in which the prohibited behavior and sanctions against it are specified. The law is extremely important for understanding deviance because it represents a major societal response to a particular behavior. It is also important because those who break laws are generally fully aware of the deviance in their behavior and continue with it anyway.

Criminal behavior is as varied as the number of laws on the books. For purposes of this discussion we will break down crime into four basic categories. We will look first at juvenile delinquency and the role of young people in crime. Second, the "standard" crimes, including murder, robbery, burglary, larceny, and so on, will be examined. Third, we will look at an interesting collection of activities commonly known as *white-collar crimes.* These crimes are distinctive because they are generally nonviolent and committed only by middle- or upper-class people. Finally, we will look at a group of crimes that is in some ways the most interesting; victimless crimes, which include gambling, prostitution, and drug use.

Juvenile Delinquency **Juvenile delinquency** includes all illegal behavior committed by individuals who are legally minors (usually under age eighteen). Much of this behavior is identical to crimes committed by adults, though some of it is criminal behavior only if committed by a juvenile. Adults, for example, cannot get into legal trouble for running away from their parents' home. Crimes such as this, which are illegal only for people in a certain social status, are called **status crimes.**

Young people in general make up far more than their share of arrests in the United States. There are roughly the same number of individuals in the sixteen- to eighteen-year-old age bracket as there are between the ages of forty and forty-four, yet there are three times more arrests from the younger group than the older one. This proportion of young people in the arrest records has been growing steadily in the United States. Moreover, the age at which young people have their first encounter with the police has been dropping steadily. Though some of this change is due to a growing number of status crimes by juveniles, a good part of it is the result of juvenile involvement in what the FBI calls *index crimes.*

Index Crime **Index crimes** are those crimes considered by the FBI to be major crimes; the list includes murder, forcible rape, robbery, aggravated assault, burglary, larceny/theft, and motor vehicle theft. In 1989 over 14 million such crimes were reported. Table 5.1 gives a breakdown by offense. And 14 million is certainly not an accurate figure of how many such crimes were committed, as a great many of these crimes are not reported. The level of inaccuracy varies somewhat from crime to crime. The 21,500 murders reported probably comes very close to the total number; murders are hard to hide, as people are missed and bodies are found. At the other extreme, no doubt there were a great many more than 94,500 forcible rapes

TABLE 5.1

INDEX CRIME REPORTED IN THE UNITED STATES, 1989

Crime Index Offenses	Number of Offenses
Violent	1,646,000
Property	12,605,000
Murder	21,500
Forcible rape	94,500
Robbery	578,330
Aggravated assault	951,710
Burglary	3,168,200
Larceny/theft	7,872,400
Motor vehicle theft	1,564,800
Total	14,251,400

Source: Federal Bureau of Investigation (1990).

committed; it is estimated that only about 55 percent of all rapes are ever reported to the police (U.S. Department of Justice, 1983). People dislike the publicity that follows rape, and perhaps more important, the rape victim often finds herself on trial along with the rapist.

Who is responsible for index crime? We have already seen that young people are heavily represented in all arrest records. Arrested individuals are also much more likely to be black than white based on their percentages in the population; in 1985 blacks made up almost 36 percent of the arrests for index crimes while making up slightly more than 12 percent of the overall population (U.S. Department of Justice, 1989). Perhaps most important, individuals arrested for index crimes are poorer than the rest of the population. It has been estimated that 80 percent of prisoners in the United States are ranked in the lowest 15 percent of the population in terms of income (Reiman, 1984). Among inmates in state prisons in 1986, over 60 percent had incomes less than $10,000 for the year preceding their incarceration. For those who had been incarcerated at some time during that year, 40 percent had a monthly income less than $500 (U.S. Department of Justice, 1990). These figures provide a rough idea of the impact of poverty on the commission of index crimes.

Who is victimized by index crime? For the most part, the victims of index crime are much like the people arrested for it, particularly when it is violent crime. Table 5.2 shows the victimization rates from a variety of index crimes in the United States during 1988. Looking first at age, we can see that young Americans have much higher victimization rates than older Americans. While almost 200 of every 1,000 Americans in the 16-to-19 age group were victimized, only 50 of every 1,000 Americans in the 50-to-64 age group were. If we look only at crimes of violence, the difference becomes even more extreme, with 72 younger victims against only 10 in the older age group. Race and ethnicity are only mildly important in terms of all crimes (blacks have slightly higher rates than whites or Hispanics), but both blacks and Hispanics have higher rates of victimization from violent crime than do whites. Perhaps the most striking figure in Table 5.2 is the importance of family income in victimization. While high income does not make one immune from index crime, it does apparently protect those fortunate enough to have it from violent crime. Looking at the violent crime total column again, we can see that those with family incomes less than $7,500 were victimized at a rate of 50 individuals for every 1,000 Americans in that income category; by comparison, for Americans making more than $50,000, only 21 of every 1,000 were victimized by violent crime. The income levels between are perfect stair steps between the two extremes; as income goes up, violent crime victimization drops. Much of the explanation for all of this is hinted at by the differences in crime rates between central cities and other areas; when you have money, you can move away from the poor people who, as we've seen, are the index criminals. Safety seems to come to us, one way or another, in our pay envelopes. We could add two more statistics to this summary: A black man is almost seven times more likely than a white man to be murdered, and a black woman is over four times more likely than a white woman to be murdered (U.S. Bureau of the Census, 1990b).

White-Collar Crime American sociologist Edwin Sutherland popularized the idea of white-collar crime in his book by that name published in 1949. **White-collar crime** refers to specific types of criminal behavior typical of middle-class and upper-class people. Crimes such as tax

TABLE 5.2

VICTIMIZATION RATES BY TYPE OF CRIME FOR SEX, AGE, RACE, ETHNICITY, INCOME, AND RESIDENCE OF VICTIM, 1988*

	Victimizations from personal crimes per 1,000 persons						
		Crimes of violence					
				Assault			
	Total	Total†	Robbery	Total	Aggravated	Simple	Crimes of theft
Sex							
Male	109.2	35.9	6.9	29.3	12.0	17.3	73.3
Female	91.7	23.8	4.1	18.6	5.7	12.9	67.9
Age							
12-15	169.2	56.9	7.2	49.4	14.9	34.4	112.3
16-19	192.9	72.0	11.3	58.8	22.1	36.7	120.9
20-24	182.2	58.9	8.9	48.4	20.0	28.4	123.3
25-34	117.5	35.2	6.3	27.8	10.2	17.6	82.3
35-49	87.2	21.8	4.2	17.3	6.1	11.2	65.4
50-64	49.6	10.2	2.9	7.0	2.9	4.1	39.4
65 or older	22.4	4.1	1.7	2.4	.8	1.6	18.3
Race							
White	98.9	28.2	4.7	23.0	7.9	15.1	70.7
Black	109.8	40.4	9.4	29.6	14.7	14.9	69.4
Other	97.4	30.0	5.5	23.8	9.9	13.8	67.4
Ethnicity							
Hispanic	98.4	34.9	10.1	24.7	8.9	15.8	63.5
Non-Hispanic	100.2	29.3	4.9	23.7	8.7	15.0	71.0
Family income							
Less than $7,500	123.7	50.1	10.0	38.3	14.9	23.4	73.6
$7,500-$9,999	109.8	44.8	6.4	35.9	13.4	22.5	65.0
$10,000-$14,999	90.2	31.4	6.4	24.3	9.9	14.4	58.8
$15,000-$24,999	93.4	29.1	4.2	24.3	8.0	16.3	64.3
$25,000-$29,999	99.8	27.1	3.9	22.6	7.5	15.1	72.7
$30,000-$49,999	94.2	21.7	3.6	18.1	6.9	11.1	72.4
$50,000 or more	104.1	21.1	3.0	18.0	6.0	12.0	83.0
Residence							
Central city	130.0	40.7	10.0	29.4	11.0	18.4	89.3
Suburban	98.0	26.6	3.9	22.3	8.3	13.9	71.4
Nonmetropolitan areas	70.7	22.3	2.1	19.9	6.9	13.0	48.4

*Persons age 12 and older.
†Includes data on rape not shown separately.
Source: U.S. Department of Justice, 1989.

evasion and antitrust violations fall into this category; some sociologists also include crimes with harsher penalties such as embezzlement, fraud, and forgery. These crimes are essentially closed to lower-class people, who don't have the skills or the access to commit them; you can't embezzle until you get access to the company funds, and you can't evade taxes until you earn some money. Upper-class people, on the other hand, are unlikely to hold up a liquor store when they can engage in a little insider trading and earn millions.

There is no question that white-collar crime results in far greater losses of property each year than index crimes. Estimates are that white-collar crime amounts to from three to ten times the dollar loss than all the index crimes put together (see Wright, 1973; Reiman, 1984). Estimates are necessary here since a large proportion of white-collar crimes go undetected, unreported, or unprosecuted. Tax evasion and price fixing are difficult to detect, employee theft is often not reported, and the influence of wealthy criminals often prevents prosecution. When white-collar criminals are prosecuted, penalties are either nonexistent or minimal compared to the sentences imposed on those accused of index crime. One famous example is the 1961 conspiracy trials of forty-five executives from twenty-nine major American electrical equipment companies (including General Electric and Westinghouse). These men were convicted of price fixing—they had met regularly for a period of time and agreed to set prices artificially high on the items their companies produced. As a result, consumers paid around $1.75 billion extra over a period of eight years (Shoemaker and South, 1974). After pleading *nolo contendere* (no contest) to the charges, the men were sentenced to thirty days in jail (Reiman, 1984). Between 1955 and 1975, 1,027 corporate executives were tried for white-collar crimes; only 5 percent went to prison (Clinard and Yeager, 1980). If the figure were higher, American business would presumably have to shut down; about half of the leading five hundred American corporations have been convicted of various crimes (Simon and Eitzen, 1986). It will be instructive to view the aftermath of the savings and loans scandals of the 1980s and the revelations of crime and mismanagement stemming from B.C.C.I. in the 1990s.

Victimless Crimes Now we come to the interesting and somewhat peculiar topic of crimes without victims. **Victimless crimes** are those crimes in which the criminal is the only victim (if there is a victim) (Schur, 1965). Whereas most laws, such as those relating to murder and robbery, seem designed to protect innocent victims, laws relating to homosexuality, prostitution, drug use, and gambling have a different intent. The implication seems to be that society in general is the victim of these behaviors and so they should be prohibited. With drug use, for example, we seem to feel that certain drugs are so bad for people that those who use them should be put in jail to prevent them from becoming victims of their own behavior.

The behaviors that fall under this heading are a curious group. Prostitution is often called "the oldest profession," yet it is illegal in most of the United States. Gambling is illegal unless the state itself chooses to run it, with lotteries or horse racing; casino gambling is permitted in only two states. Sexual relations between consenting adults of the same sex are still illegal in many states, although gay rights organizations are attempting to change such regulations through political action. Like prostitution and gambling, homosexuality is as old as human memory. In addition, like the other two activities, there have been many times and places where it was fully legal. Finally, drug use is perhaps the most curious of the group. Which drugs?

As we've seen, heroin was legal in the United States until 1914. It was once one of the most popular ingredients (along with chloroform and chloral hydrate) in a variety of nineteenth-century infant remedies for coughs and teething (Douglas and Waksler, 1982). It is now illegal on the grounds that it is dangerous to health, yet cigarettes and liquor, which are both clearly severe health hazards, are both legal (although somewhat restricted).

The existence of victimless crimes tells us more about a society than it does about the people who commit them. Though all laws make a statement about which behaviors a society approves and disapproves, crimes without victims are the clearest examples of this process. When we return, later in this chapter, to look at the role of deviance in society, a closer examination of these "crimes" will provide some insight. When we look at these victimless crimes later, however, remember that the scope of "victimhood" is a matter of dispute. Prostitutes, for example, sell a service to people who want it, but some could argue that the legal presence of prostitutes in a society also affects those who choose not to patronize them. And a prostitute who carries the AIDS virus raises a series of complex questions not only for the sociological study of deviance but also for legislators.

Noncriminal Deviance: Alcoholism, Mental Illness, and Mental Retardation

Alcoholism refers to the behavior of an individual who is not able to control either the frequency or the amount of alcohol consumed. It has been estimated that there are over 5 million Americans of whom this behavior is typical (U.S. Bureau of the Census, 1987). *Mental illness* is not so easily defined, for it refers to a wide variety of human behaviors. The common threads that run through these behaviors are that (1) other people are unable to imagine themselves engaging in the behavior with any rational purpose, and (2) the behavior is thought to be a danger either to the individual or to others. *Mental retardation* refers to the apparent inability of an individual to exhibit intellectual characteristics thought typical of his or her age. Generally, these characteristics are measured through the use of some standardized intelligence test.

These apparently strange bedfellows can share the same heading because of their similarities in the sociological study of deviance. First, the individuals engaging in each of these types of behaviors are assumed to be either temporarily or permanently incapable of behaving any other way; the fact that both alcoholism and mental illness are commonly thought to be "diseases" suggests this perspective. None of these behaviors can therefore be considered criminal since the individual is presumed not responsible for his or her behavior. Second, each of these behaviors breaks social norms and often results in a social control response from some sector of society. Alcoholics receive tremendous informal social pressure and often find their way into alcoholic treatment groups or facilities. The mentally ill may be incarcerated (voluntarily or involuntarily through a court order) in a mental-health facility, where attempts are made to alter their behavior. The mentally retarded are often removed from a standard school curriculum in favor of a program designed specifically for their category. In each case the individual is set apart from others. These examples of noncriminal deviance will help us later to understand more about deviance in general.

Types of Deviance: How Many?

One danger of typing anything is that it leads you to forget things not included in the types. Keep in mind that deviance is a general concept; behavior that breaks norms can vary from some of the extreme forms we've looked at here to a vast number of milder forms. People who are too tall or too short, too fat or too thin can be deviants in the eyes of others. Some people are considered deviant because they are mentally retarded, but how about people who appear to be more intelligent than the rest of us? The physically handicapped are often forced into forms of behavior that others consider deviant (see Sagarin, 1971). How about people with extreme political views? The list is endless—just as endless as the social norms that apparently exist only to be broken. Too close a focus on the more extreme forms of deviance can make us lose track of the way deviance is integrated into everyone's behavior and into every social situation.

THEORIES OF DEVIANCE

Theories that attempt to explain deviance can be separated into two basic types. *Deviant-centered theories* attempt to understand deviant behavior by learning more about the deviant himself or herself and trying to explain why individuals engage in acts of deviance. *Society-centered theories* attempt to explain deviance by understanding the social groups within which deviance occurs. Not surprisingly, most sociologists fall into the second category. When we look at this second collection of theories, you'll note a variety of different questions being asked. Some will focus on those factors within the social group that encourage individuals to engage in acts of deviant behavior, while others will be concerned less with the deviants themselves and more with the social group whose members find the behavior deviant. By the end of this section you should understand deviance as a complex interplay between the individual and the social group on a battlefield of social norms.

Deviant-Centered Theories

Traditionally, notions about deviance have focused on the individual deviant. In the Middle Ages unusual individuals were often thought to be possessed by the devil, and aggressive individuals were thought to have inherited their tendencies. Today, most deviant-centered theories are found in the fields of biology and psychology.

Biological Explanations It is both an appealing and a sobering thought that our biological makeup directs much of our behavior. It is appealing in the sense that it gives hope to the idea that severe mental disorders, for example, might be "cured" by a particular drug. It is sobering because too much knowledge in this area could be used to turn us all into robots. In any case, biological theories and experimentation related to behavior continue.

One of the earlier and more colorful efforts in this area was the work of criminologist Cesare Lombroso (1836-1909). He assumed that criminal deviance was inherited and that this inheritance was visible in the shape of the human skull. He isolated particular jaw structures and the like that he claimed illustrated inherited deviance. Though none of Lombroso's work is applied today, it does explain why most butlers in murder mysteries have close-set eyes and weak chins.

A more modern example of biology applied to criminal behavior focuses on chromosomes. There are two kinds of sex chromosomes, the X and the Y. Women have two Xs (or XX), while men have one of each (or XY). Some men have an extra Y chromosome, giving them an XYY configuration. Working on the assumption that men are naturally more aggressive than women, it seemed possible that an extra male chromosome might make men still more aggressive, which would lead to criminal behavior (see Witkin et al., 1976; Wilson, 1978). However, research has not supported this theory. If any consensus is forming, it is that the XYY chromosome combination is not directly related to behavior.

The more general recent interest in sociobiology (see Chapter 4) has also influenced current research in criminology. Van den Berge (1974) argues that aggressive behavior should be studied from a biosocial standpoint. Rowe and Osgood (1984) are in the process of applying this directive to juvenile delinquency in their work with twins raised separately. In a similar vein, Gabrielli and Mednick (1983) studied over 14,000 adopted children to see whether their criminal (or noncriminal) behavior more closely followed the behavior of their natural parents or their adoptive parents. While they found a significant relation between adopted children and their natural parents with regard to property offenses, they found no relationship between the two with regard to crimes of violence. If aggressive behavior is inherited, it should *least* likely appear in property crime.

Biological explanations of deviance have generally been more popular in the study of mental illness than in criminology. Part of the reason is that mental illness is often viewed as a sickness (a position known as the *medical model* of mental disorder), whereas crime is generally seen as rational and conscious behavior. And an illness, after all, should have some basis in biology. Considerable research has focused on the biological basis of schizophrenia, a common but poorly understood disorder (see Meehl, 1962; Rosenthal, 1968). Some researchers, such as Thomas Szasz (1986), have criticized the medical model; what other illness, Szasz asks, turns out differently with each individual who "catches" it?

Psychological Explanations The most famous of the psychological explanations of deviance come from the psychoanalytic tradition of Sigmund Freud (see Chapter 4). Freud's theory of the inborn id, the superego with its internalized values, and the rational ego provides one possible explanation of deviance: The deviant might be someone who has never properly internalized social group values; with little restraint, the id would run wild into deviance. Or the deviant might have internalized group values *too* strongly, leading to almost total repression of the id's desires and subsequent mental disorder. In either case the deviance would be the result of forces within the individual. Freud's *Civilization and Its Discontents,* published in 1930, started the ball rolling in this direction.

Other psychological approaches, particularly in the study of criminal behavior, have sought to isolate "psychopathic" personalities. The idea behind this approach is that many criminals have basic personality defects, which become reflected in criminal (and other antisocial) activities. Hirschi and Hindelang (1977) have sought to forge a link between the lack of intelligence and criminal activity. With regard to juveniles, for instance, they argue that low IQ leads to frustrating school experiences, which in turn leads to delinquent behavior.

From the sociological point of view psychological and biological explanations overlook much of the meaning that deviance has for the people who engage in it. Most deviant behavior is, in fact, just like any other ongoing patterned social behavior, governed by its own set of norms and values. In short, for sociologists deviance is a phenomenon of social groups.

Society-Centered Theories

Sociological, or society-centered, theories of deviance are distinctive in that they call attention to the deviant's social groups, to the social groups whose norms the deviant breaks, or both. Although the theories in this section vary considerably, they all have in common one point of similarity: They all place the deviant firmly in a social context.

Differential Association The idea of **differential association** was introduced by the American criminologist Edwin Sutherland (1962). The core of this theory is both simple and important: Deviants generally learn to be deviant from ongoing deviant social groups. The juvenile learns to steal from other juveniles who have stolen before and who support the behavior; the prostitute learns her (or his) trade from those with experience in the field. People become deviants, says Sutherland, because they associate with deviants.

The theory of differential association focuses on changes in the thinking of the prospective deviant as he or she associates with established deviants, the most important change being in definitions of legal and illegal, right and wrong. As the prospective deviant associates with established deviants, he or she may acquire a new set of attitudes that condone or even promote criminal activity, thus motivating the newcomer to future deviant acts.

Subcultural Theory As we saw in Chapter 3, a **subculture** is a social group or collection of social groups that exists within a larger culture yet has distinctive norms and values that set it off from the larger culture. Any subculture might be somewhat deviant since its members might have to break the larger culture's norms in order to follow their own. The question is: How different are the subculture's norms? A **deviant subculture** is a subculture viewed by both its members and outsiders as having fundamentally, and often threateningly, different norms and values. To become part of such a subculture is to enter the world of deviance. Aside from that, the processes of socialization and internalization are much the same as those that occur when any individual encounters a new social group.

Subcultural theorists tend to view criminal deviants as coming from a fundamentally different culture and, as a result, adhering to a fundamentally different set of values. Walter Miller (1958) explains the large number of lower-class criminals by such logic, suggesting the existence of a "lower-class culture" with values supporting toughness, excitement, trouble, and the immediate gratification of desires. Such values tend to lead individuals into criminal activity.

Labeling Theory **Labeling theory** looks beyond the social groups to which the deviant belongs and focuses attention on the groups whose norms the deviant breaks. As Howard Becker (1963:9) describes it,

> . . . social groups create deviance by making the rules whose infraction constitutes deviance, and by applying those rules to particular people and labeling them as outsiders. From this point of view, deviance is not a quality of the act the person commits, but rather a consequence of the application by others of rules and sanctions to an "outsider." The deviant is one to whom that label has successfully been applied; deviant behavior is behavior that people so label.

From this definition we can extract the basic ideas of labeling theory:

1. No action or behavior is ever inherently deviant, and no individual is ever inherently a deviant.
2. Deviance exists only when members of social groups label the violation of their norms as deviance.
3. Deviants exist only when individuals are labeled as such by members of social groups.

Let us look at these ideas one at a time.

First, the reason no act or behavior can ever be inherently deviant is that norms change from group to group and from time to time. Actions considered to be deviant today or in the eyes of a certain group may well be considered "normal" behavior tomorrow or somewhere else. We have already seen some of this variation across cultures in Chapter 3, but the same variation occurs within one culture. During Hitler's leadership in Germany, murdering Jews and burning books were considered normal, while going to certain churches or supporting programs to aid the mentally retarded was considered deviant. Probably an even better example would be the early Christian movement. In the eyes of the state (as it then was) Jesus was considered a supreme deviant and suffered the ultimate sanction—execution. Today, of course, belief in Christianity is highly respectable in the Western world. Times and people change. It is a sobering thought to realize that some of the people we think of as deviants today may be looked upon in the future as the greatest figures of our time.

Second, certain violations of certain social norms must be labeled as deviance before deviance exists. Becker's argument here is that the members of social groups must reach some kind of consensus as to which kinds of behavior are deviance and which are not. They must also decide how deviant that behavior is in relation to others. In the United States during the 1920s, for example, alcohol was illegal but marijuana was legal; today it is just the reverse. Such changes are indicative of the group decision-making process and the manner in which consensus can change. In a court of law you cannot be prosecuted for an act you committed before a law was passed declaring it illegal. By the same token, you cannot count on being released from prison should your offense be subsequently removed from the law or the penalties lessened.

Finally, individuals become deviants (in the sociological sense) only when they are labeled as such by members of social groups. According to this aspect of labeling theory, you are not a deviant until people think of you as a deviant and, more important, treat you as a deviant. If you are a mass murderer who has never been caught, you are not strictly speaking a deviant. At the other extreme, if you have been unjustly accused of a deviant act and are believed by others to have committed it, you will be treated as a deviant (even though you've done nothing). As far as Becker is concerned, a deviant is an individual who is treated as a deviant and forced by others into a deviant role. Deviance belongs to the group, not to the individual.

This last idea offered by Becker is in keeping with Edwin Lemert's (1967) distinction between primary and secondary deviance. **Primary deviance** involves the commission of an act that has been labeled as deviant. Primary deviance is a behavior that only you know about; the fact that others treat you as if it hadn't occurred minimizes its importance in your everyday life. (You can probably think of a few deviant acts out of your past that you would just as soon

Being poor in the United States unavoidably leads to deviant behavior and to a variety of deviant labels.

not have spread around.) **Secondary deviance** begins when you get caught, when others become aware of your behavior. Secondary deviance gains its importance from the nature of the social self (as described in the last chapter). If others treat us as deviants, that treatment will become a very real factor in our everyday life and will ultimately change the way we look at ourselves.

Because of its focus, labeling theory directs our attention away from the deviants themselves and toward the people who do the labeling. We must now ask several new questions: Whose norms are being broken? Why are those people in a position to label others effectively—why are they "respectable" and deviants "deviant," instead of the other way around? What is the process by which they apply labels to actions and to the people who engage in those actions? These questions can draw our attention to the people who hold power and authority in society (the people who make their labels "stick"). They direct us further to examine police, courts, judges, prisons, psychiatrists, mental hospitals, educators, and everyone else who takes an active part in the labeling process. We become aware, through labeling theory, of which people are caught, processed, and labeled, as opposed to those who aren't. We become aware of why certain behaviors may be labeled as deviance today but not tomorrow. In short, labeling theory calls our attention to deviance as a *label* that is created and applied *in social groups.*

A role with authority in a social group is a role with, among other things, the right to label. Typically, such rights are specific to certain kinds of labels; that is, a judge can label you a criminal, a psychiatrist can label you as mentally ill, and a teacher can label you as a poor student. The label can act as a self-fulfilling prophecy: If everyone (including the person labeled) treats the label as accurate, ultimately it may become accurate. Mental institutions often turn people into excellent mental patients, and prisons are famous for producing more and better criminals. As labeling theory tells us, the label carries its own reality.

Anomie Theory French sociologist Emile Durkheim (1858-1917) used the term **anomie** to describe a state of normlessness in society, when many people are unclear as to the expectations others have of them (Durkheim, 1951). Durkheim applied this concept to his famous study of suicide (see Chapter 2), explaining that suicide rates went up with increased anomie. The importance of his study for an understanding of deviance is his focus on the way a society can actually create strains in the lives of its individual members. Labeling theory examines the manner in which deviants are labeled but ignores the question of what causes deviance. **Anomie theory**, as it has been applied in the study of deviance, offers one solution to the question of what causes deviance: Deviant behavior is encouraged by strains built into the very fabric of society.

Durkheim's concept was borrowed by American sociologist Robert Merton in his study of deviance. Merton was particularly interested in the problems people had in adapting to certain cultural goals (or values) and their ability or inability to acquire certain goals through established means (or norms). For example, all Americans are socialized to value success and material goods, but not all Americans can achieve those goals through the legitimate means that are available in our society. If you want a new car and a fine house but can't find a job that will allow you to acquire them, you might find some creative (deviant) way of achieving the same ends.

Merton (1956) analyzed societal strains by pointing out the variety of ways that people might respond to such strain. As the strains occur in all walks of life, so too do the (often deviant) adaptations. Consider how each of Merton's types of adaptation occurs in the world of everyday work.

1. *Conformity.* By far the most common response, conformity occurs when individuals adhere to cultural norms and values in spite of strain. A janitor might prefer to have his or her occupation better thought of and better paid but, failing that possibility, learns to live with it and do the job. The strains are still there, but they don't appear in behavior.
2. *Innovation.* A clear deviant response, innovation occurs when individuals accept cultural values (such as success) but find alternative means for achieving them. The quiet bank teller who has been cleverly removing bank funds for years has found an alternative to the promotion that didn't happen. We can also see innovation in the actions of a bureaucrat who, frustrated with organizational graft and ineptitude, steps outside the organizational role by blowing the whistle to authorities. Innovation is a clear case in which the structure of society encourages actions of individual deviance.
3. *Ritualism.* The ritualist response to strain involves giving up goals that seem impossible to achieve in favor of adhering to the standard means (or norms). The once-dedicated high school teacher who now settles for just law and order in the classroom is a classic ritualist. Rules concerning student behavior were instituted in public schools with the idea that they would lead to more effective education. If that more effective education does not appear forthcoming, the ritualist can nevertheless cling to the ritual of following the established

means. Under this heading we also find the bureaucrat more interested in following rules than helping people or the librarian who is only really happy when all the books are safely on the shelves and the doors locked. A great many occupations appear to have unreachable goals built into them. One response to this strain is to forget them and concentrate on "doing your job" even if the point of the job seems forgotten.

4. *Retreatism.* The retreatist responds to strain by giving up on both cultural values and norms. Not even criminal occupations would fit in here since most criminals are interested in making money illegally (an innovative response). Merton's example is the "occupation" of hobo—the individual who thumbs a deviant nose at the whole society. The hobo wants none of society and has no desire to change it.
5. *Rebellion.* The last response, rebellion, rejects both cultural norms and values but seeks to change both. A radical political activist who makes bombs and plans of revolution in his or her spare time is a classic example. The Irish Republican Army in Northern Ireland and the Palestine Liberation Organization in Israeli-occupied territory in the Middle East both seek major changes through whatever means may be necessary.

All of Merton's adaptive types (except for conformity) can be thought of as deviant responses to societal strain. In each case the "cause" of the deviance lies outside the individual and in the state of anomie that exists in society. If these deviant individuals also have "personality disorders" or choose to associate with deviant subcultures, those attributes are only symptoms of more general social forces.

Anomie theory has found particular application with regard to juvenile delinquency. Cloward and Ohlin (1960) point out that lower-class juveniles are subject to acquiring the same values as middle-class juveniles but with far fewer legitimate means of acquiring them. The delinquent subculture is not so much an ongoing part of lower-class culture (as subcultural theories suggest) as an adaptive form of social organization designed to meet the needs of otherwise frustrated juveniles. Criminal behavior thus becomes a reaction to their feeling of injustice at being deprived of what middle-class youths are given.

Cohen (1955) offers a similar view of the juvenile gang. Lower-class juveniles feel a sense of material deprivation compared to middle-class juveniles, but they also feel a status loss. Middle-class juveniles, for example, are likely to acquire favorable evaluations of their self-worth from established social institutions, such as schools, whereas lower-class juveniles are likely to acquire negative attitudes about themselves from those same institutions. The gang becomes a source of self-esteem for the lower-class juvenile, providing a sense of "fitting in" somewhere. If you don't get respect at home or at school, you can always get it from fellow members of the gang.

Social Control Theory Like anomie theory, **social control theory** attempts to explain why individuals engage in deviant behavior. Unlike anomie theory, however, social control theory explains why only certain deprived individuals turn to criminal behavior while others in remarkably similar situations resist the temptation. The answer focuses on the standard sociological concept of social control—the means by which individuals are convinced (or coerced) to follow the norms of respectable (and certainly noncriminal) behavior.

Reckless (1967) separates these mechanisms of social control into outer containment and inner containment. *Outer containment* comes from the strength of the social group and its commitment to noncriminal behavior. If members of the social group are bound together tightly enough, they will police each other's behavior, thus prohibiting individual members from attempting any criminal behavior. *Inner containment* stems from the process of the internalization of values—individuals come to police their own behavior through a desire to live up to their (socially constructed) conscience. According to Reckless, when either of the social control processes breaks down as individuals interact within their social groups, deviant behavior will result.

Radical Theories The **radical theories** of deviance follow in the tradition of Karl Marx (1818-1883), whose ideas will be examined more fully in the next chapter, on social stratification. Marx's concern with social stratification has a definite bearing on deviance for, as we've already seen, the rich and the poor in the United States have very different experiences with the criminal justice system.

Marx's primary interest was to gain an understanding of capitalist industrial society—a society based on private property in which the means of production and distribution (all economic power) were in the hands of a few—the capitalists, or, more simply, the ruling class. Marx was particularly curious about how the ruling class, a very small percentage of the population, could control most of the wealth. He was also interested in the reasons that the rest of the population (who worked for members of the ruling class) would either decide to put up with their situation or seek to change it. These decisions, Marx felt, had a lot to do with actions taken by members of the ruling class. They were in a position to control the living situations of those who worked for them and even control the ideas that these people had by controlling the flow of information in society. According to the modern radical theories of deviance, one of the ways they exercised this control was through the way they defined and responded to "crime."

Jeffrey Reiman (1984), one of the modern radical theorists, raises a very interesting question. What kind of criminal justice system would you form, he asks, if you wanted to "*maintain* and *encourage* the existence of a stable and visible class of criminals" instead of eliminating crime and rehabilitating criminals? First, he says, you would need "irrational" laws on the books (such as laws against heroin) that would encourage people to engage in other forms of criminal activity (such as burglary, in order to support an expensive habit). Second, give police, prosecutors, and judges broad discretion as to which people go free and which people go to prison. Third, make the prison experience painful and demeaning. Fourth, make sure the prisoners acquire no skills while in prison and have no jobs when they get out. Finally, make sure that a prisoner's record colors the rest of his or her life, separating the individual socially, economically, and politically from those who have never been to prison. In short, says Reiman, you would set up a criminal justice system exactly like the one we have.

Reiman's radical criticism is that our criminal justice system is designed to maintain a certain percentage of the population, mostly of the lower class, involved in activities labeled *criminal* so that they may be presented to the rest of the population (the middle class) as an ever-present danger. If the middle class is concerned about lawbreaking among the lower classes, they will favor a strong government and, more important, won't come to recognize the upper classes as a danger to them. For example, middle-class Americans are afraid of being murdered. As a matter of fact, two Americans die every hour as the victims of homicide, whereas eleven Americans die in the same time period from diseases brought about by unhealthy conditions in the workplace (Reiman, 1984). Where, Reiman asks, is the real danger?

Perhaps an even more telling example (following Reiman's preceding example about drug laws) comes from attitudes held by Americans about the degree of severity of the drug problem in the United States. According to a recent Gallup Poll, 27 percent of Americans list drug abuse when asked, "What do you think is the most important problem facing this country today?" No other single category (including "unemployment," "poverty," "fear of war," "crime," etc.) surpasses drug abuse as a perceived social problem (Gallup, 1989). The percentage listing drug abuse rises to 58 percent when Americans are asked, "What is responsible for crime in the United States today?" (By comparison, only 14 percent cite unemployment as a cause of high crime rates.) The 58 percent figure is up from 13 percent in 1981, when 37 percent of those polled felt unemployment to be the greater cause of high crime rates (Gallup, 1989). While public perceptions about the importance of unemployment are no doubt affected by business cycles and unemployment levels, changes in perceptions as between 1981 and 1989 about a deviant act (such as drug use) are often cited by radical theorists to show how public opinion can be shaped by those in authority. If our attention has been refocused on drugs (and the people who use them), we will perhaps be less aware of other threats to our liberty and safety.

Why is armed robbery or assault a serious crime, while ignoring an industrial safety regulation that results in a death is only breaking a regulation? The difference, says Reiman, is in the criminal. In the first case the criminal will usually be poor; in the second case the criminal will never be poor. This is very similar to the difference between index crime and white-collar crime we've already noted. Any behavior by the middle and upper classes somehow doesn't seem quite as criminal as the things lower-class people do. Yet, as Reiman points out in his analysis of occupational hazards and unnecessary surgery, the upper classes are often far more dangerous than the lower classes.

A serious example of corporate disregard for the health of workers is presented by Paul Brodeur (1985) in his history of the lawsuits spawned by the actions of the major U.S. manufacturers of asbestos. Asbestos is a mineral that causes serious health problems when it enters the lungs; even a brief exposure can produce cancer thirty years later. For years, workers knew nothing of the danger they were in as they worked with this product. As they began to die and as lawyers began to gather evidence, it turned out that the major manufacturers had known (in some cases) for fifty years about the dangers of their product. Rather than notify their employees (which might have resulted in lawsuits) or institute safer work situations (which would have been expensive, producing a drop in profits), they chose to prepare themselves by taking out more insurance. The insurance companies investigated, also discovered the risks of asbestos exposure, and then sold more insurance at higher premiums rather than tell anyone. All these actions were motivated not by the evil intent of the individuals involved but rather by the way the business world is structured around the profit motive. From the perspective of radical theory, it is the structure of the corporate world that produces such abuses.

Another radical theorist, Richard Quinney (1980), points out a service that criminal justice provides for the economy. Capitalists, says Quinney, often have a problem coping with workers as the economy fluctuates downward and people are put out of work. What do you do with all the people? Many go on one or another government program (food stamps, unemployment compensation, etc.) until things start looking up. One of these unemployment programs, says Quinney, is prison.

Figure 5.1 shows a striking similarity between the number of people out of work and the prison population fifteen months later. Quinney points to such information to defend his theory: One place for the surplus population, apparently, is in prison. Prison certainly keeps people off the streets, and if you are a member of the ruling class, the last thing you will want is a large number of unhappy unemployed people out on the streets.

In sum, the radical theorists argue that criminal justice is a far more pervasive means of social control than we normally think. Crime is defined in such a way that potentially dangerous members of the lower class are the only people truly affected. In addition, these lower-class criminals are held up to the rest of us as a threat to our well-being; if we accept this picture, we are more likely to prefer a strong protective government and less likely to notice other threats to our health perpetrated by members of the ruling class.

POWER AND AUTHORITY IN SOCIETY: THE ROLE OF DEVIANCE

As noted in earlier chapters, **power** is the extent to which you can control the behavior of others, while **authority** is the right that others give you to exert that control. Both of these concepts are important in the study of deviance. Social control techniques that are common responses to deviance are generally backed by raw power. The police and prison systems in the United States, for example, operate through armed might. Authority may be even more important than power, however.

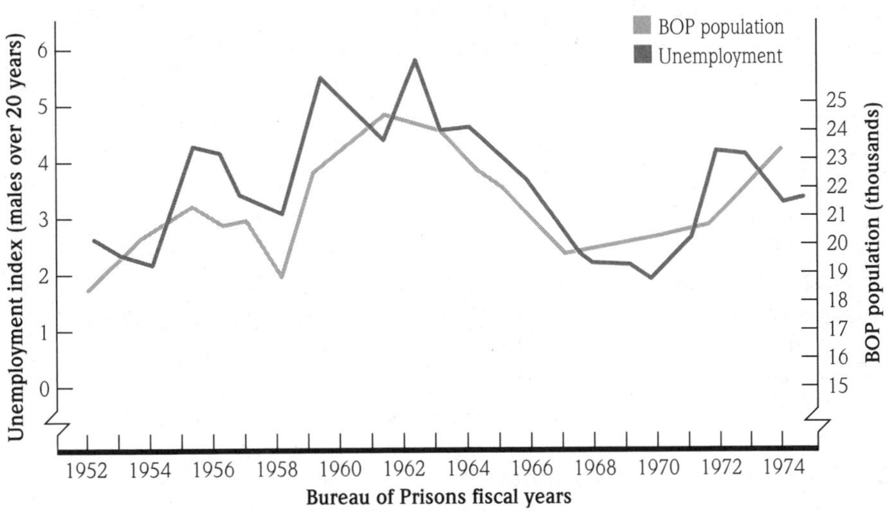

Figure 5.1 Bureau of Prisons inmate population, matched with unemployment index from fifteen months earlier. (Data from U.S. Bureau of Prisons, 1975.)

Authority was threatened mightily by the civil rights movement of the 1960s and its leaders. Militant blacks—even though avowedly and actually acting in nonviolent ways—appeared deviant to many authorities in both North and South. Here, Dr. Martin Luther King, Jr., is shown during one of several jail stays. Dr. King, of course, was eventually acknowledged as an American hero; there is a national holiday honoring him.

The theories of deviance we've examined thus far bring us naturally to the role of authority. When social groups that violate each other's norms come into conflict—police and burglars, for example—only one group ends up with the label *deviant.* Clearly, some groups have the authority to label, and others do not. The burglars find the behavior of the police highly unattractive, but that opinion does not become a societal label. Similarly, when our legislators and courts tell us that car theft is a "crime" but that industrial deaths are "safety violations," we abide by the labels; legislators and courts have the authority to make those decisions for us. The kinds of behavior that are labeled as deviant obviously have a lot to do with the positions of authority in a society.

In this section we will look at the role of deviance in relation to power and authority with two basic questions in mind. First, to what extent is deviant behavior labeled as such because it in some way threatens positions of authority? Second, how does the label of deviance become a social definition that most of us accept without question?

Deviance as a Threat to Authority

People come and go from positions of authority, and the positions themselves have been known to come and go as societies change. When Richard Nixon resigned the presidency, he lost the authority he had been receiving from that position. If a revolution had occurred as well, the position itself might have been replaced by a new position of authority. In short, authority can be a somewhat slippery social possession. And the more slippery it becomes, the more avidly it will be sought after and clutched. Not surprisingly, therefore, the quickest way for behavior to earn a deviant label is for it to threaten authority or to be perceived as a threat to authority.

Probably the clearest example of this aspect of deviance is the distinction between index crime and white-collar crime. Burglary (which is a nonviolent index crime) results in prison sentences twice as long as embezzlement and almost four times as long as income-tax fraud (Reiman, 1984). The irony is that the two white-collar crimes each result in a far greater dollar loss each year than burglary. Why the difference? As an index crime, burglary is typically a crime of the lower classes and represents an attempt to move wealth from haves to the have nots. On the other hand, white-collar crime shifts wealth from one set of haves to another. Perhaps more importantly, the people who commit white-collar crime are typically in positions of authority themselves and are the same "kind of people" as others in positions of authority (such as judges) who may be called upon to label the act (see Box 5.1).

Perhaps an even better example comes from the history of labor relations in the United States. The success and respectability of labor unions today makes it easy to forget the long period of extreme violence in the early history of unionization. Whereas a strike today attracts a federal negotiator, a strike at the end of the last century usually attracted the police, the National Guard, or the U.S. Army. Such repressive responses lasted well into the 1930s and are still not unheard of with some unions today. Why the violent response? Unions were not just asking for money and better working conditions; they were demanding some authority over their lives. Once an industry was unionized, management would thereafter always have to consider the union in all decisions. This pill has been well swallowed and digested by American industry, but it was an extremely bitter pill at the outset.

Of all the labor history that could serve to illustrate this violent response from a threatened authority, one of the most interesting incidents is the Sacco-Vanzetti execution on August 23, 1927. Nicola Sacco and Bartolomeo Vanzetti were Italian-American members of a radical labor organization. They had both had brushes with the law because of their labor activities; they were finally arrested, charged with, and convicted of the robbery and murder of a paymaster and guard at a shoe factory in South Braintree, Massachusetts. Even though another prison inmate subsequently confessed to the murders, Sacco and Vanzetti were executed anyway (Rolle, 1972). They were on trial for their labor activities, which had little to do with the crime of which they were accused.

Other examples of threatened authorities could be cited from any situation where social authority exists. Jesus was crucified not so much for his religious beliefs as for his rebellion against Roman authority. In turn, the Catholic Church, which formed in response to the teachings of Jesus, came to a position of authority itself and responded with hostility to scientific advances, such as Galileo's idea that the sun (and not the earth) was at the center of the universe. Examples are abundant in our own time, too. Doctors often want you just to take the pills without wasting their time with questions. Students who want decent grades must use care not to impugn their professor's knowledge and expertise. Employees of all descriptions must show proper deference to their employers if they wish to remain employed. In each case those in positions of authority jealously guard their right to decide and will label as deviance any behavior that gets in the way.

BOX 5.1

THE SAINTS AND THE ROUGHNECKS

William Chambliss (1973) offers us a view of deviant labeling through his study of two teenage boys' gangs: the Saints and the Roughnecks. These gangs had two striking differences between them: (1) The Saints were all middle class or upper class, while the Roughnecks were all lower class. (2) The Saints engaged in a variety of deviant acts equal to or surpassing the delinquency of the Roughnecks, yet they were seldom in trouble with the police and were well thought of in the community. The question is: How does social class play a role in the way behavior is interpreted?

The primary difference between the Saints and the Roughnecks was in style. The Saints presented an image of middle-class respectability by following middle-class norms, of which they were well aware, while the Roughnecks violated these norms. For example, the Saints were good students and were involved in school activities. They managed this even though they were truant much of the time. They always managed to leave school "legitimately" (forging excuses, etc.) so that their behavior was not widely known among teachers. When their grades did fall as a result of truancy, teachers always gave them the benefit of the doubt because they were "good students."

When truant or on weekends, the Saints got drunk, drove their cars recklessly, shouted obscenities at passing women, and engaged in acts of vandalism. If, for example, they found a street being repaired, they enjoyed removing the barriers and watching cars drive into the open holes. Abandoned houses were also considered fair game for vandalism. They were careful, however, to limit all this activity to a nearby city so as not to lose their "good name" in their home town. They generally were able to avoid the police. When caught, they were extremely polite and contrite and were generally let off with a warning.

The Roughnecks had little money for liquor and seldom had cars. They generally hung around a town street corner, regularly getting into fights among themselves or sometimes with rivals. They engaged in acts of theft, although the community was not aware of their extent, thinking the boys were primarily drinkers and fighters. The Roughnecks' drinking, though limited by their lack of funds, was highly visible when it did occur since the boys had no place to go and no cars in which they could achieve some privacy. Ironically, most of the Roughnecks attended school regularly, but they were not particularly successful students and had a bad reputation among the teachers.

The Saints were viewed by the community as good boys who sowed a few wild oats from time to time. The Roughnecks were viewed as a bad bunch. Not only were the Saints given the benefit of the doubt because of the prestige of their social class, they were able to use that class position to manage the impression they made on others. They used their knowledge of middle-class norms to appear respectable and their money to obtain privacy for their delinquent behavior. The Roughnecks had neither advantage. The different perspectives on these two gangs is almost identical to the more general distinction in the United States between index crime and white-collar crime—both the crimes and the criminals are viewed differently.

Deviance as a Social Definition

American sociologist W. I. Thomas (1863-1947) is best remembered today for his concept of the **definition of the situation.** Thomas meant by this that social reality (norms, values, knowledge, etc.) is largely a matter of definition; if we all agree that something is real, then it will become part of social reality, as it will be real in its consequences for all concerned. Consider the situation of the American college classroom. What makes that situation real? A collection of people making noise in a room becomes a college classroom as soon as everyone decides it should be. When employers tell you that you must spend time in a college classroom (or two or three) before they will hire you, they help give that situation reality. If you then go through the experience and subsequently get a job, you will taste the real consequences of an agreed-upon social definition. Note that it's not important that you actually learn anything; it's only important that you and others agree that you have. You could become very well educated through your experiences outside the classroom but never get credit for it if no one will treat your learning as "real." Similarly, the separation of people by race is an agreed-upon definition in American society; we could just as well separate people by eye color. If we all agree that the definition is real, then it will have very real consequences for all of us. Those consequences create social reality.

The function of labeling in deviance is similar to Thomas's definition of the situation; like other aspects of social reality, deviance is an agreed-upon definition of reality. We have seen that positions of authority have the right to label, but we have yet to see why most people accept the decisions of authorities without question. Why are we more apt to accept someone else's definition of the situation as opposed to creating our own? For sociologists this is the question of how authorities maintain legitimacy.

"Legitimate" Definitions of Authority Authority is not authority without legitimacy. The sense of legitimacy we feel when confronting an authority comes from the right we feel the authority has to make certain decisions that affect us. As authorities decide, they also define social reality. To decide that burglary is more serious than embezzlement is to define burglary as a more socially dangerous act than embezzlement. If you engage in either of these acts, you will experience the reality of that definition in the responses of others to your behavior; those who accept the definitions of authority will reflect that acceptance in the way they treat you. Knowing what keeps the decisions of authorities legitimate will therefore also tell us what keeps their definitions legitimate.

In a modern industrial society such as the United States the predominant type of authority is legal/rational authority (see Chapter 3). A distinctive feature of legal/rational authority is that it is attached to positions and not to individuals; individuals can exercise it only while they occupy positions of authority. If we search out these positions of authority in the United States, we find they are firmly imbedded in the dominant institutions of the society. Judges are part of the criminal justice system, which is tied into the political institution (judges are elected by the people or appointed by politicians) and the economic institution. Teachers, psychologists, and others who make decisions about students are part of the educational institution. Your spiritual conduct will be evaluated by religious officials, who are part of the institution of religion. Your ability to sell your labor will be decided upon by employers, who are part of the economic institution. In short, disputing the decisions (and definitions) of authorities gets you into a fight with a societal institution.

Institutions represent huge hunks of society; it is difficult to imagine their scope or their influence. We can see part of that scope and influence, however, in the unquestioning way that most of us accept their reality. People in prison look dangerous *because* they are in prison; the very environment gives you that feeling (Reiman, 1984). People in mental institutions look crazy *because* they are in mental institutions (Goffman, 1961b). The Rosenhan study described in Box 5.2 shows that anyone and any behavior becomes suspect just by existing within a mental hospital. Presumably, professors look knowledgeable *because* they are standing in the front of a classroom.

Social Definitions in Action: The Case of the Mentally Retarded What do we mean by the term *mentally retarded,* and who decides when it should be used? Both questions have almost the same answer: We generally accept the meaning provided by educational psychologists (the position with authority over that particular label), and educational psychologists decide when the term should be used. Typically, a mentally retarded individual is thought to be intellectually handicapped, unable to grasp certain concepts or master certain mental operations. We also usually think of this trait as inherent in people; no matter how much they learn or what kinds of experiences they have, they will always be "slow."

Sociologist Jane Mercer became suspicious of this label in her research with the Riverside, California, school system (Mercer, 1973). Her suspicions came from the ethnic membership of classes for the mentally retarded; Mexican American children had been placed in those classes in far greater proportions than their numbers in the school system should warrant. Why? Either Mexican Americans were racially (and therefore genetically) inferior to the rest of the (Anglo) school population, or being mentally retarded actually meant that one was just culturally different from the people who labeled one as retarded.

When she looked a little more closely at the situation, Mercer discovered that one of the main reasons children were placed in classes for the mentally retarded was their score on an intelligence (IQ) test. How can a test measure intelligence? A test can measure what you know about something, your ability to handle certain kinds of problems, and (perhaps most significantly) your ability to take tests. But if you don't know about something or can't handle a problem, does that mean you're retarded or simply that you're lacking a certain experience? In looking more closely at the IQ tests themselves, Mercer found that they were based almost entirely on the experiences typical of a middle-class white American child. If you had any other ethnic background, your experience with the content of the test items would be limited and, ultimately, so would your score. Children were being labeled as mentally retarded because they lacked some of the cultural experiences common to other children in their school system.

Like other deviants, the mentally retarded have been judged and labeled by an established societal authority—in this case, the school educational psychologist. And as with all such labeling situations, a social definition is created that most of us come to accept.

Boundary Maintenance: Victimless Crimes and Respectability One of the most important social realities created by the deviant label is separation between groups. Sociologists refer to this phenomenon as **boundary maintenance** (as we maintain the boundary between us "good" people over here and you "bad" people over there). Labels of deviance are very effective in maintaining boundaries in that the label givers are able to contrast the wonderfulness of themselves with the horribleness of the deviant. Just as you seldom become aware

BOX 5.2

BEING SANE IN INSANE PLACES: THE ROSENHAM STUDY

How do people get into and out of mental hospitals? How do they acquire the label mentally ill? Psychologist David Rosenhan (1973) set out to study this question by sending eight "sane" people to twelve different mental hospitals with the complaint that they were hearing voices saying things like "empty," "hollow" and "thud." Rosenhan knew these symptoms to be standard symptoms of schizophrenia that would gain these pseudopatients entry into the hospitals. From that point on, the pseudopatients were under instructions to tell no more lies and to declare the symptoms vanished. They were also instructed to take notes of their experiences for the experiment.

None of the pseudopatients was correctly identified to be sane by the hospital staffs, despite their public display of their sanity on the hospital wards after their admission. The length of hospitalization ranged from seven to fifty-two days, with the average being nineteen days. Ironically, during all this time only the other mental patients recognized pronounced symptoms of sanity among the pseudopatients, with 35 of 118 real patients questioning their "craziness"; the hospital staff members tended to view the pseudopatients as cooperative but sick. The pseudopatients told their true life stories when asked, detailing the good and bad parts of their experiences and relationships such as we all have. These stories were generally viewed in a negative light by the mental health staff so as to better "explain" the mental illness they were sure existed. One nurse even took notes on the pseudopatient's note taking, placing on the nursing record "Patient engages in writing behavior." On a mental health ward all behavior looks pathological.

Upon release the patients were labeled *schizophrenia in remission*. The implication of "remission" is that they were not cured; rather, the illness was quieted but might reappear at any time. Such a label, in these cases applied incorrectly, colors the remainder of one's life, affecting both personal relationships and public activities. Would you vote for a vice president with this label or even want such a person to teach your child?

Some mental hospital administrators told Rosenhan they doubted whether such mistakes could occur in their hospitals. Rosenhan told them he would send some pseudopatients to see how accurately they were able to pick them out. He sent none. After 193 real patients had been admitted to the hospitals, Rosenhan questioned the staff as to which were real and which were pseudopatients. Of the 193 patients, 43 were selected by at least one staff member (with a high degree of confidence) to be pseudopatients.

Rosenhan's study tells us about labeling the mentally ill and also provides some more general insights about our society. The fact that the pseudopatients looked crazy to the hospital staffs suggests the ease with which we accept the "rightness" of our institutions. An individual's existence under a label tends to be accepted as truth when an entire institution operates on that basis.

of your culture until you meet someone from another culture, you seldom become aware of your norms until you meet someone who breaks them. Then you (and all who share those norms) can communally label the deviant, reaffirm your common membership in one social group, and remind yourselves where your group ends and the other begins. It is, in fact, essential for members of social groups to maintain their boundaries in this way. The label of deviance will be created from thin air if necessary just to have something to point to as a violation. In short, group members create deviance; deviant individuals are but pawns in the game (Erikson, 1966). In Peggy Bendet's article on homosexuality on college campuses following this chapter, this battleground between deviant and nondeviant comes more into focus.

Of all the laws on the books in the United States, those that most clearly serve this function are laws against victimless crimes. These, you'll recall, are those forms of criminal behavior in which no one "gets hurt" unless you want to count the criminal. Consider a case that could be made for heroin. Contrary to popular opinion, there is actually very little evidence that heroin is as physically damaging as laws against it suggest, especially compared with cigarettes and alcohol. Heroin is more addictive than cigarettes, and addiction isn't a pleasant idea to most of us, but why is that the governments business? The physical problems we most generally associate with heroin are in fact withdrawal symptoms, and those symptoms wouldn't occur if heroin weren't illegal and were, on the contrary, inexpensive and readily available. Most deaths due to overdoses (except those that are intentional suicide) are caused by variations in the strength of heroin bought on the street. By making the possession or sale of heroin a serious crime, the government has managed to push the price of heroin sky high, which leads those who use it to commit crimes to earn money. The cost of this drug-related crime plus the cost of drug-related law enforcement easily runs into billions of dollars a year. American taxpayers (most of whom would rather not consume heroin personally) are apparently willing to pay this price to keep current drug laws on the books. Are they getting their money's worth? To the extent that such expenses provide the satisfaction of boundary maintenance, it would seem reasonable to assume that boundary maintenance is a very valuable commodity indeed.

Similar arguments could be made concerning laws against homosexuality, gambling, prostitution, and other activities entered into by consenting adults. Note the difference in the way the law deals with alcohol (which is currently respectable in the United States). Alcohol use becomes a crime only when it threatens someone besides the user (such as in drunk driving) or when the "criminal" is too poor to have a classy place to drink and gets arrested for public intoxication at the corner of Tenth and Main. Crimes without victims such as those mentioned above are illegal anywhere under any circumstances, even if kept totally private and off everyone's toes. Such laws represent a public statement about our group's norms and values and, ultimately, allow us to define "respectability." An example of these sorts of values in action is reflected in American attitudes toward various aspects of homosexuality. According to a recent Gallup Poll, 71 percent of Americans believe homosexuals should have equal rights in employment opportunities (compared with 59 percent in 1982 and 56 percent in 1977); lest you think that all attitudes regarding homosexuals reflect such a "liberalization," however, only 47 percent of that same sample believes that homosexual sexual relations should be legalized, that figure up a scant 4 percentage points since 1977 (Gallup, 1989b). Since these laws involve consenting adults in the privacy of their own homes, public attitudes supporting restricting relations suggests something of the lack of respectability that continues to be associated with homosexuality.

Respectability means being well thought of by others, but we'll need a more precise definition to capture the real meaning. An expert safecracker may be well thought of by other

Prostitution is sometimes called "the oldest profession," yet it continues to be thought of as a deviant activity in the United States. Those who hire and pay prostitutes, however, are rarely considered deviant. There appears to be a boundary maintained here between sellers (female) and buyers (male).

safecrackers, but is that really respectability? We return once again to the question of authority. To be respectable, you must be well thought of by the "right" people because you exemplify the "right" norms and values. As we've seen, being "right" means being in power and having authority. Since victimless crimes are defined by those in authority (as is all criminal behavior), such laws serve to define respectability at the same time they define deviance. And that is why they are so important. The exercise of authority that creates victimless crimes becomes necessary to justify the lifestyles of the very people who currently hold that authority. It reiterates their moral right to hold that authority. Boundary maintenance is just one aspect of the overall process through which social reality is created.

RESPONSES TO DEVIANCE: COURTS AND PRISONS

Some form of social control is the standard response to deviance. Group members typically take a dim view of having their norms broken, and their response will generally be in keeping with the importance they place on the norm(s). Acts of deviance considered mild (becoming too loud at a party, for instance) will receive more mild forms of social control (such as not being invited back). All of us commit such acts of deviance every day and are used to these forms of social control. As acts of deviance violate increasingly important norms, however, social control escalates accordingly. If your social blunders become too severe, you may face general ostracism from your community. At some point in this progression informal means of social control will give way to formal means of social control. If your behavior becomes seen as criminal, the police, courts, and prisons will intervene. If it becomes seen as dangerous and irrational, the police, courts, and mental health practitioners will intervene. This section will examine some of these formal means of social control.

In dealing with criminal behavior, courts are entrusted with determining guilt and assessing a penalty on guilty parties. Prisons are entrusted with carrying out the penalties involving incarceration or execution, the most severe penalties currently employed in the United States. All citizens are supposed to be equal before the law and should therefore receive treatment consistent with others charged with the same law violations. In addition, most people have hopes that the system of criminal justice might play some role in the rehabilitation of lawbreaking individuals it processes. As we look more closely at the system of criminal justice in the United States, however, we will find considerable variation from these goals.

Whatever else they may or may not do, courts and prisons serve to keep large numbers of people off the streets. At any point, roughly 1 of every 400 Americans is incarcerated (U.S. Department of Justice, 1989). Many of these people have not even been convicted of a crime but are merely waiting for their trials. The dominant orientation of jails and prisons is custodial. Prisoners generally learn how to play the role of prisoner and, perhaps more important (and it almost goes without saying), they get very angry.

Beyond their inability to turn convicted criminals into law-abiding citizens, there is also some question as to the fairness of both courts and prisons as far as who goes through the system and who doesn't. This question focuses in part on racism in the criminal justice system. Black Americans make up a little more than 12 percent of the U.S. population, yet they account for 30 percent of all arrests, 38 percent of the federal prison population, and almost 47 percent of the state prison population (U.S. Department of Justice, 1989). Moving these statistics to more individual terms, a black individual is eight times more likely to be in prison on any given day than a white individual. Perhaps most striking, of all the prisoners executed since 1930 in the United States, 1,760 have been white and 2,068 have been black; if you look just at executions for the crime of rape, only 48 whites have been executed compared with 405 blacks (U.S. Department of Justice, 1983). Such evidence was brought before the U.S. Supreme Court in 1986 in the case of *McCleskey* v. *Kemp.* The justices were further informed that any defendant who killed a white was 4.3 times more likely to receive the death penalty than a defendant who killed a black. The Supreme Court ruled in 1987 that the death penalty was constitutional anyway (U.S. Supreme Court Reports, 1987). Such a finding is of additional interest considering that there is little evidence that capital punishment has any effect whatsoever in reducing acts of murder (see Bowers, Pierce, and McDevitt, 1984).

A further look at particular arrest statistics (U.S. Department of Justice, 1989) shows that while blacks accounted for 30 percent of all arrests, they accounted for 40.8 percent of arrests for prostitution and vice and 47.5 percent of arrests for gambling. These victimless crimes may well indicate a certain amount of harassment on the part of the police. When was the last time you witnessed an upstanding white member of your community hauled off to jail for betting on a football game? On the other hand, blacks also dominate many of the FBI's index crimes—black arrests account for 62.6 percent of robbery arrests, 53.5 percent of murder arrests, and 45.8 percent of forcible rape arrests.

A bystander happened to film the savage beating inflicted on Rodney King by the police. Mr. King had not committed any violent crime. When the news media showed the film, the public reacted in outrage. Would the beating have taken place if Mr. King were white? And how many such beatings take place where the only witnesses are the police?

How do we account for these statistics? Are the police and judges racists who discriminate in their treatment of blacks? That's a possibility, although it's difficult to know for sure. The vast majority of American judges are white, and the majority of American police are white; the racial separation in the United States has created widespread distrust between whites and blacks, and racism could well be a factor. While there is some indication that police patrol more heavily in black areas (and arrests tend to go up and down with the degree of policy activity), blacks almost certainly commit a much higher proportion of index crimes (based on their percentage in the population) than whites. And since we've already seen that index crimes result in the stiffest prison sentences, this fact could account for the high percentage of blacks in prison.

Perhaps, not surprisingly, the most accurate explanation for these statistics lies somewhere between criminal justice system discrimination and a high degree of black criminal activity. In past years blacks clearly faced massive discrimination, as the execution rates for rape point out. Much of this discrimination is no doubt still with us. On the other hand, blacks probably do commit more than their share of index crime. Looking more closely, however, we see that most of these statistics concern lower-class blacks as opposed to middle- and upper-class blacks. Since blacks are proportionately poorer than whites in the United States, their large numbers in the criminal justice system might indicate that the system discriminates not so much against black people as against poor people (many of whom are black). Who, then, are the white people who are arrested and end up in prison?

Prisoners in the United States represent pretty much a cross-section of poor people in the United States. Part of this apparent discrimination against poor people may be due to active discrimination by individuals in the criminal justice system; to middle-class judges and juries poor people just "look" more guilty, and poor families don't "seem" a proper environment for the return of a juvenile offender. Much of the discrimination against poor people, however, results from the general workings of the criminal justice institution itself. We've already seen that poor people tend to commit more index (as opposed to white-collar) crime and that index crime is viewed as being more serious and hence entails longer prison terms. Beyond that, we find the bail system.

The bail system in the United States provides a means for individuals to remain free between arrest and trial by posting bond (leaving a specified amount of money) with the court. If they do not appear for trial, this bond is forfeited; if they appear, it is returned. The amount is set by the judge according to the crime and its potential penalty, the theory being that an individual is more likely to skip town on a murder charge than a shoplifting offense. Individuals who own property are obviously more able to post bond than poor individuals. Wealthy individuals, in fact, are sometimes not even required to post bond; they are released on their "own recognizance" on the grounds that their property holdings in the area will ensure their presence. In addition, individuals able to make bail are also more likely to be acquitted when they do come to trial (Reiman, 1984). In short, the bail system benefits people with money and penalizes those without it.

One of the reasons individuals who can afford bail are more likely to be acquitted is that they can also afford lawyers. In the past poor people simply did without legal representation. This practice was declared unconstitutional by the Supreme Court, and today in the United States anyone indicted for a felony crime has access to a public defender, a lawyer paid by the court. Public defenders are notoriously undertrained, underpaid, and overworked. Not surprisingly, the representation they provide is not usually the best. One of the reasons (and one of the ways they cut down on their work load) is the practice of plea bargaining.

Plea bargaining is the result of a bargaining session between the public defender (or any defense lawyer) and the prosecution. The prosecution agrees to lessen the charge against the defendant in exchange for a guilty plea. The vast majority of all American criminal proceedings operate with a plea of guilty achieved through plea bargaining. The courts, which are already overworked, could not function without this system, as jury trials are very time consuming. Depending on jurisdictions reviewed in a 1979 study, guilty pleas were found to range from 81 percent to 97 percent of the total cases coming to court (U.S. Department of Justice, 1983). The poorer defendant, threatened with the possibility of a long sentence at the end of a trial, may be pressured to accept the plea bargain even if the evidence against any criminal activity is inconclusive. A paid lawyer is likely to weigh the evidence more than the work, since the amount of work will be paid for; the public defender earns the same income either way and has little free time to be creative.

The American criminal justice system responds most clearly to those acts commonly considered to be the most deviant. It also responds to those lawbreakers commonly considered to be the most dangerous: lower-class individuals. Although new kinds of rehabilitation programs are developed and tried from time to time, little funding is available for them; most taxpayers would rather see their tax dollars go elsewhere. Most of the people who end up in prison are poor, and they come out of prison the same way. As ex-offenders, they must face society's reaction to the label of their deviance—problems in finding jobs, housing, and friends. One response, of course, is to return to whatever lifestyle brought them to prison in the first place. This brings us back to an observation about prisons made at the beginning of this section—they keep people off the streets. But they also put people back on the streets, usually in worse condition than they found them.

DEVIANCE AND SOCIAL CHANGE: WHEN DOES CREATIVITY BECOME DANGEROUS?

Deviance exists only because norms and values exist; if rules are made to be broken, deviance is the behavior that does it. We've looked thus far at some of the behavior labeled as deviant in the United States and some responses to that behavior. It is important to keep in mind, however, that if deviance never occurred, norms and values would, by definition, never change, and we would have a pretty stagnant society. In this sense deviance is creative, as individuals try out alternatives to the status quo. Without deviance a society would be unable to adapt to changing circumstances. The question is: When do people find this creativity useful and when do they find it dangerous?

There is unfortunately no one answer to this question. Many of the greatest advances in the worlds of art, music, science, religion, literature, and certainly politics met extremely hostile responses in their day. It is almost tempting to suggest that, the greater the level of genius, the greater the likelihood the genius will be labeled deviant. Creativity seems acceptable only when it moves slowly, giving others suitable time to get used to it. The paintings of van Gogh, unappreciated during his lifetime, now sell for record sums. The first doctor to suggest the possible presence of "germs" as a cause of disease died in a mental institution. And of course Christianity, like almost all religions, developed amid persecution and attacks upon its followers.

In part, then, deviance exists because of our adherence to norms and values coupled with the need for social change that is always present in human societies. Creative behavior in response to those needs becomes deviance almost by the very nature of its creativity. Culture, in short, encourages creativity while simultaneously encouraging that creativity to be labeled deviant. The study of deviance rests on the fine line between cultural stability on the one hand and social change on the other. The relativity of deviance makes this study very difficult. We know that today's deviant may be tomorrow's savior. However, today's deviant also may be tomorrow's deviant.

SUMMARY

Deviance is any behavior that breaks the norms and violates the values of a social group. Such behavior acquires the label of deviance when the social group in question possesses the power or authority to dominate those engaging in the deviance and to control their behavior.

Although the varieties of deviance are as boundless as the norms and values they violate, they may be divided into criminal and noncriminal forms. Criminal behavior is any behavior formally proscribed in a society by law or custom. The content of behavior has no relation to its label as deviance, as is indicated by the existence of victimless crimes—crimes in which the criminal is the only victim. Noncriminal behavior as deviance includes even the smallest violation of folkways, but major forms include alcoholism, mental retardation, and behavior considered to be irrational by societal authorities (labeled mental illness in the United States).

Theories explaining the existence of deviance may be separated into those that focus on the deviant individual (deviant-centered theories) and those that focus on society (society-centered theories). The former include theories that view biological and personality disorders as causes for individuals to vary from established norms. The latter include theories that point out the encouragement individuals receive from society for deviance (differential association theory and anomie theory) and others that find the source of deviance in the authorities that label it as such (labeling theory and the radical theories).

Behavior considered to be deviant could not exist without the existence of authorities in society that have acquired the right (in the eyes of most societal members) to determine deviance. Such authorities often respond with such a label when the behavior in question not only breaks norms but attacks their right to label. As ongoing parts of societal institutions, authorities are in an excellent position to present their labels and to have them accepted as part of social reality by most societal members. These "social definitions" are taken for granted along with the legitimacy of the authority. One particular function of these definitions is to set boundaries between social groups, separating those who adhere to the social definition from those who are labeled by it as deviants.

Deviant behavior that is considered extreme by authorities is commonly responded to formally. Criminal behavior is responded to through the criminal justice system, which in the United States tends to focus almost entirely on poor people. Noncriminal deviant behavior is responded to in appropriate institutions; "irrational" behavior may be dealt with by mental health authorities, while unusual intellectual behavior may be labeled retardation by educational institutions.

Finally, deviance is an important source of social change. Deviance is often, in effect, creative behavior—some of which is necessary for adaptation to changing circumstances.

GLOSSARY

Anomie A state of normlessness in a society, when many people are unclear of what is expected of them.

Anomie theory A theory of deviance that explains varieties of deviant acts as responses to the socially produced strain of anomie.

Authority The right to control the behavior of others.

Boundary maintenance Any behavior that reminds the members of a social group of the boundaries between their group and others, distinguishing between "us" and "them." Boundary maintenance increases group solidarity.

Definition of the situation As defined by W I. Thomas, the concept that social reality is a matter of definition; if members of a social group agree to the reality of anything, then it will be real in its consequences.

Deviance Behavior that violates the norms of a social group.

Deviant subculture A subculture viewed by both its members and outsiders as having norms and values fundamentally, and often threateningly, different from those of the general culture.

Differential association theory A theory of deviance that explains deviant acts as involving a change in attitudes of the deviant acquired through association with other deviants.

Index crime Crime considered as major by the FBI, including murder, forcible rape, robbery, aggravated assault, burglary, larceny/theft, and motor vehicle theft.

Juvenile delinquency Illegal behavior committed by individuals who are legally minors (usually under age eighteen).

Labeling theory A theory of deviance that views deviance as a label assigned to behavior and individuals by particular figures of authority.

Power The probability for control over the behavior of others.

Primary deviance The commission of a deviant act without the knowledge of others, particularly those with the authonty to label deviance. The primary deviant is not treated as a deviant.

Radical theory As applied to deviance, a theory that sees social control as an attempt by the ruling class of society to maintain its dominance. A criminal justice system, for example, is viewed as both protecting the current distribution of property in society and focusing the attentions of the middle class on lower-class lawbreakers and away from upper-class lawbreakers.

Secondary deviance Deviance that is labeled as such; the individual is treated as a deviant.

Social control theory A theory of deviance that explains deviant behavior as either a breakdown in the socialization process (as constraints on behavior are not internalized), or a loosening of ties within social groups to the point that others do not constrain the acts of the deviant individual.

Status crime Behavior considered criminal only when performed by members of a particular social status (for example, only a minor can be a runaway).

Subcultural theory A theory of deviance that explains deviant behavior through the existence of ongoing deviant subcultures that socialize deviant attitudes and behavior into their members.

Subculture A social group or collection of social groups that exists within a larger culture yet has distinctive norms and values that set it off from the larger culture.

Victimless crimes Crimes in which there is no victim but the criminal, including prostitution, drug use, gambling, and homosexual acts.

White-collar crime Crime committed by middle-class and upper-class people in the course of an otherwise legal occupation, including fraud, tax evasion, and antitrust violations.

SUPPLEMENTARY READINGS

Balkan, Sheila, Ronald J. Berger, and Janet Schmidt *Crime and Deviance in America: A Critical Approach.* Belmont, Calif.: Wadsworth, 1980.

A well-organized and clearly presented discussion of deviance and social control in the United States from the perspective of critical sociology. The authors focus on crime and the criminal justice system in America and also include sections on mental illness and the role of women as deviants and the victims of crime.

Becker, Howard S. *Outsiders: Studies in the Sociology of Deviance.* New York: Free Press, 1963.
A modern classic in the study of deviance. Becker presents the labeling theory of deviance as applied to several case studies, most notably marijuana users and jazz musicians.

Erikson, Kai *Wayward Puritans: A Study in the Sociology of Deviance.* New York: Wiley, 1966.
A study of deviance among American Puritans that presents the Durkheim perspective on the functions of deviance in boundary maintenance. According to this perspective, deviance is necessary as a means for preserving group identity.

Farrell, Ronald A., and Victoria L. Swigert (eds.) *Social Deviance* (3rd ed.). Belmont, Calif.: Wadsworth, 1988.
Farrell and Swigert offer a selection of readings to introduce the topic.

Georges-Abeyie, Daniel (ed.) *The Criminal Justice System and Blacks.* New York: Boardman, 1984.
As the title suggests, a collection of readings that focuses in particular on how the American criminal justice system treats blacks. Within that basic framework, a wide variety of topics are covered.

Mercer, Jane *Labeling the Mentally Retarded.* Berkeley: University of California Press, 1973.
An analysis of the process of labeling the mentally retarded, covering common conceptions of mental retardation and including a special focus on the labeling process itself in institutions of public education. Mercer shows how certain students are more likely to acquire the label, particularly Mexican Americans.

Mitford, Jessica *Kind and Usual Punishment.* New York: Knopf, 1973.
A description and analysis of American prisons and American prisoners, written for the layman.

Quinney, Richard *Class, State and Crime: On the Theory and Practice of Criminal Justice* (2nd ed.). New York: Longman, 1980.
A classic example of applying the radical perspective to the study of deviance.

Reiman, Jeffrey H. *The Rich Get Richer and the Poor Get Prison: Ideology, Class, and Criminal Justice* (2nd ed.). New York: Wiley, 1984.
As the title suggests, this book discusses the importance of wealth (or its lack) for staying out of (or getting into) prison in the United States. This lively and readable book presents a highly critical perspective on the American criminal justice system.

Traub, Stuart H., and Craig B. Little *Theories of Deviance* (3rd ed.). Itasca, Ill.: Peacock, 1985.
A variety of essays that provide a good overview of a wide range of deviance theories.

READING

Hostile Eyes

PEGGY BENDET

The sociological outlook on deviance is a dual one. On the one hand, it focuses on individuals who commit acts thought to be deviant and attempts to explain why they commit such acts. On the other hand, it also turns its attention on nondeviants in society and attempts to understand their accepted definitions of which acts are respectable and which are deviant. In the following article, Peggy Bendet takes this second perspective in attempting to understand why many heterosexual Americans seem to hate homosexuals so much. Unlike many deviant acts, homosexuality has no clear victim, yet antihomosexual attitudes (known as homophobia) are extremely strong. In tracing these attitudes, Bendet focuses on American university campuses today, where homophobia appears to be rampant.

A chilly breeze cut through the autumn twilight as Dennis and Steve, shouldering their way out of the crowded deli, headed back across campus to their dorm. Dennis was busy buttoning his padded jacket, a thrift-shop find, so he didn't notice the young man who hurried past them into the lengthening shadows. Steve would remember later that the guy had stood behind them in line at the deli.

Dennis and Steve (not their real names) were both sophomores at a large south-eastern state university. They had been friends for a year and roommates, at that point, for just two weeks. Outgoing, tall, and lean, Dennis was a psychology major with a deep appreciation of people's differences, including his own. He loved to dress in flashy clothes that stood out as badges of nonconformity in this conservative town. Other students thought he was a little strange, but that was more than okay with Dennis: better to celebrate being different than to pretend he wasn't.

Steve, an advertising major, admired the ease with which his friend embraced life, but he couldn't quite pull off the nonchalance himself. Fair-haired and muscular, Steve emulated Dennis, but with restraint. His clothes were colorful but coordinated, and although he was friendly at parties, he couldn't just go up to a stranger and strike up a breezy conversation the way Dennis could.

As the two friends walked through the courtyard of their dorm on this night in 1984, they noticed someone leaning beside the glass doors that led to the lobby. When they reached the door, the guy straightened up, surveyed them from head to foot, and spat out one word: "Faggots."

Steve and Dennis froze. The man merely strode through the lobby to the elevator without looking back.

"I don't even know him," Steve said, bewildered. But in his heart he knew that didn't matter. He and Dennis weren't lovers, but they were, in fact, gay. Verbal assaults weren't new to either of them.

"People always react when they find out you're gay," Dennis said later. "Even people who know you well."

But the incident would soon become more than an unprovoked insult. Over the following months, at least twenty young men in the dorm participated in a deliberate and escalating campaign of harassment. Scores of other students witnessed the abuse and did nothing either to curb it or to offer support to the victims. And no one seemed to notice that anything was

From *Campus Voice*, August/September 1986, pp. 31-37. Reprinted by permission. Copyright 1986 *Campus Voice* magazine, Whittle Communications, 505 Market Street, Knoxville, TN 37902.

wrong—no one, that is, but Steve and Dennis. This is their story.

Hostility toward lesbians and gay men has long been taken for granted by most heterosexuals as a natural response to "sick and dangerous" behavior. A decade ago, the American Psychiatric Association removed homosexuality from its list of mental disorders, but even as recently as June [1986], the U.S. Supreme Court upheld state laws that deny the right of lesbians and gay adults to express themselves sexually.

However, such homophobia is beginning to be closely scrutinized by researchers who wonder why homosexuality threatens so many people so deeply.

Homophobia is defined as an irrational fear of homosexuals. But that description is inadequate, according to Dr. Gregory M. Herek, a psychology professor at the City University of New York (CUNY) who has written numerous articles on the subject. Fear is involved, he says, but it's not the most telling component.

"Something like agoraphobia—the fear of leaving your house or even of getting up out of your chair—that's a phobia," says Herek. "But with homophobia, you're also talking about hostility and prejudice, housing and job discrimination, and threats—even *acts*—of violence."

As a lecturer at Yale University, Herek last spring conducted a survey of 200 gay and lesbian students there. Ninety of the students—nearly 50 percent—reported that they'd experienced some kind of antigay harassment. A majority of the 200 said they feared for their safety on campus because of the threat of violence.

One Yale student, a lesbian, reported being followed on campus by five men in a car who told her they wanted to teach her about sex. They then graphically outlined what they wanted to do to her and what they wanted her to do to them. Another student said a group of men accosted her and a lesbian friend at a campus party and demanded that they kiss each other. A third student said that he regularly received obscene phone calls and that one time his jacket was taken from the common room and trampled in the dirt. It was a jacket he'd marked with an inverted pink triangle—the symbol homosexuals were required to wear in the Nazi death camps.

The survey's results were presented to Yale's governing body in support of a request that the school include sexual orientation in its official antidiscrimination policy, for which gay students and faculty members had been lobbying for 15 years. Last spring, the measure finally passed.

"Rule changes aren't the most effective way to deal with prejudice," comments Herek, "but they *are* an important step."

An even bigger step is education. Homophobia, for those who think of homosexuality is unnatural, is often rooted in sheer ignorance. Sexuality, like skin and eye color, is not a choice. Researchers say that sexual orientation is set in place by a series of genetic and environmental cues so complex that no one understands why one person is homosexual, another heterosexual, and still another bisexual.

According to studies conducted by the Kinsey Research Institute, at any one time between 4 and 12 percent of the American population is primarily homosexual; about 50 percent is primarily heterosexual; and the rest of us fall somewhere in between.

The statistical probability of reversing any of these orientations, say experts, is zero. It's been tried. Through the centuries, homosexuals have been subjected to everything from electroshock treatment to exorcisms in attempts to "cure" them of their so-called deviant behavior. If you are heterosexual, try imagining what could possibly move you to become permanently and genuinely attracted to others of your own gender, and perhaps you'll understand why records fail to show one instance of such "cures" achieving their goal. Homosexuality is not the norm, experts say, but it *is* normal.

Even people who know this, however, experience homophobic feelings ranging from outright disgust to smug tolerance of gays as long as they keep their homosexuality out of public view. Why does homophobia seem so deep-seated? Researchers are only now beginning to piece together some answers.

Immediately after the incident in the courtyard, Steve and Dennis began finding explicit photographs of female body parts tacked up on their dormroom door. Other times they'd come home to find condoms filled with hand cream, or globs of shampoo smeared on the doorknob. One night someone pounded on their door. When Steve answered it, he found an article about AIDS lying on the floor outside.

As fall passed into winter, each day brought some new offering from their nameless, faceless antagonists. Dennis's natural buoyancy protected him, but Steve found his frustration building, as if he was barely holding his own in an all-too-serious game of psychological warfare. He wanted to confront someone, to stand up for himself, but Dennis talked him out of it; why ask for more trouble? For all his forthrightness, Dennis tended to extend himself only when he felt safe. And this wasn't one of those times. Reluctantly, Steve agreed to lie low.

Then, one evening in January, the situation worsened.

They were walking through the dorm lobby where students habitually hung out. Just as they reached a table full of students playing Trivial Pursuit, one of the players called out, "Faggot!"

At this point Dennis and Steve made what they later realized was a tactical error—they pretended they hadn't heard the slur. To the other guys, this just meant it was open season.

At least once a day, a group of men (but not always the same men) would eye Steve and Dennis as they walked through the lobby on their way to the elevator. Just as they passed, the men would simultaneously cough. Or they would abruptly stop talking until someone broke the heavy silence with the one-word epithet. "Faggot!" Or for variety, "Queer!"

Other times the men would turn their heads in unison to watch Steve and Dennis walk past, the two friends swallowing hard as they ran the gauntlet of hostile eyes. That little torture was the hardest to bear because it seemed to encompass everyone in the lobby. There were 500 men and women living in the dorm that year. Steve and Dennis felt that all the students knew what was happening and that their very silence was an expression of approval.

The two men started taking the stairs instead of the elevator, walking four flights up and four flights down several times a day just to avoid the lobby. When the harassment moved to the cafeteria, Steve and Dennis began eating in another dining hall clear across campus. Surely, they thought, it would all end soon.

Noting that lesbians and gay men will always be a minority group, CUNY's Herek says that "there is a high correlation between homophobia and a reluctance to accept other minority groups. People who are homophobic are more likely to be prejudiced against blacks, against Jews, against anything other than the norm in gender roles." That is, against anything that's perceived as different.

Herek's view is backed up by the work of the man who coined the word "homophobia": Dr. George Weinberg, a psychologist and author of *Society and the Healthy Homosexual.* According to Weinberg, homophobia is partially the result of a condition he calls "acute conventionality."

"Those who condemn homosexuals are really giving you a Rorschach test of their own shakiness, their own lurking fear that there is another way to live [than what they consider normal]," Weinberg says. "The rigidity is a reaction to a fear that they are losing their grip. The insistence that they have *the* way to do it is really a response to a terror that their way may not be the only way."

This societal pressure to conform is felt even by those who champion the right of lesbians and gays to live as they choose but who find themselves uncomfortable when a gay person gets too close. Many friendships have been lost when one friend tells another he's gay. As one heterosexual man says of a former friend who told him he was gay, "The other guys started giving me grief about it. Everyone knew he was gay, and I didn't want anyone to think *I* was gay. I don't feel right about it, but I stopped being his friend."

But fear of the unconventional is only one basis for homophobia. As Herek says, "Homophobia is not a monolithic phenomenon. People react negatively to lesbians and gay men for many different reasons."

One reason Herek and other researchers cite is the common discomfort felt by many heterosexual people regarding their own fleeting, natural homosexual impulses. Most people don't want to acknowledge these feelings, much less explore them, so anything remindful of them is unconsciously threatening. This is *not* to say that all homophobes are latent homosexuals. Only in extreme cases might a severely homophobic person be a homosexual who cannot bear the existence of those feelings and who will act with hatred against anyone who represents them.

Sex itself is a threatening subject in American culture. Homophobic people, ignoring the emotional and intellectual ties lesbians and gay men sustain with their partners, tend to react to homosexuality as a purely sexual issue.

Another tributary to homophobia is the difficulty people have in giving up cherished ideas that seem vital to their sense of selves. For example, Christians who believe that the Bible condemns homosexuality as a sin often cannot reconcile their love for a gay relative or friend with their love of God. Unless such people are willing to reexamine their beliefs in light of new information concerning homosexuality, they will hold onto their homophobic feelings on moral grounds.

Homophobia comes from many sources; it is also expressed in many different ways. Gay-bashing has always been a favorite pastime of more violent homophobes, and as Herek's Yale study showed, it's a problem on college campuses as well. But on a day-to-day basis, homophobia assumes other forms.

Only 47 universities bar discrimination on the basis of sexual orientation (as does only one state, Wisconsin). Admittedly, lesbian and gay studies are offered at about 30 schools, and there are nearly 300 lesbian and gay student organizations. But many of these groups function under a cloud of controversy, and most exist without the official recognition necessary for office space and funds.

At Georgetown University in Washington, D.C., for example, a lawsuit brought against the school by the student group Gay People of Georgetown University (GPGU) is holding up the sale of city bonds needed for the construction of a long-awaited $43 million student center. The administrators refused to officially sanction GPGU, despite a vote in its favor by the student government and despite a city civil rights law banning such discrimination. Administrators contend that recognition would put the Jesuit school in the untenable position of condoning a "homosexual lifestyle."

Georgetown students, originally tolerant of GPGU, have been struggling with a rising tide of homophobia now that some students blame the gays for the construction delay. Last spring, angry letters filled with antigay rhetoric showed up weekly in various student publications. But the homophobic atmosphere at Georgetown has been mild compared with that at some other schools.

Students at the University of Kansas still talk about the vicious campaign launched two years ago against Gay and Lesbian Services of Kansas (GLSOK). In September of 1984, a KU student distributed T-shirts emblazoned with the slogan FAGBUSTERS. A campus political party, Young Americans for Freedom, ran a slate of student government candidates on a platform that included the promise to stop GLSOK's funding, which the organization had only started receiving after five years of petitions to the administration.

At the height of the conflict, a disc jockey in a popular student hangout played the *Ghostbusters* theme over and over again one night, turning the volume down on the chorus while he screamed "*FAAAG*-busters" into the microphone. One of the bartenders there, who was gay, left in disgust only to be pelted with rocks outside a gay bar in another part of town.

Another gay KU student barely avoided major injury that autumn when he suddenly lost a wheel while driving his car. Upon inspection, the student found that the lug nuts had been loosened. After that, he started receiving phone calls from people threatening his life. When he complained to the campus police they told him it would "take some time" before they could get to the case.

He dropped out of school. As he told a friend, "I'm a student here. I'm trying to get an education. Somebody's trying to kill me, and nobody cares."

The Saturday before finals week late in the winter semester, Steve and Dennis decided to turn in early. They wanted a good night's rest so they could study all day Sunday. About 11 P.M., Steve, a light sleeper, heard a noise at the door.

"Who's there?" he called out. Instead of an answer, he heard the scuffling of running feet. He opened the door. No one was there, so he went back to bed.

A little later, Steve heard another sound. This time he tiptoed to the door and tried to open it without making any noise. But the lock clicked as he tripped it, alerting whoever was outside.

This went on until 3 A.M. Dennis, as usual, wanted to ignore the whole thing, but Steve decided he'd had enough. He picked up a can of hair mousse and leaned toward the crack under the door, intending to give whoever was outside a good dousing. Just then, a flame shot up through the crack, brushing a poster tacked to the door and, more alarmingly, coming within inches of the aerosol can in Steve's hand. Outside the door, a group of men ran away; it had taken them a while, but their handmade acetylene torch had gone off as planned.

Badly shaken, Steve called downstairs to report the torching of the door. But the student on desk duty that night neither recorded the call nor notified anyone else. Three days later, Steve and Dennis came home to find that the lock on their charred door had been filled with glue. It was only while they were arranging with the floor's resident assistant to have the lock changed that a report on the fire itself was finally filed. Eventually at least one student was expelled in connection with the arson attack. The exact number isn't known because few people within the administration today will confirm any details.

The administrator who was responsible for prosecuting the case in the student judiciary system refuses comment. "Any students who are charged with a violation like this have a right to the university's protection," he says.

The dorm's chief resident assistant, the student responsible for discipline and morale in the building, likewise refuses to discuss the case.

One housing official at first claims not to remember the incident, then says, "It was a very stupid prank." He smiles wryly at a reminder that the handmade torch had been fashioned from a prophylactic, but seems surprised when told that Steve and Dennis were never contacted about the incident by any representative of the university.

"Naturally it's our policy to follow up on something like this," he says. "I don't know why we didn't in this case.

"Of course, it wasn't because they were homosexuals."

In the fall of 1984 a group of students at the University of Massachusetts at Amherst launched a "Heterosexuals Fight Back" rally. They also tried to get finals week designated as "Hang a Homo" week and put up posters that read THE GAYBUSTERS ARE COMING. Instead of interpreting these actions as pranks, members of the administration took some unusual steps to confront and deactivate the tension.

Felice Yeskel of the student affairs office spent the next several months looking at causes of homophobia at UMass. She published a report the following June in which she called for a series of fifteen actions, including the creation of a visiting faculty position to teach gay and lesbian studies; the acquisition of relevant library materials; and the welcoming of lesbians and gays to an alternative dorm floor devoted to those wishing to live with others of diverse backgrounds.

The thrust of the report was that the school had the responsibility for establishing healthy communication between gay and lesbian students and the rest of the student body.

"That's really vital in this issue," says Kevin Berrill, the manager of an ongoing project on violence for the National Gay and Lesbian Task Force (NGLTF). "The notion that gay and lesbian students ought to be carrying the ball, educating the people who are prejudiced against them, handling the acts of violence that come up, is simply wrong. Homophobia is not a gay problem. It is a societal problem."

By spring, Dennis was coping with his dormmates' relentless animosity by planning a move to off-campus housing at the end of the semester.

But Steve was feeling the heat. His grades began dropping. His concentration was diffused by vague depression. No matter what he tried, he just couldn't seem to keep the climate of hostility from seeping into and corroding even the little pleasures of his daily life. Maybe, he thought, he should just drop out of school.

In a final effort to reclaim his peace of mind and salvage his education, Steve spent two hours talking with the director of the school's student-counseling service, a crusty old man who convinced Steve that he had everything to gain by meeting his tormentors head on.

And so he did. For Steve, the pivotal confrontation began like so many others. A young man heading down in the elevator called out contemptuously just as the door was closing on Steve's floor, "You faggot!"

This time Steve raced down the stairs and stopped the guy as he left the elevator for the lobby.

"What did you call me?" he said loudly, looking his adversary in the eye. Students milling nearby couldn't help noticing the exchange.

"Never mind," the man said. He started to walk away.

"I'm talking to you!" Steve yelled. "What did you call me?"

The other guy kept walking.

"You coward!" Steve yelled.

That got him. "Don't you call me that," the man said, turning around with an unexpectedly fragile look on his face.

Steve was a little taken aback; the man looked as if he was about to cry.

"Well, what did you call me?" Steve said in a calmer voice. "How do you think I felt about that?"

The man didn't exactly apologize, but he never hassled Steve again and even took to saying a friendly "hello" on occasion. After two more confrontations—and after the school's investigation into the arson attack—Steve discovered that an unspoken truce had been established. The harassment ended as suddenly as it had begun.

Today, in their senior year, Dennis lives on the outskirts of campus and Steve rooms without trouble in an upperclassmen's dorm. But though their particular time of trial may be over, the campus atmosphere remains unchanged.

Just last spring, in the same dorm courtyard where Steve and Dennis were first harassed, a pre-election rally was held for several student-government hopefuls. One vice-presidential candidate stood up and made a campaign pledge to tear down a gay bar near campus in order to create more parking.

"I'm sorry," he told the crowd. "But I'm not a homosexual. These guys can take their AIDS and get out. Burn them. Execute them. I want no part of them."

He didn't win the election, but he did get 7 percent of the votes—more than his presidential running mate.

Even highly educated people can be homophobic, as proven by the U.S. Supreme Court's 5-to-4 decision in June 1986 to uphold a Georgia law prohibiting sodomy. Although sodomy is defined legally as oral and anal sex, not uncommon among heterosexuals, laws against sodomy are almost exclusively applied to gay men. In fact, Justice Byron R. White, who wrote the decision, specifically stated that the court was addressing the issue of "homosexual sodomy."

"This decision is a legal and moral disgrace," says Kevin Berrill of NGLTF. "I think it's an attack on the entire basis of our civil rights laws, not just for gay Americans, but for all Americans. It is a blatant act of prejudice by the five justices who voted for it."

The U.S. Justice Department has also dealt a blow to enlightened public treatment of gays and lesbians. The department ruled last spring that an employer can fire someone who has AIDS if the employer fears that the person will spread the disease to other workers.

Given that AIDS is transmitted only by semen or large amounts of blood, Berrill points out that the fear of its being spread under normal working conditions is starkly irrational—a hallmark of homophobia. "The ruling will be used as a tool to discriminate not only against AIDS victims but also against anyone who is gay or lesbian," he says.

When it comes to America's campuses, Berrill says that the climate for homosexuals has never been better—and it's never been worse.

"It's good,' he says, "in that more gay and lesbian student organizations are forming, more schools are adopting nondiscrimination clauses, more schools are offering gay and lesbian courses. But the violence is getting worse."

In a 1984 NGLTF survey of 2,074 gay men and lesbians in eight cities, 82 percent said they'd been threatened with physical violence. In 1985, another survey found that 20 percent of gay men and 10 percent of lesbians polled had been the victims of antigay physical abuse. Berrill, who oversees a national hotline for college students concerned about such violence, has noticed a change since the 1985 survey was conducted.

"There were almost no calls before that time, and now it's a deluge," he says. Whether there is actually more violence or merely better reporting of it is unclear, but Berrill's hunch is that increased media attention to gays in the wake of the AIDS crisis has given more homophobes the excuse to attack homosexuals.

"But the increased visibility doesn't cause the violence," he emphasizes. "That's the same flak women get when they're told that they bring rape on themselves. It's antigay prejudice that causes the violence."

If the fear of violence doesn't drive lesbians and gay men further into obscurity, perhaps their increased visibility will eventually work in their favor. Herek cites a simple lack of exposure to gay friends, family members, or co-workers as another important factor in homophobia.

Visibility is a funny thing, however, when you're talking about some 20 million Americans. Notes Ron Najman, the media director for NGLTF, "It's not that people don't know someone who is gay. Everybody knows someone who is gay.

"It's just that they don't know they know someone who is gay."

Discussion Questions

1. Bendet says that homophobia is not a true phobia in the psychiatric sense but a form of social prejudice. What sources does she suggest for this prejudice?
2. Dennis and Steve were often harassed by groups of individuals; at the University of Kansas, students proudly wore "fagbuster" T-shirts. These and other examples in the article suggest that people often go to a considerable amount of trouble to express their prejudices in group settings. How does such group behavior support the boundary maintenance theory of deviance?
3. The fear of AIDS has often been cited as a contributing factor to growing homophobia. Do you think that AIDS has created homophobia or just provided an excuse for its expression?
4. Based on the reactions of Dennis, Steve, and other gays mentioned in the article, what kinds of reactions are deviants likely to have to their deviant status?

READING

The Social Organization of Serial Murder: The Story of Theodore Robert Bundy

JOHN CURRA

Serial murder refers to a succession of murders committed over time by one person. Typically, victims are unrelated and usually unknown to the murderer prior to their violent contact. The apparent pointlessness of the crime coupled with its violence combine to fascinate and attract interest in American society on a variety of levels. The electrocution of Theodore Robert Bundy—one of the most famous of America's serial murderers—provided only temporary respite from the crime; the discovery of Jeffrey Dahmer's victims in Milwaukee during the summer of 1991 suggests that serial murder is to be an ongoing occurrence in American society.

From the point of view of social science, serial murder raises some interesting questions. On the one hand, the apparently deranged mental perspective of the serial murderers would seem to call for the services of the psychiatrist who might be the most adept at explaining the existence of such extreme mental states. On the other hand, serial murder, as with most deviants, does not occur in a social vacuum. Curra blends the perspectives of psychology and sociology in the following reading, describing the peculiar mental states of the serial murderer and simultaneously examining the social organization of this crime. The fact that serial murder does not occur in all societies at all times suggests that social change may provide the necessary breeding ground for killers like Bundy.

Theodore Robert Bundy. He was described as the "Deliberate Stranger," the "Stranger Beside Me," or the "Boy Next Door" by the authors who chronicled his life story.[1] To the woman with whom he lived for several years, he was the "Phantom Prince."[2] To journalists, he was the "love-bite killer." To the FBI, an "organized serial murderer."[3] To his victims, he was a charming, witty conversationalist who reverted to a brutal, sadistic murderer once they were under his control. To family members of his victims, he was a monster.

Who was Theodore Robert Bundy? He was born November 24, 1945, in a home for unwed mothers in Burlington, Vermont. His mother had traveled there from her home in Philadelphia to spare her family the embarrassment of an unmarried woman giving birth. Mother and son eventually moved to the state of Washington and settled in Tacoma. Ted Bundy killed his first victim, Ann Marie Burr (age 8), when he was fifteen. He abducted her from her home, strangled her, and threw her lifeless body into a ditch that was eventually covered over by a road construction crew. When he was 20, he savagely attacked two other women as they slept (one of whom died). The killings from 1974 to 1978 are the ones that brought him to the attention

[1] Ann Rule, *The Stranger Beside Me* (New York: W.W. Norton, 1980). Richard Larsen, *The Deliberate Stranger* (1980).
[2] Liz Kendall, *Phantom Prince: My Secret Life with Ted Bundy* (Seattle: Madrona Publishers, 1981).
[3] FBI. "Crime scene and profile characteristics of organized and disorganized murderers." FBI Law Enforcement Bulletin: 18-25 (August, 1985).

of authorities and established his notoriety. Authorities believe he killed at least 10 women in the Washington area (1974), 4 women in Utah (1974), and four women in Colorado (1975). Other apparent victims were found in in Idaho, Minnesota, Pennsylvania, Michigan, and Georgia. In 1978, he committed his most outrageous crimes. While in residence in Tallahassee, Florida, he attacked two college women at the Chi Omega house at Florida State University in the middle of the night as they slept (Margaret Bowman and Lisa Levy). They were bludgeoned, strangled, and savagely killed. He also assaulted and permanently injured three other women: Kathy Kleiner and Karen Chandler, both of whom were in residence in the Chi Omega house, and Cheryl Thomas, who lived in an apartment near the sorority house. About three weeks later (February 9, 1978), Bundy abducted and killed a 12-year-old girl from Lake City, Florida: Kimberly Diane Leach. Her decaying body was found under a hog shed in Northern Florida on April 15, 1978, by a Florida State Trooper. Bundy was arrested February 15, 1978, in Pensacola, Florida, for driving suspiciously. He was eventually charged and tried for three of his killings and his assaults. At his first trial, he was sentenced to two death penalties for the killing of Margaret and Lisa and ninety years for the three assaults. Approximately 6 months later (February 12, 1980), Judge Jopling sentenced him to die for the killing of Kimberly Diane Leach.

Serial killings are of interest to sociologists because they reflect characteristics of American society. Social and cultural factors in the United States make acts of criminal violence a likely occurrence.[4] In fact, Jane Caputi argues that we live in the age of sex crime:

> Sex crime in the form of the serial mutilation murder is a modern practice. By claiming the current period to be an "age of sex crime," I claim sex crime to be a key sign of the times, a root paradigm, a practice that expresses precisely what the patriarchal world in which we are living and dying is doing.[5]

What Caputi means, specifically, is that the murder, torture, and rape of women by men are very understandable (she says "eminently logical") correlates of the development of patriarchy and male dominance. The sexual mutilation and killing of women are manifestations of American culture's deep-seated contempt for women.

Serial killers may very well be acting out themes of their societies.[6] In the transition from feudalism to capitalism in the 1400s, the aristocracy and landed gentry came to fear and dislike members of the newly emergent capitalist class. This led them to commit serial murders. They didn't kill members of the capitalist class, however; they misdirected their wrath toward laboring peasants, who could be killed more easily. In the early stages of capitalism, serial killers came from the ranks of the middle class, and they killed people from the lower classes whom they viewed as disreputable or insignificant: prostitutes or servants.[7] From the end of World War II until the 1960s, America was characterized by prosperity and upward mobility for most people, and there were few multiple murders. By the late 1960s, there was a slowdown in the economy and more and more people were finding it difficult to achieve the standard American dream. Some of these individuals became resentful and hostile and wanted to get revenge against those people who they felt were responsible for their misery and lack of mobility. Their selection of a victim was governed by their beliefs about what was valuable in society and their quest for revenge: They preyed upon people—women and children —who they felt were highly prized in American society. Serial killers often turned to torture, brutality, and murder as a way to get even with a society that they felt had excluded them socially

[4] Ronald M. Holmes and James E. DeBurger, "Profiles in Terror: The Serial Murderer." Federal Probation 49, #3:29-34 (1985). P. 29.

[5] Jane Caputi, *The Age of Sex Crime* (Bowling Green Press, 1987). P. 158.

[6] The following paragraph is based on Elliott Leyton, *Compulsive Killers: The Story of Modern Multiple Murder.* (New York: New York University Press, 1986).

[7] Ibid. p. 277.

and economically. The increase in multiple killings between the 1950s and the 1980s in the United States may partly reflect these deteriorating social and economic conditions.[8]

In some respects, serial killing is like most other kinds of violence. The aggressor must formulate appropriate motives and the necessary intent; he must find available targets for his aggression; and he must neutralize constraints against violence and overcome any inhibitions he may have. At times a serial killer wouldn't think of hurting the person he's with, and at other times it is all he can think of doing.

Occasionally, the constraints against violence are neutralized through the use of alcohol or other drugs. More often, the killer uses a "special" set of verbalizations that allows him both to kill and then to rationalize his killing after it occurs. The killer depersonalizes his victim. He believes, at least temporarily, in the redundancy, equivalency, and insignificancy of people. To the killer, there are too many people (redundancy), one person is much the same as another (equivalency), and it is not a problem when people disappear (insignificancy). Ted Bundy felt that people vanished all the time: one person wouldn't be missed in a hundred years.[9] He felt he could kill anyone he wanted to, and no attention would be paid to the person's disappearance. In his own words: "I mean, there are *so* many people. This person will never be missed. It shouldn't be a problem."[10] These vocabularies of motive and rationalization mean that the killer can value human life in general but still brutalize and kill a *specific* person in a *specific* situation. A killing can be very rational and caused by the killer's feelings of necessity: it is a way to remove witnesses who might testify against him at some later date.

Serial killing is also of interest to sociologists because it shows that collective definitions of deviance and crime have a history of their own. In the United States, from 1983 to 1985, serial killing became the focus of public attention, and serial murder was portrayed as an "epidemic."[11] In 1983, a subcommittee of the United States Senate held public hearings on serial murder.[12] Sociologists study the social factors that are responsible for the prevailing interpretation of deviance.[13] Serial murder became the focus of attention during the 1980s because of changing political, economic, cultural, and social factors. The preoccupation with it was partly a reflection of the prevailing conservative climate that endorsed the view that crime and deviance were caused by evil, ruthless individuals.[14]

Ted Bundy is of particular interest to sociologists because he acted out cultural themes of power and dominance. While some killers are angry and frustrated, psychotic, or antisocial, the power/control serial killer is fascinated by the prospect of controlling another person. The pleasure for this kind of killer comes from the stalk, the capture, and the total control and possession of a helpless person.[15] The killing, and the sex that usually accompanies it, enhance the killer's feelings of power and potency. In the killer's mind, the abduction of a victim is often little different from the stealing of a car or stereo. The abduction and murder is a way for the killer to seize and possess something that he feels is highly valued by society. He took a life, a form of possession, and he then possessed the remains for a while.

[8] Elliott Leyton, *Compulsive Killers: The Story of Modern Multiple Murder,* ibid.

[9] Stephen Michaud and Hugh Aynesworth, *Ted Bundy: Conversation With a Killer* (New York: Signet, 1989). P. 188.

[10] Ibid., p. 135.

[11] Philip Jenkins, "Myth and murder: The serial killer panic of 1983-5." Criminal Justice Research Bulletin 3, #11:1-7 (Huntsville, TX: Sam Houston State University, 1988).

[12] Serial Murders. Hearing Before the Subcommittee on Juvenile Justice of the Committee on the Judiciary. United States Senate. 98th Congress. First session on patterns of murders committed by one person, in large numbers with no apparent rhyme, reason, or motivation. July 12, 1983. U.S. Government Printing Office. Washington, 1984.

[13] Laurie Taylor and Ian Taylor, "Changes in the motivational construction of deviance." Catalyst 6:76-99 (Fall, 1972). P. 81.

[14] Jenkins, op.cit., p. 5.

[15] Ron Holmes and James DeBurger, *Serial Murder* (Newbury Park, CA: Sage, 1988).

Power/control serial killings are the most organized of all serial murders. Usually, the place where the victim is killed and the place where the body is found (if it is found at all) are different. In fact, they may be many miles apart. The killing is done partly out of necessity (to avoid detection by authorities) and partly because it is the ultimate form of control. The usual method of killing is by strangulation, knife, or club because the killers prefer a slower form of killing requiring flesh-to-flesh contact. Conversation occurs but it is limited, and the killer has a controlled mood throughout the killing. The victim is quickly subdued, and she is physically restrained. Control killers tend to be of average or above-average intelligence; they are socially and sexually competent; they have a high birth order (e.g., first born); and they are geographically mobile and have cars in good condition.[16] Hickey insists that serial killers embody the "Golem syndrome"; a person who can destroy another human being without remorse or guilt and who feels no need to justify to others what he has done is a golem.[17]

On January 24, 1989, Theodore Robert Bundy was led to the electric chair at Florida State Prison ("Old Sparky") for the killing of Kimberly Diane Leach. He was strapped in at 7:06 A.M., and 2000 volts of electricity were sent through his body as hundreds of people outside the prison, sporting signs like "Burn, Bundy, Burn" and "Roast in Peace," cheered. His body arched, his hands clenched, and after a minute the electricity was turned off. At 7:16, Ted Bundy was declared "dead" by the attending physician. The final entry on his "Inmate Record" sheet reads: "Destination: Unknown."

[16] This profile was developed by the FBI to explain murderers like Bundy. See FBI, op.cit.

[17] Eric W. Hickey, *Serial Murderers and Their Victims* (Pacific Grove, CA: Brooks/Cole, 1991). P. 24. A Golem is a "killing machine." The term come from a Jewish medieval legend where a "golem" was a robot, a machine-like person or a clay figure supernaturally brought to life.

Discussion Questions

1. Curra quotes Jane Caputi, who argues that the serial murder of women reflects America's patriarchal society with its contempt for women. Other cited authors argue that serial murderers feel the need to strike out at society and select women as victims because they (along with children) are highly prized in American society. Are these two perspectives contradictory or can they coexist within the same theory?
2. Curra argues that Bundy acted out American cultural themes of power and dominance. Is Bundy just a perverse and out-of-control version of the heroes we venerate on the football field? Does it seem likely that he wouldn't have committed these crimes if he had grown up in some other culture where he didn't face such ideals of dominance at every turn?

RAIN
ic
TRAV
YO

PART Three
SOCIAL INEQUALITY

CHAPTER 6 SOCIAL DIFFERENTIATION AND SOCIAL GROUPS

In the United States today it is very possible for you to be born in New York City, grow up there, move to Los Angeles as an adult, and meet a native of that city with whom you have much in common. You may find, for example, that you enjoy the same movies or television programs, that you have the same attitudes toward religion and politics, that you enjoy the same music, and that in general you understand each other very well. Meeting someone with whom you share so many things is an exciting experience in communication, and it is all the more exciting when it occurs in an unlikely place. Strangely enough, the more "likely" places may be full of people you don't understand and can't stand; there are probably people who grew up a few blocks away from you with whom you have nothing in common and whose tastes and interests may be very different from yours. These two situations could be written off as coincidence. With so many people in American society, it stands to reason that many of them would be different from you (even if they live nearby) and some would be very much like you (even if they grew up far away). The coordination of society leaves little to chance, however, and these two occurrences are not exceptions.

As we have seen in previous chapters, individuals grow up as social creatures and are to a large extent shaped by their social experiences. The norms you follow, the roles you play, the knowledge you acquire, and the values you hold are all products of the experiences you have. Through socialization you come to internalize all of this and accept it as part of yourself. When you meet someone else who seems to share a lot of your behaviors, ideas, and values, it is undoubtedly because that individual had many of the same social experiences you did. Two individuals who like caviar, for example, must have grown up around or associated with other people who also liked caviar and introduced them to it. Two individuals who crack safes for a living must both have had associations with safecrackers. These similar social experiences can occur in very different places—like New York City and Los Angeles. Of even more interest to sociologists is the fact that *clusters* of experiences tend to happen to the same individuals. Eaters of caviar are likely to be highly educated, listen to classical music, and be employed as lawyers or corporate executives, for example. Safe-crackers, on the other hand, are more likely to be less educated, to prefer country-western music, and to be more fond of hamburgers than caviar. Two individuals who share one important experience with each other usually also share just such a cluster of experiences. That clustering is part of the coordination in society.

This chapter will explore some of the ways that clusters of experiences occur in the lives of members of society. Such an exploration would be interesting in its own right since it would tell us something about why people turn out as they do. But there is an added dimension to this study that is of particular importance to the sociologist: Individuals who share clusters of experiences often note or feel the things they have in common and form social groups around those points of similarity. Individuals with the same hobby may form a club. Individuals with the same religious beliefs may form a church. Individuals with the same problems may form a political party to do something about those problems. We tend to feel that our association with such social groups is voluntary and the result of individual decision. The sociological outlook, however, suggests that our previous experiences have primed us to be attracted to certain people and repulsed by certain other people. Just as our clusters of experiences are part of the coordination of society, so, too, are the social groups we form. Sociologists refer to this overall variation in society as *social differentiation.* As we look at social differentiation in society, we will pay particular attention to the ways differences among us influence the social groups within which we interact. We will also look at the variety of forms those groups may take, finishing the chapter with a close examination of a particularly modern form of social group—the formal organization.

SOCIAL DIFFERENTIATION: CATEGORIES AND GROUPS

Social differentiation refers to the general process by which differences are created among individuals as a result of the different experiences they have as members of society. Because these experiences come in clusters, individuals turn out being different in a great many ways. In modern American society people are differentiated, for example, by the amount of wealth they possess. Rich people have a wide variety of experiences that only rich people have, and poor people have a wide variety of experiences that only poor people have. Depending on your level of wealth, you will likely eat different food, live in a different neighborhood, enjoy different music, go to different schools, speak and think differently, spend your leisure time differently, work at a different occupation, and have different kinds of problems in living your everyday life from people at other levels of wealth. You will have these experiences not because you choose to have them but because American society is structured so that you will be thrust into them. In any society, social differentiation exists when different sets of experiences occur in the lives of different collections of individuals. Though wealth is one of the more important such differences in many societies, it is only one of the many attributes that lead individuals into different sets of experiences. Sociologists refer to these attributes as social categories.

The Category and the Group

A **social category** is a collection of individuals who have something in common. Technically, that something could be anything that an outside observer, such as a social scientist, might emphasize—for example, being left-handed and blue-eyed. The point of categories, however, is to call attention to some significant similarity among individuals that is useful in understanding other things about those individuals, and the category of being left-handed and blue-eyed does not particularly do that. If the category instead included all black women in the United States, its usefulness would be more apparent. Being black and being female in the United States are both factors that shape the experience of the individuals who are so defined. In fact, we could say that individuals in the category of black females encounter certain situations and experiences that no one outside the category could ever share. In short, the idea of the category helps us understand how collections of individuals both share experiences with each other and differ in their experiences from other collections (or categories) of individuals Perhaps most important, the idea of the category emphasizes that individuals share common experiences not because they go out of their way to share them but because society, by its structure, "sees to it" that they share them. The category calls attention to the ways that society shapes our experiences.

Though individuals who share a category may have much in common, there are two things they do not share. First, they do not usually know each other or even necessarily care to know each other. Second, they may not share the observer's enthusiasm for the category itself. They may, in fact, think that they share nothing with the other individuals with whom the observer has grouped them. This disagreement does not matter because the concept of the category belongs to the observer not to the observed. If the disagreement continues, however, the concept of *group* cannot be applied, for that concept belongs to the people.

Unlike a category, a **social group**, in the usage of social science, is a collection of people who (1) know each other (or know of each other), (2) agree that they share something (at least their groupness and the goals of their group), and (3) have continuing interactions with each other. A group exists in the hearts and minds of the people involved; if it does not exist there, it does not exist. When groups do exist, their actions can change the course of human societies—a result that a lone individual can never hope to attain. It is not surprising, therefore, that one of the primary questions in social science is how the idea of groupness develops simultaneously in a collection of individual minds.

Members of a group feel that they have much in common. Members of a category alo have at least one very important thing in common. If the category is a significant one in a given society, the individuals' common membership in that category will lead them to a number of common experiences in their everyday life. It is just such common experiences that can form the basis of a group. All that is needed is for the individuals in the category (or some of them, at any rate) to recognize their shared situation. In a circular way, the nature of a society itself (which forms the categories) can lead to the formation of social groups, which, through their actions, can change the nature of society.

In most complex societies a great many categories work at cross-purposes. For instance, one important category in the United States consists of all people who are poor—obviously a significant shared feature of their lives. But within the category of poverty are other, conflicting categories. Some poor people are white and others are black, for instance. A poor white person may not want to form a group with all other white people since many of them do not share the common experience of poverty; nor will he or she want to form a group with all other poor people since many of them do not share the common experience of being white. That example only begins to explore the contradictions and conflicts between and among categories.

Types of Social Groups

Once categories of individuals decide that their points of common experience are important enough to warrant further interactions, and they form groups, the kinds of social groups they form may vary considerably. One of the most important distinctions is between primary and secondary groups. **Primary groups** are typically small and characterized by a great deal of face-to-face interaction and extremely strong emotional ties among the members. The family is perhaps the best example of a primary group (although kin relationships are not the only way to achieve the strong emotional ties; a group of close friends is another). Primary groups are very important in any society because of the tremendous impact they have on the lives of their members (Cooley, 1902). Socialization and social control within the primary group are generally more effective than similar social pressures coming from any other source; a loved one's threat to withhold affection may change your behavior more quickly and more completely than a formal law and the threat of imprisonment. Because our roles within primary groups are usually the most important roles we play, our dominant view of ourselves tends to come from these groups on the basis of those roles. Others may think you are a worthless individual, but the love of family members can counteract that to a large extent and help you maintain self-respect.

Secondary groups are basically any social groups that are not primary groups. Secondary groups are typically larger than primary groups and are characterized by less intense emotional ties among the members and usually more specific roles. Examples of secondary groups would include political parties, voluntary clubs or associations, the people you work with or play with, collections of acquaintances, and so on. Your emotional commitment to a secondary group will generally be less than to your primary groups. In addition, your secondary group roles will usually be more specific than those found in primary groups; you may be a precinct worker in your political party, a secretary for your club, a fellow office worker within your occupational group, a member on a bowling team, and a friend to your neighbors. In each case you are in a specific role in which only a part of yourself will be involved.

Social groups vary in a number of other ways:

1. Groups can be either **formal** or **informal**. Any bureaucratic organization (such as the military) would be extremely formal; a group of friends or your family would be far more flexible and informal. The formal organization, a social group with a clear structure of roles and norms consciously designed for the achievement of particular goals, will be discussed in detail in the last section of this chapter.

2. Groups can be **voluntary** or **involuntary**. Some groups are a little hard to classify: A family, for example, can be either, depending on whether you married into it or were born into it. A group of friends formed from inmates within a prison would be a group voluntarily entered into by individuals who were involuntarily placed in a common environment.

3. Groups can be **open** or **closed**. Open groups are those open to new members; closed groups accept no new members. Many groups are a little bit of both, being open to some individuals while closed to others. The Ku Klux Klan, for example, is a group that seeks new members but is closed to Jews and blacks.

4. Groups can be **horizontal** or **vertical**. Horizontal groups contain members who all occupy the same social class; vertical groups contain representatives from a variety of social classes. In American society voluntary or informal vertical groups are very rare. Some reasons for this rarity will be examined later in this chapter as well as in Chapter 7.

5. Groups can be **in-groups** or **out-groups**. In-groups are social groups in which the individual feels at home or with which he or she identifies. The out-group, on the other hand, is any group to which the individual does not belong. The out-group is perceived as "they" by the individual; the in-group is perceived as "we." One person's in-group is therefore another persons out-group, and vice versa.

6. Groups can be **reference groups** for their members or even for their nonmembers. Reference groups provide standards against which individuals may measure themselves and their accomplishments. Ultimately, individuals develop a self-image from their reference groups; we come to know more clearly who we are when we identify ourselves with specific norms

As Alexis de Tocqueville pointed out a century and a half ago, America is a vast collection of social groups. We join together for reasons that vary from a shared hobby to a social cause. Many groups, from Shriners to street gangs, call attention to group membership through distinctive clothing. These "uniforms" contribute to identification with the group and to group cohesion.

and values found in specific social groups. Your circle of intimate friends may be a reference group for you; members of an occupational group to which you aspire may also provide a reference, acting as models for what you hope to see in yourself one day.

These classifications of social groups do not exhaust all the ways groups can differ, but they do call attention to some of the more important variations. Social groups are ultimately the product of human sociability, but the decisions people make about exercising that sociability have a lot to do with the social categories created within a society. Social groups are often the product of experiences shared by individuals who occupy the same category.

How Individuals Recognize Their Category Membership (with a little help from their friends)

As we saw earlier, in a complex society such as the United States any individual belongs to many social categories simultaneously. One individual might be a white, middle-income, Jewish male who works in an office and is confined to a wheelchair. Each of these characteristics is significant in the United States; the individual in question will have different kinds of experiences as a result of each: Whites have different experiences from people of other races, middle-income people live different lives from people of greater or lesser income, Jews are distinguished from other religious and ethnic groups, men are treated differently from women, office workers have experiences unique to office workers, and people in wheelchairs experience a world unknown to those who can walk. This individual will share at least *some* experiences with other people who share *even one* of his categories. He will, for example have something in common with all other American men since many experiences are parceled out by sex in American society. He will also, however, have many common experiences with women who are confined to wheelchairs—an experience most American men do not have. Thus arises a basic question for the sociologist: Under what conditions does a given category membership become important enough to individuals that they are drawn together into a social group?

Most individuals become convinced to emphasize one category over another with a little help from their friends Other people (with whom you share the category in question) will maintain that that category is more fundamental than others. If our hypothetical individual knows other Jewish people, they will likely attempt to convince him that he has more in common with them than he does with non-Jews in wheelchairs. His Jewish friends can call upon the long Jewish tradition and the importance of religion to everyday life. They can also point to the large number of existing Jewish groups and organizations; if other members of the category feel that it is important enough to warrant grouping together, who is our hypothetical individual to object?

The informal pressure from friends to maintain loyalty to a category becomes most effective when already existing social groups and organizations back them up. The existence of synagogues, Jewish social clubs, Yiddish-language newspapers, weddings, funerals, and so on all serve to reinforce the importance of the social category for our Jewish individual. In the case of many such organizations (religions, political groups, labor unions, and the like) it will be in the interests of the organization to attract as many category members as possible into the group. Our hypothetical individual will find himself being systematically bombarded with the importance of his religious and ethnic background.

While our "friends" help call attention to social categories, events and life experiences can be just as important. Our individual in the wheelchair will have a variety of important experiences that only people in wheelchairs have. Some of these experiences may be physical (the difficulty in getting from here to there), and some may be social (job discrimination based on the handicap, for example). The importance and vividness of these experiences cannot help but call attention to the category of the physically handicapped, leading individuals in that category to recognize their similarity to other members of the category. In fact, these very kinds of experiences led many handicapped Americans to organize politically; their efforts resulted in the passage of the Architectural Barriers Act of 1968 and the Rehabilitation Act of 1973. These pieces of legislation require, among other things, that public buildings be accessible to people in wheelchairs.

Other events such as disasters or economic depressions play major roles in calling attention to social categories. A hurricane calls attention to geographical categories, separating people in its path from those who live safely distant. An economic depression will likely affect some economic categories more than others and will call attention to economic differences in a society. Inflation affects the poor and people on fixed incomes more than it does others. A war coupled with a draft calls attention to age categories, separating those of draft age from those who are younger or older. If only men are drafted, it also calls attention to sexual categories. Events such as these all play a part in making certain social categories more or less important to their members at different times. The points of similarity among members of the category may be present all the time, but certain events may call attention to those points of similarity and lead people to act *in groups* based on the category.

Social Group Processes

Social Groups and Boundary Maintenance **Boundary maintenance** refers to efforts by group members to keep track of who is in the group and who is not in the group—or, more basically, to keep "them" separate from "us." The most obvious and pervasive example of boundary maintenance occurs with family "titles" (son, daughter-in-law, cousin, and so on), which specify both that you are a group member and the kind of group member you are. The family is an important group to its members, and membership requirements are generally quite strict. New members can join through marriage, and a great deal of attention is generally paid to the prospective new member before the ceremony. Other groups and organizations accomplish the same boundary maintenance through initiation ceremonies, membership cards, and group or organizational titles.

Boundary maintenance thrives on less formal techniques as well. Every family, for example, has traditional family stories, jokes, and ways of doing things that exist only within the family unit. When outsiders confront these activities, they are reminded of the fact that they are outsiders. Groups or organizations can also have secret hand-shakes, distinctive clothing, specific mannerisms, or even a separate and distinctive vocabulary or style of speaking. All of these activities or attributes serve as constant reminders to both insiders and outsiders exactly where the group boundary is located.

Social Groups and Social Control As a rule, group members don't need rational reasons for insisting on conformity to their norms. Humans are social animals and all that they do is in some way related to their sociability. A number of studies by sociologists and psychologists have demonstrated this aspect of human behavior quite clearly.

An experiment by Solomon Asch (1958) provides a striking illustration of group pressure. Asch constructed a test consisting of a set of lines of three lengths (lines 1, 2, and 3) coupled with an additional, single, line (A) that obviously corresponded in length to line 2 (see Figure 6.1). When he asked subjects individually which line in the set corresponded to line A, no one had any difficulty answering the question correctly. He then moved his experiment into a group setting in which a number of people had been instructed to answer the question incorrectly in front of a naive subject before that subject was asked the same question. In this group situation a significant number of subjects agreed with the group rather than trust their own eyes. Thus we either keep our differences from the group to ourselves or, just as likely, we come to see things differently over time due to our desire to be part of the group.

Social control by the group appears just as strikingly in the world of everyday life. Where do fads come from? How can we explain large numbers of people simultaneously deciding to buy hula hoops, swallow goldfish, or add colors and spikes to their hair? Perhaps hula hoops are fun and live goldfish are tasty, but that still doesn't explain why so many people first discover

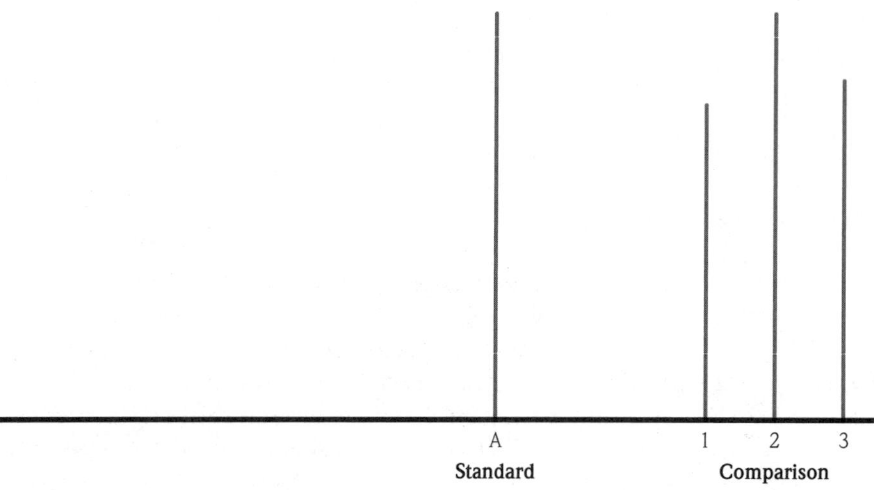

Figure 6.1 Standard and comparison lines in the Asch experiment. (Adapted from Asch, 1958.)

and then forget those facts simultaneously. One of the most fascinating aspects of fads is the power they exert on individuals during the fad's life span and how quickly fads can become out of date. Fads and fashions are clearly an example of group pressure and the desire of many individuals to do whatever the rest of the group is doing.

Social Groups: Conflict and Cooperation Individuals generally feel that their acts of conflict and cooperation are motivated by their own feelings and attitudes: Anger and hostility can lead to conflict, while warm and friendly feelings lead to cooperation. But where do the feelings and attitudes come from? As our social groups give us norms, encourage us to color our hair and alter our perceptions, they also influence our feelings and attitudes toward others.

Georg Simmel, a German sociologist who wrote at the turn of the last century, focused a good deal of attention on the ways that social groups generate conlict and cooperation among individuals. His primary insight was that increasing conflict *between* two groups leads to increasing cooperation *within* each group (Simmel, 1955). A social group torn by internal differences can immediately be unified in the face of an outside threat. This principle can be witnessed in either small or large groups. A sports team builds unity through the experience of meeting other teams that seek to defeat it. A nation-state becomes more unified when attacked by the military forces of another country. The Japanese attack on Pearl Harbor in 1941 and the taking of hostages in Iran in 1979 both served to generate intense feelings of patriotism among Americans.

An outside threat to a group can be real or imagined. A leader faced with dissension can manipulate the group by convincing members they face some outside threat. One of the most graphic examples is Adolf Hitler's attempt to unify the German people by convincing them that their problems were the result of an international Jewish conspiracy. Similarly, American politicians have for many years rallied the electorate around their candidacies with pledges to counter the threat to the United States from the Soviet Union. If a social group can be convinced

Social control by the group has an iron grip on young Americans. What chance would there be for a boy who couldn't skateboard to join this group?

of an outside threat, they are likely to forget their individual differences in the name of group solidarity and follow their leader. Under such circumstances individuals in the group will experience feelings of friendship and warmth for other group members along with feelings of hostility toward individuals in the group that threatens them.

Simmel's insight into group conflict and cooperation was studied experimentally by Muzafer and Carolyn Sherif (1956). They separated a group of preadolescent boys at a summer camp into two competing groups and then organized a series of sporting contests in which the boys competed *as groups.* Points were awarded to each group at the end of each contest. Individuals in the winning group received a pocketknife as a prize, while individuals in the losing group received nothing. The Sherifs also fanned the flames a bit beyond the built-in competition. For example, they organized parties but gave different starting times to the two different groups, knowing that the members of the first group would eat all the ice cream before the other group arrived. The experimentally produced competition led to degrees of conflict even beyond the expectations of the Sherifs. The two groups began with name calling and soon escalated the conflict to threatening posters, group pranks (such as spreading cocoa and syrup over an area to be cleaned by the other group), and finally physical violence. By the time the staff stepped in, conflict between the two groups was well on its way to becoming an accepted fact of everyday life, and individuals within each group identified very strongly with their group.

AGE AND SEX DIFFERENTIATION

Age and sex are two ways that humans can vary. Almost all human societies provide different life experiences for men and women and for people of different ages. Most commonly, different roles are assigned to people on the basis of their sex and age. In most societies (including the United States) the most highly rewarded and influential roles are occupied by people of middle age who are men. Some societies provide better roles for women, and still more societies treat the aged better than they are treated in American society, but the generalization holds.

The assignment of different roles according to age is necessary to some extent. Humans mature very slowly; younger members of society must necessarily occupy dependent roles for quite a number of years. Most age and sex differentiation reflects general cultural values, however, rather than such practical considerations. People of both sexes and a variety of ages could fill far more roles than most societies permit. In American society a woman could easily fill the role of president, and a man could be a fine homemaker. Similarly, old people could continue to do a great many jobs beyond the age of retirement, and young people could no doubt handle more responsibility than they are usually given. If such situations existed, age and sex would be far less important social categories, and an individual's everyday life experience would not vary greatly on the basis of either sex or age. As it is, however, men and women grow up and live in different worlds with differing role expectations, and people of different ages are thrust into very different experiences and often live in isolation from each other. Not surprisingly, Americans often feel most comfortable in social groups containing others of their own sex and age. Considering that individuals are placed in age and sex categories involuntarily, these categories provide a fundamental starting point for the understanding of social differentiation.

Age Differentiation in American Society

Age as a Social Category Biology requires that in any society the very young occupy somewhat different roles than older members. Even this basic statement must be qualified, however. Only in industrial societies such as the United States is "childhood" a fairly lengthy stage of life. In most nonindustrial societies children enter adult roles (especially work roles) quite early in life. American prohibitions against child labor may look much more humane, but the fact is that we have few jobs for unskilled child labor. Our industrial economy provides more skilled and fewer unskilled jobs with each passing year. It is important, therefore, to extend the period of childhood to keep young people out of the economy and in training programs (such as formal education) as long as possible. As the institution of education grows in response to this need, children are increasingly oriented away from their families and toward their peer group at school. The emphasis on their being children and not adults further serves to separate young people from older people. The "generation gap"—a very popular concept in the 1960s—reflects the consciousness of both generations of this increasing isolation.

An industrial society also promotes rapid social change, which has many important repercussions at the top end of the age spectrum. In nonindustrial societies older people often receive respect because of their accumulation of knowledge and experience. In a rapidly changing industrial society, however, their knowledge may well be out of date and their experience may be considered irrelevant. And since values change at a similar pace, the young and the old wind up miles apart and often distrustful of each other. It is instructive that older people are often looked upon as being similar to children and are often treated as such; like children, older people are commonly out of the workforce and lack many of the skills and knowledge common to the wage-earning generation.

In between young and old is the wage-earning generation—the age group most actively tied into the economy. The demands of a modern industrial economy make children an expense and older people a nuisance to this middle category. Industrial employment requires the middle generation either to limit or to cease having children and to look elsewhere than the family structure if the grandparents need additional care. Not surprisingly, industrial employment leads to smaller families, day-care centers, formal institutions of education, and an increase in nursing homes. In addition, the geographical mobility required of employees in an industrial economy tends to separate generations within a family as each new generation faces the possibility of having to move to find work.

One of the most basic characteristics of industrial societies is rapid social change in all aspects of culture. Beyond making the knowledge and experience of the aged irrelevant, rapid social change means that each generation will "come of age" in a fundamentally different environment from the previous generation. Norms and values favored by parents may only partially apply to the world facing their children. In such a situation each generation comes out culturally a little different from the one before. Consequently, age as a social category gains importance.

Age as a Basis for Group Formation The importance of age as a social category in modern American society is reflected in the growing number of social groups that form around the common experience of age. The term *youth culture,* for example, was popularized in the 1960s, but its roots go back several decades before that. The change can perhaps be seen most clearly in the world of popular music. Popular music used to be ageless in its audience; Bing Crosby appealed to a variety of age groups. In the 1940s, however, Frank Sinatra began his career amid the screams of teenage girls. By the 1950s and the rise of rock and roll, certain kinds of music were clearly directed at audiences of specific ages. Today you need only to look at a tape or c.d. collection to know the age of the collector, no matter what his or her social position.

As younger people cluster together at one end of the age spectrum, so older people cluster together at the other end. All cities have senior citizen centers, and all states have varieties of retirement communities and apartment complexes that specialize in housing for the aged. Special magazines, such as *50 Plus,* are directed specifically at older Americans just as *Rolling Stone* is directed at younger Americans. Mandatory retirement places the aged in a similar relationship to the world of work; magazines like *50 Plus* devote considerable space to articles on how to fill the hours of the day, how to deal with loneliness, and how to have fun on a reduced income. The underlying thread behind many of these experiences common to the aged in the United States is ageism.

Ageism is prejudice toward the aged as well as acts of discrimination against them on the basis of age (Barrow and Smith, 1979). The United States has become a youth-oriented society in which baldness, gray hair, and wrinkles are feared as if they were diseases. Looking, acting, and thinking young have become highly valued and form the basis of a prejudice against the aged simply because they are old. This prejudice is often coupled with discrimination, particularly

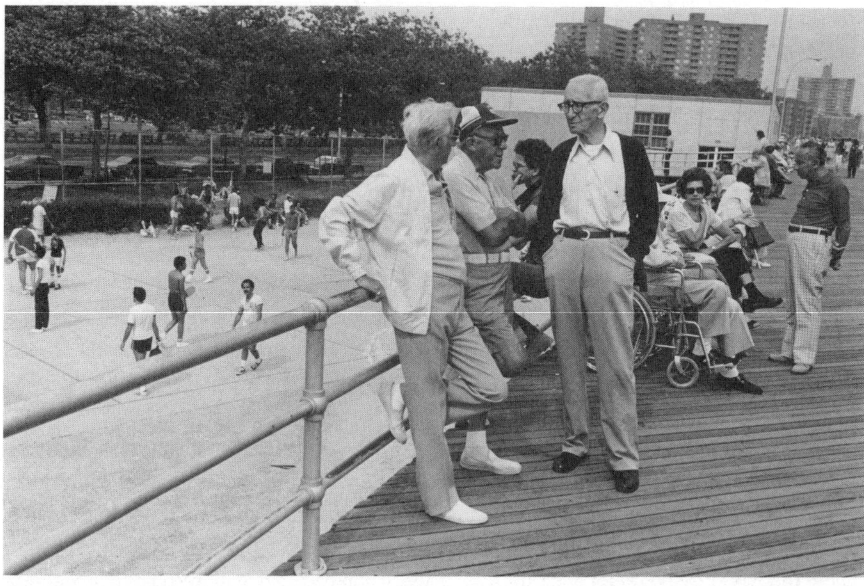

Many of our social roles depend on the age group we belong to. In American society, most older people experience a restriction in social roles, as they have left the workforce and have fewer family responsibilities.

in the area of employment. Unemployed older workers find work very hard to come by when facing younger competition, and in spite of seniority systems older workers are often the first to be laid off (Sheppard, 1976). Contrary to popular stereotpes, however, old people are not uniformly poor; better retirement programs coupled with Social Security have produced economic stability for older Americans and have insulated them from some of the economic changes that have thrust younger Americans into economic hardships (O'Hare, 1985).

The various manifestations of ageism have called attention to the category of old age and have stimulated the formation of political groups organized to protect the rights of the aged. One of the earliest political organizations of the aged was the Townsend movement of the 1930s, the main program of which was to provide $200 a month for elderly Americans from federal government funds. The plan was never instituted, but parts of it were not that different from the provisions of the Social Security Act (passed shortly thereafter), which provided incomes for most aged Americans. Of the more modern political organizations for the aged, the largest is the coalition of the National Retired Teachers Association and the American Association of Retired Persons. A more radical and more loosely organized group is the Gray Panthers, founded by Maggie Kuhn. These and other organizations were instrumental in the passage of the 1967 Age Discrimination Act and recent amendments to that act, which, among other things, broke the iron rule of mandatory retirement in many sectors of the economy. The growth of these organizations in recent years reflects the increasing importance of age as a social category and the need of the aged to have their interests represented.

Like all social categories, age is a social category in the United States today because the modes of coordination we live by constantly call attention to our age. The roles we play and the norms we are expected to live by vary considerably as we grow older. As this occurs, our attention is drawn to others who are similarly affected. We are apt to feel most comfortable with these people and have interests in common with them, so we are also apt to form social groups with them. Human biology requires some of this differentiation, but much of it is forced upon us by the nature of our society. Sex differentiation operates similarly.

Sex Differentiation in American Society

The ever-popular "battle of the sexes" is probably fought in every human society in one form or another. The differing biological make-ups of men and women are certainly responsible for some of the behaviors and interests that differentiate the sexes. But as with age differentiation in society, the biological basis of the differentiation cannot come close to explaining the experiences and expectations we confront depending on our sex.

The vast majority of human societies—and certainly American society—place a great importance upon sexual differences. Boys and girls are raised in very different manners in order to make them suitable occupants for the sex-specific roles they will encounter later on. In American society it has traditionally been thought that women should be kind and nurturing so they will make better wives, mothers, nurses, and kindergarten teachers, while men should be aggressive and rational to become better corporation executives, football players, brain surgeons, and college professors.

Sex-Role Socialization Johnny finds a truck, a football, and a six-gun under the Christmas tree, while Mary receives a doll, a frilly pink dress, and a set of play pots and pans—even Santa Claus believes that little boys and little girls are fundamentally different. Children in American society receive a clear message practically from birth as to just which sorts of thoughts, beliefs, and actions are appropriate for their sex. Adults even treat newborns differently depending on their sex; thus, to some degree sex roles have an impact in even the first few weeks of life (Condry and Condry, 1976). Parents, relatives, teachers, other kids, and even total strangers appear to conspire in sex-role socialization. A boy cannot cry in front of any of these people without running the risk of being labeled a "sissy"; a girl should not climb trees or start fights unless she's willing to face taunts of "tomboy." By the time boys and girls are old enough to reflect on what's happening to them, they are already very different kinds of people.

The growing child and young adult becomes increasingly aware of the outside world, and much of what is encountered there supports the earlier messages. Men are generally portrayed in movies, fiction, and television as strong, independent, and self-confident; they are also usually the most important characters. Women, on the other hand, have usually been portrayed as weak, fearful, and dependent on some male figure. Even school textbooks carry a similar message. In a recent study of children's books, it was found that male characters outnumbered female characters and engaged in more diverse social activities (Best, 1985). The six o'clock news contains information about the activities of important men in the world and is generally reported by men. Men paint great paintings, write great books, invent important things, introduce great religions, and lead great revolutions; they exist everywhere as models for role behavior for the growing boy. Little girls, on the other hand, must hunt for such role models.

Just as with any form of socialization, sex-role socialization does not end with childhood. Adults are subject to much of the same socialization through the media, and they also spend a good portion of their time socializing each other. The "American date" is a classic situation in which sex-role expectations become reinforced through the established roles that are played. A woman can easily test this by not only making the "date" in the first place (which is becoming acceptable) but also by continuing to play the "male" role throughout—she could drive the car, select the entertainment, pay for everything, and then aggressively seek a sexual reward in return for the money she has spent on the evening. She would most likely receive a negative response to this dating behavior: Roles must be followed, with men and women staying on their own sides of the fence.

Sex Discrimination and Sexism As with age differentiation, more than simply role differences makes sex an important social category. Women clearly face discrimination in the United States. When we look at the economic marketplace, we find that women have been largely kept out of occupations thought unsuitable for them. Some job discrimination is tied closely to the stereotypes that guide sex-role socialization. Women have, for example, generally been kept out of the sciences because they are stereotyped as "not good at that kind of thing." If parents and teachers pass on the stereotype to little girls who then come to believe it, they will, in fact, not do well in science and will not go on to seek careers in scientific fields. (Sociologists call this circular process a **self-fulfilling prophecy**, in which a belief that something will happen makes it happen.)

Other forms of job discrimination are more blatant. Several leading American religions refuse to allow women to occupy the dominant roles within their organizations. The Catholic Church, for example, has long insisted that only men may fill the role of priest. Other jobs have been closed to women by male employers simply choosing not to hire them. Even on the job, discrimination exists in the form of sexual harassment, when women are expected to provide sexual favors in exchange for advancement or even to keep the job they have.

In the past, women were largely limited to such occupations as grade-school teaching, semiskilled factory work, nursing, and secretarial, clerking, and household work. Defined as "women's work," most of these occupations have traditionally been poorly paid. This kind of "double standard," in which traditionally female-dominated occupations are by and large lower paying than male-dominated occupations, has led to demands for comparable worth laws. These laws would provide comparisons between male and female occupations in terms of years of training required, difficulty of the work, and amount of responsibility inherent in the occupation. Occupations deemed similar by such standards would then be required by law to provide equal pay (Feldberg, 1984). The segregation of women into low-paying jobs coupled with hiring discrimination has maintained a considerable income gap between men and women that has changed little over the last two decades.

Sexism refers to stereotyping on the basis of sex and to the prejudice and discrimination that are directed by sex. It's a useful concept to the sociologist for it weaves together the various aspects of sexual differentiation. As with age, people experience their sexual category in all walks of their existence; the experiences we have as children on the playground or around the Christmas tree are reflected later in life when we look for jobs. To argue that the United States is a sexist society is to argue that the male experience in this society is fundamentally different from—and more positive than—the female experience. Not surprisingly, the individuals involved notice these differences and group together accordingly.

Discrimination against women on the job reveals itself in sexual harassment, which is sometimes blatant, sometimes fairly subtle. This boss might appear to be simply discussing the work on the drawing board, but his arm is enclosing and pressing the young woman, who does not appear to welcome such attentions. If she tells him to back off, however, how likely is it that she will get the next promotion that comes up?

Sex as a Basis for Group Formation As we saw with age differentiation, an important social category usually becomes a basis for the formation of social groups. The social category of sex is particularly interesting in this regard for, unlike different generations, people of both sexes must group together to some extent if the society is to continue beyond the current generation. This tie between the sexes is obviously a strong one; marriages and families are probably the strongest social groups that individuals form in any society. Yet different experiences based on sex work somewhat at cross-purposes. A man and woman may be drawn together in marriage, yet both may actually have more experiences in common with other members of their own sex than with their spouse. Years of sex-specific experiences can make understanding within a marriage very difficult. The early separation into Boy Scouts and Girl Scouts appears later in life in the husband's nights out with "the guys" and the wife's shopping trips with her friends—the social category of sex apparently makes us not want to go scouting or shopping with members of the opposite sex. Old habits are hard to break. When parties of married couples dissolve into a men's group in the living room and a women's group in the kitchen, it is clear that social categories are at work. Box 6.1 illustrates something of the sexual isolation in American society. When and if sex-role specification breaks down in the way we learn our appropriate roles, our interests should be more similar and these voluntary social segregations less likely to occur.

A great many of the voluntary social groups in American society are sex-specific. Many churches, which contain members of both sexes, have sex-specific social groups within the

BOX 6.1

CONFESSIONS OF A FEMALE CHAUVINIST SOW

American society differentiates greatly on the basis of sex. Males and females are treated differently from birth and face a variety of expectations specific to their sex as they grow older. This differentiation isolates men and women, giving them experiences they find difficult to share and creating communication problems should they try. Moreover men have traditionally received most of the advantages in this differentiation, leading many women to feel envious and bitter.

The following extract presents a few childhood memories and a few thoughts on this issue from writer Anne Roiphe (1972):

> I remember coming home from school one day to find my mother's card game dissolved in hysterical laughter. The cards were floating in black rivers of running mascara. What was so funny? A woman named Helen was lying on a couch pretending to be her husband with a cold. She was issuing demands for orange juice, aspirin, suggesting a call to a specialist, complaining of neglect, of fate's cruel finger, of heat, of cold, of sharp pains on the bridge of the nose that might indicate brain involvement. What was so funny? The ladies explained to me that all men behave just like that with colds, they are reduced to temper tantrums by simple nasal congestion, men cannot stand any little physical discomfort—on and on the laughter went.
>
> The point of this vignette is the nature of the laughter—us laughing at them, feeling superior to them, us ridiculing them behind their backs. If they were doing it to us we'd call it male chauvinist pigness; if we do it to them, it is inescapably female chauvinist sowness and, whatever its roots, it leads to the same isolation. Boys are messy, boys are mean, boys are rough, boys are stupid and have sloppy handwriting. A cacophony of childhood memories rushes through my head, balanced, of course, by all the well-documented feelings of inferiority and envy.

membership. Men's organizations such as the Masons, Elks, or Knights of Columbus are still very strong, and many maintain parallel organizations for women (such as the Eastern Star for the Masons and Emblem Club for the Elks) rather than permit female membership in the organization itself. On a less organized scale Americans also belong to many sex-specific groups such as bowling leagues, softball teams, poker parties, cooking clubs, and so on; while many of these associations are increasingly becoming coed, for the most part the sexual separation is still there. Perhaps the most interesting example comes to us from the world of warfare. Traditionally, only American men have gone to war, and they have followed that experience by forming veterans' organizations such as the American Legion and the Veterans of Foreign Wars. When the question of drafting women arose in 1980, most members of these organizations were opposed, suggesting a desire to keep a male domain male.

As sexual differentiation has encouraged men to form men-only groups, it has had a similar effect on women, particularly in recent years. The separation of men and women over the right to vote led directly to the women's suffrage movement. Other forms of discrimination against women have led to the formation of a wide range of women's groups and organizations pursuing feminist issues. These groups have taken direct aim at economic discrimination against women as well as at the prejudices and stereotypes that define a woman's place as in the home, playing second fiddle to her husband. The effects of this movement have been far reaching. Rigid sex-role socialization is less prevalent today than it was only ten years ago. Women can now be found playing strong roles in movies and on TV, reporting the news, and—perhaps most important—making the news.

We cannot choose our sex at conception, nor can we keep ourselves from growing older (although we spend millions every year trying). Both sex and age, however, are human attributes that are integrated into the coordination of most societies in such a way that the roles open to us and the norms that govern us will vary depending on age and sex.

Just as sex and age separate people, differences in wealth, prestige, and ancestry create walls between people in American society. We will turn now to a brief examination of these aspects of social differentiation in American society, looking first at social class and social status differentiation and finally at racial and ethnic differentiation. These topics will be covered in fuller detail in the next two chapters, for which these short sections will serve as an introduction.

SOCIAL CLASS AND SOCIAL STATUS DIFFERENTIATION

Unlike sex and age, your social class and your social status have nothing to do with human biology; they are both purely creations of society. In a modern society such as the United States both exist within the more general structure of social stratification. Although all of these concepts have been introduced in earlier chapters, it might be useful at this point to review them. **Social stratification** refers to the arrangement of different activities (or roles) into a hierarchy in which activities ranked high are highly rewarded and activities ranked low are poorly rewarded. The rewards generally consist of money, prestige, and influence over others. **Social class** refers to collections of individuals whose activities (or roles) are similar in terms of the rewards they bring to their participants. **Social status** refers to your social position, particularly with respect to prestige. In some societies social status might be entirely determined by how others thought of your parents. Although this is an important part of social status in any society, a modern society generally also associates high or low social status with roles (particularly occupational role) and is therefore something an individual can achieve (or not achieve). Your occupational role within the system of social stratification generally has a major impact on your social class (your occupation is generally the source of most of your "rewards") and on your social status (people often think well or ill of you depending upon "what you do"). In short, these three concepts are highly interrelated.

The introduction of a social stratification system makes social differentiation more organized and quite a bit more rigid. In an agricultural society, for example, farmers with 50 acres might not only be better thought of than those with 10 acres, but very likely they will also have more wealth. If their society is such that their children are able to inherit this wealth, a system of social stratification is born; social status then becomes more closely associated with "what you do" and the wealth that activity brings you (your social class). As new generations are born into this society, they will likely step into the shoes waiting for them, becoming high or low in both social class and social status as they inherit their parents' wealth and "good name" (or poverty and "bad name") simultaneously. Note the similarity between this form of differentiation and sexual differentiation. You cannot choose your sex, nor can you choose the wealth or prestige of your parents; in both cases, the differentiation is there waiting for you and will place you into a specific social category. Just as being born a male leads you into experiences different from those of individuals born female, so being born into the upper classes leads you into experiences different from those of people born into the lower classes.

In comparison with age and sex, social class and social status would seem to be far more flexible. Social status, in particular, is basically a matter of how well you are thought of by other members of your society; such opinions should be more easily changed than the aging process. Similarly, social class is largely determined by where you tie into the economy, and people have been known to change jobs, make fortunes, and lose fortunes during a lifetime. The sociological idea that social groups will forrn out of social categories assumes that the categories will remain somewhat constant. Only then can a collection of individuals share a common body of experiences over time that might lead them to group together. If social class and social status are social categories, our first question must relate to their stability: How common is it for people to change in class and status?

For most societies (including American society) this question can be answered in a very straightforward manner. It is in fact quite *uncommon* for people to change very much in social class or social status, not only during one lifetime but even from one generation to the next. This fact runs contrary to the American "rags to riches" ideal and the belief that "anyone can make it" by working hard enough. Obviously, some individuals do move from rags to riches; we are very aware in particular of professional athletes and movie stars who make this jump. We also read stories of little-known inventors who make millions through one of their creations. But keep in mind that these people are in the news *because* they are unusual. The individual who wins the Irish Sweepstakes is written about only because most of us do not win it. The same is true for movie stars and athletes. For every individual who makes it, a great many more try and fail. Most of us in fact wind up in a social class very similar to that of our parents. For reasons we'll look at in more detail in Chapter 7, a social stratification system generally makes it fairly easy to avoid falling much below your family's rank and fairly difficult to move much above it. Since social status has become so closely tied to social class in the United States, both status and class tend to remain constant for most of us, just like our sex.

We have looked previously at how the coordination of American society is such that people are thrust into very different experiences depending on their age and sex. The same is true for social class and social status. Just as men and women are to some extent isolated from each other, so people from different social classes and statuses are isolated from each other, and to an even greater extent. Social interaction across class lines tends to be sporadic and superficial. The reason is partly the financial differences between one class and the next. Large, expensive homes are effectively prohibited to the lower classes. This means that lower- and upper-class neighborhoods will be separated, which in turn means that children of different classes will not meet and play with each other. To the extent that schools serve particular neighborhoods or that wealthier children attend private schools, children will continue to be separated by class during their school years. Should they meet through a device such as busing, they will still not necessarily socialize beyond the superficial level required by attending the same school. Their parents will, by definition, be engaged in different kinds of work, so they are not likely to meet, either. All of these people are separated; they will be living, working, and playing with very little input from other classes. In short, all aspects of their lives, from the most important to the most trivial, will develop in relative isolation and, therefore, in different directions. And whatever that development is, it will be passed from one generation to the next. A growing child learns to shoot craps, go bowling, or play polo because that activity is prevalent in his or her social environment. The same is true of modes of speaking, ways of worshiping, attitudes toward education, and so on. As differences develop through isolation, so they persist through isolation. The article by Fusell following this chapter offers a whimsical view of this differentiation.

When individuals do meet each other across social class lines, usually they either follow rigid roles (such as master and servant or, to some extent, any employer and employee), or they become uncomfortable. Without those roles people of different social classes discover how little they have in common and how their expectations for behavior (which had always worked well within their own social class) don't seem to be working. This kind of experience tends to make people return to the more comfortable realm of their own social class, usually bringing with them negative stereotypes such as "Poor people are rude, ungrateful, and slovenly," or "People with lots of money are snobs who'll step on anyone just to make a few bucks." The communication difficulties that often exist between men and women occur between members of different social classes as well, and for exactly the same reasons—different experiences make people different.

RACIAL AND ETHNIC DIFFERENTIATION

Ethnicity is cultural; an **ethnic group** is a group of people who share a common culture, claim to share a common culture, or are defined by others as sharing a common culture. *Race,* on the other hand, refers to biological similarity; a **racial group** is supposedly a group of people who share a biological heritage that is specific to them and distinct from other groups. *Supposedly* is necessary because not all biologists agree that race is a useful biological concept. People obviously inherit different genes and, among other results, look different. The question is, do they inherit different genes in *groups*? Can we argue, for example, that all black people are genetically more like each other than any of them are genetically like white people? No, we can't, for it's not true.

Whatever the biological questions involved in race, however, it has a quite particular social definition: A racial group is a group of people who *are generally believed* to share a biological heritage that is specific to them and distinct from other groups. In short, a race exists whenever a lot of people think it exists. This addition to the biological definition is important for, as we shall see in Chapter 8, race is a term that has been used very loosely throughout history; a group believed racially distinct this year might not be thought of that way next year. Conveniently, groups that are labeled racial groups at any point in time are also typically ethnically different from whichever group is doing the labeling; hence, racial groups either are or contain ethnic groups.

The United States has grown tremendously in its 200-year history, and massive numbers of people have come to its territory from other places. Sometimes called the "nation of

One group of immigrants—the Chinese—set up tightly knit communities in cities all over the United States. Here, Chinese New Year is celebrated in Boston's Chinatown.

immigrants," the United States is a truly unique society for the ethnic diversity within it as well as for the way that diversity occurred.

There is nothing like meeting someone from another culture to make you become aware of your own. Normally, people take their cultures for granted, but when you meet people whose diet consists mainly of raw fish, unleavened bread, tortillas, rice, or pasta, it makes you look at your meat and potatoes in a new light. Since people from any culture will be ethnocentric, the coming together of different ethnic groups makes ethnicity a natural characteristic with which to differentiate. As the United States grew and as its ethnic diversity increased, ethnic differences came to be seen as increasingly important; encountering all that ethnic diversity out on the street might make you want to get home to your family where you feel warm and secure. This experience was especially strong for immigrant groups to the United States, who felt totally overwhelmed by the new culture they had entered and almost always formed tight immigrant communities where much of their old culture was maintained. The experience of immigration made the category of ethnicity stand out.

The immigrant brought not only a new culture to the United States but job competition as well. Particularly in times of economic recession the immigrant was viewed with fear and distrust by those already here, who saw the newcomers as threats to their economic security. One response to this kind of threat is the prejudice and discrimination that always seem so common between racial and ethnic groups. Acts of discrimination, such as a refusal to allow members of the immigrant group to live in certain areas or work at certain jobs, makes your neighborhood and job all the more secure. Prejudice and stereotypes point out the supposed shortcomings of the immigrant group and their culture, thus justifying the discrimination against them. Slavery in the United States is a good example of this process. It helped whites in that (1) white slaveowners gained wealth through the labor of black slaves, and (2) all whites were spared having to compete with blacks for jobs since slavery kept them out of the job market. After the emancipation of slaves many other forms of discrimination against blacks were developed to serve the same purpose. Along with the discrimination went a variety of forms of prejudice and stereotypes, not the least of which was the basic belief in racial superiority that justified (in the minds of white people) a domination of black people.

Both setting up discriminatory processes against an ethnic group and facing those discriminatory processes call attention to ethnic differences. Slavery, for example, made whites very aware of being white and blacks very aware of being black. As a mode of social coordination, slavery served to differentiate people on the basis of skin color, thus making skin color an extremely important human characteristic. Although slavery is probably the most extreme example in American history (matched only by the near extermination of American Indians), most ethnically different immigrant groups faced some forms of prejudice and discrimination in the United States. And prejudice and discrimination added to cultural difference makes race or ethnicity an important social category.

FORMAL ORGANIZATIONS AND BUREAUCRACIES

As we've seen, social groups vary in a great many ways; they can be large or small, primary or secondary, and varied in the kinds of people who form them. One of the most important variations in social groups is the degree to which they are formal or informal. A group of you and your friends, for example, is informal in that you do different things at different times and places and probably permit a wide range of behavior among yourselves. If your social group decided to form a charity, produce a salable product, or elect a political candidate, however, you would very soon discover a need for more organization. Who would do what and when? Who would make decisions? Who would be responsible for getting things done? In short, you would need to transform the informal organization of your social group into a formal organization. The formal organization is one of the clearest cases of a social group that reflects the coordination of society; informal groups take their social organization for granted, but formal organizations approach the question of coordination in a very self-conscious and conspicuous manner.

A **formal organization** is a social group with a clear structure of roles and norms consciously designed for the achievement of particular goals. It is characterized by a division of labor and a hierarchical chain of command. Formal organizations can be small and relatively simple, like a local election campaign committee, or they can be large and extremely complex, like Exxon or ITT. The more industrial and complex a society becomes, the more informal social groups will be replaced by formal organizations. If you are currently going to school or working, you have almost daily dealings with formal organizations. Since formal organizations are obviously much larger and more powerful than individuals, you will necessarily have to adapt your behavior to the organizations' demands. If you disagree with those demands, you might try fighting by forming your own formal organization; labor unions were formed for just that purpose. But the folk wisdom that "you can't fight city hall" indicates something of the difficulties you will have (see Box 6.2, for example).

BOX 6.2

FINKING ON THE BOSS: GRIEVANCES IN A FORMAL ORGANIZATION

Formal organizations are characterized by a hierarchy (or chain of command) in which authority is very specifically divided. What do you do if your immediate superior is dishonest, incompetent, or simply unbearable? According to the rules of the formal organization, you take all problems to the person in the office immediately above you—but obviously you can't do that when that person is the problem. Deena Weinstein (1979) describes some instances of workers in this difficult situation and some of the results they achieved by "informing" on their bosses to those higher up the chain of command.

> Some counselors in a drug abuse clinic found out that the vice-directors of the agency had been "skimming money from federal funds for their own personal use. . . . The scheme was camouflaged nicely, by talented 'bookjuggling' by the culprits. Funds, supposedly used for drug purchases, improving 'job-readiness,' and counseling tools were confiscated by the vice-directors." A statement detailing the malfeasance was drawn up by the counselors and given to the director, but no action was taken. The oppositionists soon learned that the director was also dishonest: "Therefore, we had to make an appointment which finally got through, to enlighten the Executive-Director to the present conditions. This was fairly difficult to do, because of his 'isolated position' he kept himself in. Finally, after three weeks of trying to get through we got that appointment, by one day barging in his office and announcing we needed to talk to him." In this case, the information was appreciated and action was taken.
>
> Informing over the heads of one's immediate superiors can also backfire when they are told about it. A weapons analyst in the U.S. Air Force, physicist Kenneth S. Cook, broke the chain of command in the course of his bureaucratic opposition. His immediate commanding officer informed him that he had a copy of his "confidential" letter to the higher brass: "What followed was a Kafkaesque nightmare. Cook's top-secret security clearance was summarily removed without explanation. . . . Then, before a military medical panel . . . he was found mentally and physically incapable of performing further service . . . within the government."
>
> Similarly, after his superior held up a report about air charter abuses for more than five weeks, a Federal Aviation Administration employee, P. I. Ryther, went over the official's head to the deputy administrator. When he did not take the report seriously, Ryther tried to contact the administrator of the agency. He did not respond and passed the word that he would not comment on the report. Shortly afterwards Ryther was forced to resign when he was "called on the carpet at a special meeting of his superiors for ignoring proper channels."
>
> Working one's way up the organizational chart, even if gaining access is not a problem, does not always make sense. The official chart may not coincide with the way that power is really distributed. The more that the oppositionists are familiar

BOX 6.2 (continued)

with the "shadow table" (the actual hierarchy of influence), the better they can target their activities. At one university it is well known that one of the several vice-presidents controls or can control all areas of the administration. Several bureaucratic oppositions which began with informing strategies went directly to him, by-passing chart-relevant deans.

Information may be ignored, used against those proffering it, or used to further the goals of the bureaucractic opposition. Monarchs were known to kill bearers of ill tidings and, while not nearly as severe, administrators rarely welcome the bad news that oppositionists bring. Officials more or less correctly feel that improprieties are their responsibility, because they have formal authority over the situation. Often they were responsible for the hiring, promotion, or good ratings of the rule violator. Anthony Jay, author of *The Corporation Man,* writes: "The hardest and most thankless task is to tell the higher managers in the corporation that your immediate boss is no good. In the first place, they appointed him, so you are implicitly criticizing their judgment. In the second place, maintenance of corporate authority demands that they take his word against yours. In the third place, no one much wants to employ the sort of person who is liable to go behind his back to a superior and vilify him, even (or especially) if the person is telling the truth. In the fourth place, your motives are bound to be suspected." (Reprinted by permission.)

Bureaucracies

Most modern formal organizations contain some elements of bureaucratic organization. A **bureaucracy** is a formal organization characterized by a set of positions arranged in a hierarchy of authority governed by specific procedural rules designed to accomplish specific tasks. Because it is often claimed that bureaucracies work better on paper than in practice, it would be useful to begin this examination by looking at the ideal form of the bureaucracy presented by sociologist Max Weber.

According to Weber (1946), the ideal bureaucracy (or a bureaucracy as it might logically function) would have the following characteristics:

1. The bureaucracy should be based on a body of laws or rules intentionally constructed and specifically designed to meet the goals of the organization. This body of laws or rules should represent an impersonal order to which all members of the bureaucracy should be subject. This means, in short, that rules should operate consistently on a day-to-day basis and that no one in the bureaucracy would be "above the laws." The successful working of the United States Constitution during the Watergate episode and the Iran-Contra affair suggests an approximation of the ideal implementation of a bureaucracy's rules.
2. The offices of the bureaucracy should be organized according to a division of labor in which there is clear hierarchy of authority. Specific tasks should be assigned to specific offices to provide maximum efficiency of operation, and there should be no doubt as to which offices have the authority to give orders to the occupants of which other offices. In a university,

for example, a professor has the authority to assign certain kinds of educational tasks to students and to test the completion of those tasks according to acceptable testing procedures. That same professor does not have the authority, however, to assign killing as an educational task or to schedule tests on Sunday morning.

3. Individuals should exercise authority or be subject to authority according to the position they occupy within the bureaucracy. In a bureaucracy no one "owns" his or her position and the authority that comes with it. This is the basis of Weber's legal/rational authority type (Chapter 3), in which authority is clearly attached to positions and not to individuals. As we've seen, individuals very easily forget this as they commonly get caught up in their positions and come to identify with them.
4. Individuals should have specialized training for the particular tasks involved in their offices and should be appointed to those offices only on the basis of their technical qualifications. The specialized training is designed to provide for qualified bureaucratic officers. Appointment on any other basis (such as family relations or political connections) would make the bureaucracy less efficient.
5. There should be a separation between ownership of the bureaucracy (its property or profits, for example) and the offices within it. Bureaucratic officers should receive fixed salaries for the work they do and not have their decisions motivated by personal profit.

Weber's ideally efficient bureaucracy has some shortcomings even beyond frequent human unwillingness or inability to abide by it; indeed, Weber did not intend his ideal type to be a bureaucracy as it actually exists but as an extreme case. The most important shortcoming lies in the nature of the tasks performed by the bureaucracy. A bureaucratic organization is at its peak of efficiency when the tasks at hand are repetitive and do not require creative responses on a day-to-day basis. If specific tasks are assigned to specific offices whose occupants have specialized training, the introduction of new and different tasks acts as a monkey wrench in the workings of the organization. As we'll see shortly, bureaucratic structure often varies from Weber's ideal type in anticipation of such needs for flexibility.

Two semihumorous criticisms of bureaucracies attempt to explain why bureaucratic actions fall short of Weber's ideal conception. The Peter Principle states, "In a hierarchy every employee tends to rise to his level of incompetence" (Peter and Hull, 1969:25). The explanation of this principle is that an employee who does well at a particular level of the bureaucracy will receive a promotion when a vacancy opens up above. (Note how this violates Weber's rule concerning specialized training.) Individuals who don't do well, on the other hand, will not receive promotions but will not be fired. The logical result of this practice, say Peter and Hull, is that every employee will ultimately arrive at a position beyond his or her level of competence—the level of *in*competence—and will stay there forever, doing an inadequate job.

As a second criticism of bureaucracies, we encounter Parkinson's Law: "Work expands to fill the time available for its completion" (Parkinson, 1957). If carried out, Parkinson's Law leads to waste and inefficiency instead of the hoped-for efficiency of the bureaucracy. The source of this observation lies in the tendency of all bureaucracies to continue over time and to grow in size. It is not in the interests of bureaucrats either to terminate their activities or to reduce the size of their staffs. It is, in fact, in their interests to *increase* the size of their staffs, as that adds prestige to their positions. Whatever work there is to do must be expanded to fill the time of the current staff in order to justify a later increase. One way to fill this time is to increase the amount of paperwork—a noted characteristic of all bureaucracies.

Finally, at the individual level, we come to one of the most basic problems confronted by all bureaucracies: Individuals in the offices may choose not to follow the rational organization of the bureaucracy. Individual officers may ignore or circumvent rules, refuse to do the work in their job description (and then cover up that fact), or form alliances with other officers of the bureaucracy to expand their section at the expense of another (and perhaps vital) section. In short, individuals may choose not to comply with the rules or the goals of the bureaucracy.

Organizational Alienation and Compliance

Alienation, a concept popularized by Karl Marx, refers to an individual's inability to control the forces that affect his or her own life. The individual consequently experiences these forces as "alien." In the world of work (and formal organizations) alienation occurs when individual members of the organization, usually those at the bottom of the bureaucratic hierarchy, cease to feel any connection to the work they do. One result is that they may choose not to comply with the rules of the organization.

The hierarchy of authority that exists in any bureaucracy rests upon its members' acceptance of its legitimacy. Authority is differentiated from power by the willingness with which people take orders. Weber's notion of legal/rational authority (which exists in bureaucracies) depends on this sense of legitimacy. If individual workers come to feel alienated from the organization as a whole, they will lose this sense of legitimate authority.

The idea of worker compliance entered the discussions of American sociologists in the 1920s, largely as the result of a famous study of workers at the Western Electric plant in Hawthorne, Illinois (Roethlisberger and Dickson, 1964). The goal of the researchers was to find ways to increase worker productivity. Their findings were not at all what they expected. First, they separated two groups of workers into an experimental and a control group (see Chapter 2). In keeping with the rules of the formal experiment, they left the control group alone in one room and tried raising the level of lighting for the experimental group. The result? Productivity went up in *both* groups. After many more similar studies they came to the conclusion that the very fact of being studied (or the presence of the experimenters) was creating the differences in levels of productivity; unlike plants and single-celled animals, people know when they're being watched. (This effect of the social scientific investigator on the object of study has come to be called the *Hawthorne effect,* after this study.)

The Western Electric investigators were in for a few other surprises as well. They found, for example, that informal groups of workers conspired to hold down production so that assembly line rates would not be increased or piece-rates changed. In short, the Western Electric investigators concluded that worker productivity had a lot to do with the workers' attitudes about the work they were doing. This conclusion largely founded that perspective on formal organizations known as the *human relations school.*

Other students of formal organizations have criticized the human relations school on the grounds that it makes value judgments biased on the side of management; workers who comply are viewed as good, whereas those who don't are viewed as bad. A bureaucracy that is efficient and rational from management's point of view may result in worker layoffs. To workers, an efficient bureaucracy is one that maintains their jobs and may require an informal restriction of output.

David Mechanic (1962) continued this criticism of the human relations school in his study of the "lower participants" (or lower-level workers) in bureaucracies. Observing the differing perspective that lower participants have, he pointed out the kinds of control available to these positions for influencing the higher-ups. Secretaries, for example, can withhold administrative information from superordinates in an office situation or even slow down their work in order to change the way they are treated. Even prisoners have some control over guards. A guard who turns in too many rule infractions will appear not to be doing a good job as a guard. It is in the interests of guards, therefore, to exchange a few favors with prisoners in return for their general cooperation in not breaking too many rules. In short, lower participants can often control persons, information, or behavior to which those higher up require access. Bureaucracies often operate on just such a system of negotiation (see Strauss et al., 1964).

Although lower participants have some control over those above them in the authority hierarchy, there are factors that make them comply with that authority. Amitai Etzioni (1961) pointed out that, beyond the lower participant's belief in the "rightness" of the authority structure, he or she may be forced or induced with rewards to comply. If the lower participant believes in the authority hierarchy, the power of the formal organization is *normative;* that is, lower participants comply because they adhere to norms of compliance. Failing such norms, power can be *coercive;* that is, the lower participants are forced against their will to comply. Finally, organizations can be *utilitarian:* Lower participants may not love their work or their boss, but they may need the job and will comply to keep it. Coercive organizations include concentration camps, prisons, prisoner-of-war camps, and some mental institutions; utilitarian organizations include most unions, most occupations, most occupational organizations, and the peacetime military; normative organizations include religious organizations, colleges and universities, hospitals, some fraternal organizations, and some political organizations (Etzioni, 1961).

Etzioni gave some attention to the lower participant in his analysis of different formal organizations. A coercive organization, he argues, leads to alienation among the lower participants; prisoners may follow orders, but they certainly have no extra love for their guards or the warden. Utilitarian organizations produce calculating workers; if you comply only for the money, every act of compliance will be figured out carefully in terms of "what's in it for me." Workers are often more concerned with their job and income than they are with the financial health of their employer. Finally, normative organizations produce moral compliance; members of religious or extreme political organizations may act according to a strict moral code inherent in their organization. As with all social groups, individuals who value the norms highly will also have a high level of loyalty to the group.

Organizational Structure

Figure 6.2 illustrates schematically a typical bureaucratic hierarchy of authority. Different levels of the hierarchy represent different levels of authority, the boxes represent different offices, and the lines between the boxes follow the paths by which orders are given and received. Though most real bureaucracies would be much larger, consider the effect this structure would have

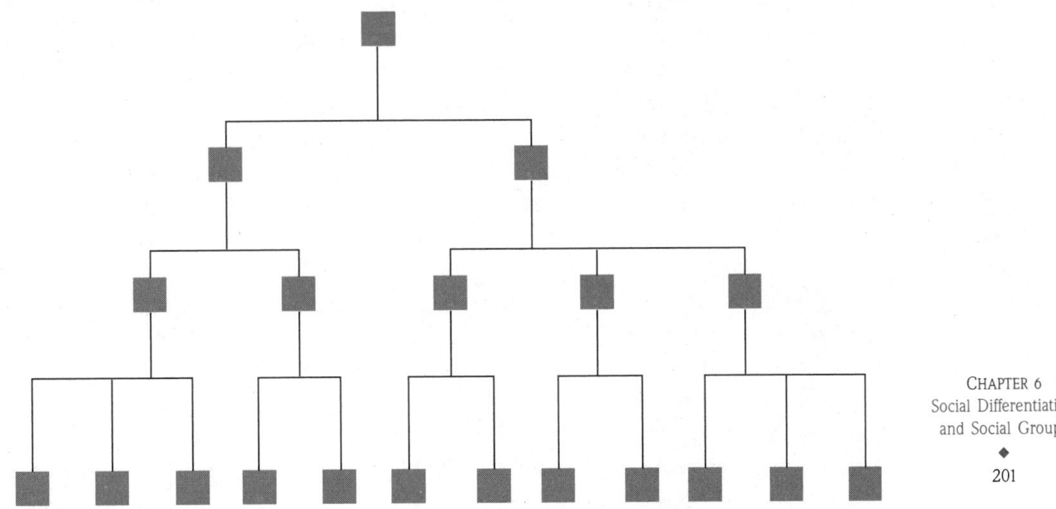

Figure 6.2 Bureaucratic hierarchy of authority.

on the people who filled the offices. The lower participants, for example, would find themselves divided into five sets, or work groups, and would probably have very little interaction across those groups. The middle-level officers would (perhaps) have to keep a close eye on their underlings while being careful to "look good" to the boss at the top. In addition, the middle-level officers might (a) not know each other, (b) not understand each other because of the different kinds of work they do, or (c) be locked in intense competition, each trying to prove that his or her arm of the organization is the most important.

Consider the differences you might find in an organizational hierarchy like that in Figure 6.3. This organization has a head officer, as Figure 6.2 had, but beyond that there is little similarity. All of the lower participants (if they can be called that) in Figure 6.3 are on an equal footing with each other. They may be doing totally different kinds of work, or, more likely, different versions or aspects of the same work. The fact that they cannot give orders to each other might encourage them to cooperate rather than to compete (although other factors might be equally

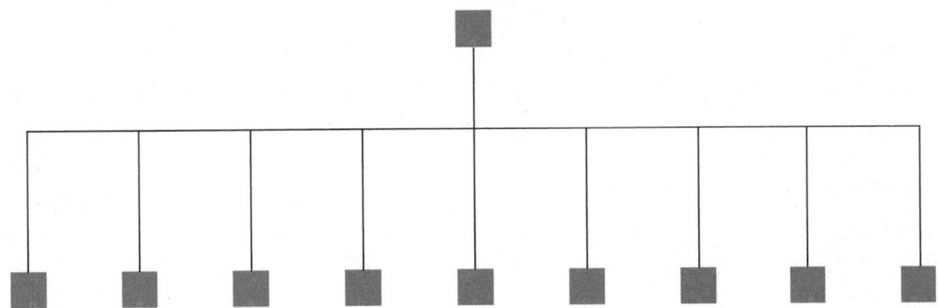

Figure 6.3 An organization of professionals.

important in determining this). Perhaps more important, the organization in Figure 6.3 would probably be less methodical but more flexible than the organization in Figure 6.2. The Figure 6.3 organization would be able to adapt easily to changing circumstances and different work because of its simple structure, whereas the organization in Figure 6.2 would require more time changing its structure to adapt. Figure 6.2 is a standard kind of bureaucratic structure used, for example, in routine office work; Figure 6.3 is the kind of organization found, for example, in a university department, where each professor is equal and under the authority of the chairman. Professors and office workers do different kinds of work; the organizations that hire them can help or hinder that work by their very structure.

The need for flexibility and creativity in a formal organization can perhaps best be seen in the role of the doctor in the modern hospital. The problem is made even more complicated by the fact that the hospital requires large amounts of routine work completed and, in addition, is often administered by an officer who lacks medical training; doctors may feel that they should not be given orders by an individual who doesn't understand their work (a feeling doctors share with a great many other occupations) (Perrow, 1986). One solution to this problem is to create a hospital organization that combines Figures 6.2 and 6.3. With such a combination business officials, nurses, janitors, cooks, and receptionists can be placed in a Figure 6.2 structure for their routine work, while doctors can be placed in a Figure 6.3 structure, existing parallel to and separate from the rest of the hospital staff. This allows doctors to have considerable control over their work. Meanwhile, routine tasks are carried out, and the hospital runs efficiently.

Organizations and Their Environments

Formal organizations do not exist in vacuums. They operate in an environment that includes natural forces, technology, people, and perhaps most important, other formal organizations. Organizations of American scientists who study volcanoes benefited from the 1980 eruption of Mt. St. Helens in the state of Washington because interest in volcanoes led to increased resources available for research. In the early twentieth century formal organizations that mass-produced automobiles had a major impact on other formal organizations that refined gasoline, paved roads, engineered bridges, and designed roadside restaurants. People can affect formal organizations through such basic things as their ages, their numbers, or their concentrations. Formal organizations are commonly located in cities where large numbers of people are concentrated. If men go off to war, women will have to fulfill different positions (as during the World War II movement of housewives to factories). Americans today are having fewer babies and living longer; that means that soon the majority of Americans will be quite old. Such a change places considerable pressure on the Social Security Administration. We will look at some of these changes in more detail in Chapter 9.

Probably the most significant environmental element for the formal organization on a day-to-day basis is the **organizational set**—the collection of other formal organizations with which the organization in question interacts (Evans, 1966). Philip Selznick (1949) studied the Tennessee Valley Authority (TVA) and the organizational environment within which it grew. The TVA was designed by the United States government in the 1930s to produce power, control flooding, build dams, and manufacture fertilizer. It was also supposed to preserve forests, help poor farmers, and create recreational areas. With all of these goals the potential for stepping on other organizational toes within the TVA's organizational set was tremendous. Some of the crushed toes belonged to the Department of Agriculture, the Farm Bureau Federation, local land-grant colleges and universities, agricultural extension workers and county agents, and local political and business leaders in general. Selznick describes the battles that took place as the TVA attempted to fulfill its mandate while other organizations attempted to stop it. Since one of the goals of the TVA was to involve local people in its activities, it not surprisingly accumulated large numbers of people from the stepped-on organizations who sought to turn the TVA around from the inside. As the TVA adjusted to its environment, it was required to give up many of its original programs.

As organizations are affected by their organizational set, so do they affect it. Formal business organizations, in particular, look out for their own interests and attempt to change their environment to further those interests when possible. Corporations give money to political candidates (sometimes illegally), hire lobbyists to promote their interests in Congress, engage in industrial espionage, bribe local and international officials, and attempt to control the markets for their goods (Perrow, 1986). Large modern governmental bureaucracies tend to become permanent figures on the social landscape as their functionaries work to maintain the official structure of the organization come what may. Labor unions—which once were small, radical bands of workers with socialistic goals—are now commonly much larger and more interested in maintaining a secure institutional place for their members. The growth of multinational corporations in recent years has made these possibilities for environment shaping more feasible and a little more frightening. Formal organizations that are larger than most countries and practically beyond the legal jurisdiction of any one country are in an excellent position to structure their corner of the world to make it as comfortable as possible for themselves.

SUMMARY

The coordination involved in any human society involves patterns of activities in which different people often fulfill extremely different functions. Doing different activities provides for different kinds of experiences and, consequently, makes people different from each other. This overall process is referred to as social differentiation. When differentiation occurs in a society, sociologists speak of the differentiated parts as social categories; individuals find themselves categorized according to their specific characteristics that make up the basis for the differentiation. Since being similarly categorized provides for similar experiences, people in the same social category are often much like each other and/or have similar interests; these points in common often lead them to form social groups.

Both the importance and the power of social groups become apparent through studying boundary maintenance and social control. Through the unlimited number of social interactions that produce boundary maintenance, group members remind one another about the distinction between group members and nonmembers. Social control becomes apparent through the need many group members have to conform to group standards, even at considerable personal cost so as to not jeopardize their membership. This attachment to the group becomes stronger whenever the group is threatened from the outside.

While any human characteristic could conceivably become the basis for social differentiation, each society contains only a few categories that its members think significant. In the United States the major social categories are formed around social differentiation of sex, age, social class, social status, race, and ethnicity. We examined these important social categories in terms of (1) how American society creates them as categories, and (2) how individuals respond to sharing these categories by forming social groups.

Formal organizations are social groups with a clear structure of roles and norms consciously designed for the achievement of particular goals. If the organization contains offices arranged in a hierarchy of authority, it may be described as following the principles of bureaucratic organization. Organizations typically face problems in obtaining the compliance of lower participants, creating a structure that is conducive to organizational goals, and defending themselves (or furthering their interests) in an environment of other potentially competitive formal organizations.

GLOSSARY

Ageism Prejudice toward the aged as well as acts of discrimination against them on the basis of age.

Alienation A worker's lack of interest in and identification with his or her job and a feeling of powerlessness in general over the conditions that affect his or her life.

Boundary maintenance Efforts by social group members to separate one group (typically their own) from another by focusing on differences in group members or typical group behavior.

Bureaucracy A formal organization characterized by a set of positions arranged in a hierarchy of authority and governed by specific procedural rules designed to accomplish specific tasks.

Closed group A social group that allows no expansion in membership.

Ethnic group A social group whose members share a common culture, claim to share a common culture, or are defined by others as sharing a common culture.

Formal organization (Formal group) A social group with a clear structure of roles and norms consciously designed for the achievement of particular goals. It is characterized by a division of labor and a hierarchical chain of command.

Horizontal group A social group whose members share a common social class.

Informal group A social group in which norms, roles, values, and goals are agreed to tacitly and are subject to some flexibility.

In-group A social group that an individual feels "at home" with or identifies with.

Involuntary group A social group to which members belong involuntarily (for example, the family you are born into, a group of prison inmates).

Open group A social group open to new members.

Organizational set The collection of formal organizations with which a particular formal organization interacts.

Out-group Any social group that a particular individual does not belong to or identify with.

Primary groups Social groups that are small and characterized by considerable face-to-face interaction and strong emotional ties (for example, a family or a group of close friends).

Racial group A collection of individuals who define themselves or are defined by others as sharing a particular and distinctive biological heritage.

Reference group A social group against whose standards a particular individual measures himself or herself and his or her accomplishments.

Secondary groups Social groups that are typically larger and less emotionally based than primary groups. The individual's tie to the secondary group is generally through a specific role played within the group.

Self-fulfilling prophecy A social occurrence in which the belief that something will happen helps make it happen.

Sexism Stereotyping on the basis of sex and prejudice and discrimination based on sex.

Social category A collection of individuals who have something (characteristics, attributes, abilities, etc.) in common.

Social class A collection of individuals whose activities or roles are similar in terms of the rewards they bring to their participants.

Social differentiation The process by which differences are created among individuals as a result of the different experiences they have as members of society. The differentiation occurs along the lines of socially important attributes such as (in American society) sex, race, income, occupation, and so on.

Social group A collection of people who (1) know each other (or know of each other), (2) agree that they share something (at least their groupness and the goals of the group), and (3) have continuing interactions with each other, resulting in patterned behavior.

Social status An individual's social position within the social group, particularly with respect to his or her prestige.

Social stratification The arrangement of different activities or roles into a hierarchy whereby activities ranked high are highly rewarded and activities ranked low are poorly rewarded. The rewards generally consist of money, prestige, and influence over others.

Vertical group A social group whose members occupy a variety of social classes.

Voluntary group A social group to which members belong voluntarily.

SUPPLEMENTARY READINGS

Barrow, Georgia M., and Patricia A. Smith *Aging, Ageism and Society.* St. Paul, Minn.: West, 1979.
A clear, concise picture of age separation in American society, covering such topics as the psychological experience of aging, age discrimination, the political organizations of the aged, and special medical problems of the aged.

Blau, Peter M., and W. Richard Scott *Formal Organizations: A Comparative Approach.* San Francisco: Chandler, 1962.

Although somewhat dated, this is a standard in the study of formal organizations. It emphasizes organizational structure and comparisons between organizations.

Collins, Randall *Sociology of Marriage and the Family: Gender, Love and Property.* Chicago: Nelson Hall, 1985.

A general introduction to the sociology of the family that employs a conflict perspective and focuses on the importance of sex roles in understanding the family. In particular, Collins emphasizes how sex roles learned in the family help reinforce male dominance in American society.

Etzioni, Amitai *A Comparative Analysis of Complex Organizations: On Power, Involvement and Their Correlates.* New York: Free Press, 1961.

Like Blau and Scott's, this book is a little old, but it is also one of the standards in the field of formal organizations. In particular, Etzioni focuses on the power relations in formal organizations and the abilities of various positions within organizations to get their orders carried out.

Foner, Nancy *Ages in Conflict.* New York: Columbia University Press, 1984.

Foner offers a view of age cohorts in the United States, emphasizing the inequality among them as viewed through a conflict perspective.

Kaufman, Michael *Beyond Patriarchy: Essays by Men on Pleasure, Power and Change.* New York: Oxford University Press, 1987.

Essays on a variety of topics relating to sex differences and sex roles, including biology, homosexuality, changing sex roles, and images of sex roles as portrayed in the media.

Kephart, William *Extraordinary Groups: The Sociology of Unconventional Life-Styles* (3rd ed.). New York: St. Martin's Press, 1987.

A collection of essays on such groups as the Amish, gypsies, the Shakers, Mormons, and others who have formed clearly distinct subcultures within American society.

Luhman, Reid, and Stuart Gilman *Race and Ethnic Relations: The Social and Political Experience of Minority Groups.* Belmont, Calif.: Wadsworth, 1980.

This book focuses on racial and ethnic groups in the United States, with a particular emphasis on the ways social and political occurrences encourage group formation along the bases of race and ethnicity.

Nielsen, Joyce McCarl *Sex in Society: Perspectives on Stratification.* Belmont, Calif.: Wadsworth, 1978.

Nielsen provides a clear picture of sex discrimination in the United States and ties it to existing prejudices and stereotypes against women.

Perrow, Charles *Complex Organizations: A Critical Essay* (3rd ed.). New York: Random House, 1986.

Perrow summarizes the major theoretical perspectives used in the field of complex organizations, calling attention to both their strengths and shortcomings.

Podhoretz, Norman *Making It.* New York: Random House, 1967.

A fascinating semiautobiography of Podhoretz, the editor of Commentary magazine. He grew up in a poor Jewish neighborhood in New York City and moved from "rags to riches" with the help of an aggressive teacher, some well-placed scholarships, and a lot of hard work.

Tuchman, Gaye, Arlene Kaplan Daniels, and James Benét, eds. *Hearth and Home: Images of Women in the Mass Media.* New York: Oxford University Press, 1978.

A look at the world of stereotypes directed against women through the mass media. Contains separate sections on the role of TV, the nature of women's magazines, newspapers (especially their "women's sections"), and the effect of TV on children.

A Dirge for Social Climbers

PAUL FUSSELL

Social class is an important social category, marked by degrees of wealth, prestige, and influence over others. Your social class is one of the most important determinants of your life. But what makes one social class truly different from the next, and, more important, how do individuals experience the different lifestyles that characterize social class differences? Paul Fussell offers his answers to these questions in the following essay.

If the dirty little secret used to be sex, it is now social class. No subject today is more likely to offend. Thirty years ago Dr. Kinsey generated considerable alarm by disclosing that 25 percent of the male population has enjoyed at least one homosexual orgasm. A similar alarm can be occasioned now by asserting that despite the much-discussed mechanisms of social mobility and the constant redistribution of income in this country, it is virtually impossible to break out of the social class in which one has been nurtured. Bad news for the ambitious as well as for the bogus, but there it is.

Defining class is difficult, as sociologists and anthropologists have learned. The more data we feed into the machines, the less likely it is that significant formulations will emerge. What follows here is not based on interviews, questionnaires, or any kind of scientific technique but on perhaps a more trustworthy method—observation. Theory may inform us that there are three classes in this country: high, middle, and low. Observation will tell us that there are at least 10, which I would designate and arrange like this:

Top Out-of-Sight
Upper
Upper Middle
Middle

High Proletarian
Mid-Proletarian
Low Proletarian

Destitute
Bottom Out-of-Sight

In addition, there is a floating class with no precise location in this hierarchy. We can call it Class X. It consists of well-to-do hippies, "artists," "writers" (most of them write nothing), floating bohemians, politicians out of office, disgraced athletic coaches, residers abroad, rock stars, "celebrities," and the shrewder sorts of spies.

The quasi-official division of the population into three economic classes called high-, middle-, and low-income groups misses the point, because as a class indicator the source of money is almost as important as the amount. Key distinctions at both the top and the bottom of the class hierarchy arise less from degree of affluence than from the people or institutions to whom one is beholden for support. For example, the main thing distinguishing the three top classes from one another is the amount of money inherited in relation to the amount currently earned. The Top Out-of-Sight class (Rockefellers, du Ponts, Mellons, Fords, Whitneys) lives entirely on inherited capital. There, money is like the hats of the Boston ladies who, asked where they get them, answer, "Oh, we *have* our hats." No one whose ample money has come from his own work, like film stars, can be a member of the Top Out-of-Sights, even if the size of his current income and the extravagance of his expenditure permit him temporary social access to it.

© 1980 The New Republic, Inc. Reprinted by permission of *The New Republic*.

Since extremes meet, it is not surprising to find the very lowest class, Bottom Out-of-Sight, similar to the highest in one crucial respect: it is given its money. It is kept sort of afloat by either the welfare machinery or the prison system. Members of the Top Out-of-Sight class sometimes earn money, as directors or board members of philanthropic or even profitable enterprises, but the amount earned is insignificant in relation to the amount already possessed. Membership in the Top Out-of-Sight class depends on the ability to flourish without working at all, and this is what unites the classes at the top and the bottom of the scale. This also is what distinguishes members of the Upper class from their superiors in Top Out-of-Sight. The Upper class lives on both inherited money and a salary from their attractive, usually slight, work, without which, even if it could survive, or even flourish, it would feel bored and a little ashamed. The next class down, the Upper Middle, may possess virtually as much as the two above it. The difference is that the Upper Middle class has earned most of it, in law, medicine, or the more honorific sorts of trade. The Upper Middles are afflicted with a bourgeois sense of shame, a conviction that to live on the earnings of others, even forebears, is not entirely nice.

The Out-of-Sight classes at top and bottom have something else in common: they are literally all but invisible. The facades of Top Out-of-Sight houses never are seen from the street, and such residences (like Rockefeller's upstate New York premises) often are hidden away deep in the hills, safe from envy with its inseparable attendants, confiscatory taxation and expropriation, or at least disapproval. The Bottom Out-of-Sight class is equally invisible. When not hidden away in institutions, monasteries, lamaseries, nunneries, or communes, it is hiding from creditors, deceived bail-bondsmen, and merchants intent on repossessing cars and furniture. When you see a house with a would-be impressive facade addressing the street, you know it is occupied by a mere member of the Upper or the Upper Middle class. The White House is an example. Its residents, even on those occasions when they are Kennedys, never can be classified as Top Out-of-Sight; they are only Upper class. Temporary residence in the White House, just because it presents itself so conspicuously to the street, usually constitutes a comedown for some of its occupants. It is a hopelessly Upper- or Upper-Middle-class place.

Another shared feature of the Top and Bottom Out-of-Sight classes is their anxiety to keep their names out of the papers. This too suggests that socially the president is always rather vulgar. All the classes in between lust for personal publicity; this, almost as much as income, distinguishes them from their top and bottom neighbors. The High and Mid-Prole classes can be recognized by their pride in advertising their physical presence, a way of saying, "Look! We pay our bills and have a place in the community." Thus hypertrophied house numbers, or house numbers written "Two Hundred Five" instead of 205, or flamboyant house or family names blazoned on facades, like "The Willows" or "The Polnickis." If you go behind the facade into the house itself, you will find the kind of wood there an instant class indicator. The top three classes invariably go in for hardwoods for doors and paneling; the Middle and High-Prole classes, pine, either plain or "knotty." The knotty-pine "den" is an absolute stigma of the Middle class, one that never can be overcome or disguised by temporarily affected higher usages.

Facade study is a badly neglected anthropological field. As we work down from the (largely white) bank-like facades of the Upper and Upper Middle classes, we find such Middle and Prole conventions as these, which I rank in order of social status:

Middle

1. A potted tree on either side of the front door.
2. A large rectangular picture-window in a split-level "ranch" house, displaying a lamp table between two side drapes. The cellophane on the lampshade must be unviolated.
3. Two chairs, usually metal, disposed on the front porch as "a conversation group," in dramatic disregard for the traffic thundering past.

High-Prole

4. Religious shrines in the garden, which, if small and understated, are slightly higher class than

Mid-Prole

5. Plastic gnomes and flamingos, and blue or lavender shiny spheres supported by fluted cast-concrete pedestals.

Low-Prole

6. Defunct truck tires painted white and enclosing flower beds. (Auto tires are a grade higher.)
7. Flower-bed designs worked in dead light bulbs or the butts of beer bottles.

The Destitute have no facades to decorate, and of course the Bottom Out-of-Sights, being invisible, have none either, although both these classes can occasionally help others decorate theirs—painting tires white on an hourly basis, for example, or even watering and fertilizing the potted trees of the Middle Class. Class X also does not decorate its facades, hoping to stay loose and unidentifiable, ready to relocate at the slightest sign that its cover has been penetrated.

As we move down the scale, income of course decreases, but income is less important to class than other seldom-invoked measurements: the degree to which one's work is supervised by an omnipresent immediate superior, for example. The more free from supervision, the higher the class, which is why a dentist ranks higher than a mechanic working under a foreman in a large auto shop, even if the mechanic makes considerably more money than the dentist. The two trades may be thought equally dirty: it is the dentist's freedom from supervision that confers class upon him. Likewise, a high school teacher obliged to file weekly "lesson plans" with a principal or "curriculum coordinator" thereby occupies a class position lower than a tenured professor, who reports to no one, even though the high school teacher may be richer, smarter, and nicer. It is largely for this reason that even the highest members of the naval and military services lack high social status.

Class is thus defined less by bare income than by constraints and insecurities. It is defined also by habits and attitudes. Take television watching. The Top Out-of-Sight class doesn't watch at all. It owns the companies and pays others to monitor the thing. It is also entirely devoid of intellectual or even emotional curiosity. The Upper class watches, but prefers camp offerings, like the films of Jean Harlow or Jon Hall. The Upper-Middle class regards TV as vulgar except for the high-minded emissions of the Public Broadcasting System, which it watches avidly. Upper-Middles make a point of forbidding children to watch more than an hour a day and worry a lot about violence in society and sugar in cereal. The Middle class watches, preferring the nicer kinds of non-body-contact sports, like tennis or acrobatics or figure skating. With High, Mid-, and Low Proles we find heavy viewing of the soaps in the afternoon and rugged body-contact sports (football, hockey, boxing) in the evening and on weekends. The lower one is located in the Prole classes, the more likely one is to watch "Bowling for Dollars." Destitutes usually "own" about three color sets, and the problem is what three programs to watch at once. Bottom Out-of-Sights have no choice at all, the decisions being made for them by institutional personnel.

The time at which the evening meal is consumed defines class as well as anything. Bottom Out-of-Sights eat dinner at 5:30, for the Prole staff on which they depend must clean up and be out roller-skating or bowling early in the evening, and so eats at 6:00 or 6:30. The Middles eat at 7:00, the Upper Middles at 7:30, or, if very ambitious, at 8:00. The Uppers and Top Out-of-Sights dine at 8:30 or 9:00 or even 9:30, after nightly protracted "cocktail" sessions lasting, usually, at least an hour and a half.

Similarly, the physical appearance of the various classes defines them fairly accurately. Among the top four classes thin is good, and the bottom two classes appear to ape this usage, although down there thin is seldom a matter of choice. It is the three Prole classes that tend to fat, partly as a result of convenience foods and beer. These are the classes too where anxiety about slipping down a rung generates nervous overeating, resulting in a fat that can be rationalized as advertising the security of steady wages and the consequent ability to "eat out" often. A recent ad for a diet book aimed at Proles stigmatizes a number of erroneous assumptions about body weight, proclaiming with some inelegance that "They're all a crock." Among such vulgar errors is the proposition that "All Social Classes Are Equally Overweight." This the ad rejects by saying, quite accurately:

> Your weight is an advertisement of your social standing. A century ago, corpulence was a sign of success. But no more. Today it is the badge of the lower-middle-class, where obesity is *four times* more prevalent than it is among the upper-middle and middle classes.

It is not just four times more prevalent. It is at least four times more visible, as any observer can testify who has witnessed Prole women perambulating shopping malls in their brightly colored tight jersey trousers. Not just obesity but the flaunting of obesity is the Prole sign.

Another physical feature with powerful class meaning is the wearing of plaster casts on legs and ankles by members of the top three classes. These casts, a sort of white badge of honor, betoken stylish mishaps with costly toys like horses, skis, snowmobiles, and mopeds. They signify a high level of conspicious waste in a social world where the question of missed work days does not apply. But on the matter of clothes, the Top Out-of-Sight is different from both Upper and Upper-Middle classes. Top Out-of-Sight prefers to appear in new clothes, whereas the class just below it affects old clothes. Like Top Out-of-Sight, all three Prole classes make much of new garments. The question does not arise in the same form with Destitutes and Bottom Out-of-Sights. They wear used clothes from the thrift shop or the prison supply-room.

"Language most shows a man," writes Ben Jonson. "Speak, that I may see thee." As all acute conservatives like Jonson know, dictional behavior is a powerful signal of a firm class line. Nancy Mitford so indicated in her hilarious essay of 1955, "The English Aristocracy," based in part on Professor Alan S. C. Ross's more sober study "Linguistic Class-Indicators in Present-Day English." Both Mitford and Ross are interested in only one class demarcation, the one dividing the Upper class (or "U," in their shorthand) from all below it ("non-U"). Their main finding is that euphemism and genteelism are non-U. People who are socially secure risk nothing by calling a spade a spade, and indicate their top-dog status by doing so as frequently as possible. The U-word is "rich," the non-U word "wealthy." What U-speakers call "false teeth" non-U speakers call "dentures."

In America the situation is similar, although more classes are distinguishable here than in England. Here U-speech characterizes some Top Out-of-Sights, Uppers, Upper-Middles, and class Xs. All below is a wasteland of genteelism and jargon, sad evidence of the upward social scramble which inevitably fails.

One especially American linguistic class line divides those who persist in honoring the 19th-century convention that advertising, if not commerce itself, is reprehensible, and those proud to identify themselves as consumers, happy when they can imagine themselves as happy members of the system by responding to advertisements. For U-persons a word's success in advertising is a compelling reason never to use it. But possessing no other source of idiom, the subordinate classes are pleased to appropriate the language of advertising for personal use, dropping brand-names all the time and saying things like "They have some lovely fashions at that store," where "fashions" means "clothes."

Those who employ the vacuous commercial "Have a nice day" and those who wouldn't think of saying it manifestly belong to different classes, and it is unlikely that those classes will ever merge. (One visiting Englishman of my acquaintance, a U-speaker if there ever was one, has devised the perfect U-response to "Have a nice day": "Thank you," he says, "but I have other plans.") The same ultimate divide separates the two classes which, when introduced, say respectively, "How do you do?" and "Pleased to meet you." There may be comity between those who say "prestigious" and those who don't, but it won't survive much strain. Members of these two classes can sit in adjoining seats on the plane and get along fine (although there's a further division between those who talk to their neighbors in elevators and planes and those who don't), but once the plane has emptied, they will go toward different destinations. The pretense that either person can feel really comfortable in the presence of the other is essential to the presiding American fiction.

Some people invite constant class trouble because they believe the official American publicity about these matters. The official theory, which experience is constantly disproving, is that one can earn one's way out of one's original class. Richard Nixon's behavior indicates that this is not so. The sign of the Upper class to which he aspired is total psychological security and freedom, expressed in loose carriage, saying what one likes, and an entire imperviousness to what others think. Nixon's vast income from law and politics—the San Clemente property aped the style of the Upper but not the Top Out-of-Sight class, for everyone knew where it was—could not alleviate his original awkwardness and meanness of soul or his nervousness about the impression he was making.

What, finally, marks the higher classes? Primarily a desire for privacy, if not invisibility, and a powerful instinct for freedom. It is this instinct for freedom that may persuade us that inquiring into the American class system and some of its signals is an enterprise not entirely adventitious and silly and merely amusing. Perhaps, after all, the whole thing has something to do with ethics and aesthetics. Perhaps a term like "gentleman" still retains some meanings that are not just sartorial and mannerly. Freedom and grace: it would be nice to believe those words still mean something, and it would be interesting if the class system should turn out to be a way of paying those concepts a due respect.

Discussion Questions

1. Fussell describes major differences in lifestyle among people who occupy different social classes in the United States. Why would such differences exist? Do you think his descriptions are accurate? Why or why not?
2. What are members of different classes saying (or trying to say) about themselves through the way they live and the styles they follow?
3. How many social classes are there in the United States? Compare Fussell's ten divisions with others described in this chapter.

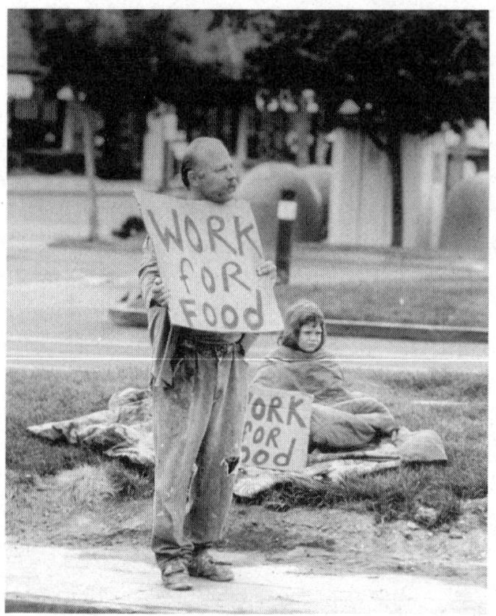

CHAPTER 7 SOCIAL STRATIFICATION: SOCIAL DOMINANCE AND SUBORDINATION

The supposedly unsinkable British ocean liner *Titanic* sank rapidly after colliding with an iceberg in 1912. Like most luxury liners, the *Titanic* was divided into different "classes" in which the passengers could purchase the amount of luxury they wanted in their accommodations. Of the female deaths 3 percent were first-class passengers, 16 percent were second-class passengers, and 45 percent were third-class passengers. Even though women and children were supposed to be first into the lifeboats, more third-class women perished than first-class men (Lord, 1955). Consumers are frequently lectured that "you get what you pay for"; the statistics on *Titanic* survivors are just one case in point. Even survival can be purchased.

The separation of people into rich and poor through a system of social stratification permeates every aspect of life in a modern society such as the United States. It is one of the most distinctive features of such societies; it is also one of the most important features in the everyday lives of their members, including those who are sociologists. Sociologists have very few thoughts that don't wander into the realm of social class differences sooner or later. That subject has run as a common thread throughout every chapter of this book so far. This chapter will pause to hold it down for examination.

Let us recall once again that **social stratification** refers to the arrangement of different activities of a society into a hierarchy whereby activities ranked high are highly rewarded and activities ranked low are poorly rewarded. Individual people fulfill those activities and receive those rewards (or lack of rewards) as long as they occupy the position. In a manner of speaking social stratification is a vast game board (not unlike Monopoly) on which we are forced to play. Corporation executives are more important than janitors, just as Boardwalk is more important than Baltic Avenue; the game board is there, and you must do what you can according to the rules of the game. If you don't happen to land in the executive's position (or on Boardwalk), you will have to take orders from those who do.

Our system of social stratification has almost the impact on our lives that the game board and rules of Monopoly have on Monopoly players, constantly offering us reminders of our place in it and coordinating our behavior. This chapter will examine the "game board" of social stratification, paying particular attention to the effects of the game on the players. We will look first at the basic features of the social stratification hierarchy, emphasizing the arrangements of the positions and the degree to which it is possible for individuals to move among them. Second, we will examine some of the theories offered by sociologists that attempt to explain why social stratification exists and who its beneficiaries are. Finally, we will take a close look at social class differences as they exist today in the United States; as with the sinking of the *Titanic* in 1912, it is still true that being upper class adds years to your life. The sociological outlook on social stratification will allow you to place yourself within this competitive situation and show you some of the forces beyond your control that affect your life chances.

BASIC FEATURES OF SOCIAL STRATIFICATION

The separation of rich and poor in the United States is immediately obvious to any observer of society who opens either eye slightly. The United States does not have the extreme social class divisions found in some countries, yet the differences in living conditions between rich and poor in our country are nevertheless dramatic. However, many fine lines separate the positions in the hierarchy, making it difficult to tell just which social classes contain which positions. "Rewards" also come in many different packages: Money or property is clearly a reward, but so is the respect you receive from others. Which is more important? If you give up your job as a traveling salesperson to become a college teacher, you will probably make less money but receive more respect. Are you now in a different social class or the same one? This section of the chapter will introduce the basic concepts sociologists use to answer these and other confusing questions about social stratification. By the end of this section we will at least be able to organize our confusion.

Class, Status, and Power

The rewards our positions bring us in a social stratification hierarchy are generally separated by sociologists into economic rewards (your **social class**), social rewards (your **social status** or prestige), and political rewards (**social power**, or your ability to influence the behavior of others). Different positions and activities in a society can be ranked in terms of how much of each kind of reward they produce for their occupants. Positions at the very top of the hierarchy will by definition bring their occupants large amounts of money, prestige, and influence over others; positions at the very bottom will also by definition bring their occupants poverty, ridicule, and the privilege of taking orders. The positions in the middle of the hierarchy (which most of us occupy) will bring their occupants varying amounts of each kind of reward. Traveling salespeople, for example, rank a little higher economically but proportionately lower socially than college teachers.

Class, status, and power are three dimensions of social stratification—or parallel hierarchies within the overall hierarchy—along which any given position might be ranked. There is a good deal of dispute in sociology, however, as to how these dimensions should be measured. There is also dispute over how independent the dimensions are. Are they three separate aspects of social stratification, or are they just three different ways of measuring the same thing? Money, after all, usually generates respect and certainly can be used to purchase influence over others. In looking more closely at different positions on this question, we will discover that these concepts change meaning depending on the side of the dispute being argued.

Karl Marx: A Theory of Social Class Karl Marx was one of the first sociologists to single out social stratification as a fundamental and important feature of human society; in fact, to Marx it was the most important feature. Marx saw the forms of coordination in any society as reflections of the economic arrangements employed in that society. Social stratification, as a form of coordination, is the most direct reflection of the economy since it organizes people by their economic roles (or their social class).

Marx studied class within the framework of **capitalism**, an economic system in which most of the wealth is the private property of individuals. This wealth (or *capital*) can be invested and can be increased through *profit*, the difference between the cost of production of a marketable item and what it can be sold for. The most distinctive feature of capitalism for Marx was that it is a system in which wealth can accumulate in a few hands—in short, a system that produces and maintains social inequality (see Marx, 1956, 1976).

Karl Marx (1818-1883). Marx is best remembered for his ideas on revolution, but most of his time was spent analyzing economic relations in industrial society. His views on social stratification and social class provided many insights into the power relationships that govern social order.

Marx defined social class in terms of the degree of inequality that exists within the economic system. Capitalist societies contain business enterprises that produce and distribute goods and services (the *means of production and distribution,* in Marx's terms). Individuals either own these enterprises or work for those who do. Those who own the enterprises are the **bourgeoisie** (or ruling class), while those who work for them are the **proletariat** (or working class).

Marx's concept of social class was clearly an economic concept. He was aware of differences in prestige and power within societies, but he believed these differences to be determined by social class. In his view, the control of capital by the employer leads directly to power over the worker. Marx thought that social class also determines prestige, although in a less direct manner. The ruling class of a capitalist society not only controls the economy but also controls the government, the arts, the sciences, religion, philosophy, education, and practically every other aspect of social life. Those in the ruling class are in a position to define themselves as important and convince others (the proletariat) to accept that social definition. (We've already seen one example of this idea in the study of deviance: Those in authority in a society are in a position to define deviance and convince others to accept their definition.) The proletariat is trained to accept the status quo under capitalism and to believe that those who rule *should* rule by virtue of their social superiority. If social status and social power are the direct results of social class, there is no need to study them as separate aspects of social stratification. Thus, according to Marx, once you understand social class, you will understand the other two as well.

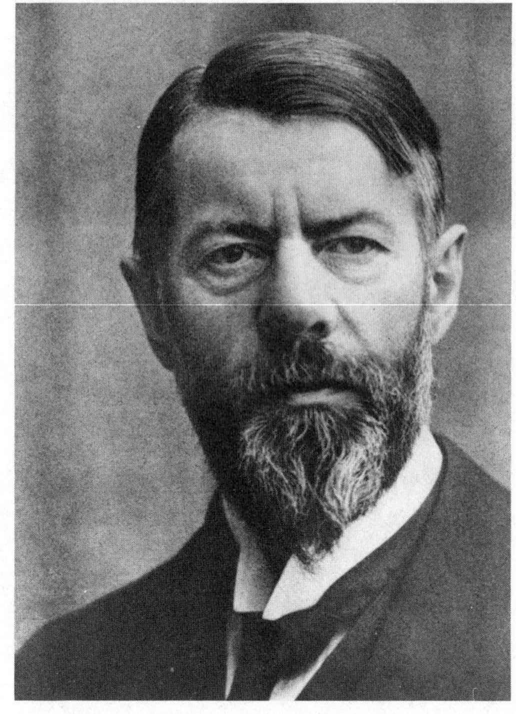

Max Weber (1864-1920). Weber's wide-ranging interests in sociology included a particular focus on social stratification. In opposition to Marx's focus on social stratification, Weber suggested a three-dimensional approach in which an individual's social position consists of social class, social status, and political influence.

Max Weber: Class, Status, and Party Max Weber (1946) was almost as interested in social stratification as Karl Marx was. Where Marx placed all his eggs in the economic basket, however, Weber took a more general approach. With his concepts of class, status, and party, Weber began the three-dimensional approach to social stratification that dominates American sociology today.

Like Marx, Weber felt that social class is the most important dimension of social stratification; unlike Marx, Weber did not see it as the only dimension. Whereas Marx thought that social status would automatically follow social class (either up or down), Weber suggested that status might have a life of its own. There are some wealthy people, he said, who do not command the respect in their communities that some of their less wealthy neighbors do. Although these two aspects of social coordination—the economic and social—are highly related and affect each other, they do not totally determine each other.

The dividing line Weber perceived between social class and status runs parallel to the line between the everyday norms of social exchange and the rich life of cultural values. The economy operates more or less rationally (as individuals figure their advantages and disadvantages), but culture operates according to its own logic. A successful individual in the world of economic give-and-take might not exemplify cultural standards of honor and therefore receive respect. Shared lifestyles, geography, ancestry, or a variety of other attributes can bind together those with property and those without. Weber suggested, in fact, that such points in common would be much more likely to attract people together into groups or communities than a common relation to wealth (social class). On the other hand, Weber admitted, two individuals with the same relation to wealth (two rich people, for instance) would be more likely to share common lifestyles, geography, or ancestry with each other than either would with a poorer person. Status can live a life of its own, but it also tends to vary along with social class. Weber's conception is less rigid than Marx's but not all that different.

Weber referred to social power in terms of political parties, using the term **party** to refer to political action or interest groups of any size in any social arena. In the United States this would include traditional political parties as well as special-interest political pressure groups such as the National Rifle Association (which opposes gun control), the Right to Life movement (which opposes abortion), and Amnesty International (which fights to protect civil liberties around the world and publicizes violations). The purpose of the political party is to concentrate power and direct it to represent the interests of members of the party. Who are the party's members? Most of the time they will share social class, social status, or both with each other; it is common, he says, for people with a common social class to have common political interests and to form a party to represent those interests. A labor union would be a case in point. However, says Weber, this is not always the case, which is the reason for discussing party and power separately from class. Parties are not always mere reflections of social class or of social status; people can come together for a variety of reasons to exert political pressure.

Socioeconomic Status In the 1930s Weber's notion of class, status, and party was borrowed and put to work by American sociological researchers who wanted to measure these dimensions in the lives of the people they studied. They came up with the measure of socioeconomic status.

Socioeconomic status (or SES as it is commonly abbreviated) is an average score assigned to an individual on the basis of (1) income level, (2) level of education, and (3) occupational prestige. Such a measure doesn't measure the dimension of social power too accurately, but it does include a measure of wealth (income) and social status (occupational prestige). Educational level usually is an index of both, since education often leads to better paying, more prestigious jobs and, in addition, by itself increases social status. We might note in passing that a measure such as SES is much farther away from Marx than Weber ever intended to be. Using income as a measure of social class, for instance, takes into account the amount but ignores the source of the income, which was for Marx of central importance.

Income and education are pretty straightforward attributes to measure, but how do you measure occupational prestige? The easiest way is to ask people to rank lists of occupations from those they most respect to those they least respect. If you ask enough people to do this, you can produce an average ranking that reflects a social consensus on occupational prestige (Davis and Smith, 1984). As Weber suggested, more than just occupational income produces occupational prestige. How else could college professors be ranked above dentists and plumbers (Merton, 1968)?

Status Inconsistency How do you average all the measures that come together to form an SES score? Does an individual who makes $40,000 a year with a third-grade education average out the same as an individual who makes $20,000 with two years of college? Once you accept the different dimensions of social stratification, it is possible to talk about an individual's consistency across all the dimensions (see Lenski, 1956). Sociologists call this *status consistency.*

Status inconsistency describes individuals who are *not* consistently high, medium, or low across *all* the dimensions of social stratification. A janitor with a Ph.D. would be status inconsistent, as would an impoverished dentist or a Nobel Prize winner with a grade-school education. The idea behind status inconsistency is that being different from most of the people with whom you associate would put a strain on you. If you were a janitor with a Ph.D., for example, the janitors you worked with wouldn't share your educational background and interests and the people who shared your educational background would not share your occupational experiences; you would be a marginal member of both groups. Greater degrees of status inconsistency can often lead to fewer opportunities for economic advancement (Lorber, 1984).

Many research studies have attempted to test hypotheses relating status inconsistency to a great variety of factors, including psychological stress (see Rossides, 1976). The results are inconclusive. Part of the problem is that many social circumstances can result in apparent status inconsistency, with very different attitudes and feelings among the individuals affected. Whatever its effects, however, status inconsistency is strongly related to industrial societies. A simple stratification hierarchy characteristic of agricultural societies is generally highly consistent where different dimensions of stratification develop and ultimately diverge from a single ranking system. But even the existence of these different dimensions would probably not produce status inconsistency if it were not possible for individuals to move up and down within them.

Social Mobility

Social mobility is the movement of groups or individuals within the ranking system of social stratification. Just as geographical mobility represents a change in physical space, social mobility represents a change in social "space," whereby you become a changed social creature in the eyes of other social group members (Abrahamson, Mizruchi, and Harnung, 1976). **Vertical social mobility** is mobility up or down the stratification hierarchy; to achieve it you must move from an activity or position at one social class level to an activity or position at another social class level. Going from "rags to riches," or, less dramatically, from office clerk to head of the accounting department, illustrates upward vertical social mobility. Going from "riches to rags" would be downward mobility. **Horizontal social mobility** is a change from one activity to another within the same social class. A clerk/typist who becomes a keypunch operator is moving horizontally, as is a drugstore clerk who gets a job as a waitress in a coffee shop. The vast majority of activity changes are of the horizontal variety; it is much easier to change jobs within one social class than to move upward in social class.

Vertical social mobility is the most important kind of social mobility for the study of social stratification. Horizontal mobility represents relatively minor changes in society ("You wash and I'll dry tonight for a change"), but the existence of vertical mobility suggests a stratification system in which the rulers and the ruled change places. This one-sided emphasis is so strong that many sociologists leave out the word *vertical* in their writings without fear of being misunderstood; unless otherwise specified, social mobility means vertical social mobility.

Vertical social mobility can be either intragenerational or intergenerational. **Intragenerational vertical social mobility** is a change in social class that occurs within the lifetime of one individual (or within one generation). If you start your occupational career as an office clerk and work your way up to the top of the company, your mobility is intragenerational.

Intergenerational vertical social mobility is a change in social class that occurs across generations. For example, your father might have worked a lifetime as a mail carrier, and you might have gone straight through law school to a position as a successful corporate lawyer. Within your experience no mobility has occurred, yet a definite change has occurred from one generation to the next; your social class is very different from your father's social class. As we will see in the final section of this chapter, both of these types of vertical social mobility are difficult to achieve.

Problems in Measuring Vertical Social Mobility Unfortunately, vertical social mobility is difficult to measure. One reason is that sociologists lack agreement as to just how many different social classes exist or exactly where the boundaries between them should be drawn. We will look at this dispute in more detail when we turn to the class structure of American society in the final section of this chapter, but consider the differences we've already seen between Marx and Weber. Marx states that there are two social classes, determined by their relation to capital. Weber isn't as specific, but it's clear he has a more general conception of relation to wealth. For Marx professional baseball players haven't changed classes even if they triple their income from one year to the next; for Weber (and for most American sociologists), such a change would be a clear-cut example of upward social mobility.

Measuring intragenerational vertical social mobility is difficult without knowing quite a bit about the individual cases being measured. Consider the following two examples:

1. Jim drops out of Harvard in his freshman year after a fight with his parents and frustrating experiences with school requirements. He works for two years as a construction worker doing unskilled work. Tiring of this, he returns to Harvard, finishes law school, and goes to work for a prestigious Wall Street firm.
2. Jeanne goes to work as an office clerk after receiving her high school diploma. Her supervisor notes the attention she pays to her work and is impressed. Jeanne makes some suggestions for making the office run more smoothly that turn out to work very well. She is promoted. After observing her new work environment and doing a little reading on business administration, she makes more suggestions, which successfully revolutionize the organizational structure of the business. She is soon a vice-president.

Are Jim and Jeanne equal? Obviously not, for Jeanne has worked much harder and started with much less. But on paper they both appear to be examples of dramatic upward intragenerational mobility.

How do you compare the occupations of parents and children? A child may take a job that didn't exist in the parent's generation, so how can you tell whether it represents a movement upward or downward? This problem becomes increasingly difficult when you look at overall occupational changes that have occurred in the United States over time. Most significantly, every year sees fewer unskilled and manual jobs and greater numbers of white-collar office and service occupations; the changes that occur in industry and technology make such occupational changes necessary. A white-collar offspring of a blue-collar worker would normally be considered intergenerational upward mobility, but when you consider the overall shift in occupations, the change does not appear so great. A similar problem has occurred in measuring educational levels: Each generation goes to school longer than the one before, so the younger you are, the more likely you are to have a higher level of education. Have you moved up from your parents, or have you simply flowed with the currents of your generation? Your college degree will probably get you the same level job your parents achieved with a high school diploma. Degrees inflate right along with dollars.

In short, vertical social mobility is difficult to measure, much less explain. Nevertheless, sociologists have tried their best. We'll look at some of those attempts in the final section of this chapter.

Class and Caste Societies: Social Mobility and Group Formation Class societies and caste societies are largely products of the sociologist's imagination (or "ideal types," such as Weber's conception of the bureaucracy described in Chapter 6). **A class society** is a society that permits wide-scale vertical social mobility; positions in the social stratification hierarchy are open to all and achieved through an open competition process. A **caste society** is based entirely on ascribed status and permits no vertical social mobility at all; social positions are inherited as a right of birth. Neither of these two descriptions provides a very good fit for any real society, although it's possible to find fair approximations of caste societies in the real world. The term *caste,* which refers to a totally closed social level, comes to us from India, where the population used to be rigidly separated into specific groups of social roles; the Brahmin caste was at the top of the hierarchy and the "untouchables" were at the bottom, with no possibility of change. The American system of slavery came close to a caste system as children born to a slave mother were automatically slaves. A similar caste system operates in South Africa today.

True class societies are much harder to find in the real world. Modern industrial societies such as the United States have just about as much vertical social mobility as you'll find anywhere, yet access to positions is clearly limited. Even though many positions (or jobs) are technically open to anyone, it still often helps to "know somebody." Less obvious but perhaps more important advantages come as an accident of your birth. Your parents automatically pass on to you certain skills, abilities, resources, and knowledge. If your parents are upper class, that "inheritance" will get you admission to good schools, the abilities and skills to get through those schools, the confidence to get ahead, the social skills for leaving a good impression on employers at interviews, and a great many other advantages too numerous to mention. If your parents are lower class, you will receive an "inheritance" of equal size but you will find its content less useful for attacking dominant American institutions and becoming successful; those institutions are largely under the control of the upper classes. To form a true class society, you would have to remove children from their parents at birth, give them all an equal background at a state-run orphanage, and then fill jobs through a competition that would be truly open.

Sociologists use the concepts of class and caste in order to better understand the range of vertical social mobility that occurs between the two extremes. Different societies can be placed at different points between the extremes and compared accordingly. The same society can also change location between these extremes over time, as with the emancipation of slaves in the United States. Class and caste societies provide some insight into the ways people form social groups.

Consider first a caste society. How would such a stratification system affect the individual? First of all, the individual would become extremely aware of his or her caste. Most individuals would probably accept the caste system as a basic and unchangeable fact of existence since they would have no experience with alternatives. Members of the bottom castes might feel a lot of hatred and envy of the castes above, but they probably wouldn't try to do much about it; the possibility of change might not even occur to them since they had never witnessed it. This description fits the American system of slavery fairly well, even though those slaves born in Africa had a clear picture of an alternative society. Slaves were extremely aware of the color line (as are most Americans still today), but they only rarely attempted to do much about it. Slave revolts were very unusual, as most slaves apparently felt there was little hope for success. Such a response is characteristic of a caste system.

An ideal class society would produce very different kinds of individual thoughts and behavior. The rapidity with which individuals moved into and out of social positions would prevent groups of individuals from becoming aware of a shared situation, and, unlike the caste system, there would not be strong senses of group identity. On the other hand, members of a class society would be engaged in constant acts of individual competition. The openness of the stratification system would encourage individuals to do something about their current positions but would discourage them from acting as groups. Your best shot at getting ahead would come from working alone. It's harder to find a real-world illustration of this case, but a classroom of students graded on the curve provides a rough approximation. A "grading curve" means that certain percentages of the class will receive certain grades, *regardless of the quality of the work they do.* Their work must only be equal in quality to the best work in the class for them to receive high grades; if that best work is of poor quality, then poor quality will receive top grades. This system is designed to encourage individual competition. What would you do if you found the answer sheet to a final examination in a class graded on the curve? Assuming you would be unscrupulous enough to use it at all, the most rational course would be to share the answers with no one; the lower the other grades, the better yours will look by comparison. You might want to share the answers with a few close friends (thereby competing as a group), but consider that the more people you help, the worse your grade will be by comparison. If you share the answers with the entire class, it will help you not at all. A class system, like a grading curve, encourages individual competition but discourages people from competing in groups.

The United States falls somewhere between a caste system and a class system. These extreme ideal types help us understand the kinds of competition and group formation that come from such a stratification system. Because vertical mobility is possible to some extent in the United States, many Americans are competitive; where there is great potential for vertical mobility, they are even competitive as individuals. But American society is not all that open. As we've seen, the children of the upper classes enter the competition with advantages that children of the lower classes don't have. This inequality tends to keep the same families at the top or the bottom, a castelike situation that makes individuals aware of others who share the boat with them and leads to strong feelings of group identity (see Chapter 6). When you combine the competition characteristic of mobility with the group formation characteristic of a caste system, you find the compromise characteristic of American society—group competition.

Americans have the idea and see the possibility of advancement, but they also see the hurdles set in front of their particular group. The labor union is a typical response to such a situation as individuals seek to advance by improving the overall status of the group to which they belong.

If social stratification were in fact turned into a board game like Monopoly, social mobility would be one of the strategies you could use to change the play of the game. When we look later at the effects of social class membership on the individual, this variable will become extremely important.

WHY STRATIFICATION AND WHO BENEFITS? OPPOSING THEORIES

Not all human societies are stratified, but most of them are. Some very small societies don't even have an organized division of labor, and since social stratification organizes labor activities into a hierarchy, the division of labor must come first. In attempts to explain why stratification exists, these facts are hard to interpret. Apparently, social stratification is not absolutely essential to all human societies since some of them get along quite well without it. On the other hand, the vast majority of human societies employ some kind of social stratification hierarchy in their social organization; most human societies, in short, thrive on inequality. Stratification thus appears essential for all practical purposes.

Why does social stratification exist in so many human societies? Does it benefit all members of the society or just those who occupy the top rungs? Sociologists are divided in the way they answer these questions. The structural-functionalist, or "order," theorists believe that social stratification is necessary for the existence of human society and, for that reason, benefits all members of society. The conflict theorists, on the other hand, argue that social stratification is an organized system of thievery in which one segment of the population benefits at the expense of another. While we looked at both of these perspectives in Chapter 2, this section will compare these two opposing perspectives on social stratification.

Structural-Functionalism: The Order Theorists

Many general theories of society are derived from the school of structural-functionalism; it was a particularly popular perspective among American sociologists between the 1930s and 1950s, when it was largely unchallenged. During that period structural-functionalism was specifically applied to the question of social stratification. If all parts of society have developed because they fulfill some specific function and are important for the functioning of the whole, then mustn't social stratification be necessary and have a specific function? Two American sociologists, Kingsley Davis and Wilbert Moore, set out to answer that question.

According to Davis and Moore (1945), social stratification is necessary for getting the right people into the right jobs. Since parts of society fulfill different functions, it stands to reason that different jobs fulfill different functions. It also stands to reason that some jobs must fulfill more important functions than others, just as your heart is more vital than your gallbladder and both are more useful than your appendix. Davis and Moore suggested that jobs that fulfill the most important functions for society are likely to be highly regarded in the social stratification hierarchy. Furthermore, since they are the most important, it is important that they be filled by competent members of society. One way to ensure that competence is to provide more rewards for these more necessary jobs; these rewards encourage the most competent members of society to seek them. These people would be willing to undergo whatever training might be necessary for the job since the future rewards will make up for whatever deprivations they experience in the present.

Thus, for Davis and Moore, stratification exists for two basic reasons. First, some positions in society are more important than others. Second, there may be a scarcity of personnel to fill these important positions (since most important positions require a lot of training). Simpson (1956) raised the question of garbage collectors, whose work is essential to the health of societal members yet poorly rewarded. Davis and Moore would point out the lack of specialized training involved in the occupation; important jobs that anyone can do may not be highly rewarded. Since almost all societies with a division of labor face differences in functional importance and the scarcity of personnel for many of those important positions, social stratification is necessary.

The structural-functionalists are sometimes called *order* theorists. This label suggests that the perspective of structural-functionalism focuses attention on maintaining social order and the status quo at the expense of understanding social change. The structural-functionalists have been accused of looking at social change as a sickness in society rather than as a common process, like seeing change in your body as a sign that you are probably sick. Particularly in looking at social stratification, the structural-functionalists tend to accept the current state of affairs as being "right" or natural. The functional importance of a position in society is at least partially determined by how highly rewarded it is; thus, functional importance is the same as success in convincing others of the importance of your position. The structural-functionalists are accused of not appreciating that success can vary from time to time. These accusations come from a perspective on society known as conflict theory.

The Conflict Theorists

The general perspective on society known as conflict theory is traced from the theories of Karl Marx. As an overall perspective, **conflict theory** suggests that conflict, rather than order or consensus, is the usual state of affairs in society because of the inequality imposed by social stratification. Since the hierarchy of social stratification gives more to some people than to others, it is natural that individuals at one level of the hierarchy should be in competition and conflict with individuals at other levels. That conflict, when it occurs, leads to social change.

Conflict theorists tend to view social stratification as an organized way for certain members of society to gain wealth at the expense of certain others. In the stratification system of the United States, for example, garbage collectors have to give up a larger portion of their earnings for medical care than physicians must give up for garbage collection (in addition to the different incomes they have in the first place). The system therefore benefits physicians at the expense of garbage collectors. Benefiting garbage collectors more would involve benefiting physicians less. The stratification system works this way not because there is consensus (even among garbage collectors) over the arrangement (the structural-functional position) but because those who benefit are in a powerful enough position to keep the system going.

Where structural-functionalists see consensus and agreement over basic norms and values, conflict theorists see social power coercing those at the bottom into obedience. Power is one of the critical factors in the stratification hierarchy from any perspective; the conflict theorists emphasize its existence and the way it is used. One of its primary uses, according to this position, is to cover its own tracks as much as possible. Those at the top of the hierarchy prefer to have those at the bottom in as much agreement as possible with the status quo; they may therefore use their power to socialize those at the bottom into that acceptance through their

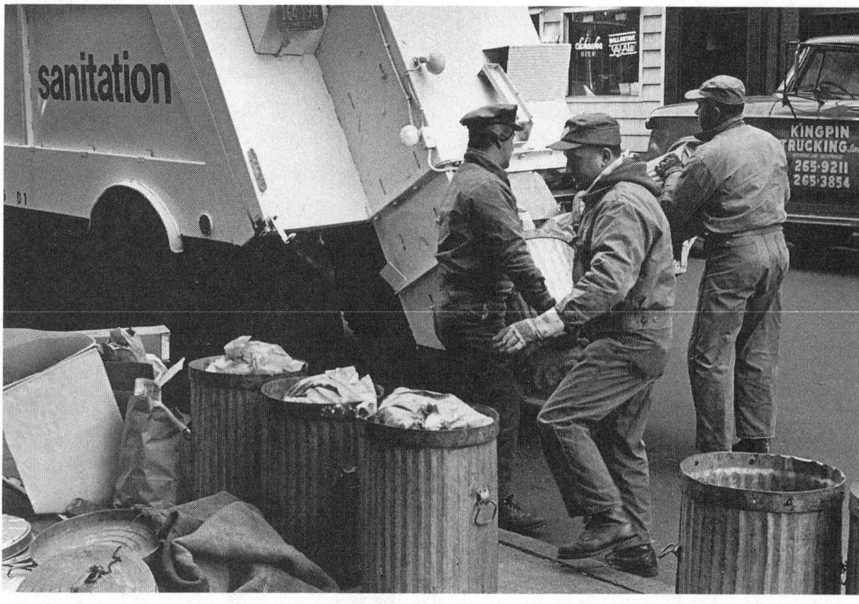

Modern methods of sanitation have saved more lives than physicians could ever hope to, yet garbage collectors receive relatively little respect for the work they do. They also receive much less financial reward than doctors—and incomparably less than professional athletes, who are not expected to save any lives. The order theorists argue that this sort of discrepancy is the result of the minimal specialized training needed for garbage collecting; conflict theorists argue that garbage collectors suffer from a lack of political clout.

control over schools ("Stand in straight lines and don't talk back to the teacher"), religion ("Blessed are the meek for they shall inherit the earth"), and general folklore ("The head of the sales department has so many worries and responsibilities, I'm just as glad I didn't get the promotion"). If the socialization fails, there is always military might to fall back upon (Verba, Oren, and Ferree, 1985).

Karl Marx: The Father of Conflict Theory We've already looked at Marx's theory of social class, but it is better understood within the context of his theory of social stratification, from which it came. As we saw, Marx viewed social stratification within a capitalist society as consisting of two social classes: the ruling class and the working class. Marx viewed capitalism as the latest stage in a long history of economic development in which a ruling class exploited a lower class according to whatever economic arrangements were currently in practice. Under feudalism, for instance, the serf was tied to the lord's land.

Exploitation, in Marx's terms, refers to the unequal manner in which the ruling class benefits from the working class. Under feudalism the lord becomes wealthy while the serf toils on the land; under capitalism the capitalist becomes wealthy through profit while the worker creates all the value in the product from which the profit comes. Since the serfs or the workers do not receive the value of their labor, they are exploited. A system of social stratification, therefore, is nothing more than organized exploitation; it has no other purpose, says Marx.

The ruling class is in a position to exercise great control over all aspects of society. Marx claimed that most of the forms of social organization we live by were constructed by the ruling class to maintain its position in society. A government, for example, is constructed to enforce the status quo and to punish those who seek to change it. Laws, such as those regulating the right to private property, benefit those who currently own property (the ruling class) while working against individuals who own none or very little (the working class). Even though much of society is organized for this purpose, many members of the working class don't understand their disadvantage and accept what they are told. What they are told, according to Marx, are ideologies of the ruling class.

An **ideology** is an idea or set of ideas that represents a particular interest of a particular social group; for Marx it is a set of beliefs that specifically represents the interests of the ruling class in a society. The American belief that private property is a good thing, for example, is an ideology of the ruling class; it is an idea that reflects the interests of the ruling class but not the interests of the working class. You may feel that the laws protecting private property are in your interest because you own a TV and car that you would rather I not steal. You would be better off, says Marx, giving up your right to your TV and car to gain access to the billions and billions of dollars of private property currently closed to you in the hands of the ruling class. If you don't agree, says Marx, you are suffering from false consciousness.

False consciousness occurs when individuals in a particular social class are not aware of the true interests inherent in their class position. (If they *are* so aware, they have a **class consciousness.**) False consciousness occurs primarily among members of the working class when they accept the ideologies of the ruling class. If, for example, you are currently a member of what is generally called the middle class in America and believe you benefit from the current system of stratification, you have a false consciousness. The ruling class, says Marx, does everything in its power to perpetuate false consciousness, as it is in its interest to have willing obedience from the working class. Racial or religious hatred, for instance, keeps members of the working class from grouping together; thus it is useful to the ruling class, which will attempt to keep such divisions alive (see Box 7.1). Perhaps most important in false consciousness are all the different income levels and status symbols that exist in a society. People who drive Cadillacs feel superior to those who drive Fords; people who wear expensive clothes feel superior to those who wear less expensive clothes; people who make $20,000 a year feel superior to those who make $15,000, who feel superior to those who make $10,000, and so on. From the point of view of the ruling class, all these differences are trivial, but the members of the working class are trained to believe them to be significant. They come to believe that they live in a great many different social classes instead of just the one large class that Marx claims they occupy. If the differences continue, they will prevent class consciousness and, ultimately, class action.

We come finally to Marx's idea of revolution, the part of his theory most roundly criticized today because his predictions have not come true. According to Marx, class action by the working class would ultimately take shape as revolutionary action when the working class came to recognize their exploitation. This recognition would be bound to occur, according to Marx, for it is in the nature of capitalism for wealth to become increasingly concentrated in fewer and fewer hands. This concentration would limit the ability of the ruling class to spread false consciousness around, which would force more and more members of the previous "middle class" into the poverty of the working class. In Marx's terms capitalism contains the "seeds of its own destruction" as it would force the working class ultimately to rise up against the ruling class, overthrow the capitalist system, and finally substitute a system Marx called communism. Ironically, Marx barely spoke about *communism,* as he claimed he was in no position to truly understand what it might be. All he knew for sure was that it would have no exploitation, no social classes, and, as follows, no system of social stratification (see Marx, 1956).

Marx predicted that revolution would occur first in the most industrial nations of the world. As it happened, those revolutions that have carried his name have occurred in the nonindustrial nations and, in fact, have not led to classless societies in spite of some claims to the contrary. This apparent failing in Marx's theory should not, however, lead us to ignore the bulk of his work. His emphasis on power and conflict in society and, in particular, his theory of ideology have had a major impact on political and sociological theory.

Modern Conflict Theory Most of the modern conflict theorists (although not all) ignore Marx's predictions of revolution in favor of advancing his other ideas. One of the most influential in this effort is Ralf Dahrendorf (1959), who shifted focus somewhat from Marx's idea of economic class to the idea of social power. Modern industrial society, says Dahrendorf, is no longer as clear-cut with regard to class as it was in Marx's day. Marx witnessed the early days of the industrial revolution, when workers lived in abject poverty and the members of the ruling class who placed them in that situation owned the factories in which they worked. Today corporate enterprises are owned by stockholders but run by managers hired by the corporation. The managers don't own the means of production, but they are often in conflict with workers because they have authority over the workers.

BOX 7.1

U.S. STEEL VERSUS THE UNIONS: THE STORY OF GARY, INDIANA

Gary, Indiana, is a company town. Before 1905 it wasn't there; it was constructed by U.S. Steel Corporation right at the foot of Lake Michigan as an ideal location for steel mills. Between 1905 and 1907, $40 million was invested in the construction of Gary. All it needed then was workers.

The initial methods used by U.S. Steel to locate workers for Gary might have come directly from a page written by Karl Marx. How does the ruling class control the working class? By making sure that the working class stays divided among itself. As Edward Greer (1971:31) describes it:

> The corporation planned more than the physical nature of the city. It also had agents advertise in Europe and the South to bring in workers from as many different backgrounds as possible to build the mills and work in them. Today over 50 ethnic groups are represented in the population.
>
> This imported labor was cheap, and it was hoped that cultural differences and language barriers would curtail the growth of a socialist labor movement. The tough, pioneer character of the city and the fact that many of the immigrant workers' families had not yet joined them in this country combined to create a lawless and vice-ridden atmosphere which the corporation did little to curtail. Gary is indelibly stamped in the mold of its corporate creators.

Dahrendorf has focused his attention on the ways authority is exercised and maintained in modern society. Individuals are not limited to one social class, as Marx maintained, but are in fact involved in a wide variety of authority relations in many social arenas. A corporate executive, for example, may have authority in a work arena but lack authority in a political arena such as a court of law. The executive can give orders in one arena but must take them in another. The "boats" that people see themselves sharing, therefore, will be determined by the way authority operates in all these different arenas; being on the same side of an authority relation gives you something in common, but only with others in that particular arena of society. If individuals form social groups based on these points in common and become involved in conflict, that conflict will be largely limited to the arena in question. Marx's theory is approximated only by the very top and very bottom of the stratification hierarchy; the very rich may give orders in every social arena, while the very poor find themselves taking orders every time they turn around.

Other modern theorists in the conflict tradition have directed their analyses closely to the Davis and Moore argument and to the world of work in general. Melvin Tumin, who made a career of attacking Davis and Moore, pointed out that, within the logic of structural-functionalism, social stratification could even be shown as a dysfunctional (or nonfunctional) system. Because social stratification has such limited routes of upward mobility, Tumin (1953) argued, very talented members of the lower and working classes will never be recognized and made use of by the society; they will, in fact, remain in their social classes while less talented members of the upper class compete for medical school and other high-status training programs. Bucher and Stelling (1969) pointed out that highly rewarded occupations may not necessarily be more important; rather, their members have simply "played their cards right." Professional status, they argue, has more to do with political processes through which the occupation gains prestige than with the nature of the work itself. Physicians, for example, have been much more successful in creating a positive image than chiropractors (Verba, Oren, and Ferree, 1985).

In general, modern conflict theory accepts Marx's notion of exploitation and the inherent nature of power and conflict within social stratification. Social stratification is viewed as a very tempting form of social organization that occurs whenever a society can produce more than it requires for survival; in such a situation some members will surely attempt to appropriate the surplus for their own use. When such appropriation becomes institutionalized over time, social stratification is born. This structured inequality is accepted much of the time by many of the participants, but conflict is always a potential beneath the surface of the smooth interactions of everyday life.

Order and Conflict Theories: A Final Look

An interesting philosophical difference between order and conflict theories may be a key to the way they interpret the world. That philosophical difference lies in the conflicting ways they view humans in their societies. The order theories, such as structural-functionalism, tend to view humans as inherently bad or disruptive creatures who are held in check by social norms and social power. Within this perspective society becomes a vast civilizing force that is necessary to prevent our animal selfishness from taking hold. The conlict theories, on the other hand, tend to view humans as inherently good creatures who become surly and competitive only in societies that encourage such behavior. To the order theorists social stratification is necessary to motivate people to work and to keep the society functioning in some sort of orderly fashion; inequality is the necessary price we must pay for that service. To the conflict theorists social stratification is the cause of many of the less redeeming human qualities we see every day; a more orderly society might be possible if we removed the causes of hatred and conflict that currently keep us at each other's throats.

SOCIAL CLASS IN THE UNITED STATES

All modern industrial nations have elaborate systems of social stratification, and the United States is no exception. The activities we engage in every day are firmly embedded in a class hierarchy. Social class is a very real factor in the life of every American. It is probably the single most important social factor in explaining the differences among Americans; people in different social classes are different from each other in almost every way imaginable. This section will explore some of those differences and the reasons for them: inequalities in wealth distribution and barriers to upward social mobility.

Inequality in the United States

Systems of social stratification introduce structured inequality into any society. By *structured,* sociologists mean that the inequality is not just the result of individual differences in talent or ability but is built into the roles people play and the rewards they receive. Any stratification system therefore produces inequality in that those at the top receive more rewards than those at the bottom. One question to be answered in regard to any particular stratification system is the degree of inequality. How much difference is there from top to bottom and just how unequal is the distribution of rewards?

Figure 7.1 shows how income was distributed among citizens of the United States in 1987. It arbitrarily divides the population into five equal segments, ranging from the wealthiest 20 percent of the population to the poorest 20 percent. The wealthiest 20 percent of the population received 43.7 percent of all the income earned, while the poorest 20 percent had to get by with 4.6 percent of the available income. If we look more closely at the top 20 percent (and at a statistic not included in Figure 7.1), we find that in 1987 the top *5* percent of the people earned 16.9 percent of all the income earned. These statistics provide specific support for a fact already familiar to anyone who lives in the United States: we live within a system of social stratification.

Table 7.1 presents income distribution statistics for the years 1950-1970. Comparing this table with Figure 7.1 may tell you something you didn't know: The distribution of income in the United States has changed virtually not at all since 1950. The top 20 percent went from 42.7 percent of the income in 1950 to 43.7 percent in 1985, a change of less than 1 percent; the bottom 20 percent barely moved, from 4.5 percent of the income to 4.6 percent. American culture and technology changed quite a bit during that thirty-seven-year period (and average yearly income jumped from about $4,000 to about $25,000), but the ratio between the haves and the have nots stayed essentially the same. Different people are certainly involved in the

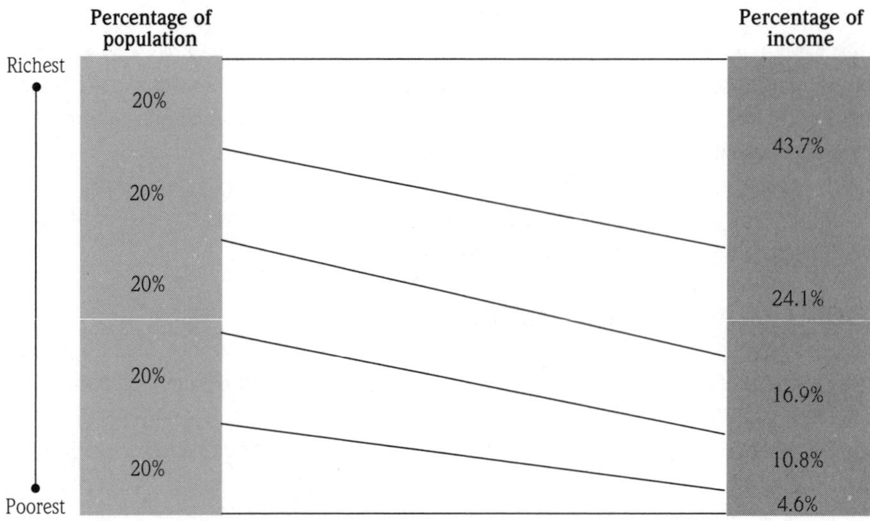

Figure 7.1 Percent of income received by fifths of population in the United States, 1985. (Data from U.S. Bureau of the Census.)

stratification system today than in 1950, but the system itself is no different; the same percentages of rewards are still dispersed to the same segments of the population.

To say the least, social stratification in the United States is structured inequality. But how is it structured? Income distribution can be arbitrarily examined across five equal segments of the population, but that does not necessarily mean there are five social classes of equal size. Some sociologists who focus on the very top of the stratification system argue that .3 percent of the population makes up one social class (see Domhoff, 1983). There have to be at least two social classes, but beyond that, sociologists are in disagreement as to exactly how many there are.

TABLE 7.1

FAMILY INCOME AS PERCENTAGE OF INCOME IN THE UNITED STATES, 1950-1970

Year	Lowest Fifth	Second Fifth	Middle Fifth	Fourth Fifth	Highest Fifth	Top 5 Percent	Mean Income
1970	5.4	12.2	17.6	23.8	40.9	15.6	$11,106
1965	5.2	12.2	17.8	23.9	40 9	15.5	7,704
1960	4.8	12.2	17.8	24.0	41.3	15.9	6,227
1955	4.8	12.2	17.7	23.4	41.8	16.8	5,010
1950	4.5	11.9	17.4	23.6	42.7	17.3	3,832

Source: U.S. Bureau of the Census, 1976, p 37.

Social Classes in the United States: How Many?

In 1949 Richard Centers asked people to label themselves as to their social class. From that group of labels, which Centers had provided, people organized themselves as follows:

Upper class	3%
Middle class	43%
Working class	51%
Lower class	1%
Don't know	2%

In 1976, the National Opinion Research Center received the following responses to the same question:

Upper class	1.5%
Middle class	47.7%
Working class	46.4%
Lower class	4.4%

One possible conclusion is that one generation answers the question in much the same way as the generation before. Can other conclusions be drawn?

One of the problems with such research is that it forces people to use the labels provided by the sociologist. Some people, for example, like to think of themselves as upper middle class. A more serious problem, however, is that the research doesn't tell us how important or how real most of the respondents consider their own social class to be. The concept *social class* is a social category not a social group. It is a concept sociologists employ to understand or explain other things about people; it is therefore not absolutely necessary that the people themselves recognize the importance of the category. Unfortunately, sociologists are as confused and divided over the meaning of social class as the people to whom the concept is applied.

Thus far we've looked at social class through the eyes of Karl Marx and Max Weber. Marx left little doubt as to the meaning of the term. Weber spoke of social class in terms of "life chances"; the higher the social class, the more life chances (or opportunities) one would have to acquire possessions and control one's existence. He didn't specify how many social classes there might be. Some modern American sociologists—Cuber and Kenkel (1954), for instance—have argued that social classes don't have boundaries and therefore can't be counted; they should instead be measured as temperature is measured by a thermometer. With Cuber and Kenkel at one extreme and Marx at the other, it is not surprising that most sociologists slide into the middle ground. If there is any consensus at all, it is that the number of social classes varies from community to community and, perhaps more important, that the sociologist might want to assume different numbers of social classes for different kinds of research. For some research questions you might care only about approximate social class divisions; for other questions (such as social mobility research) you might want to focus more closely on class boundaries. American sociologists have had a variety of research concerns related to social class and, as a result, have used a variety of ways to measure it.

One approach to social class is the *community study,* which involves in-depth interviewing and observation to determine how members of the community see themselves and each other. W. Lloyd Warner and Paul Lunt (1941) pioneered this work in a small New England community they called Yankee City, concluding there were six social classes: the upper upper class, the lower upper class, the upper middle class, the lower middle class, the upper lower class, and the lower class. A. B. Hollingshead (1949) did similar research in a community he called Elmtown and collapsed the two middle classes into one. Warner described his classes as follows:

Upper upper class: This class was very small (about 1 percent of Yankee City), was very wealthy, and thrived on strong family traditions; proper ancestry was necessary for membership. The members of this class did not need to work and were oriented toward the proper pursuit of leisure.

Lower upper class: This class was distinguished from the upper class primarily by its absence of prestigious family background. Sometimes referred to by other community members as the "new rich" or as having "new money," this class contained many doctors, lawyers, and businessmen, many of whom tried to emulate the members of the upper upper class.

Upper middle class: One of Warner's tongue-twisting terms that found a firm home in the American vocabulary, the upper middle class contained about 10 percent of the Yankee City population. This class included many professionals, but they clearly differed in lifestyle and amount of money from the members of the lower upper class. This class also included many wholesale and retail businessmen.

Lower middle class: The lower middle class contained a variety of white-collar workers such as clerks and a number of skilled workers. This class differed from the one above in both income and lifestyle; its members valued hard work, morality, and regular church attendance.

Upper lower class: The largest class in Yankee City, the upper lower class contained unskilled or semiskilled workers involved primarily in construction and factory work. Many of them were foreign born. They made up the "poor but honest" population of Yankee City.

Lower class: Finally, we come to the unemployed and poorly thought of members of Yankee City. Members of this class were believed to be lazy and responsible for their own condition.

The most interesting aspect of both Warner and Lunt's research and Hollingshead's Elmtown project is the emphasis on noneconomic factors in social class. Warner's distinction between the upper upper class and the lower upper class, for example, has turned up time after time in sociological research as being significant in most American communities. The only difference between the two classes is social status, not economic standing; in other words, it's not how much money you have but where you got it and the style with which you spend it. This old rich-new rich distinction lends support to Weber's multiple-dimension approach of class, status, and power.

Daniel Rossides (1976) sums up much of American sociological thinking about social class in America in Table 7.2. Leaving out Warner's new rich, or lower upper class, Rossides breaks down class attributes and lifestyle differences according to Weber's dimensions. Many of the class differences he details cross class boundary lines, making the table more accurate although a little more difficult to read. The implication, following most sociological research in the United States, is that social classes do not have rigid boundaries, the only major exception being the "old rich" of the upper class, whose members have a clearly ascribed status to go along with their wealth (see Domhoff, 1983). Other social classes have definite differences on the whole but spillover occurs when it comes to particular differences. However, note the great differences

TABLE 7.2

THE AMERICAN CLASS SYSTEM IN THE TWENTIETH CENTURY: A COMPOSITE ESTIMATE*

CLASS

Class (and percentage of total population)	Income	Property	Occupation	Education	Personal and Family Life	Education of Children
Upper class (1-3%)	Very high income	Great wealth, old wealth	Managers	Liberal arts	Stable family	College education
Upper middle class (10-15%)	High income	Accumulation of property through savings	professionals, high civil and military officials Lowest unemploy- ment	education at elite schools Graduate training	life Autonomous personality Better physical and mental	by right for both sexes Education system biased
Lower mid- dle class (30-35%)	Modest	Some	Small busi- nesspeople and farmers, lower profes- sionals, semi- professionals, sales and clerical workers	Some college High school	health Longer life expectancy	in their favor Greater chance of college than working-class children
Working class (40-45%)	Income Low income	savings No	Skilled labor Unskilled labor Highest	Some high school Grade school Illiteracy	Unstable family life Conformist	Educational system biased against them Tendency toward voca- tional pro- grams
Lower class (20-25%)	Poverty income (des- titution)	savings	unemploy- ment Surplus labor	especially functional illiteracy	personality Poorer physi- cal and men- tal health Lower life expectancy	Little interest in education, high dropout rates

PRESTIGE

Class (and percentage of total population)	Occupational Prestige	Subjective Development	Consumption	Participation in Group Life
Upper class (1-3%)	High	Consistent	Tasteful	High participation

*This estimate is based on a variety of sources: the federal government, especially the Census Bureau; community, metropolitan, and national studies; and interpretive works. The proportion of the total population represented by each class is given as a percentage range to emphasize that this is an estimate. For expository purposes, racial and ethnic minorities are not included.

(continues)

PRESTIGE (continued)

Class (and percentage of total population)	Occupational Prestige	Subjective Development	Consumption	Participation in Group Life
Upper middle class (10-15%)	occupational prestige	attitudes Integrated self-perception	consumption Affluence and comfort	in groups segregated by breeding, religion, ethnicity, race,
Lower middle class (30-35%)			Modest standard of living Consumption of mass	and function
Working class (40-45%)	Low occupational prestige	Inconsistent attitudes Unrealistic self-perception Greater	"material" and "symbolic" culture Austere consumption	Low participation in group life
Lower class (20-25%)	Stigma of worthlessness on the labor market	prevalence of mental illness	Physical suffering Acute economic anxiety	Social isolation

POWER

Class (and percentage of total population)	Participation in Political Processes	Political Attitudes	Legislative and Governmental Benefits	Distribution of Justice
Upper class (1-3%)	High participation	Belief in efficacy	Greater governmental	Legal order biased
Upper middle class (10-15%)	in voting and other forms of political participation	of political action Support for civil rights and liberal	benefits than classes below despite smaller numbers	in support of their interests and rights Much greater
Lower middle class (30-35%)	Monopoly on governmental positions	foreign policy Negative attitude toward governmental intervention in economy and toward welfare programs		utilization of legal processes than classes below
Working class (40-45%)		Tendency to discount value of political action Except for	Governmental	Legal order biased against lower classes

POWER (continued)

Class (and percentage of total population)	Participation in Political Processes	Political Attitudes	Legislative and Governmental Benefits	Distribution of Justice
	Tendency not to vote or	minorities, opposition to civil	neglect, some repression, some	
Lower class (20-25%)	participate in politics	rights Support for more nationalist foreign policy and governmental programs that provide economic help and security	paternalism	Little utilization of legal processes

Source: Daniel W. Rossides (1976), pp. 24-26. Copyright © 1976 by Houghton Mifflin Company. Used by permission.

between, for example, the upper middle class and the working class; there is practically nothing in common between those two classes on any of the dimensions. As we will see in the section on social mobility, most research on mobility suggests that many Americans are upwardly mobile but that few move very far. Table 7.2 makes it easy to see some of the economic and cultural roadblocks waiting for the unwary stratification traveler.

The Myth of the Classless Society

American culture contains strong values regarding equality and democracy. Even though there are numerous exceptions to both, one consequence of these values is that many Americans prefer not to think of the United States in terms of class structure. It is more pleasant to think that some people accomplish more with the opportunity America offers and that economic success or failure need not separate people in terms of their more human concerns. One of our favorite movie plots, for example, is the romance between the rich boy and poor girl (or vice versa), in which love always triumphs over lifestyle differences and family objections. Actually, only rarely do people marry outside of their social class. Love is only one of the many activities that most people confine to their own social class.

If a sociologist asked to predict some human behavior is allowed only one question about the people involved, the sociologist will want to know something about their social class. Beginning with birth, the classes are different. Lower-class women have more babies than upper-class women. The reason for this difference is that lower-class women are less likely to have detailed knowledge of birth control techniques and are more likely to have a cultural bias toward large families. Upper-class women, on the other hand, have access to birth control, may prefer to have careers, are more likely to look upon children as an economic drain to the family, and are less likely to value large families.

Once born, the children of the different social classes will be raised differently. Urie Bronfenbrenner (1958) found that lower- and working-class parents employed repressive forms of socialization in which child obedience was highly valued and discipline was harsh. Middle-

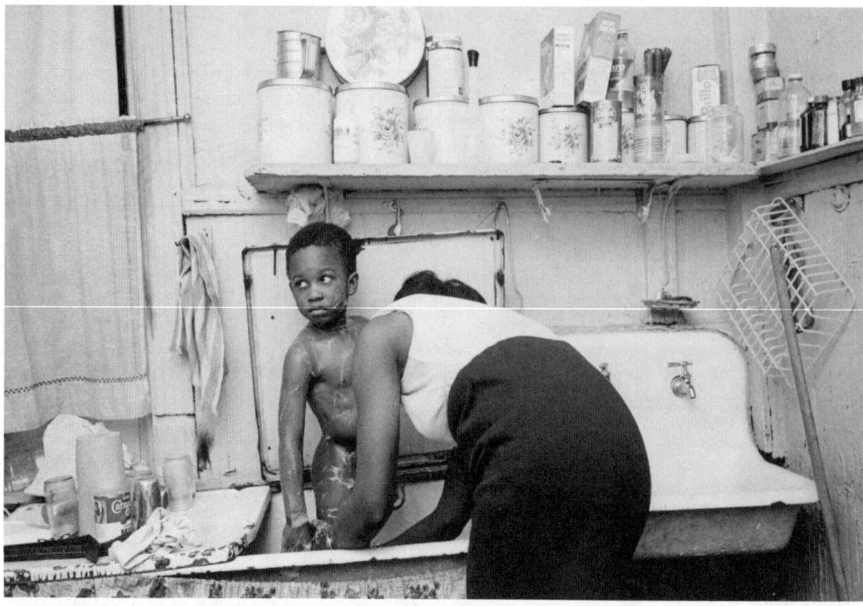

Social classes in the United States live in different worlds in all senses of the word. The trappings of their lives, from the physical surroundings to daily routines, vary in significant and not-so-significant ways.

and upper-class parents, on the other hand, were much more likely to spare the rod and to deal verbally with their children over differences of opinion regarding behavior. Children in the latter families were treated much more democratically and given considerably more freedom. Kohn and Schooler (1983) explain these differences in socialization in terms of the occupational circumstances of the different classes. Middle-class people have more autonomy on the job and pass this independence along to their children; working-class jobs, on the other hand, are more likely to stress obedience on the part of the employee. Since people tend to marry within their social class, methods of raising children continue across generations as parents raise their children in the same way they were raised.

Roach and Gursslin (1965) noted the high incidence of lower-class children arrested for acts of delinquency. We've already seen the relationship between social class and the American criminal justice system in Chapter 5 (see particularly Box 5.1). Whatever the explanations offered, your parents' social class has a major impact on the number of your encounters with the police and the courts.

On the whole, social class is the greatest single predictor of educational success, IQ scores, or anything else associated with educational expectations. William Sewell (1971) found that lower-class children did much more poorly in school than middle- and upper-class children: Their grades were lower, and they were much less likely to attend college. Lower-class children are less likely to be prepared for teacher expectations when they enter school and less likely to become responsive to those expectations as they continue, falling farther and farther behind their middle-class peers. Education seems to have a double relationship to social class. We have

already seen that there is a definite relation between an individual's education level and subsequent earnings. As with childrearing techniques, class patterns in relation to education tend to continue across generations as lack of education limits social class, which will limit education in the next generation.

Social class also affects a wide variety of social behavior in adults. In such everyday matters as the people you choose to invite into your home, middle-class people are more likely to socialize with an assortment of friends (many of them work or business relations) than lower-class people, who are more likely to contine their socializing to relatives (Cohen and Hodges 1963). The upper classes are much more likely to belong to voluntary associations than the lower classes (Hodges, 1964). There is also a difference in the kinds of associations that receive the participation of different classes; the upper classes are more likely to be involved in professional or charitable organizations, while the middle and working classes are more likely to belong to fraternal organizations (such as the Masons or the Knights of Columbus). A similar pattern of participation occurs in the world of politics; the higher the social class, the more likely the individual is to vote and the more likely he or she will vote Republican (Krauss, 1976).

Social class is highly related to race or ethnic status. When racial or ethnic groups face discrimination, one of the many results is that routes of upward social mobility are cut off for their members; in other words, discrimination locks members of affected groups into the lower classes. Figure 7.2 illustrates the income levels of white families, blacks, and Hispanics in 1988. If we look at net worth as opposed to income, the differences become even more striking. In 1988, the median net worth of white American households was $43,279; in that same year, the median net worth for black and Spanish-origin American households was $4,169 and $5,524, respectively (U.S. Bureau of the Census, 1990). The vast difference is caused by the fact that

Percentage of families with income under $10,000 a year
Percentage of families with income over $25,000 a year
Median income
White 8.5 65.8 $33,915
Hispanic 20.3 43.9 $21,769
Black 27.3 39.3 $19,329

Figure 7.2 Family income levels in the United States, 1988. (Data from U.S. Bureau of the Census, 1990b.)

many minority families owe more than they own; over 30 percent of black households and almost 24 percent of Spanish-origin households fall into that category as compared with around 8 percent of white households. The disproportionate presence of racial and ethnic groups in the lower social classes is a major cause of many of their problems as well as the conflicts they become involved in with others. This distribution of racial and ethnic groups within social stratification is called **ethnic stratification**. It will be a key concept in Chapter 8, on racial and ethnic groups.

Apparently, social class also affects people's happiness. Norman Bradburn and David Caplovitz (1965) found that individuals described themselves as "very happy," "pretty happy," and "not too happy" in direct relation to their income, education, and occupational status; the higher the social class, the happier people were. They will also be happier for longer; being in the lower classes takes six to eight years off one's life because of higher infant mortality, poorer nutrition, higher rates of homicide, poorer sanitation, and poorer medical care in general (see Luhman and Gilman, 1980). From start to finish low social class can be hazardous to your health.

This brief discussion only scratches the surface of the differences among people that sociologists attribute to social class. The research included was selected for its range, particularly with respect to the different stages of life affected. One basic point is apparent: If people have so many differences due to social class, a great many individual experiences must be shaped by social class. In order for that to occur, however, the social classes must be relatively stable. The implication of the research we have looked at is that social classes differ from each other culturally as well as financially. Such cultural differences would not exist if people did not stay in social classes over generations for the most part, or if people in different classes had more social contact with each other—which brings us back to social mobility and the way social class shapes individual experience.

Avenues and Barriers to Social Mobility

As near as most researchers can tell, American society contains quite a bit of both inter- and intragenerational mobility compared to other countries. However, as we mentioned, it also appears that few individuals move very far (Vanfossen, 1979). There is enough movement to provide for some social change but apparently not enough to alter the basic class differences in American life.

Perceptions versus Reality in Social Mobility Social mobility refers to an overall change in social class, but one that is very difficult to measure, as we saw earlier in this chapter. As a result, most sociological research on social mobility focuses on occupational change and, in particular, the prestige of occupations. The same occupation can actually entail two different kinds of work in two different places; it can also result in two different incomes. In addition, recent research into the "underground economy" of the United States, where earnings are unreported and products are exchanged, indicates that there is a hidden side to the economy that sociologists have just begun to explore (see Denton, 1985). On the other hand, even if it is not the very best measure of social class, occupational prestige remains relatively stable.

Stephen Thernstrom (1964), studying occupational changes between fathers and sons among nineteenth-century workers in New England, found (perhaps not surprisingly) that the good old days in the land of opportunity were not all that good, due to lack of opportunity. Sons tended to follow pretty closely in their fathers' footsteps.

The most famous study of social mobility by American sociologists is *American Occupational Structure,* a 1967 study by Peter Blau and Otis Duncan. Working closely with census data, Blau and Duncan sought to determine just how much mobility occurred in the American occupational structure and, just as important, what caused it. They discovered, as we have noted, a fair amount of social mobility but most of it fairly limited; both inter- and intragenerational mobility occurred, but generally the improvements were slight. Hauser and Featherman (1976) found a relation between father's occupational prestige and son's occupational prestige during the 1960s and 1970s; the most common occurrence was for white-collar fathers to have white-collar sons and for manual-working fathers to have manual-working sons.

The father's occupation appears to have a definite effect on the son's occupation, but Blau and Duncan wanted a more complete explanation. Using sophisticated statistical techniques designed to unearth such relationships, Blau and Duncan concluded that a variety of factors determined the son's occupation. The most important direct factor was the son's education. More education led to better jobs. But what determined the son's education? The more education and the higher the occupational level of the father, the more education the son would get (Blau and Duncan, 1967). Similar results have been found by more recent research. Jencks et al. (1979) found that an individual's income and occupational status are best explained by looking to the educational level of the individual's family and, in particular, at the skills and values for achievement acquired from the family. In short, social mobility is possible, but a variety of factors in family background have a strong impact on keeping the same kinds of jobs in the same kinds of families.

The avenues and barriers to social mobility have complex and intertwined roots that trail back into the overall workings of the social stratification system. Why, for example, should the father's level of education affect the son's level of education? Part of the answer, no doubt, is that a father who went to college might be more apt to encourage the same behavior from the son, but the full explanation is more complicated. Fathers who went to college will make more money and will be more able to send their sons to college. Fathers who went to college have acquired certain skills necessary to doing well in school that they will pass on to their sons. Fathers who went to college will probably have jobs that require a college degree and have friends with similar jobs; the sons will grow up in this environment, become aware of those kinds of occupations, and probably want to work in one themselves (for which college will be necessary). Fathers who went to college may belong to alumni associations and have some pull in getting their sons accepted; this is particularly true with high-prestige universities. Such explanations could continue indefinitely. The coordination of life within social stratification tends to keep values, skills, abilities, personal contacts, general information, and individual motivations passed on as a cluster from one generation to the next. This coordination is loose enough to allow for some social mobility but tight enough to prevent very much. Overall, the barriers to social mobility are high enough to give the United States clear differences in social class that persist over generations. As a result, individuals in different classes are very different from each other.

Changing Opportunities in the United States

As we've seen, many aspects of the social stratification system in the United States have changed little in many years. The rich and poor will always be with us and in approximately the same proportions. There have, however, been some major changes in both the United States economy and in the world economy over the past twenty years that have brought about profound changes in the experiences of American workers and their families. We seem to have fewer jobs in the steel industry and more jobs in the computer industry. Another part of that change comes from economic competition from abroad. The trade deficit (the difference between what we export and import) has grown steadily throughout the 1980s to the point where Americans are now consuming far more foreign products than exporting American products. This deficit threatens the value of the dollar and plays a major role in the elimination of jobs in the United States.

Many of these changes have been described by Bluestone and Harrison (1982) as the "deindustrialization" of America. The United States now has far fewer jobs available in the semiskilled and nonskilled categories; there are now fewer places to "start out" if one lacks basic occupational skills. In addition, much of America's basic heavy industry cannot compete with lower prices and, in many cases, superior products from abroad. Hence many of the traditional blue-collar occupations, such as in the steel and automobile industries, are turning into dead-end careers. Given these changes, economic recessions now affect different Americans than they used to. In the recession of the early 1980s, for example, a new kind of poor emerged. Most notably perhaps, they were young and not old (O'Hare, 1985; Harrington, 1984). Older Americans were either well situated within the American economy or retired with income such as Social Security with built-in protections from economic changes. It was young workers just starting out who found few opportunities. Another change has been termed the "feminization" of poverty; as more and more American families have become female headed (and as female occupations tend to be more poorly paid), a growing number of the poor have been women and their children (Pearce, 1983; Harrington, 1984). During the recession of the early 1980s, however, men slipped into poverty at a greater rate than did women. Changes in the American economy may be more important in the long run than demographic changes in the American family (O'Hare, 1985).

We noted earlier in this chapter that racial and ethnic minorities tend to be clustered toward the bottom of the social stratification system. Not surprisingly, we find that blacks and other minorities also disproportionately occupy poverty status in the United States. While most poor in the United States are white (due to the fact that most Americans are white), the poverty rate among both black Americans and Hispanic Americans is over three times that of white Americans (U.S. Bureau of the Census 1990b). These figures have changed little over the last twenty-five years. The unskilled and semiskilled industrial jobs that allowed so many European immigrants to climb out of poverty early in this century are no longer available. For many of those immigrants, better jobs for one generation led to better education for the next generation and still better jobs for the third generation. Black Americans and Hispanic Americans appear to be locked into a cycle of inadequate training leading to limited opportunities.

The Individual Experience of Social Class

We come finally to the individual's perspective on social stratification. How exactly does social stratification make us so different from each other? This very important question is unfortunately diffcult to answer through any kind of systematic research. Your social class is a part of your life that affects every aspect from the moment you are born. Because of it, every day you will have slightly different experiences from those of people in other social classes. You will see different places and people, acquire different skills and abilities, be treated differently by others, learn different norms, and acquire different values. By the time you are an adult, this accumulation of experience adds up to making you a different kind of person, just as the accumulation of experience of growing up in London would make you different from those who call New York home. How do you then go back through research to determine just which of those experiences played the major role in making you the person you are today? Social class is a general concept. Because it is so general, it is very difficult to nail down. Its generality also makes it very important.

Even if we don't know all we need to about the exact causes of social class differences, we can see many of the effects. Some of these were examined earlier in this chapter, but many are not easily expressed as research results. For example, people of different social classes are generally uncomfortable around each other in social situations. Of course, there are social settings where people of different classes commonly meet, but most of them are formal. Interactions between an employer and employee, for example, are necessary to get on with the business at hand, but do the two individuals ever really come to know each other very well? Most such settings have fairly strict rules as to how each person should talk and the kinds of topics that may be discussed. If the employer were to invite the employee to a party (or vice versa), both would probably be uncomfortable. The different classes have different kinds of parties, for one thing, but they also have different kinds of interests and different styles of expressing those interests. There is often not enough common ground for such interactions to occur easily.

Most of us don't consciously see our experience as shaped by our social class. We encounter people and situations, some of which we like and some of which we don't. We rarely say, "I'm comfortable with these people in this situation because both are part of my social class." Instead we say, "They are good people and a lot of fun." Part of the reason they are "good" and "fun," however, is that they fit in with the way we see the world and the people in it. And we acquired that world view as part of our social class. Left to our own devices, we will organize our life so that we can spend as much time as possible with the people and situations we prefer. Considering that the people we like are doing the same thing, it's not surprising that people cluster together within social classes, rarely venturing out into the chaos and uncertainty that lies beyond.

The tendency for people to group according to social class has been a primary concern of sociological research on social stratification from the very beginning. Marx was waiting for the day when class consciousness would replace false consciousness, leading the working class into the revolution he predicted. Weber thought this wouldn't happen because people would form groups based on similarities of power or social status as well as on economic concerns. But even Weber recognized that class, status, and power operate together more often than they operate independently; most of us are ranked at more or less the same point on each hierarchy. Nevertheless, people may often group according to class similarities without being aware of it; a neighborhood association, a labor union, or a fraternal organization may represent more common interests than its members realize. This is one of the most confusing yet most interesting questions raised by the study of social stratification: How do individuals perceive their place in the system? These perceptions can change drastically, and sociologists are still searching for the reasons why.

SUMMARY

Social stratification refers to the arrangement of different activities of a society into a hierarchy whereby activities ranked high in the hierarchy are highly rewarded and activities ranked low are poorly rewarded. These rewards consist of economic privilege (social class), respect from others (social status), and influence over others (social power). These three dimensions overlap considerably, as activities that receive economic rewards generally also receive respect and are allowed to influence others. Individuals acquire these rewards by virtue of their engaging in one of the activities and only as long as they engage in it.

The movement of individuals from one activity to another is called social mobility. If the activities are within the same social class, the social mobility is horizontal; if the activities are in different social classes, the mobility is vertical. Societies that permit no vertical social mobility are called caste societies, while societies that permit open vertical mobility are called class societies. The former encourage the formation of large social groups based on caste, while the latter encourage individual competition. Societies located somewhere in between the two extremes, such as the United States, are characterized by group competition and conflict.

The structural-functional theory of social stratification maintains that stratification is necessary to place competent individuals in the activities most important to the society. This theory maintains that highly ranked activities are by definition more necessary to society and that high levels of rewards will encourage individuals to compete for those activities. The conflict theory maintains that social stratification is a form of social organization designed to benefit certain members of society through the organized exploitation of other members. This theory maintains that social stratification forces competition and inequality on the society and benefits only those who occupy the top positions of the hierarchy.

The United States has a clear system of social stratification in which a very few members of society control most of the wealth and power. There is consistent social mobility of individuals one social class boundary. To the extent that barriers to social mobility exist, individuals tend to remain in given social classes across generations, living in social and spatial isolation from each other. This class isolation creates distinctive class cultures or lifestyles, which further serve to separate the members of different social classes. As a general and important sociological concept, social class defines a wide variety of social experiences that people have. No social category has as great an impact on separating individuals as social class.

GLOSSARY

Bourgeoisie As defined by Karl Marx, the social class that owns the means of production and distribution in a capitalist economy (the ruling class).

Capitalism An economic system in which most of the wealth is the private property of individuals. This wealth (capital) can be invested and can be increased through profit.

Caste society A society with a social stratification hierarchy in which no vertical social mobility occurs.

Class consciousness As defined by Karl Marx, the ability of individuals in a particular social class to recognize the true interests of that class.

Class society A society with a social stratification hierarchy in which vertical social mobility occurs.

Conflict theory A school of sociological theory that focuses on the inherent strains and conflicts in social relations and the use of power by members of society to further their interests in the light of that conflict.

Ethnic stratification The clustering of ethnic group members at certain class levels of social stratification, with the result that members of certain ethnic groups will be found disproportionately in certain social classes.

Exploitation As defined by Karl Marx, the unequal manner in which the ruling class in society benefits from the working class.

False consciousness As defined by Karl Marx, the inability of individuals in a particular social class to recognize the true interests of that class.

Horizontal social mobility The movement of groups or individuals from one activity to another within the same social class level.

Ideology An idea or set of ideas that represents a particular interest of a particular social group. As defined by Karl Marx, it refers specifically to the set of beliefs that supports the interests of a ruling class in society.

Intergenerational vertical social mobility Vertical social mobility occurring between generations (as differences between the social class level of parent and child).

Intragenerational vertical social mobility Vertical social mobility occurring within the lifetime of one individual (or within one generation).

Party As defined by Max Weber, a political action or political interest group.

Proletariat As defined by Karl Marx, the social class that does not own the means of production and distribution in a capitalist economy but works for those who do.

Social class A collection of individuals whose activities (or roles) are similar in terms of the rewards they bring to their participants.

Social mobility The movement of groups or individuals within the ranking system of social stratification. (See vertical and horizontal social mobility.)

Social power The ability to influence the behavior of others.

Social status An individual's social position within the social group, particularly with respect to his or her prestige.

Social stratification The arrangement of different activities (or roles) into a hierarchy whereby activities ranked high are highly rewarded and activities ranked low are poorly rewarded. The rewards generally consist of money, prestige, and influence over others.

Socioeconomic status A sociological measure of social class, representing a combination of income, education, and occupational prestige.

Status inconsistency A social situation in which an individual is *not* consistently high, medium, or low across all the dimensions of social stratification.

Structural-functionalism A school of sociological theory that focuses on the interrelations among the elements of a society, emphasizing how elements of the social structure function to maintain the society.

Vertical social mobility The movement of groups or individuals up or down the stratification hierarchy, from one social class level to another.

SUPPLEMENTARY READINGS

Bendix, Reinhard, and Seymour Martin Lipset, eds. *Class, Status and Power.* New York: The Free Press, 1966.
A collection of essays on social stratification from both theoretical and empirical perspectives.

Gaventa, John *Power and Powerlessness: Quiescence and Rebellion in an Appalachian Valley.* Urbana: University of Illinois Press, 1980.
In this award-winning book, Gaventa describes how outside corporate interests use their influence to control economic development in areas they are exploiting in order to keep the labor force weaker.

Lenski, Gerhard *Power and Privilege: A Theory of Social Stratification.* New York: McGraw-Hill, 1966.
A view of social stratification from the developmental perspective. Lenski views the development of power and privilege in terms of different types of societies, showing how they change together.

Mills, C. Wright *White Collar: American Middle Class.* New York: Oxford University Press, 1951.
A classic American study of occupations and social stratification. Mills focuses on the rise of white-collar occupations in American society in the light of overall social change.

Rose, Stephen *Social Stratification in the United States.* New York: Pantheon, 1986.
Rose provides a good introduction to the sociological study of social stratification along with a quantity of recent data on inequality in the United States.

Rossides, Daniel W. *The American Class System: An Introduction to Social Stratification.* Boston: Houghton Mifflin, 1976.
As the title suggests, this is a general introduction to the sociological study of social stratification. More particularly, it is a source of good information concerning social class in the United States. Rossides presents a well-documented picture of modern social inequality.

Ryan, William *Blaming the Victim.* New York: Vintage, 1976.
In this easy-to-read book Ryan points out how many of the "failures" in American society are blamed for their own misfortune. Ryan suggests a sociological alternative by pointing to the structures of American society that create "victims" from the population. This book is appropriate both to the study of the lower class within a social stratification system and to the study of deviance.

Who Is the Underclass?

WILLIAM KORNBLUM

In this first of two articles on the underclass and income disparity within the American social stratification system, William Kornblum distinguishes the underclass from what he terms the "merely impoverished." While the latter group exceeds 13 percent of the U.S. population, he limits the term "underclass" to a segment of the population of perhaps 3 million or less that is hopelessly locked into poverty by forces beyond the individuals' control. He defines the term as applicable only to those people who "have fallen or been pushed into a world of suffering they can escape only *with help from others* in the larger society (Kornblum's emphasis)." In the course of examining the underclass in the United States, Kornblum takes us into the worlds of welfare, drug use and sales, AIDS, and homelessness.

The Underclass and the Merely Impoverished

All writers on the underclass agree that no matter how defined, its numbers are smaller than those of the poor. The most often used "official" U.S. government definition of poverty nets about thirty-two million Americans (13.1 percent of the population) who live below the threshold annual income of about $12,500 for a family of four. But included among these 32 million (and among the millions of others whose incomes hover just above this low figure) are Native Americans on impoverished reservations; people in households where there is a full-time (low) wage earner, where the household is composed of graduate students, where the household is composed of elderly persons on fixed incomes; and many others. So mere poverty, no matter how calculated, may be a necessary qualification but is not a sufficient measure of what the underclass might be.

The leading cause of poverty in the United States is low wages. Throughout the entire decade of the 1980s and continuing into the 1990s (despite the rather paltry 1990 increase in the minimum wage), a family of four with one full-time wage worker earning at or slightly above the minimum wage did not come even close to bringing home enough to exceed the official poverty threshold. Among the fifty million two-parent families in which one or more parents works full time, there are about three million families below the official poverty threshold. Much is written about the dramatic rise in poverty among single-parent families, and the large majority of children in single-parent families are living in poverty; but there are still far more children growing up in two-parent families and many of these are quite poor. In his book *Poor Support*, an invaluable study of contemporary poverty, David Ellwood shows that at least half the children in poverty in the United States are living in two-parent homes suffering the hardships of low wages and lack of employment. And an additional heavy proportion of the children growing up in single-parent homes once lived in two-parent homes that disintegrated because of severe economic hardship.

Separate the working poor, the unemployed, and the handicapped from the underclass, and what remains are people whose behavior, rather than unemployment or low wages, seems to some observers to be the cause of their woes. In *Science* (April 27, 1990), the nation's most prestigious

William Kornblum's article "Who Is the Underclass?" appeared in *Dissent* magazine, Spring 1991 issue. It is reprinted here by permission of both author and publisher.

scientific journal, economists Ronald Mincy, Isabel Sawhill, and Douglas Wolf point out that if one subtracts only those among the impoverished in America who have been down for a long count—eight years or more—"then about one fifth of the poor or about 6 million people could be considered members of the underclass." And if one considers the underclass as only those who have been impoverished over their entire lifetimes, the total would be perhaps no more than one or two million (their "educated guess"). But these authors go further and choose, as many who write on this subject do, to define the underclass in "behavioral terms." This "behavioral underclass" could be measured, they assert, by counting "the number of people who engage in bad behavior or a set of bad behaviors." Crime (especially in the drug industry), failure to work when not physically or mentally handicapped, teenage pregnancy, dropping out of school, and long-term welfare recipiency, are the actual bad behaviors they cite, arguing that these are typical of people who do not conform to norms of work, family, and morality. Using a methodology developed by Erol Ricketts and Isabel Sawhill, which counts the population in neighborhoods predominantly composed of people with such "bad behaviors," the authors come up with an estimate of a "behavioral underclass" composed of about 2.5 million people (based on the 1980 census) who live in 880 neighborhoods in American cities where there are high concentrations of other such ill-behaved people.

Middle-class Americans often cite the growth in teenage pregnancy and illegitimacy as indicators of the growth of a moral underclass. Between 1960 and 1986 expected births to teenage females actually declined by 50 percent among whites and by almost that much among blacks. Illegitimacy, however, has increased dramatically in the same period, so that about 16 percent of white babies and about 60 percent of black babies will be born to unmarried women. Much of the precipitous increase in illegitimacy among blacks can be attributed to joblessness among men. There is even evidence among whites and blacks with jobs and income of an increase in male unwillingness to take on family responsibilities; but, as Christopher Jencks notes, "as women earn more they become less willing to marry and more willing to divorce men who are hard to live with." In any event, because illegitimacy is increasing among middle-class people as well as among the poor, it is difficult to make the case that the increasing prevalence of illegitimacy is evidence of growth in a moral underclass.

In education, finally, trends in school achievement offer little support for the idea that there is a growing educational underclass, especially among African Americans. In 1960 almost 44 percent of whites and 76 percent of blacks between 25 and 27 years of age had not finished high school. By 1985 the proportions had declined to 13 percent for whites and 17 percent for blacks, and in fact white graduation rates have leveled off since the mid-1970s while black graduation rates continue to improve steadily. The same trends apply to college completion. In 1960 only 8.2 percent of whites and 28 percent of blacks (aged 25 to 29) had completed college. By 1985 the proportions were 23.2 percent for whites and 16.7 for blacks. Considering their extremely low "cultural capital" at the start of desegregation (as economists like to say), blacks made extraordinary gains in this period, and their rate of gain is now faster than that of whites.

These figures do not lend support to the idea of an educational underclass (especially not a black one), but neither are they cause for celebration. If rates of college completion have been increasing (only slowly, if at all, for whites), we still have far to go before we will be educating enough young people with the technical and cultural capabilities required in a rapidly altering economy.

Falling into the Underclass

Men who unload trucks for daily cash and other casual laborers and those who still seek to become part of the more stable working class ought not be included, I believe, in a general definition of the underclass. If we must speak of an underclass I hope the term may be narrowed to include only people who barely survive below the legitimate class system of capitalist society and below the lowest ranks of the criminal-class system as well. If it must be used at all, I think the term underclass ought to refer to people who have fallen or been pushed into a world of suffering they can escape only *with help from others* in the larger society.

We can reasonably use the concept of the underclass, for example, to understand such familiar scenes as this:

It is about midnight, on a wintry early Spring night quite near the beginning of the twenty-first

AIDS: COMMUNITY OF THE DAMNED

Victor Ayala directs the SEEK program in one of New York City's community colleges. A native New Yorker of Puerto Rican heritage, Victor himself "came up" through the City University system and knows hundreds of ways to help children of the inner city to a more solid educational footing. The work is exhausting. Budget cuts, tired staff, kids frustrated with school and expecting the worst from the bureaucracies; but Victor dwells on the successes, and this gives him energy to do his night work.

For the past two years Victor has worked four nights a week in the AIDS unit of a large public hospital in Brooklyn. He counsels homeless and indigent AIDS patients. His vast knowledge of the bureaucracies can help ease their anguish. In doing this work day after day Victor has become an expert on how this epidemic is experienced in the bottom depths of the city's poorest neighborhoods and in its embattled public hospital wards.

AIDS is rapidly becoming the scourge of the down and out. Its incidence is highest among intravenous drug users and their lovers and among the regulars in the crack dens, where young women, "crack bitches," often trade sexual favors for the drug. Many of the babies born into this community of the damned will also develop AIDS symptoms.

Victor does this work because he believes more people need to know what occurs inside the changing AIDS epidemic. Often the first, the last, and the most persistent hospital worker to speak with the AIDS patients, Victor writes copious notes on each case. Here is a sample, a typical vignette among the hundreds he has collected:

> "Dolores" is a 43-year-old black female diagnosed HIV positive, wih PCP pneumonia, tuberculosis, and high fevers. She has been homeless for four years and has lived in women's shelters or on the streets, occasionally with friends. She has a twenty-year history of substance abuse, including alcohol, heroin, and crack.
>
> After a month of avoiding me, Dolores finally speaks about her family. She has four children ages eight, ten, fifteen, and eighteen. Two of them live with her aunt. The oldest is in prison for attempted murder. By her standards she has been a neglectful mother. Her past eighteen years are a blur of drug abuse, prostitution, petty robbery, and homelessness. Almost everyone in Dolores's immediate family circle is involved with drugs. An intravenous drug-addicted brother, who frequently shared needles with her sister, died from AIDS-related illnesses. Dolores used to share needles with her sister, too. She has learned recently that her former husband, absent for five years, has died from AIDS-related illnesses.

When Dolores feels some strength she likes to socialize with other AIDS patients and with the hospital staff. The patients share cigarettes and often find ways to secure drugs. Victor finds Dolores an SRO (single-room occupancy) room and she prepares to leave the hospital. Shortly before her discharge the fever returns. A spinal tap reveals that she has cyptococcis meningitis, often a terminal illness in the AIDS patient. Victor describes how Dolores seeks more street drugs in the last two weeks of her life while she denies her impending death. Victor concludes on this note:

> Although Dolores is surrounded by other AIDS patients in various stages of dying, she believes there is time to live before she goes through the same things. As the end approaches, people avoid her room. Her doors remain closed, lights turned off, less and less routine care is provided.

century. A line of sedans and taxis, here and there a stretch limo, inches across Manhattan from the Midtown tunnel toward the Lincoln Tunnel on the West Side. I am in the fitful procession on my way to a college lecture scheduled for early the next day. Once past Fifth Avenue and into the garment center, the cars stopped at red lights are approached by gaunt men holding cans of window spray. They do not wait to see if the drivers want their windshields cleaned but immediately begin their sullen work. Some drivers wave them away, others are more offended. Shouts and insults fly. I take either the more socially conscious or cowardly path (depending on your politics) and spend a few quarters to have my window washed over and over again. Three times in three blocks I put coins in a man's hand. Each time I touch well-calloused fingers or a work-hardened palm.

The windshield washers are not the street urchins who ply this annoying trade uptown. They are adults who haunt the streets of midtown below the bus terminal. In cold weather they sleep in packing crates and cardboard boxes. By day they may seek casual labor, unloading trucks, moving merchandise, sweeping up, anything for immediate pay. At night many drink themselves to sleep. Some have crack or other dope habits to support. Most, but not all, are black or Puerto Rican.

If, then, we must have an underclass category, these men and others like them are good candidates for it. The bottom ranks of the working class always have men and women who are the most exploited and who, despite their hard work, cannot keep body and soul together. Sometimes such people are called wage slaves (Alec Wilkinson's book *Big Sugar* is a moving account of rural and migrant wage slavery). But homelessness and destitution in addition, as George Orwell showed in *Down and Out in Paris and London,* become a form of prison (with wage slavery) in the bosom of civil society. The homeless person can become locked into a round of daily survival behaviors, the search for food, for coins, for warmth, for an anodyne, for sleep. Increasingly most kinds of work except the most casual come to be out of reach for one reason or another, apart from how well the economy is doing. Life on the street soon destroys most people. Sleep deprivation, hunger, cold, sickness, and depression quickly take a toll. Men (and women) like these windshield wipers inhabit a despised street world intimately tied to the "regular economy," which that economy in fact produces in the backs of restaurants and in all the growing markets for casual labor and "lower overhead."

What about the children these men may have fathered along the way to their precarious adulthoods? Are they also to be thought of as part of the underclass? Suppose, as is often likely, the children are living with mothers who are on welfare. Some of their mothers may have had a few children by different fathers and been on welfare for years. Are "chronic" welfare mothers and their children also part of the underclass?

In most definitions of the term, welfare mothers who are on public assistance for more than three years and have additional children while on assistance are classified as "chronic welfare recipients" and are considered as part of the underclass. I reject this idea.

A mother of dependent children has real work to do and a mother with no regular male help has even more work. This should not be a controversial assertion. Middle-class mothers who choose to stay home in order to raise children often zealously defend their choice. They do not look kindly on suggestions that their lives are leisurely even if they also admit their good fortune in not "needing to go to work right away." Welfare mothers have even more obstacles to surmount since just existing on welfare is hard work itself. And few welfare mothers can actually exist on AFDC benefits, Medicaid, and food stamps. Almost all seek additional income, from off-the-books work, like caring for others' children along with their own, or in innumerable "hustles." And if receiving welfare payments was such a cushy way of life, welfare mothers would be expected to migrate from states with lower benefits to those with higher ones. But there is no evidence that such migration occurs. Instead, the women typically plan ways of improving their education or finding a decent job or forming a stable relationship, all the things any of us would try in order to "get on our feet." Now the welfare laws increasingly push women to get back into the labor market when their children are old enough to be in day care, but of course we have yet to develop anything like an adequate day-care system.

Yet to exclude all mothers on welfare from even my narrow and reluctant definition of an underclass would not well reflect the suffering and neglect we see around us in cities like New York and Chicago and in hundreds of other American communities large and small. Women without homes, mothers and children without homes, all run the risk that homelessness itself becomes an insurmountable and debilitating obstacle. Welfare mothers who become addicted or who become entrapped in a world of prostitution and unsuccessful petty crime, or whose material and emotional lives have disintegrated to the point that they neglect and abuse their children, all can be thought to have fallen into the lowest ranks of poverty and misery. AIDS workers like Victor Ayala (see box) would agree that indigent AIDS patients, surely down and out, might also be counted among an underclass, but he believes the term serves little purpose except to excuse our ignorance of the AIDS epidemic.

There are also children who fall into extreme poverty and risk living out brutally shortened lives at the bottom. One of the best recent books about this subject is Terry Williams's *Cocaine Kids,* a detailed ethnography of the lives of teenagers in upper Manhattan who become involved in the world of crack dealing. Williams and others have shown that existing drug laws encourage adult dealers to recruit children into the underground drug industry. There are a few cases of teenagers who become wildly successful and even more cases of teenagers who make some money for a while before getting into trouble with the authorities or within the drug underworld. Williams shows that those who begin using drugs, other than marijuana, quickly decline and are cast out, often to drift into trouble or violence. Kids with records of arrest, failure in school, histories of drug abuse and depression, and with only limited training for employment and few contacts in labor markets are prime candidates for lives as windshield washers and street-corner junkies. But if they are not trapped into such lives because of homelessnes or severe debilitation, they should not be counted among those who are down and out. Though at risk of falling, they have not yet dropped into the underclass. Whether they do so or not will depend a good deal on the opportunities our society makes available to them to help themselves. It will also depend on the kind of adult mentors it provides them.

In sum, as I use the term, the underclass includes those people who are trapped in a netherworld at the bottom of both the legal and illegal class systems. The major traps are addiction, homelessness, mental illness, destitution, and usually a combination of these conditions. Although their numbers are growing steadily, especially in central cities and segregated ghettos, the size of this population is far lower than the overall poverty population (which has also been growing). The idea that the underclass is relatively small and is composed of people who have fallen out of the working or criminal classes (or who never made it up before becoming trapped at the bottom) will help emphasize the special programs of emergency housing, supported work, drug rehabilitation, enhanced schooling in low-income communities, and other measures that could reduce destitution and homelessness. If the down-and-out make up no more than three million people (including the nation's present homeless population), we ought to be able to immediately reduce that number.

We ought to be able to help, that is, if we can ever overcome the consequences of all the theft of public funds and the vicious attacks on our social institutions that has marked the past decade. In fact, by my definition of the underclass there is not a major new social class to trumpet about or to blame on welfare institutions. There is instead a significant growth in old-style misery, due in some part to industrial restructuring and in another and more evil part to the cupidity of the nation's elite. History will show that for some time toward the end of our American Century the nation's upper class, or the part of it in power, embraced a philosophy of narrow self-interest first elaborated by Bernard Mandeville in his tract of 1705, *The Grumbling Hive* (later expanded into *The Fable of the Bees*). Mandeville coined the phrase, "Private vice makes public virtue." Someone might want to offer this profound insight to the corner windshield washers or to the homeless people huddled outside the gates of the White House.

Discussion Questions

1. Some observers define the underclass in largely behavioral terms, focusing on what they perceive to be immoral behaviors (drug use, the birth of illegitimate children, etc.) that keep people who perform those behaviors in poverty. Kornblum rejects this characterization. What arguments can be made on both sides?
2. Kornblum recommends help for the underclass, including emergency housing, supported work programs, drug rehabilitation, and better schools. What arguments does he offer that allow him to predict success for such programs? What arguments could be made in opposition to such programs? If, as is likely, such programs would grow from tax-supported government spending, what would increase or decrease political support for such programs?

READING

The Income Distribution Disparity

PAUL KRUGMAN

Paul Krugman examines poverty in America in a historical perspective, showing how inequality has increased since 1980, after several decades of decreasing inequality. He lays the blame for part of this change on policies initiated in 1980 by the Reagan administration, which simultaneously cut taxes for the wealthy and reduced spending on the poor. He lays another part of the blame on a growing drop in productivity in the American economy—a factor that he feels is particularly important in understanding the working poor (who currently face fewer job opportunities and lower incomes) and the underclass (who seem hopelessly cut off from any kind of opportunity). In short, Krugman paints a picture of the American social stratification system since 1980 in which the rich have clearly gotten richer and the poor have clearly gotten poorer.

Although the typical American family had about the same real income in 1988 as it did in 1978, this was not true of untypical families: the rich and the poor. The best-selling novel of 1988, Tom Wolfe's *Bonfire of the Vanities*, portrayed an America of growing wealth at the top, a struggle to make ends meet in the middle, and growing misery at the bottom. The numbers bear him out. During the 1980s, the rich, and for that matter the upper middle class, became a great deal richer, while the poor became significantly poorer.

In making this comparison, it is important to be careful about starting dates. The great bulk of the population is better off now than it was in the last year of the Carter Administration or the first two years of the Reagan Administration, when the economy was in a deep recession. That recession, however, was transitory—as we will see later, it was part of a deliberate, bipartisan policy of temporarily raising unemployment in order to reduce inflation. The recession years, therefore, provide a misleading base for comparison. The more appropriate comparison is with a time of more "normal" unemployment, which puts us back to 1979. When one does this, the growth in inequality is startling.

One recent study concludes that, after adjusting for changes in family size, the real income before taxes of the average family in the top 10 percent of the population rose by 21 percent from 1979 to 1987, while that of the bottom 10 percent *fell* by 12 percent. If one bears in mind that tax rates for the well-off generally fell in the Reagan years, while noncash benefits for the poor, like public housing, became increasingly scarce, one sees a picture of simultaneous growth in wealth and poverty unprecedented in the twentieth century. The same study estimates that the fraction of Americans who are "rich" (defined by an arbitrary but constant standard) nearly doubled from 1979 to 1987, even while the fraction of families defined by the U.S. government as living in poverty simultaneously increased by 15 percent.

Even these numbers probably fail to capture the full extent of what has happened, because they miss the real extremes. The ranks of the extremely well-off were reinforced by the vast fortunes made by traders and investment bankers on Wall Street, and by huge increases in executive compensation. Meanwhile, the amount of

Paul Krugman is Professor of Economics at the Massachusetts Institute of Technology. This article is excerpted with permission from his book, *The Age of Diminished Expectations: U.S. Economic Policy in the 1990s*, published in 1990 by The Washington Post Company.

sheer misery in America has surely increased much faster than the official poverty rate, as homelessness and drug addiction have spread.

Long-term comparisons of income distribution are fraught with difficulties, but for what it is worth, standard calculations show that the surge in inequality in the United States after 1979 reversed three decades of growing equality, pushing the income shares of the top and bottom categories to their highest and lowest levels, respectively, since 1950. Since measures of inequality in 1950 were magnified by widespread rural poverty, it is probably safe to say that income distribution within our metropolitan areas is more unequal today than at any time since the 1930s.

While some conservatives do not consider income distribution a valid issue for public concern, the changes in that distribution in the 1980s had a far more important effect on people's lives than any deliberate government action. After all, even a disastrous policy blunder is unlikely to lower the real incomes of 25 million Americans by more than 10 percent; yet that is what happened to the poorest tenth of the population during the 1980s. Not everyone agrees that the soaring inequality of the 1980s was a bad thing, but it is a simple fact that the growth of both affluence and poverty in the 1980s largely reflected changes in the distribution of income, rather than in its overall level.

An Extra $1,000

There are at least two reasons for arguing that the increased inequality of the 1980s changed *overall* welfare for the worse. First, most Americans do care at least a little bit about how well-off others are, and it is hard to argue with the conclusion that an extra thousand dollars of income matters more to a poor family than to someone whose income is already in six digits. Second, the income distribution colors the whole tone of society: A society with few extremes of wealth or poverty is a different, and surely more attractive, place than one with a yawning gulf between rich and poor.

In the long run, income distribution is not as imporant a determinant of economic well-being as productivity growth, but in the 1980s increasing inequality in income distribution, rather than growth in productivity, was the main source of rising living standards for the top 10 percent of Americans. And the 1980s were the first decade since the 1930s in which large numbers of Americans actually suffered a serious decline in living standards.

Yet income distribution, like productivity growth, is not a policy issue that is on the table. This is partly because we don't fully understand why inequality soared, but mostly because any attempt to reverse its trend appears politically out of bounds.

One reason that action to limit growing income inequality in the United States is difficult is that the growth in inequality is not a simple picture. Old-line leftists, if there are any left, would like to make it a single story—the rich becoming richer by exploiting the poor. But that's just not a reasonable picture of America in the 1980s. For one thing, most of our very poor don't work, which makes it hard to exploit them. For another, the poor had so little to start with that the dollar value of the gains of the rich dwarfs that of the losses of the poor. (In constant dollars, the increase in per family income among the top tenth of the population in the 1980s was about a dozen times as large as the decline among the bottom tenth.)

To tell the story of what happened in the 1980s, it is necessary to paint a more complicated picture. At least three separate trends have combined to make our society radically less equal. To begin with, at the very bottom of the scale, the so-called "underclass" grew both more numerous and more miserable. Entirely unrelated, as far as anyone can tell, was a huge increase in the incomes of the very rich. In between, among those who work for a living, the earnings of the relatively unskilled fell while the earnings of the highly skilled rose.

Let's start with the underclass. While there is no generally accepted statistical definition of the underclass, we all know what it means: that largely nonwhite hard core of people caught in a vicious circle of poverty and social collapse. Attempts to measure the size of the underclass, like those of Isabel Sawhill at the Urban Institute, suggest that it began growing during the 1960s, and has continued to grow, perhaps at an accelerating rate, since then. In the 1960s and 1970s, social programs were expected to cure persistent poverty; in the 1980s they were widely accused of indirectly perpetuating it. At this point it appears that if you increase spending on the poor, they have more money; if you reduce it, they have less; otherwise, it doesn't make much difference. That is, neither generosity nor niggardliness seems to make much difference to the spread of the underclass OSC by making it more difficult for the poor to climb out of poverty. Both could be right. The most important causes of the growth in the underclass, however, like the sources of the productivity slowdown, lie more in the domain of sociology than of economics.

The increased incomes of the rich and very well-off present less of a puzzle than the growth of the underclass. While high incomes have been made in a variety of ways, one source stands out above all: finance. The 1980s were a golden age for financial wheeling and dealing, and the explosion of profits in financial operations has helped swell the ranks of the really rich—those earning hundreds of thousands or even millions a year.

Most Americans live between the stratosphere and the lower depths, and for them the growth in inequality has been yet a different story. First, there was the yuppie phenomenon: the rise of two-income families with $50,000 or more in annual income. Second, wage differentials among occupations widened: the real wages of blue-collar workers have declined fairly steadily for the past decade, and earnings of highly educated workers have risen rapidly. (The ratio of earnings of college graduates to those of high school graduates declined during the 1970s from 1.5 to 1.3, then rose to 1.8 during the 1980s.)

What we really don't know is why these phenomena have all happened now. The rise of two-income professional couples reflects the lagged effects of the women's movement, plus the aging of the baby boom generation. The surges in pay differentials and in market manipulation are more mysterious. Politics may have had something to do with it. The Reagan years provided a tolerant climate both for tough bargaining with workers and for financial wheeling and dealing. Other forces, like the decline of smokestack America and the consequent restructuring of the U.S. economy, may also have played a role.

What to Do?

Whatever the reasons for soaring inequality in the 1980s, what can policy do about it? In particular, can anything be done about the extremes of wealth and poverty that have emerged in the past decade?

The problem with poverty, as an issue, is that it has basically exhausted the patience of the general public. America launched its War on Poverty in the 1960s—a time of rising incomes and widespread optimism about government activism. This "war" was supposed to be social engineering, not merely charity. It was intended not simply to raise the living standards of the poor, but to help them work their way out of poverty. Yet poverty did not decline. Despite sharp increases in aid to the poor between the late 1960s and the mid-1970s, poverty remained as intractable as ever, and the underclass that is the most visible sign of poverty grew alarmingly. Today, relatively few people believe, as so many did in the 1960s, that government can do much to help the poor become more productive; all that it seems able to do is raise their standard of living by giving them more money (and influential books, like Charles Murray's *Losing Ground,* deny even that).

But if aid to the poor is simply charity, then its political base is nothing more than public generosity. In a time of budget deficits and largely static living standards for the average American, such generosity does not come easily. There are some modest signs of a resurgence of social activism; money may eventually become available to deal with the conspicuous poverty of the homeless; and Congress has made an effort to reform the tax system to help the working poor. But any systematic initiative to raise the incomes of the poor seems unlikely for many years.

As for the rich, a few public policy initiatives might cut down on some of their sources of income. For example, tighter regulation of financial markets might limit the number of people with incomes in the tens of millions, and a cooled-off financial market might indirectly put some limits on executive pay. For the most part, however, the only way to make the rich less so is to tax them. Yet this conflicts, or is perceived to conflict, with other policy goals—such as encouraging risk-taking and entrepreneurship. Given that the deepest problem with the U.S. economy is slow productivity growth, it is difficult to argue for tax increases that might reduce incentives, even if some people make large sums in return for dubious contributions. In effect, there seems to be a public consensus that Donald Trump is the price of progress.

So income distribution, like productivity growth, is a policy issue with no real policy debate. The growing gap between rich and poor was arguably the central fact about economic life in America in the 1980s. But no policy changes now under discussion seem likely to narrow this gap significantly.

Discussion Questions

1. Krugman argues that the rich in America got richer during the 1980s despite a decrease in the level of economic productivity. How does he support that assertion? Where did the money come from?
2. Krugman suggests that spending money on poor people will provide them with more money temporarily but will not cure their poverty. How does he connect this assertion with declining productivity in American society?

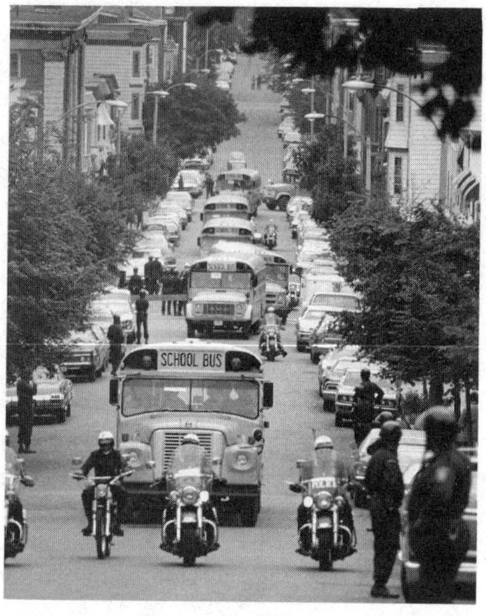

CHAPTER 8 RACIAL AND ETHNIC RELATIONS

Imagine a scene somewhere in the country. A farmer is standing on a country road looking fondly at his most prized possession—several hundred acres of good farm land. A stranger comes walking down the road and strikes up a conversation.

"That's a mighty nice piece of land there," says the stranger.

"Yup," replies the farmer.

"Belongs to you?" asks the stranger.

"Yup," replies the farmer.

"How did you come by it?" asks the stranger.

"Well," replies the farmer, "I got it from my father, who worked it all his life and left it to me."

"Well, how did he get it?"

"From my grandfather."

"But how did he get it?"

"From his father before him."

"But how did he get it?"

"Well," replies the farmer, "he fought for it."

"That's fine," counters the stranger, "I'll fight you for it."

Why doesn't the stranger have a right to fight for the land? No piece of land on the face of the earth is occupied by its original owner or even the descendants of the original owner. All ownership is initially or subsequently fought for. At some point following the fight, the state takes over to maintain the status quo. In the case of the story above, the farmer's great-grandfather took the land by force, but he subsequently received a legal deed to the property from the state. That deed means that the next person who wants to fight for the land will have to fight the state as well as the farmer. Like a vast game of musical chairs, the state has the power to stop the music and award the chairs to whomever it chooses. Throughout American history, for instance, most land was awarded to European immigrants, while very little was awarded to American Indians. Box 8.1 provides an example of similar loss of land by Spanish settlers in New Mexico following the Mexican War in 1848.

As this example suggests, the study of racial and ethnic groups in any society will also be the study of power. This chapter focuses on the racial and ethnic groups in the United States, paying particular attention to the power relations among them. As we will see, those power relations are organized within a system of ethnic stratification in which different racial and ethnic groups disproportionately occupy certain class levels in the stratification hierarchy. A major focus of this chapter is thus the way ethnic stratification encourages the formation of stereotypes, prejudice, and discrimination. We will also examine the different cultures that ethnic groups bring to a society and what happens when those cultures meet. Finally, we will take a more specific look at some of the racial and ethnic groups that make up the population of the United States. Racial and ethnic diversity in any society adds an important wrinkle to its basic social coordination. Our ideas about racial and ethnic groups change the meanings we have about specific forms of social interaction and specific roles; a black policeman, for example, is somehow different from a white policeman in both black and white community perceptions. The sociological outlook will help you understand why those perceptions are different.

BOX 8.1

MINORITY STATUS AND PROPERTY OWNERSHIP: LAND GRABS IN NEW MEXICO AFTER THE MEXICAN WAR

The parable that opens this chapter is designed to show the relationship between power and property ownership. Ultimately, the group in power gets to make the rules, which typically favor itself. But while that parable is fictional, there are many historical cases that provide clear illustrations of the principle in practice. One such case occurred in the state of New Mexico in the last half of the 19th century, as land ownership moved from Spanish settlers to Anglo speculators.

Prior to the 1846 war between Mexico and the United States, northern New Mexico represented the largest Spanish settlement in what was then northern Mexico. Some 60,000 people lived there. The much weaker Mexico was easily defeated and was forced to turn over its northern provinces to the United States according to the terms of the Treaty of Guadalupe Hidalgo signed in 1848. (Incidentally, the United States had less claim to this land than Iraq had to Kuwait in 1990, but the victors do get to write the histories.) The interesting aspect of the Treaty is that it pledged to respect the land-ownership rights of current settlers even though they would now be living in American territory instead of Mexican territory. The United States government was under no constraint to be so gracious, but, as it turned out, the pledges were not honored in any case.

Between 1848 and 1900, approximately four-fifths of land formerly owned by Spanish citizens passed into Anglo hands (Barrera, 1979). The methods used were as varied as the human imagination. Many Spanish settlers could not prove specific land ownership because of differences in surveying methods between the two countries (Westphall, 1965). Much land was held as communal grants by settlers, so no one person owned the land; American courts recognized no such form of land ownership (Knowlton, 1967). When land ownership was challenged, Spanish settlers were required to hire lawyers; having little money but much land, the settlers were forced to pay lawyers with land (so that even a successful court outcome resulted in land loss) (Knowlton, 1967). Property taxes were introduced. Since most land owners did not operate on a cash economy, they had little money to pay such taxes; in some cases, they were not even told about the existence of taxes until their land had been taken for nonpayment (Swadesh, 1974). And finally, records were forged, government officials were bribed, and an assortment of other clearly illegal methods were employed when none of the above "legal" methods was successful. Some Spanish resistance was stimulated by all of this. Most notable was Las Gorras Blancas—a secret society that operated near Las Vegas and Santa Fe in northern New Mexico around 1890 and that specialized in destroying fences and railroad property (Larson, 1975). Nevertheless, the economic and legal clout of Anglos (coupled with their growing numbers as the Old West was settled) proved too strong an enemy. Today, the descendants of those early Spanish settlers still live in northern New Mexico but most in minority status and most without their land.

KEY ISSUES AND CONCEPTS IN RACE AND ETHNIC RELATIONS

The sociological study of racial and ethnic groups is typical of the sociological outlook in general. Though racial and ethnic groups are social groups that adhere to different norms and values, much like social groups anywhere, there are a few distinctive aspects to this study that have led sociologists to create some specific concepts to explain them. It's not always clear, for example, just what difference there might be between the concepts of racial group and ethnic group. And what makes either a minority group or a majority group? Perhaps the most important concept is ethnic stratification, which explains much of the hatred and conflict we're so used to seeing between racial and ethnic groups.

Racial and Ethnic Groups

As we saw in Chapter 6, an **ethnic group** is a group of people who share a common culture, think of themselves as sharing a common culture, or are defined by others as sharing a common culture. Another way of putting it is to say that they share common ethnicity. Ethnicity is not a complicated concept to apply, since culture is observable and that observation is often agreed upon by both the observer and the observed. The concept of a racial group, however, is not so easily defined.

Since an ethnic group is a group of people who share a common cultural heritage, we might suggest that a **racial group** is a group of people who are socially defined as sharing a common genetic heritage. Genetic heritage could be roughly defined as a cluster of genetic information that, *as a cluster,* differs from other clusters of genetic information. Thus, a given individual in one racial group might have the same shape of nose or the same blood type as an individual from another racial group, but, on the whole and as groups, they would have different characteristics. This seemingly simple definition appears to make sense in everyday observation. Most people think they can distinguish between white people and black people, for instance, by looking for a cluster of physical characteristics that are supposed to separate the races. White people are supposed to have lighter skin, finer hair, thinner noses, and so on. If a particular individual happens to have somewhat darker skin, he or she might still be classified as white because of the presence of other "white race" characteristics. The problem, however, is that parents who are classified as black could have children who might be classified as white (as long as the children do not challenge the new classification). Conversely, "white" parents might have children classified as black purely on the basis of appearance.

The real problem with the concept of race is that, although we think it is a biological term, its meaning derives from the social interactions of nonbiologists. When people become convinced that two or more races exist, then those races do, in fact, exist in the everyday lives of the people who are labeled accordingly (Trillin, 1986). We thus have at least two possible definitions of race: a scientific definition and a social definition. With regard to the scientific definition, biologists do not unanimously agree on the meaning or even the existence of race. As interesting as that dispute is, it does not directly affect us, for our concern forces us to the second, or social, definition of race. We must be concerned with what nonbiologists think of race, for it is their decisions that affect individual lives in society.

A brief look at history suggests that nonbiologists are more confused by the concept of race than biologists are. For example, some Americans of northwest European ancestry suggested in the early part of this century that they belonged to a different (and, of course, superior) race from Poles, Italians, Greeks, and other southeast Europeans. The latter group they thought to be, at best, feebleminded. This idea, which seems ridiculous today, is little more than fifty years old; one wonders how our ideas of race will stack up fifty years from now.

Consider a tentative solution to this confusion. Returning to our original concept of ethnic group, we find that groups of people who are said to differ racially invariably also usually differ ethnically from whoever is doing the labeling. Thus, racial groups are also usually ethnic groups. This is true for a remarkably simple reason: The term *race* is usually used in justifications for doing something unpleasant to someone else. It becomes less upsetting to do that unpleasant thing if the victim can first be defined as unworthy or in some way unequal. It is much easier, for instance, to enslave someone who is defined as ignorant by reason of belonging to an inferior race. This makes it easier to give human beings the status of farm animals; like the black slave, farm animals are not thought capable of handling a more independent situation. In a strange twist of logic the slave owner can even conjure up the belief that he is doing the slave a favor. In short, people do not face discriminatory treatment because they are racially different; rather *they are defined as racially different to justify discriminatory treatment.* The function of these kinds of social situations is to keep people separate from each other. If the people did not enter such a situation already ethnically different, a relatively short stay would create that difference. Racial groups are also usually ethnic groups or contain several ethnic groups as a result of this social separation.

Minority and Majority Status: A Question of Dominance and Subordination

The terms *minority group* and *majority group* are used for reasons more of tradition than of science. Traditionally, a minority group was a relatively small ethnic group living within the country of a much larger ethnic group. The minority often found itself getting the short end of the stick because the majority group would help itself to whatever was valued in the society before giving the minority group a chance. The majority group's ability to dominate the minority appeared at first glance to be the result of its larger size; hence the names *minority* and *majority.* The problem, however, is that although power can come with larger group size, it can be achieved in other ways as well. Smaller groups can dominate larger groups if they are more powerful. That power is more important than group size leads to the following definitions: A **majority group** is a social group that controls the organization and distribution of rewards in a society. A **minority group** is a relatively powerless social group that is subject to the decisions of the majority group. The general term *rewards* here refers to the wide range of possessions and activities within a society that its members might value, such as jobs, prestige, and power. Access to rewards in any society is always a matter of utmost concern, and control over that access is perhaps the ultimate measure of power. A majority group, by definition, is the ethnic group that has that power. A minority group, by definition, is one that does not. More accurately, then, we should perhaps call a majority group a **dominant group** and a minority group a **subordinate group.** If that dominance becomes structured into the society in an ongoing manner, the result is a system of ethnic stratification.

Ethnic Stratification: The Exploitation of Minority Groups

Ethnic stratification refers to a specific arrangement of ethnic groups within an already established system of social stratification; it is therefore a special type of social stratification. The "specific arrangement" of the ethnic groups refers to the location of a disproportionate number of people from a given ethnic group in particular social classes. For example, in the United States we have never had a black U.S. president nor are you likely to find many blacks running major corporations; there is, in fact, a definite lack of black people occupying upper-class positions in American society. (When individual black Americans do move into high-level positions, their race seems to come to the forefront and to overshadow their other accomplishments; when Jesse Jackson ran for the Democratic presidential nomination he was viewed as a *black* candidate by *both* black and white voters.) If you look at the other extreme, however, you will find that black Americans make up more than their share of people below the poverty level in the United States. That is ethnic stratification.

We have already looked at social stratification in general and the routes (or barriers) to social mobility within it (see Chapter 7). Lower-class people in general find it difficult to move up in social class; lower-class *nonwhite* people find such obstacles even more insurmountable. Certain ethnic groups have been placed into specific jobs at certain levels of the stratification hierarchy and tend to remain there across generations.

The upper classes in the United States have long been dominated by white Protestant Americans descended from northwest European immigrants (popularly called white Anglo-Saxon Protestants, or WASPs). When you think of a typical upper-class American, such a person immediately springs to mind, as our system of ethnic stratification continues to place such people (and their offspring) in those top positions. When you think of a household servant or a garbage collector, on the other hand, a very different image will spring to mind. Depending on where you live, that image may very likely be a nonwhite person (provided there are enough nonwhite people where you live to do those jobs).

Ethnic stratification is a very useful system for those at the top (the dominant group). Its primary use is that it structures exploitation into the everyday business of society. **Exploitation** is a concept with many definitions, but, according to most definitions, it describes a situation where an individual does not receive the full value for his or her labor. Such situations occur when individuals have few options in their lives. If, for example, your choice is to starve or to take a difficult and/or dangerous job at low pay, you will probably take the job. Historically, that is what most people have done. Those individuals doing the hiring (again, members of the dominant group) are therefore in a position to benefit since their employees have no choice but to work on their terms. Ethnic stratification exists when routes to upward social mobility are cut off for particular ethnic groups. This situation leaves them little choice but to work at the jobs left over (see Box 8.2).

The most obvious example of exploitation through a system of ethnic stratification is the American system of slavery. Under slavery blacks were legally locked into their economic position; having no other choice, they worked. White slave owners, of course, benefited greatly from this system. As a more recent example, many American employers today specialize in hiring illegal aliens, individuals who dare not object to working conditions or pay scales for fear of being deported. Exploitation depends upon the exploited individuals' having limited

BOX 8.2

AMERICAN ETHNIC MINORITIES AND THE WORLD OF PROFESSIONAL BOXING

Occupying the bottom rung on a stratification system generally means you have to do the work that no one else wants to do for whatever they want to pay you; lower-class jobs are typically poorly paid and unpleasant. One unusual example of a lower-class job that fits that description generally is professional boxing. It does not fit the description perfectly, however. Although most boxers make little money, there is always the possibility of "making it." In addition, the obvious physical unpleasantness of the job is lessened somewhat by the necessary skill and social status involved. Nevertheless, boxing is and always has been an occupation of the lower classes.

S. Kirson Weinberg and Henry Arond (1952) studied the ethnic groups that were professional boxers in America between 1909 and 1948. Their findings offer some interesting insights into the interplay between social class and cultural differences that occur within ethnic stratification. Some ethnic groups, for example, seem to have a cultural bias against boxing. The Irish became boxers but not the Scandinavians; Filipinos became boxers but not the Chinese or Japanese. Of the ethnic groups that did favor boxing their members went in for the sport only during the time their particular group occupied the lowest classes of American society. The year 1909 saw boxing dominated by the Irish, and by Germans; 1909 was the middle of the southeastern European immigrant influx, and these new groups had yet to settle into the occupational world of boxing. By 1928, however, two southeastern European groups, the Jews and Italians, had displaced the Irish and Germans in boxing as well as in the lower classes in American society in general. By 1948 black Americans and Mexican Americans came to dominate the sport—a trend that is still with us today.

Like most lower-class jobs, boxing is an occupation shunned by those with other (and presumably better) options. As one 1950 statement from a boxing promoter suggests,

> They say that too much education softens a man and that is why the college graduates are not good fighters. They fight emotionally on the gridiron and they fight bravely and well in our wars, but their contributions in our rings have been insignificant. The ring has been described as the refuge of the under-privileged. Out of the downtrodden have come our greatest fighters. . . . An education is an escape, and that is what they are saying when they shake their heads—those who know the fight game—as you mention the name of a college fighter. Once the bell rings, they want their fighters to have no retreat, and a fighter with an education is a fighter who does not have to fight to live and he knows it. . . . Only for the hungry fighter is it a decent gamble. (Weinberg and Arond, 1952: 461-462)

options, and ethnic stratification provides that situation by keeping those individuals locked into the lower classes through some means of discrimination.

Discrimination appears in society in many manifestations: Individuals may be denied housing, forced to ride at the back of the bus, refused employment, denied the vote, or have their

Migrant farm workers coming from Mexico to harvest crops in the United States have no rights as citizens and so are prime candidates for exploitation. The wages they receive may be extremely low by American standards, but the money is still more than the workers could earn in Mexico.

land taken away from them. In each case there is a common core that defines the concept. **Discrimination** is any action that shows a bias against an individual on the basis of his or her group membership; it is typically designed to hinder the competitive abilities of individuals in that group. Discrimination, in short, closes routes of upward social mobility and allows ethnic stratification to survive from one generation to the next. Instances of discrimination that do not appear to hinder competitive abilities directly (such as requiring blacks to ride at the back of the bus) tend to serve this purpose indirectly: The act of discrimination may do psychological damage to members of the affected group, and, furthermore, segregated buses are usually accompanied by segregated employment. As one of the central concepts in the sociological study of race and ethnic relations, discrimination will reappear throughout this chapter. For the present it is important to grasp the relationship between the system of ethnic stratification within which we live and the discriminatory actions with which we respond to that system. As we will see, discrimination is not the result of a bigoted person's blindly striking out at members of other ethnic groups; it is rather a coldly rational and highly effective weapon for achieving success. Ethnic stratification encourages the use of many such weapons.

STEREOTYPES, PREJUDICE, AND DISCRIMINATION: RESPONSES TO ETHNIC STRATIFICATION

Stereotypes

A *stereotype* is a piece of knowledge (an idea or a belief) about a piece of the social world. By "piece of the social world" we mean the way in which we subdivide an otherwise overwhelming confusion of human beings into manageable pieces, such as black or white, men or women, rich or poor. A term such as *black people* refers to many different human beings who share one trait that is important to the user of the term, ignoring differences in favor of calling attention to similarities that are thought important. In this sense any descriptive term does damage to the thing it describes by only partially describing it, but this kind of mental organization is necessary so that the vast variety of experience can be made manageable (for example, see Levin, 1975; Schutz, 1970).

Now we can return to the first part of our definition of stereotype: A stereotype is a "piece of knowledge." A piece of knowledge is simply an idea or belief that the holder of that piece of knowledge finds convincing. The "knowledge" is usually nothing more than a collection of adjectives that the user of the stereotype believes is an accurate description of some group of people. Most stereotypes can in fact be reduced to the following simple form: "(*insert name of human group here*) are (*insert adjective here*)." For example, blacks are lazy, women are illogical, Poles are dumb, Jews are cheap. Enough of these statements will tell you all you think you need to know about some group of people. If their group is in the way of your group or threatens your group, you can make sure that all of the adjectives are negative, as in the examples. In practice, therefore, a **stereotype** becomes a generalized description (usually negative) of a specific social group and applied to its members (see Luhman, 1990).

The Psychology of Prejudice

Prejudice is a negative attitude toward a group of people. It is built upon stereotypes, which specify the boundaries between groups of people (enabling you to find the people you dislike) and which provide a handy set of reasons for your negative attitudes. A dislike of black people can be rationalized with the stereotype "They are lazy and stupid"; a dislike of Asian people can be justified with the stereotype "They are ambitious, clever, and inscrutable." Almost any adjective can fuel a negative stereotype if it is thought of and said in just the right manner. As Gordon Allport pointed out, Abraham Lincoln is admired for being thrifty, hard-working, ambitious, and devoted to the rights of the average person. Jews, on the other hand, are hated for being tight-fisted, overambitious, pushy, and radical (Allport, 1954).

The Prejudiced Personality Since prejudice is an attitude or belief, it seems to fall at least as much within the province of psychology as of sociology. Not surprisingly, therefore, much research has attempted to determine the nature of prejudice and its psychological roots. One direction this research has taken is a search for what might be called the prejudiced personality. Two assumptions behind this research are (1) that prejudice is a general orientation toward the world rather than a specific set of ideas or beliefs regarding particular groups of people, and (2) that prejudice is somehow pathological and indicates an emotional disturbance in the prejudiced individual. The most famous research on the prejudiced personality was done by T. W. Adorno and his associates.

The years immediately following World War II saw considerable reflection on the fascism and anti-Semitism that had characterized Nazi Germany. Adorno and his colleagues concluded that there existed a group of personality characteristics that, as a set, might be described as "potentially fascistic," and that this set of characteristics might further be linked to prejudice (Adorno et al., 1950). They came to label this potentially fascistic personality as the *authoritarian personality,* and they explained it as the result of particularly harsh and restricted childhood socialization.

A supporting piece of research within this tradition is E. L. Hartley's (1946) study of prejudiced attitudes. Hartley found that individuals prejudiced against ethnic or racial groups showed the same prejudices when confronted with questions about fictional ethnic groups such as Wallonians, Pirenians, and Danerians. The implication is that an individual who displays prejudice against even a nonexistent group (which precludes having rational reasons for the dislike) must be considered as having a prejudiced orientation toward the world.

Maintaining Self-esteem Self-esteem is an individual's subjective evaluation of his or her self-worth. That worth can be measured against some objective standard (such as success in following the Ten Commandments) or against the performance of others in the individual's immediate environment. In the first case the individual's self-esteem can rise only through personal achievements; in the second case self-esteem can rise *either* through personal achievements or through the failure of others: when others fail, one's own performance looks superior. Individuals whose self-worth is measured relative to others therefore may choose between expending their energy on succeeding themselves or on helping others fail. For those who choose to help others fail, prejudice is an excellent tool; it downgrades others, making the prejudiced individual feel superior by comparison. The important point is thus not so much the maintenance of self-esteem (since everyone must do that) but the extent to which individuals measure it through comparison with others.

Jack Levin (1975) related this line of research directly to questions of prejudice. He first separated his subjects into "self-evaluators," who tended to evaluate themselves against fixed standards, and "relative evaluators," who relied more on the immediate competition. Levin exposed the subjects to situations in which their performances and abilities were questioned and then tested their prejudice against Puerto Ricans. He found that the individuals labeled as relative evaluators responded to attacks on their abilities with increased prejudice, but the self-evaluators showed no such increase. Thus, it appears that prejudice can be a way to increase self-esteem if the individual involved measures that self-esteem against the performances and abilities of others rather than against a fixed standard. But even relative evaluators must first feel a threat to their self-esteem before they will defend themselves with prejudice.

The Sociology of Prejudice

Prejudice can also be used as a social weapon within a system of ethnic stratification. Prejudice, and the stereotypes that accompany it, discredits whole groups of people who might otherwise be a social threat. If you are a white person and a black person is competing for your job, you may be able to save your job by convincing others (especially your employer) that blacks are lazy and irresponsible. Losing your job (or even the threat of losing it) can lower self-esteem

Prejudice gets passed along from generation to generation in a culture.

and create frustration. If your employer is too strong to be the object of your aggression, prejudice becomes all the more useful as a weapon in fighting the secondary source of the frustration. In more general terms, prejudice is the natural outcome of the competition inherent in social stratification; prejudice helps maintain a social position when the potential social mobility of others threatens that position.

Prejudice produced by social competition becomes most noticeable when the individuals or groups involved are of similar rank. This puts those individuals or groups into competition for the same jobs, housing, education, and any other rewards that people get more or less of, depending on their class level. It is therefore not surprising that most antiblack prejudice in the United States is found among working-class whites, for they are in direct competition with blacks (who are similarly ranked, for the most part) and feel threatened by them (Levin, 1975).

Prejudice can also become part of the culture of a group, passed from parents to children along with the rest of their culture. The world view, as transmitted, takes an "us versus them" form, making each individual feel even further from the opposing group and, at the same time, more firmly rooted in his or her own group.

Discrimination

Attempts by groups either to improve their class position or to defend it from another group usually extend well beyond the realm of ideas to acts of discrimination. As we've seen, such acts are designed to hinder the competitive abilities of individuals in another group, thus giving the group doing the discriminating a competitive advantage within some arena (or arenas) of the stratification system (Bonacich, 1972). The appeal of discrimination stems from an interesting fact: Competition can encourage excellence, but it requires only being "better than." One can be better either through excellence or through hindering the opponent. Discrimination, of course, does the latter. It can operate directly—as in refusing employment to members of certain groups—or indirectly—as in constructing biased employment tests that require information not present in the culture of certain groups.

Discrimination is basically an attempt to control unrestricted social mobility by introducing elements of a caste society into a class society. Rather than allowing individuals to compete for mobility *as individuals,* it forces them to compete *as groups.* Discrimination separates those groups so that members of higher-ranked groups can achieve and hold their position against intruders. Those who discriminate give in to the temptation to load the dice. The higher a group is ranked, the more power it has, and therefore its ability to enforce its brand of discrimination is increased. The lower-ranked groups are forced to play with the dice provided for them.

Just as prejudice and stereotypes can become part of a group's culture, thereby keeping that group apart from others, so discrimination can maintain group separation and lead to further conflict. At the outset, discrimination maintains groups on separate ranks in the stratification system, which tends to keep groups separate. But, in addition, discrimination rubs salt into the wound. The we-they orientation that is begun by prejudice is nourished by the continued experience of discrimination. Recognizing that another group has loaded the dice to ensure your loss tends to solidify your group; discrimination convinces the affected group that the only hope for improvement is group action rather than individual effort.

Institutional (Covert) Discrimination

Institutional discrimination consists of the *indirect* forms of discrimination that affect a certain group because of certain attributes or abilities most of that group's members have (or lack). More often than not, institutional discrimination operates through the situation already provided by ethnic stratification: Since minority group members are disproportionately poor, institutional forms of discrimination that affect the poor disproportionately affect minorities. In this case poverty becomes the "attribute" possessed by the minority that leads to their being affected by discrimination. To the extent that they are culturally different from the dominant group, minorities often have different kinds of skills and abilities from the dominant group. Should the dominant group decide to discriminate on the basis of certain abilities, the minority group might easily be disproportionately affected. The use of intelligence (or IQ) tests (which measure similarity to the dominant group in knowledge and style of thinking) has prevented minorities from obtaining jobs and education. This is because their different cultural background makes it difficult for them to pass the tests, and passing the tests is the key that opens the door to such opportunities.

Institutional discrimination that affects minorities because of their cultural background can be intentional or unintentional. The dominant group employer, for instance, may insist that a prospective employee have certain abilities because the employer knows that a given minority is not likely to possess them. On the other hand, the employer might simply value those abilities for their own sake, with no intention of discriminating. Unlike overt discrimination, intent is not inherent in the act of institutional discrimination, and it cannot be proved by the existence of the discrimination. For that reason it is a tempting alternative for members of the dominant group who wish to discriminate in the face of laws prohibiting such actions.

Dominant groups are in a position to organize social relations; not surprisingly, they tend to shape social relations to their benefit. Thus, social institutions develop along lines that emphasize and reward the values and abilities of dominant group members; simultaneously, those institutions deemphasize and do not reward the values and abilities of other ethnic groups that share the society. For example, all major institutions in the United States today operate in (and reward the speakers of) Standard American English. Individuals who speak other languages or other dialects of English are at a disadvantage, whether they are going to school, to court, to work, or to vote, or are attempting to fill out an income tax return (a good example is provided in the essay by H. M. Murai at the end of this chapter).

For the minority group individual, institutional discrimination seems to be a conspiracy that places barriers at every turn. There is seldom a single discriminator who can be held personally responsible, and institutional discrimination, from whatever source, cannot be proved. As black leader Whitney Young (1964:18) described it:

> I go to the employer and ask him to employ Negroes, and he says, "It's a matter of education. I would hire your people if they were educated." Then I go to the educators and they say, "If Negro people lived in good neighborhoods and had more intelligent dialogue in their families, more encyclopedias in their homes, more opportunity to travel, and a stronger family life, then we could do a better job of educating them." And when I go to the builder he says, "If they had the money, I would sell them the houses"—and I'm back at the employer's door again, where I started to begin with.

Blacks encounter overt forms of discrimination in employment, education, and housing that intensify their problems in overcoming poverty. But institutional discrimination by itself (which we might call the cycle of poverty) accounts for a good number of the barriers against them. Box 8.3 discusses one social response to this situation.

RACIAL AND ETHNIC GROUPS IN CONTACT: SOCIAL AND POLITICAL ARRANGEMENTS

So far we've emphasized the competition between ethnic groups brought about by ethnic stratification. This emphasis provides us with a picture of people using every social trick in the book as they attempt to maintain or better their social position. It is a useful emphasis in the study of racial and ethnic relations, as competition certainly plays a major role, but it does not present the whole story. In fact, it emphasizes the *group* of ethnic group while glossing over the *ethnic*. Ethnic groups are culturally distinct entities beyond their different economic interests. The cultural changes that occur when two ethnic groups meet are highly related to the economic arrangements they hammer out—and vice versa. As you read on, keep that relationship in mind.

The results of culture contacts between ethnic groups are as varied as the ethnic groups themselves. For convenience sociologists have divided the primary types of culture contacts

BOX 8.3

EMPLOYMENT DISCRIMINATION AND AFFIRMATIVE ACTION

Of all the forms discrimination may take, one of the most far-reaching is discrimination in employment. Jobs are basic to quality of life for most of us, and being denied access to them directly affects the way we live. For many years, certain occupations have been closed to certain social categories. Blacks have been kept out of many labor unions and training programs over the years, while women have met a similar fate in the male-dominated occupations. Affirmative action programs were designed to change all that.

Affirmative action refers to any program designed to bring more members of a previously discriminated-against group into a job or training program. Because blacks have traditionally been kept out of the craft unions and apprenticeship programs for craft occupations, an effort to train more blacks for craft occupations would be an affirmative action program. There is a certain degree of political resistance to such programs, however. Getting more blacks or women into an occupation, for example, is simultaneously *not* getting more whites or men. Members of the latter social categories sometimes charge that affirmative action is actually reverse discrimination—the same kind of treatment previously given to minorities but now directed in reverse. And the Civil Rights Act of 1964 made occupational discrimination on the basis of sex, race, or ethnicity illegal.

One of the first challenges to affirmative action came from Allan Bakke, a white male whose application had been turned down by the University of California (Davis) Medical School. The medical school allowed 100 new students to enter their program every year; of those 100, 10 slots were set aside for the most qualified minority applicants. As it turned out, Bakke was not qualified enough for the top 90 slots, but his grades and test scores were superior to those of the 10 minority students. Bakke went to court, charging illegal discrimination. The U.S. Supreme Court finally decided that (1) the extreme quota system employed by the medical school was unfair and that Bakke should be admitted, and (2) affirmative action was still a good idea in some form if not in this one.

The next challenge came from Brian Weber, a white male worker in a Kaiser Aluminum Plant near New Orleans. Kaiser had instituted a new training program to raise the ratio of blacks in the craft occupations in their plant; blacks made up 39 percent of the workforce but only 1.83 percent of the craft workers (Luhman and Gilman, 1980). The training program was to consist of 50 percent white workers and 50 percent black workers. Weber, a white worker, was not admitted and went to court. The U.S. Supreme Court found against Weber, arguing that the program employed by Kaiser was in keeping with the intent of the 1964 Civil Rights Act.

The implications of affirmative action programs affect all aspects of the world of work. For example, what about seniority? Unionized workers are commonly laid off in order of seniority, and plants with affirmative action programs will have many women and ethnic minority employees with little seniority. The Supreme Court has argued that seniority should come along with the affirmative action program, with new workers being given credit for several years of work (when, presumably, they would have been working had not discrimination kept them out of work) (Time, 1976). This would mean that a white male worker with several years' experience would find himself

(continues)

BOX 8.3 (continued)

out of a job in a recession, while more recently hired women and minority workers would be kept on. Such actions have created considerable conflict within America's labor force.

Affirmative action programs represent an attempt to alter the structure of ethnic stratification in American society. It is hard to say at this point what their long-term effects will be, but they certainly illustrate an important lesson about ethnic and social stratification: There is only so much to go around, and your gain will be my loss. The conflict is built in.

into a few basic categories. In this section they are grouped under three basic headings: first, the melting pot, presented here as largely a myth (for reasons to be explained shortly); second, the dominant group's response to culture contact (those cultural results generally preferred by the stronger of the two groups); and third, the subordinate group's response (those cultural results sometimes fought for by minority groups).

The Myth of the Melting Pot

The **melting pot** refers to the mixing and blending of cultures through intermarriage (see Gordon, 1964a; Newman, 1973). While the melting pot depends on intermarriage to mix people from different ethnic groups, intermarriage by itself does not result in a melting pot. The cultural elements, when blended, must produce a new culture. For example, two languages could combine vocabulary and grammar to form a new language; two religions could combine their beliefs and rituals to form a new religion; two styles of dress could merge into one new style; and two styles of cooking could combine to form one. Though they do not begin to catalog the many facets of culture, these examples provide some idea of the give and take involved in blending different cultures into one. The result would be a totally new culture, composed of equal parts of the individual cultures that blended to form it.

The key words are *equal* and *give and take.* The problem with the melting pot is that the meeting of ethnic groups usually results in more taking than giving, and whatever cultural mixing occurs is usually anything but equal. It is an advantage to any ethnic group in any society to have its culture dominate that society's institutions. When ethnic groups come together, each will generally attempt such a domination. A melting pot situation can therefore occur only when no single group is able to dominate—a situation that usually occurs only when the groups involved are remarkably similar in power and no one group can get the upper hand. The odds of such similarity are not great, making the melting pot a rare situation.

The Response of the Dominant Group

We turn now to less mythical descriptions of cultures in contact—specifically, to a variety of descriptions that are either promoted by or generally acceptable to the dominant ethnic group in the society. One could argue that *any* variety of cultural contact must be more or less acceptable to the dominant group; if it were not, they could probably alter the situation. That argument has a great deal of merit, but we prefer to emphasize degrees of acceptability. This section deals with situations either promoted by the dominant group or generating at least the tacit

A century of immigration has turned the United States into a multi-ethnic society, and, as politicians know well, every ethnic group contains voters. These banners in New York's Chinatown show that people running for office will always find ways to appeal to voters.

acceptance of the dominant group. The next section examines situations that usually achieve, at best, the grudging acceptance of the dominant group and that are never promoted by them.

Genocide and Expulsion **Genocide** is actions by the dominant group that cause the deaths of most or all members of a given subordinate group. These actions might be systematic and intentional, as they were in Nazi extermination camps; they might also be largely unintentional, as was the spread of smallpox among American Indians after the arrival of the Europeans. We focus here only on intentional genocide.

Expulsion refers to the physical removal of most or all members of a subordinate group from within the boundaries of a nation-state. Under this heading we might include the removal of eastern American Indian tribes to reservations west of the Mississippi before that land was part of the United States.

Genocide and expulsion are both relatively rare, at least in the modern industrial world. These tactics are usually not highly desirable from the standpoint of the dominant group, which will clearly prefer some form of exploitation; faced with the alternatives of murder or exile, most minority groups will accede to that preference.

Perhaps because they are extreme, genocide and expulsion are clear and simple concepts. They may be employed for different reasons, but they are always a tactic of last resort. As we look next at the various continuing relationships that minority and majority groups work out, keep in mind the consequences when those relationships do not work out.

Segregation **Segregation** is the dominant group's decision to separate itself, either socially or physically, from a given minority group. When that separation occurs, the minority group may be described as segregated. Remember that the term *segregation* refers only to group separation instigated by the dominant group; when separation is the minority group's choice, it is separatism, which we will discuss later. The two are very different.

Social segregation is a situation in which two ethnic groups live near each other and interact with each other regularly but only on a highly formalized basis. For example, in a master-slave relationship there is considerable interaction, but all interaction follows rigid cultural norms of formality. Master and slave interact in terms of limited social roles and not as individuals who might aspire to a more well-rounded relationship. They are not and cannot be friends in any sense of the word. In such a situation, people can talk to each other every day without ever knowing each other. This situation occurs between many blacks and whites in the United States today.

Physical segregation is a situation in which two ethnic groups live spacially apart from each other within the same political boundaries. For example, the decision of the dominant group has placed American Indians in reservations. By its very nature, physical segregation includes social segregation; for this reason it is a more extreme measure on the part of the dominant group. In fact, there is only a very fine line between physical segregation and expulsion.

Assimilation **Assimilation** is the incorporation of one ethnic group into the continuing culture of another ethnic group. For example, one ethnic group (usually a relatively weak one) intermarries with members of another ethnic group, losing or giving up its cultural distinctiveness in favor of the culture provided by the stronger group. In a less extreme form of assimilation, the weaker ethnic group might not intermarry with the stronger, but after several generations it takes on most of the culture of the stronger. The original culture of the assimilated ethnic group is no longer recognizable or distinct. None of its component parts (its members) have been lost; they have simply become part of a very powerful system through taking on its culture.

Assimilation in one form or another is one of the most common outcomes when two cultures come into contact. This is particularly true in the history of the United States, in which a basically English culture has become the dominant way of life to which all newcomers must conform. It is always in the interest of any ethnic group to promote its culture when it comes into contact with other ethnic groups. The more its culture comes to dominate a society, the more competitive advantage its members will have in that society. In the United States people of English descent had the power to promote their culture as the dominant one in the early days of the nation, and the English culture has not lost that domination since; over 200 years later, it is still people of basically English descent who hold a competitive advantage in the United States. Social assimilation is a long process requiring a series of stages (Gordon, 1964a, 1978).

The Response of the Minority Group: Cultural Pluralism and Separatism

Members of minority groups may be quite happy with a cultural arrangement like assimilation, which was the stated goal of many immigrants to the United States. However, assimilation destroys the ethnic group by requiring conformity to the host culture. It may not be unpleasant overall, but it certainly occurs beyond the control of the minority group. Nevertheless, it is an option usually taken if available.

Ethnic groups locked into the bottom of the ethnic stratification system have created other options, the two dominant (and related) ones being cultural pluralism and separatism. **Separatism** requires the political separation of land occupied by members of the minority ethnic group so that they may govern themselves. A number of French Canadians in Quebec became interested in separatism for Quebec in the mid-1970s and advocated that the province should leave Canada to become a separate French-speaking country (See, 1986). Separatism changes a *minority* ethnic group into the *only* ethnic group and ends the minority group-dominant group relationship. Box 8.4 discusses Marcus Garvey, an advocate of black separatism.

Cultural pluralism is a similar but less extreme route for the minority group. As it is much more common than separatism, especially in the United States, we will focus on it in this section. **Cultural pluralism** describes a social situation where two or more ethnic groups share one society, in which (1) each ethnic group maintains its separate cultural distinctiveness, and (2) no one ethnic group dominates the other(s). In a society such as the United States, which is already ethnically stratified, cultural pluralism becomes a political movement in which the minority group attempts to maintain its ethnicity while gaining power for the group. Its success as a political and cultural goal can be viewed through ethnic groups such as the Amish (Kephart, 1987) or Hasidic Jews (Harris, 1985)—two very distinct groups that have managed to maintain clear cultural separation between themselves and the outside dominant society.

As an ideology, cultural pluralism has found varying popularity with almost every ethnic group in the United States in recent years. American Indians have organized and begun fighting for tribal land; Hispanics have fought for bilingual education; Japanese Americans recall the years of internment during World War II as they learn to speak Japanese in night school; and, perhaps most interesting, some European ethnic groups, such as Polish Americans and Italian Americans, are rediscovering roots well covered by years of assimilation. In terms of ethnic identity and goals, cultural pluralism was clearly the most visible if not the dominant ideology of the 1970s and 1980s.

If further evidence is needed for pluralism as a trend, we can look outside the world of ethnic politics. The variety of movements making up feminism and women's liberation all suggest a pluralistic basis. There are separate magazines intended for women only and women's legal and social services (rape counseling centers and organizations to help abused wives, for example). Similarly, many homosexual rights organizations that seek gay liberation have a pluralistic emphasis. Many homosexuals in the past chose to keep their lifestyles as private as possible while "passing" as heterosexuals. But it is more common today for homosexuality to be stated openly, coupled with the demand that homosexuals be accorded all the rights that heterosexuals enjoy. One important goal of gay liberation is to convince everyone (especially homosexuals) that homosexuality is perfectly normal and that individuals have a right to that

BOX 8.4

MARCUS GARVEY: EARLY SEPARATISM IN BLACK AMERICA

Marcus Garvey was an extremely controversial black political leader in the United States in the years following World War I. Speaking largely to the new urban blacks of the 1920s, Garvey advocated racial separation and a black return to Africa. His organization, the Universal Negro Improvement Association, grew rapidly, publishing a newspaper and seiling shares in the Black Star Steamship Line, which would one day make the trip back to Africa. Garvey's politics worried white political leaders. He was imprisoned in 1925 for using the mail to defraud (by selling steamship tickets) and was finally deported to his native Jamaica in 1927. Perhaps Garvey was a con man, but, considering that blacks were never prosecuted in the 1920s for victimizing other blacks, his legal problems were no doubt motivated by feelings other than a love of justice among white political leaders.

Garvey may have been personally unsuccessful, but his ideas survived in one form or another. Though few American blacks advocate a return to Africa today, the following statement made by Garvey in 1923 sounds much like the ideas of cultural pluralism now common in the black community:

> Some Negro leaders have advanced the belief that in another few years the white people will make up their minds to assimilate their black populations; thereby sinking all racial prejudice in the welcoming of the black race into the social companionship of the white. Such leaders further believe that by the amalgamation of black and white, a new type will spring up, and that type will become the American and West Indian of the future.
>
> This belief is preposterous. I believe that white men should be white, yellow men should be yellow, and black men should be black in the great panorama of races, until each and every race by its own initiative lifts itself up to the common standard of humanity, as to compel the respect and appreciation of all, and so make it possible for each one to stretch out the hand of welcome without being able to be prejudiced against the other because of any inferior and unfortunate condition.
>
> The white man of America will not, to any organized extent, assimilate the Negro, because in so doing, he feels that he will be committing racial suicide. This he is not prepared to do. It is true he illegitimately carries on a system of assimilation; but such assimilation, as practiced, is one that he is not prepared to support because he becomes prejudiced against his own offspring, if that offspring is the product of black and white; hence, to the white man the question of racial differences is eternal. So long as Negroes occupy an inferior position among the races and nations of the world, just so long will others be prejudiced against them, because it will be profitable for them to keep up their system of superiority. But when the Negro by his own initiative lifts himself from his low state to the highest human standard he will be in a position to stop begging and praying, and demand a place that no individual, race or nation will be able to deny him. (Garvey, 1968:26)

lifestyle. Like many efforts toward pluralism, gay liberation has been countered with demands for conformity. Local elections in several states in the 1970s indicated a desire that certain kinds of discrimination against homosexuals continue, particularly with regard to employing teachers and other educators. On the other hand, several Supreme Court cases of the 1980s have strengthened the rights of gays, particularly in the military.

Along with "gay power" (not to mention the earlier white, black, brown, red, and yellow forms) we now have "gray power." This new minority is made up of old people who feel that American society has a negative stereotype about the nature and abilities of old people and constantly discriminates against old people. Probably the most colorful of the political organizations that represent the interests of old people is the Gray Panthers, organized by Maggie Kuhn (see Hessel, 1977). The Gray Panthers condemn American society for putting its old people out to pasture and emphasize the virtues of being old and the right of old people to be free from discrimination based on their age. Those organizations that come under the label *gray power* or the *gray lobby* have taken on the task of protecting the special interests of old people, working against discrimination ranging from individual acts to the acts of Congress. Once again, we see political organizations defending the right to be different, while insisting that American society be altered so as not to abridge those rights.

Organizations of the physically disabled also use pluralism as the basis for their political action. Such groups initially formed to eliminate the kinds of discrimination their members faced because of particular disabilities. People confined to wheelchairs, for example, could not engage in activities that took place in buildings with stairs. The Architectural Barriers Act of 1968 and the Rehabilitation Act of 1973 were passed in response to those needs; federal funds can now be withheld if structural accommodations are not made for the physically disabled. In addition, the Rehabilitation Act of 1973 mandates the creation of affirmative action programs for the benefit of the physically disabled (*Newsweek,* 1976). However, such programs often run up against the sense of pride in difference that is characteristic of pluralism. For example, Jim Gashel of the National Federation of the Blind, assessing the supposedly model program for the handicapped at the University of Illinois, Champagne-Urbana, criticized its "medical model" aspect. Just as early black power advocates hated being "taken by the hand" by whites who wanted to help them, Gashel criticized programs for the disabled that focus only on their physical disabilities while ignoring their strengths (*Science,* 1976).

Among the physically handicapped the most striking parallel with ethnic pluralistic politics is found among the deaf. In the past deaf people were encouraged to learn lip reading, which can be considered an effort at assimilation by conforming to the mode of communication favored by hearing people. Today, however, many deaf people favor the use of sign language and take pride in its use. Institutions such as Gallaudet College in Washington, D.C., which accepts only students with serious hearing impairment, have become centers for the development of group pride. This pride erupted in early 1988 when a hearing president was appointed at Gallaudet over a popular deaf candidate. The students went on strike, closing down the campus until their demands were met (Brand, 1988). The touring National Theater of the Deaf (in which the actors communicate in sign language coupled with spoken "subtitles" for people with communication impairment in understanding sign language) has helped turn sign language into an art. In short, there is a growing pride among the deaf based on the strengths inherent in their difference from those who can hear.

Such examples of organizations that form to build group pride and to work for the right of the group to be different, in whatever way, suggest a reevaluation of conformity among Americans. Instead of viewing differences in sex, sexual preference, age, ethnicity, or physical ability as unfortunate, many Americans now call attention to those differences and challenge the rest of society to accept them.

RACIAL AND ETHNIC GROUPS IN THE UNITED STATES

The United States is often called the "nation of immigrants." This is a more fitting title than you might think, for even our "native" American Indians were themselves immigrants, coming from Asia some 20,000 to 40,000 years ago. As human history goes, that's relatively recent history, but compared to the other people who moved to what is now the United States, they are clearly the "native" oldtimers of the area. The first non-Indian immigrants (responsible for calling its inhabitants *Indians*) were the Spanish explorers. The Spanish were followed in short order by the English, Dutch, French, and Portuguese. The English soon gained control over the eastern coast of what is now the United States and were joined over the next several centuries by one of the wildest mixes of ethnic groups the world has ever seen. But as diverse as that ethnic mix became, descendants of those original English colonists maintained control over the basic coordination of social life that characterizes the United States today. Everyday life in the United States today is largely an experience of an Americanized English culture.

The Growth of Racism

The English Pilgrims arrived in Massachusetts in 1620; they were beaten by one year by the first African arrivals in the colonies: twenty Africans who were sold from a Dutch freighter in Jamestown, Virginia, as indentured servants. The Africans weren't yet permanent slaves, and ideas of racism were still very much in their infancy in the new land, but both slavery and racism were already on the horizon.

Racism can describe either a belief or a way of life. As a belief, it represents the social separation of people into two or more races coupled with the idea that different races are biologically inferior or superior to each other. As a way of life, racism describes the individual experience of living within a system of ethnic stratification in which the groups at the bottom of the hierarchy are defined as racially inferior. Racism is an idea peculiar to the minds of Europeans over the last several centuries; previously humans had been guilty of all kinds of atrocities against each other, but they never defined their victims as biologically inferior while having them drawn and quartered. More modern Europeans became increasingly attracted to the ideas of racism that were popularized throughout the 1700s and 1800s. The central idea (later to be dusted off by Adolf Hitler) was that northwestern Europeans ("Aryans") were a separate race and superior to all others; southeastern Europeans (such as Slavs, Italians, and so on) were thought to be of a clearly inferior race. With such fine distinctions in operation among types of Europeans it's no wonder that the peoples of the rest of the world soon found themselves the possessors of increasingly derogatory labels. Asians were in one race, Indians in another, and Africans in still another. No finer idea than racism could ever be found to justify exploitation.

European Immigration

The English and Africans were not the only immigrants to the New World in the 1600s; ever since the beginning of colonization in North America, a variety of European ethnic groups made up the immigrants (even though those of English descent generally were the most influential). Of these early non-English immigrants, probably the most notable were the Germans and the Scotch-Irish. It is noteworthy that all the early European immigrants were both Protestant and from countries in the northwest of Europe. Their cultural differences, in short, were not really very great.

The first major non-Protestant immigrant group was the Catholic Irish, who fled the potato famine in Ireland in the late 1840s. These Irish faced some of the most vicious prejudice and discrimination ever to appear on the American scene. Black Americans faced worse discrimination through slavery, but in that case the white Americans had such complete control that they were not moved through fear into angry acts of protest and hatred. Almost any northern American newspaper of the 1850s would include a cartoon portraying the Irishman as an ape with interests only in drinking and fighting. Many neighborhoods and occupations were closed to the Irish. Such discrimination led them to work on the canals and railroads, where cheap labor was needed. While black Americans were being exploited in the South through slavery, Irish Americans were being exploited in the North through less organized means of discrimination.

If the Irish looked culturally different to white Protestant Americans in the 1850s, imagine the shock touched off by the coming of the southeastern Europeans in the 1880s. As we saw, racist ideas of the day placed southeastern Europeans in a separate race from northwestern Europeans. Moreover, southeastern Europeans were either Jewish or Catholic—never Protestant. But probably most important was the manner in which they came: Huge numbers of southeastern European immigrants poured into the eastern cities, especially New York City, and formed ethnic communities. Figure 8.1 illustrates this change in the source as well as the volume of immigration beginning in the late 1800s.

The surge of southeastern European immigrants into the United States altered the society greatly; suddenly the Irish didn't look so bad. The early 1900s saw increasing racism directed against the newcomers from Europe. Early IQ tests determined that most Jews and Italians were "feebleminded." Popular books were written about the ruining of good old Yankee stock with the entrance of inferior genes into the population. The result of all this was a 1924 law that essentially cut off immigration to the United States from anywhere except northwestern Europe.

The descendants of most European immigrants cannot properly be termed minority groups in the United States today. The Irish, who were locked into labor exploitation in their early years, are today largely in the middle class and working class of American society. The Italians and Poles present a similar picture. On the whole, however, the descendants of northwestern European immigrants dominate the upper classes of American society, reflecting their domination of a hundred years ago.

Asian Immigration

Just as the northeastern United States was becoming home to waves of European immigrants, the West Coast was becoming the focal point of Asian immigration. The largest group was the Chinese, who began to enter the United States in 1850. The vast majority of the Chinese

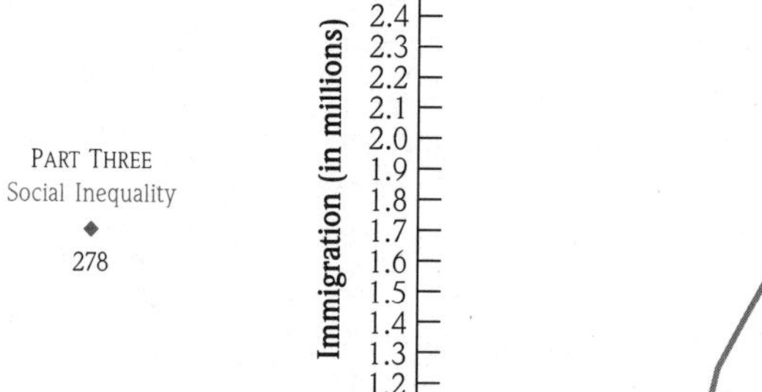

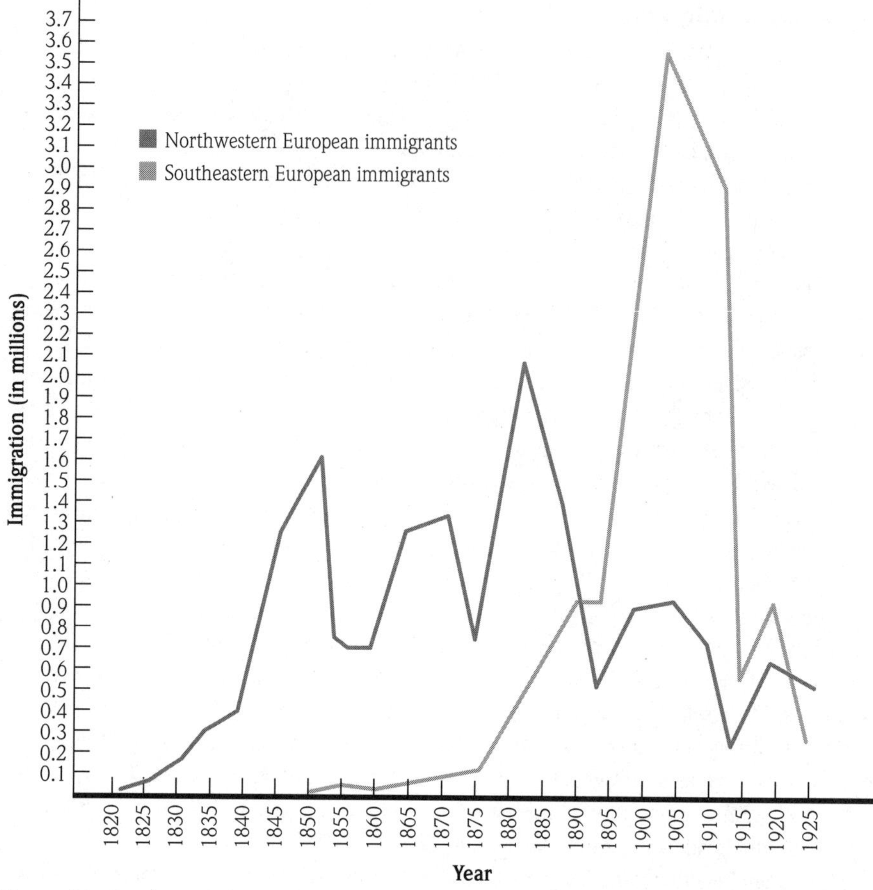

Figure 8.1 European immigration to the United States, 1820-1930. (U.S. Bureau of the Census.)

immigrants were men from southern China who perceived the move more as a temporary expedition than as permanent immigration. Their goal was to accumulate wealth and then return to their families in their native land. As unskilled laborers, they were immediately useful to the railroad companies in building the transcontinental railroad. They soon became the object of racist attacks from non-Asian westerners who, among other things, did not appreciate the competition for jobs. In an 1871 Los Angeles riot twenty-two Chinese were hanged, and the 1885 Rock Springs, Wyoming, massacre claimed twenty-nine Chinese (Kitano, 1976). Less physical attacks took the form of attempts to end Chinese immigration, which bore fruit in 1882, when the door from China was closed. In the meantime the "Chinatown" pattern in western cities had begun, as Chinese male immigrants banded together for mutual support, protection, and pleasure. The lack of families greatly hindered the establishment of an ongoing Chinese community.

The second largest Asian immigrant group, the Japanese, began to arrive soon after Chinese immigration ended. They found anti-Asian sentiment already established and readily transferable to them. The Japanese emperor had not permitted emigration until 1885, when increasing population density on the islands plus favorable earlier Western contacts made the idea more appealing. Between 1885 and 1898 Japanese immigrated to Hawaii, and, in 1898, when Hawaii was annexed to the United States, Japanese began coming to the West Coast states. California, the most popular destination, had little over 1,000 Japanese in 1890, but their numbers increased to over 10,000 by 1900 and over 40,000 by 1910 (Kitano, 1976). Unlike the Chinese, many Japanese immigrated as families; in other cases families selected wives in Japan and sent them over to join waiting grooms. In either case the early Japanese communities were family centered and industrious. Though industriousness was as American as apple pie, in this case it incited racist attacks on the Japanese from those sectors of the non-Asian population that feared competition. As the Japanese became successful at truck farming, such fears led to the passage of the California Alien Land Law of 1913, which prohibited aliens (which is to say, Japanese) from owning land. Although this law could be circumvented by Japanese fathers who could transfer ownership to their American-born children, it indicates the building resentment and racism that would erupt at the outbreak of World War II.

The entrance of the United States into World War II, and in particular the Japanese attack on Pearl Harbor in Hawaii, resulted in widespread fear and distrust of the Japanese American communities in the western United States. Ironically, there was no such fear in Hawaii itself (which then and now has the largest Japanese American population of any state), because there had been so much cross-cultural contact. Nevertheless, the western states convinced the federal government to "relocate" the Japanese American population through the auspices of the United States Army. Beginning in early 1942, all persons of Japanese descent (who of course included a great many American citizens) were sent for the duration of the war to what can only be called concentration camps. An important exception to this rule were the young men in the camps who volunteered for military service. They were combined with Hawaiian Japanese Americans to form an all-Japanese American army unit. Sent to Europe, this unit—the 442nd—compiled one of the finest records in the history of the American military. After the war these men, along with relocation camp inmates, returned to their former communities, where they faced much of the same racism they had left four years before and went to work to overcome the setback of lost property and time.

With the passage of the Immigration Act of 1965, the door to Asian immigration was once again open. New Chinese immigrants arrived along with Koreans, Filipinos, and, with the ending of the Vietnam War, Vietnamese and Laotians. During the 1970s, Asians made up 34 percent of the total legal United States immigration and since 1980 have accounted for a full 48 percent of the total. There are currently 6.5 million Asian Americans and Pacific Islanders in the United States (U.S. Bureau of the Census, 1990b). Of this number, Chinese account for 21 percent; Filipinos, 20 percent; Japanese, almost 15 percent; and Vietnamese, 12 percent. Some groups, such as the Vietnamese, are largely immigrants, while other groups, such as the Japanese, are largely native born.

It is difficult to make generalities about many of the Asian groups, as there are many internal divisions within each group. A Chinese American, for example, may be descended from many generations of American citizens or may have arrived last week. Nevertheless, most statistics regarding Asian success in the United States are impressive. Consider high school graduation. A high school diploma is achieved by 87 percent of the white population, 75 percent of the

The 1942 "relocation" of West Coast Japanese Americans from their homes into guarded camps in the interior of the country was a dark moment in American history. Anti-Asian racism at the time led many to view all of Japanese descent as threats to security after the bombing of Pearl Harbor. This Japanese American family has been tagged and waits for transportation to a camp for the duration of the war.

black population, and 59 percent of the Hispanic population; by contrast, the same achievement is accomplished by 96 percent of Japanese, 88 percent of Chinese, 90 percent of Asian Indians, and 87 percent of Filipinos (Gardner, Robey, and Smith, 1985). In addition, family income for Asian Americans is higher than for Americans as a whole.

Of course, not all Asians are wealthy; positive stereotypes can be just as inaccurate as negative stereotypes. On the other hand, the history of Asian immigration to the United States suggests that much can be accomplished, even in the face of racism and discrimination. Asian cultural orientations, such as strong family ties and positive values toward work, have aided Asians considerably in the competitive struggle that all immigrant groups face. Continued immigration should enlarge the Asian community in the United States in coming years.

American Blacks: A History of Discrimination

The institution of slavery in North America began inconspicuously in 1619 and grew steadily larger and more oppressive before its demise during the Civil War. Slavery in the United States was unusually cruel because the captured Africans were systematically separated from members of their families or tribes when they were sold. The slave owners' purpose was to break down native cultures more quickly and to replace them with a tailor-made slave culture more suitable for the work and lifestyle demanded by the system. All children born to slaves were automatically slaves, and families thus formed could be broken up if the owner had economic or punitive reasons for doing so. In short, slaves were not legal persons in the United States except for the strange way they were counted (one slave equaled ⅗ of a man) to help the slave owners increase their numbers in the House of Representatives. Slaves could not own property, they could not enter into a contract of any kind, and they had no legal recourse whatsoever. They were pieces of property and could be used and disposed of as their owners saw fit. The one small advantage the slaves did have was that they were relatively expensive property, which provided them protection from some grosser abuses.

Beyond the legal restrictions, blacks were also limited socially. The most notable restriction concerned education: It was generally against the law to teach a slave either reading or writing. Once again, the rationale behind the law was that slaves could thus be more easily controlled. The law certainly served this purpose. It also placed blacks at an extreme disadvantage upon emancipation, when they had few skills to use to improve their situation. The inferior education most blacks have received since emancipation has not made their task any easier.

The end of slavery did little to improve the situation of blacks in the United States. While it was a necessary condition for improvement, many other obstacles stood in the way. The vast majority of blacks had been slaves; therefore the vast majority of free blacks after the Civil War found themselves unskilled and living in the rural South. The relatively short period of Reconstruction was of temporary benefit to those blacks, but the end of Reconstruction and the return of political control to white southerners placed the blacks once again in a situation of powerlessness. With options severely limited, the only viable alternative to starvation appeared to be sharecropping.

As practiced in the South at the end of the nineteenth century, the system of sharecropping kept blacks with almost as little power as slavery had. Typically, a sharecropper farmed land belonging to someone else and shared the profits from the crop with the owner. The sharecropper took the risks, however, and was responsible for buying such necessities as seed and farm tools. Since former slaves had no available capital, they purchased on credit, with the understanding that they would pay debts out of their profits from the expected crop. Food and clothing were purchased the same way. More often than not, all these purchases were made from the land owner himself, who arranged prices so that the sharecropper's profit would never be enough to pay back the debt. When the crop came in, the sharecropper's remaining debt was listed against the next year's crop. In the process of producing the next year's crop, however, more debt was incurred. In short, to sharecrop was to be forever and increasingly in debt. Furthermore,

NEGROES
FOR SALE.

I will sell by Public Auction, on Tuesday of next Court, being the 29th of November, *Eight Valuable Family Servants*, consisting of one Negro Man, a first-rate field hand, one No. 1 Boy, 17 years of age, a trusty house servant, one excellent Cook, one House-Maid, and one Seamstress. The balance are under 12 years of age. They are sold for no fault, but in consequence of my going to reside North. Also a quantity of Household and Kitchen Furniture, Stable Lot, &c. Terms accommodating, and made known on day of sale.

Jacob August.
P. J. TURNBULL, *Auctioneer.*

Warrenton, October 28, 1859.

Printed at the *News* office, Warrenton, North Carolina.

This 1859 handbill offers property for sale, human as well as "household and kitchen furniture." Three of the slaves offered for sale were "under 12 years of age." One may assume that these were children of the "Negro Man" or "excellent Cook" or the other slaves mentioned, but if it suited the owner, all could have been sold separately so that parents and children would never see each other again.

it was against the law to attempt to leave the area while in debt. Sharecroppers were almost as effectively tied to the land as slaves, but now no one cared whether they starved to death in the process (Daniel, 1972). As immigrants from southeastern Europe moved into the northern cities and gained footholds in the industrial economy, 90 percent of the black Americans were still living in the South, many locked into the sharecropping system (Pinkney, 1975).

The same period of American history that witnessed the legal slavery of sharecropping also saw the final institutionalization of racial segregation through what have come to be called the Jim Crow laws. These laws, as a group, forced racial separation in practically all aspects of life, from separate drinking fountains and washrooms to separate schools and neighborhoods. Perhaps ironically, such laws originated in the North before the Civil War in response to growing numbers of free blacks. Free blacks, though free from the bonds of slavery, nevertheless faced severe restrictions on their activities in almost every northern state. Such laws were, of course, unnecessary in the South until the Civil War, since slavery provided a far more complete form of domination. With the emancipation of the southern black population, southern whites began looking for alternative means of domination. They found those means in the Jim Crow laws. During the later years of the nineteenth century the southern states enacted a vast collection of Jim Crow laws, and by the turn of the century American blacks found themselves once again firmly and legally placed in a situation of subordination. In the legal sense this subordination lasted until 1965.

There are now over 30 million black Americans (U.S. Bureau of the Census, 1990f). The Jim Crow laws are no longer with us, but those political changes have not been matched by economic changes in the black-white relationship. As the statistics show, blacks are much more likely than whites to live in the central cities, be poorly educated, be unemployed, work at blue-collar jobs, make less money, and wind up below the poverty level. Perhaps even more significant is the lack of change over time in many of these areas. The gap between black and white income, for example, has remained about the same since 1950 (Luhman and Gilman, 1980; Farley, 1984). The gap in unemployment rates has also remained the same during the same period (Newman et al., 1978). The gap in life expectancy between blacks and whites has actually *widened* since 1930 and has widened more in just the last few years; being born black in the United States takes about six years off your life (U.S. Bureau of the Census, 1990b).

The picture of black America that emerges is clearly one of ethnic stratification. Blacks face discrimination in all of the dominant American institutions; that widespread and built-in discrimination is reflected in the range of problems that blacks face today. For instance, 81 percent of all American households are located in segregated neighborhoods (Newman et al., 1978). The segregation in housing is reflected in segregated (and unequal) educational facilities, in which blacks lag far behind whites. And even when blacks do catch up to whites educationally, the same rewards do not as automatically follow. As Figure 8.2 shows, black men lag behind white men (and to a lesser extent behind Hispanic men) in yearly median income at all educational levels. As these figures only apply to full-time, year round workers, the results are all the more striking in that blacks are more likely than whites to work part time and to be laid off more frequently. The income gap at each educational level suggests a factor of discrimination that is still very much with us as presumably qualified black workers are either not getting the jobs or not getting the promotions that white workers get. The left side of Figure 8.2 is interesting on two levels: On the one hand, there appears to be less discrimination against black and Hispanic women than against their male counterparts; at each educational level, the median income levels are very similar. On the other hand, sexism in the American economy is very clear here: no women of any ethnic or racial group can compete with similarly qualified male employees in terms of earnings. We will examine the gender gap in American education and the economy in fuller detail in Chapter 10.

Within the black community, other changes are at work. O'Hare et al. (1991) report that the widening gap between rich and poor in the United States that occurred in the 1980s has hit the black community especially hard. After making some gains in the 1960s and 1970s, poorer, unskilled blacks faced a particularly bleak decade in the 1980s, with no hope of improvement in the near future. At the same time, middle-class blacks with skills and education have benefitted from changes in the economy and, to some extent, from affirmative action policies. With middle-class blacks moving up and lower-class blacks moving down, the black community in the United States today is looking increasingly polarized. The remarkable unity that has characterized black politics over the years, particularly in party affiliation, may well be threatened by the growing disunity in black economic positions.

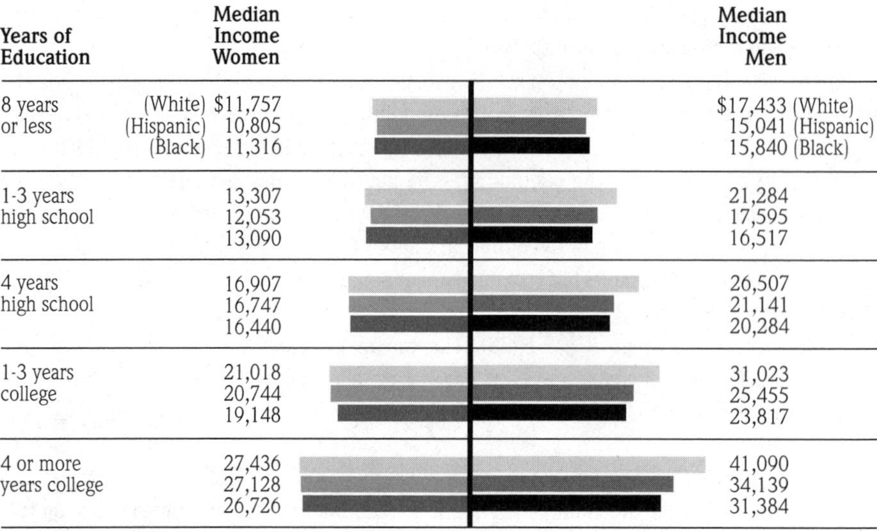

Years of Education
Median Income Women
Median Income Men
8 years or less
(White) $11,757
(Hispanic) 10,805
(Black) 11,316
$17,433 (White)
15,041 (Hispanic)
15,840 (Black)
1-3 years high school
13,307
12,053
13,090
21,284
17,595
16,517
4 years high school
16,907
16,747
16,440
26,507
21,141
20,284
1-3 years college
21,018
20,744
19,148
31,023
25,455
23,817
4 or more years college
27,436
27,128
26,726
41,090
34,139
31,384

Figure 8.2 Median income for year-round, full-time workers by years of education and sex, 1989. (Data from U.S. Bureau of the Census, 1991.)

Hispanic Americans

Hispanic Americans (or Americans of Spanish origin) is a category that includes a wide variety of people. Altogether, there are over 20 million Hispanic Americans. Of that 20 million, almost two-thirds are Mexican Americans, over 2 million are Puerto Ricans, and the remainder are Cuban and an assortment of Central and South Americans (U.S. Bureau of the Census, 1990e). Most Mexican Americans live in the Southwest, about two-thirds of the Puerto Ricans live in New York City, and most Cubans live in Florida; thus, these people vary in geography as well as culture, home country, time of immigration, and reason for immigration. In the case of Mexican Americans some are not even United States immigrants—their ancestors already occupied the territory when the United States came to them. Hispanic Americans are, as a category, a minority group in the United States today. In many areas, especially education, they are behind black Americans and far behind white Americans. We will look at the history of Mexican Americans in the United States as a representative of Hispanics; not only are they the largest ethnic group within this overall category, but they illustrate typical patterns of discrimination faced by minority ethnic groups in the United States.

Mexican Americans originally joined the United States under the terms of the peace treaty that followed the United States' war with Mexico in the 1840s. Before that war the area that is now the entire southwestern United States was controlled by Mexico, which had been controlled by Spain. Spanish settlement of the area began around 1600. As happened with other Spanish settlements, the original settlers soon found themselves in varying degrees of isolation. When Spanish control passed to Mexico, the isolation continued; few Mexicans could be convinced to move north and strengthen the Mexican hold over the land. As the Mexican government watched European settlers pour into what is now the state of Texas, it became obvious

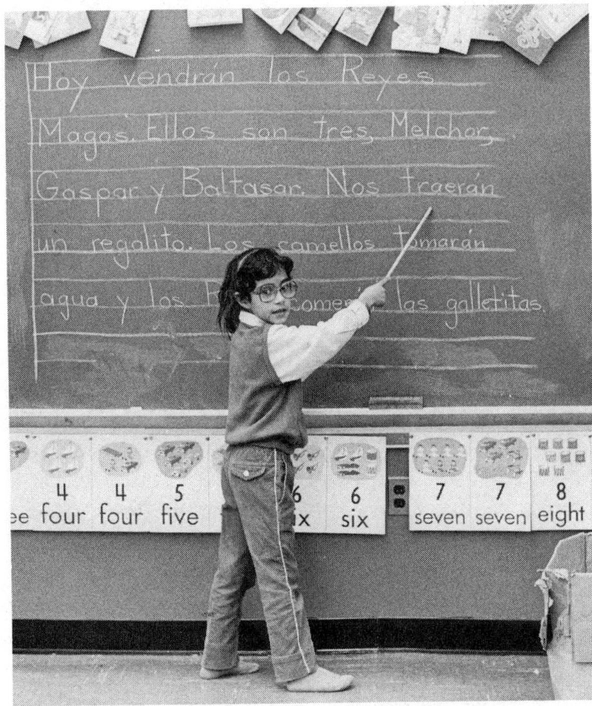

In the past, non-English-speaking immigrants had to more or less sink or swim in the dominant English culture of the United States; most such groups faced considerable pressure to conform. A more modern alternative is the bilingual classroom. Here, Spanish-speaking children learn English through their native tongue.

that Mexico would soon lose control over the northern provinces. Heroics of the Alamo aside, the result of the war with Mexico was a largely foregone conclusion at the outset.

At the end of the war there were about 60,000 Mexicans in New Mexico, 5,000 in Texas, 7,500 in California, 1,000 in Arizona, and a few settlements in what is now Colorado (Moore, 1976). Each of these areas entered the United States somewhat differently. In New Mexico, for example, the basic activities of the people remained relatively stable although considerable changes in power and the economy took place (see Box 8.1). Texas, on the other hand, was the scene of much of the conflict of the war. Even though many Texas Mexicans had favored the formation of the Texas Republic, they were soon very far from the seats of power and commerce as Texas entered the Union. California, of course, became engulfed in the gold rush. The old Mexican ranchos could not survive the rush of the forty-niners to the gold fields and the rush of merchants to the forty-niners. However different the various situations, there was one important point in common: In no territory did the Mexican population really maintain political control. It did for a while in New Mexico, but even there the Spanish language passed out of use in the legislature, and control over land and power slowly slipped from Mexican hands. The same transfer occurred more quickly and more completely in each of the other territories. Only recently has any political power whatsoever been in the hands of Mexican Americans.

There is an important second chapter in the history of Mexican Americans in the United States, the story of immigration from Mexico after the treaty of 1848. This immigration of primarily poor and rural northern Mexican peasants did not occur on a large scale until the early 1900s.

In the half-century between the end of the war with Mexico and the beginning of large-scale migration from Mexico, European dominance was established throughout the Southwest. Only New Mexico still had a numerical majority of Mexicans, but even that advantage was no match for incoming settlers or, more important, for the power of the United States government, which had firm ideas on how the territory should operate. By the time Mexican immigrants began arriving, the minority status of Mexican Americans was well established in the area. The newcomers, almost entirely unskilled, found work, when it was available, primarily on railroads and in agriculture. When work was less available, during the Great Depression, for instance, the familiar pattern of ethnic group competition over employment repeated itself, and Mexicans joined the ranks of so many other ethnic groups pronounced racially different from Europeans. Such clashes followed the ups and downs of the economy, major flare-ups occurring in the 1930s (when more than 400,000 Hispanics were deported) and again in the 1950s (Davis, Haub, and Willette, 1983). In both periods many Mexicans were deported to Mexico under the charge of being illegal aliens. Many no doubt were, but welfare and immigration officials were not concerned with absolute accuracy on that point. In times of prosperity, on the other hand, Mexicans were more than welcome as industrial and agricultural workers. In short, Mexican Americans fell into the familiar pattern of the involuntary immigrant. Even though many were technically voluntary, their low status had already been established in the course of conquest, and their lives were very much at the mercy of the dominant Europeans, who alternately used them and discarded them as the situation required.

Today, Hispanic Americans make up varied components of the ethnic scene in the United States. Cubans, who are concentrated in Florida, are economically better off than other Hispanics and have also been more successful in maintaining a thriving Spanish cultural community as an island within English culture. Mexican Americans, who are also becoming increasingly urbanized, have maintained strong cultural ties, particularly with regard to family loyalty (Keefe and Padilla, 1987). Nevertheless, most Hispanics trail white Americans in economic, educational, and occupational indicators. In 1988, 28 percent of Hispanics were below the poverty level, compared with 10 percent of the white population; median family income was $20,306, representing less than 70 percent of white family income—a percentage that has remained unchanged since the 1970s (Davis, Haub, and Willette, 1983; U.S. Bureau of the Census, 1990b). As we can see from Table 8.1, the pattern of discrimination with regard to Hispanic men is similar to that with regard to black men; at every educational level, Hispanic men earn less than their white counterparts. Table 8.1 shows an occupational breakdown for 1989 of different Hispanic groups with comparisons to the total United States population; in the two top occupational categories, Cubans make the best showing but all Hispanics fall significantly behind the national average. Perhaps the worst socioeconomic gap between whites and Hispanics comes in the field of education. In 1987, only 60 percent of the Hispanic population ages twenty-five to twenty-nine completed high school compared with 86 percent of the white population and over 83 percent of the black population (National Center for Education Statistics, 1990a). All of these statistics are all the more important considering demographic predictions for the Hispanic population. A high birth rate coupled with growing immigration have led to predictions that Hispanics will move from their current 7.9 percent of the United States population to 14.7 percent by 2020. If these population predictions are accurate, Hispanics will become the largest

Table 8.1

Occupations of Hispanic and All Workers, by Sex, 1989*

	All workers		Total Hispanics		Mexican origin		Puerto Rican		Cuban	
	Women	*Men*	*Women*	*Men*	*Women*	*Men*	*Women*	*Men*	*Women*	*Men*
Managerial and professional specialty	26.4	26.3	12.2	14.9	8.7	12.8	10.6	20.0	25.2	22.3
Technical, sales, and administrative support	19.5	44.1	14.5	38.4	12.0	36.8	22.3	43.3	25.3	43.1
Service occupations	9.7	17.5	17.7	24.1	17.7	24.6	21.2	18.1	10.2	17.1
Farming, forestry, and fishing	4.0	.9	7.7	1.4	11.1	1.9	.3	—	1.6	.8
Precision production, craft, and repair	19.4	2.3	19.3	3.1	19.8	3.0	20.2	2.9	15.2	2.4
Operators, fabricators, and laborers	21.0	8.9	28.6	18.2	30.7	20.9	25.4	15.7	22.5	14.3

*Numbers in percent of total workers.
Source: U.S. Bureau of the Census, 1990e.

minority group in the United States, surpassing blacks, who will make up 14 percent of the overall population in 2020 (Davis, Haub, and Willette, 1983).

American Indians

A complete history of American Indians would have to be long and complex to capture the uniqueness of each tribe. Despite their uniqueness, however, they have seldom been in a position to express it in the face of the overwhelming power of the Europeans, who exercised their domination in a manner highly standardized for all tribes. That power was used to place almost all American Indians in a common situation, and it is that common situation that concerns us.

From the point of view of Europeans, American Indians have always had two grave drawbacks. First, they could never be successfully exploited as a labor force. Attempts in the early days failed because tribal cultures proved to be too strong an obstacle, and returning to the tribe was too easy. The latter problem was not, of course, a factor in the control of Africans, which made them far more desirable as laborers (Noel, 1968). Second, Indians were physically in the way as European settlement expanded westward. In light of these two facts, Europeans had the choice of either killing Indians or moving them to undesirable land. Both solutions were adequate from the European point of view. The magnitude of their domination is perhaps best expressed by statistics. There are today approximately 1.7 million American Indians living in the United States, making up 0.6 percent of the overall population (U.S. Bureau of the Census, 1990b). As Figure 8.3 indicates, that number is a considerable drop from the estimated 5 million

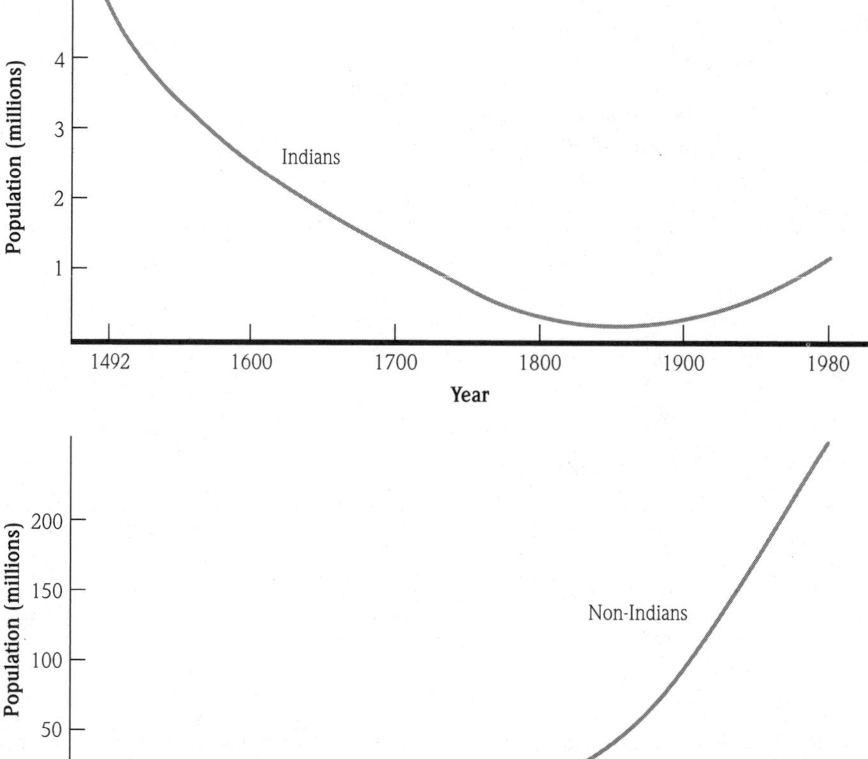

Figure 8.3 American Indian population decline and recovery in the United States, 1492-1980, compared to population growth of U.S. non-Indians. (Data from Thornton, 1987.)

Indians living in what is now the continental United States in 1492. Contact with Europeans had left many tribes completely extinct and the overall numbers of Indians in general reached near extinction around 1900. Since that time, there has been a rapid population growth among Indians due to a lowering of the death rate. The greatest killer of Indians through European contact was disease, particularly smallpox, typhus, and cholera, against which Indians had no natural defenses. While smallpox killed around 10 percent of a European population in the early days, it could completely eliminate an Indian tribe (Thornton, 1987). There are even documented reports that Europeans intentionally spread the disease through donating infected blankets to Indians (Thornton, 1987; McNeill, 1976). While the disease needed little such help, such actions indicate something of the total disregard for Indians common to many Europeans.

The Indians who were moved (and many tribes were moved more than once) found themselves in the curious limbo of the United States government-created reservation. The reservation was and is a no-man's-land between two cultures. It is organized along the lines of tribal autonomy and group activity that made up so many Indian tribes. However, the tribe has no real political control; the U.S. government has taken up the position of legal guardian, supposedly acting in the interests of the tribe. More often than not, government actions were and are designed to make the Indian as European as possible, imposing European forms of education and political processes from without. The result was that many Indians became non-Indians, but very few became Europeans.

Since 1924 American Indians have been legal citizens of the United States, yet they are still caught between two worlds. On the reservation all control is in the hands of the Bureau of Indian Affairs, part of the executive branch of the federal government. There is no legislative recourse to actions by the Bureau. Off the reservation American Indians have the rights of a United States citizen—but legal freedom is only part of the battle. The non-Indian, non-European culture of the reservation, coupled with the lack of political control by Indians, gives the contemporary Indian little future on or off the reservation. Indians have no power in either place and cannot compete economically in the modern industrial world. The use of political pressure as a group, with which other cultural groups have achieved so much, is, for Indians, nonexistent. Their group has been defused by the powerless institution of the reservation. Off the reservation, they are largely on their own.

Today, less than half of the American Indian population remains on reservations. Those who leave tend to have higher levels of education and higher incomes, but, as a group, Indians have the lowest median income of all the ethnic groups discussed in this chapter. Alcoholism and suicide are chronic problems, infant mortality rates are high (although improving rapidly relative to whites), life expectancy is low, and diseases such as tuberculosis that specialize in lower-class victims have extremely high rates (Thornton, 1987).

The one shining light that may be on the horizon for American Indians beams from political processes. The United States government has, over the years, signed a great many treaties with American Indian tribes and has subsequently broken almost all of them. Many of these treaties granted land to Indians, land that was later taken back for other uses. Today the U.S. government faces a barrage of legal claims from various tribes as Indians are taking the government to court over old treaties. A number of cases have been settled in the Indians' favor, resulting in payments of large sums of money from the government to the tribes in question (Brodeur, 1982). It is perhaps ironic that the government's reservation system helped keep tribes intact, making these court cases possible today.

CHANGES IN U.S. IMMIGRATION POLICY

The 1924 National Origins Act limited U.S. immigration to the white Protestant countries of Northwest Europe. This highly discriminatory law remained in effect until replaced in 1965 with new criteria for admission that focused on the presence of members of the immigrant's family already in the United States and on occupational skills of the immigrants. Beyond these criteria, exceptions had been made all along for refugees from selected foreign countries (usually those with communist governments) whose entrance into the United States supported its foreign policy. The major difficulty following 1966 concerned the large number of illegal immigrants who found their way into the United States. The majority of them came from Mexico, but there were representatives among them from all over the world. Of the estimated 2.1 million illegal immigrants that appeared in the 1980 census, 55 percent were from Mexico and 22 percent were from other Latin American countries; of those arrested, ninety-three different countries were represented (Bouvier and Gardner, 1986).

Illegal immigrants come to the United States primarily for economic reasons. Particularly for those from nonindustrial countries (such as Mexico), wages in the United States are far superior to what they could make at home. There is considerable debate as to the costs or benefits of their presence in the American workforce. Some observers argue that they do work other Americans don't want and at low wages, which helps some industries (such as clothing and agriculture) remain competitive with foreign products. These observers also point out that illegal immigrants give more than they take, considering taxes paid and social services received. The alternative perspective to illegal immigrants is that they swell the workforce and thereby keep wages low for other Americans; the more potenial workers present in the marketplace, the lower the wages that will be offered. These observers also point out that many illegal immigrants fill skilled and semiskilled occupations in construction and elsewhere that many other Americans would like. From all the debate, one fact remains clear: American employers favor the presence of illegals and American employees do not (Alexander, 1985; Bouvier and Gardner, 1986).

In response to the growing numbers of illegal immigrants in the United States, Congress passed immigration reform legislation in 1986. Under the new law, employers will be held responsible for checking on the legality of their employees. If they fail to do so, they will face fines ranging from $250 to $10,000 and the possibility of prison terms for persistent offenders. On the other side of the coin, illegal immigrants who have been in the United States since 1982 will be granted amnesty and given legal residency status and the future possibility of applying for citizenship. Even more lenient standards will apply to agricultural workers in response to those American employers who claimed they would be hurt the most through the end of illegal immigrant labor. Thus far, the impact of the new law is difficult to judge. There is a thriving business in providing counterfeit identification to illegal immigrants, which when checked by prospective employers, relieves those employers of liability. Few American employers have faced sanctions to date. On the other hand, relatively few illegal immigrants have come forward to take advantage of the amnesty program. They may be confused about eligibility requirements (which have changed several times) or they may simply not trust the government. In any case, a flood of illegal immigrants continues to enter the United States on a daily basis and shows no sign of stopping soon (Bouvier and Gardner, 1986).

SUMMARY

Ethnic groups are social groups whose members share a culture, think of themselves as sharing a culture, or are defined by others as sharing a culture. If two or more ethnic groups share a society and one ethnic group controls the distribution of rewards so as to benefit itself with upper-class membership, a system of ethnic stratification exists. Within this system the ethnic groups with power are majority (or dominant) groups, and the ethnic groups without power are minority (or subordinate) groups. A system of ethnic stratification is maintained through discrimination, which may operate either overtly or covertly (institutional discrimination). Whichever form it takes, discrimination closes routes to upward social mobility for the ethnic groups it is directed against.

Social stratification in general and ethnic stratification in particular produce competition between individuals and among groups in society. This competition is potentially threatening to all members of society. Prejudice, or a negative attitude toward a group of people, is a natural outcome of this threatening situation as individuals seek to support their sense of individual worth and their social position. Prejudice generally contains stereotypes—generalizations (negative in this case) about the group that is the recipient of the prejudice.

When ethnic groups come together, a variety of social arrangements and cultural outcomes are possible. One American dream has always been the "melting pot," in which individuals would intermarry and intermingle their cultures so as to produce new people with a new culture. Closer to reality are some alternatives such as genocide (the physical extermination of an ethnic group) and expulsion (the physical removal of an ethnic group from a society). Segregation may also be employed as a means for keeping two ethnic groups culturally separate (on the dominant group's terms) while sharing the same society. Separatism is separation of a minority group by their own choice.

Assimilation, one of the most common outcomes, occurs when the minority group's culture fades away, and simultaneously, the dominant group accepts the minority group's individual members into dominant group activities and, ultimately, families. A social and cultural alternative generally proposed by minority groups is cultural pluralism. Cultural pluralism is the peaceful coexistence of two or more ethnic groups within the same society in which (1) they maintain their cultural differences and (2) all ethnic groups share in the power and rewards of the society.

The United States has been a center of immigration for centuries. The dominant ethnic group today is made up of descendants from northwestern European immigrants. Although a great many different ethnic groups have faced racist situations and discrimination at varying times in American history, the three ethnic groups currently facing the most difficulties are black Americans, Hispanic Americans, and American Indians. Each of these groups is defined as racially different, occupies the lower classes disproportionately, and faces discrimination as a part of everyday life.

GLOSSARY

Affirmative action Any program designed to alter the racial, ethnic, or sexual composition of a social group (students, employees, etc.) by actively seeking minority group members.

Assimilation The incorporation of one ethnic group into the continuing culture of another ethnic group.

Cultural pluralism A social situation where two or more ethnic groups share one society; each ethnic group maintains its separate cultural distinctiveness and no one ethnic group dominates the other(s).

Discrimination Any action that shows a bias against an individual on the basis of his or her group membership; it is typically designed to hinder the competitive abilities of individuals in that group.

Ethnic group A group of people who share a common culture, think of themselves as sharing a common culture, or are defined by others as sharing a common culture.

Ethnic stratification The disproportionate location of ethnic group members in particular social classes of a social stratification system.

Exploitation The situation of an individual who does not receive full value for his or her labor.

Expulsion The physical removal of most or all members of a subordinate group from within the boundaries of a nation-state.

Genocide Actions that result in the deaths of most or all members of a given subordinate group.

Institutional (covert) discrimination Indirect forms of discrimination (intentional or unintentional) that affect a certain social group because of certain attributes or abilities most of that group's members have (or lack).

Majority group (dominant group) A social group that controls the organization and distribution of rewards in a society.

Melting pot The mixing and blending of two or more cultures through the intermarriage of their members.

Minority group (subordinate group) A relatively powerless social group that is subject to the decisions of a majority (dominant) group.

Prejudice A negative attitude toward a group of people.

Racial group A group of people socially defined as sharing a common genetic heritage.

Racism (1) The belief that people are separated into different races and that those races are biologically inferior or superior to each other. (2) The individual experience of living within a system of ethnic stratification in which the groups at the bottom of the hierarchy are defined as racially inferior.

Segregation The dominant group's decision to separate itself, either socially or physically, from a given minority group.

Separatism The physical and political separation of a minority group, by their own choice, from a dominant group.

Stereotype A generalized description (usually negative) of a specific social group, applied to its members.

SUPPLEMENTARY READINGS

Allen, James Paul, and Eugene James Turner *We the People: An Atlas of America's Ethnic Diversity.* New York: Macmillan, 1988.
That's right, this is an atlas of who lives where, compiled from the 1980 census. Every ethnic group counted in the census appears graphically on color maps. This book can be a very useful resource.

Brown, Dee *Bury My Heart at Wounded Knee: An Indian History of the American West.* New York: Holt, Rinehart and Winston, 1971.

An extremely easy-to-read history of the western Indian tribes in the last half of the nineteenth century, focusing on the conflict between the incoming Europeans and the American Indians.

Josephy, Alvin M. *Now That the Buffalo's Gone: A Study of Today's American Indians.* New York: Knopf, 1982.
A general and sympathetic portrait of the place of Indians in contemporary American society.

Kessner, Thomas, and Betty Boyd Caroli (eds.) *Today's Immigrants: Their Stories.* New York: Oxford University Press, 1982.
A collection of essays that offers a wide perspective on modern U.S. immigrants, including such groups as West Indians, Koreans, Latin Americans, Asians, and Russian Jews.

Levin, Jack *The Functions of Prejudice.* New York: Harper & Row, 1975.
A readable discussion of sociological and psychological perspectives on racial and ethnic prejudice. Levin takes a functional perspective on the subject.

Luhman, Reid, and Stuart Gilman *Race and Ethnic Relations: The Social and Political Experience of Minority Groups.* Belmont, Calif.: Wadsworth, 1980.
A general introduction to racial and ethnic groups in the United States from the dual perspective of sociology and political science.

Malcolm X *The Autobiography of Malcolm X.* New York: Grove Press, 1966.
As an early leader of the Black Muslim movement in the United States, Malcolm X is an important figure from many points of view. His life story provides a description of growing up black in the United States as well as an insight into minority political movements in general and the Black Muslims in particular.

Shibutani, Tamotsu, and Kian M. Kwan *Ethnic Stratification A Comparative Approach.* New York: Macmillan, 1965.
A substantive work on ethnic relations and the importance of ethnic stratification that draws significantly on the international realm. It is not designed as an introductory work, yet its readable style places it within the grasp of any serious beginning student.

Sowell, Thomas *The Economics and Politics of Race.* New York: Morrow, 1983.
Sowell is often characterized as a conservative black sociologist. The characterization fits only partially. Sowell offers some keen insights on the economics of racism in the United States.

No Can Geeve Up: Crossing Institutional Barriers

H. M. Murai

Institutional discrimination is discrimination that affects particular racial or ethnic groups not because of their group membership but because of skills or abilities that tend to distinguish them from dominant group members. When our institutions discriminate on the basis of such skills or abilities, particular racial or ethnic groups may be adversely affected just as surely as if their group had been singled out for unequal treatment. In the following article, H. M. Murai tells the story of his childhood and his experiences as a university freshman. Growing up in a distinctive Japanese American community in Hawaii, he differed in many ways from the dominant group (which conceived and operates the University of Hawaii). Of those many differences, Murai focuses on his language. He grew up speaking a form of language known as a pidgin (which combines and simplifies elements of two or more other languages). A pidgin language accomplishes the task of communication (which is all a language really need do), but Murai found it less than acceptable to his freshman English teacher at the university; to Murai, freshman English might as well have been freshman Greek. Since he wrote the following article, he must have succeeded, but many in his place wouldn't have.

I grew up in a sugar plantation community near Hilo on the "Big Island" of Hawaii. In spite of its size, it is still considered to be one of the "outer islands" of Hawaii; i.e., not the center of industry and especially the tourist industry, which thrives on the island of Oahu and more recently, Maui and Kaui. Growing up in a plantation community one was considered to be "from the country(side)." People from the country are often considered lower class and lower in "class."

Plantation language, which was my first language, was closer to the pidgin spoken by the original immigrant workers, somewhere between a Creole and a dialect of English. You were likely to find interaction between ethnic groups in the plantation camps in spite of management's attempts to keep the groups separate and ununited. The integration of ethnic groups contributed to the perpetuation of the original pidgin created for communication across languages. On any given Sunday you would find Filipinos, Japanese, and Portuguese gathering at the local cockpit and billiard hall. Growing up in this environment made it difficult to identify the sources of words borrowed from Filipino, Japanese, Portuguese, Hawaiian, and so on in the local dialect.

I believe that the majority of the children coming from the camps were proud of their roots. Being proud of our backgrounds I believe further contributed to our maintenance of the language and culture of the camps. Life in the camp was rarely dull. One could always go "pick cane" from the cane fields or "catch cane" from the flumes delivering the cut sugar cane stalks to the mill. There was also "poking crayfish" and opu (mudfish) in the rivah (river), catching opai (river shrimp), picking wild guava and rose apple, or just following the rivah. In my case there was also body surfing with scraps of board at one

Copyright © 1988 by H. M. Murai. Used by permission of the author.

of dah bes beaches in the islands. During the summer months, baseball and the Japanese bon dances (commemorating the deceased) provided more weekend recreation and entertainment. Entrance into the middle and secondary schools located in the city provided for a broadening of one's cultural-linguistic circle; however, the foundation of the personalities of the kids from the camps was formed in the camps, and Hilo, Hawaii is indeed a country town when compared to Honolulu.

Leaving the warmth and security of home for the first time to venture off to school in the big city, Honolulu, provided as much cultural-linguistic conflict as I could handle. The institutional barriers to being successful in college were many.

I had heard about how one-third of the freshman class failed English composition at the University of Hawaii and how failure in composition usually led to flunking out of school. English comp. was known as the screening class for those who could and those who couldn't. This was especially true of students with my background; i.e., students who were from the rural areas of the islands and who spoke "pidgin" English (actually a dialect of English). I was from one of the "outer islands" (islands other than Oahu, where Honolulu, the capital, is located). Adding to my fears was the self-doubt that haunted me throughout my first year—self-doubt that was set in motion by my almost total failure during my final two years in high school and by a counselor who thought I would be "wasting time and money" by pursuing a university degree. I am quite sure that my father had the same sense of doubt when he waved me off at the airport with the somewhat ambiguous, "No can come home" (may be interpreted as "You can't come home" or the intended, I believed, "If you can't make it, come home"). In fact, till this very moment it is still not clear to me how I was able to attend the university out of high school. I had taken college preparatory courses such as chemistry, geometry, and a second year of algebra, but I would have been the first to admit that I had no demonstrable proof that I had learned anything in these classes. Nearly straight D grades were an accurate reflection of my near total neglect of academics. Attitudinally, I learned that I was not capable of anything beyond the usual requirements for high school graduation. I definitely felt much more comfortable playing for extra spending money in the pool room or drinking beer "wid dah boys" than in any classroom.

Perhaps my greatest fear during the first semester was that someone would discover that I was mistakenly admitted to the university and that yes, my high school counselor was correct in suggesting that it was a waste of time and money for me to pursue a university education. This led to more than a bit of paranoia. I felt that I was being watched and could not afford to attract any attention through failure. Failure on any examination and definitely failure in any class I was sure would lead to immediate discovery. Visiting the office of any instructor was thus out of the question. My inability to speak "good English" would surely lead to my being spotted as an imposter. Much to my relief none of my professors required individual meetings. In fact, I do not recall any professor mentioning office hours much less inviting students with problems to come in for consultation.

I can still recall, after 25 years, what my first semester freshman schedule was like. I know I felt compelled to enroll for 18 units, which was the maximum allowed. I thought (incorrectly) that I had to do this in order to graduate in four years, just as the catalog had illustrated. I recall speech class, where I was obviously in deep trouble trying to pronounce the "th," "ed," short "i" and "schwa" sounds and vainly attempting to speak "like one haole" (anglo). Western civilization class was at 7:30 A.M., Tuesday, Thursday, and Saturday and freshman English was Monday, Wednesday, and Friday at 2:00 P.M. Western civ. was a memorable class not simply because of the time and the 300 or so students packed in an auditorium, seat numbers assigned, but because of the difficulty I had in note taking. Note taking was a skill I had never acquired in high school. I assumed that my notes had to be accurate and thought that someone might ask to read them. I wrote in pencil, filling every line and margin as though I had spent my last penny on the notebook. I also erased words while desperately trying to record lectures verbatim. Someone forgot to tell me that I was only supposed to capture the main points (assuming I could determine what they were). Needless to say, when it came time to review my notes I had difficulty deciphering my own handwriting and could barely make sense of the little that I was able to decipher. I received a well-earned D in the first semester of Western civilization. But ah, English composition, there was the ultimate challenge.

The instructor for English 101 was, I learned later, a former high school English teacher. She had what may be referred to as a "no nonsense" approach with an emphasis on actually writing rather than grammar or the how-to of writing. In correcting papers, my papers at least, Mrs. C. tried to interpret what I, more frequently than not, was unable to clearly express. She was a risk taker. She was not afraid to substitute words or rewrite sentences in attempting to clarify my compositions. During the first half of the semester, Mrs. C. came close to totally rewriting my compositions. More often than not, she was, as far as I could ascertain, on the money. I was impressed, amazed, astonished even, to see how clearly she could represent my deepest thoughts and feelings without ever consulting with me. Nevertheless, I managed to receive straight F's on my first six compositions. We were at midterm and I thought, "You in real trouble bruddha. How you going do dis!" There were no remedial classes offered. It was the prototype of the "sink or swim," "give up or geev um!" (show what you can do) situation.

Receiving graded papers, due on Monday and returned on Friday, was the most demoralizing and embarrassing part of that first semester. In high school I could laugh at the fact that I did not try to do well and thus expected poor grades, but this was the big time and I was indeed trying my utmost to succeed. Thus when I received my straight F's, I simply slid my papers into my notebook so they would not be revealed to my classmates. I also averted looking at any of my classmates who spoke aloud about their disappointment in receiving B's or C's and even A minuses! Even the gal with the friendly smile sitting next to me who did not say anything about the straight A's she was receiving was a threat to my ego. Surely these people realized that I did not belong in the same room much less the same university. Surveying the class of twenty-five or so students, it was difficult not to conclude that I was the one of three who were destined for failure. "I just gotta show um (them)" (that I could do it).

As soon as we were given the topic for the next composition on Friday, I headed for the library. Thanks to the good advice of two older students, I had left time after each of my classes to review notes or conduct the research necessary to clarify points in doubt. Although it was extremely painful, and partly because it was required, I immediately began the rewrite of my paper. Because of the detailed correcting by Mrs. C., this was not a terribly difficult task. During the first few weeks, library work included looking up words that were part of the assigned topics. After the very first class, the first word I had to look up was "composition." I was not sure what was being required. I also looked up "plagiarize" (I knew the "Don't" part of the phrase). Although my dictionary never left my side, I frequently found it necessary to look up more detailed descriptions of words in the encyclopedia or unabridged dictionaries in the library. Then began the writing process, outlining, and starting the rough draft. Because the composition class was my last class on Friday, I could spend two to three hours in the library before heading back to my apartment for dinner. My goal was to write the exact number of words required for the composition.

The writing continued immediately after dinner and ended sometime around midnight. As reward for my hard work, I would often treat myself to a bowl of crisp kau chee mein (Chinese noodles with vegetables) and several cups of tea in a restaurant sparsely patronized mainly by people who had closed the local bars. This was a treasured time for meditation and contemplating my world view. Friday evening or early morning at the Golden Duck and martial arts practice during the week were the few breaks in my daily academic routine. I was always happy to get out of the studio apartment I shared with two working brothers. Although only fifteen minutes from Waikiki, I never spent time on the beach that first year in school. Saturdays were devoted to Western civilization, so the final draft on the composition was not completed until Sunday. Until my teacher hinted that it would not be a bad idea to either write the composition with a pen rather than a pencil or even type the final draft, I did not have to spend a lot of time producing the final draft. In spite of the usual ten to fifteen hours of writing spread over three days, I seemed to make little progress during the first six weeks. None of my classmates seemed to be experiencing any difficulty in the class.

I vividly recall standing outside the classroom a half hour before class began, listening to students who were actually completing their compositions before class! These were students who were receiving A's and B's. All I could think of was "You in beeg trouble bruddha!" There were many days of loneliness and discouragement during which times, for some reason, I refused to accept failure, thinking that all I had to do was work ten times as long and hard as my classmates, a hundred times if necessary. "No can geev up!" was always my final thought.

Then, alas, during the seventh week of class, I was asked to read my paper to the class, an honor given to the chosen few each week. I panicked and hesitated. I was also having serious problems in my speech class at that time. In addition, I had been turned down as a volunteer reader for a blind student because of my inability to read English fluently, and I was not at all confident about getting up in front of the class. The kind teacher obliged by reading my composition for me while I listened with ambivalent feelings of pride and shame. I made it through English composition with a C grade the first semester and a B for the second semester.

I often wonder how and why I persisted during that first semester, especially during the first half of that first semester. I had no one to turn to except myself and a sister-in-law who sometimes read my papers for obvious flaws. I can think of some obvious reasons, such as the fact that I was able to survive without a great deal of effort in my Spanish and psychology classes and of course, P.E. and the required ROTC. However, it was also clear to me that by any combination of grades that I could expect, failing English composition would definitely lead to disenrollment from the university. Reflecting back into that time, I can see numerous reasons for my survival.

I come from a family background where it was assumed that anything could be achieved through effort. I think I felt that failure in school was worse than death. "No can come home" was an ever-present thought throughout my four years as an undergraduate. Hereditary limitations in intellect were not considered important. My father, who I greatly admired, had himself risen from the ranks of a plantation laborer to a supervisorial position. During my junior year in high school he had been selected to join a team of engineers and horticulturists to help modernize sugar mills in a third-world country. Daddy, though extremely strict in discipline, always provided a loving arm around the shoulders in a timely manner, and obviously put the needs of his children over and above his personal needs. He had an eighth-grade education. My mother I admired for her determination to provide for the family through hard work and persistence under difficult economic, sociocultural, and oftentimes highly stressful psychological conditions. She was the model of the nurturing mother always there in times of need and never punitive. She, too, put her children's needs ahead of her own. Relatives, especially Uncle and Aunty Y, Roy and Kay, also impressed upon me the importance to success of hard work and the willingness to suffer through hard times. These values were reinforced by participation in the martial arts from an early age and by Japanese samurai films that my aunt and uncle introduced to me early on.

Participation in sports must have had some influence on my attitude about persistence in the face of difficult odds. Although never an outstanding athlete, I had experienced some success in baseball, track, and football and even tried swimming and amateur boxing during my junior year when I was injured and unable to participate in football. I had the experience of competing under teachers and coaches who were, for better or for worse, sometimes sadistic in their training methods. Being able to run the last wind sprint and stand up for the final tackle drill and experiencing some success throughout all of the trials I am sure contributed somewhat to my belief that hard work could conquer all.

Although academic successes were few and far between throughout my early school years, I recall reminding myself that I had had some moments of success achieved through hard work. I had vague memories of being fairly successful in challenging social studies, science, and English classes during my junior high school days just prior to being initiated into one of the local gangs. I also had memories of being able to learn Spanish without too much effort and elementary algebra, which did not seem to come too easily for some of my classmates who I thought were higher achievers. It is funny how a few successful experiences can be so meaningful in times of doubt and carry you over hurdles.

I have always attributed some of my success to a cousin whose intelligence I respected although he had not completed his college work. He had told me that I would never fail if I attended classes faithfully and kept up with my daily work. For the first two years I took his words to heart, never missing a class even though I suffered through several bouts of illness during that time period. I could think of absolutely nothing that could keep me from attending classes, an extreme contrast with my attitude during my high school days when I missed more classes than I attended. This was all in spite of the fact that attendance was never applied as a factor in grading in any of my classes.

My financial situation must be included as a factor that encouraged me to persist and survive. It was my feeling that I would have no second chances in any of my classes; my financial situation, I believed, did not allow for second chances. Although my parents were able to help me with cost of room and board during my first year, I had saved from my part-time job in high school and from several summer jobs including work with a trucking company and in a fertilizer factory.

There is little doubt that the teacher of my composition class was of primary importance in helping me persist. Although the grades she gave me were not encouraging, the fact that she obviously took the time to correct my errors gave me hope that I could improve if I could learn to self-correct as she had been modeling for me. In fact, I think I spent time committing most of the corrections she modeled for me to long-term memory. I was determined never to make the same error more than once, and though I was not always successful, I knew that I was improving by my fourth or fifth failure. I wonder if Mrs. C knew how her comments and grading of my papers affected me. She gave me no indication that she did, yet she must have surely wondered how I ever managed to get into the university and why I kept coming back for more punishment.

Any one of the reasons discussed above could account for my persistence in English composition. I am of the opinion that, as with most of human behavior, only a complex combination of many reasons, including but not limited to the above, must be considered. Nevertheless, today, as I relate my experience to my students who seem to be in similar situations, I emphasize that one can only fail if one lacks the desire to succeed, the willingness to sacrifice for one's goals. No can geeve up.

Discussion Questions

1. Do you think that Murai's problems in his freshman year were due to his cultural differences from the university or his lack of attention to school during high school? Are the requirements of freshman composition just to learn to communicate effectively, or do they also include that one do so in a certain approved language? What would have happened if Murai had written clearly but in pidgin?
2. Murai describes his frustration and embarrassment in getting such low grades during his freshman year. How is failure made more difficult to bear when you are surrounded by others to whom success comes so easily?

3. Murai's story is one of surmounting the barriers of institutional discrimination. If he could do it, why can't everyone? How high a barrier is institutional discrimination when we broaden our vision from one person's story to large numbers of people who have important cultural differences from dominant societal institutions?

PART Four
SOCIAL INSTITUTIONS

CHAPTER 9 Social Change and Industrialization: The Growth of Social Institutions

Sociologists look at societies in terms of the way human behavior is coordinated. Societies produce this coordinated behavior in endlessly creative and often complicated ways. A society can consist of twenty people who agree to share a specific place to gather berries together or it can consist of a vast industrial giant like the United States. This chapter will explore some of the variation to be found in human societies, with a particular focus on the elaborate separation of different activities—which sociologists refer to as *institutions*—found in industrial societies.

TYPES OF HUMAN SOCIETIES (AND TYPES OF HUMANS)

So far we have looked at the ways humans coordinate their activities into the social patterns of society. We have also looked at the ways people become socialized into those patterns so that their thinking and their behavior are appropriate for the particular patterns by which they live. Sociologists examine this interplay between societies and people, paying particular attention to the different kinds of people that result from different kinds of societies. Comparing society to playing a game can help you understand how this happens. The game of Monopoly makes people competitive, methodical, envious, anxious, and very alert—you may well wind up hating your best friend before the game ends. By contrast, playing catch with a Frisbee on a sunny afternoon makes people noncompetitive and relaxed. Societies differ just as games do. Some, like modern American society, require competition; because of their socialization, Americans tend to be competitive people (and may find the casual tossing about of a Frisbee somewhat unfulfilling as a result). Other societies, such as some American Indian tribes, require cooperation among their patterned activities, and their members thus tend to be less competitive (and likely to favor more cooperative games). Observations of such differences have led sociologists to examine the range of human societies.

Technological Change in Society

Of modern sociologists, Gerhard Lenski has examined the range of human societies in the most detail (Lenski, 1966; Lenski and Lenski, 1974). He separated societies into types according to the dominant forms of technology. One advantage of using technology as the organizational principle is that it reminds us that the basic problem of any society is survival; a society's technology is a key to survival and thus affects all other elements of the society. Lenski organized the types of societies into a hierarchy ranging from those with the simplest forms of technology to those with the most complex forms. As a result, two interesting relationships appeared: First, as technology becomes more complex, the social division of labor becomes more complex. This is not too surprising, since a complex technology would require a complex organization of labor, and a division of labor is fairly efficient. The second relationship, however, is not as obviously necessary and is in many ways more interesting: As technology becomes more complex, a gap opens between the "haves" and the "have nots" in society.

Let us simplify Lenski's typology down to its four most basic types. We first encounter the *hunting and gathering society,* the extreme of rudimentary technology, in which relatively small nomadic groups are constantly on the move in search of food. This type of society is usually characterized by group cooperation, as the difficulty of life requires that the group work together if they are to survive. If there is any division of labor at all in the hunting and gathering society, it is a basic one based on sex, in which men specialize in hunting activities and women specialize in gathering activities. The amount of the time spent in procuring food plus the need to keep on the move limits both the physical and social development of culture. (More recent researchers, such as Richard Lee (1979), have studied modern hunting and gathering societies such as the !Kung bushmen and have noted that less than full-time attention is paid to food procurement, leaving the people with considerable leisure. Lee explains their lack of accumulated wealth by the need for constant mobility.)

Moving up one step in technology, we encounter the *horticultural society.* The primary technological difference between the hunting and gathering society and the horticultural society is an extremely important one: The horticultural society *produces* its own food rather than depending solely on the environment for it. The horticultural society can stay put, grow larger (as more people can be fed by the same amount of work), and develop other forms of technology, which further increases the division of labor. In addition, the horticultural society is advanced enough to produce a *surplus* of goods, more than needed for the immediate survival of group members. It is this surplus, says Lenski, that first opens the gap between the haves and have nots. It becomes possible for some members of the society to take more than their fair share without starving the remainder of the society. As acquired goods, land, and so on are passed along in families, ongoing patterns of social inequality are intensified and perpetuated.

The third basic type of society is the *agrarian society.* In most ways the agrarian society is an extension of the social patterns begun in the horticultural society. The agrarian society is characterized by introduction of the plow. Still more people can be fed with less work, leading to larger societies (and governments), more leisure, more technology, an increasing division of labor, greater surpluses, and an increasing gap between the haves and the have nots.

The fourth basic type of society is the *industrial society.* The industrial society still produces food through farming, but the overall society is characterized by manufacturing, elaborate technology, large cities, elaborate and highly organized divisions of labor (such as the modern bureaucracy), large and powerful governments, and a continuing gap between the haves and the have nots (although not as rigid a gap as in some of the other societal types, according to Lenski).

Modern American society could be considered a prime example of Lenski's industrial society. Some sociologists, however, have created an additional type of society known as the *postindustrial society.* A postindustrial society is one in which workers primarily produce information and services. A staple of that information is technological knowledge that can be used to increase profits in local industry as well as to export for foreign industry. Such a new focus in industrial activity relegates much of the heavy industrial activity to other countries (which often provide cheaper labor) and changes the labor needs of the society; unskilled workers are no longer in demand (see Toffler, 1980; Harrington, 1984; O'Hare, 1985).

The parallel development of the increasing division of labor and the gap between the haves and have nots in Lenski's scheme points to one of the fundamental concepts used by sociologists in understanding modern society and the people in it: **social stratification**. As Lenski observed about the beginnings of the gap between the haves and have nots, for the most part these activities run in families; the children of large stockholders tend to have many options in society and can generally locate a highly rewarded activity, while the children of welfare recipients are more likely to become welfare recipients.

Social stratification makes people competitive. The hope of moving to a more highly ranked activity and the fear of moving down in the hierarchy make people highly conscious of how they're doing in relation to others; they watch out for their own interests in order to succeed. We give our children grades when they begin school and give them Monopoly games to play in order to prepare them for competition later in life. If we turn our attention to the kind of cooperation necessary for the survival of a hunting and gathering society, we can see how societies differ and, ultimately, how people differ from one society to the next.

Gemeinschaft and Gesellschaft: Traditional and Industrial Societies

Ferdinand Tönnies, a German sociologist writing around the turn of the last century, looked at the same variation in human societies that would later interest Lenski, but from a slightly different perspective. Rather than emphasize the variations in technology, as Lenski did, Tönnies focused more on changes in the basic ways people related to each other. He organized this focus by isolating two extremes in human societies, which he labeled Gemeinschaft and Gesellschaft (Tönnies, 1957).

Gemeinschaft is best translated into English as a traditional or communal society. It is characterized by small size and very little division of labor. In addition, the activities are in one way or another tied to family or kin relationships; families tend to be quite large, and they stay together not only because they pray together but because they work together, fight together,

German sociologist Ferdinand Tönnies (1885-1936). Tönnies was an important figure in the early growth of sociology but is best remembered today for his twin concepts of Gemeinschaft and Gesellschaft, which compare small communities with large modern societies.

learn together, raise children together, and settle personal disputes together. Individuals have a variety of highly personal encounters with the same people on an everyday basis. As a result of this close interaction and the low division of labor, Gemeinschaft individuals tend to be relatively similar to each other. When people constantly do the same things with the same people and group cooperation is strongly emphasized, people tend to turn out pretty much the same. In a Gemeinschaft, the group comes first and the individual second.

At the other extreme is **Gesellschaft**, best translated as an industrial society. More specifically, the German word *Gesellschaft* refers to commercial activities (as opposed to personal or non-money-related activities), and it is that business relationship that Tönnies wished to emphasize. In an industrial society the family becomes far less important as more and more of the individual's activities occur with nonrelatives. The personal and emotional basis of human interaction that characterizes Gemeinschaft is replaced by impersonal and formal relationships in Gesellschaft. These new relationships develop as the society becomes larger and develops a complex division of labor involving a wide variety of activities. The diversity of activities in the society leads to a diversity of individuals who follow different norms and hold different values. In a Gesellschaft the individual places himself or herself first; the group comes second.

No individual society is ever likely to be 100 percent Gemeinschaft or 100 percent Gesellschaft; the two concepts represent extremes in the organization of human societies. Even the most basic hunting and gathering societies would probably have some kind of division of labor, the beginnings of social stratification, and nonfamily relationships conducted on a formal basis. At the other extreme, a Gesellschaft society like the United States has many Gemeinschaft features, particularly in the more traditional or rural corners of the society. The terms are designed to call attention to general features of society and, most important, to help us understand something about social change. Whereas Lenski directed our focus to technological change, Tönnies concentrated on the growing complexity of the division of labor in society as we move from Gemeinschaft to Gesellschaft.

In Gemeinschaft, the same people (usually your relations) take care of all your needs; in Gesellschaft, the complex division of labor means that a wide variety of people (usually not your relations) take care of your needs, and different groups of these people specialize in different needs. For example, in Gemeinschaft socialization occurs within the family. In Gesellschaft, on the other hand, the process of socialization happens in the family, in school, with friends and acquaintances, from the media, at church, on the job, and so on. Even more significantly, these different spheres of activities may be populated by very different people, who are not necessarily in agreement as to what you should be learning. In order to make some sense of this complexity, sociologists attempt to look at these spheres of activities, or institutions, one at a time. Complex societies such as the United States contain elaborated social institutions that provide a specific kind of social organization for the society. As we encounter institutions in everyday life, we may feel that we are in fact living everyday *lives* (as opposed to one single life) as our experience becomes separated into different arenas.

THE DEVELOPMENT OF SOCIAL INSTITUTIONS

Most people think of an institution as a mental hospital or, perhaps, a prison. That meaning of the term has nothing whatever to do with the way sociologists use it. To a sociologist, an

institution is a cluster (or sphere) of interrelated activities within a society, coupled with the knowledge, beliefs, and objects that relate to those activities. Institutions are typically stable configurations of social forms that meet social needs in specific areas. For example, the family (though not *a* particular family) is an institution in modern American society. Within that institution are included mothers, fathers, brothers, sisters, aunts, uncles, cousins, beliefs about family togetherness, attitudes toward divorce, family reunions, marriage ceremonies, in-law jokes, family Bibles, genealogy tracing, and Thanksgiving dinner (even the turkey). For all its variety, this list just scratches the surface of the family. Understanding any one item on the list requires understanding the other items as well; because they are all part of the same institution, they are all interrelated. *Brother* cannot be defined without *sister, divorce* must be defined with *marriage,* and the Thanksgiving turkey sacrifices all in the name of family togetherness.

Of all the activities, ideas, and objects that cluster within institutions, one element that is not limited within the institution is the individuals who act out the activities, think the ideas, and use the objects. A woman who is a mother/daughter/wife/sister in a family can think thoughts of family togetherness and cook a Thanksgiving turkey, but she can also attend church, hold a job, join the PTA, and run for political office. These activities take her outside the institution of the family and into the institutions of religion, the economy, education, and politics, respectively. Each time she moves into an activity in a different institution, she confronts the other activities, ideas, and objects that cluster within that new institution; just as mothers, fathers, and Thanksgiving dinners exist within the family institution, teachers, students, examinations, and classrooms exist within the educational institution.

In a manner of speaking, an institution is like a miniature society, complete with roles, norms, values, objects, and so on. The major difference between an institution and a society is that a society takes care of a wide variety of human needs, while institutions (as parts of larger societies) take care of just a few needs. The institution of education, for example, specializes in socialization and does little along the lines of providing food, shelter, and protection to societal members. Those needs are taken care of by other institutions.

As societies change from Gemeinschaft to Gesellschaft, the development and separation of institutions become evident. Figure 9.1 illustrates how a Gemeinschaft might take care of the variety of human needs. A Gemeinschaft is structurally a fairly simple society; if it can be said to have institutions, it has only one—the family. But to imagine any modern meaning to the term *family* as applied to Gemeinschaft will cloud the real functions of the family in such a society. As suggested by Figure 9.1, the Gemeinschaft "family" satisfies the needs of religion, protection, survival, and socialization at the same time that it provides companionship and oversees the raising of children. We might call it a government as well as a family for, in the modern sense of those words, it has the functions of both. In Gemeinschaft, all needs are met by the same people.

At the other extreme a Gesellschaft might be represented by Figure 9.2. The institutional separation characteristic of Gesellschaft can be viewed as a kind of gradual "eating away" of the importance of kin relationships. As the institutions develop into separate spheres of activities, they come to specialize in taking care of certain needs, and as they specialize, the family provides less and less for the individual. It is important to realize, however, that individuals do not necessarily choose to relieve their families of importance in these areas. As the overall

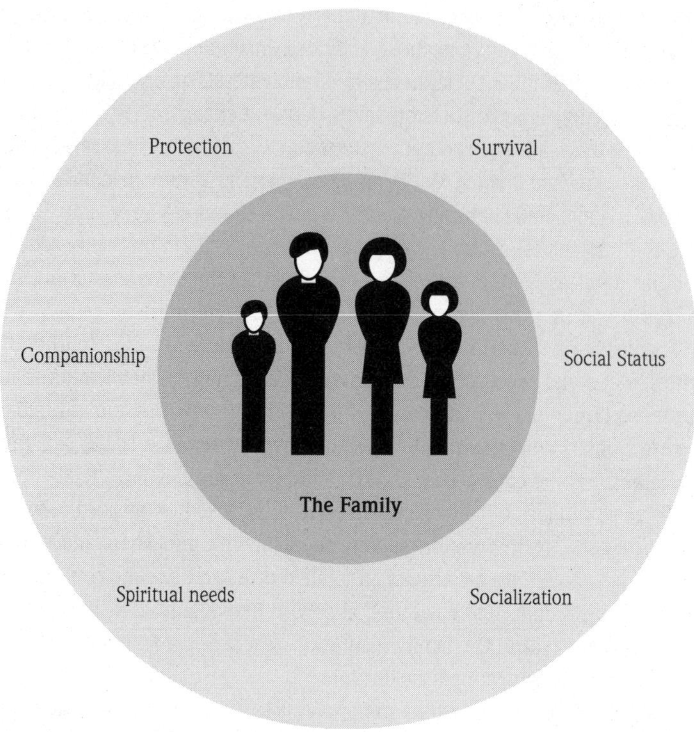

Figure 9.1 Individual needs in Gemeinschaft. The multifunction family.

society changes, it becomes increasingly impossible for individuals to depend upon their families for everything; institutions take over the business of caring for human needs.

Social change often forces changes in the lives of many individuals who are unable to withstand them. The reading by Alan Banks at the end of this chapter illustrates this clearly with a case study of the change in Kentucky from an agricultural society to an industrial society. More than most changes, industrialization causes widespread disruption in almost all aspects of life; the ultimate result is institutional separation. We can perhaps best understand this development by looking individually at the major institutions that develop: education, economics, politics, religion, and the family in its modern sense. These institutions are the focus of the rest of this chapter.

Education and the Family

Industrial societies require literate and skilled employees to cope with the technological sophistication on which they run (Apple, 1982). Relatives may do well at teaching the young how to farm and manage simple crafts, but they fall short when the society needs fewer farmers and more computer technicians. The efficient way to meet this need is to relieve relatives of their educational duties and to encourage the young to consult the specialists of education, who, presumably, know more about the things that need to be learned. The modern institution of education in a typical industrial society consists of teachers, students, classrooms, books, ideas

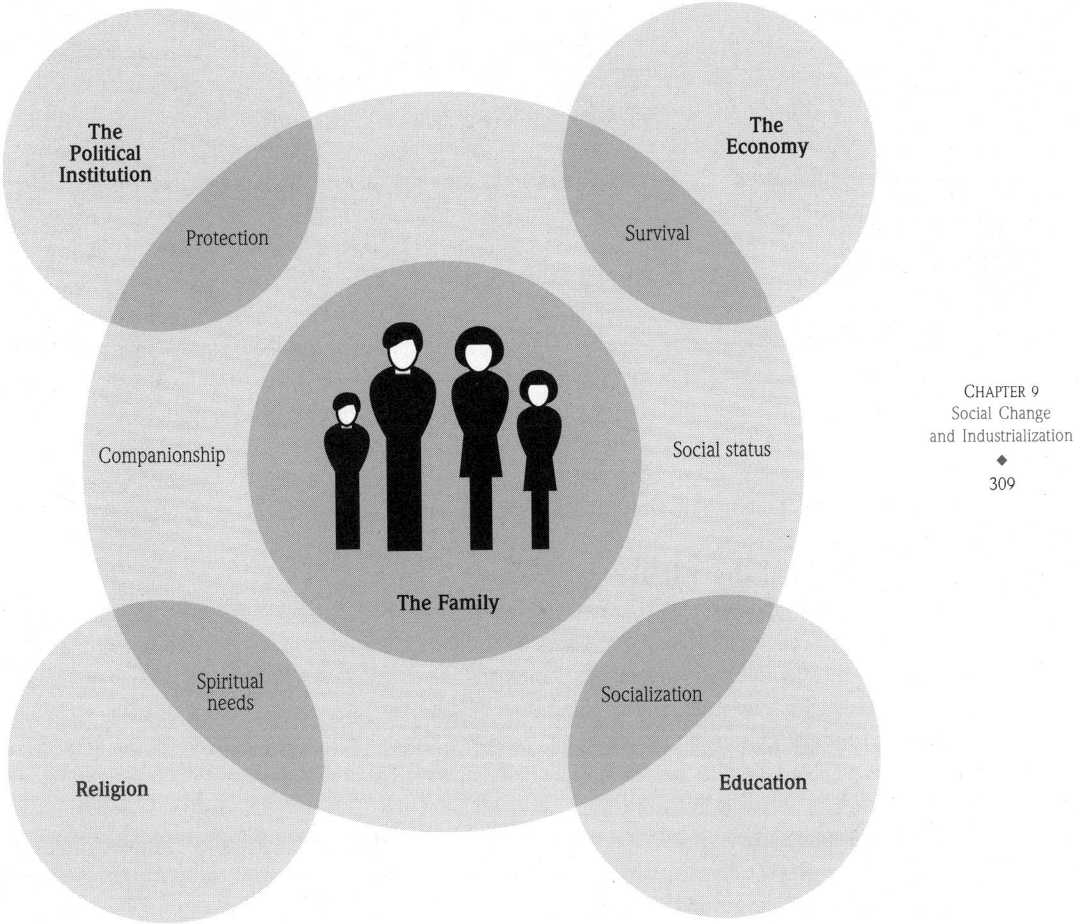

Figure 9.2 Individual needs in Gesellschaft. Institutional separation.

and beliefs concerning the whys and hows of learning, and many more such elements. As it exists today in the United States, the institution of education has become a vast enterprise (both public and private) that is structurally separate from families. Education is left to families for only the first five years of a child's life; after that, by law, responsibility for a child's education must be surrendered to the state or a private institution acceptable to the state.

As with all institutions, the separation is not complete. Schools are ultimately controlled by school boards, the members of which are elected by the public. In addition, parents may opt for a variety of forms of private education (if they can afford it) that may add religion to the curriculum or even alter the basic curriculum itself. In 1974 parents in Charleston, West Virginia, organized a protest over the religious and political content of school textbooks. A similar event occurred in Tennessee in 1986; parents went to court arguing that standard school textbooks violated the religious instruction they were attempting to instill at home. In both cases, the parents felt that the texts taught socialism and atheism; the teachers, of course, felt that the textbooks were educationally valuable. Such disputes help sociologists locate the boundaries between institutions—usually right on the battle lines where the different activities and ideas collide.

As the institution of education physically removes children from family settings, it places them into educational settings with other children of their own age. The old one-room schoolhouse with all ages mixed together closely approached a family-style arrangement; modern education, however, uses larger facilities and organizes children by age. As a result of this age segregation, children focus their attention on others of their own age and away from individuals of different ages. Viewed in this light, modern education is in large part responsible for the growth of the "youth culture" in the United States since World War II. Young people come to develop distinctive lifestyles, habits, and tastes through their age isolation, becoming a distinctive market for certain music, clothes, movies, and other products (both legal and illegal). The more young people focus their interests and activities upon their own age group, the less dependent they will be on their families, not only for socialization but for affection and companionship. Needs that once were solidly within the family domain are now partly, if not largely, satisfied by the institution of education and social groups associated with that institution.

Work and the Family

Physical survival is clearly a fundamental human need. If a society cannot provide survival for its members, its existence will soon be a faint memory. Recognizing this fact, Lenski organized his society types according to the dominant means employed for survival. Whether humans hunt, gather, grow, raise, or manufacture their food, they still must have the means to stay alive. Traditionally, the real strength and necessity of the family lay in providing for the survival of its members. Families may or may not have been sources of love and affection for their members, but they were always work units.

Perhaps the ultimate ideal of the family work unit is the family farm characteristic of an agricultural society. In a society where everyone is responsible for his or her food needs, the family becomes a workable organization for producing that food. It is not so large that the organization of work and the distribution of food become complicated, yet it is not so small that the work cannot be done. The family is not as useful a work unit in an industrial society. As every year goes by in the United States, we find fewer and fewer people engaged in agricultural work as the family farm becomes replaced by the agricultural corporation. People do not necessarily leave the family farm out of choice but because their changing society forces that choice upon them; the small-scale family farm is simply not economically competitive.

The problems of the family farm in an industrial society represent more than just a change in agriculture; they represent a fundamental change in the way people survive. The family has ceased to be an effective work unit in all areas of industrial society. In the United States today the "mom and pop" grocery store cannot compete with the supermarket; in general, the family-run business cannot compete with the corporation. As a result, most modern American families have no direct role in the productive economy at all. Income within the family comes from outside the family unit as its members enter the institution of the economy, most typically in a job.

As an institution, the economy is made up of a vast variety of "work" activities, both public and private, and a vastly complicated system of capital that controls investment, credit, interest

In highly industrialized societies, the division of labor gives rise to highly specialized jobs. These groundskeepers, for instance, know exactly what is required to maintain a baseball field and to build a pitcher's mound to exact specifications.

rates, profits, and wage scales. Even more clearly than with education, to enter the world of the economy is to leave the family behind. The emotions and loyalties that characterize family relations seem out of place in the world of work. Corporations may fire an individual with little thought of the effects of unemployment on that individual's family. They may also subject the individual to hazardous work conditions or insist on a transfer across the country if it serves the interests of the corporation. The world of the economy seems to follow its own momentum; individuals may get on or off at their own risk.

Perhaps the greatest irony in comparing the family with the institution of the economy comes from the needs of the economy itself. Whereas the family used to be an economic necessity for an individual, it is now actually a hindrance. Children on a family farm were necessary for getting the work done, but children in an industrial society become a large expense for their wage-earning parents. Not surprisingly, industrial societies, wherever they are found, result in smaller families. In addition, the flexibility demanded by the economy in an industrial society can be a problem to the marriage relationship, particularly if both partners work. Consider the problems, for example, if one spouse is transferred when the other isn't. Beyond being a source of new workers, the family is not highly important in keeping the economy alive;

instead of producing goods, the modern family relates to the modern economy more by consuming goods.

Families, Protection, and the Rule of Law

Next to survival—perhaps a fundamental part of it—protection is a basic human need. Food was probably the first necessity of early humans, but having a sheltered place to eat it probably came second. Considering that we need shelter from both the elements and other humans, protection can be seen as a fundamental human need for society to fill.

In a hunting and gathering (or Gemeinschaft) type of society one of the basic tasks of the family unit is to provide protection for its members. Very large extended families often attain their size for the same reason societies raise large armies—the more soldiers you have, the more protection you can provide. Individuals can live through the day relatively safely knowing that a great many other individuals will be at their side should they need help. The loyal ties characteristic of family relations make that help particularly valuable since it is dependable. In particular, the large family provides protection against the worst foe that humans have—other humans. A potential enemy will be less likely to attack knowing that an attack on one person will bring about the retaliation of a great many relatives.

The protective aspect of the family can be most clearly seen in the institution of marriage, and many such aspects still remain (at least symbolically) in marriage in modern industrial societies. Some societies require their members to select a spouse from a neighboring community. Such rules keep family size up by constantly bringing in new relations. This function of marriage can be seen today in the traditional marriage ceremony, where the groom's family sits on one side of the aisle and the bride's family on the other side; as the bride and groom are joined, the two parts of the community are joined together. In the past, the marriage partner's family was really of more importance than the marriage partner himself or herself. In the United States today we leave marriage largely up to the bride and groom. One reason we do is that the family is no longer important for protection.

In an industrial society the political institution provides official protection for the individuals. The political institution in such a society consists of any activities, beliefs, or ideas that relate to what we generally call *government*. Thus, we would include police, laws, jails, judges, constitutions, elections, prisoners, and, to some extent, feelings of patriotism. Like every other institution, it also limits the rights of persons or other institutions to fulfill its function. If you have a complaint against another individual in the United States, your only legal recourse is to turn your complaint over to some official in the political institution. Taking care of the problem yourself (better known as taking the law into your own hands) will result in your society having a complaint against you, no matter how justified you might have been. Your government does not see fit to allow you to make that decision without its help. If you have been robbed, its representatives will catch and punish the culprit (if they wish), but you may not.

Like education and the economy, governments specialize in fulfilling a few basic needs and develop a whole sphere of activities and ideas that are separate from those of other spheres. The simplicity of turning to your uncle for help has been replaced by elaborate systems of laws and legal procedures that specify the ways individuals and groups of individuals may legally relate. As is typical of Gesellschaft, your help now comes from strangers.

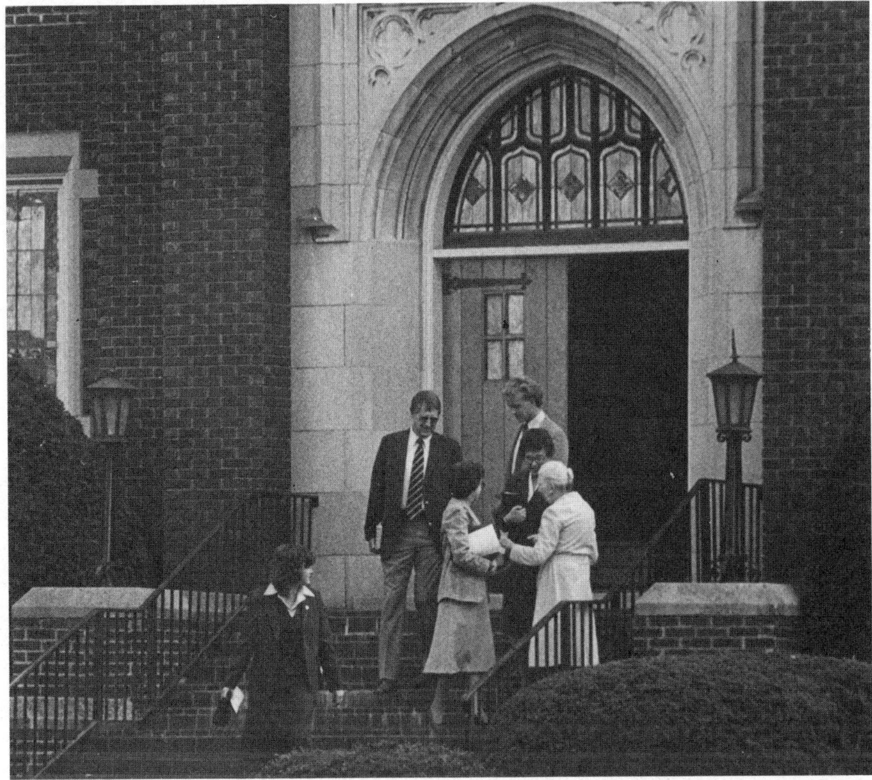

Religion in the United States has become highly institutionalized into large organizations that control property, exert political influence, and decide matters of theology. In spite of this institutional separation, religious institutions still depend on families to make up their congregations and give them strength.

Religion and the Family

Whereas the institutions we have looked at so far respond largely to the physical and practical needs of humans, religion responds to our spiritual needs. In an industrial society such as the United States the institution of religion would include religious functionaries (priests, ministers, rabbis, and the like), lay people, churches, beliefs, Bibles, hymns, parochial schools, and church socials, to name just a few elements. The United States offers a variety of religious activities and beliefs, but they are all remarkably similar in the way they provide their activities and beliefs as a separate sphere outside the family.

In the United States religion is more closely tied to the institution of the family than education, the economy, or the government (although it is tied to all). Religions generally support (while attempting to influence) the family structure and are in turn dependent on families for their support. Many significant family activities and events occur through or with the aid of religious functions, including baptisms, Bar Mitzvahs, marriage ceremonies, and funerals. Nevertheless, there is a fundamental boundary between family activities and religious activities in our society. When the family blends its activities into religious activities, it must follow the rules and regulations of the religion it follows; like other institutions, religion provides "specialists" who presumably know what's best.

In a Gemeinschaft-type society without institutional separation, religion is typically a family concern, like the other needs we've been discussing. Religious activities and beliefs are integrated through the daily lives of the people who adhere to them. By contrast, it is possible in the United States, for example, to preach charity on Sunday and then return to cut-throat business dealing the other six days; institutional separation makes this possible and even reasonable to the individuals concerned. In Gemeinschaft, religion is inseparable from everyday life, as part of an agricultural endeavor or basic to a social gathering.

If religious specialists developed in a Gemeinschaft, the first such specialists might typically be certain family members. For example, the religion might specify that a father, an aunt, or an uncle should be in charge of religious education. The family individual in charge of economic and protection decisions (likely an elder) might also be in charge of religious decisions. In fact, these three decisions would probably be seen as one, for it is only our institutional separation in the United States that makes us see such things as separate. Today, religions generally request that religious decisions be made by religious people who specialize in such decisions. The family turns outside itself for religious leadership.

The Changing Family

We come finally to the family, the last of the five basic social institutions. Though the needs it fulfills have steadily dwindled, the family is still the most basic institution and probably still the most important. It is still the strongest socialization force in society. Before the school sees the child, the basic work of socialization (whether good or ill) has been accomplished. Even with the increasing use of day care, the family unit is still the greatest force in socialization.

Families provide for the creation as well as the raising of children; however, they are not necessary for either. Children have always been born out of wedlock, and in the United States today illegitimacy is far from the social stigma it once was. Furthermore, single-parent families are increasing continually as divorce rates rise. As remarriage occurs, complex multiple families are constructed, frequently including one or two sets of stepparents and stepsiblings (see Cherlin, 1983). Although this may sound confusing, it is hardly as complicated as some of the extended families characteristic of Gemeinschaft-type societies. Clearly, our traditional definition of a family as mom, dad, and the kids is in for some change.

In the United States today we generally treat children in relation to the status of their parents. Thus, the children of rich parents are often seen as more valuable and important than the children of poor parents. (These conceptions are particularly important when teachers hold them.) Although the family determines the *entering* (or beginning) status of the child, the child may be able to change status during his or her lifetime through achievement; industrial societies are typically less rigid in this regard than more traditional societies where no one ever forgets your roots.

Families are also still an important source of affection and companionship. Though they are no longer the only such source, the growth of voluntary associations and singles apartments doesn't appear to be capable of replacing the family. This function of the family seems all the more apparent today with the rise in the number of childless marriages in the United States; individuals presumably enter such marriages for the sole purpose of companionship.

Finally, the family also fulfills part of a wide variety of needs, although it sometimes creates as many problems as it solves. When no one will lend you a dollar, not even the friendly loan company on TV, perhaps a relative will. On the other hand, a relative may want to borrow from you and never pay you back. When your physical well-being is threatened by a fellow citizen, perhaps a family member will give you a hand before the police arrive. Family members may also, however, be responsible for threatening you in the first place. Many homicides and assaults are committed by relatives; research indicating increasing child abuse is often cited as responsible for the 2 million teenage runaways each year (Gelles and Cornell, 1985).

When your teacher has neither the time nor the interest (or maybe even the skill) to teach you something, perhaps a wise relation will share some knowledge or a skill. And when you doubt the meaning of it all, the caring of your family may have more impact on you than the ministrations of an organized religion. As Figure 9.2 suggests, the family may have lost primary control over the satisfaction of many needs, but it has not lost total control over any of them. The family is perhaps the only institution still searching for its area of specialization and willing to do a little of everything in the meantime.

UNDERSTANDING SOCIETY THROUGH INSTITUTIONS

Institutions provide the sociologist with units of manageable size for analysis. The complex division of labor that characterizes any Gesellschaft-type society complicates the sociologist's job. We know something about how people are affected by their group affiliations, but how do we trace those effects when the individual seems lost in the sea of affiliations? The wife and mother who works, prays, joins the PTA, and runs for political office as well as cleaning house and cooking the Thanksgiving turkey is an increasingly common phenomenon in the United States. The concept of institution directs the sociologist to separate the spheres of those activities along their natural boundaries, allowing for a clearer perspective on the division of labor as well as providing some insight into the effects on individuals of each part of it. If the wife and mother becomes obsessed with political injustice, for example, the concept of institution would suggest not only where she probably got those ideas but also the arenas of her life in which she is likely to express them.

Chapters 10 and 11 will take us through an exploration of the five major institutions of American society, providing a more detailed picture of how those institutions function and the problems that occur within them. As we explore them, the interrelations among them will also be more apparent. Chapter 10 takes us back to the family for a closer look and is followed by an examination of education. Chapter 11 completes the series with sections on the economy, the political institution, and religion. Taken together, these chapters will give you a view of sociology "at work" on understanding social problems within their institutional contexts.

SUMMARY

Technology plays a major role in the kinds of organization found in a society. Societies that live by hunting and gathering are typically small because of the physical mobility required by their technology. Horticultural and agrarian societies—those that produce their own food—

typically grow much larger and develop more elaborate forms of social organization based on an increased division of labor. The greater efficiency of food production that characterizes them permits the growth of social differences in society as certain members of the society gain control over the surplus produced. Industrial societies are characterized by urban life, an extremely high division of labor, large size, powerful governments, and elaborate technology.

As technology changes, so do forms of social organization. The smaller, less technologically developed societies may be classified as Gemeinschaft; the larger, more technologically developed societies may be classified as Gesellschaft. The change from the former to the latter results in an increase in purely economic social arrangements and impersonal social relationships.

Gesellschaft-type societies are characterized by institutional separation. Institutions are spheres of interrelated activities within a society that focus on the satisfaction of specific human needs. The five basic institutions in a modern industrial society are education, religion, the economy, politics, and the family. Each contains a separate body of activities, ideas, values, and physical objects that differentiate it from other institutions. The modern individual acts within all institutions. At the same time that institutions are separate, however, there are definite interrelations among them so that changes in one result in changes in the others.

GLOSSARY

Gemeinschaft As defined by Ferdinand Tönnies, a traditional or communal society characterized by small size, a low division of labor, and a strong sense of shared values.

Gesellschaft As defined by Ferdinand Tönnies, a society characterized by an emphasis on economic interests, considerable group diversity, and impersonal social relationships.

Institution A cluster (or sphere) of interrelated activities within a society coupled with the knowledge, beliefs, and objects that relate to those activities. Institutions are typically stable configurations of social forms that meet social needs in specific areas.

Social stratification The arrangement of different activities (or roles) into a hierarchy whereby activities ranked high are highly rewarded and activities ranked low are poorly rewarded. The rewards generally consist of money, prestige, and influence over others.

SUPPLEMENTARY READINGS

Adams, Bert N. *The Family: A Sociological Interpretation.* (4th ed.). New York: Harcourt Brace Jovanovich, 1986.
A good general introduction to the sociology of the family with a focus on family roles and the changes that have occurred in the modern American family.

Allan, Graham *Family Life: Domestic Roles and Social Organization.* New York: Basil Blackwell, 1985.
An introduction somewhat similar to the Adams work but with emphasis on the interactions between family structure and economic changes in American society.

Cox, Harvey *Religion in the Secular City.* New York: Simon & Schuster, 1984.
An analysis of religions and religious beliefs in the 1980s in the United States with a particular focus on Protestant fundamentalism.

Dahl, Robert A. *Dilemmas of Pluralist Democracy.* New Haven, Conn: Yale University Press, 1982.
Dahl is perhaps the main proponent of pluralist perspectives on power in the United States.

Domhoff, G. William *Who Rules America Now? A View for the 80s.* Englewood Cliffs, N.J.: Prentice-Hall, 1983.
An analysis of the distribution of power in American society, emphasizing the important role played by the small percentage of people who control much of the wealth in America.

Hurn, Christopher *The Limits and Possibilities of Schooling* (2nd ed.). Boston: Allyn & Bacon, 1985.
Hurn focuses on the relations between education and the rest of society. In particular, he considers the ability of schools to bring about change in the social positions of students.

Jencks, Christopher, et al. *Inequality: A Reassessment of the Effect of Family and Schooling in America.* New York: Basic Books, 1972.
A somewhat technical but highly influential study of the effect of family on educational achievement and the effect of education on future income.

Johnstone, Ronald L. *Religion in Society: A Sociology of Religion.* (3rd ed.). Englewood Cliffs, N.J.: Prentice-Hall, 1988.
An examination of religion within the United States with particular emphasis on the relations among religion, politics, and the economy.

Kozol, Jonathan *Illiterate America.* Garden City, N.Y.: Anchor Press, 1985.
In spite of its major emphasis on education, the United States contains more illiterate people than many other industrial societies. Kozol brings this issue to light along with analyses of its cause and suggestions for its alteration.

Lenski, Gerhard *Power and Privilege: The Theory of Social Stratification.* New York: McGraw-Hill, 1966.
An analysis of social stratification from a developmental perspective. Lenski discusses the development of power and privilege as they occur in several types of societies.

Mills, C. Wright *The Power Elite.* New York: Oxford University Press, 1956.
In this modern American sociological classic, Mills presents the elitist perspective on political power distribution through a discussion of power in American society.

Ritzer, George, and David Walczak *Working: Conflict and Change.* (3rd ed.). Englewood Cliffs, N.J.: Prentice-Hall, 1986.
Ritzer and Walczak provide a general introduction to the sociological perspective on occupations and organizations.

Saxon, Lloyd *The Individual, Marriage and the Family* (6th ed.). Belmont, Calif.: Wadsworth, 1985.
A basic introductory text in this area.

Stark, Rodney, and William Sims Bainbridge *The Future of Religion: Secularization, Revival and Cult Formation.* Berkeley: University of California Press, 1985.
An overview of religion in the United States today with particular attention paid to some of its more extreme manifestations (such as cults), along with the relation between religions and other institutions of society.

The Transition to an Industrial Economy in Eastern Kentucky

ALAN BANKS

The societywide view of social change presented in Chapter 9 is beyond the control of any one individual or even any group of individuals. Nevertheless, individuals do play a role in social change by placing their energies in support of social changes already in progress. Alan Banks describes the changes that occurred in Kentucky over the last century as a basically rural society was pulled (sometimes kicking and screaming) into the modern industrial world. The political and industrial leaders who made it happen profited greatly, but their success was probably mostly due to being in the right vocation at the right time. As for the natives of Kentucky (who woke up one morning and found their agricultural existence displaced by logging companies and coal mining camps), the changes must certainly have seemed well beyond their control.

For a variety of reasons, many sociological accounts of the transition from preindustrial to industrial society remain rather vague and general. What many writers offer are thumbnail sketches of very important changes in social structure and daily life. These descriptions often hang loosely on abstract terms such as Gemeinschaft and Gesellschaft, organic solidarity and mechanical solidarity, or folk and urban society. While undoubtedly useful, these sorts of descriptions can best illuminate patterns of social change when they are combined with concrete-historical analyses of specific localities. Such studies demonstrate that the transition from preindustrial to industrial society does not happen because some technological advance makes wage labor relations inevitable or because people join together in the spirit of harmony to herald the onset of a new age. Whether in advanced nations in the past or developing nations in the present, the emergence of modern industry involves a complex interplay of activities carried out by individuals who are influenced by their class interests. No classical sociologist emphasized this more clearly than Karl Marx. For him, the first step in the emergence of modern industry involved the separation of workers from real control over the productive resources of a society. Whether through political, economic, or cultural practices, the first days of capitalism are marked, for Marx, by the separation of workers from control over the means of production.

In eastern Kentucky, capitalism emerged against a background that was characterized by small-scale production carried out by independent commodity producers. Small, family-owned farms and workshops predominated. Each worker had access to the means and product of labor. There were, of course, other forms of production. Some wage and slave labor existed, but independent commodity producers predominated. What follows is a brief description of the transition to industrial

I would like to thank Appalachian State University/Appalachian Journal for permission to reprint portions of previously published materials. A longer version of this article can be found in Alan Banks, "The Emergence of a Capitalistic Labor Market in Eastern Kentucky," *Appalachian Journal* 7(3): 188-199, and "Land and Capital in Eastern Kentucky," *Appalachian Journal* 8(1), 8-18. Copyright 1980 by the *Appalachian Journal*/Appalachian State University. Used by permission.

capitalism in eastern Kentucky. The guiding question is: What social practices or social forces led to the transformation of eastern Kentucky from a society dominated by independent commodity producers to one of industrial wage laborers?

Preindustrial Setting

Prior to the 1860s, Kentucky was primarily, though not exclusively, rooted in an agricultural economy, or rather in two agricultural economies. Outside eastern Kentucky in the Bluegrass portion of the state, where the majority of the population lived, a production system based upon large land holdings and black slave labor predominated. Planters settled large tracts of land and surplus slave labor set the economy in motion. Slave labor in the Bluegrass was made possible (and profitable) by rights to the legal ownership of black slaves and long-distance trade connections along the Ohio and Mississippi rivers, which provided an avenue for trade and the realization of profits. As early as 1787 and 1788, under a trading treaty with the Spanish authorities in New Orleans, substantial exports of tobacco, hams, butter, and flour were floated downstream from Frankfort. From its inception, this trade proved extremely lucrative and thereby led to the expansion of the use of slave labor. Trade with the southwest continued and was stimulated by the use of steamboat navigation around 1820. A limited railroad system built in the 1830s also proved beneficial to planters and their way of life.

In the mountain regions of eastern Kentucky, production rested upon a wholly different foundation. Production in these eastern counties consisted primarily of a self-reliant style of farming common in many areas of North America in the eighteenth and nineteenth centuries. This style of production rested on the labor of small landowning farmers, not slaves. There was little reliance on wage labor and very little currency in circulation. Regular household needs ranging from clothing and food to soap, lamp oil, sorghum, hand tools, and stoneware were satisfied through a local trading network based upon exchange of products from household manufacture, limited farming, and artisanship. The producers and consumers in this setting were virtually one and the same people.

So long as the mountains were not penetrated by the railroads and independent commodity producers retained control of productive resources, this mode of production predominated in daily life. Even if mountain producers could accumulate sufficient surplus goods for export, the mountains themselves presented a formidable barrier, even to the most daring and enterprising individuals. Roads in the region were wholly inadequate for the reliable transport of large quantities of goods and amounted, in many cases, to little more than paths. Even the major transmountain routes were virtually impassable during the seasons of rain and snow. The only feasible trade links were provided by rivers and streams. But the principal river system of the region presented a whole set of obstacles to trade. The Kentucky River was only navigable for six months of the year. Moreover, the whole region was prone to flash flooding, which was exacerbated by the fact that the Kentucky River is generally low-lying between steep hillsides or cliffs. On short notice, the river could be transformed into a raging torrent. Other geographical factors, such as the random flow pattern of the area's water systems, provided even more obstacles to the development of trading networks with the Bluegrass and beyond. These impediments, in turn, provided temporary barriers to the emergence of either slave or industrial production for several years.

The Emergence of Industrial Capitalism

For eastern Kentucky, the transformation of independent commodity producers into wage laborers employed by giant, nonresident corporations was a complex process which began immediately following the Civil War and continued into the first two decades of the twentieth century. The transformation involved fundamental changes in the everyday life of the region which cannot be dismissed lightly as the inevitable result of social change. The occupational structure, modes of work, distribution of laborers throughout industries, and relations between people, resources, and land underwent fundamental alterations. The complexity of this historical process arises from the fact that the producers of the pre-1860 period were neither employed by others nor employers of labor to a significant extent. Yet, by the end of this process, a large portion of the workforce was employed by large industrial firms. What induced, cajoled, or forced workers into this change? And what prevented them from succeeding at alternative forms of subsistence? More generally, what led to the decline of preindustrial society and the dominance of an industrial economy fueled by investment from large multinational corporations?

The Politics of Transition

As early as 1828, some Kentucky politicians displayed dissatisfaction with the policy of granting land to small settlers at nominal prices. Land, they argued, should be granted to "monopolizing capitalists" for the "purpose of speculation."[1] Restrictive land legislation, they believed, would benefit the state by promoting industry. The logic behind these arguments was very simple. Land was visualized as a commodity in that, like other commodities, it was (a) bought and sold in a marketplace, and (b) priced in accordance with the laws of supply and demand. From this vantage point, it was further argued that *land* policy had a direct influence on the forces of supply and demand in the capitalistic *labor* market. If a potential worker had the opportunity to acquire land cheaply, the likelihood that that worker would permanently enter the labor market was greatly reduced. Cheapness of land, in other words, was linked with the price and availability of wage labor for hire. An industrial economy would grow more quickly if working people had fewer alternatives.

While discussions about the connection between land and labor policy were commonplace, systematic attention was not given to the labor question until after the Civil War. The major reason for the growth of concern over labor policy after the war was the destruction of the slave labor system in the Bluegrass portion of the state. As a result of the war, the whole agricultural and industrial system of a large and economically important part of the state was brought to a halt. One document, dated 1871, listed the evils inflicted by the war in the following way:

> Kentucky had an efficient and reliable system of labor. During the war . . . portions of her territory were ravaged and property of her citizens destroyed or consumed; the tranquil pursuit of agriculture was violently disrupted; living in the country remote from cities and military stations became perilous; the citizen and his family were subject to perpetual alarms; cattle and other livestock were slaughtered; horses were pressed into service; slaves were insubordinate and after several years of such demoralization the colored people were freed.[2]

The "sudden emancipation" of 205,781 slaves valued at over $100,000,000 "struck our industrial system down," said one politician.[3] The bitterness of these slaveholding politicians was increased by the fact that the "General Government, notwithstanding the formal obligation to pay for them [the slaves], was guilty of repudiation, and slaveholders received nothing for their property." At the very least, the slaveholders felt, the "General Government" could have slowly phased in the blackman's freedom, permitting him to become "somewhat habituated" to his new privileges and responsibilities. After all, the government should clearly see that "their interests [the slaves and slaveholders] were identical, not antagonistic." But such was not the case and the efforts to rebuild a labor system in the Bluegrass would profoundly influence the eastern Kentucky mountain economy. It would open the entire state to outside industrial capital, and many resource-rich eastern counties would figure prominently in plans to lure workers and investments into the Commonwealth.

The tone for the new flurry of labor policy discussions which followed the Civil War was established in the Governor's Message on January 6, 1868. "A change in the domestic policy of Kentucky," the governor remarked, "has become forced upon her people by a fundamental alteration in her domestic institutions." The governor warned that the policy changes were inevitable and permanent and that lawmakers had to meet the challenge with reasoned and enlightened temperaments. Then, he stated the problem and his proposed solution bluntly: "The present need of the state is a sufficient supply of efficient labor. It can only be obtained by largely increased foreign emigration." Kentucky, the governor argued, should have little difficulty in attracting its share of prospective laborers, provided that sufficient information was available to them. In his message, the governor described Kentucky as "the Garden of the American Union" and suggested that this alone would attract immigrants. Then, as if to underline the importance of the issue, he remarked that immigration "is now an essential requisite of our prosperity. It lies at the root of all social and material wealth. It is a question which towers in importance at this time over any, except revenue . . ."[4]

Appeals for a more sound labor policy were the subject of much discussion over the next few years. In Louisville, at the Commercial Convention, businessmen took a position on what they believed to be the best method to encourage immigration. For them, it seemed more practical, and less costly, to establish a general immigration agency for the whole South. The agency, jointly financed by the southern states, would be authorized to prepare, distribute, and translate propaganda favoring the South as a place to settle. White, European immigrants were targeted as the most acceptable labor recruits. Advertisements, therefore, were to be prepared in English, French, German, Italian, Dutch, Swedish, and Norwegian. Several Kentucky politicians saw merits of such a program, but they did not seem overly enthusiastic about a multistate agreement and therefore decided to forge ahead with their own separate policies. Near the end of 1869, Governor Stevenson of Kentucky announced that an effective labor policy must be broadened to include both labor and capital inducements. "For a sufficient supply [of labor]," he remarked, "we must look to foreign immigration. But our need does not stop there. We must look to Europe also for capital . . . if we desire to increase our population and develop our industrial and mineral wealth. How then, is the tide of European immigration [and capital] to be induced to flow into Kentucky?"[5] Stevenson proposed a program which included the systematic promulgation of information favoring Kentucky as a place for laborers to settle and as an area for capitalists to invest. For labor, propaganda sought to remove prejudice from the minds of immigrants and instruct them as to the resources and advantages of permanent settlement in the state. For capital, several propaganda vehicles were proposed. Messages to specific interests would be one means to familiarize outsiders with conditions in Kentucky. "The iron-masters of Europe," for instance, "must become acquainted with our industrial and mineral wealth." The distribution of geological surveys showing that "Kentucky possesses a greater area of coal of good quality than is contained within the limits of any other State in the world" would leave a favorable image in the minds of European capitalists. Another vehicle suggested was the promulgation of information at industrial expositions in England, France, Germany, and Russia. Specimens of Kentucky coal, iron, timber, and fireclay—accompanied with geological survey statements—could demonstrate the superiority of Kentucky resources.

Governor Stevenson used an 1870 letter from a Colonel Blanton Duncan to underscore the importance of his proposals. While in Europe, Duncan had made the observation that conditions for inducing labor to Kentucky were favorable but would soon change. Kentucky politicians, he stated, must act quickly. Duncan suggested that a state agency, headed by "influential men," be set up and that government assure immigrants employment and finance their trip to Kentucky. His reasons for prompt action were rather straightforward. "The war now raging [in Europe] affords an additional argument. We have no powerful neighbors, no possibilities of entanglements, no danger of conscription to take off the laboring classes . . ." The war in Europe had created favorable conditions for emigration, but its prolongation would only worsen these conditions. Speaking of Germany, Duncan wrote that "there will be no surplus population for the next ten years. The dead, the maimed and the useless population . . . will not reach less than 500,000 adult males before the close of the war. . . . The labor market will be so depleted that there will be ample occupation for every remaining laborer . . . and their government would feel bound to throw obstacles in the way of continued emigration."[6]

And so, by early 1871, a bill was passed to set up a Bureau of Immigration for the State of Kentucky. In this bill, the legislature set forth a fairly comprehensive statement of its position on the question of labor and its vision of economic development. The drafters of the bill recognized immigration as "not inferior . . . to any question that may come before the Senate." The "development of this country is not due to the labors of the gentle classes of England . . . but rather to the sturdy frames and strong arms of the humble and needy who have been hardened by a life of toil and privation." In other words, members of the legislature were recognizing the "immense capital value of immigration [labor]." To support this idea, they went so far as to offer a statistical analysis to demonstrate that the increase of wealth in the nation proceeds in exact ratio to the increase in labor, which, they argued, has resulted largely from immigration.

Besides recognizing labor as the source of wealth in society, the bill to establish a Bureau of Immigration reflected the racist tone which characterized much of the debate leading to its passage. After the war, "the colored people flocked to the cities, herded in tenements and ate the rations of idleness and indolence. . . . The result was the general derangement and paralysis of our system of labor." The problem facing Kentucky politicians was a tricky one. They wanted to state the problem in a way that suggested Kentucky had all the components of production but was a little short in the areas of labor and capital. In reality, there were considerable numbers of surplus black laborers who were clearly recruitable. The problem, then, was not a lack of labor but rather one of politicians/industrialists who were reluctant to hire people who they previously owned. The old labor system was found unsuitable, and an alternative was sought out in Europe where "an exhaustless supply" of labor existed, "where land is scarce . . . where people are crowded, wages low and living difficult." Immigration was viewed as the surest remedy to the disintegration of the old system of labor relations and it also promised to furnish "men of our own race" for the laboring classes.[7]

Labor policy continued to evolve into the 1880s and 1890s, but images of labor as well as the role of the state in internal improvement/development of the Commonwealth were clearly established by 1875. The view embraced contained the following key elements:

1. Labor was recognized as crucial for the development of industrial production. In the Governor's Message of 1876, we find the statement that "labor makes capital and labor and capital together give life and impetus and strength to a State or nation." Without reasonably priced labor, it was assumed that all the interests of the Commonwealth were endangered as the production of social wealth would be discontinued. The role of the state, therefore, was to protect all interests of the state by encouraging the growth of wage labor so that an adequate surplus labor pool would guarantee the proper balance of forces of supply and demand in the wage labor market.

2. Kentucky's economy needed more than labor. It also needed capital investments *and* a correct balance of power between labor and capital. To achieve this balance, Kentucky politicians followed two general policies. First, they sought to entice investments and labor through generous tax laws and through information peddling outside Kentucky. Such was the purpose of the Bureau of Immigration, attendance at commercial conventions, and other activities to attract specific industrial interests. Second, to assure the development of a labor market, politicians resolved to prevent immigrants from flowing into nonindustrial modes of living. They sought out immigrants who had little resources to set up as independent commodity producers and they had little intention of granting them land

at reasonable prices.[8] The guiding rule appears to have been this: the more desperate the immigrant the better. Also, passage to Kentucky was often financed, which meant that new immigrants were in debt upon arrival and thus compelled to seek wage labor. Even in this age of so-called laissez-faire economics, Kentucky politicians believed that some government intervention was advantageous—namely, to assure a continuing supply of cheap wage labor for hire.

3. Politicians generally took a favorable stand toward the question of outside investment. They realized that, weakened by the war and by the loss of its labor system, Kentucky would have to look elsewhere for the means to build a new economy. Kentucky politicians actively solicited outside investment as the preferred avenue to economic development. This preference for outside investment encouraged patterns of absentee ownership which would characterize the eastern portion of the state throughout the twentieth century. Moreover, the vast coal, timber, iron, and clay resources of the eastern portion of the state proved to be attractive enticements in political plans for industrial development.
4. Finally, Kentucky politicians felt it their duty to provide essential services for those who owned the means of production by functioning as a sort of clearinghouse for the distribution of labor power. A distribution center was set up in Louisville where leaders of commerce and industry could send requests for laborers in the mines, factories, and fields of Kentucky.

From the standpoint of Kentucky politicians, these policies were presumed to be good for all the interests of the state. For the absentee owners of large holdings in Kentucky, this assumption proved valid. For the interests of those who worked for many of these corporations, for independent commodity producers, or for local political independence, these assumptions seem dubious, at best.

The Economic Transition

Experts and businessmen had been familiar with the lucrative resource potential of eastern Kentucky since the 1870s at least. Geological surveys, carried out by the state, combined with the private reports of industrial and railroad corporations, offered detailed estimates of iron, timber, and coal reserves. These reports also contained careful analyses of coal quality, timber varieties and uses, and iron deposits. When Kentucky politicians formulated their policies to encourage outside investments and guarantee an adequate supply of exploitable labor for hire, promoters and industrialists responded with predictable excitement and interest. What happened next involved a period of consolidation wherein the new investors sought to position themselves in a manner to ensure their future success.

A key element in this process involved large-scale land acquisitions. For decades, land speculation in eastern Kentucky had been mainly a sort of sport for high society in the Bluegrass. Land was cheap, surveys indicated future potential, and much land was not even registered. This casual speculation of the pre-1880 period was soon replaced with a qualitatively different form of investment. The "new" investors typically operated on a much grander scale. In this region where the only towns consisted of a few hundred souls, complete cities were built. Some were designed to include parks, luxury hotels, hot springs, theaters, and resorts. The pace and volume of these investments varied from place to place. They did not all occur at the same time. But, whatever their timing and exact form, these investments contributed in a major way to (1) the establishment of an industrial economy as the dominant form of subsistence, and (2) the transformation of land into capital.

In 1892, these new investors had made considerable headway into the region and were clearly identifiable. In the tax lists for various counties, the names of large, often international, corporations, usually land/coal/development/mining companies, became commonplace. The penetration of these corporation investments into eastern Kentucky can be seen in a cursory way

LAND CONCENTRATION IN SELECTED EASTERN KENTUCKY COUNTIES, 1892

County	Number of large taxpayers	Total assessed acreage (X)	Acres held by large taxpayers (Y)	Acres held by large nonresidents (Z)	Y as % of X	Z as % of X
Bell	29	375,404	303,343	197,374	80.5%	52.6%
Harlan	38	315,564	194,728	n.a.	61.7	—
Leslie	33	239,899	149,768	115,580	62.4	48.2
Letcher	31	287,067	119,774	n.a.	42.0	—
Perry	40	410,803	263,480	194,367	64.1	47.3

in the accompanying Table. In 1892, the last year in which the tax lists for all eastern Kentucky counties are available, the amount of land concentrated in the hands of the top twenty to thirty taxpayers was quite impressive.

It would be twenty years before the railroads and coal operators would overtly appear in Harlan, Letcher, and Perry counties in the southeastern portion of the state. Bell County, the most "developed" of these southeastern counties at the time, had been involved in *commercial* coal production for only one year. Yet a virtual land monopoly already existed. As the Table indicates, over 80 percent of Bell County surface land was owned outright by a few large landowners. Harlan, Letcher, Leslie, and Perry counties were all approximately 60 percent in the hands of large taxpayers. And in counties where nonresident data were available, nonresidents controlled in the neighborhood of 50 percent of the total assessed acreage.

While the data in the Table appear rather exaggerated, there are two good reasons to believe that they are more likely *underestimates* of the true level of land concentration. First, there are indications that a number of these "large" taxpayers underestimated their true land ownership for tax purposes. In Bell County, for instance, there are at least two examples of this practice. In the tax lists, the American Association, Ltd., owned by a group of British investors, claimed ownership to 19,000 acres for tax purposes. Yet in their public statements to investors, they claimed ownership of 80,000 acres and an additional 5,398 acres through their subsidiary, the Middlesboro Town Land Company. That leaves 66,398 acres of land for these two firms which were not figured into the calculations in the Table. Another Bell County example of this practice is the Log Mountain Coal, Coke and Timber Company. For tax purposes, this corporation claimed title to 20,204 acres in 1892. Based upon the company's correspondence, however, it is clear that true land ownership exceeded 26,000 acres. Second, there is good reason to believe that the "nonresident" category in the Table is understated. According to tax procedures of that time, if a company had an office in the county in which it held land, then that company was considered as a resident by the tax assessor. The British investors behind the American Association, therefore, are listed as resident land owners in the Bell County tax lists, as is the Middlesboro Town Land Company.[9]

Another key element in the transition to an industrial economy in eastern Kentucky involved the dominance of the new investors over the everyday lives of the new labor recruits through the systematic development of interlocking firms. Another look at Bell County, where the famous Cumberland Gap lies, provides us with an illustration of how these developments emerged in southeastern Kentucky.

In 1885 or 1886, Alexander A. Arthur, a representative of Scotch and English investors who owned and lumbered a large tract of land in North Carolina, entered Bell County to examine firsthand the famous tracts of timber there as well as coal and iron deposits which were clearly visible through cursory observation. Within a year, Arthur was in London, England, giving glowing accounts of what he had seen to the directors of the Baring Brothers banking house, the stockholders of the Watts Iron and Steel Company, and other prominent investors. After receiving supporting reports of other experts, the American Association, Ltd. was capitalized with a stock valued at $2,000,000. In the Mine Inspector's Report of Kentucky, the name of the American Association appeared for the first time in 1887. A branch line of the Louisville and Nashville Railroad was completed in 1888 from Corbin to Pineville, Kentucky. By the following year, the railroad reached Middlesboro, the heart of American Association activities in Kentucky. What this marked was a significant moment in the reshaping of social institutions and daily life in the area. Soon the predominantly rural family economy of independent commodity producers would be replaced by an urban-industrial economy of wage laborers. Middlesboro would grow from a town of 50 families in the spring of 1889 to an industrial city of over 10,000 in 1892.

These changes were accomplished through a combination of land acquisitions and the systematic development of a number of closely related business organizations. The centerpiece of this business network was the American Association, Ltd., through which resource rich land was owned. The second piece of the puzzle was the Middlesboro Town Company, which owned the land upon which the city of Middlesboro was built. Another company, the Cumberland Gap Park Corporation, was formed in 1890 to commence the building of a luxury hotel, a sanitarium, and a casino. Still other companies were formed to exert control over valuable infrastructural support projects necessary for resource extraction operations. The Middlesboro Belt Railroad, for instance, circled the town with branch lines leading to mine sites. The Knoxville, Cumberland Gap and Louisville Railroad operated 73 miles of track leading to Knoxville, Tennessee. And the Knoxville Southern Railroad operated 110 miles of track between Knoxville and Atlanta, Georgia. Five miles south of Middlesboro near a town named Arthur, Tennessee, the Watts Steel Syndicate controlled more large tracts of land containing iron and coal deposits. The point is simply this: The transition to an industrial economy in and around Bell County was achieved through exclusive, interlocking control of key business organizations, including railroads, resource extraction firms, transportation and financial services, land ownership, and control over the means of consumption.

A glance at the accompanying Figure illustrates how this business network was held together. The names of English investors behind the scenes appear only in information dealing directly with the American Association, Ltd. The names listed in the figure are those of American representatives who acted as directors and executives in the other firms in this network.

While the emergence of capitalist social relations in Bell County was limited, in some respects, by conditions on the world market, few restrictions posed much of a problem at the local level. Here, the hidden secret of development involves understanding the absolute domination of the means of production and consumption by the new investors. Through a combination of resource monopoly, overlapping business organizations, and help from friendly politicians, a social condition in which workers were separated from any real control over their means of existence was socially constructed.

Similar tales of development can be told about other southeastern Kentucky counties. Between 1900 and 1910, heavy investments were placed "in Harlan and other mountain counties by Eastern and Northern capitalists." These investments were viewed as "the forerunner of a railway extension into one of the richest regions of the state." The Kentenia Corporation boasted ownership of over 100,000 acres, although only 39,000 were declared for tax purposes. Wisconsin Steel, a subsidiary of the Morgan-McCormick International Harvester Corporation, purchased over 20,000 acres on which

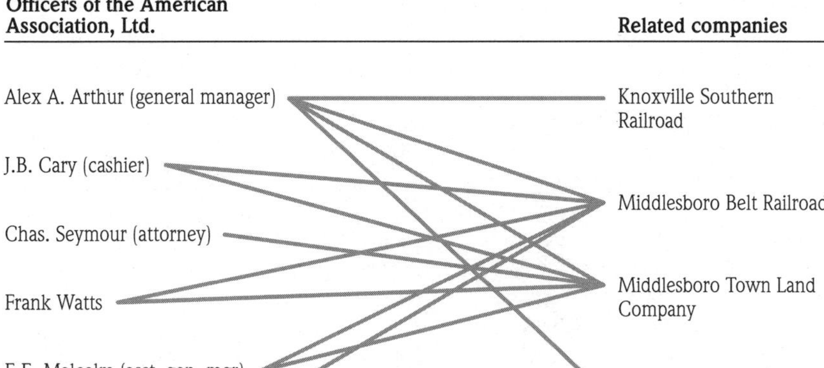

Interlocking executive relationships in selected enterprises in and around Middlesboro, 1890.

it was equipping its mines with "electrical machinery . . . for a daily output of 2,000 tons of coal and constructing 300 coke ovens."[10] In nearby Leslie County, the Fordson Coal Company (Henry Ford) was allegedly in the process of acquiring approximately one-half of that county's acreage.[11] Consolidated Coal was fast becoming the largest land owner and coal producer in Letcher County.

By 1914, the L & N Railroad had built its own branch line into Harlan and several other counties (it entered Harlan in 1911). At that time, over 70 percent of the total assessed acreage of Harlan County was concentrated in the hands of twenty-six landowners. Over 61 percent was owned by nonresident resource extraction/development companies, which included some of the largest firms in the world. One further indication of the influence of these new investors can be found in coal production data. In Harlan County, Wisconsin Steel produced 43 percent of the total county output in 1911. And when Wisconsin Steel output is combined with Wallins Creek Coal Company, another Morgan controlled corporation, the percentage changes to 76 percent. In Letcher County, the Consolidated Coal Company produced 1,273,248 of the total 1,539,070 tons for 1914; that's 82 percent of the county total. Only Perry County had a different pattern; in 1914, seven major coal companies, none of which produced more than 60,000 tons, operated.

Comments

The conquest of eastern Kentucky's productive resources was a profound development that may have been little comprehended by the local population. The monopolization of land/resources weakened the material basis upon which many independent commodity producers operated. It generated irrepressible tendencies which led to a situation where workers had little control over productive resources. Land, coal, and timber, along with the infrastructural network for social development, was tightly controlled by the new investors for their own purposes. Land and power were closely interconnected; those who controlled the land were well positioned to set the terms for development. And with the coming of the railroads, workers for the new mine and forest industries of Kentucky could be drawn, with the aid of friendly politicians, from surplus labor populations throughout the world.

The transition to an industrial economy in eastern Kentucky varied from place to place, but, for individuals, the general effects were clearly evident. The consolidation of control over land/resources and infrastructural organizations by outside investors who operated on a scale unimaginable to most local inhabitants set limits on the courses of action available to eastern Kentuckians. Whether by force or not, many independent commodity producers entered a labor market which offered money income in the form of wages, often script, to purchase the means of subsistence from company stores. Whole families left the farm or workshop/home to live in company housing where job dismissal meant automatic eviction and partying with the wrong people could get you fired and houseless. Every aspect of family life was mediated, in some respect, by the structure of the company town and the new investors' exclusive control over jobs, stores, housing, towns, recreational facilities, and police, who were often paid by the companies.

Notes

[1] "Governor's Message," *Kentucky Senate Journal,* 1828.

[2] *Kentucky Senate Journal,* 1871, 208.

[3] *Ibid.*

[4] "Governor's Message," *Kentucky House Journal,* 1868, 21.

[5] "Governor's Message," *Kentucky House Journal,* 1869-70, 23.

[6] Letter from Colonel Blanton Duncan to Governor Stevenson, August 28, 1870, reprinted in *Kentucky House Journal,* 1871.

[7] These quotes can be found in the "Bill to Establish a Bureau of Immigration," *Kentucky Senate Journal,* 1871, esp. 207-215.

[8] Kentucky politicians were generally more interested in offering inducements to labor which did not include land grants. In 1871, Governor Stevenson wrote that "in new counties the grand feature is their ability to endow the immigrant with a free homestead, which overcomes the reluctance to encounter hardship and to give up the comforts and protection afforded by more civilized settlements. To meet this difficulty, Kentucky, *having no lands to give,* might substitute other inducements to labor." This statement regarding the inability of Kentucky to offer cheap land to prospective immigrants is highly suspect. During the same year and in the same document, it was pointed out that Kentucky had a population density per square mile of less than any of the midwestern or southern states, except West Virginia. *Kentucky Senate Journal,* 1871-1872, "Governor's Message" and page 211.

[9] Information on the land claimed for tax purposes can be found in the Tax Lists for Bell County, 1892, State Archives, Frankfort, Kentucky. The other claims of land ownership can be found in "A Prospectus for Investors, American Association, Ltd., 1892," and "Letter from Log Mountain Coal, Coke and Timber Company to Investors, 1891," Special Collections, University of Kentucky.

[10] One of the best sources of information concerning investments in the southern coalfields between 1900 and 1910 is *Manufacturers Record: A Weekly Southern Industrial, Railroad and Financial Newspaper.*

[11] Cited in Harry Caudill, *Night Comes to the Cumberlands,* Boston: Little, Brown, 1963, 65.

Discussion Questions

1. Banks describes an alliance between political and business leaders in the early days of industrialization in Eastern Kentucky. What made their interests similar enough to produce such cooperation?
2. America was a growing nation at the turn of the last century due to massive immigration from Europe. What role did population growth play in changing the economy, politics, and lifestyles of Kentucky citizens?
3. Kentucky joined the industrial world primarily because of natural resources, particularly coal and timber, that outsiders wanted. Who were these outsiders, and what changes were occurring in their world to motivate them to interfere in Kentucky?
4. How does the situation in this reading illustrate the distinction between Gemeinschaft and Gesellschaft?

CHAPTER 10

THE FAMILY AND EDUCATION

Our intensive examination of the five basic social institutions that were briefly introduced in Chapter 9 begins with a focus on the family—arguably the most important institution in any society—and then we study the educational institution. The family was the basic social unit before the development of modern complex societies with their institutional separation. Family members were usually a child's only educators. Institutional separation created a new form of society, in which individuals' needs became satisfied in public settings. The modern family still retains great importance, however; as we saw, it fulfills important functions in terms of child-rearing, providing emotional support for its members, and bestowing an entering social status on its members as they venture out into the wider world.

THE FAMILY

Sociologists study the family as an institution in order to better understand how its structure and the changing activities that occur within it affect its members' lives. As with all institutions, the family does not exist in a vacuum. At the same time the family affects members' lives, it is affected in turn by the wider society and must change in response to those more general social forces. As just one example (which we will examine further), changes in the economy can make it necessary for women to spend more and more of their time outside the home in the labor force. Such changes in role affect not only the women directly involved but their husbands and children as well. In its approach to the modern family as an institution, sociology attempts to provide a better understanding of why families change and how those changes change individuals.

Elements of Family Life

No two family structures are ever exactly alike, but their variation seems to occur along certain dimensions rather than randomly. Among other things, families vary in size, authority relations, numbers of spouses involved, and how spouses are selected. We will first discuss some general patterns that appear cross-culturally in family structures, then examine the centerpiece relationship of the family—marriage.

Patterns of Family Life Variation in size is perhaps the most basic dimension of family life encountered in cultures around the world. In the smallest unit, the **nuclear family** contains only two spouses and their immature offspring. An increasingly common variation on the nuclear family is the single-parent family, in which one of the parents (usually the father) is missing. Although nuclear family members typically note and give importance to other kin relationships, the primary focus of attention is on the marriage relationship and the parent-child relationship. Another form of family structure is the **extended family**, which includes a number of related nuclear families that live together as one unit. Extended families can become quite large. Some cultures, such as that of the United States, lean toward the nuclear family as the common unit, whereas other cultures contain more extended families. In general, nuclear families are more typical of industrial societies; extended families provide many services for their members (such as economic support and protection) that are provided by other sources in industrial society. Moreover, the urban life and high geographical mobility characteristic of

Family patterns vary greatly from culture to culture. In the United States and most Western cultures, the basic pattern is the nuclear family—parents and children. The Yagua Indians of Brazil consider everyone in the community as a family member.

industrial societies make stable extended families difficult to maintain. It should be remembered, however, that kin ties outside the nuclear family can be very important in even the most industrialized societies (we will explore this importance later in this chapter).

Individuals alter their relationship to the family unit as they age, whether they reside in a culture that emphasizes the nuclear family or the extended family. The child is a member of a **family of orientation**: parents and siblings provide for the child's basic socialization, thereby "orienting" him or her to life in the wider society. Although it becomes less important as the child grows into maturity, its early central role in shaping the individual gives it a critical importance throughout the life course of that individual. For example, child abuse in the family of orientation can lead that child to grow into a parent who in turn abuses children. The family of orientation is often complemented in later life by the **family of procreation**, in which the individual raises children; this parental role is typically (although by no means always) coupled with the role of spouse.

Authority within the family unit is of critical importance and varies cross-culturally. In a **patriarchal family** men (sometimes the oldest male) have the authority; in a **matriarchal family** women govern; and in an **egalitarian family** men and women share the decision making. The patriarchal family is by far the most common across cultures. Matriarchies are rare in that few (if any) cultures provide women with such regularized institutional authority. However, matriarchies often arise when male authority figures must be absent. The egalitarian family is found most typically in industrial or post-industrial societies where new economic roles have been extended to women. Economic independence for women tends to weaken the monopoly on authority characteristic of a patriarchy. American families have traditionally been patriarchal but are becoming increasingly egalitarian.

The tracing of descent within the family varies from one culture to another. In cultures that practice a **patrilineal** tracing of descent, one's identity is defined entirely through the father's line and, perhaps more important, inheritance is passed along only through the father's side. Such systems are fundamental for the status-bestowing function of the family. By contrast, a **matrilineal** system bestows identity and wealth through the mother's side. While it might appear that matrilineal tracing of descent would be coupled with matriarchal authority in the family, there is no necessary connection. In a matrilineal system, wealth may always be in the hands of men but simply passed along through the woman's line. For example, a boy might inherit from his mother's brother. Finally, a **bilineal** system uses both lines for tracing identity and bestowing inheritance. Typically, the American family uses the bilineal system, even though our surnames come to us in a patrilineal fashion because women change their names upon marriage. A woman who keeps her maiden name (her father's surname) simply moves the process back one generation without fundamentally altering it. Naming is symbolic of descent tracing, but bilineal naming can become extremely cumbersome.

Finally, the residence of newly married individuals varies cross-culturally from **patrilocal** residence (in which the newlyweds move in with or near the husband's family) to **matrilocal** residence (in which the happy couple locates with or near the wife's family). **Neolocal** patterns of residence find the bride and groom in a new place of residence separate from either of their families. The norm in American culture is for neolocal residence for newlyweds whenever possible.

Patterns of Marriage and Mate Selection Perhaps the most fundamental variation found cross-culturally in marriage is the number of spouses involved. **Monogamy** is a marriage between one man and one woman. Extra participants produce **polygyny** (the marriage of one man and two or more women) or **polyandry** (the marriage of one woman and two or more men). Of the three, polygyny is by far the most common. One study found that polygyny was permitted in 83 percent of the cultures surveyed, while monogamy was the ideal in less than 20 percent (Murdock, 1967). It should be noted, however, that permitting polygyny does not necessarily mean that it will be the most prevalent form of marriage in a given culture; typically, only the wealthiest men have more than one wife. At the other extreme, polyandry is very rare, even in those societies in which it is permissible. And when it does appear, it is not typically in a matriarchy. It is more common in polyandry for women to be shared among men who, more often than not, have kin ties to one another. Finally, monogamy makes up for its lack of historical and cross-cultural popularity by being the dominant marriage form found in industrial societies.

All cultures regulate mate selection to some degree. Rules of **exogamy** specify the group *outside* of which an individual must choose a mate. In American society, these rules coincide with cultural norms concerning incest (see Chapter 3); that is, the rules name individuals deemed too closely related for consideration as marriage partners. An American is supposed to look beyond his or her first cousin for a prospective spouse. Rules of exogamy in other cultures are often more extensive; in fact, one's whole community may be declared off-limits for marriage. Such rules, which force individuals to look elsewhere, can create important economic and political ties for the community through its members' marriages.

Rules of **endogamy** specify the group *inside* of which an individual must choose a mate. In American society, it was once illegal in most states to marry anyone not in one's racial group. While such laws are no longer around, many of the same cultural expectations remain. In 1988, for example, only 956,000 of 52,613,000 married couples in America were interracial. And that figure represents a significant increase since 1970, when only 310,000 of the then 44,597,000 total married couples were interracial (U.S. Bureau of the Census, 1990c). While the rules of endogamy prohibiting interracial marriage in the United States are weakening, they are still clearly in force for most people. We also find rules of endogamy specifying marriage inside of one's religious group and even within one's social class. In short, any expectation that you marry someone "like yourself" represents a rule of endogamy. Marriage between people with the same social characteristics is termed **homogamy**. Rules of endogamy in concert with the structure of American society (such as the isolation of social classes described in Chapter 7) tends to place most of us in homogamous marriages. Cupid is apparently quite selective about the destinations of his arrows. Figure 10.1 provides a graphic representation of how the rules of exogamy and endogamy structure the social world of spouse selection.

In many cultures, mate selection is deemed far too important to be left in hands of the prospective mates. As we have seen, the family is an institution with many functions, and when parents select spouses for their children, they keep many of those functions in mind. Whether or not mate selection is in the hands of the prospective mates, not all cultures

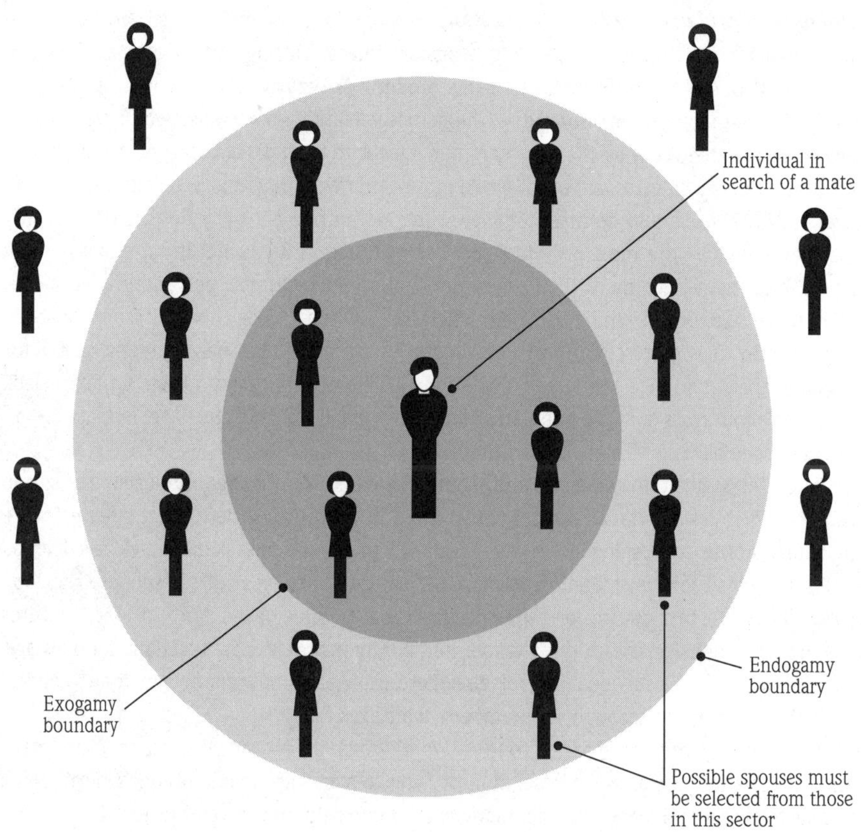

Figure 10.1 Rules of exogamy and endogamy in mate selection.

accept the notion of romantic love that dominates mate selection in the United States. Romance is hardly new to the world, but its spread as a value to all social classes (not just the elite with time to write sonnets) plus its connection with mate selection is a modern phenomenon, arising in industrial society. Romantic love is probably not the best basis on which to build a marriage because it seldom lasts in face of the fundamental day-to-day demands of family life. In any case, society's hand tends to point Cupid's arrow at "suitable" partners. People very different from ourselves more often irritate than fascinate us, making romance and marriage an unlikely outcome.

Social Change and the American Family

Social change in American society directly affects the American family. Most notably, changes in the economy have created new opportunities for (and demands on) American women. And as women have changed, so have the men to whom they are married. Sociologists of the family have been extremely interested in tracing some of these changes in an attempt to understand the new family patterns that have resulted. In this section, we will examine some of the impacts of social change on sex roles within the family and changes in the value placed on children.

Changing Roles in the American Family The average age of Americans at their first marriage has been steadily rising since the mid-1960s. In 1989, the median age at first marriage was 26.2 for men and 23.8 for women—higher than any previously recorded level (U.S. Bureau of the Census, 1990c). This increase has been greater for women than for men, which suggests that some of the social forces creating this change are focused on women. One of the sex-specific forces that has caused women to delay marriage is greater economic opportunity (Oppenheimer, 1988; Gottfried and Gottfried, 1988; Teachman and Schollaert, 1989). The same opportunities that encourage women to delay marriage for education and career advancement also encourage them to remain in the labor market after marriage. Today, close to 70 percent of all American married couples have both members in the labor force. Nevertheless, women typically earn 60 percent of what their husbands earn, and most couples live with the assumption that the husband's work is more important when priorities come into conflict (McRae, 1986). The most poorly paid of these working women are those with the least education and fewest career possibilities, yet economic necessity propels them into the labor force in spite of the gender wage differential.

Women who spend more time at work have less time to spend on the home activities of the traditional women's role. Since women have traditionally had primary responsibility for childrearing, their unavailability has created a near-crisis socially—at least in the United States. The United States is distinctive among industrial nations for the exceptionally small role the federal government plays in providing child care facilities or subsidizing their costs. Regulations to ensure the quality of such facilities are also minimal, and some psychologists were concerned that children's social and intellectual development might suffer. In spite of these obstacles, however, all indications are that the children of working mothers develop with few differences from the children of traditional mothers who stay at home; the key factor in producing normal development in such families, however, appears to be a combination of adequate funds in the family plus a parent's spending of "quality time" with the child (Kinnon and King, 1988; Gottfried and Gottfried, 1988). Although some of that "quality time" is provided by fathers, many fathers are selective in form of their involvement; they prefer to specialize in the less routine aspects of child care—a trip to the zoo rather than changing diapers (Pleck, 1985).

If the husbands of working women have a somewhat checkered record with regard to childcare, their efforts at housework are even less impressive. One of the most common findings of research on the two-breadwinner family is that women still do most of the housework (Blumstein and Schwartz, 1983; Fuchs, 1986). An interesting study of this issue discovered that men who help the most with housework are those whose income is the closest to their wife's income (Ross, 1987). In light of all of these findings, it is not surprising to discover that women in top executive positions in the American labor force are over ten times more likely to be single and childless than men in those same positions (Fraker, 1984).

Bernard (1982) argues that, for many of the reasons outlined above, modern marriage is beneficial for men but detrimental to women. Ross, Mirowsky, and Huber (1983) pursued that question in an interesting piece of research relating types of marriage to levels of depression experienced by the participants. Figure 10.2 summarizes their findings. At first glance, it seems apparent that marriage in any form is associated with higher levels of depression in women than in men, with the lone exception of the husband who would prefer his working wife to remain at home. Bernard's assertion seems to have some basis in fact. For women, working outside the home has little association with depression regardless of whether the working woman

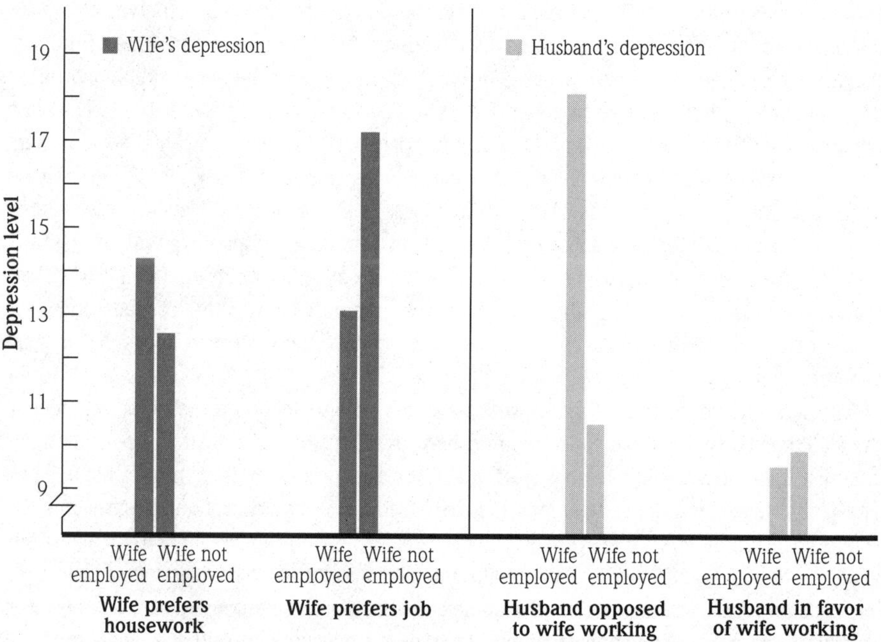

Figure 10.2 The interactive effects of preferences for wife's employment and wife's actual employment on the depression levels of husbands and wives. (From Ross, Mirowsky, and Huber, 1983.)

herself prefers being employed to remaining at home. The highest levels of female depression are associated with confinement to the home when the woman would prefer to be employed. When husband support with housework for working wives was examined, high support produced (not surprisingly) the lowest levels of female depression. Since such male support with housework is still a rare occurrence, the marriage relationship seems in need of additional change before it functions as well for women as it does for men.

The Value of Children: Childless Marriages In the preindustrial world, children were an economic asset, but industrialization removed their economic potential and replaced it with additional costs (Zelizer, 1985). Children also place considerable stress upon the marriage relationship. Sociological research has shown that couples without children are happier than those with children and that those whose children are grown are happier than those with younger children (Morgan, Lye, and Condran, 1988; Adams, 1988). It is not surprising, then, that attitudes about ideal family size have changed over the years. Currently, the majority of Americans consider two or less children to be ideal. Most couples now carefully consider the costs before having children.

In fact, the number of couples choosing to remain childless has increased notably in American society. In most cases, these are couples with higher-than-average income and education, and both have careers to which they are dedicated. Because they foresee that childrearing would interfere with those careers, many couples delay having children or eliminate them altogether. The same forces that affect general attitudes about the ideal number of children have helped support decisions to remain childless. As the expense of raising children continues to increase, voluntary childlessness should become increasingly common.

The Family and Inequality An individual's entering status into society is determined solely by his or her family. You can alter your status during your lifetime through your own efforts, but your first status will be that of your family. If your family is of low social status and is looked down upon by others, it follows that those same observers will not expect much of you. If such observers are teachers or police officers or judges, their prejudgments can have a significant impact on your life. Since your family's income level will determine what options are open to you, your family can also have a fundamental effect on your economic well-being as an adult.

The issue of economic inequality interests sociologists—in particular, the increase in the number of children in the United States being raised by a single parent. Figure 10.3 shows the growth in the percentages of children being raised by a single parent from 1960 to 1989, comparing white, black, and Hispanic populations. If we view this over the years of childhood for individual children, we find that 40 percent of white children and 85 percent of black children spend at least some years with a single parent (Rawlings, 1989). Since almost all single parents are women, these children are more likely to live in poverty than children with two parents. In 1989, the mean income for families with two parents present was $42,488, compared to a figure of $15,681 for families headed by single women. Only 9.3 percent of the two-parent families lived below the poverty level, while 51.7 percent of the families headed by women did so (U.S. Bureau of the Census, 1990c). Part of the reason for the large difference in income

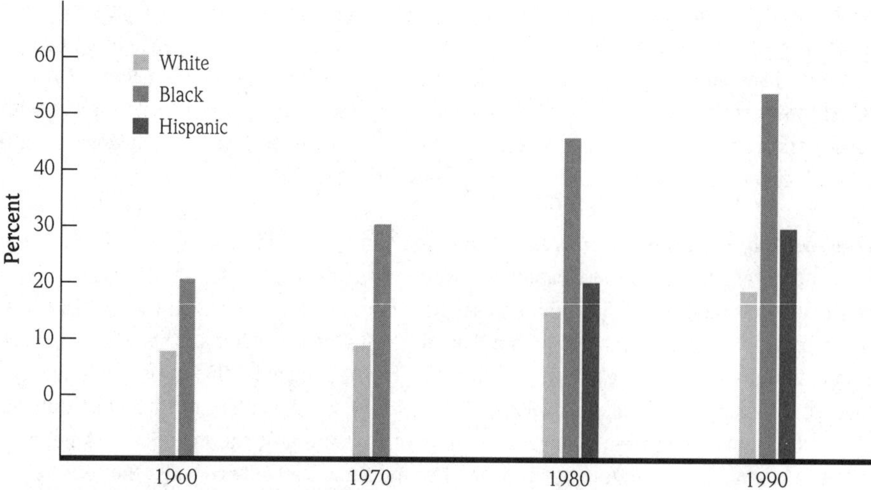

Figure 10.3 Percent of children raised by a single parent, 1960-1989. (Data from *Marital Status and Living Arrangements: March 1989.* U.S. Bureau of the Census, Current Population Reports, Series P-20, No. 445. U.S. Government Printing Office, 1990.)

is the presence of two wage earners in many of the two-parent families. Another part of the reason, however, is the lower pay that American women receive relative to men. If we compare the 1989 families headed by single women with those headed by single men, we find that the mean income of the families headed by males was $26,706; consequently, only 20.3 percent of male-headed families fell below the poverty line, whereas over 50 percent of female-headed families did so (U.S. Bureau of the Census, 1990c). The yearly income for male-headed families is still well below that earned by two-parent families but significantly higher than that earned by women.

Another concern sociologists have with single-parent families headed by women is the disproportionate number of nonwhite women involved. Figure 10.3 suggests much of this difference; in 1989, only 18.8 percent of white children lived with one parent, compared to 54.5 percent of black children and 30.5 percent of Hispanic children. If we combine ethnic differences with the income differences noted above (displayed graphically in Figure 10.4), the relationship stands out clearly. While all families headed by single women tend to be poorer, that fact is even more true of black and Hispanic families than of white families.

The growth in single-parent families, especially in nonwhite populations, has been explained in a variety of ways by sociologists. One of the more controversial was a 1965 study by Daniel Patrick Moynihan entitled "The Negro Family." Pointing to some of the statistics cited above (which were far less pronounced in 1965), Moynihan concluded that the rise of the female-headed family in the black community indicated a cultural breakdown within that community and would, in itself, be a cause of poverty for the upcoming generation of blacks because of a lack of proper male role models. The implication of this study was that black Americans would have to clean up their own act before they could expect anything better from life.

Critics of Moynihan's study (and subsequent restatements of the conclusions in various forms) have argued that the lack of two-parent families is a product of poverty rather than a cause.

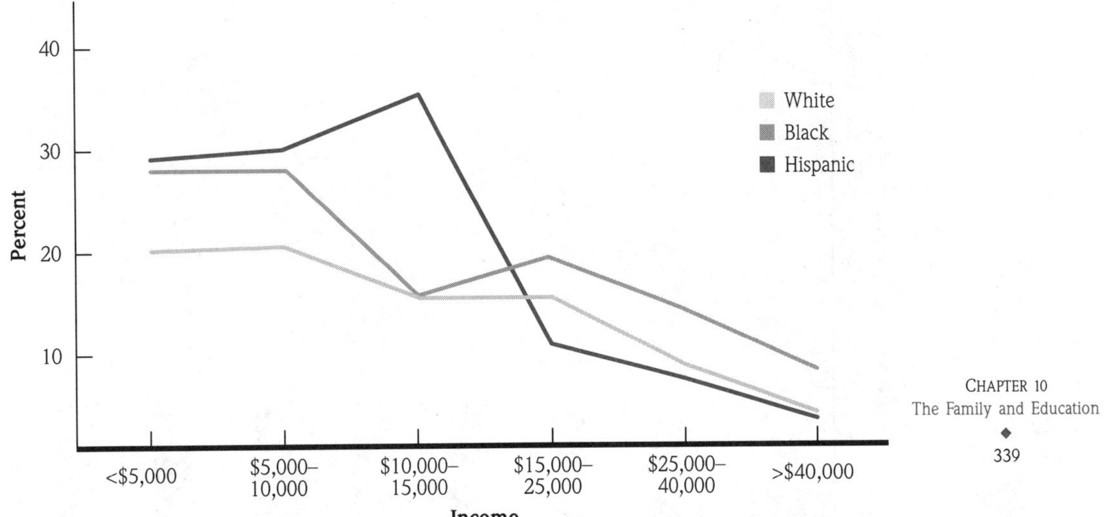

Figure 10.4 Percent of families headed by a single woman, by income level and ethnic background. (Data from *Marital Status and Living Arrangements: March 1989.* U.S. Bureau of the Census, Current Population Reports, Series P-20, No. 445. U.S. Government Printing Office, 1990.)

The pressures of low-income jobs and frequent unemployment make stable family life difficult, to say the least. Moynihan traced these aspects of the black family to the disruptions of family life caused by slavery, but other observers have noted that the rise of the female-headed family has been more a response to the problems of poverty in an urban environment than a result of history (Wilson, 1987). There is also considerable debate as to whether the black family is indeed weak (see Stack, 1975). Fathers may be absent, but ties to other relatives in an extended family sense are quite strong. In 1988, for example, 7.4 percent of black children were being raised by someone other than either parent, as compared to 2.2 percent for whites and 3.6 percent for Hispanics (U.S. Bureau of the Census, 1990c). This loosely defined category is in most cases composed of other relatives of the children, who have stepped in to help. The bottom line of Moynihan's critics, however, is that poverty must be ended if the nuclear family is to grow. And even economic change may not be enough, given the many factors that have combined to increase divorce rates in the United States. (The reading by Thompson following this chapter explores the black family in much greater detail.)

Marriage and Divorce The relationship between marriage and divorce in the United States is a curious one. Divorce rates have risen steadily in recent decades (see Figure 10.5) to the point that there is now a ratio of about one divorce for every two marriages. One estimate is that half of all marriages occurring now will not last beyond thirty years (Weed, 1989). We have already seen that Americans who do marry are marrying at older ages now than at any recorded time. There is also an increase in the number of Americans who choose not to marry at all. Figure 10.6 (page 341) shows the changes over the last twenty years for three different

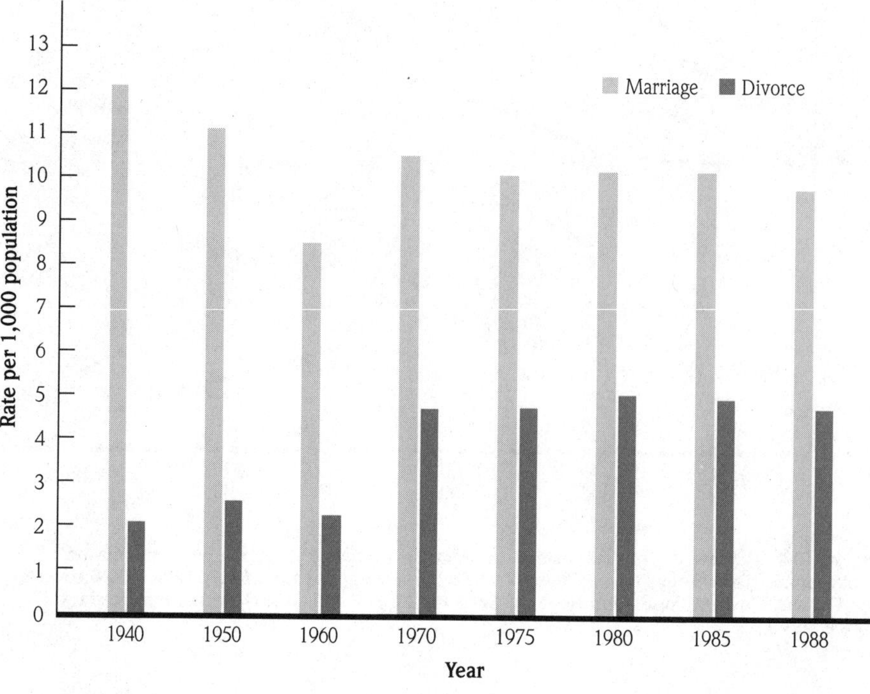

Figure 10.5 Marriage and divorce rates in the United States 1940-1988.

age groups for both men and women. Nevertheless, 90 percent of all Americans marry at some time in their lives. The higher divorce rates seem to indicate a greater ease and willingness to terminate a marriage relationship but not a widespread disenchantment with marriage itself. We have already seen evidence that suggests the marriage relationship is more beneficial to men than to women. On the other hand, both suicide rates and overall death rates are higher for divorced people than for married people (Emery et al., 1984).

The higher divorce rate in itself is not easily explained, but certain changes in American society seem to have played an important role. As noted earlier, the marriage relationship and the family are no longer the practical necessity for life they once were. Individuals can earn a living outside of the marriage relationship; increasing occupational opportunities for women, in particular, mean that they are much less likely to be trapped economically in an unpleasant marriage. Furthermore, since children have changed from an economic asset to an economic drain, there may be fewer of them—or none—so "staying together for the children" loses its force. Remarriage introduces stepchildren, and the presence of stepchildren on both sides in a remarriage increases the likelihood of divorce (White and Booth, 1985). Stresses of modern life and, in particular, the problems faced by lower social classes play a role; unemployment, frequent moving, low levels of education and low income are all linked with high probabilities of divorce (Raschke, 1987). Finally—and perhaps as a result of these other changes—divorce no longer carries the social stigma it once had or presents the legal difficulties formerly involved.

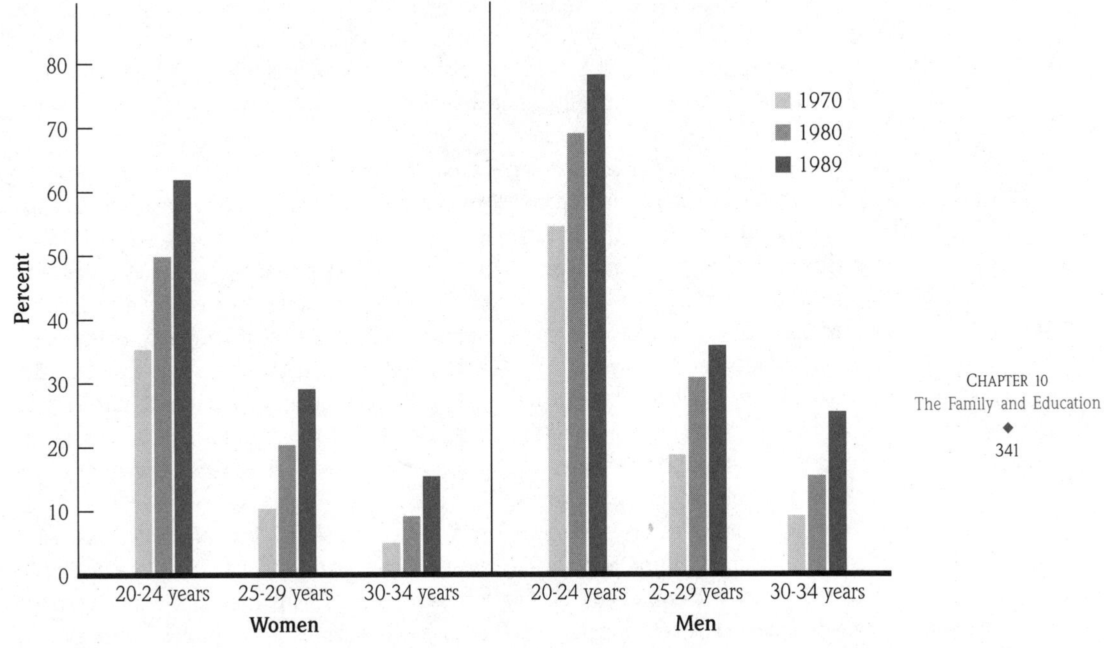

Figure 10.6 Percent of Americans who never married, by age and sex: 1970, 1980, and 1989.

When we contemplate divorce, our friends are less likely to discourage us than a generation ago (Gerstel, 1987). Almost all states now have no-fault divorce laws (originated in California in 1970), which ease the legal process. Divorce is now generally accepted as a rational and often beneficial way to cope with an unpleasant marriage relationship.

While the ease of divorce today may save some individuals from an unhappy life married to the wrong person, it also creates significant economic problems, particularly for women. Sociologist Lenore Weitzman (1985) studied the effects of California's no-fault law and found that most women face severe financial problems following a divorce. One year after a typical divorce, a woman's standard of living *decreases* by 73 percent while her ex-husband's standard of living *increases* by 42 percent. Part of the reason for this change is that most women are awarded custody of children following a divorce. Even if the ex-husband pays court-ordered child support (and many do not), the average amount of child support is generally not enough to cover the costs of raising a child. Probably a more important cause of women's financial problems following a divorce is that women generally have fewer job skills and/or a less solid career history from which to become self-supporting. Courts are currently evaluating findings such as these in order to make divorce settlements more equitable. (The reading by Okin following this chapter examines the issue of no-fault divorce and the economic disadvantages it has for women.)

Family Violence At the same time that the family is the source of warmth and affection, it is also sometimes a setting for incredible violence. Some violence against relatives may be misdirected; people may really want to strike out at individuals who are the source of their frustration—a boss, a tax collector, a policeman—but it is family members who are nearby and relatively defenseless. Nevertheless, the family also promotes some of the frustration that explodes as family violence. It is one of the most important social groups to which we belong. The family deals with matters of utmost importance to its members, where intense emotions may be combined with economic relationships. It is not surprising, therefore, that members often come into conflict over the obligations and responsibilities they have to each other (see Shupe et al., 1987).

Spouse abuse is typically the abuse of women by men (although the opposite does occur). It is estimated that 1.6 million wives are beaten each year in the United States (Straus and Gelles, 1986). Andrews (1984) estimates that 25 percent of all wives have been slapped, 15 percent have had sex forced on them by husbands, and 10 percent have been beaten. Child abuse involves either the physical or sexual abuse of children by adults. It is estimated that between 1.5 and 2 million children are beaten each year (Straus and Gelles, 1986). Physical abusers are about 90 percent men and sexual abusers are almost entirely men. Evidence indicates that most child abusers were themselves abused as children (Gelles, 1985; Gwartney-Gibbs, Stockard, and Bohmer, 1987; Seltzer and Kalmuss, 1988).

While this violence occurs in all social classes (particularly sexual abuse of children), it appears to be more common in the lower social classes (Gelles and Straus, 1988). Once again, the stresses of poverty are generally blamed for the added tensions they create among family members. It should be kept in mind, however, that all the figures and estimates available reflect only those cases that come to the attention of authorities. Spouse abuse is commonly hidden by women who are unable or unwilling to stand up to their husbands. (The rapid growth of battered women's shelters is an attempt to make this kind of reporting easier for women.) Families also conceal physical child abuse and, of course, the sexual abuse of children. The child victims of sexual abuse (who are almost always female) often feel shame, and the adult female members of the family are typically fearful or passive; the result is that the crime goes unreported. Family violence incidents in the lower social classes are more likely to come to the attention of police and social workers than similar incidents in the middle or upper classes; we should therefore use the available figures with some caution.

The rape of a spouse and "date rape" have only recently received the attention they deserve from the media, the law, and social scientists. One study of college students found that 12 to 36 percent of college undergraduates surveyed had experienced dating violence (Carlson, 1987). Muehlenhard and Linton (1987) found that 15 percent of college women surveyed had been raped while in a dating relationship. In general, one-third of rape victims know the individual who rapes them (Makepeace, 1986). As with the crimes discussed above, date rape is generally not reported. The rape of one's spouse has only recently come to be recognized as a crime independent of other forms of spouse abuse. The fact that many legislators traditionally held that a husband's "rights" precluded any question of rape indicates something of male insensitivity to the rights of women, which is reflected in many laws governing family violence.

The Family: A Last Look

Increases in the divorce rate plus rising numbers of Americans avoiding marriage do not indicate a "death of the family," as some observers fear, but rather a reflection of changes in other social institutions. As we have seen, institutions are always in the process of change, and changes in one inevitably lead to changes in the others. The future of the family will no doubt involve increasing attention to issues such as artificial insemination, *in vitro* fertilization, surrogate mothers, and homosexual marriages. One of the most striking events of the 1980s and 1990s for the American family may well be the rapid growth of AIDS and the threat of its spread into the heterosexual community (Nichols, 1986). All indications are that fear of AIDS has produced the best public relations that monogamy has seen for some time in the United States (Altman, 1986). The modern American family is a new creature in many ways, but it is far from extinct.

EDUCATION

In industrial societies such as the United States, the institution of education provides children with their first major step outside the family. From the child's point of view, whole new sets of human relationships await in new physical settings called schools. From the sociologist's point of view, however, education represents one of the separate social institutions that warrants an individual look in the process of understanding the structure of an industrial society. As with all institutions, it operates with some degree of isolation, carried along by its own logic, as teachers, students, and school administrators go through their respective motions in their respective roles. But as with all institutions, the institution of education has important connections with other institutions. Its connection with the family is obvious as it removes children from one set of caretakers and socializers to place them in the hands of others. Its forceful intervention into the family, however, stems primarily from other important institutional forces that help shape education's goals and functions. Specifically, the institution of education responds to the political institution, which, in turn, is highly responsive to the needs of the economy (two institutions we will look at in more detail in Chapter 11). In this section, we will begin by looking at the goals and functions of educations (as influenced by politics and the economy); this discussion will provide a basis for understanding some of the important outcomes of this institution, such as its effect on social inequality and its effectiveness in reaching its stated goals.

Education and Society: Goals and Functions

There is certainly some overlap in the stated goals of education and the sociologically observed functions of education. Goals that are achieved, for example, represent functions that the institution fulfills. Education attempts to make Americans literate, for example, which is a skill the economy requires in the workforce. Although schools are not completely successful in accomplishing this goal (see Box 10.1), they achieve at least a modest success with most of us. This goal is part of the function of imparting knowledge to each generation, as we will explore in just a moment. On the other hand, schools sometimes achieve ends for which they not only do not strive but perhaps might prefer to avoid (such as the thrusting together of large numbers of youths the same age who subsequently form a youth culture in which drugs and gangs may be promoted). Such non-goals are functions nonetheless (often called latent functions) in that the institution produces them on an ongoing basis. A first step in understanding this institution is to explore its impact on those who pass through it and its functions for the wider society.

BOX 10.1

LITERACY IN THE UNITED STATES

Can you pass this test? Read the following advertisement for a rental house and then answer the questions.

> Attractive house in excellent condition. Three floors. Full basement. Large living room. Backyard with garden. Two-car garage.

1. Would you tell me how the ad describes the living room of the house?
2. How does the ad describe the backyard?
3. How does the ad describe the basement?

If you have read ten chapters in this book with no problem, this test is unlikely to be much of a challenge, but many Americans would have difficulty with it. Since literacy is a fundamental skill for most jobs in an industrial society, the idea that some 20 to 30 percent of the American population might have trouble with such a simple reading task makes one wonder how work ever gets done (Stedman and Kaestle, 1991; Kozol, 1985).

Literacy is the ability to extract meaning from the written word. Our schools teach this skill and then teach other skills that require literacy. This kind of "school literacy" requires even higher-level skills than the preceding test of "functional literacy," which measures the ability to read in everday life contexts. As Kozol (1985:4) points out, "Twenty-five million American adults cannot read the poison warnings on a can of pesticide, a letter from their child's teacher, or the front page of a daily paper. An additional 35 million read only at a level which is less than equal to the full survival needs of our society."

The initial inclination of most Americans is to blame the school system. Bumper stickers that read, "If you can read this, thank a teacher," also invite the public to blame teachers for those who cannot read. Over one-third of the member nations of the United Nations have higher literacy rates than the United States (Kozol, 1985). Many of those same countries also require more months in the school year and more homework. Some think they have more dedicated teachers and students. But such statistics and surmises do not necessarily give us a complete picture. Spending more money and time on formal education cannot hurt our literacy statistics but neither does it offer a guarantee of a magic solution. Most illiterates are found among the poor and minorities, who have never been well served by the American system of formal education. While some of the difference between black and white literacy rates in the United States can be accounted for by economic differences alone, some of those differences seem to be connected to more general causes, such as prejudice and alienation (Stedman and Kaestle, 1991).

Kozol (1985) believes that the best cure for illiteracy is to employ less formal, community-based programs. The poor and minorities have had too many negative experiences with formal bureaucracies, argues Kozol, to be responsive to programs housed in such environments. Yet the 1980s and 1990s have not been periods of excess funds for domestic programs in the United States. The adult illiterate described by Kozol, who, from embarrassment, attempts to navigate through life while hiding a lack of reading ability is likely to be a large and often invisible portion of the American workforce for some years to come.

Americanization of Immigrants In the early nineteenth century, education was privately provided, and generally only the rich could afford it. Most occupations did not require any of the fine points of learning, and most workers did not have the leisure to pursue education, no matter what its cost. In the nineteenth century, industrialization began its spread in the United States, and it created demands for basic literacy. The nineteenth century also brought large numbers of immigrants to the United States and they brought considerable cultural diversity (see Chapter 8). Power in the United States, then and now, was held largely by Protestant Americans of European descent; this power elite felt that their values were threatened by these new arrivals. Compulsory public education appeared to be a solution: teach the new arrivals American values.

If you saluted the flag in elementary school, you were participating in a ritual that had its roots in the Americanization concerns of the last century. That pledge of loyalty was originally designed to teach the children of foreign immigrants that they could no longer have any allegiance to a political entity other than the United States. In addition, the schools were also viewed as a method for promoting the basic Protestant values that were seen as central to all other American values. Public schools were structured as a way to counteract the force of other religions whose memberships were growing rapidly through immigration, especially Catholicism (see Soltaw and Stevens, 1981). The goals behind the public school movement in the late nineteenth century were not lost on the newcomers; one major response came from the Catholic Church, which placed a major emphasis on the growth of parochial schools so as to isolate the children of Catholic Americans from the anti-Catholic forces behind the public school movement (Gabriel, 1948). Less powerful groups, most notably Native American Indians, were unable to structure alternative schools and found themselves at the mercy of imported public education, which ignored or downgraded their cultures while promoting American culture. Still today, public education promotes American culture to new immigrants.

Cultural and Political Integration The goal of "Americanization" in the United States has its counterpart in all multi-ethnic states, and educational institutions are typically used to implement the goal of integrating immigrants (and others) into the mainstream culture. An area in which goals and functions clearly overlap is cultural and political integration. Integration becomes an issue because multi-ethnic states are not nations in the true sense of the word. A *nation*-state would be a state with only one ethnic group so that the political boundaries of the state would be the same as the boundaries of the group to which individuals attached their personal loyalties and sense of belongingness. But is a given Native American likely to see himself or herself as an American first or a Navajo first? One goal and sometime function of education is to produce the first result.

Cultural and political integration means that a state's citizens are enough alike for the state to function as a unit. This does not mean that they have to be cultural clones of one another but that they are able to communicate with one another and share both a political loyalty to and knowledge of their government. As with the Americanization of immigrant children described above, education also provides this function for each generation. In the United States, for example, all public schools either are taught in English or use other languages (as in the case of bilingual schools) only to pave the way for children to master English at some point

The school experience of children in this 1920s one-room schoolhouse had to be vastly different from that of children in today's strictly age-graded schools. In the one-room schoolhouse, the older children were often expected to help teach the younger ones (an arrangement announced a few years ago as an innovation in instruction). Those children were probably socialized to value cooperation more and competition less.

in their student career. Courses in government are also generally required so that no child can leave the system without encountering the United States Constitution and learning some of the basics of the political structure that has grown from it. This process of education does not eliminate cultural differences among Americans but it does give them common ground at some level. Even industrial nations with minimal cultural diversity (such as Japan) maintain a higher level of cultural and political integration through the institution of education.

Imparting and Creating Knowledge The most obvious goal of education is also probably its most obvious function. As we saw in Chapter 9, there are many ways to acquire knowledge besides the formal process of education, but industrial societies have found formal education to have a number of advantages. The most important is that compulsory education produces literacy (see Box 10.1). As we have seen, an industrial economy cannot function without most of its citizens having at least some basic skills. Beyond that, the wide range of skills that characterize the occupations in a society with a high division of labor are generally beyond the capabilities of most parents or other family members to teach. Finally, the institution of education also plays a major role in the creation of new knowledge. A primary goal of the modern American university is professorial research designed to expand the various disciplines represented.

Screening In the process of providing knowledge, the institution of education also evaluates those who seek it, separating the successful from the unsuccessful. Education can be viewed as a series of hurdles that must be jumped en route to the finish line of graduation. A missed hurdle at any point creates a nonfinisher; some students drop out of high school while others acquire a diploma. Some stop with that diploma while others enroll in a college or university. And some of those who enroll will fail or quit while others receive degrees. Of those, the elite will pursue still more education in search of advanced degrees. The farther along the hurdles, the fewer the number of students who will still be in the running. Employers therefore have their applicants already screened for them. Simply placing an educational requirement on a given occupation will automatically eliminate certain kinds of people who missed the hurdles prior to that requirement. Sociologists examine the institution of education carefully to understand this screening process and, most important, to understand just why some kinds of people falter at hurdles so easily jumped by others (see the reading by Murai following Chapter 8). A common observation is that education tends to preserve the system of social stratification from one generation to the next (see Colclough and Beck, 1986; Mingle, 1987). We will examine this process more closely in the next section of this chapter.

Socialization (and the Hidden Curriculum) When the topic of discussion is socialization we normally think of the family, but the institution of education plays a significant part in the socialization of all who pass through it. Socialization includes the imparting of knowledge discussed above, but schools provide a much more wide-ranging experience to students than simply the opportunity to acquire knowledge and skills. They create social arenas within which children have their first major encounters with both adults and peers outside the family. The child's ability to develop social relationships thereby grows. The school experience also imparts more general cultural values, as students are encouraged to admire and dislike specific cultural objects, people, lifestyles, forms of government, and so on. Children who spend considerable classroom time studying the Founding Fathers but very little time on the history of nonwhite Americans, for example, acquire a clear picture as to what is important and what is not.

Instruction in values is an intended goal of education, but the institution imparts many values that are not found in textbooks or teacher training programs but rather are built into the basic structure of school systems. These values have been termed the **hidden curriculum** (Jackson, 1968). For example, one of the most notable aspects of the educational system is the competition it requires of students. The grading system is only the obvious sign of the competitive pressures that exist everywhere in school. When a child fails to answer a teacher's question correctly, for example, other children who know the answer cannot contain their enthusiasm in their desire to show up their fallen comrade. Schools cannot take all the credit for the student desire to be "better than," however, since competition colors all aspects of life in an industrial society. As part of that society, the institution of education is consistent with the dominant values. The emphasis it places on competition makes it an important factor in the socialization of children. Being a student is learning to compete—a lesson for later life that may be more important than much of the specific subject matter of education.

In American society the school has become one of the most important socializers in the early life of its members. Children learn to sit quietly, walk in straight lines, salute the flag,

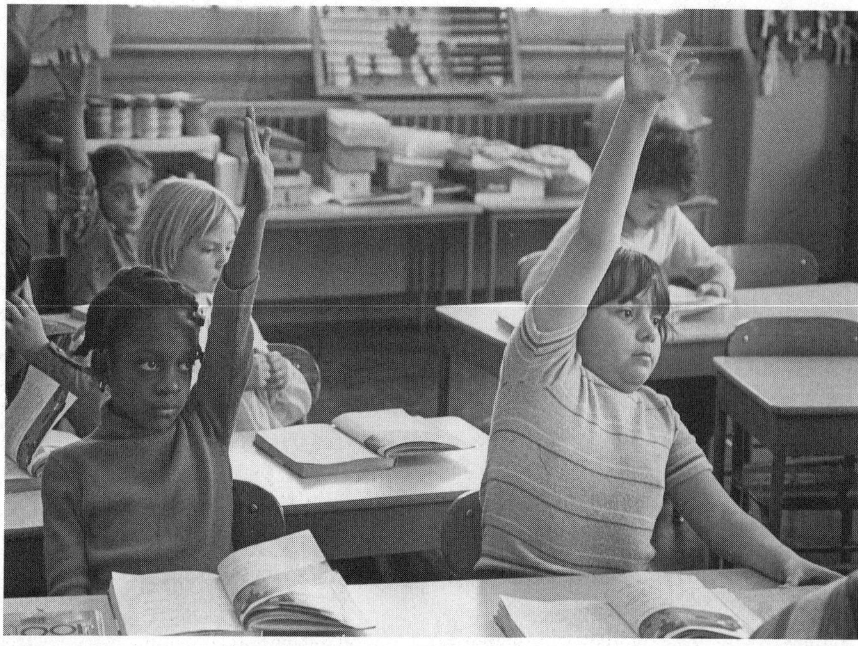

Along with reading, writing, and arithmetic, children learn all sorts of things in school. One of the most obvious is competition—which is not surprising, since the American culture is a very competitive one. The vigor of some hand-raising in elementary school is saying, "Call on me so I can show off and give the right answer and get one up on my classmates."

and take orders from authority figures. They learn to "get along" with each other in socially approved ways, following norms typically different for boys and girls. Boys, for example, learn to act more aggressively on the playground and dominate in math, science, and social studies in the classroom; girls, on the other hand, do better in writing, reading, and literature. Children become adults during the school years. The kinds of adults they become can be traced in large part to the impact of their many years spent in the classroom, playing the student role.

Equality of Educational Opportunity

As we saw earlier, one of the major reasons public education grew in the United States in the nineteenth century was to respond to the growing cultural diversity brought about by immigration. Schools face that same diversity in the 1990s as immigration continues and as ethnic and racial groups of longstanding in the United States still bring cultural diversity to the classroom. In addition, lifestyle differences from one social class to the next are profound enough (see Chapter 7) that lower class and middle class students from the same ethnic or racial group bring strikingly different backgrounds to school. Looking beyond school, levels of education have traditionally been connected to the level of occupational advancement an individual later achieves (Blau and Duncan, 1967). As diplomas and degrees have become increasingly tied to specific kinds of work in the economy, jobs that once one could "work into" are now formally connected to particular educational expectations and credentials; workers who lack that education cannot even be considered (Collins, 1979).

With education such an important route to success in the economy, the ability of schools to provide that opportunity to their diverse student population becomes increasingly important. In general, American schools have not provided that opportunity on a large scale. The schools are there, but most students who have significant cultural differences from the school curriculum do not succeed. As noted in the reading by Murai (Chapter 8), they usually have so much catching up to do that the task becomes insurmountable. In looking at how schools respond to those differences, sociologists have given us a much more complete picture of how the education institution responds to group differences.

Teacher Stereotypes and Expectations Most elementary school and secondary school teachers come from the middle classes of American society. Predictably, they hold many middle class values and stereotypes about people significantly different from themselves. While most teacher training programs attempt to sensitize prospective teachers to the cultural differences they will encounter in the classroom, such sensitizing can only go so far. As with most of us, teachers respond more favorably to students who are culturally more like themselves, and teachers have higher academic expectations of them. They respond less favorably to students who vary in social class, race, or ethnicity (Alexander et al., 1987; Farkas et al., 1990). Such differences in responses and expectations are not lost on the children who receive that different treatment.

Much of the concern with teacher expectations was generated by a 1968 study by Robert Rosenthal and Lenore Jacobson. They told the teachers involved in the study they had a test that would predict "late bloomers," students who might or might not have done well in the past but who should do exceptionally well during the coming year. Then they randomly selected some students from the classrooms and gave their names to the teachers as the individuals from whom big things should be expected. Returning at the end of the year, the researchers discovered that the children randomly selected had done significantly better than other children in the classroom. The only plausible explanation for this outcome was a change in the teachers' behavior; a teacher who conveys to a child that more is expected may well behave in ways that cause the child to fulfill that expectation. Efforts to replicate this study of positive teacher expectations have not produced identical results (see Boocock, 1978), but researchers have been able to show clearly that negative teacher expectations hinder the academic progress of students (Dusek, 1985).

Tracking The school experience communicates a definite message to children about their individual abilities and inabilities, good points and bad points. When elementary school reading groups are separated into the "bluebirds" and "robins," for example, children in the robin reading group soon discover that they are moving through their reading book much more slowly than the bluebirds. Later, in high school, those same slow readers may be placed into classes not designed to prepare them for college. This process of placing different students into different classes according to a measure of their ability is called **tracking**. It is used in over half of all American elementary schools and is a common element in most high school programs (Eyler, Cook, and Ward, 1983). The idea behind it is that students learn best in classes whose content is geared to their abilities and in which other students have similar abilities; advocates say that the higher-achieving students will not be held back by slower learners, while those with less ability will not face frustration. Tracking affects a student's achievement in two ways. First, students on the lower track receive a different course content which, over the years, will give them a substantially different education. Students who do not receive college preparatory classes, for example, will have less background in necessary subjects should they ever decide to venture into the ivory tower. Second, students in all tracks respond to the expectation that their track placement communicates. Students on the high track will presumably think well of themselves (since school officials obviously do) while those tracked in slower programs will get that message as well (Oakes, 1985). In short, tracking affects both the quality and, ultimately, the amount of education that students receive (Froman, 1981; Gamoran and Mare, 1989).

Which students are placed in which tracks? Students whose parents have a high level of education are much more likely to be placed in the higher tracks, aiming toward the same educational level as their parents (Kerbo, 1983). Students from families with a low income and minorities are much more likely to be found in the lower tracks than would follow from their proportion of the school population (Boocock, 1978). And, as we saw in Chapter 6, minorities are also likely to be overrepresented in the ultimate of low tracks—classes for the mentally retarded (Mercer, 1973). Students are initially separated through tracking, and tracking fosters continued separation. Ironically, tracking also affects the friendships of students. Since most students draw their friends from their classes, tracking assures that most students will select their friends from a pool of students much like themselves (Hallinan and Williams, 1989). Even schools that contain considerable diversity in social class, race, or ethnicity may have very little socializing across those boundaries if students never meet in classes. Tracking is clearly one of the ways in which the institution of education helps to maintain the current system of inequality in the United States: poor students are placed in low tracks, which lead to more poorly paid jobs, which make them poor adults, soon to be parents of poor students as the cycle begins again.

Inequality in School Funding Public schools in the United States have traditionally served the neighborhoods surrounding them. Since schools receive a large share of their funding from property taxes and since the value of property varies considerably from neighborhood to neighborhood, some school districts receive considerably more money than others. And since neighborhoods often contain many representatives from one racial or ethnic group, schools have traditionally reflected very little diversity in social class, race, or ethnicity. This was one of the first observations made by sociologist James Coleman and a team of researchers in 1966, who were seeking answers to questions about educational inequality in the United States. Although schools were not segregated by law in the United States by 1966, most of them experienced *de facto* segregation; that is, ethnic neighborhoods coupled with neighborhood schools produced segregated schools.

Coleman and his colleagues were primarily interested in finding out why good students excelled. They concluded that the most important factor in student success was *not* the amount of money spent in their school district but rather the student's attitude toward school, work habits, and socioeconomic background. Furthermore, they found higher test scores among black students who attended schools with high levels of racial and economic diversity, as compared to black students in largely segregated schools. Their overall conclusion was that unequal school funding was not the primary cause of educational inequality; the blocks to success were poor school attitudes coupled with a poor cultural background among segregated black students. The logical solution seemed to be compensatory education and busing.

Compensatory education assumes that certain students come from cultural backgrounds that ill prepare them for the demands of the public school system; compensatory education is designed to fill in the gaps in that background so that those students will be able to compete on an equal footing with other students. The best known such program is Head Start, which attempts to prepare preschool children for the demands of first grade and beyond. Early studies on the efficacy of Head Start were somewhat inconclusive; it obviously helped students in the short run but it was less clear how much it helped in the long run. Such questions are difficult to answer because so many factors affect school achievement. Nevertheless, some recent studies suggest that Head Start graduates do make long-term gains (Brown, 1985; Carmody, 1989).

Busing is the attempt to create student bodies with diversity in race, ethnicity, and social class through the movement of students within and across school district lines. Busing within a district may produce few results if all schools within the district contain mostly poor non-white students. In fact, many American cities today lack diversity since increasing numbers of middle class families have moved from cities to suburbs. When busing plans cross district lines between city and suburb, the goals of diversity become possible to achieve. Although busing created considerable political conflict when it was first introduced, there is less conflict in the 1990s, partly because other approaches to integration, such as magnet schools, have been introduced. Busing does help minority students achieve higher grades and test scores, when buses bring them to schools containing white students from a higher socioeconomic background (Mahard and Crain, 1983). The fact that efforts such as busing are dependent upon increasing contact among students from different classes suggests that much of the inequality we see in student performance stems from inequality outside the classroom and probably cannot be removed through even the most innovative educational experiments. It may be asking too much of our schools that they do more than mirror the society that created them.

The Structure of American Primary and Secondary Education

Primary and secondary education comprise grades one through twelve, commonly with kindergarten at the outset. For most American children, this process begins at the age of 5 or 6 and continues until eighteen. Although many children spend more hours watching television than attending classes during those years, it is still easy to make a case for the tremendous impact of the educational institution on the child. We have already looked at some of those effects, but we should also remember that not all schools (and school experiences) are the same. There are a number of traditional options for how to spend those twelve years—especially the choice between private or public education. Recent times have produced new choices within the public system. In this section of the chapter, we will first look at the differences between public and private education, then take a look at new programs in public education, such as magnet schools, bilingual and multicultural education, and the mainstreaming of disabled students.

Public and Private Schools There are currently over 83,000 public schools offering primary and secondary education in the United States; they educate over 88 percent of American children enrolled in schools. The remaining 12 percent primarily attend over 27,000 private schools, of which almost 20,000 are run by religious institutions. Half of those religious schools are

In public schools, especially schools in big cities, classes may consist of thirty to forty students. With so many children in a classroom, it is usually necessary to arrange desks or tables in rows and make fairly rigid rules of conduct, just to keep some semblance of order. Many private schools can offer smaller class sizes, some small enough so that students can sit around casually and discuss things with each other as well as with the teacher.

run by the American Catholic Church, and half are organized by other religious institutions (National Center for Education Statistics, 1989). While it might appear at first glance that the relatively large number of private schools enrolling so few students would result in many fewer students per teacher, class sizes in those private schools are only slightly smaller than in public schools. Private schools tend to be much smaller than public institutions and to have smaller staffs. But while the student-teacher ratios are similar, the results of student achievement vary considerably. Private schools are doing a better job.

Figure 10.7 shows the difference between public and private school students in their scores on the Scholastic Aptitude Test (SAT) in 1988. Not surprisingly, a higher percentage of private school students also attend college than do graduates of public schools (Falsey and Heyns, 1984). A logical explanation for this difference might seem to be the difference in costs between the two forms of education. Since private education creates direct costs for parents, the students would be economically screened, producing far fewer lower class children in the private school classrooms. That economic explanation certainly accounts for some of the differences in educational achievement, but it does not explain all the differences. If we compare private and public school students whose parents are similar in social class and education, students in the private schools still achieve more than their matched comrades in the public schools (Coleman et al., 1982; Coleman and Hoffer, 1987). If we narrow that comparison down to just Catholic schools

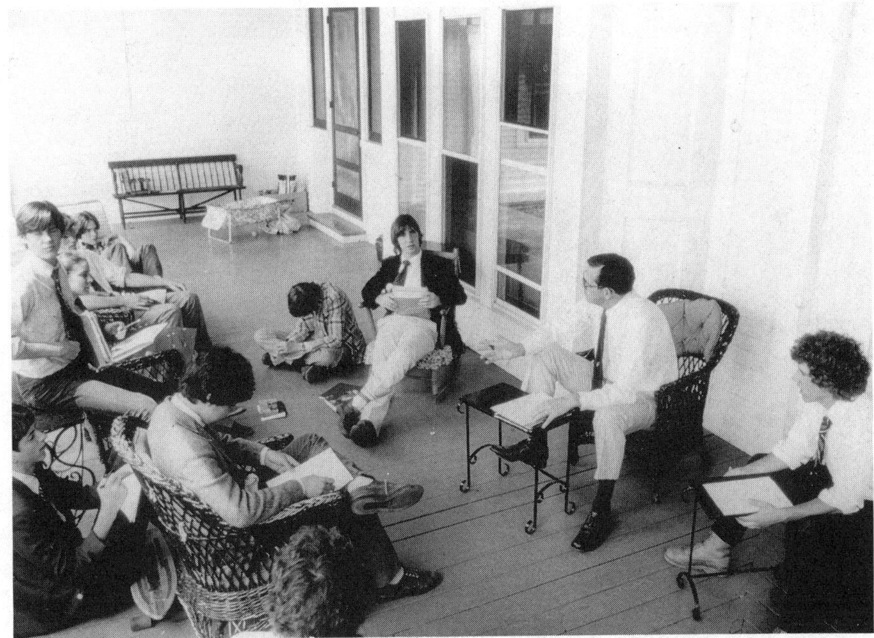

and just minority students, the private school again appears to be doing a superior job of both educating and motivating students (Greeley, 1982). As we have seen, there are no major differences in student-teacher ratios between public and private schools, but there are differences in other areas. Catholic schools tend to have both higher discipline and higher educational standards for their students than do public schools; presumably, their students are willing and capable of responding (Jensen, 1986).

Public schools are unlikely to make major economic inroads on private education. Public schools now receive about half of their funding from state sources and the other half from local property taxes. The latter source produces school inequality, as we have seen, and their overall dependence on the American taxpayer (who has not been inclined lately to favor higher taxes) suggests that economic difficulties for public schools will continue. The less tangible factors that seem to favor private education are more difficult to assess. Could, for example, public schools effectively raise both academic standards and standards for discipline to create an environment approximating Catholic schools? There may be other factors involved as well. Even inner city Catholic schools with predominantly nonwhite students may be able to create higher motivation because of their distinctiveness amidst a public school environment. Private schools may also be attracting students from those parents who are most committed to and supportive of their children's education. Nevertheless, the relative success of private schools suggests what is possible in education. Even though a child's socioeconomic background has a major impact on school success, educators are not completely helpless in counteracting that impact.

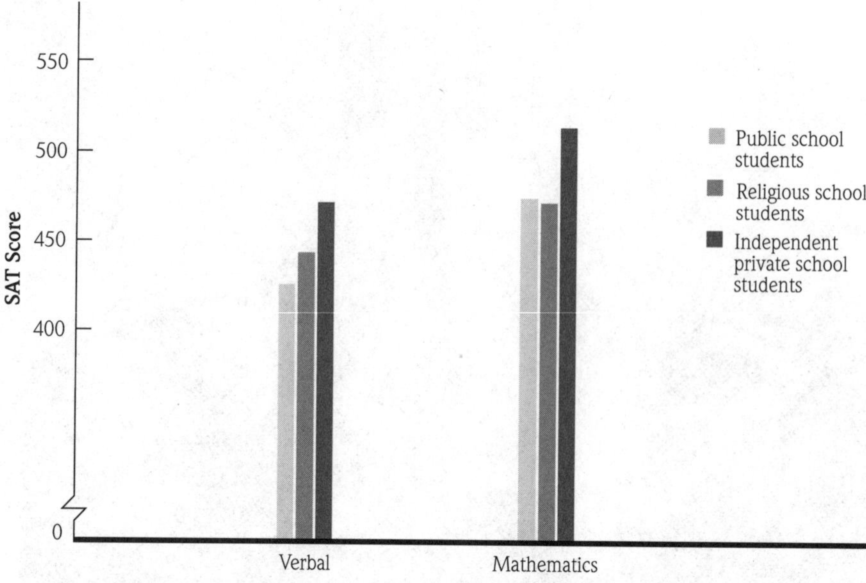

Figure 10.7 Differences between public and private school students in SAT scores, United States, 1988. (Data from *The Condition of Education, 1989: Volume One—Elementary and Secondary Education.* U.S. Department of Education, Office of Educational Research and Improvement. U.S. Government Printing Office, 1989.)

Magnet Schools American cities have been physically expanding over the last several decades as residents have moved beyond city limits into suburban areas (see Chapter 12 for a more complete discussion). Those who moved are largely middle class and white, while those left behind are largely lower class and nonwhite. This population change has left the inner city schools underfunded (because of declining property values surrounding them) and often segregated by race or ethnicity. Many school busing programs now operate across school district lines so as to mix the predominantly nonwhite students of the inner city with the predominantly white students of the suburbs. Since busing is mandatory and is often resented by suburban white families, efforts have been made to entice suburban students to return voluntarily to inner city schools. One of the more successful experiments has been the creation of magnet schools.

Magnet schools are secondary public schools that specialize in a particular area of the curriculum, providing students with focused (and presumably excellent) instruction in classes with other students who share their interests. A school might specialize in the humanities, science, the performing arts, or foreign language and culture. A school might even choose traditional studies, emphasizing the basics of education in a highly disciplined environment. By providing such a focus, the schools attract not only the best and most highly motivated students but also dedicated teachers to whom that educational environment is appealing. In general, magnet schools have been very successful in attracting white students back to the inner city. In some cases, they have been perhaps too successful, as inner city nonwhites have had some difficulty in competing for enrollment space. In spite of their value, magnet schools are only

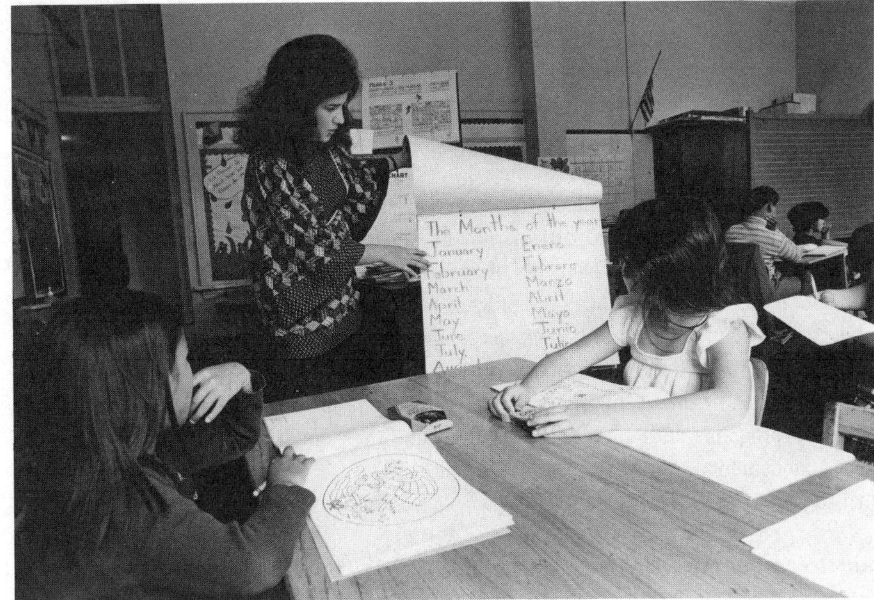

A bilingual classroom for Spanish-speaking students.

a partial answer to the problems of unequal and segregated public schools in the United States, since there is not enough funding to provide such facilities for all students.

Multicultural and Bilingual Education Although public schools have generally been under local control, the general form of instruction and curriculum content has been largely standardized, so children throughout the country have received a remarkably similar experience. The schools, not surprisingly, have reflected the predominantly English culture that characterizes American life, with an emphasis on English language and literature couched within a generally Eurocentric view of the world. In the past, students who brought non-English or non-European cultures with them to school faced a large gap between who they were and what their teachers wanted them to become. Traditionally, public schools have been less than tolerant about such student problems, sometimes punishing students for speaking languages other than English in class or even on the playground. Such treatment has helped to eliminate certain non-English cultural traits on the American landscape, but it has not always been successful at replacing those traits with the skills promoted by the school curriculum. Minority children often fail to learn what schools teach, and a significant number drop out before receiving a diploma. Beginning in the 1960s, American schools have tried to respond to these shortcomings through bilingual schools and multicultural programs.

Schools providing bilingual education and/or multicultural programs vary both in form and in degree. Some provide additional course content designed to match the cultures children bring to school, while others devote a significant portion of the curriculum to non-English content and to classes taught in a language other than English. The official goal of such programs is to provide children with an easier route to traditional American educational objectives. For example, children who do not speak English are first taught to read in their native language while simultaneously learning to speak English; once they have accomplished both of those ends, learning to read in English should be easier. Such programs have been geared primarily to Spanish-speaking children in the Northeast, Florida, and the Southwest, and to Asian children who have immigrated to the United States over the last twenty-five years (see Chapter 8). An unofficial goal of such programs, particularly with regard to Spanish-speaking populations, has been to maintain some of the elements of Spanish culture through the institutional support of the educational system. Although the programs and schools have been in place for a number of years, it is difficult to fully assess their success in achieving either goal. Factors beyond school curriculum also have a major impact on students' attitudes toward school achievement and toward mainstream American culture. Under the circumstances, it is difficult either to fully credit such programs with success or to fully blame them for failure. Nevertheless, they do reflect a fundamental change (if they remain permanently in place) in how open the educational institution is to other cultures.

Mainstreaming the Disabled American public education has theoretically been open to all since its inception, but not all students have had equal access. As we saw in Chapter 8, certain ethnic and racial groups have been singled out for special (and unequal treatment) at various times in American history. In addition, individual students thought to be incapable of handling the standard school curriculum because of mental or physical disabilities have either been denied access to public education or have been relegated to separate classes. In 1975, the United States Congress passed the Education of the Handicapped Act, which provided for a "free and appropriate public education" to all children with handicapping conditions.

Between 1977 (when the law was implemented) and 1988, the number of special education students rose from 3.7 to 4.4 million, primarily as a result of an increase in the number of students classified as "learning disabled." Learning disabled students now make up over 43 percent of all special education students; the other major categories include speech impaired students (21 percent), mentally retarded students (13 percent), and seriously emotionally disturbed students (8 percent). Special education students as a whole jumped from 1.8 percent of all students enrolled in the United States in 1977 to 4.8 percent in 1988 (National Center for Education Statistics, 1990a).

Traditionally, special education students were handled in segregated classes or facilities. In recent years, however, efforts have been made to **mainstream** these students, that is, to integrate them in normal public school classes whenever possible. One goal of mainstreaming is to undermine the stigma connected with segregated "special" classes. In addition, educators hope that integration will benefit disabled students educationally through their increased contact with a wider variety of students; they also hope that "normal" students will gain a wider perspective. Such efforts are of particular importance considering that close to half of all special education students have been labeled as "learning disabled" and that this label has been criticized as being subjectively applied (Carrier, 1986). The fact that poor and minority children are more likely to acquire this label lends credence to the argument that these children should not be isolated from the more general school curriculum and population.

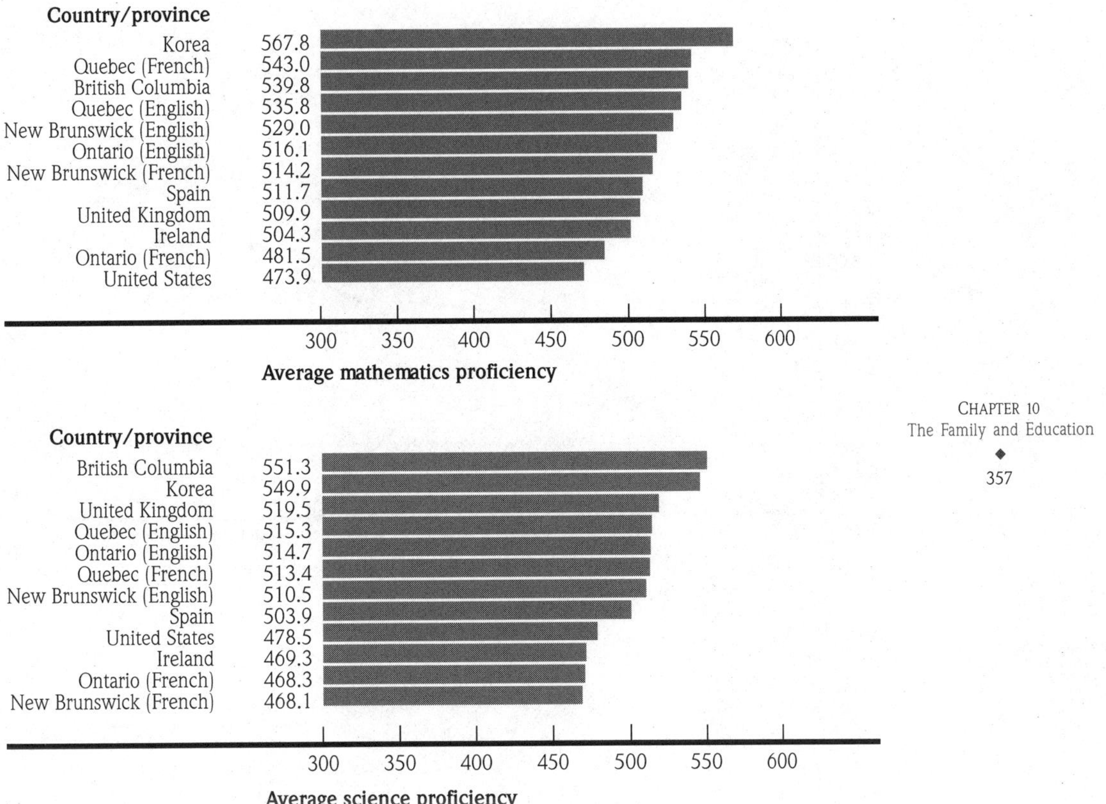

Figure 10.8 Mathematics and science proficiency at age 13 in selected countries/provinces, 1988.

School Effectiveness In April of 1983, The National Commission on Excellence in Education presented their conclusions as to the effectiveness of public education in the United States. They concluded that America's schools were failing in their mission to educate America's youth with the skills necessary for dealing with a technological society. They cited such facts as the 23 million American adults who are functionally illiterate (see Box 10.1), the drop of student scores on standardized achievement tests, and the poor showing of American students on tests relative to scores achieved by students in other industrialized societies. The Commission concluded that if such an educational system had been imposed on us by a foreign power, we would have viewed it as an act of war (National Commission on Excellence in Education, 1983).

Figure 10.8 shows some of the differences in student abilities in various nations noted by the Commission. In tests of mathematics and science skills among 13-year-old students conducted in the United States, Canada, Korea, Spain, Ireland, and the United Kingdom in 1988, American students scored at or close to the bottom on both. Considering that students from industrial powerhouse nations such as Japan and Germany were not included in this test, the results are all the more alarming. Part of this difference is explained by improvements in education achieved by other countries. It is interesting to note, for example, that teachers in Japan

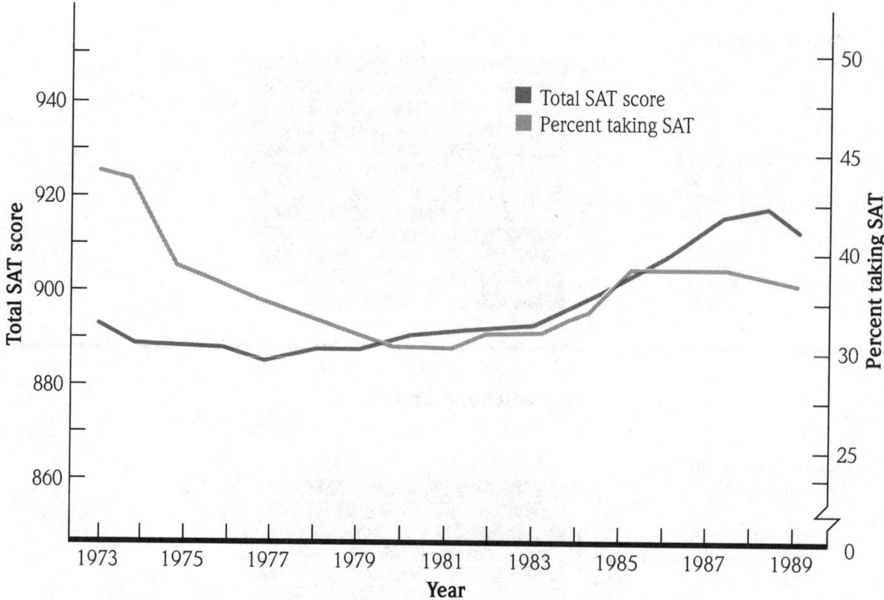

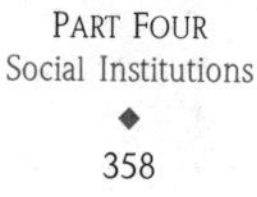

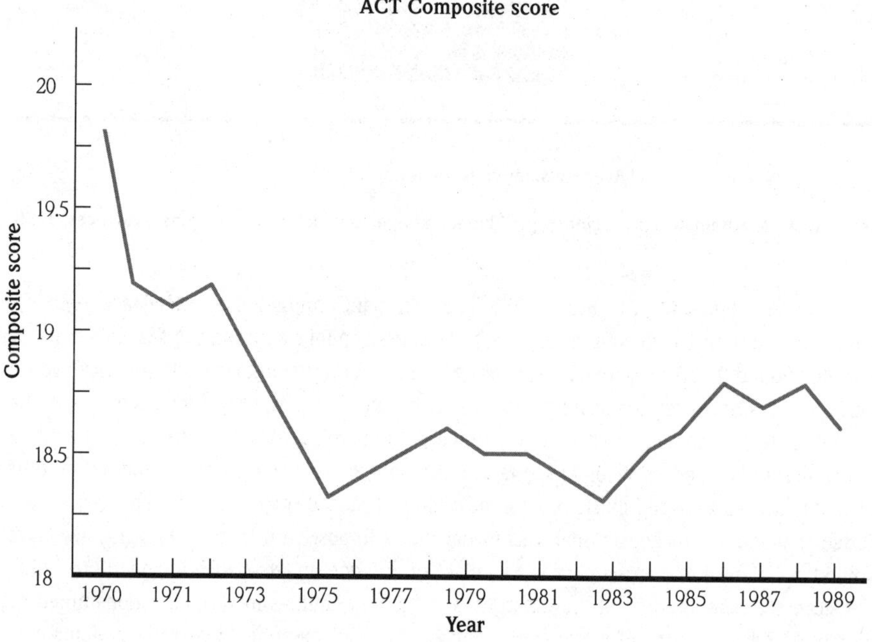

Figure 10.9 Changes in SAT and ACT scores by American high school graduates, 1973-1989.

are in the top 10 percent of all wage earners, whereas in the United States, teachers rate about average with regard to other occupations (Baker, 1987); such differences suggest the relative importance placed on education by the two countries. But part of the difference between

American students today and those of other countries appears to be the result of changes in American education over time as well. American students today may not be the equals of American students a generation ago.

Figure 10.9 shows some of the changes in test scores in recent years by American students on the two common college entrance examinations—the Scholastic Aptitude Test (SAT) and the American College Testing Program (ACT). Scores by college-bound American students were at their peak on both tests a generation ago; they dropped noticeably until leveling out in the late 1970s and early 1980s. It is often argued that these changes in scores are due primarily to changes in the numbers and kinds of American students who take them. If we look at the percentage of American high school graduates taking the SAT, however, we find that scores dropped from 1973 to 1980 while the percentage of graduates taking it remained about the same; the rise in that percentage since 1980 has been followed by a rise in test scores. Assuming that the higher percentage indicates that more poor and nonwhite graduates are taking the test, it cannot be argued that score changes are totally the result of there being increased numbers of lower class students with presumably poorer educational and test-taking skills (see Owen, 1985).

In response to charges of failure from critics, some public schools in the United States have turned to minimum-competency tests for high school graduates. The purpose of such tests is to require high school graduates to have acquired at least a minimum level of competency in certain skills. Students who fail that exam will be denied their diploma until they are able to pass it. The proponents of such tests argue that schools will no longer have incentives to give "social promotion" without course mastery, since a diploma is not guaranteed. Those who oppose such mandatory testing for diplomas argue that (a) tests are not always the best measure of one's knowledge but also measure other things (such as cultural background or test-taking skills), and (b) ethnic minorities in the United States will be unfairly affected and rejected by such tests, thereby blocking them from moving forward in their educational pursuits.

It is difficult to measure academic accomplishment by students or, when measured, to assess blame or credit for the results. As we saw earlier in this chapter, schools in the United States vary considerably from district to district. Poorly funded schools tend to be filled with lower class students who, on any measure, tend to exhibit poor academic accomplishments regardless of their racial or ethnic background. Beyond that, American students today may lack the levels of dedication of previous generations, and that change may be reflected in changing standards at public school institutions. It is difficult for a teacher to keep his or her attention on nouns or verbs if students are bringing violence or drug sales to the classroom.

Higher Education in the United States

Postsecondary education in the United States currently faces a declining population of 18-year-old high school graduates but benefits from a higher percentage of those graduates enrolling in college plus increasing numbers of older students returning to college after years in the labor market. More and more jobs require specific college degrees; also, a number of jobs have come to require more advanced degrees than they once did. This "degree inflation" (sometimes termed credentialism) occurs as the employment sector comes to evaluate individual qualifications more on the amount of training than on demonstrable skills and abilities (see Collins, 1979). In short, higher education in the United States is healthy, but the interest of sociologists in its structure and processes stems from its connection to the labor market. As higher education becomes increasingly the route to occupational advancement, sociologists want to know which Americans benefit from it and which do not. In this section, we will take a brief look at the structure of higher education and then examine who has access to it.

Higher Education: Public and Private There are currently over 2,000 4-year institutions of higher learning in the United States, along with almost 1,500 2-year institutions. Current enrollment stands at around 13 million students, and it is projected to remain at that level through the year 2000. (As recently as 1967, only half that number was enrolled.) Of that 13 million, approximately 75 percent are enrolled in public institutions; the remainder attend private institutions. Forty percent of that number are students over the age of 25 (U.S. Bureau of the Census, 1990b; National Center for Education Statistics, 1989a). Currently, 37 percent of high school graduates enroll in college within the next year (U.S. Bureau of the Census, 1990a), and that figure has been increasing gradually over the years as college degrees have become increasingly important for occupational success. In short, higher education is a major enterprise in the United States that touches many of our lives in one way or another.

Institutions of higher learning in the United States vary in more ways than their public or private status. Universities offer 4-year degrees but also provide graduate education in a variety of liberal arts and professional programs. Some universities are research oriented; that means that their primary aim is the production of new knowledge and technology through the efforts of their faculty, who are required to contribute toward that end. In such institutions, some faculty members become so engrossed in research that they rarely, if ever, see the inside of a classroom. Research is supported in part by the universities themselves but primarily through grants provided by outside agencies, often those of the federal government. These institutions are typically the homes of doctoral programs, through which new generations of researchers and faculty members are produced. By contrast, other universities and almost all 4-year colleges are teaching oriented. That means that research may or may not occur but that the primary aim of the institution is to provide a complete and stimulating educational environment for students.

Two-year colleges include a wide variety of private colleges; also, there is an ever-growing community college system in the United States through which low-cost education is provided. These schools provide for the enrollment of over 37 percent of American higher education students (U.S. Bureau of the Census, 1990b). Their low cost, availability, and open admissions policies make them the logical choice of many lower income Americans, who often lack the income and/or the educational skills to attend more prestigious (and more expensive) institutions. While community colleges were initially viewed as a stepping stone to 4-year colleges, the majority of their students do not take that step but enter the labor force after completing 2-year programs. According to some research, community college education is perceived as less valuable in the occupational marketplace (Monk-Turner, 1988).

Access to Higher Education While educational degrees provide the credentials essential for occupational advancement, it is also true that the *absence* of educational degrees effectively blocks occupational advancement. Education clearly has a pivotal role in modern American society. Therefore, an important sociological quest is to find who has access to the institutions that bestow these valued goods. In particular, sociologists are interested in the availability of education to those most in need of advancement—poor Americans, in general, and racial and ethnic minorities in particular.

The first step toward higher education is high school graduation. In 1988, over 82 percent of white Americans between 18 and 24 years old had graduated from high school. This figure reflects only a slight increase from 1968, when almost 78 percent of this group had diplomas in hand. By contrast, the 75 percent of black Americans in the same age group who had graduated from high school in 1988 represented a major improvement over the 58 percent who had graduated in 1968. Figures on Hispanic Americans have been collected only recently, but their 55 percent graduation rate in 1988 suggests a less successful experience with educational institutions (U.S. Bureau of the Census, 1990a). Figure 10.10 sheds more light on this experience by comparing these American ethnic groups of all ages in 1988 by the percentage of each group failing to finish high school. All the major Hispanic groups have higher failure rates than either white or black Americans; the largest Hispanic group—Mexican-Americans—have the most difficulty, over half of them failing to achieve a diploma. For many black and Hispanic Americans, therefore, access to higher education is cut off before they can even get to the admissions door.

Of all Americans who do receive high school diplomas, over 56 percent enroll in a college or university in the following year. If we break that figure down into its ethnic components, we find that 57.7 percent of white high school graduates continue their education immediately, as compared to 44.1 percent of black Americans and 45 percent of Hispanic Americans. They do not all enroll in the same schools, however. While black Americans make up 8.7 percent of all college students nationwide, they make up 8 percent in 4-year institutions as compared to 9.7 percent in 2-year institutions. For Hispanic Americans, those same figures are 3.6 and 7.9 percent (National Center for Education Statistics, 1990b). Unless they graduate and transfer, therefore, both black Americans and Hispanic Americans are less likely to achieve a 4-year college degree than white Americans.

Figure 10.10 also shows the differences in 1988 in the percentage of different American ethnic groups of all ages who had received a 4-year college degree. Black Americans graduated at a rate of only 54 percent of whites while Hispanics fared less well, graduating at 48 percent of the white rate. These figures, however, are for all Americans of all ages. If we consider

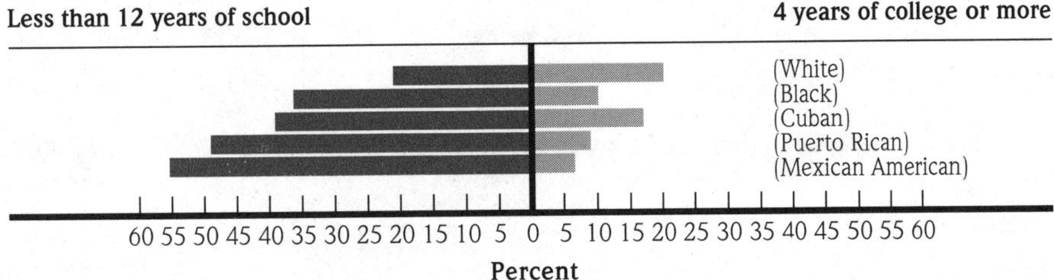

Figure 10.10 Percent of American population with less than twelve years of school and with four years or more of college by race and Hispanic origin, 1988. (Data from *Statistical Abstract of the United States, 1990.* U.S. Government Printing Office, 1990.)

the possibility that more black Americans and Hispanic Americans are of high school and college age than whites due to higher birth rates (and, for Hispanics, immigration), a clearer picture would emerge if we looked only at Americans between the ages of 20 and 29. This narrower focus would also eliminate any effects of past educational discrimination on these groups by removing older members from the sample. In looking at these figures for 1988, we find that 13.6 percent of whites have completed 4 years of college, compared to 7.1 percent of blacks and 5.8 percent of Hispanics. While blacks of all ages earn 4-year degrees at 54 percent of the white rate, these younger blacks achieve that end at only 52 percent of the white rate; for younger Hispanics, the rate drops to 43 percent from the 48 percent achieved by Hispanics of all ages. These results could indicate that lower percentages of whites are returning to college after the age of 29 than of blacks or Hispanics, but that is not true. Equal percentages of older students appear from all groups (National Center for Educational Statistics, 1989a). In short, younger Hispanics and blacks are doing *less* well in achieving 4-year degrees relative to young whites than their parents did in competition with older whites. The last ten years in American society represents a *downward* trend for black and Hispanics in higher education relative to white successes.

Lack of success with higher education by ethnic minorities in the United States has many causes. A good part of the problem is simply money. Ethnic stratification in the United States guarantees that ethnic minorities will be disproportionately poor (see Chapter 8). Money buys higher education directly but it also buys experiences and environments throughout life that add to success later in higher education. Table 10.1 contains SAT scores for different American ethnic groups in 1987-1988. Only Asian-Americans can outdistance white Americans, and they do so only in mathematics. High SAT scores, which open doors to colleges and scholarships, also indicate something about the familiarity that members of different groups have with the skills expected for college education. Individuals with lower scores will be in the situation of Murai in the reading following Chapter 8, facing frustration in the classroom because the course material is unfamiliar.

Ethnic minorities have less access to higher education because they have less income, but poorer whites face many of the same limitations. Hodgkinson (1986) found that wealthier

TABLE 10.1

SAT SCORES BY SELECTED AMERICAN ETHNIC GROUPS, 1987-1988

Ethnic Group	Verbal	Mathematics
White	445	490
Asian	408	522
Mexican-American	382	428
American Indian	393	435
Puerto Rican	355	402
Black	353	384

Source: Digest of Education Statistics, 1989. National Center for Education Statistics, U.S. Department of Education, Office of Educational Research and Improvement. U.S. Government Printing Office, 1989.

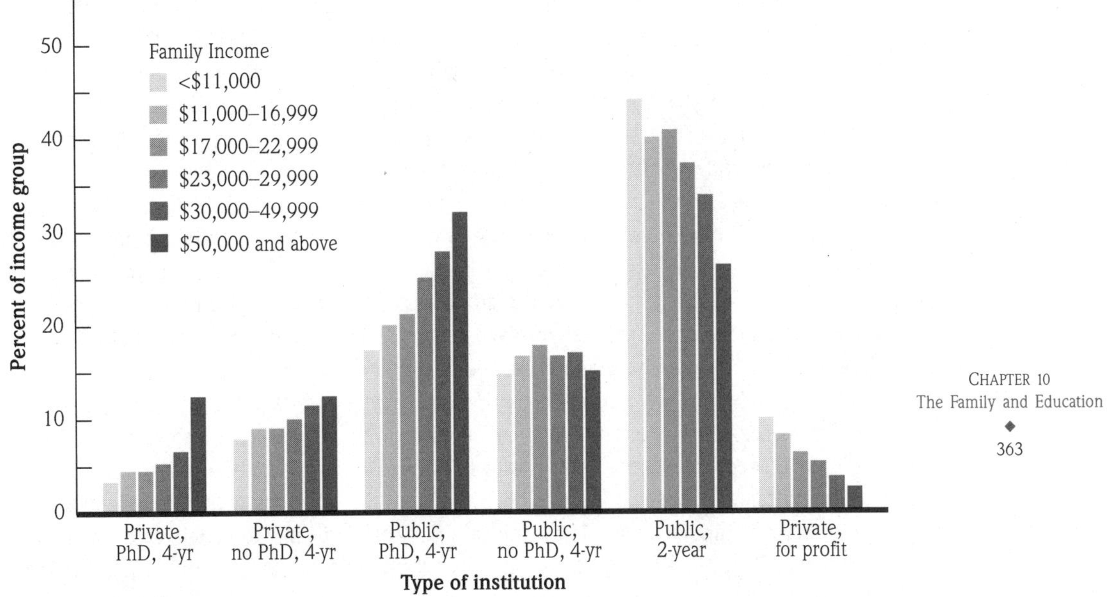

Figure 10.11 Percent of postsecondary students enrolled in different types of institutions by family income, fall 1987. (Data from *The Condition of Education, 1990: Volume Two—Postsecondary Education.* U.S. Department of Education. U.S. Government Printing Office, 1990.)

young people with only medium scholastic abilities were more likely to enroll in college than were lower-income young people with high scholastic ability. When poorer white students do enroll in college, they are likely to enroll in 2-year institutions, as are ethnic minority students. Figure 10.11 shows the distribution of American students in Fall, 1987, according to their family income level and the kind of institution they were enrolled in. While the public 2-year institutions enroll large numbers of all students, their specialization in lower-income students is obvious. As with ethnic minorities, poorer students in general are less likely to be in 4-year institutions or in institutions with graduate programs.

Education is not the only determinant of economic success in American society. Nevertheless, as education becomes increasingly formalized in the United States and as degrees become increasingly connected to routes of economic mobility, education becomes a significant institution in determining the quality of life for most of us. As the data presented above suggest, education may be available in the United States but it is not accessible equally to all. To the extent that poor Americans and minorities do not benefit from education, it can be argued that formalized education justifies the current system of social stratification by convincing those whom it fails that the responsibility for failure is theirs and not the institution's.

SUMMARY

As an ongoing form of social organization based on kin ties, the family is a universal social phenomenon, although its structure varies considerably from one culture to another. This variation includes differences in size, decision making power, lineage tracing, and number of spouses involved in the marriage relationship. Spouse selection is always restricted to some degree, so as to ensure selection from the appropriate group.

In the United States, the traditional family structure is undergoing change in response to other social changes that affect the institution. Important among these is changing roles for women in the wider society, which have led to important changes in women's roles within the family. Changes in the industrial world have also led to fewer (or no) children, higher divorce rates, increases in the number of people who choose not to marry, and a significant rise in the number of single-parent families, most headed by women. Such families, which are particularly common among some minority groups, are associated with lower income levels and fewer opportunities for the children involved. Family violence is also apparently on the increase in the forms of spouse abuse and child abuse.

The growth of the educational institution has occurred in large part as a response to the changing needs of an industrial economy. In addition to passing along knowledge and skills needed in that economy, schools also serve to provide social and cultural integration (through both intended and less obvious forms of socialization that accompany the school experience) and to "screen" the population in the allocation of certain people to certain areas of employment. Research on the educational institution indicates that the social class of incoming children is the strongest predictor of educational success, this relationship produced through a variety of influences, including teacher expectations, tracking, and cultural differences among incoming students. In addition, inequality of funding from one school district to another has provided fewer resources for poor children than for middle class children. Compensatory education and busing have both been tried in the last few decades to minimize the results of such inequality.

Besides public education in the United States, there are private educational institutions (some independent, some sponsored by religious organizations), which, on the whole, appear to be more effective in reaching their educational goals, as measured by standardized tests of student achievement. The public school system has responded to critics with new approaches, such as magnet schools (in which individual schools specialize in their curricula) and bilingual education (in response to the growing numbers of new immigrants who are not English speaking). Efforts have also been made to "mainstream" the disabled so as to end their segregation from the general school population.

Many other industrial nations appear to be surpassing American schools in their success, as measured by student achievement. Also, American students appear to be less well prepared than in the past, again as measured by standardized tests.

Higher education has become increasingly necessary because American occupations are demanding better training for entry-level positions. Growth in higher education, both public and private, has been considerable in response to this change; in particular, enrollment in 2-year institutions has increased. As with primary and secondary education, social class is the best predictor of student success in college. Non-white students compete even less effectively among their white college counterparts than they do in the earlier grades, and this gap in achievement in higher education appears to have been growing in recent years.

GLOSSARY

Bilineal descent A system of descent tracing that combines both the mother's and the father's line for descent purposes.

Busing The attempt to create school populations with diversity in race, ethnicity, and social class through the movement of students within and across school district lines.

Compensatory education Programs, such as Head Start, that aim to give children from "deprived" backgrounds the same skills that middle class children start school with.

Egalitarian family A family unit in which men and women share the decision making.

Endogamy Cultural norms that specify the group inside of which an individual must choose a mate.

Exogamy Cultural norms that specify the group outside of which an individual must choose a mate, those norms often coinciding with cultural rules regarding incest.

Extended family A family unit consisting of a number of nuclear families that live together as one unit.

Family of orientation The family into which an individual is born and which provides for the basic socialization for that individual.

Family of procreation The family with which an individual raises children.

Hidden curriculum Basic cultural values imparted indirectly to students through the school experience; generally acquired through the requirements of the role of student.

Homogamy Marriage between two people with the same basic social characteristics.

Magnet schools Secondary public schools that specialize in a particular area of the curriculum, providing students with focused instruction in classes with other students who share their interests.

Mainstreaming The integration of physically, mentally, or emotionally disabled students in normal public school classes.

Matriarchal family A family in which women have the authority and are responsible for most of the decision making.

Matrilineal descent The tracing of family lineage through the mother's family as opposed to the father's family.

Matrilocal residence The practice through which newly married individuals reside with the wife's family.

Monogamy A marriage between one man and one woman.

Neolocal residence The practice through which newly married individuals reside in a location apart from both husband's and wife's families.

Nuclear family A basic family unit consisting of only two spouses and their immature offspring.

Patriarchal family A family in which men have the authority and are responsible for most of the decision making.

Patrilineal descent The tracing of family lineage through the father's family as opposed to the mother's family.

Patrilocal residence The practice through which newly married individuals reside with the husband's family.

Polyandry The marriage of one woman with two or more men.

Polygyny The marriage of one man with two or more women.

Tracking The process of placing different students into different classes according to their measured ability.

SUPPLEMENTARY READINGS

Adams, Bert N. *The Family: A Sociological Interpretation* (4th ed.). New York: Harcourt Brace Jovanovich, 1986.
A good general introduction to the sociology of the family with a focus on family roles and the changes that have occurred in the modern American family.

Allan, Graham *Family Life: Domestic Rules and Social Organization.* New York: Basil Blackwell, 1985.
An introduction somewhat similar to the Adams work but with emphasis on the interactions between family structure and economic changes in American society.

Ballantine, Jeanne H. *The Sociology of Education* (2nd ed.). Englewood Cliffs, NJ: Prentice Hall, 1989.
A general overview of how sociologists approach the institution of education along with relevant research.

Coleman, James S., Thomas Hoffer, and Sally Kilgore *High School Achievement: Public, Catholic, and Private Schools Compared.* New York: Basic Books, 1982.
This study focuses on differences in students and differences in student achievement in public and private education in the United States, relating school structure and requirements to student outcomes.

Gelles, Richard J. *Family Violence* (2nd ed.). Newbury Park, CA: Sage, 1987.
An overview of a wide variety of family violence including a review of relevant current research.

Havemann, Ernest, and Marlene Lehtinen *Marriages and Families: New Problems, New Opportunities* (2nd ed.). Englewood Cliffs, NJ: Prentice Hall, 1990.

Hurn, Christopher *The Limits and Possibilities of Schooling* (2nd ed.). Boston: Allyn & Bacon, 1985.
Hurn focuses on the relations between education and the rest of society. In particular, he considers the ability of schools to bring about change in the social positions of students.

Jencks, Christopher, et al. *Inequality: A Reassessment of the Effect of Family and Schooling in America.* New York: Basic Books, 1972.
Somewhat technical but highly influential study of the effect of family on educational achievement and the effect of education on future income.

Kain, Edward L. *The Myth of Family Decline: Understanding Families in a World of Rapid Social Change.* Lexington, MA: Lexington Books, 1990.
An analysis of changes in family structure in response to social changes in other institutional sectors.

Kozol, Jonathan *Illiterate America.* Garden City, NY: Anchor Press, 1985.
In spite of its major emphasis on education, the United States contains more illiterate people than many other industrial societies. Kozol brings this issue to light along with analyses of its cause and suggestions for its alteration.

Weitzman, Lenore J. *The Divorce Revolution: The Unexpected Social and Economic Consequences for Women and Children.* New York: Free Press, 1985.
Weitzman offers a view of the results of divorce, particularly on women, as a result of no-fault divorce laws.

READING

Boy, You Better Learn How to Count Your Money

AARON THOMPSON

Aaron Thompson is an African-American sociologist who will soon receive his Ph.D. Such times of transition are often times to reflect. In the first section of this article, Thompson describes his early childhood, focusing on the importance of his family in influencing him to work hard and to be successful in a newly integrated school system that was often less than hospitable to him. "Little Aaron" responded to those influences and succeeded, but his story is not the story of all African-Americans in the American educational institution. In the second part of this article, Thompson examines some of the differences between white and black families, tracing those differences to the history of discrimination, particularly job discrimination, faced by blacks. His overriding message is clear: Social institutions are connected to one another in significant ways. Here we see how the economic institution affects the family which, in turn, influences the success of children in the educational institution.

The closer I come to the pinnacle of educational achievements, the Ph.D., the more I hear the remark, "Your family must really be proud of you." That remark always brings me pause because the word "pride" does not adequately accommodate the range of feelings that accompany my approach to the Ph.D. You see, this guy had extremely humble roots, and it is precisely the family institution that made my academic success possible.

Two words best describe my childhood days: poverty and discipline. Love played a major role in our household, but at times other things needed to come first, such as food. Being African American and living in southeastern Kentucky, the heart of Appalachia, did not provide for the grandest of living styles. Even though my father worked twelve hours a day in the coal mines, he earned only enough pay to supply staples for the table; our family also worked as tenant farmers to have enough vegetables for my mother to can for the winter and to provide a roof over our heads.

My father, Aaron Senior, was born in October 1901 in Clay County, Kentucky, with just enough African ancestry to be considered black. My mother, on the other hand, was a direct descendant of slaves and moved with her parents from the deep south at the age of 17. My father lived in an all-black coal mining camp, into which my mother and her family moved in January 1938. It wasn't long before the dark, beautiful lady met the tall, light-skinned, handsome man and married him. At age 37 this was my father's first marriage, and he was marrying a woman half his age. I remember asking him why he waited so long and why he chose to marry my mother. He answered, "How many eligible black women who are not your kin do you know?" I said, "Very few," and he replied, "There were even less then."

My father always seemed an extremely logical person; he was also quiet, reserved, and somewhat shy. I'm not sure my mother ever really appreciated these attributes in him. The one thing I remember the most about my father was his ability not to let anything or anyone

Copyright © 1992 by Aaron Thompson. Used by permission of the author.

antagonize him to the point of interrupting him in the pursuit of his goals. He often tried to pass this attitude along to his children. He would say to me, "Son, you will have opportunities that I never had. Many people, white and black alike, will tell you that you are no good and that education can never help you. Don't listen to them because soon they will not be able to keep you from getting an education like they did me. Just remember, when you do get that education, you'll never have to go in those coal mines and have them break your back. You can choose what you want to do, and then you can be a free man."

In early adolescence, I did not truly understand what he meant, but as a Ph.D. candidate in sociology, I believe that I can finally grasp what he was trying to tell me. My father lived through a time when freedom was something he dreamed his children might enjoy someday, because before the civil rights movement succeeded in changing the laws African Americans were considerably limited in educational opportunities, job opportunities, and much else in what is definitely a racist society. My father remained illiterate because he was not allowed to attend public schools in eastern Kentucky. The eight brothers and sisters who preceded me also had many barriers to attaining a higher level of education, and many did not exceed the level of my father.

In the early 1960s my brother, my sister, and I were integrated into the white public schools. Since there were so few blacks in our small community, we three seemed to get the brunt of the aggression that so many whites felt toward a race they considered inferior. Physical violence and constant verbal harassment caused many other blacks to forgo their education and opt for jobs in the coal mines at an early age. But my father remained constant in his advice to me: "It doesn't matter if they call you nigger; it doesn't matter if they hate you with all their might; they probably will never know how to be your friend anyway. What really matters is that you are the hope of this family to achieve something better than breaking your back in these coal mines. If it gets too unbearable, get one of them alone and beat the shit out of him, but don't you ever let them beat you by walking out on your education."

My father died at the age of 77, after I had finished my undergraduate degree. He was truly proud that I had made it beyond the coal mines. Now, my mother is another story. You see my mother's method for motivating me was vastly different from my father's. My father was a calm, wise man who conscientiously searched for the right things to say and do. My mother, on the other hand, had no verbal or physical reticence. I can still hear her voice, "Boy, I'm gonna get your ass when we get home." My mother was fire and brimstone, and now in her 70s, her ardor has cooled very little. Mother was the true academic in our house, with an eighth-grade education, which made her truly proud. An eighth-grade education represented quite an achievement in the 1930s to a southern black woman.

My mother would tell me stories of how blacks were treated in the "old South" and what to watch out for with the white man. She would say, "They don't want you to have an education because then you would have a way to get money; they definitely don't want you to have money." This attitude was part of my mother's philosophy, and it colored mine, since she started my childhood education early. In my preschool years she taught me writing, reading, and, most importantly, how to count money. By the time I was 4 years old, I could walk to the little country store to buy small amounts of groceries, and I knew to the penny how much change was due me. This feat was not so much a credit to my learning abilities but rather a credit to my mother's belief that people will take your money if you don't watch them closely.

When I was ready to start school, the representative from the three-room, all-black school came by our house to talk to my mother. I was 5 years old and listened closely to the conversation. The representative said, "Mrs. Thompson, we would like to start Aaron in school early because we think that in the next several years the schools will be integrated, and we want him to be able to have enough skills to perform with the little white children."

I vividly remember my mother's classic response to this person. She said, "Shit, my son can read and write better than you can and will someday make a whole lot more money than you. You don't need to get him ready, just don't hold him back." So I started school that year, and from then on "Little Aaron" could do no wrong academically in his mother's mind. If I ever had any problems, it was someone else's fault because she made sure I did my homework, attended school every day, and did everything the "No-Goods" down the hollow didn't do.

When I graduated from college, my mother was present and very happy. She often said, "He made it through school without our help. We had no money to help him, but he worked hard and made it. Reckon how much money he's going to make with this degree." My mother definitely appreciates my educational achievements, and the more she can empirically measure it monetarily, the prouder she becomes. She has always been my biggest cheerleader, and my achievements could not have happened without those cheers.

These circumstances help explain why I have trouble using adjectives like "proud" to express how my family truly felt about my education. I believe that most families are proud of their own, but it takes a truly special family to overcome such monumental social obstacles and continue to see hope for the future of their offspring. I look at the negative conditions that my brothers and sisters lived through, knowing how my mother and father wanted opportunities for them, and I understand the frustrations and sadness my folks experienced when the opportunities were not there and some did not achieve. But I lived in my own little world when my parents were giving me those motivational encouragements.

Many black families throughout the United States face seemingly insurmountable obstacles, and the future seems to be a shadow rather than a reality. Many live in conditions of poverty and many in one-parent households. But as my mother always said, "If you listen to the morals that are being taught to you, throw out the ones with hatred, and just learn how to count your money; then you will do okay in life." My mother seems to have the perfect answer to many of the problems of our society in this one statement. But as we all know, when many of us were growing up, there was very little money to count. Today, with both mother and father in the workplace, it is harder for the parents to give as much direct attention to the children as my mother showered on me. This issue could become problematic since socializing our children to understand that education is the important element to success usually starts in the family at an early age. Economics can be the culprit in the successes and failures of our children in this society. With education, success is not assured, but without education, failure seems virtually assured. Being poor, black, and Appalachian did not offer me great odds for success, but constant reminders from my parents that I was a good and valuable person helped me to see beyond my deterrents to the true importance of education. My parents, who could never provide me with monetary wealth, truly made me proud of them by giving me the gift of insight and an aspiration for achievement. Insight and knowledge are the paths for success in people of all races and classes. The family is where these paths begin.

* * *

Black Americans and their families have faced segregation, discrimination, and inequalities throughout the history of industrial America. When compared to whites, blacks were more often faced with discriminatory laws, individually and in the family structure. Under slave law, black women, black men, and their children were the property of slave owners. Family units under slavery did not exist for blacks. People could marry, but property could not, and slaves were considered property. Although many slaves defied this law and were married within their own community, slave owners could destroy this bond at any time they saw a need to do so by merely selling one or both of the partners to different slave owners.

After slavery, whites created formal and informal laws for the domination of black labor, a labor they once owned. These laws were enacted in the late 1800s. These laws, as much as anything else, fostered a division of labor by sexes in the black family, as well as a barrier to the existence of black families. For example, if a black woman married a black man, then the property she owned would go to him. Since the laws stated that property could only be owned by males, women did not relish the idea of working to give property to a male, so many decided to remain unmarried. If the black husband did not have a job, then the state could take his property. Of course, there was a good chance that the black male would not have a job, so many marriages did not take place. With such barriers to the intact black family, there was a greater chance for poverty in the black community. Black women faced a dismal prospect for survival above the poverty level because they needed to find a job that could support them and, in many cases, their children. The state made laws saying that if black parents could not afford to care for their children, then the children could be apprenticed out as free labor. When girls were apprenticed out, most went to white households as domestic help. When boys were apprenticed out, they went as outside manual laborers such as blacksmiths. These divisions reflected a labor market distinction between men and women as well as the distinctions made by outsiders about workers in the African-American community (Boris and Bardaglio, 1987).

Historically, there is a difference between the family structures of black Americans and white Americans. The work roles inside and outside the households seem to be one of the major differences. American plantation slavery did not make a distinction between the work performed by black men and that done by black women. Both worked in the fields and both worked within the household doing domestic labor. Gender role expectations were very different for black and white women. Black women were not seen as weak: in fact, they were seen as being able to work in the fields, have a baby in the evening, and cook breakfast the next day. White women, on the other hand, were viewed as weaker than black women, unable to deal with the normal stresses of the day-to-day activities of the plantation. A woman's duties centered around pleasing her husband, whatever his wishes might be.

In the late 1800s, when there was a need for more females in the work force, laws were loosened to accommodate this need. These laws had a significant effect on the white family but very little effect on the black family. Later, when black family members began moving into jobs in the industrial sector, they went into the paid labor market at a different pace and level than the white family. Black women most often were paid less than black men or white women, and they always maintained jobs in the paid labor market as servants, seamstresses, laundresses, and other domestic positions. Black women were not allowed to serve as salesclerks, cashiers, etc., jobs being filled by many white women in the labor market. In 1900, black women constituted approximately 20 percent of the female population and were 23 percent of the servant population. By 1920 they were 40 percent of the servant population. As the twentieth century got older, the proportion of black female servants continued to grow (Kessler-Harris, 1981).

Black men who had job skills in many cases could not practice those skills. For example, blacks were not allowed to join many of the trade unions in the South, where most blacks lived. The United Mine Workers Union in the South had many problems getting black members accepted as regular union members. Thus, in many cases blacks who worked as miners remained outside the union, with inadequate pay when compared to the white union members (Gutman, 1975). Black women therefore could not depend economically on their men. The black female came to see the black male as a liability to her and her children, which further broke down the black family structure.

Early in industrialization, a family wage system was enacted. A family wage system is one that is designed to pay enough money to the male to support him and his family. This system allowed the female to stay in the household and the male to stay in the paid labor force with the title of "head of household." Although laws stated that men were head of households, black men could not assert themselves as the undeniable heads of their households if they did not have the economic ability to back their claims. Thus, a pattern of households headed by single females started in the black family. Black men clearly did not and could not make a family wage for their family, and so black women continued to work. Since black men did not have the political or economic power structure on their side to help keep their families intact, the patriarchal father was not as dominant in the black household as he was in the white family.

White women and black women shared the burden of being forced to be in domestic positions both in the home and, when they had to get paying jobs, in the labor market. The difference here is that the family wage that the white women depended on was considerably higher than the one black women enjoyed or expected. Without a doubt, black women from the beginning have not been able to depend on a constant family wage; thus, they never have.

Black women have headed their households for most of this century and have been accustomed to accepting all kinds of jobs throughout their lives to support their families. Black men are still experiencing unemployment and underemployment; when they do get jobs, the majority of jobs are in the secondary labor market or in work that many white men would not accept. Black female-headed households comprise approximately 44 percent of all black families (U.S. Bureau of Census). This percentage is almost as high as the total black male paid labor force participation. Though it is harder for the black woman to obtain enough education to increase her chances in the labor market, she still surpasses the black male in gaining these necessary resources. With the black male's inability to break the barriers of institutional racism, the idea of a dual-career black family as the norm is not in the foreseeable future.

Women as a whole are getting more education, and dual-career marriages are the norm in America now instead of one-career marriages. Children expect to see their mothers as well as their fathers working outside the household and supporting the family in financial ways. This change will likely bring about a change in the structure of the family. Hopefully, more egalitarian conditions for males and females will emerge. However, the black family still is not at a level of stability capable of dealing with these structural changes. Black women are not experiencing the same level of new-found freedom in the job market or the family that white women do. The black men are still underemployed or unemployed. Until black workers reach a point in our society where they are operating on the same footing as the white workers (equal education, equal employment, equal pay), blacks will be hard pressed to move into the twenty-first century with more of an egalitarian balance in the family and work.

In conclusion, labor market participation, low wages for both sexes, and discriminatory laws have affected the black family structure, producing what many percieve as problems: in particular, the large number of households headed by a female, with no husband present. Although I have no instant solutions to any problems suggested in this paper, as a sociologist I do believe there are some directions we can follow, and they can be stated in three simple steps. The family is the primary institution for socialization in our society, and this is where we should start looking for answers and providing solutions: (1) teaching our children the importance of education for the sake of knowledge as well as for economic survival; (2) setting forth a pattern of appreciating cultural and economic diversity (understanding that race and class are social mechanisms for prejudice and discrimination); and (3) teaching our children to look beyond the limitations that society might have placed on them and build on steps one and two.

References

Boris, Eileen and Peter Bardaglio. 1987. "Gender, Race, and Class." Pp. 132-152 in *Families and Work*, edited by Naomi Gerstel and Harriet E. Gross. Philadelphia: Temple University Press.

Gutman, Herbert G. 1975. *Work, Culture & Society*. New York: Vintage.

Kessler-Harris, Alice. 1981. *Women Have Always Worked.* Old Westbury, New York: The Feminist Press.

Discussion Questions

1. Thompson argues that sex role expectations have traditionally been different for white and black Americans. How are these expectations connected to economic and family roles in both the white and black family?
2. Single-parent families make up a greater proportion of black families than of white families. How does Thompson explain this difference?
3. Thompson describes the economic and social forces that have created a lack of stability within the black family. Did his family reflect this lack of stability? Why or why not?

READING

Economic Equality After Divorce: "Equal Rights" or Special Benefits?[1]

SUSAN MOLLER OKIN

No-fault divorce in the United States was designed to eliminate some of the hypocrisy of earlier laws, but as some observers (notably Lenore Weitzman) have pointed out, no-fault divorce commonly leaves women and young children poverty stricken. The reason for this, which Okin explores in this reading, is the tacit agreement in most American marriages that the man's career will come first and that the woman will take over most home and nurturing duties (often to the detriment of her own career). Consequently, divorce leaves men with enhanced earning power and women with half-finished education and little work experience. Marriage assets are divided in half according to no-fault laws, but how do you divide education and earning power? Susan Okin has some suggestions.

Family law has become highly controversial in the last two decades. Child custody, child and spouse abuse, and surrogate motherhood are the issues most likely to capture the attention of the media. But these are not the only troubling issues. The differences in economic impact of divorce upon men, women, and children have also become increasingly visible.

By the late 1980s half of all single parents in the United States lived below the poverty line, and 70 percent of these poor families were headed by divorced or separated women. The feminization of poverty has proceeded at such a pace that, if present trends continue, all of those below the poverty line in the year 2000 will be women and children. Even for many who are not poor by official standards, the sudden drop in standard of living that often follows separation or divorce is extremely disruptive. Family homes are often ordered sold upon divorce, so that there can be an immediate division of the couple's assets. Not only wives but children too are subjected to undue physical and economic dislocation, at the very time they are likely to be psychologically vulnerable. Ex-wives with few recognized skills and little experience of wage work are unrealistically expected to be able to support themselves and their children within a few years. And what is often the family's most valuable asset—the man's future earning power—is entirely ignored when the "family property" is divided up. Divorce, because it disrupts the lives of women and children, can have shock effects lasting for the rest of their lives.

This problem has raised controversy among feminists, as well as between feminists and non-feminists. Some claim that in order for divorce settlements to be fair, and to save divorcing women and their children from poverty, women need special treatment, not just equal rights. Treating divorcing women just the same as men, they claim, is not a solution; rather, it is a large part of the problem. Because of women's special capacities and their customary role as mothers, such critics of current law argue, alimony for women is justified—as is maternal preference in custody disputes.

Others, arguing for equal treatment, claim that such laws reaffirm the very roles and assumptions that have caused so many problems for women in the first place. The law should be

[1] Thanks to Jean Cohen and Deborah Rhode for helpful comments on an earlier draft of this article.

Reprinted by permission of *Dissent* magazine and the author.

sex blind. Later I will argue that, on this issue, equal treatment is not a problem. Women's difficulties after divorce can be greatly alleviated without laws that are gender-specific or protective of women only. What is needed are laws that protect those of either sex who have forgone economic advancement because they have been wholly or primarily responsible for the unpaid work of their families. The (rare) male homemaker or the highly involved father who scales back his work because of nurturing responsibilities deserves the same fair treatment as the women who, far more often, undertake these roles.

Part of the controversy about the economic aftermath of divorce concerns facts and causes. Part is about solutions. These latter disagreements are both about the likely effectiveness of changes in the laws themselves or in the ways they are applied, and also about what is fair in the economic outcomes of divorce.

Has the economic situation of women and children substantially deteriorated since the enactment of no-fault divorce, now at least an option in all fifty states? If so, is there a causal connection between no-fault divorce and any deterioration that has occurred? Might further reform of the divorce laws alleviate the problem of maternal and child impoverishment in the United States? What is the problem—the laws themselves, the ways they are applied in the courts, or the larger socioeconomic inequality of women and those who depend on them? Harvard sociologist Lenore Weitzman, in her influential book *The Divorce Revolution* (New York: The Free Press, 1985), answered "yes" to the first three questions and "all three" to the last one.

Weitzman argues that, with no-fault divorce, women lost the considerable bargaining power they often had either as the "innocent" or the more reluctant party in fault-based divorces. Having lost their power to prevent or delay an unwanted divorce by holding out for economic equity, they are now less frequently being awarded the family home and are unlikely to be awarded more than short-term alimony, if any. And since in 90 percent of divorces, children live with their mothers, one can see why, as Weitzman puts it, "for most women and children, divorce means precipitous downward mobility—both economically and socially." Weitzman's most striking finding is that, in the year after divorce, the standard of living of the ex-wife's household (adjusted for need) falls by 73 percent, whereas that of the ex-husband rises by 42 percent.

Critics have charged that Weitzman overgeneralizes from California, an atypical state; that she focuses too much on the minority of divorces in which there is a home owned and in which spousal support is awarded; and that the disparity in standards of living she finds is not borne out by her own data and is far greater than that found in other studies. They also argue that because, in many states, the shift to no-fault coincides with other changes in divorce laws—those having to do with the distribution of property and alimony—it is almost impossible to isolate the effects of no-fault. However, later studies, both in other states—Vermont and Connecticut, for example—and of national samples, have also found large disparities in economic well-being between men and women after divorce. And they confirm that under no-fault regimes these disparities have at least somewhat increased.

Some of Weitzman's critics seem far removed from the actualities of contemporary family life. One study[2] assumes that a household consisting of one parent and two small children will require less income to achieve a given standard of living than a household with two parents and two small children. But, in making this assumption, the study pays no attention to how the children are cared for while the income is earned! This is a clear case of the simultaneous assumption and neglect of "women's work" that is prevalent in many branches of scholarship. For the two-parent family, unlike the one-parent, has the option of allowing one parent to stay home with the children "for free" while the other goes out to paid work, or of having each work different shifts or part-time, thereby saving considerable child-care expenses. Anyone who has ever paid

[2] Saul D. Hoffman and Greg Duncan, "What *Are* the Economic Consequences of Divorce?" *Demography* 25:4, November 1988.

for child care of reasonable quality in order to earn an income (at the very least, $5,000 per child per year in a regulated setting) will immediately perceive this oversight in the study. Those surprised by or skeptical of Weitzman's findings would do well not to "forget" women's unpaid work, and to keep in mind the extent to which the traditional division of labor still prevails in most marriages. Weitzman's findings are far less surprising than is the fact that people have been so surprised by them.

Regardless of the disagreements about the extent and causes of divergent standards of living after divorce, there is little doubt that, on average, men fare significantly better than do both women and the almost 90 percent of children who are, usually by mutual consent, in the mothers' custody. The situation has become even worse in the last two decades. Sometimes the blame is laid on feminists and their drive for equal rights. It is said they spearheaded the no-fault "revolution" and argued for the equal, gender-blind treatment of divorce that has allegedly caused the problems. But such charges distort history. As the authors of several chapters in Stephen Sugarman's new volume, *Divorce Reform at the Crossroads* (New Haven: Yale University Press, 1990), make clear, it was not feminists who initiated or fought for no-fault divorce. Neither did they claim that it would improve women's post-divorce situations. No-fault divorce, rather, was promoted primarily by law reformers who wanted to eradicate the fraud and hypocrisy often present in fault-based divorce and by advocates for men who considered themselves abused by unfair awards of alimony. As Deborah Rhode and Martha Minow point out: "In part, the absence of "women's concerns from the debate reflected the absence of women." So it is ironic that the worsened situation of women after divorce should now be blamed on feminists.

What is happening to women and children after divorce is clearly unfair. But what would be fair, and how might it be achieved? Change must begin with the recognition that *future earning power* is the principal asset of most marriages. Fewer than 50 percent of divorcing couples have any tangible assets at all, once debt is taken into account. Moreover, in Weitzman's sample of divorces, the average assets were worth what the husband earned in ten months. Given this, the solution aimed at by much divorce reform so far—a "clean break" as soon as possible after division of the family's tangible assets—is simply inconsistent with fairness. Future earning power, as a crucial asset of a marriage, must be fairly distributed in the event of divorce. Because of the typical division of labor in the family, the husband has usually developed his earning capacity to a far greater extent than the wife. But divorce settlements all too seldom take account of this central disparity. Weitzman reports the responses of forty-four California judges to the following hypothetical case: A nurse, married at eighteen, and her doctor husband are divorcing, eleven years later. She supported them for ten of these years, while he finished college and his medical training. They have few material assets and no children, but at the time of the divorce the doctor is earning a substantial income. The nurse now wants to go to medical school. The judges were asked whether they thought it was fair to require her former husband to support her while she did so. Only 31 percent said they would require such support. The great majority maintained that it would be unfair to thus encumber him, since she was capable of supporting herself.

What explains this approval of such blatant injustice? In part, women's increased participation in the paid labor force has encouraged the assumption that they can adequately provide for themselves and their families. It is often claimed that they therefore need not receive spousal support, regardless of the division of labor within a marriage. This belief is ill-founded in most cases, and especially when a couple has had children. Despite the considerable increases in women's wage labor, fewer than 30 percent of wives work full-time outside the home, and the average wife who works for pay (full- or part-time) earns 42 percent as much as the average full-time working husband. This is partly due to a sex-segregated labor market that discriminates against women, but it is also directly tied to the typical marital division of responsibilities. Women's greater domestic contribution has been estimated to account for 70 percent of the earnings differential between husbands and wives.

Few husbands substantially alter their wage working hours after the birth of a child, whereas wives' employment or education is in the vast majority of cases greatly affected. Few husbands, but many wives, choose occupations or jobs on the basis of location or flexibility of hours, in order to accommodate the needs of children. Few husbands are willing to move so that their wives can pursue new work opportunities, whereas wives do this routinely. (In some states, until recently, they could be divorced on the grounds of desertion if they did not!) As well as providing support while he trains for a more prestigious career, as in the above case, a wife often contributes even more directly to her husband's work. Sometimes she works without pay for his business or practice, or contributes to his commercial networks or his scholarly or creative achievements. This is seldom publicly acknowledged, except sometimes in the prefaces of books.

Partly in acknowledgement of the ways in which wives contribute to the career advancement of their husbands, the courts in some states have recently begun to treat professional degrees and qualifications as marital property. Where one spouse has significantly helped the other to achieve such qualifications, in the expectation that the resulting income would be shared by the family as a whole, it seems only reasonable for courts to insist that, in the event of divorce, the contributing spouse be adequately compensated. How this should best be done is likely to depend on the circumstances. In some cases, what will most benefit the relatively untrained spouse is to be supported through an equivalent training. Where this is inappropriate or not desired, it seems fair that such past contribution be taken into account in determining spousal support.

Some commentators have expressed concern that treating education and training as marital assets may hurt many divorcing *women* who have completed their education or retrained after raising children, and will then be perceived as being indebted to their husbands. Given the division of labor in most marriages, this would be unjust. The most recent research suggests that even when wives are full-time wage workers or students, they continue to perform most of the family's housekeeping and nurturing tasks. It would scarcely be fair for a wife who had trained as a teacher after raising her children, and had meanwhile continued to assume most of the household responsibilities, to owe her higher-earning husband for her training, should they divorce. Career assets should be perceived as marital assets only, it seems, when the non-training partner can show that his or her potential for work advancement has been sacrificed in contributing to that training.

One problem with the focus on degrees and professional qualifications is that it can benefit only a minority of ex-wives and children—and not necessarily those most badly affected economically by divorce. The larger issue, cutting across class lines, concerns not just professional training but future earning potential and employment benefits in general. About this moral issue of what is a fair distribution of income after marital breakup, there is also disagreement. As the doctor and nurse case demonstrates, many of those who exert considerable power over the outcome of divorce think that each ex-spouse should become self-sufficient as soon as possible, leaving the other unencumbered by long-term financial responsibilities. But is this fair? Surely not. Marriage involves a commitment to the collective well-being, and given our gendered patterns of socialization, it is hardly surprising that many couples still choose to divide up the earning and nurturing responsibilities of a family unevenly. Even within a marriage, though, this does not dictate that the nurturing spouse must be economically dependent on the wage-earning spouse. I have recently argued in *Justice, Gender, and the Family* (New York: Basic Books, 1990), that such dependence should be minimized by legally mandated sharing of the earner's paycheck. It is far more harmful, though, in the event of a divorce, for the spouse who has had (usually) his earning power at worst unaffected and in most cases enhanced by the marriage to be allowed to walk away with this enhanced capacity. Arrangements after divorce should aim to equalize the standards of living of both postdivorce households.

How long should such equalization continue? That depends on the length as well as the practices of marriage. It should certainly last as long as children are dependent and until the previously dependent spouse is educated or trained to support her- or himself. In the case of long-term marriages, it should continue permanently. Most displaced homemakers aged forty-five or more have very little chance of earning more than a small fraction of what their ex-spouses can earn. While placing considerably more demands on some divorcing men than is now customary, such arrangements seem eminently fair. There can be no good reason that one should suffer vastly more economically than the other from the breakup of a relationship whose uneven division of labor was mutually agreed on. From now on, those who wish to avoid or at least minimize such possible future responsibilities can do so by practicing a division of labor within marriage in which each shares equally in wage work and nurturing work.

The legal and policy changes I have suggested here can all be achieved within the equal rights framework. They do not require special rights for women, even though in the vast majority of cases women would be those who benefit from them. Laws written in these terms would be fair in two senses: they would protect from economic vulnerability those who now actually need such protection (almost all women), and they would not discriminate against or leave unprotected those men who do now or wish to break with the prevalent sex roles.

To what extent can changes in divorce law help to alleviate the economic distress experienced by so many women and children after divorce? Most students of the problem agree that changes in family law alone cannot completely solve it. The education of family court judges will have to play a major role. And one of the biggest remaining problems is that of enforcement. The 1984 Child Support Amendments and 1988 Family Support Act require the states to enforce spousal and child support laws more stringently. Automatic withholding from paychecks has helped to some extent, but levels of nonpayment are still intolerably high. More than half of divorced men fail to meet the (inadequate) payments asked of them. And, except in Wisconsin, states have failed to address the problem of family support when the earnings of both ex-spouses are inadequate to keep the two resulting households out of poverty. Some argue that a social insurance scheme akin to Social Security should be available to supplement income after divorce when the parties are not making enough to provide adequately for both postdivorce households.

It is probably true that the economic effects of divorce cannot be wholly alleviated without a complete solution to women's generally disadvantaged position in the economy. This will come about only if and when we radically revalue the presently unpaid domestic contributions of women. It will come about only if and when we insist that workplaces take into account real-life concerns, such as parenting and the care of elderly parents. For now, however, reforming the terms of divorce and insisting on their enforcement are good places to begin. This action might also eventually result in the reallocation of responsibilities within marriage.

Discussion Questions

1. Okin poses a hypothetical question to judges about a divorce between a doctor and nurse, the latter having sacrificed to put her husband through medical school. After the divorce, the wife wants to go to medical school. Should the ex-husband support her? Why or why not?
2. Okin argues that "career assets" be part of a divorce settlement when one partner can show that his or her work advancement potential has been harmed through sacrifice for the spouse's career. What problems of measurement of such assets might arise?

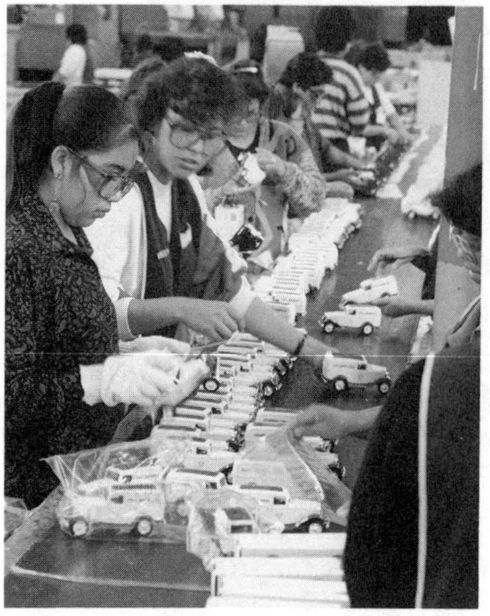

CHAPTER 11 THE ECONOMY, THE POLITICAL INSTITUTION, AND RELIGION

When we compare the modern industrial society with agricultural and less complex societies, the family is one of the most recognizable holdovers, in spite of the many changes it has experienced in the name of progress. As we've seen, it is no longer feasible to rely on our kin for our survival; it is not that the kin are necessarily unwilling but that the institutional changes in society serve to thwart the best intentions in the world. In looking only at the development of the educational institution (as we did in the previous chapter), knowledge transmission and much of basic socialization has clearly moved from stories at grandfather's knee to mass-produced, culturally approved "knowledge" served up in highly structured classroom situations. But two institutions cannot be viewed in isolation. As we already saw, the relationship between the family and education is firmly connected to other major institutions in society. We cannot understand the educational institution, for example, without also understanding the politics that control its operation, the economy into which its graduates leap (or are pushed), or the religions that sometimes feel compelled to offer their own versions of the truth. This chapter will explore three other major institutions in society in order to complete the story begun in Chapter 10. If the family and education represent the first two major institutions we confront in the life cycle, the economy, the political institution, and religion shape our experiences as adults.

THE ECONOMY

Societies satisfy many basic needs of their members, but perhaps the most basic need is survival. If that need is not met, little else matters. Some sort of coordinated system is necessary to create and distribute the essential means of survival so that members of society can live long enough to accomplish other ends. As we saw in Chapter 9, hunting and gathering societies typically have a fairly loose (although still coordinated) system. At the other extreme, industrial societies employ a complex system that requires elaborate forms of coordination and extreme specialization of tasks (a high division of labor). If farmers, truck drivers, and grocers unknown to you don't do their jobs, you will find yourself without food. Sociologists refer to this complex form of coordination as the economic system. An **economic system** is the organization of social activities that produces and distributes goods and services within and between societies. All individuals in an industrial society have some connection to this institutional sector of activity, whether they live off occupational income, inherited wealth, or public assistance. Sociologists are interested in the different kinds of economic systems and how individual activities and social interactions are affected by them.

The economic system is typically divided into three sectors, to specify differences in goods and services produced. The **primary sector** of the economy refers to activities associated with the production of raw materials. These would include farming, fishing, mining, harvesting timber, and so on. The **secondary sector** of the economy refers to manufacturing activities that transform these raw materials into usable goods, such as food, clothing, fuel, lumber, machines, and all consumer goods. The **tertiary sector** refers to the production and distribution of services—such activities as law making, house cleaning, teaching, running a grocery store, and frying potatoes at the local fast-food outlet.

All three sectors must be active and coordinated with one another for the economic system to function properly, but coordination can become very complex. When economic systems operate between societies (international trade), it becomes possible for one society to engage in largely primary sector activities while other societies emphasize secondary or tertiary sector activities. Changes in such relationships affect the overall wealth of societies, and consequently the quality of individual life within a society as people respond to changes in the economic system.

Types of Economic Systems

While all economic systems produce and distribute goods and services, there are different ways of organizing the system. Different systems create differences in such basic areas as who does what job; how decisions are made as to what will be produced; and how benefits of the system are distributed to members of society. An important variable that affects all these areas is the degree to which a given society's political institution directs the economic system. Economic systems with lower levels of political direction are **capitalist economies**, which are characterized by private ownership of property and a form of coordination based on a market system of exchange; in the market system, the value of goods and services is determined by supply and demand. When economic systems are subject to high levels of political direction, they are referred to as **socialist economies**. In these economies property is owned by the state, and the state coordinates the production and distribution of goods and services. A **mixed economy** represents a compromise between capitalist and socialist types: some property is privately owned and some is controlled by the state. The privately owned property is coordinated through a market system in the capitalist mode, while the state-owned property is managed by the state as in the socialist mode. As we look at each type of economic system in more detail, it will become apparent that the structure of a society's economic system affects almost every aspect of life for the people who live and work within it.

Capitalism The cornerstone of capitalism is capital. Capital is any kind of wealth or property that can become productive as income. A factory, for example, is capital since it can earn income for its owner through its products. Money in the bank is also capital in that it draws income through interest. It draws that income, of course, because it can be used elsewhere in the economy (through the bank's investment) to create other income (it might be borrowed by someone to start a business, for example). In this sense, all capital is interchangeable, since any form of it can be turned into any other form of it. The hallmark of capitalism is that capital is privately owned by individual members of society. Its value to those individuals is determined by the market, which coordinates its exchange.

The free market is the system of exchange through which the value of property is determined. As goods and services are exchanged, supply and demand will regulate their values. Supply refers to the amount of a given good or service available to those who might want it. Demand refers to the number of people who desire that good or service. If you are trying to sell shoes to an already well-shod population, you will probably find few buyers. Your response may be to lower prices on your shoes enough so that potential buyers might be induced to purchase a pair anyway, perhaps to save for later when their current footwear wears out. Full supply coupled with low demand acts to lower prices (or value) of the goods or services in question.

At the other extreme, if you have the only supply of shoes in a market of desperate barefoot consumers, you will be free to raise prices on your goods considerably since demand is high while supply is short. But if you raise prices beyond the ability of these consumers to pay, they will go without your product, even though they desire it. In a free market, the price (or value) of your product will level off at a point low enough where the shoes still sell but high enough so that they do not all sell out in the first hour of business. As other manufacturers notice your success, they will turn to shoe production themselves, hoping to cash in on this bonanza. As more of them do so, the supply of shoes will rise and slowly the price will begin to drop. This is how supply and demand determine value in an ever-changing balance in a market economy.

The driving force in capitalism is the motivation of individuals to use their capital in order to increase their wealth. The increase created through productive capital is called profit. The market's mechanisms offer the incentive to invest capital toward this end. An early observer of this economic system was Adam Smith (1723-1790) who published an explanation of capitalism in 1776 called *The Wealth of Nations*. He argued that the market system through which capitalism operated would balance itself naturally and encourage investors to fill demand in response to rising prices. In this way, he argued, all necessary goods and services would automatically be produced. Since the market was subject to a natural balance, he pointed out, it was important that no outside force (such as government) should interfere; any such interference would artificially force investors to (for example) stop creating a product if a government prevented the product's prices from rising even though demand for the product was high. The principle of no government interference in the market is referred to as *laissez faire*.

The market's response to the forces of supply and demand sometimes causes it to respond inadequately to other social concerns. For example, high prices in the wake of low supply and high demand often puts prices for goods or services above the ability to pay of many individuals. When a society prices medical care by that means, the free market determines that the rich will remain healthy and live while the poor will be ill and die. The high prices encourage great advancements in medicine but make its benefits less available throughout society (see Box 11.1). The free market therefore ensures that there will always be goods and services available but at a cost too high for many.

A second problem of the free market involves business cycles. The fluctuations of supply and demand do not always fall into a state of equilibrium instantly. If demand falls too far for too long, investors will stop producing. Factories will close, which creates unemployment, which gives consumers less money to spend, which lowers demand yet further, which cuts down further on production, and so on. Such downturns in the business cycles are recessions or depressions, depending upon their degree and length. During such downturns, many investors lose their wealth and many members of society who depend on their labor for subsistence lose their income through unemployment. When the cycle ends and a business upturn occurs, those investors who withstood the downturn (usually the holders of relatively large amounts of capital) return to increasing their wealth through creating profit, and laborers return to the newly created jobs caused by expanding production. In short, the supply and demand business cycle often creates considerable misery in society while it is sorting itself out.

There are no economic systems today that could be characterized as purely capitalist. No industrial society is willing to follow Adam Smith's directions entirely by keeping government

BOX 11.1

FREE TRADE AND HEALTH CARE IN CANADA

In 1988 the Conservative party in Canada won a landslide victory, and a free trade agreement with the United States became law. The Canadian government believed the free trade agreement would help Canada in three areas. The agreement would: (1) increase the market for Canadian goods in the United States; (2) create new jobs in the Canadian economy; and (3) stem the growing tide of American economic protectionism. However, Canadians were asking whether their government could enter into a free trade agreement and still maintain existing social and economic programs that are distinct from American systems. One of the programs Canadians were particulary interested in protecting was public health care.

The Canadian medical system is organized around five basic principles: (1) *universality*—the system must cover *everyone*; (2) *accessibility*—everyone must have equal access to health care; (3) *comprehensiveness*—health care services must include all basic health and hospital services; (4) *portability*—people travelling or moving to another province must be able to take their health care coverage with them; (5) *public administration*—the system must be run on a *nonprofit* basis by a public agency of government.

Health care coverage in the United States does not follow such principles, and for the most part, American health care is privately funded. While the Canadian system guarantees universality, it has been estimated that 60 percent of America's poor are ineligible for medical services (Guest, 1988). In light of such differences, Canadians pride themselves on their system. However, the free trade agreement has the potential to change that system. American doctors receive notably higher fees, and Canadians worry that if the financial opportunities for their doctors are better in the United States, they may move. With free trade, there would be little to stop them.

hands off the economy and away from productive ownership. Nevertheless, the United States comes close to this form, with a major part of its industrial wealth in private hands. Even in this society, however, government does run a number of enterprises, including the postal service, the military, education, various social services, and so on, employing approximately 15 percent of the labor force; it also interferes greatly in business cycles through its control of interest rates and tax rates, in an effort to manipulate the wide swings that would otherwise take place.

Socialism Socialist economic systems place productive capacity in the hands of the government. This means that production of all major goods and services will be state owned and controlled; individual members of society will work for the state in some capacity, either through the administration of this elaborate system or through direct labor within it. The driving force in a socialist economy is intended to be the welfare of society's members rather than the search for profits. Decisions as to what goods and how much of them should be produced, as well as the prices of products, are made by government administrators rather than by market forces. Thus, demand cannot create supply unless the government approves. If prices are not allowed to rise as demand rises, consumers will continue to buy, supply will quickly run out, and shortages will occur. A typical government response in such a situation would be to introduce rationing

The socialist economy of the Soviet Union simply failed to deliver to Soviet citizens the goods and services to be expected from a rich and powerful nation. Russians spent hours almost every day in lines to buy food and clothes, often goods that were shoddy and unfashionable—wardrobes designed by a commissar.

of the good or service in low supply until government directives can create more of it. While capitalism deprives low-income members of society of some goods and services through price rises when shortages start to occur, socialism spreads that deprivation around more easily. Also, shortages in supply are more resistant to government directives than they are to market forces, which generate investment in that area of the economy. Shortages can thus become a common problem in socialist economic systems.

As with capitalism, there are no perfect examples of socialist economic systems in societies around the world, but countries such as the Soviet Union, Cuba, and China have represented efforts to achieve this ideal. Recent changes in the Soviet Union's political structure, including its name change to the Commonwealth of Independent States, have been coupled with a move toward a market economy, which suggests that the country will have more of a market economy in the future. In socialist societies, most enterprises are state run. In general, socialist economic systems have been less successful than capitalist systems at achieving high levels of productivity. The huge governmental bureaucracies required to make economic decisions have been unsuccessful at responding efficiently to the economic needs of socialist societies, and the result has been less production and more shortages.

Mixed Economies Mixed economies represent the middle ground between the two economic systems just discussed. In mixed economies, the government wields considerable economic power, particularly with regard to major industries and social services; this government activity is coupled with a sizable private sector in which market forces operate. The goal of such mixed systems is to achieve the economic growth of a free market and at the same time to protect workers, as in socialist economies. For example, medical care in the United States receives some government support, but the majority of medical bills are paid through private insurance companies. Individuals unable to afford such insurance are therefore likely to receive medical care of poorer quality. In societies such as Great Britain, France, or Sweden, which have mixed economies, basic medical care is subsidized by the government for all citizens regardless of income. Similarly, such other services as day care, basic utilities, and even transportation services may be government run. This kind of governmental support prevents the extremes of social inequality that result from an unrestricted market economy—the rich are less rich and the poor are less poor.

Mixed economies may well be the economic form of the future. Although the United States was clearly a capitalist economy at the turn of the last century, it has been moving steadily toward increasing the government's control over economic fluctuations and its support of basic social services. Programs such as social security, which seemed radical to Americans in the 1930s, are taken for granted today by almost all Americans; government provision of basic medical care may not be far behind; in fact, the United States is one of the few industrialized nations in the West that does not provide it. At the other end of the continuum, the introduction of elements of the free market into the Commonwealth of Independent States and China, coupled with the democratic and economic reforms in Eastern Europe, suggest a steady move away from the extremes of state socialism.

Corporations

A **corporation** is a legal entity that functions in the economic sector of a capitalist or mixed economy with rights of ownership and potential liabilities much like those of an individual; on the other hand, it is legally separate from the individuals who own it in the sense that they do not personally own what the corporation owns, nor are they personally liable for what the corporation does. Corporation ownership is typically held through shares of stock, which may be held by a very few individuals or a great many. The actual business operations of the corporation are conducted by various levels of managers, organized bureaucratically (see Chapter 5), who are answerable to the shareholders for their decisions.

Corporations were developed in the United States toward the end of the nineteenth century. By 1905, 74 percent of domestic production in the United States was corporate production (Roy, 1983). As the United States became a growing industrial power, corporations helped increase both the size and efficiency of business operations. The open ownership of corporate stock gives the illusion that American capital is in the hands of many rather than the hands of a few. Indeed, over 41 million Americans own stock in at least one corporation. In spite of this, however, the vast majority of all shares of stock in the United States are in just a very few hands (Useem, 1980).

Monopolies and Oligopolies One of the assumptions of the free market is that business competition will maintain the supply-demand balance. For example, rising demand for a product forces prices to rise until supply also rises to meet the demand. If many independent producers are involved, that should happen, but a single producer could respond to that rising demand by *not* producing more on purpose so as to keep prices and profits high. It would then obviously be in the business interest of a corporation to minimize competition with their product or service. Corporations therefore often attempt to form monopolies or oligopolies.

A **monopoly** is the control over a given product or service by a single corporation. An **oligopoly** exists when a few corporations dominate the production of a given product or service. In fact, with regard to most products, only a few corporations control the vast majority of the market. For example, General Motors, Ford, Chrysler, and Volkswagen control over 70 percent of the automobile market in the United States; similar oligopolies exist in such industries as automobile tires, soap, dairy products, drugs, and petroleum refining. Outright monopolies usually face legal challenges under antitrust legislation that was designed to prevent such complete control over a given market. An oligopoly is conducive to price-fixing—also illegal—whereby the few corporations involved agree informally not to compete in their product pricing but to maintain prices at a certain level, regardless of demand (see Chapter 6).

Conglomerates and Interlocking Directorates The United States government prohibits a single corporation from buying out all of its competitors in order to form a monopoly in a given sector of the economy. It does not prohibit corporations from expanding into other sectors of the economy. A **conglomerate** is a large corporation formed through the merger of many smaller corporations that operate in different sectors of the economy. For example, R. J. Reynolds Tobacco, which grew through the manufacture and sale of cigarettes, merged with Nabisco Brands (famous for crackers and other food products) to form RJR Nabisco. Beatrice Foods expanded in the early 1980s to form a conglomerate of fifty companies, which added, among other things, luggage and cosmetics to their line of food products (Spragins, 1988). More recently, large Japanese firms have acquired numerous American business interests outside their primary product line. Conglomerates do not create monopolies per se, since they are so diversified, but their size gives them the edge when confronted by competition from smaller corporations in any of their lines.

Competition is also reduced through **interlocking directorates**. Interlocking directorates exist when the same individuals sit on the board of directors of a number of different corporations. In this way, corporations with different products but complementary interests can act in unison when making economic decisions or, more extensively, when moving into the political realm—for example, in backing political candidates. In general, such connections allow for the passage of considerable information and foster collusion. General Motors, for example, is connected to the boards of directors of twenty-nine other firms, including oil companies, banks, insurance companies, mining companies, and transportation companies. Since members on the boards of those firms sit on the boards of still other firms, General Motors is connected to 728 other American corporations (Mintz and Schwartz, 1981, 1985).

Multinational Corporations A **multinational corporation** is a corporation located in one country while owning companies based in other countries. For example, General Motors obtains 25 percent of its profits from companies that operate in twelve countries besides the United States (Madsen, 1980). Virtually all major corporations are multinational in the 1990s.

These corporations without a country represent one way in which economic systems have outdistanced political systems. While political systems still operate within separate states, multinational corporations exist in the margins between those states, often answerable to no one state; from the point of view of any given state, much of the corporation's assets lie elsewhere, beyond taxation and control. When such corporations do interact with separate political systems, the results can have major international political repercussions. For example, the multinational ITT was able to convince the American government in the 1970s to help overthrow the Chilean government of President Allende. ITT's goal was to protect its assets in that country, which had promised to move to a socialist economy and would then have nationalized telecommunications.

Corporations become multinationals for the same reason they do most things: corporate managers are under constant pressure to increase profits. A major expense of any business is labor, and labor costs in the United States have grown steadily over the years, as American workers have demanded a higher standard of living. Cheaper labor is available in the countries of the nonindustrialized world. It makes good economic sense, therefore, to shut down factories in the United States and to operate overseas in Asia, South America, or Africa, where labor costs are a fraction of what they would be at home. An added benefit of such multinational connections is that if American workers fear factory closings, they may become willing to work for lower wages (Harrison and Bluestone, 1988).

The developing nations of the third world contain 75 percent of the world's population but only 20 percent of its wealth (Haub and Kent, 1987). That makes them ripe for corporate development by multinationals, but what are the effects of such economic development? Some observers argue that bringing basically agricultural societies into the modern industrial world will ultimately have positive results by increasing the amount of wealth in those countries and helping to promote the growth of democratic forms of government, which they see as logically connected to industrial development (Berger, 1986). Other observers focus on the degree to which traditional economic relationships are destroyed by such developments; industrialization may result in the end of subsistence agriculture, for example, which may force native people into the overcrowded slums of third-world cities to compete for industrial employment. These observers also note that profits made by multinationals seldom find their way into third-world economies (Wallerstein, 1979). Few observers disagree, however, on the amount of impact such industrial expansion has on third-world cultures and on employment changes in the industrial world as the primary and secondary sectors of the economy become noncompetitive, which leads to growth in the tertiary sector.

The World of Work in the United States: Problems and Trends

How do individual workers fit into this picture? The forces that drive major corporations also drive the individual workers that produce their goods. An industrial society such as the United States contains fewer and fewer "traditional" occupational opportunities, and individual workers are pushed into the changing needs of the corporate economy. Since 1900 the percentage of agricultural workers and unskilled labor has dropped noticeably, while the proportion of service workers has increased. The extent of this change can easily be seen by looking only at changes in the farm population in the United States. In 1880, over 43 percent of the American population lived on farms; by contrast, less than 2 percent live on farms today (U.S. Bureau of the

Census, 1989). The needs of a modern manufacturing nation can be seen in the increasing numbers of professional and technical workers and substantial increases in the number of clerical workers. And all these changes (along with broader changes in the economic system) have caused changes in worker satisfaction, the rates and impact of unemployment, and the importance of labor unions in mediating between the individual worker and the employer. We will examine these issues in this section as we change course in our examination of economic systems, focusing now on how American workers cope with changes in the economic institution.

Worker Satisfaction: The Work Ethic and Alienation Although their motives differ, both workers and management are concerned with worker alienation and job satisfaction. In this situation, **alienation** refers to a worker's lack of interest in and identification with the job, coupled with a general feeling of powerlessness over the conditions that affect his or her life (see Seeman, 1972). The separateness of the economic institution from other activities often carries over into specific jobs, which the worker may see as a necessary but separate facet of existence, not connected to the things that "really matter." An individual who is extremely loyal to friends and family may care little about the corporation for which he or she works, wanting only to get the work done with as little effort as possible. Jobs such as assembly-line work may increase alienation as the individual worker loses perspective on the overall product, concentrating instead on the three bolts that must be tightened every thirty-seven seconds on each item that moves down the line. Sociological research indicates that loss of job autonomy (such as happens on an assembly line) tends to increase levels of alienation (Kohn et al., 1990). Assembly-line work is a far cry from the work of a craftsperson, who sees a task through from start to finish and can take pride in the product. But, then, the modern corporation is also a far cry from the small, intimate units within which people used to work. Nevertheless, part of the success of Japanese industry stems from the fact that Japanese workers tend to have just that kind of intimate sense of loyalty to large multinational corporations (Naoi and Schooler, 1985).

In spite of any dissatisfaction American workers might feel, they want to work, having accepted the work ethic. The work ethic is the cultural value placed on work as an end in itself, independent of its products. If you ever feel guilty for "wasting" time even though you may not have much you really need to get done, you may well have internalized this value yourself; it is one of the more commonly held values in the United States. We are socialized to value activity over inactivity, and most of us find it quite difficult to do nothing for any extended period of time. In keeping with this pattern, older Americans have recently attacked mandatory retirement rules in hopes of working just a few more years. Part of this concern is undoubtedly purely economic since, particularly with the prospect of inflation, retirement on a fixed income is frightening. But interest in prolonging the period of work also comes from the central place work has in most people's lives. Many of us acquire much of our self-identity as well as our identity in society from our jobs. Retirement can be a wrenching experience, a loss almost like a death in the family.

The level of attachment workers feel for their jobs and their employers plays a role in industrial **productivity**, the number of worker hours required to produce a given product. Since worker hours are a major expense for a corporation, low productivity is reflected in higher prices for the manufactured product and therefore a product that is less competitive than that of a more productive corporation. The productivity of American workers has been called into question in recent years because of the inability of American products to compete with foreign imports, particularly in the automobile industry.

There are other reasons for low productivity, however, that stem from more general structures in the economy. Robert Reich, director of the Office of Policy Planning at the Federal Trade Commission, has pointed out some fundamental differences between the United States and Japan. Of every 10,000 citizens in Japan, he notes, one is a lawyer, three are accountants, and four hundred are engineers and scientists. Of the same 10,000 American citizens, twenty are lawyers, forty are accountants, and only seventy are engineers and scientists. The difference, he claims, is that the American economy rewards what he calls the "paper entrepreneurs" with money, job security, and high social status, while the truly productive occupations carry fewer rewards and attract fewer people (Fallows, 1980). According to Reich, Americans may be working hard, but they are working at the wrong things. Yet they work where they work because our economic system is structured that way.

Unemployment Unemployment is a permanent part of life in an economic system based on a free market. As business cycles fluctuate, the percentage of American workers employed rises and falls accordingly. During boom cycles, production is high and jobs are plentiful; during recessions or depressions, production drops due to lack of demand and jobs disappear. Individual workers may come to experience a certain feeling of helplessness, since their employment is clearly directed by forces beyond their control. It may make clear corporate sense to sell off parts of the corporation, close plants, and move operations overseas, but corporate priorities may seem misplaced from the perspective of the individual worker. Unemployment exists even during the most productive business cycles. A 5 percent unemployment rate is generally considered to be close to full employment; unemployment is only considered to be a "problem" when it reaches 8 percent or so (Albrecht, 1983). In the recession of the early 1980s, unemployment passed 10 percent.

Unemployment rates affect the economy as much as they affect the individual workers who find themselves without jobs. When employment is high, a great many workers have money to spend, and—not surprisingly—they spend it. This increases demand, which increases prices. In short, high employment can fuel inflation. One way to stop inflation is to force a recession, which lowers employment, decreases disposable income, lowers demand, and ultimately lowers prices. The recession of the early 1980s effectively ended the runaway inflation of the late 1970s in the United States because it left many American workers without jobs. The implication of this examination of cycles is somewhat sobering. It suggests that a certain level of unemployment is necessary if our economic system is to function without inflation. The expression, "The poor will always be with us," seems to have some sound economic basis to it.

Unemployment is measured by counting the number of people who are actively seeking work at any given time. Such a tally doesn't take into account many American workers who are not exactly thriving in their employment status. For example, many Americans are underemployed. Underemployment means that a worker is employed in a job different from (and also well below) his or her previous employment and unrelated to acquired job skills. A skilled machinist unable to find work in that field might drive a taxi to make ends meet;

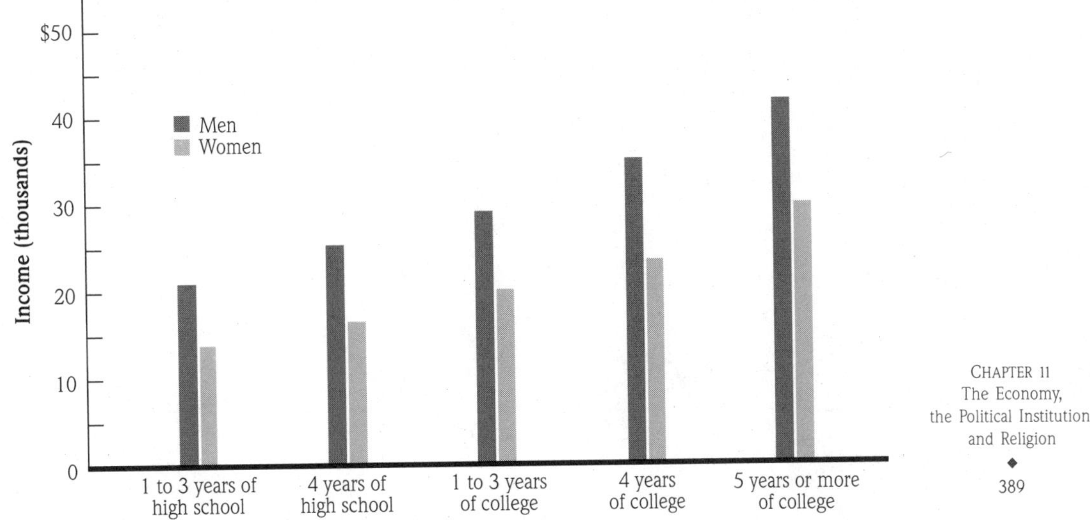

Figure 11.1 Median annual income of full-time workers age 25 and over by number of years of school completed and sex, 1987. (Data from *Money Income and Poverty Status of Families and Persons in the United States,* Bureau of the Census, Series P-60, No. 161.)

as such, he or she would not be counted in unemployment statistics. Another uncounted American would be a single mother living on public assistance. While she might prefer to work, the combined problems of paying for day care for her children plus losing the free medical coverage that comes from public assistance (but not from all jobs) would keep her on public assistance and off the unemployment rolls; she is not, after all, actively seeking work. Finally, there are many Americans who have simply given up on finding employment. Inner city black teenagers, for example, may search for work in an urban arena where there is little work for anyone and almost none for those without job skills. Even relatively low unemployment rates, therefore, miss many who are unemployed or poorly employed.

Figure 11.1 illustrates the different ways that American workers are affected by unemployment. Individuals without a high school diploma clearly stand in the greatest danger of unemployment. Beyond that, the more education you have, the more likely that your place in the economic system will be assured. As the American economy changes, with decreased opportunities in the primary and secondary sectors coupled with increases in the tertiary sector, there are fewer and fewer opportunities for the unskilled—with the exception of the most basic service jobs (such as cooking fast-food hamburgers or working as a hotel maid). We will examine this change in occupational opportunities shortly.

Another factor affecting unemployment is race. Figure 11.2 shows the difference between black and white unemployment over a number of years. Black unemployment is typically about twice that of white unemployment *regardless of whether the economy is strong or weak.* Black workers often describe themselves as last hired, first fired; these unemployment statistics suggest that there is considerable truth in that statement. More significantly, the gap between white

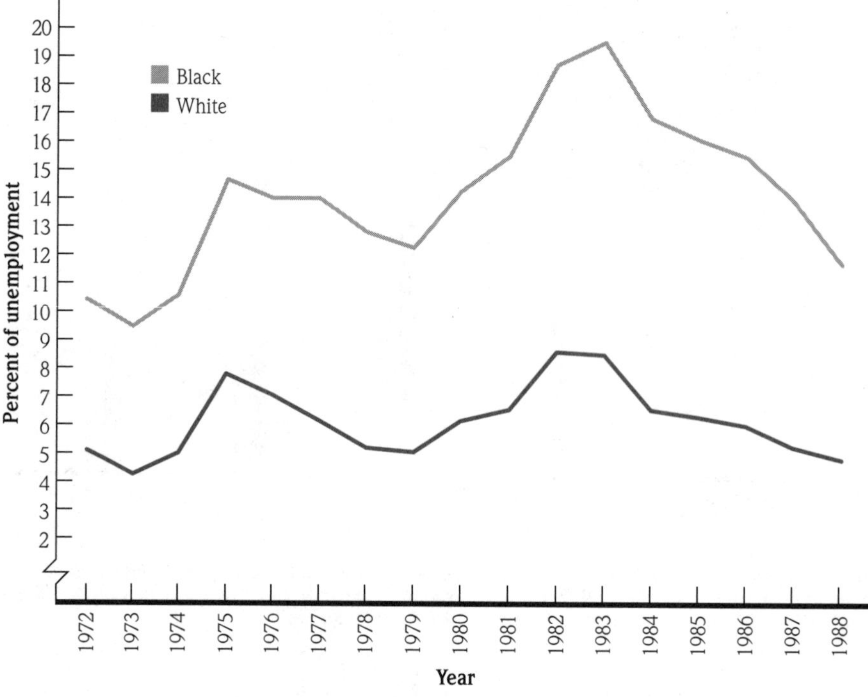

Figure 11.2 Unemployment rates of black and white American workers age 16 and over, 1972-1988. (Data from *Handbook of Labor Statistics.* U.S. Department of Labor, Bureau of Labor Statistics. U.S. Government Printing Office, 1989.)

and black unemployment has been increasing over the last twenty years rather than decreasing. The presence of more black faces in well-paid jobs previously denied them in American society leaves the impression that there have been significant economic advances for blacks in general; for most black workers, that impression is just not accurate. And these differences in unemployment are even greater if we add the factor of age. Workers under the age of twenty (many of whom obviously lack important job skills) typically have unemployment rates three times that of adults. Thus, if white employment is running about 5 percent, white youth unemployment rates will typically run 15 percent. More strikingly, black adult unemployment rates of 10 percent will result in 30 percent unemployment rates for black youths. Such statistics make it clear that the American dream of economic advancement is available only on a selective basis to American workers.

Labor Unions in the United States Labor unions have had their ups and downs in American economic history. In the early nineteenth century, most labor leaders were viewed by most business leaders as radicals intent on overthrowing the American government. Labor leaders were often denied employment (a procedure known as "blacklisting"), which denied them access to workers. Labor demonstrations were routinely put down with violence, as police were typically allied with employers. And employers found endlessly creative ways to prevent

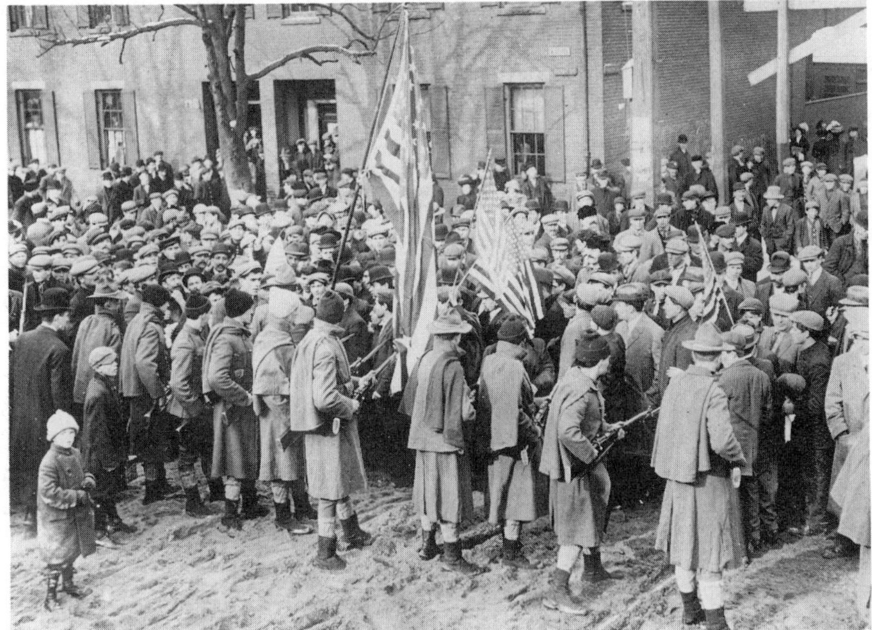

During the late nineteenth and early twentieth centuries, the U.S. government itself acted against the rising tide of labor organizing. Here, state militia troops confront mill workers in Lawrence, Massachusetts, who had struck in protest of a wage cut. The strike ended.

the growth of unions (see Box 8.1 in Chapter 8). Nevertheless, efforts by the American Federation of Labor and the newer Congress of Industrial Organizations culminated in federal legislation in the 1930s that guaranteed the right to organize, to bargain collectively, and to strike. Approximately 35 percent of the workforce belonged to unions by 1945; membership remained at that level until the early 1960s, when it began to drop, falling to around 15 percent in the 1990s.

During their period of dominance, unions achieved many rights for American workers; the medical and pension programs they put in place, coupled with job security based on seniority, made employees feel less helpless. Of course, unions did not bring down the American way of life, as feared by many employers; in fact, they often added an element of predictability to labor costs and thus promoted more accurate planning by management. The drop in union membership over the last thirty years probably has more to do with changes in the American workforce than it does with worker attitudes about unions. The strength of unions traditionally was in the secondary sector of the economy—in the major manufacturing industries such as steel and automobile production. Unions also made inroads in some areas of the primary sector, such as coal mining. The tertiary sector (which includes white collar and professional occupations) has always been difficult to unionize. As we've seen (and will examine more closely in the next section), the American economy has been changing steadily over the years to a service-oriented economy, because primary and secondary sector production has been unable to meet competition from overseas. As the children of steelworkers become clerks, considerable union membership is lost (see Goldfield, 1987).

Changes in the Labor Market: The Growth of Service Occupations The labor market in the United States has been undergoing change throughout the current century. There has been a massive decline in agricultural employment coupled with a steady decline in blue-collar employment; these losses have been roughly balanced by a massive rise in white-collar jobs in the tertiary sector, which is predicted to rise even more over coming years (Slater, 1987). As we've seen, the exploitation of cheap labor in the developing countries by multinational corporations has eliminated considerable employment in the United States in the primary and secondary sectors of the economy. This change is forcing many American workers to seek job retraining as the need for their current skills disappears. It is almost impossible today to find American-made televisions, VCRs, or cameras; the label on the clothing you are wearing right now may inform you that it was stitched together in Korea or perhaps the Caribbean; and every passing year increases the chances that your automobile either originated overseas or was produced in the United States by a foreign-owned corporation. While the United States imports so many of these goods, much of its exports involve the information technology that Americans still dominate. Growth in such new services provides strength to the American economy and sound opportunities for some skilled American workers, but not all new jobs in the service sector offer such a bright future.

For every new job in designing computer software in the United States, there is another new job handling routine tasks in the fast-food industry. Although both may be labeled as service jobs, the differences in which workers will get them and how the job will affect the worker are obvious. An important distinction that may help us understand some of these changes is that between the primary and secondary labor markets. The **primary labor market** includes those occupations that provide a range of employee benefits coupled with relatively high job status with at least some security. By contrast, the **secondary labor market** includes relatively low-skilled and poorly paid occupations that provide little if any employee benefits. Employee benefits include such essentials as medical insurance, retirement programs, and the like. But along with these benefits in the primary labor market come status, higher pay, greater security, and, most typically, greater autonomy and inherent interest in the work activity. Individuals entering the secondary labor market will lack these advantages and satisfactions; more important, they will probably be entering a world of employment from which escape may be difficult. With the exceptions of teenagers working summer jobs, these secondary labor market occupations may well represent dead ends in terms of upward mobility.

As the American economy comes more and more to consist of this split world of service occupations, there is some danger that our social stratification system may become even more rigid in terms of mobility than it has been in the past. Many of the occupations in the secondary labor market are becoming homes for nonwhite workers, while more affluent white workers live in the separate world of the primary labor market. As we have seen in this chapter and in Chapter 10, some routes for advancement have become less open than they had been. With fewer and fewer black and Hispanic youth achieving four-year college degrees relative to white youth and with the uselessness of job skills learned in the secondary labor market for advancement, it is hard to see new areas of opportunity in the American economy appearing in the 1990s.

THE POLITICAL INSTITUTION

If we focus on institutions in terms of the basic human needs they satisfy, the political institution specializes in the basic need for protection from other members of society (see Chapter 9). This need grows from the fact that people attempt to use power in their social relationships to further their own ends. As we turn to explore the operation of the political institution, we will need to first examine the ways in which power and authority operate in modern societies; we will pay special attention to the growth of the modern state. We will also examine the different types of governments, ranging from democratic to authoritarian, that direct the political system within states. Following this introduction to political systems, we will turn to politics in the United States, examining political participation in electoral politics and the role of interest groups and the media in determining who has power and how they use it. Finally, we will look at different theories of political power, each providing a different perspective on who really has power in the United States.

Political Systems: Arrangements of Power and Authority

The **political system** represents the social organization in an industrial society that distributes power within a society and governs its use. The system determines what rights and obligations citizens have to each other and to government at various levels. Much political activity is highly structured and ongoing, involving legal decisions, law enforcement, and overall government functioning; however, it also includes a wide range of "unofficial" political activities. When communities or social groups organize to protest, for example, those activities exist within the

The Pope of the Catholic Church can serve as a contemporary example of legitimation of authority through tradition, although his position does depend, as well, on other types of authority.

It was largely through charisma that Boris Yeltsin's authority first became legitimated. Later, of course, he was elected president of Russia through rational voting procedures.

political system since the protest groups seek to bring about changes in who has power or how decisions regarding social rights or obligations are made. (We will explore these types of protest groups fully in Chapter 13.) To better understand political systems, we will examine the institutionalization of power and authority in society and the different types of government within which it occurs.

Power, Authority, and the State The issues of power and authority became central issues in sociology through the work of Max Weber. As we saw in Chapter 3 (which includes a more complete discussion of these concepts), power is the ability to control the behavior of others regardless of their willingness to be dominated. By contrast, authority is a special kind of control in which the individuals who are dominated feel that the domination is legitimate in some sense. Weber identified three dimensions of the legitimation that characterizes authority: tradition, the charisma of individual leaders, and rational systems of law. Rational systems of law (such as the United States Constitution and the many laws enacted by Congress since) command respect through the acceptance of their usefulness by those who are governed by them.

While charismatic authority is often the source of social change as charismatic leaders generate respect for themselves among protest movement followers, traditional authority, rational systems of law (or legal-rational authority), and raw power often become institutionalized within a state. A **state** is a form of social organization that controls the means of coercion (or force) over a territory with specified political (or international) boundaries. (A **nation-state** is a state with only one significant ethnic group within its boundaries.) The state defines citizenship within

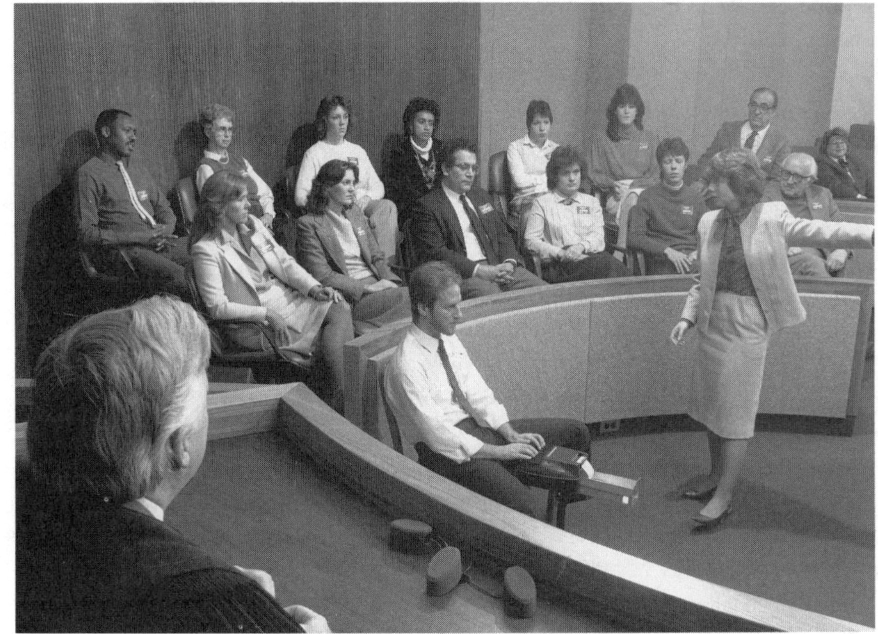

An American courtroom—legitimation of authority through a rational system of laws.

its jurisdiction, controls the use of force within its boundaries (setting and enforcing law), and defends its boundaries against other states that may wish to take control of them (see Enloe, 1981; Giddens, 1985). The state obviously controls power within its territory, but it generally attempts to generate authority among those it governs; no state can survive if it must hold its entire citizenship (or even a sizable portion of it) at gunpoint. Leaders of states develop traditional authority over time, but a more immediate source of authority stems from the acceptance among its citizens of the utility of its legal system plus its maintenance of a monopoly over the right to alter that system. In this sense, there is no difference between the acceptance by Americans of their rule of law and the acceptance by Germans of Hitler's decisions during the early days of Nazi Germany. In both cases, the laws are perceived to be legitimate and this perception gives the state authority.

States have grown in territory as industrialization has progressed; they have also become more formalized. The large scale of commerce characteristic of industrialization becomes more efficient in a large state. One can produce goods in Oklahoma, for example, and market them throughout the other forty-nine states without fear of paying tariffs or having one's assets seized by a rival state government. In addition, the federal government of the United States facilitates the export of those same goods to foreign countries through its establishment of international economic and political relations. The formalization (or bureaucratization) of states provides even more efficiency. Whatever its shortcomings, bureaucratic organization provides consistency and predictability, which are crucial to anyone attempting to make long-term business decisions (see Chapter 5).

During the twentieth century, many states have expanded their roles beyond the maintenance of boundaries, internal order, and economic relations. In particular, state concern for and action in behalf of the public welfare is now expected in all highly industrialized nations. In the United States, programs such as social security, medicare, and aid to families with dependent children reflect the intervention of the state in the personal affairs of its citizens. In the case of social security, for example, most workers participate automatically, with or without their consent. In those industrialized states described earlier in this chapter as having mixed economies, it is typical to find a much wider range of public services than found in the United States. Great Britain and Sweden, for example, provide for the public welfare from cradle to grave; this state activity eliminates much of the economic inequality found in states with less welfare orientation, such as the United States.

Democratic Governments While all states share the basic functions described above, they vary in the degree to which they permit citizens to participate in the affairs of government. A **democratic government** is a government in which citizens are permitted to participate, either directly or indirectly, in the processes of government. A **direct democracy** occurs when each citizen has an equal voice and directly participates in governmental activities. By nature, direct democracies must be quite small; for example, some New England towns call meetings to which all members of the community are invited to discuss and vote on community actions. A **representative democracy** involves the election of representatives by groups of citizens; those representatives discuss and vote on governmental actions. The representatives may be organized in various governmental bodies. In a democratic republic such as the United States, some representatives are combined into legislative bodies (as in the House of Representatives and the Senate) while an executive (the President) is elected separately. A parliamentary system, such as that in Canada, Great Britain, Israel, and most democratic governments, elects a leader (a Prime Minister) from either the majority party in parliament or some coalition of political parties in parliament who agree to form a government.

As human history goes, democracies are both new and still relatively rare on the world scene; such governments have only become common since the onset of the industrial revolution. As we saw in the previous section, the free market is the cornerstone of capitalist economies. A democratic government is clearly one way to facilitate the growth of such economic systems. In keeping with the famous quotation from President Calvin Coolidge, "The business of America is business." There is always a clear connection between the nature of the economic system and the structure of the political system. Some observers have argued that there is a necessary connection between free markets and democratic institutions (Berger, 1986). Other observers have noted that free markets have prospered under quite authoritarian forms of government and that democratic governments are particularly rare when there is considerable economic inequality within the society or disagreement among elites as to the basic value of democratic institutions (Muller, 1988; Higley and Burton, 1989). Lipset and Schreider (1973) found that high levels of economic development in general helped to maintain stable democracies.

Authoritarian Governments While democratic governments are characterized by widespread political participation in and control over the state, an **authoritarian government**

is characterized by the concentration of political control within the hands of a few members of society. A **dictatorship** is the concentration of political power in the hands of one person; an **oligarchy** is the concentration of political power in the hands of a small group of people.

Authoritarian governments differ in the degree to which they exert control over their citizens. Most allow some freedom and control outside the scope of government as, for example, in permitting religious freedom and giving some autonomy to religious organizations. By contrast, a **totalitarian government** is an authoritarian government that seeks control over all aspects of communal and individual life within its boundaries. Nazi Germany provides a clear example, as does the Khmer Rouge regime in Cambodia during the 1970s, during which hundreds of thousands of people were executed and many were relocated to the rural areas. The goal of leader Pol Pot was to completely wipe out all aspects of the previous culture so as to govern over a totally transformed society. Totalitarian regimes are typified by rigid ideologies (which justify the existence of the regime), complete control over the media, a single (and overwhelmingly strong) political party, considerable control over the economy, and extreme methods of social control in response to deviance. With regard to those controlled economies, totalitarian governments are found associated with both socialist economies and capitalist economies.

Politics in the United States

The United States has been governed by a representative democracy since its formation following the Revolutionary War. The percentage of the population represented has grown considerably since that time, however, as initially only white male property holders were allowed to vote. The right to vote was extended to black Americans in 1870, to women in 1920, and to American Indians in 1924 (see Chapter 8). The political system within which they vote has changed very little in structure for over two hundred years. The three branches of the federal government have remained intact, with offices filled as specified in the United States Constitution. But while the structure of government has changed little, there has been considerable change not only in who votes but in why they vote, their interest in voting, and the information that affects their voting. Similarly, there have been many changes in how candidates are selected, advertised, funded, and influenced after election. The framers of the Constitution would recognize their work in the current political system but would be astounded at the forces that move it and the manner in which it is manipulated.

Political Participation: Voting Behavior and Apathy Individual citizens in the United States can become involved in the political institution in many ways, including, of course, actually running for office themselves. Short of that, they may work for candidates or become involved with special interest groups and lobbying. The vast majority of people, however, limit their direct participation to voting (and many choose not even to do that). Sociologists attempt to understand some of this variety in participation by studying **political socialization**—the process by which individuals acquire values and patterns of behavior with regard to the political institution. Not surprisingly, political socialization occurs in much the same way as more general forms of socialization. The strongest influence on the political socialization of most people is the views of their parents (Jennings and Niemi, 1981). Children learn political attitudes from parents and they also acquire behavior patterns; children who watch their parents go to the polls on election day are presented with a role model that they may accept for themselves in later life. Other important factors in political socialization include education (courses in government are often mandatory) and the media (which provide us with debates, interviews, political commentary, and endless political advertising around election time). In spite of all this input, many Americans remain blissfully uninformed, not only about particular candidates or their current representatives, but about the basic structure of the American political system (Converse, 1989).

Although the U.S. Constitution is not structured around the existence of political parties, a wide variety of political parties have entered the political arena since the early days of the republic. By the Civil War, both the Democratic and Republican Parties were in place, and the two-party dominance of the political system was soon established. The parties have both gone through many changes in the course of their respective histories. The Republican Party has traditionally been the party of business, but it was also the party of the North (until the 1960s) and of black voters (until the 1930s) because of its association with Lincoln and the union forces in the Civil War. The Democratic Party gained strength in the latter half of the nineteenth century as the party of immigrant voters, many of whom were Catholic or Jewish. It was also the party of the South (again, thanks to the Civil War). President Franklin Roosevelt altered some of these allegiances in the 1930s when he built a coalition of working class, Jewish, Catholic, nonwhite, and Southern voters which lasted for over thirty years. The association of the party with the civil rights movement of the 1950s and 1960s and with assorted other liberal causes has allowed the Republican Party to make inroads among Southern voters and, to a lesser extent, among working class, Jewish, and Catholic voters. Woven through all this history is a fundamental difference between the two parties with regard to government economic and public welfare policies. The Republican Party has retained its relation to American business through its support of conservative economic policies, which has included efforts to minimize the welfare role of government. The Democratic Party has generally favored more liberal economic policies and has promoted the welfare role of government.

Many of the differences between the two parties can be seen in the data provided by Table 11.1, which allow us to analyze where support comes from in the last several Presidential elections in the United States. Turning first to income data, the support of Democratic candidates by poorer voters and the support of the Republican candidate by wealthier voters is clear. Even soundly defeated Democratic candidates such as Mondale in 1984 and Dukakis in 1988 received a majority of votes from the poorest voters. Characteristics related to income, such as level of education and occupational status, show a similar relationship: the Democratic Party receives a majority of support from less educated and low status voters while better educated and higher status voters are more likely to lean toward the Republican Party. The racial and ethnic breakdowns of voting trends show some continuities and some changes in the traditional allegiances of the two parties. Nonwhite voters still lean toward Democratic candidates to a wide degree while white voters are more likely to vote Republican. The traditional Catholic and Jewish support of Democratic candidates has dropped considerably among Catholic voters, however, and somewhat among Jewish voters; both groups used to be strong supporters of the Democratic Party. Finally, a new wrinkle in American politics has appeared in the differences in support by gender for the two parties. In every election, men have favored the Republican candidate more than women. The most probable explanation for this is the continuing support for federally

TABLE 11.1

PRESIDENTIAL VOTE BY GROUPS IN GENERAL ELECTIONS, 1980-1988

Group	Percentage of 1988 voters	1980			1984		1988	
		Democrat	*Republican*	*Independent*	*Democrat*	*Republican*	*Democrat*	*Republican*
Sex								
Men	48	36	55	7	37	62	41	54
Women	52	45	47	7	44	56	49	50
Race/ethnicity								
White	85	36	55	7	35	64	40	59
Black	10	85	11	3	89	9	86	12
Hispanic	3	56	35	8	61	37	69	30
Education								
Not high school graduate	8	51	46	2	50	49	56	43
High school graduate	27	43	51	4	39	60	49	50
College incomplete	30	35	55	8	37	61	42	57
College graduate	35	35	52	11	41	58	43	56
Religion								
White Protestant	48	31	63	6	27	72	33	66
Catholic	28	42	49	7	45	54	47	52
Jewish	4	45	39	15	67	31	64	35
White fundamentalist	9	33	63	3	22	78	18	81
Income*								
Under $12,500	12	51	42	6	54	45	62	37
$12,500-24,999	20	46	44	7	42	57	50	49
$25,000-34,999	20	39	52	7	40	59	44	56
$35,000-49,999	20	32	59	8	33	66	42	56
$50,000 and over	24	26	63	9	30	69	37	62
Total	*100*	*41*	*51*	*7*	*40*	*59*	*45*	*53*

*Income categories in 1980 were: less than $10,000; $10,000-14,999; $15,000-24,999; $25,000-49,999; and $50,000 and over.
Source: New York Times, November 10, 1988, B6 (copyright © 1988 by the New York Times Company, reprinted by permission).

funded social programs by the Democratic Party—programs that are more likely to be favored by women than men.

While party loyalty is an important result of political socialization, an equally important result is voter apathy. In every presidential election since 1920, the winning candidate has received fewer votes than the number of Americans of voting age who chose not to vote. While men and women vote in almost equal numbers, most other social-category distinctions are reflected in different levels of voting. Whites, for example, are more likely to vote than blacks, and both groups are much more likely to vote than Hispanics. Considering that Hispanic Americans are one of the fastest growing American minority groups, their current lack of political participation is of particular importance. Older Americans are much more likely to vote than younger Americans; this fundamental result of political socialization is reflected in continuing decreases over time in the percentages of voting age Americans who vote. (Eighty percent of the voting age population voted in 1896.) Table 11.2 gives us a closer look at who votes and who doesn't, using data from the presidential election of 1988. Turning to some basic elements of socioeconomic status, we find—see Table 11.2—that Americans with more education and with higher incomes (who are generally the same people) are much more likely to vote than poorer or less educated Americans.

There are a number of reasons why Americans have lower voter turn-outs than other industrial countries and why particular categories of Americans are more likely to vote than others. Most other industrialized countries make the registration process less complicated so that more voters find themselves eligible to vote when election day comes around (Glass, Squire, and Wolfinger, 1984). Looking to differences among categories of voters within the United States, we find that voting is more likely to occur among individuals who have a clear personal sense of political efficacy (Orum, 1978). These are people who perceive that individuals can make a difference in influencing the factors that affect their lives. Individuals with lower socioeconomic status are much less likely to perceive politics as a solution to the problems in their lives (Teixeira, 1987). Since low-status Americans are, by definition, going to have more problems by any objective measure, these differences are profoundly important. Perhaps the relative lack of problems provides the illusion of individual efficacy so that higher status Americans are more likely to attribute their success to their own efforts. Another possible explanation is that the political institution does in fact work better for higher-status people, who have the money and the influence to affect the system. Whatever the explanation, different levels of political participation can result in the continuation of the current inequalities in how the system works. Politicians are less likely to respond to the concerns of groups that do not vote; similarly, people whose concerns are not addressed by politicians may have less reason to think that the system can work for them and less motivation to participate.

Interest Groups: Politics and Money Candidates respond to constituents who vote, but they are likely to pay more attention to constituents who contribute to their campaigns. Private individuals do contribute, but the bulk of campaign contributions in the United States comes from special interest groups. **Interest groups** are social organizations that represent particular political interests and seek to influence the political institution to further those interests. Their actions may involve contributions and/or lobbying. **Lobbying** constitutes the provision of special information to political leaders coupled with attempts to convince them to vote in accordance

Table 11.2

Percentages of the Voting-Age Population Who Voted in the 1988 Election

	Percentage Voting
Years of education	
Elementary	36.7%
High School: 1-3 years	41.3
High School: 4 years	54.7
College: 1-3 years	64.5
College: 4 years or more	77.6
Occupational status	
Unemployed	38.6
Agriculture	53.0
Private wage and salary	54.6
Self-employed	63.3
Government worker	75.2
Not in labor force	57.3
Family income	
Under $5,000	34.7
5,000-9,999	41.3
10,000-14,999	47.7
15,000-19,999	53.5
20,000-24,999	57.8
25,000-34,999	64.0
35,000-49,999	70.3
Over $50,000	75.6

Source: U.S. Bureau of the Census, *Voting and Registration in the Election of November, 1988.* Current Population Reports, P-20, No. 440. Washington, D.C.: U.S. Government Printing Office, 1989.

with the desires of the interest group. Interest groups may range from very specialized interests of particular groups of Americans to much more general interests, which may have wide-ranging appeal. For example, the American Medical Association is an interest group that seeks to further the interests of physicians in the United States; nonphysicians would receive no direct benefits from such actions and could be negatively affected by the results of such lobbying. A somewhat more general example would be the National Rifle Association, which seeks to prevent legislation aimed at limiting access to firearms; hunters and gun enthusiasts (who belong to the N.R.A.) benefit directly from such lobbying, but other Americans who have definite opinions on gun control also have a stake in the results. Finally, very general interest groups such as consumer protection organizations may seek to require manufacturers to provide additional product information or to increase safety levels in the use of their products. Such actions directly affect all consuming Americans to some degree. (Box 11.2 traces such issues by examining the political side of responses to AIDS in the United States.)

BOX 11.2

THE POLITICS OF AIDS

Sociologists take notice when human populations increase or decrease for whatever reason. Such changes can only occur as a result of changes in birth rates, death rates, and migration rates. While population size changes affect all aspects of society, regardless of the source of those changes, the source of change often affects the portion of the society most greatly affected. For example, the illegal migration of Mexican workers to the United States affects some states more than others and some members of the U.S. employment sector more than others because of resulting employment competition. Similarly, a rise in the birth rates among poor mothers adds members to the bottom rungs of the social stratification system while leaving other levels affected only indirectly. But the rising death rates in the United States due to AIDS (acquired immunodeficiency syndrome) not only affects distinct portions of the U.S. population, it also connects with some dominant American values and challenges American governmental political response.

AIDS first appeared on the American scene in 1981, when gay men began to die from rare diseases normally found only among people with deficient immune systems. AIDS received its name in 1982 and Congress appropriated funds for research. By 1984, the virus had been isolated and scientists began to understand the difficulty of its transmission—by blood or other bodily fluids—which tended to keep the disease from spreading rapidly throughout the population. In other words, if your degree of social contact with AIDS victims was limited, so too would be your danger of contracting the disease. While many African countries suffer from widespread distribution of the virus, transmitted through heterosexual contact, the virus in the United States is still primarily limited to the homosexual and bisexual community and to those who share needles for the purpose of intravenous drug injection.

In the United States today, 60 percent of AIDS cases stems from male homosexual or bisexual contact, and 22 percent results from intravenous drug use. Another 7 percent results from the combination of those situations. Of the "respectable" ways to acquire AIDS, 1 percent comes from hemophilia/coagulation disorder, 2 percent results from contaminated blood transfusions or body tissue transplants, and 5 percent results from heterosexual contact. Of the last group, over half the cases result from sexual relations with an IV drug user (Center for Disease Control, 1990).

These figures paint a picture of affected subpopulations in the United States that share deviations from mainstream American values. Homosexuals violate some basic American values, some religiously based and some not, while IV drug users receive the negative evaluation associated with drug use in the United States. In addition, most IV drug users tend to be both poor and nonwhite. For example, black women make up just over 13 percent of American women aged 15-44, yet they comprise over 57 percent of AIDS victims within that age group. Similarly, Hispanic women account for just under 8 percent of that population but make up almost 17 percent of young female AIDS victims. We find very similar figures for black and Hispanic children, who often contract the disease from their mothers (Gayle et al., 1990). While 76 percent of AIDS within the white community is connected to the homosexual community, less than 40 percent of the disease is connected to homosexual contact within the black and Hispanic communities (Center for Disease Control, 1990.)

BOX 11.2 (continued)

All these figures have led to major political clashes in the United States in the 1990s. AIDS victims and activists argue that government is not doing all that it could because the disease has left the mainstream population (and most politicians' constitutents) relatively untouched. Unlike the situation in African countries, the disease has not yet moved into the middle class heterosexual community with significant force. That same middle class community often opposes the spread of sexual information regarding safe sex in the schools or the dissemination of sterile needles to IV drug users. Even more political disagreement occurs over the allocation of scarce federal funds to AIDS research. While all of these issues spark the current political scene, the view down the road suggests increased conflict to come. Most significantly, the growth of AIDS will almost certainly place a considerable stress on the American medical delivery system, particularly considering that so many of future AIDS patients will be poor and medically uninsured. Seldom has one virus assaulted the American economic and political institutions with such virulence.

Interest groups are often organized as political action committees. A **political action committee** (or PAC) is an organization formed to raise and contribute money to support the political aims of a particular interest group. PACs may represent any interest group but their most common form is the PAC that represents business or occupational interest groups. PACs typically provide ongoing sources of money for candidates in order to maintain a political relationship so that the politician's ear may be available when particular pieces of legislation appear that have a direct bearing on the PAC's interests. Because large PACs may contribute millions of dollars in any given election, many political ears stay tuned to PAC interests (see Table 11.3). Most PACs contribute to politicians from both major parties and from different points on the political spectrum in hopes of maximizing the number of allies for important votes. The only kind of politician generally ignored by PACs is the politician who is out of office and therefore, by definition, cannot vote. PACs are not as interested in packing Congress with sympathetic politicians as in influencing those already there. That generalization is particularly true for business or occupationally related PACs, but it should be noted that interest groups often do become involved in the election process itself. Organizations such as Right to Life (which supports legal limitations on abortions in the United States) often contribute to out-of-office politicians who support their agenda. The tendency for PACs in general to support incumbents has made it increasingly difficult for aspiring politicians to break into the political arena. Even when voter dissatisfaction is high (as measured by voter opinion polls), incumbents still win with overwhelming regularity. While a large amount of dollars in a campaign chest have always been important in waging a successful campaign, money has become even more essential with the greater expense and spreading influence of the media in modern American political campaigns.

Politics and the Media The most important elements of the media for political socialization are television, radio, and newspapers. Of these, television has clearly become the most important as it is the major source of news for most Americans. Both the inherent nature of television and its popularity with consumers have given it a major and distinctive influence on American political life.

TABLE 11.3

TOP TEN PACS IN OVERALL SPENDING AND IN CONTRIBUTIONS TO FEDERAL CANDIDATES, 1987-1988

PAC	Overall spending
1. National Security Political Action Committee	$10,279,012
2. Democratic Republican Independent Voter Education Committee	8,475,552
3. Realtors Political Action Committee	5,930,618
4. American Medical Association Political Action Committee	5,385,951
5. NRA Political Victory Fund	4,672,291
6. National Congressional Club	4,140,237
7. Campaign America	4,025,876
8. National Committee to Preserve Social Security PAC	4,013,264
9. American Citizens for Political Action	3,870,927
10. Association of Trial Lawyers of America Political Action Committee	3,870,741

PAC	Contributions to federal candidates
1. Realtors Political Action Committee	$3,040,969
2. Democratic Republican Independent Voter Education Committee	2,856,724
3. American Medical Association Political Action Committee	2,316,496
4. National Education Association Political Action Committee	2,104,689
5. National Association of Retired Federal Employees Political Action Committee (NARFE-PAC)	1,979,850
6. UAW-V-CAP (UAW Voluntary Community Action Program)	1,953,099
7. Association of Trial Lawyers of America Political Action Committee	1,913,558
8. Committee on Letter Carriers Political Education (Letter Carriers Political Action Fund)	1,737,982
9. American Federation of State, County, and Municipal Employees—PEOPLE, Qualified	1,663,386
10. Machinists Non-Partisan Political League	1,490,780

Source: Federal Election Commission, "FEC Finds Slower Growth of PAC Activity during 1988 Election Cycle," press release, April 9, 1989, 15-16.

By its nature, television cannot provide the depth and detail of political information that newspapers can provide. Time constraints on both network and local news programs force a condensation of material; newspapers have no such constraints. This lack of time affects political information in two ways. First, the details of political issues and positions cannot be reported, nor can the possible repercussions of those issues and positions. Voters receive the broad brush strokes but may be left unaware of other facets of the issues that might personally affect them and thus alter their positions and political behavior. Second, certain kinds of political issues are either too detailed or too narrow in focus to warrant the attention of television news. The news *not* shown represents important decisions made by news producers and directors with an eye toward general interest and higher viewer ratings.

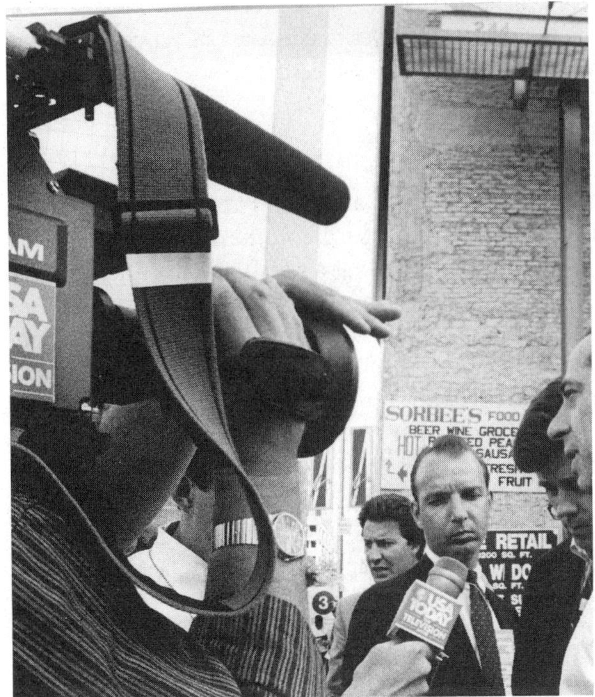

Politicians and professional campaigners are keenly aware of television's impact; most visits to neighborhoods are arranged to allow national or local TV news coverage.

The popularity of television with American consumers has fundamentally altered both the nature of political campaigning in general and political advertising in particular. Individuals who direct political campaigns are fully aware of the constraints on and desires of television news programs. As a result, campaigns are turning increasingly into a series of media events in which the politicians finds himself or herself in photogenic (and often symbolically important) surroundings uttering neat catch phrases that lend themselves to the close editing needed for balancing material on the evening news. Viewers are thus confronted by politicians at flag factories or on military bases repeating phrases that they hope will become ingrained in the political consciousness of American voters. The visual and brief nature of the medium forces campaigning to become picturesque and short, both of which tend to oversimplify complex political issues.

The amount of political advertising on television has grown enormously in recent years, paralleling the growing popularity of the medium with the public. The old fashioned stump speeches of politicians who traveled from town to town are no longer an effective way to reach large numbers of voters and survive only if film of them can be "sold" to news program directors or be included in professionally produced television advertisements. Campaigning on television isolates politicians from voters (who may have very real questions they wish to ask) and forces politicians to simplify their messages (due to the same time limitations faced by news programs). Perhaps most important, however, television advertising is extremely expensive; poorly funded candidates are therefore at an extreme disadvantage. We have already seen that incumbents have built-in advantages as a result of their increased levels of contributions. A dependence upon television by both voters and politicians creates a situation in which the more poorly funded candidates may not even be able to achieve name recognition among voters.

The Sources of Power: Pluralism versus Elitism

In industrial societies, the role of power has spread to a wide range of social activities, particularly with regard to maintaining the built-in inequalities of social stratification. Power keeps the rich in control, enabling them to remain rich. Power also plays a role in attacks upon the status quo as less favored groups use their influence to restructure the bases of power. The diversity characteristic of industrial societies creates a great number of interests that often come into conflict; when that conflict occurs, power invariably plays a major role in determining the outcome. When there is no outright conflict, the sources of power in society are not so readily apparent. Sociologists do not agree as to just how power is distributed in society. A variety of theories have been suggested, but most fall under one of two general headings—pluralism or elitism.

Pluralism essentially sees power as relatively evenly distributed among the members of society. This perspective is most clearly in keeping with representative government as it is commonly assumed to work. Democratic political representation is supposed to place power in the hands of the people through the vote. In a pluralistic society, therefore, power would appear to be evenly distributed among the voters. The essence of pluralism is that just such a distribution exists.

Elitism assumes that a small group of individuals (an *elite*) in society hold the vast majority of power, leaving little for the mass of the population. Elitist theorists point out that elected representatives don't always vote as their constituents would wish, perhaps leaning more strongly toward satisfying their most wealthy contributors. More important, however, elitist theorists question the degree to which power is directly in the hands of elected representatives. Corporate leaders, for example, may play a major behind-the-scenes role in shaping the decisions of an industrial society; elitist theorists search for just such leaders.

An example of the pluralist perspective can be found in Robert Dahl's 1961 book *Who Governs?,* which traces the history of political control in the city of New Haven, Connecticut. According to Dahl, the early leaders were descendants of the Puritans who first settled the area. The industrialization of the nineteenth century brought businessmen into the circle of power, widening the distribution of power in the area. Finally, massive immigration of southeastern Europeans into the area in the early twentieth century added still another group to the picture, widening the distribution of power still further. According to Dahl, the early elitist power structure of New Haven has given way to a pluralistic power structure; a wide variety of groups share power and contest decision making. He sees similar pluralistic power distributions in other American cities (Dahl, 1982).

Another version of pluralism offered by David Riesman introduces the concept of the **veto group**, a political group that exercises sufficient power to prevent the actions of other political groups. According to Riesman, the sharing of power under pluralism does not allow a variety of groups enough power to change society directly into the form they would prefer. These groups do, however, have enough power to limit the excesses of other groups in *their* attempts to have their way. This limitation takes the form of a veto, in which power acts in a negative way. According to Riesman, power is at least evenly enough distributed in American society for a variety of groups to defend themselves from others (Riesman, Glazer, and Denney, 1950).

A classic example of the elitist perspective is presented in C. Wright Mills's *The Power Elite* (1956). According to Mills, there are three major sources of power in American society: the executive branch of the government, business leaders, and the military. He sees these three spheres as acting in concert much of the time because of the interchangeability of their leaders; the same individuals can be found moving among major positions in the military, the government, and the business world. These "elites," according to Mills, make the decisions that govern our lives. As a unit, they form a "military-industrial complex," with elites in each area making decisions that will benefit all three. Ironically, Mills found a willing convert to this idea in President Dwight Eisenhower, who, in his farewell address to the nation in 1961, warned against just such a centralization of power in American society.

The elitist interpretation gained some additional support from the research of G. William Domhoff (1983). In his book *Who Rules America Now? A View for the 80s,* Domhoff searched for the actual individuals in the elites referred to by Mills. According to Domhoff, the "governing class" is a relatively small group of individuals (about one-half of one percent of the American population) who make most of the decisions that govern the lives of the whole population. Mostly rich businessmen and their families, they form quite a cohesive group. They seem to be interchangeable on the boards of directors of major corporations, and, perhaps more interestingly, they have clear social ties within their group, ranging from country club memberships to marriage ties. According to Domhoff, these people are not only a small ruling elite, they are also a social group *conscious* of themselves as a ruling elite. If their decisions appear to follow a pattern of providing mutual benefits within the group, it may be more than chance.

The complexities of a modern industrial society such as the United States create difficulties for sociologists in every area of study, but the number of decisions made in everyday life and the elaborate forms of social organization from which they emanate (such as bureaucracies) make the question of power truly one of the most difficult. Many Americans express the sense that they are losing control over the events that affect their lives. We seem to have a clear sense of where power *isn't* but a much less clear idea of just where it *is.*

RELIGION

Human societies around the world have created almost infinite variations on the theme of survival. Although every society, for example, must care for and socialize its young if it is to last, what constitutes the "family" varies widely from culture to culture. Families can be large or small, authoritarian or equalitarian, and so on. Even so, the universal presence of families of some description points to it being basic for survival. But is religion basic to survival? Virtually all human cultures contain shared beliefs concerning a supernatural realm, along with some expression of those beliefs in their everyday behaviors. We commonly think of those shared beliefs as religions and of those behaviors as religious ritual.

Specifically, **religion** includes those shared beliefs, associated behavior patterns, and forms of social organization that are oriented toward the supernatural. We find such beliefs, behaviors, and social organizations in practically all human cultures. In industrial societies, religion takes on the characteristics of a separate institution as those social organizations become formalized into churches; religious ritual comes to be closely associated with church doctrine and church settings. In this section of the chapter, we will examine the growth of the religious institution. First, we look briefly at some of the basic varieties of religious belief and behavior. Then we examine some theories of religion offered by sociologists, each offering a different perspective on why religions come into existence and how they affect other aspects of society. Finally, we turn to the role of religion in the United States, focusing on the interplay between religions and family behaviors, political attitudes, economic position, and a variety of other aspects of social life on which religion leaves its mark.

Religious Beliefs and Organizations

In dealing with the supernatural world, religious beliefs integrate human consciousness with forces clearly outside the individual. Other beliefs do this as well. Patriotic beliefs, for example, integrate the individual with others who share his or her nation or state. When such beliefs are intensely held, they take on many of the characteristics of religious beliefs. Nineteenth-century French sociologist Emile Durkheim (1858-1917) identified this fundamental characteristic as the **sacred**, referring to those elements of human experience which inspire awe, fear, or reverence. In Western society, for example, a Bible is a sacred object as compared to an atlas. The atlas belongs to the other realm of human experience, which Durkheim called the **profane**, including all elements of experience that are commonplace or everyday. In comparing religious beliefs with patriotism, we can see some similarities in that a flag, for example, in standing for a belief held in reverence (patriotism), takes on sacred qualities. Yet political beliefs and behaviors should not be confused with religious beliefs, however interesting the similarities may be. Religious beliefs occupy the world of the sacred but they also take us into the realm of the supernatural, providing meaning for and explanations of human existence that come clearly from beyond the scope of human dealings (such as governments).

Varieties of Religious Beliefs **Animism** refers to religious belief systems that impute supernatural forces to natural objects. For example, an animal, a river, or a mountain could be viewed as a sacred object, possessing supernatural forces that will be reflected in the lives of humans. A sacred animal might offer protection; an aspect of the environment—ground considered sacred—might seek revenge if it has been mistreated. For example, the Sioux of the American plains viewed the Black Hills of the Dakotas as sacred. When gold was discovered and pressure from miners led the U.S. government to appropriate considerable territory in the Black Hills from the Sioux, their displeasure obviously involved far more than just a distaste for losing land. Indeed, their religion had been attacked, and negative repercussions for the tribe could well be expected.

By contrast, **theism** is the belief that supernatural forces are controlled by a number of gods or a single god that are interested in and responsive to human affairs. **Monotheism** is the belief in one god, and **polytheism** is the belief in more than one god. Of major world religions, Christianity, Judaism, and Islam are all monotheistic while Hinduism (which is the oldest) is polytheistic (see Winther's reading following Chapter 3). Theistic belief systems hinge on the power of their god or gods, relating that power to a religious worldview that connects human behavior to religiously provided meanings. A given god, for example, might require particular kinds of ongoing human behavior (such as religious ritual) if those humans are to achieve particular kinds of religiously defined ends (such as salvation). Included within the belief system is the recognition that the god or gods have the power to intervene in human affairs for good or ill, depending upon the behavior of the believers.

Some major religions are not theistically oriented at all; their supernatural worldview provides goals for human behavior and encourages particular behaviors as being best suited to meeting those goals. For example, Buddhism (which originated in India) shares a belief in reincarnation (or rebirth) with Hinduism but omits the gods of that religion, turning instead to a belief in the possibility of attaining a state of enlightenment and understanding through the redirection of one's personal actions toward that end. An even clearer example of a nontheistic religion is Confucianism, which originated in China more than two thousand years ago. Confucius recommended a life of loyalty to and concern for others in place of self-interest. Confucianism thus appears to be more a moral code than a supernaturally oriented religion.

Religious rituals consist of behaviors that are defined and promoted by particular religious belief systems. All religions make demands on the actions as well as the beliefs of their adherents. We normally think of such rituals in terms of rigidly defined repetitive acts of religious significance (such as saying the same grace before every meal), yet all behaviors that carry religious significance fall under this heading. In Confucianism, for example, displaying loyalty for one's family would constitute a religious ritual, while in Christianity church attendance itself can be viewed as a ritual, independent of (but necessary for) the other rituals that occur after you arrive at the church. In making such demands on what people do as well as what they believe, religious beliefs affect society in a very tangible way. Rituals require your time; often entail some degree of sacrifice; and, perhaps most important, make your beliefs visible to others. To others with whom you share those beliefs, rituals serve to create a form of social cohesion through a shared activity. To those with whom you do not share beliefs, rituals serve to mark and maintain boundaries between groups who believe and those who do not. Rituals thus simultaneously hold social groups together and create distance between one social group and another. The more public, frequent, and distinctive the rituals, the more this is true.

Forms of Religious Organization Social organizations that grow up around religious belief systems vary almost as much as the belief systems themselves. Sociologists typically categorize those organizations under a few broad headings. Critical factors highlighted by those headings include (1) differences in organization size, (2) degree of independence of the associated belief system from other religions, and (3) the type of relationship that exists between the religious organization and political forces that control the society within which it exists.

An **ecclesia** is a religious organization that is essentially one with the state, enjoying the support of the government and claiming all citizens of that state as members. More often than not, the need for unity between the church and state will be a central part of the religious doctrine, as in the religion of Islam. The Islamic states in Iran and Saudi Arabia are examples of ecclesiae in which all governmental action occurs in accordance with the rules of Islam. Islamic beliefs concerning the consumption of alcohol, for example, become reflected in official

The social organization in today's Iran is an ecclesia: the church and the state are one. Laws exist to support religious injunctions and to punish infractions of religious dicta.

prohibition of alcohol for all citizens and even visitors. During the Persian Gulf War of 1991, American service personnel in Saudi Arabia encountered many cultural difficulties that stemmed from differences in the religious traditions of the two societies.

A somewhat less extensive form of religious organization is the denomination. A **denomination** is a large and formally organized religious organization that enjoys a harmonious relationship with the state but shares the religious sector of society with other denominations, all of which benefit from relatively high levels of social respectability. In the United States, the Roman Catholic Church, the Episcopal Church, and the Presbyterian Church are all denominations. Denominations tend to be large and have at least a minimum amount of tradition to draw on to augment their authority (see Chapter 3). Members come and go according to their acceptance or rejection of denomination doctrine. That doctrine is formulated and promoted through the activities of a formal bureaucratic organization with paid employees.

One of the major sources of change in the religious world occurs when there is a split (or schism) in the membership of a denomination and some members leave to form a new religious organization. These new organizations, called **sects**, are small, informally organized groups that follow a doctrine derived from that of the denomination which gave them birth. In general, the largest religious organizations give birth to the most sects (Liebman, Sutton, and Wuthnow, 1988). The most common scenario for such a split is for a minority within the denomination to accuse the denomination of losing sight of its original goals while striving to achieve growth and respectability; those "original goals," transformed somewhat in response

The state tried to outlaw religion in the Soviet Union and the Eastern bloc countries it held in thrall, basing its actions on Marx's theory that religion serves to divide people and to justify social inequality. Religious faith, however, did not disappear. It played an important part in the Polish workers' struggle against the Communist Party apparatus. Here striking workers, members of the Solidarity Union, are shown in 1980, praying in front of a portrait of Pope John Paul, himself a Pole.

to changes in society, then become the basis of the sect's doctrine. Although the sect's doctrine may be to some degree responsive to changes in society since the inception of the original denomination, it does not typically reflect the dominant values of the social order within which it arises; it is indeed a sect characteristic to stand against many of those dominant values. Sects therefore do not usually enjoy anywhere near the level of respectability that characterizes denominations. If the sects persist over time and grow, however, they turn into denominations themselves with amazing regularity, thereby giving birth to new sects as members again become disgruntled. During the time of Martin Luther during the Reformation, the Lutheran Church was a sect; today, it is clearly a denomination.

The final category of religious organization is the cult. Sharing many characteristics with the sect, the **cult** is a small, usually informally organized group with a generally low level of respectability in the wider society; unlike the sect, the cult's religious doctrine is not a reformulation of some established denomination's doctrine but represents a distinctively different religious orientation. In the United States, some recent cults include Scientology, Transcendental Meditation, and the Unification Church (see Chapter 4). A less easily classified organization is the Church of Jesus Christ of Latter Day Saints (or Mormons). This religious organization contains many elements of Christianity (which would suggest a sect) yet so many variations on that theme as to suggest a cult. The latter is probably a better term; other organizations such as the Unification Church also contain elements of Christianity yet with enough contradictory doctrine (such as suggesting divinity for their Korean born leader) that they are never confused with sects. The Church of Jesus Christ of Latter Day Saints clearly had cultlike beginnings, yet today it is well down the road to recognition as a denomination in the United States, particularly in Utah. It also reflects many of the changes that moving toward denomination status brings about, such as the elimination of polygamy in order to better match dominant American values. Church members opposed to such changes toward moderation have formed splinter groups in response, thus showing how a cult can become a denomination while producing sects along the way.

Sociological Theories of Religion: Origins and Functions

Sociologists have traditionally been interested in religion as a social phenomenon, focusing on the effects that certain religious beliefs have on social groups or on the variety of ways that people organize their religious activities. Religions provide meaning to life. Although they may locate the source of those meanings in another world, they apply the meanings very much in this world.

Emile Durkheim was very interested in the relation between religion and what today we would call social values (Durkheim, 1954). Society is possible, said Durkheim, because its members feel bound together by sharing common values. Since they are shared, these values exist outside the individual, thriving in the everyday interactions among the group members who share them. The more we engage in those interactions, the stronger the hold these values will have over us, and we will experience that hold as coming from an outside source. Our religious experience, said Durkheim, reflects that experience of group values. In other words, we experience the source of religious meaning, such as a deity, as existing outside ourselves; in worshiping a deity, we actually worship the social forces that bind our group together in common purpose. Religion, in short, functions to hold social groups together.

Karl Marx (1818-1883) focused more on the ways religion separates individuals in society. Religion, Marx argued, is often used to justify social inequality. Christianity, for example, states that the meek are blessed, that the other cheek should be turned, and that the poor will find a just reward in heaven. These ideas make the poor less likely to attack the rich and more likely to make the best of their current situation.

Max Weber (1864-1920) emphasized the role of religious ideas in directing other activities. In his famous work *The Protestant Ethic and the Spirit of Capitalism* he argued that early Protestantism (Calvinism in particular) glorified hard work as its followers sought proof through their worldly success that they were in God's grace (Weber, 1958). This glorification of hard work, which Weber named the *Protestant ethic,* played a major role in promoting the growth of capitalistic enterprise during the early days of industrialization. Protestant capitalists poured their profits back into their businesses to make them grow still bigger to obtain even more secure proof of their state of grace. According to Weber, the religious basis for this activity largely passed away, but the work ethic remained very much alive as a social value. As we saw earlier, Americans still value work in itself as an activity.

These early theories of religion have played a major role in directing more modern sociological research. Durkheim's observation of the connection between religion and group solidarity has been both supported and extended. Sociologists today emphasize the group cohesion function of religious beliefs and rituals. Shared beliefs and, probably more important, shared patterns of behavior associated with religious ritual provide constant reminders of group membership to those who participate. When certain evangelical religious groups in the United States speak of holding "revivals" during group worship, they are focusing clearly on the potential role of group ritual in providing a boost to group solidarity through strengthening the attitudes of individuals in a group setting (see the reading by Denton following Chapter 13). Rituals conducted in such group settings are probably the most important in this regard, but even private rituals conducted in one's home provide reminders of the larger group with which one is associated.

The religious affiliations that provide people with ties to social groups make that group a source of social control over individuals' actions. As we saw in Chapter 4, individuals and groups to which we are most closely and most emotionally attached can exert considerable influence through the threat of removal of their attention and affection. An ultimate threat is expulsion from the group. Connections to religious social groups are some of the most intense ties that exist, and this intensity makes religious groups an effective source of social control. Both the beliefs and the attachment to the group that shares those beliefs give people motivation to choose or avoid certain behaviors. Weber's work on the effects of the Protestant ethic on influencing behavior falls within this general perspective.

Marx's work on the connection between religion and inequality has also been extended. Sociologists have examined the role of religion spread by missionaries during the period of Europe's colonization in Asia, Africa, and the Americas. While the missionaries' goals were no doubt religious, the spread of Christianity played a major role in spreading Western culture in general, making people in colonies more receptive to their rulers. An even clearer example comes from the use of Christianity during the period of slavery in the United States. The "turn the other cheek" aspects of Christianity were emphasized, while the more violent and revolutionary aspects of the religion were kept carefully hidden from the slaves; since slaves were prevented by law from learning to read, most had no direct access to the Bible (see Chapter 8).

Religion in the United States

An important aspect of both Christianity and Judaism is their respective acceptance of the separation of church and state. The Judeo-Christian heritage that dominates American culture is in harmony with the democratic form of government structured by the United States Constitution, which prohibits religion from directly controlling the political institution while simultaneously protecting the rights of citizens to practice their religions without interference from either the government or other citizens who may not approve. While there have been exceptions to this generalization, most notably the oppression of several Native American Indian religions, the United States for the most part has been fertile ground for religious diversity, participation in religious organizations, and religious change. In this section, we will examine some of the ways that religious beliefs and organizations affect other social institutions and how the organizations reflect the variation among members of American society.

Organization A full 90 percent of Americans report a preference for a particular religious organization when asked if they have such a preference (The Gallup Report, 1985; The National

Opinion Research Center, 1989). While all world religions are represented in the United States, the vast majority of American religious affiliation is with Christian and Jewish organizations. Of the 90 percent with a preference, somewhere between 57 and 65 percent report a preference for Protestant Christian religious organizations; between 25 and 28 percent report a Roman Catholic preference; and 2 percent report a Jewish preference (The Gallup Report, 1985; The National Opinion Research Center, 1989).

American Protestants are dominated by a few major denominations, including Baptists (20 percent), Methodists (9 percent), Lutherans (7 percent), Episcopalians (3 percent), Presbyterians (2 percent), and the United Church of Christ (2 percent); the remainder consists of a wide variety of Protestant denominations and sects. During the last twenty years, these percentages have been relatively stable, with only the Methodist and Presbyterian denominations showing a downward trend; the others have maintained their share of the Protestant sector (The Gallup Report, 1985). (We will look at reasons for such changes in a later section.) Jewish identification is somewhat more complicated since Jews are both an ethnic and a religious group; those who identify a preference for Judaism in response to a poll question may exhibit few religious behaviors otherwise. Of those Jews who do identify with religious organizations, approximately 14 percent identify with Orthodox Judaism, 49 percent with Conservative Judaism, and 34 percent with Reform Judaism (Lazerwitz and Harrison, 1979). Table 11.4 provides more complete information about membership of the larger American denominations.

While the major religious organizations are found to some extent throughout the United States, there are some interesting geographical concentrations that have resulted from earlier ethnic migrations. The Catholic Church, for example, dominates in the northeast and north central United States, where so many southeastern European immigrants settled. It is also strong in southern Florida (home to Cuban refugees) and in the southwestern United States, with its large Hispanic population. The Baptists dominate the southern states up to the Ohio River and west through Missouri, Oklahoma, and Texas. Lutherans dominate the Dakotas, Minnesota, and some areas of Montana and Iowa, where so many German and Scandinavian groups settled. Methodists, while found in large numbers in many locations, show particular dominance in Delaware, Maryland, Ohio, West Virginia, Iowa, Nebraska, and Kansas. Finally, the Church of Jesus Christ of Latter Day Saints dominates Utah and southern Idaho, the result of Mormons' nineteenth-century search for a land free from persecution.

While 90 percent of Americans feel comfortable stating a particular religious preference, only 67 percent report themselves as actual members of a particular religious organization and 42 percent state that they attended a church or synagogue during the preceding seven days. During the last half century, these figures have shown some consistency: 76 percent reported church membership in 1947, and 49 percent reported attendance during the preceding week in the late 1950s (high points for both), but the figures have been generally up and down over the whole period. There have been only minor long-term drops in church membership and virtually no change in the percentage of Americans who attended services during the week before they were interviewed (The Gallup Report, 1989). Considering that over the same half century, church attendance in Europe has dropped considerably (particularly among the young), one might conclude that organized religion in the United States is at least holding its own (Greeley, 1989).

TABLE 11.4

CHURCH MEMBERSHIP FOR SELECTED DENOMINATIONS

Religious Body	Year reported	Members
African Methodist Episcopal Church	1981	2,210,000
African Methodist Episcopal Zion Church	1987	1,220,260
American Baptist Churches in the U.S.A.	1987	1,568,778
Assemblies of God	1987	2,160,667
Christian Church (Disciples of Christ)	1987	1,086,668
Christian Churches and Churches of Christ	1987	1,071,995
Church of God (Anderson, IN)	1987	198,552
The Church of God in Christ	1982	3,709,661
The Church of Jesus Christ of Latter-Day Saints	1987	4,000,000
Church of Nazarene	1987	543,762
Churches of Christ	1987	1,623,754
The Episcopal Church	1987	2,462,300
Evangelical Lutheran Church in America	1987	5,288,230
Greek Orthodox Archdiocese	1977	1,950,000
Jehovah's Witnesses	1987	773,219
Jews	1987	5,943,700
The Lutheran Church—Missouri Synod	1987	2,614,375
Pentecostal Church of God, Inc.	1987	88,616
Pentecostal Holiness Church, International	1984	113,000
Presbyterian Church (U.S.A.)	1987	2,967,781
The Roman Catholic Church	1987	53,496,862
The Salvation Army	1987	434,002
Seventh-Day Adventist Church	1987	675,702
Southern Baptist Convention	1987	14,722,617
United Church of Christ	1987	1,662,568
The United Methodist Church	1986	9,124,575
United Pentecostal Church, International	1988	500,000

Source: Constant H. Jacquet, Jr. (ed), *Yearbook of American and Canadian Churches, 1989.* Nashville, TN: Abingdon Press, 1989.

The Correlates of Religious Affiliation: Organizations, Beliefs, and Social Attitudes

In this section, we look at the variation of religious beliefs and social attitudes that exists across religious organizations, along with differences in the social backgrounds of their members. Differences in beliefs should, of course, be expected. But sociologists have found variations not included in the official theologies of dominant American religions. Also, beyond religious beliefs, there are significant differences among members of different religious organizations in their attitudes on such secular (or nonreligious) topics as civil liberties, race relations, women's rights, and the appropriateness of various personal behaviors. Religious affiliations obviously have an impact on many aspects of their members' lives.

TABLE 11.5

VARIATIONS IN RELIGIOUS BELIEFS AMONG MEMBERS OF CHRISTIAN SECTS AND CHURCHES IN THE UNITED STATES

Denomination	Percent indicating belief in existence of God*	Percent indicating belief in virgin birth†	Percent indicating belief in Jesus's walking on water‡	Percent indicating belief in Jesus's future return§	Percent indicating belief in miracles"	Percent indicating belief in existence of devil¶
Congregational	41%	21%	19%	13%	28%	6%
Methodist	60	34	26	21	37	13
Episcopalian	63	39	30	24	41	17
Disciples of Christ	76	62	62	36	62	18
Presbyterian	75	57	51	43	58	31
American Lutheran	73	66	58	54	69	49
American Baptist	78	69	62	57	62	49
Missouri Lutheran	81	92	83	75	89	77
Southern Baptist	99	99	99	94	92	92
Sects	96	96	94	89	92	90
Total Protestant	*71%*	*51%*	*50%*	*44%*	*57%*	*38%*
Roman Catholic	*81%*	*81%*	*71%*	*47%*	*74%*	*66%*

* Percentage of people in each denomination agreeing with the statement "I know God really exists and I have no doubts about it."
†Percentage of people responding "Completely true" to the statement "Jesus was born of a virgin."
‡Percentage of people responding "Completely true" to the statement "Jesus walked on water."
§Percentage of people responding "Definitely" to the question "Do you believe Jesus will actually return to earth some day?"
"Percentage of people agreeing with the statement "Miracles actually happened just as the Bible says they did."
¶Percentage of people responding "Completely true" to the statement "The devil actually exists."
Source: Stark and Glock, 1968. Reprinted by permission of University of California Press.

Table 11.5 shows some of the variation in religious belief across some of the major denominations in the United States. A prime example of this variation is found with the first question, concerning the existence of God. While 95 percent or more of the American public claims a belief in God or a universal spirit, that percentage does not prevail across all religious organizations (The Gallup Report, 1985). Less than half of Congregationalists indicate having that belief, compared with 99 percent of Southern Baptists. Even larger differences appear with regard to miracles associated with Jesus and the existence of the devil. These data certainly suggest that individuals might wish to investigate different denominations in order to find one that is convivial to them, but an equally important observation is the variation *within* each religious organization. With the exception of percentages close to zero or a hundred, these data suggest that most major American religious organizations contain members who have fundamental disagreements *among themselves* as to religious doctrine. If 51 percent of Presbyterians believe that Jesus walked on water, that means that 49 percent of Presbyterians harbor definite doubts about it. In each, irrespective of official church doctrine, members vary in their degree of acceptance of that doctrine. The religious diversity in American life apparently goes beyond even the number of organizations available.

Religious organizations in the United States also vary considerably in the social backgrounds of their members. Table 11.6 provides an overview of this variation. For example, the decreases in membership experienced by the Methodist and Presbyterian denominations noted earlier can be seen reflected in the age distribution of their respective memberships; more of their members are over fifty while relatively few are under thirty; these data suggest some difficulty in keeping the children of current members within the fold plus low birth rates, perhaps, among the members. By contrast, Baptists have a large number of young members, which reflects their growing membership. Another young organization is the Roman Catholic Church, but the explanation here comes from the large Hispanic proportion of their membership. Both birth rates and immigration rates are high within the Hispanic population (see Chapter 8), and these create a growing population of new members. High birth rates within the black population of the United States also play a role in the vitality of the Baptist Church.

Variations in income and education across religious organizations are particularly interesting and help explain some of the basic differences we have seen in religious practice and belief. Income and education are basic measures of socioeconomic status (see Chapter 7) and give us some indication of social class differences across organizations. The best educated and wealthiest organizations in Table 11.6 are Episcopalians and adherents of Judaism. It is rare to find a high school dropout in either group. Lutherans and Presbyterians are also both relatively high on both variables. By contrast, Baptist organizations represent the other extreme, with poorer, less educated members. While Table 11.6 does not include the more fundamentalist Protestant denominations and sects, their memberships share these characteristics with the Baptist Church. In short, the more liberal and less strict organizations (see Table 11.5) are also the wealthiest, best educated, and slowest growing (or declining); the more fundamentalist organizations are the poorest, least educated, and fastest growing. While Table 11.6 does not distinguish among the different forms of American Judaism, the least strict—Reform Judaism—contains the wealthiest members while the most strict—Orthodox Judaism—contains the poorest (Lazerwitz and Harrison, 1979). This interesting connection among the variables of social class, form of religious belief, and vitality of organizational membership makes up one of the most interesting areas for contemporary sociological research in religion.

Finally, members of different religious organizations also vary in their political affiliation. The Democratic Party gains its strength from Jews, Catholics, and Baptists. The source of this strength, as well as its expression, varies considerably, however. Catholic affiliation with the Democratic Party results from the early days of Catholic immigration, when poor, urban Catholic neighborhoods at the turn of the last century were organized by the Democratic Party in its efforts to build a power base to combat the stronger Republican Party, which had dominated American politics following the Civil War. Jews became Democrats for similar reasons, but also because the Democratic Party came to be viewed as the party of social reform, minority rights, and organized labor, all of which fit into the major political concerns of many Jews. By contrast, the Baptist Church in the American South has displayed its traditional Democratic Party affiliation mainly because the Democratic Party was *not* the party of Lincoln. But Baptists represent a clearly conservative wing to the Democratic Party, and they, along with many of the stricter Protestant organizations, are moving increasingly to the Republican Party—a trend we will examine more closely in the next section.

TABLE 11.6

VARIATIONS IN AGE, ETHNICITY, SOCIAL CLASS, AND POLITICAL AFFILIATION AMONG MAJOR CHURCHES IN THE UNITED STATES (PERCENTAGES)

	Catholic	Jewish	Total Protestants	Baptists	Methodists	Lutherans	Presbyterians	Episcopalians
Age								
Under 30	30	19	23	28	17	20	16	17
30-49 years	38	41	37	38	35	39	32	40
50 and older	31	39	39	34	48	41	51	42
Race/ethnicity								
White	93	99	84	70	92	98	97	94
Black	4	0	14	29	7	1	2	3
Hispanic	19	1	2	1	1	1	1	1
Education								
College graduates	17	44	18	10	19	29	29	44
College incomplete	26	25	24	20	24	29	30	27
High school graduates	34	24	33	37	36	32	25	21
High school incomplete	22	7	25	32	20	15	16	8
Household income								
$40,000 and over	23	36	19	14	21	25	29	39
$25,000-39,999	25	24	22	20	24	27	22	20
$15,000-24,999	21	16	22	23	22	22	22	15
Under $15,000	25	17	31	39	28	22	22	18
Political affiliation								
Republican	26	15	32	25	27	39	43	38
Democrat	42	59	38	50	27	29	27	33
Independent	28	24	27	23	18	31	29	27

Source: Religion in America 1990. Princeton Religion Research Center. Princeton, NJ. 1990.

The Republican Party gains its traditional strength from the world of Protestant America in general and from the wealthiest denominations within that world in particular. Part of that connection is most certainly related to social class. On economic issues, the Republican Party generally takes conservative stands that tend to appeal to those who have benefitted most within the economic sector. Additionally, the religious specialization noted earlier in the political parties, which began in the last century, has strengthened Protestant membership within the Republican Party. In more recent years, the Republican Party has become increasingly conservative on social issues such as abortion and prayer in school, which has strengthened its appeal to the stricter denominations within Protestantism.

Social variation such as reflected in Table 11.6 explains some of the ways that religious organizations are perceived by nonmembers and ways that members of organizations perceive themselves. The beliefs and styles of worship of the wealthier churches, for example, tend to be harmonious with the beliefs and behaviors of Americans of a higher social class, in general. In addition, when individuals attend a particular church, they respond not just to the theology of that organization but also to the current membership. An individual from a lower social class, for example, would probably feel uncomfortable attending a church whose membership came largely from the wealthier side of the tracks (and, of course, vice-versa). As we saw in Chapter 7, different social classes in American society vary in a great many cultural or lifestyle ways. People's interest in surrounding themselves with other members of their social class does not stop at the church door.

Trends in Religious Change What is the role of religion in everyday American life and how might that role be changing? Sociologists have offered different analyses at different times. Robert Bellah (1970) argued that America was headed toward being dominated by a "civil religion," a watered-down compromise of all religions that presumably would offend no one. Our money carries the motto, "In God We Trust," without specifying which God from which religion is receiving that trust. In the 1950s, the Pledge of Allegiance to the flag had its patriotism augmented with religion as "under God" was added to the "one nation" receiving that pledge. Many of our public functions involve prayers as part of the ceremony, including locker-room prayers before football games in hopes that God might throw that last block for the winning touchdown. Such a civil religion would express Americans' desire to keep religion alive, but it also would suggest a weakening of strict religious commitment.

Some sociologists predicted a growing secularization in American life (Berger, 1961; Cox, 1971). **Secularization** is a weakening of religious tradition as people turn away from other-worldly, religious concerns and focus their attention on this-worldly, secular issues. Many theorists predicted a continuing move in this direction in industrial society as a result of the increasing prominence of science and scientific method in society. Indeed, many everyday human behaviors or problems facing humans (such as deviant behavior or illness) are no longer explained by most Americans in religious terms but in social scientific terms; bank robbers are not possessed by the devil but are simply brought up improperly, having had no appropriate moral code ingrained in them. Alternately, they may suffer from chemical imbalances or have been rejected by their mothers at a tender age. When science takes over the basic business of getting us through the turmoil of life, it would seem logical that religion might be on the way out.

In addition, some of the other social changes that were brought about by industrialization seem to be at odds with traditional religious behavior. High rates of geographical mobility have tended to follow industrialization, for example, and people who move are less likely to attend religious services than those who do not migrate (Wuthnow and Christiano, 1979). As a result, certain areas of the United States with high rates of geographical mobility tend to have lower rates of church attendance. The western region of the United States, including Alaska, Washington, Oregon, Nevada, and California, has been termed the "unchurched belt" (as opposed to the traditional "Bible belt") because it has the lowest rates of attendance in the country. Interestingly, residents of these states report having the same level of religious belief as other Americans, but those beliefs are not reflected in organizational participation; this finding gives support to the migration hypothesis, as migration rates are higher in those states than in others (Stark and Bainbridge, 1985). In spite of all these changes, however, most indications are that religion in the United States is holding its own and, in some ways, even growing organizationally stronger.

As we saw earlier, 90 percent of Americans still identify themselves with a particular religion, and church attendance has been relatively steady over recent years. Most Americans still report that they believe in God. But the most interesting support for a religious revival in the United States comes from research identifying which religions are most responsible for maintaining this support. Trends in church membership indicate that the sects and denominations growing the fastest are those with the strictest adherence to religious doctrine (Flake, 1984; Bromley and Shupe, 1984; J. Hunter, 1985; Hout and Greeley, 1987). In addition, Protestant and Jewish denominations that have traditionally been more liberal are becoming more traditional in their doctrine and practices (Steinfels, 1989). The mainstream Protestant denominations are no doubt responding to growth among the more fundamentalist Protestant groups (to which we'll turn in a moment). The Jewish groups have noted a resurgence among younger Jews in their observance of more traditional aspects of their religion. The most strict of all American Jewish religious groups—the Hasidic Jews of the northeastern United States—have been attracting more liberal Jews (Danzger, 1989). The intermarriage of Jews with non-Jews (which used to result in lost members of the Jewish religion) is now producing growing numbers of conversions from among those non-Jewish spouses who have become very committed religious Jews (Cohen, 1985; Roof and McKinney, 1987). Interestingly, the forms of mainstream religion in the United States that might be viewed as most closely tied to the secular world are the very ones facing a decline in popularity.

Perhaps no aspect of the religious revival in the United States more clearly characterizes the trend than the growth of fundamentalism. **Fundamentalism** includes those forms of religion characterized by a strict and unquestioned adherence to religious doctrine and sacred writings. In the United States, fundamentalism has been a most powerful force within the Protestant religious sector. The growth of fundamentalist organizations is not easily explained. Sociological theories have focused on the appeal of both the belief systems and the organizational attractiveness. The high rate of social change in other aspects of life is often cited as enhancing the attraction of the stricter fundamentalist beliefs. Among other things, social change can include alterations in an individual's social status; such change can result in higher levels of anxiety among those affected. One might therefore expect to find that people suffering from such "status anxiety" might be those most attracted to fundamentalism (Lipset and Raab, 1981). Some support for this hypothesis comes from the fact that the most conservative Protestant sects tend to have converts with a lower socioeconomic status than the status of families that were already members (Stark and Bainbridge, 1985).

Other research indicates that belief systems may be secondary to more personal considerations for people who convert. Converts are most likely to have personal relationships with current sect members. Those relationships may well be as important as religious beliefs in promoting organizational growth (Stark and Bainbridge, 1985). In keeping with that perspective, Roof and McKinney (1987) point out that both liberal and conservative churches exhibit considerable stability in the United States today. The important factor is not their doctrine but the communal stability of their membership.

Certainly the most colorful aspect of the growth in fundamentalism has been the booming business in religious television, which has made household names of such religious leaders as Oral Roberts, Jimmy Swaggart, and Jim and Tammy Bakker. In spite of legal and ethical problems of some television evangelists, religious television continues to be a major force in American religion. Over two hundred television stations are owned by religious groups, and the growth of cable TV has increased the viewership of such programs tremendously. Over one-quarter of religious TV air time is devoted to fund raising, which is successful enough to fill collection plates beyond the wildest dreams of preachers limited to nonelectronic congregations (Frankel, 1987). Much of this growth stems from technological advancements in the medium, but it should also be noted that religious television programs were once largely managed by the mainstream denominations (Hadden, 1987). The change in viewer popularity of religion over the airwaves thus parallels the change in orientation we see in community-based religious participation.

The impact of fundamental Christianity in the United States is felt well beyond the world of the religious institution. Many fundamentalists derive a particular political agenda from their beliefs, and this agenda has resulted in some of the more hotly debated political conflicts in recent years (Stevens, 1987). Public schools have been attacked for their teaching of evolution in science classes. An alternative has been proposed, known as creationism, which attempts to make scientific data conform to the contents of Genesis in the Old Testament of the Bible. Textbook companies have also been attacked, not only for the evolution content of their material, but also for what fundamentalists perceive as a general set of values (termed secular humanism) that promotes relativity in values. But the ultimate conflict is undoubtedly the ongoing argument over the use of prayer in public schools. In 1960, the United States Supreme Court ruled that religious observances in public schools violated the separation of church and state mandated in the Constitution. The fundamental wing of American Protestantism is uniformly in favor of changing that ruling and has actively (although unsuccessfully) worked toward that end for many years.

The clearest movement on the American political scene by fundamentalists was the formation of the Moral Majority in the 1980s by Jerry Falwell. During that decade, Falwell attempted to create a political agenda based on fundamentalist Protestant beliefs that might unify and mobilize followers toward common political ends. This agenda included opposition to the Equal Rights Amendment, to pornography, to abortion rights, and to homosexual rights. Efforts were made to identify politicians who supported these issues and to work toward their defeat, either through direct political attacks or through the backing of alternative candidates whose positions were acceptable. The culmination of this effort was the candidacy of Pat Robertson for

President in 1988. While Robertson was unsuccessful and the Moral Majority is no longer an active force, the political issues of fundamentalist Protestantism remain central areas of conflict in American political life. The growth of fundamentalist Protestant sects and denominations along with growing membership in the Catholic Church and a resurgence of interest in Judaism among American Jews suggests that the secular side of American life will soon have considerable company from religious organizations.

SUMMARY

An economic system is the organization of social activities that produces and distributes goods and services within and between societies. In industrial societies (in which it is a clearly separate institution), it consists of three sectors: the production of raw materials, basic manufacturing, and the production and distribution of services. Modern economic systems vary in terms of ownership of property: largely private ownership occurs in capitalist economies, and largely public ownership of property in socialist economies. Within the former, a basic economic unit is the corporation, which operates with the rights of ownership and the liabilities of an individual but is typically owned by a number of individuals who are its shareholders. Corporations can be large (even multinational in scope) to the point where they may control whole sectors of the economy.

Modern economic systems run on the labor of workers whose efforts are obtained through contract with employers. The nature of this relationship (and, in particular, the level of satisfaction of workers) plays an important role in determining industrial productivity. Business cycles result in rising and lowering levels of unemployment as demand for products rises and falls. In response to these and other uncertainties in the workplace, many workers have formed and joined labor unions in order to gain a more forceful voice in affecting their situation in the marketplace. In the United States, industrialization has changed over the years; there has been growth in the service sector of the economy coupled with declines in raw material production and basic manufacturing (much of which now occurs in newly industrializing nations with lower labor costs). The growth of the service sector has changed the occupational structure of American society, including the formation of highly skilled and well rewarded occupations (the primary labor market) and unskilled and poorly rewarded occupations (the secondary labor market).

A political system represents the social organization in a society that distributes power and governs its use. Modern industrial societies vest such power in a centralized organization called a state, which coordinates power and comes to hold considerable authority. Membership in state governments and forms of decision making range from democratic governments (controlled through popular election) to authoritarian governments (in which power is concentrated in the hands of a few leaders). Democratic participation in the United States, particularly with regard to electoral politics, has declined throughout the twentieth century. Of the more organized forms of participation, such as lobbying, a particularly important development is the growth of the political action committee, through which considerable money and influence are channeled. Equally important is the role of the media in politics as candidates must now finance and orchestrate their activities through media, especially television. As a result, candidates are encouraged to spend more money and to maintain campaigns emphasizing symbols and often considerable superficiality.

Religion includes those shared beliefs, associated behavior patterns, and forms of social organization that are oriented toward the supernatural. In industrial societies, such organizations operate within a separate institution. They vary in form from the ecclesia (which is a religion closely associated with a state), to denominations (which are highly organized but independent of the state), to sects or cults (which are small and represent new trends in religious practice and belief). Some religious organizations function as ideologists for traditional authorities within society, while others may act as agents of social change. Within the United States, religion is organized in a wide variety of independent denominations, sects, and cults, most of which stem from the Judeo-Christian tradition. These organizations vary in terms of beliefs and practices but also in terms of the social characteristics of their members. Americans profess high levels of religious belief and exhibit high levels of religious participation as compared with other industrialized nations. In recent years, the United States has seen a growth of secularization in some sectors of society along with a growth of interest in the most fundamental forms of religious belief in other sectors of society.

GLOSSARY

Alienation A worker's lack of interest in and identification with the job, coupled with a general feeling of powerlessness over the conditions that affect his or her life.

Animism Those religious belief systems that impute supernatural forces to natural objects.

Authoritarian government A government characterized by the concentration of political control within the hands of a relative few members of society.

Capitalist economies Economic systems characterized by the private ownership of property and a form of coordination based on a market system of exchange through which goods and services are exchanged according to value determined by supply and demand.

Conglomerate A large corporation formed through the merger of many smaller corporations that operate in different sectors of the economy.

Corporation A legal entity that functions in the economic sector with rights of ownership and potential liabilities much like those of an individual but legally separate from the individuals that own it.

Cult A small, usually informally organized religious group with a generally low level of respectability in the wider society and whose doctrine represents a distinctively different religious orientation.

Democratic government A government in which citizens are permitted to participate, either directly or indirectly, in the processes of government.

Denomination A large and formally organized religious organization that enjoys a harmonious relationship with the state but shares the religious sector of society with other denominations, all of which benefit from relatively high levels of social respectability.

Dictatorship The concentration of political power in the hands of one person.

Direct democracy A democratic government in which each citizen has an equal voice and directly participates in governmental activities.

Ecclesia A religious organization that is essentially one with the state, enjoying the support of the government and claiming citizens of the state as members.

Economic system The organization of social activities that produces and distributes goods and services within and between societies.

Elitism The belief that a small group of people in a society inevitably hold power.

Fundamentalism Those forms of religion characterized by a strict and unquestioned adherence to religious doctrine and sacred writings.

Interest group A social organization that represents particular political interests and seeks to influence the political institution to further those interests.

Interlocking directorate The appearance of the same individuals on the board of directors of several corporations simultaneously.

Lobbying The provision of special information to political leaders by an interest group coupled with attempts to convince them to vote in accordance with the desires of the interest group.

Mixed economies Economic systems characterized by a compromise between capitalist and socialist economic systems whereby some property is privately owned while other property is controlled by the state.

Monopoly The control over a given product or service by a single corporation.

Monotheism The belief in one god.

Multinational corporation A corporation that is located in one country yet owns companies that are based in other countries.

Nation-state A state with only one significant ethnic group within its boundaries.

Oligarchy The concentration of political power in the hands of a small group of people.

Oligopoly The domination over the production of a given product or service by a relatively small number of corporations.

Pluralism The belief that power in a society is relatively evenly distributed.

Political action committee An organization formed to raise and contribute money to support the aims of a particular interest group.

Political socialization The process by which individuals acquire values and patterns of behavior with regard to the political institution.

Political system The social organization in an industrial society that distributes power within the society and governs its use.

Polytheism The belief in more than one god.

Primary labor market Those occupations that provide a range of employee benefits coupled with relatively high status and at least some security.

Primary sector That sector of the economy associated with the production of raw materials.

Productivity The number of worker hours required to produce a given product.

Profane All elements of human experience that are commonplace (see sacred).

Religion Those shared beliefs, associated behavior patterns, and forms of social organization that are oriented toward the supernatural.

Religious rituals Behaviors that are defined and promoted by particular religious belief systems.

Representative democracy A democratic government involving the election of representatives by groups of citizens, after which those representatives discuss and vote on governmental actions.

Sacred Those elements of human experience that inspire awe, fear, or reverence.

Secondary labor market Those occupations that are relatively low-skilled and poorly paid and that provide few if any employee benefits.

Secondary sector That sector of the economy associated with manufacturing activities through which raw materials are transformed into usable goods.

Sect A small, informally organized religious group that follows a doctrine derived from that of the denomination which gave it birth.

Secularization A weakening of religious tradition as people turn away from other-worldly, religious concerns and focus their attention on worldly, secular issues.

State A form of social organization that controls the means of coercion (or force) over a given territory with specified political (or international) boundaries.

Socialist economies Economic systems characterized by the public ownership of property and the state-run coordination of the production of goods and services.

Tertiary sector That sector of the economy associated with the production and distribution of services.

Theism The belief that supernatural forces are controlled by a single god or a number of gods that are interested in and responsive to human affairs.

Totalitarian government An authoritarian government that seeks control over all aspects of communal and individual life within its boundaries.

Veto group A version of pluralism in which distribution of power occurs because one group—a veto group—has enough power to limit any actions of another group that might result in that group's ascension.

SUPPLEMENTARY READINGS

Berger, Peter *The Capitalist Revolution.* New York: Basic Books, 1986.

Berger provides a theoretical approach to the interplay between the growth of capitalism, its resulting forms of economic development, and the growth of democracy. He concludes that the former two occurrences are necessary for the latter result.

Brown, Michael K. (ed.) *Remaking the Welfare State: Retrenchment and Social Policy in America and Europe.* Philadelphia: Temple University Press, 1988.
A comparative approach to the welfare role of the modern state with a focus on the problems of organizing and financing social welfare.

Cox, Harvey *Religion in the Secular City.* New York: Simon & Schuster, 1984.
An analysis of religions and religious beliefs in the 1980s in the United States and the prospects of change for the future with a particular focus on Protestant fundamentalism.

Dahl, Robert *Dilemmas of Pluralist Democracy.* New Haven, CN: Yale University Press, 1982.
Dahl is perhaps the main proponent of pluralist perspectives on power in the United States.

Domhoff, G. William *Who Rules America Now? A View for the 80s.* Englewood Cliffs, NJ: Prentice Hall, 1983.
An analysis of the distribution of power in American society, emphasizing the important role played by the small percentage of people who control much of the wealth in America.

Johnstone, Ronald L. *Religion in Society: A Sociology of Religion* (3rd ed.). Englewood Cliffs, NJ: Prentice Hall, 1988.
An examination of religion within the United States, with particular emphasis on the relations among religion, politics, and the economy. Designed as a textbook, this work provides one of the more general overviews available.

Mills, C. Wright *The Power Elite.* New York: Oxford University Press, 1956.
In this modern American sociological classic, Mills presents the elitist perspective on political power distribution through a discussion of power in American society.

Orum, Anthony *Introduction to Political Sociology* (3rd ed.). Englewood Cliffs, NJ: Prentice Hall, 1989.
This text on political sociology provides a good place to start on a further exploration into sociological research and relevant theories on the political institution.

Ritzer, George, and David Walczak *Working: Conflict and Change* (4th ed.). Englewood Cliffs, NJ: Prentice Hall, 1990.
A textbook on the world of work, this volume provides an overview of the interplay of the economy, the structure of the occupational world, and individual responses to the work environment.

Roof, Wade Clark, and William McKinney *American Mainline Religion: Its Changing Shape and Future.* New Brunswick, NJ: Rutgers University Press, 1987.
Roof and McKinney offer an excellent overview of the major denominations in American society, with particular attention paid to changes in religious behavior, the demographic composition of different denominations, and the impact of religion on individual attitudes.

Stark, Rodney, and William Sims Bainbridge *The Future of Religion: Secularization, Revival, and Cult Formation.* Berkeley: University of California Press, 1985.
An overview of religion in the United States today with particular attention to some of its more extreme manifestations (such as cults) and to the relation between religions and other institutions of society.

Woronoff, Jon *The Japan Syndrome: Symptoms, Ailments, and Remedies.* New Brunswick, NJ: Transaction, 1986.
An examination of the modern Japanese workplace and its relation to the overall economic growth of Japan and its domination of world trade.

READING

As We Go into the Nineties: Some Outlines of the Twenty-first Century

DANIEL BELL

How will international politics and economics shape the coming decade? Bell offers some interesting predictions based on changing political structures (most notably in the Soviet Union and Europe), changes in the political posture of the United States in international relations, and growing economic competition from the Pacific Rim countries, with Japan in the forefront. Bell begins with an examination of internal events in the Soviet Union, offering his explanation for the economic problems and ethnic conflict that developed in that country in the late 1980s and early 1990s. While events have moved extremely quickly in that country (which has reverted to a commonwealth of individual republics) it seems clear that the cold war will no longer dominate international relations. Bell continues with an examination of the growing strength and unity of Europe and the Pacific Rim, suggesting a continuing role for the United States in technology and innovation coupled with a diminishing political role in foreign affairs.

As we enter the 1990s, the outline of the twenty-first century, with respect to the configuration of issues and forces, already seems clear. We can identify four:

1. The collapse of communism
2. The reunification of Europe
3. The end of "The American Century"
4. The rise of the Pacific rim

Beyond these are other, more inchoate and indistinct forms, whose outlines are not as clear, though this does not mean they are of lesser importance. In some instances, as the twenty-first century unfolds, they may, indeed, prove to be the most disruptive. These issues are the following: the problems of poverty in the Third World (exempting east Asia now from that configuration), the fratricidal rivalries in the Middle East, and the rising ethnic and nationalist rivalries in many different parts of the world, as the older issues of class and imperialism recede.

How can we understand these new forces in some systematic way? Is there some framework that allows us to order them in some explanatory fashion? More than fifteen years ago, in seeking to provide a coherent picture of the world at that time, I set forth four "axes" along which the alignments might be understood. These were, schematically put:

1. *East* vs. *West*. This rivalry was principally between the United States and the Soviet Union and the forces grouped behind them in the NATO and Warsaw Pact alliances. The rivalries here were political and ideological, with the constant threat of military confrontation. This was the cold war.

2. *West* vs. *West*. This rivalry was principally between the United States on the one side and, on the other, Japan (putting her in this context within the West) and Germany. The rivalry here was economic.

3. *North* vs. *South*. Here were the OECD, or industrialized countries, versus the newly industrialized societies, the "Group of 77" within the United Nations, who were demanding a redistribution of world manufacturing capacity. The issues here were economic and ideological.

Reprinted by permission of Daniel Bell and *Dissent* magazine.

4. *East* vs. *East.* This rivalry was the Soviet Union against China, where the competitions were ideological and political with a thin threat of military conflict.

It was, and still is to some extent, a useful frame of reference.* The intention was to see which axis was salient, at what time. When this was first presented it was obvious that the East vs. West axis dominated all others. The West vs. West was only a dim cloud, and some writers thought it improbable. North vs. South was very strident. And East vs. East was very strained.

Today it is likely that the cold war is finished. West vs. West, in particular the rivalry between Japan and the United States on economic issues, has become highly salient. But there is also now the rise of the various East Asian "tigers," such as Korea, Taiwan, and Thailand, to add to that competition. North vs. South at the moment is somewhat muted. And East vs. East is, for the while, quiet.

That analytical framework may still have some limited use. But there is now a new intellectual challenge to provide a different, coherent framework to encompass the new alignments as they are emerging. Whether this can be done remains to be seen. But before we can do so, there is much detailed analysis to explore.

Events of the Past Decade

For almost fifty years after the Russian Revolution of October 1917, it seemed as if Marxism would sweep the world. Nothing so blazing as revolutionary Marxism had been seen, as some historians compared it, since the rise of Islam more than a millennium before. Here was a new faith system that had inspired working-class movements in Europe, sparked a revolution in China, become a model for intellectuals in Latin America and new elites in Africa, and so on. And now it has collapsed, in less than a decade, like a house of cards. It would take many volumes to analyze the reasons why. For the moment, let us deal with two related groups, one the Soviet Union, the other Eastern Europe.

*Much of this scheme was elaborated in my essay "The Future World Disorder" (1977), reprinted in my book *The Winding Passage* (Basic Books, 1980).

There are, I would say, three factors, now conjoined, that account for the crisis in the Soviet Union:

1. *The failure of the economic model.* Soviet planning was rigid and inflexible and, beyond an initial start, it could not manage a large and complex economy. In an early essay Lenin said that planning was a simple affair. If there were 200 million Russians and each one needed two pairs of shoes, one produced 400 million pairs. There is, paradoxically enough, a *surplus* of shoes today in Soviet warehouses. But nobody wants them. They are too ungainly, shoddily constructed, and of poor quality. What the Soviet Union had, in the early five-year plans, was not "planning" but a *mobilized* economy based on *physical* targets. But there was no price mechanism to judge whether resources were being used efficiently. In fact, for dogmatic reasons, Soviet planners did not use the mechanism of interest rates (since interest was usury and exploitative) as a measure of the relative efficiency of capital. At the same time there were heavy subsidies on such items as bread and housing rents. But no one knew the true costs; more resources were devoted to bread, and because it was relatively cheap, the product was misused. Lacking a true cost and accounting system (and using a double-ruble system to divert resources for military use) Soviet planners had no measures of the deficits they were running and the inflation that was hidden. Today the economy is in shambles.

2. *The failure of ideology.* Ideologies are worldviews (weltanschaunungen) that mobilize their believers for a "cause" and provide a set of justifications on the basis of the "higher" goals. But the "revolutionary" goals of egalitarianism and of a classless society, and the ideas of socialized property, gave way, increasingly, to a "new class" of privileged, the *nomenklatura;* and the regime, particularly under Stalin, resorted to terror as a means of forcing compliance with its demands. The failure of ideology, when there are no other justifications, means a loss of legitimacy and the beliefs of the rulers and the ruled in their "right" to rule. For a period of time, the "patriotic war" against Nazi Germany

provided a social cement. But the resumptions of terror and privilege eroded those commitments.

3. *The crumbling of "empire."* What was little known is that the Soviet Union was the *only* nation that came out of World War II with extensive territorial gains, at a time when almost all the other imperial and colonial powers were surrendering their control over lands in Asia and Africa. Since 1940, starting with the Nazi-Soviet pact, the Soviet Union annexed Finnish Karelia, the Republics of Estonia, Latvia, and Lithuania, the Koenigsberg district of East Prussia, the eastern provinces of Poland, the sub-Carpathian district of Ruthenia from Czechoslovakia, Bukovina and Bessarabia from Romania, and the Sakhalin and Kurile islands from Japan.

In addition, badly drawn boundary lines within the older Soviet Union have left large pockets of ethnic rivalries, such as the Caucasus territory of Nagorno-Karabakh, which is heavily Armenian and Christian within the republic of Azerbaijan, which is Muslim. On the Black Sea, the small area of Abkazia wishes to secede from neighboring Georgia, while Georgia itself wants autonomy within the Soviet Union. And, more to the point, the most successful economic region of the Soviet Union, the Baltic republics of Estonia, Latvia, and Lithuania, are now demanding, if not freedom, then almost complete autonomy.

Almost twenty years ago, the Soviet dissident and writer Andrei Amalrik (who spent many years in the gulag and was killed tragically in an automobile accident) wrote a tract, *Will Russia Survive Until 1984?* It seemed odd and fanciful at the time. Now Russian politicians such as Boris Yeltsin (himself somewhat of an opportunist and demagogue) ask seriously whether the Soviet Union can last until 1994.

No one can provide an answer. It has been the genius of Mikhail Gorbachev that he has recognized all the problems and sought to provide reforms through *perestroika.* He has, at the same time, recognized that the party cannot rule alone and has begun to create political structures with a degree of independent power. Even if Gorbachev succeeds, it is evident that the Soviet Union cannot remain an effective superpower and that the military and ideological threat it once posed, especially to Europe, has now largely receded. If he fails? There was once an old Soviet joke that said that when Stalin died he left two envelopes. One said, "In case of trouble, open this." Trouble arose and the envelope was opened. In it was a message that said, "Blame me." The other envelope said, "In the event of more trouble, open this." More trouble came and the second envelope was opened. It said, "Do as I did."

That is now impossible. Deng Xiaoping could still have the authority among the veterans of the Chinese revolution to give an order to shoot. Gorbachev cannot. His destruction of Stalin and the legitimacy of that "revolution" makes it impossible. Yet if Gorbachev fails, the greater likelihood is that of a right-wing, nationalist reaction, using the symbols of old Russia and seeking to mobilize the Soviet people on the basis of traditional symbols. But such a move would alienate the intelligentsia and the modernizing elements in the Soviet Union, and even if a right-wing force came into power, its economic base would still be weak.

About Eastern Europe: the news has been electrifying. Within a few months the communist regimes of Poland, Hungary, Bulgaria, East Germany, and Czechoslovakia have crumbled. The reasons are fairly clear. In almost no country had there been strong, indigenous communist forces. The regimes were *imposed* almost entirely from the outside and reinforced by Soviet troops. More than that, in the first decade after World War II, Stalin purged the leadership of most of the native Communist parties in a sweeping set of trials. In Czechoslovakia, there was the Slansky trial. In Hungary, The Rajk trial. In Bulgaria, the Petkov trial, and so on. In 1956, an independent Hungarian regime led by *communists,* such as the premier Imre Nagy, was suppressed by Soviet tanks, and Nagy was executed and buried in an unmarked grave until the poignant moment last summer when his remains were given a public, ceremonial funeral. In 1968, the Prague Spring, the effort of Alexander Dubcek to put forth the new idea of "socialism with a human face," was smashed by Soviet tanks.

Once *glasnost* and political reforms had begun in the Soviet Union, how could the older regimes hold out against change? They could not. In Hungary, the Communist party has dissolved itself, and only *5 percent* of its former members have joined a new Communist party. In Poland, the Communist party, though nominally guaranteed a majority of seats in the lower house, could not even gain enough votes to ratify that agreement, and a non-Communist is the prime minister of Poland, received with amiable greeting by Gorbachev himself.

From all that political rubble, one thing is clear. Whatever the formal adherence to the Warsaw Pact may mean, Eastern Europe is no longer a reliable force for the Soviet Union. Nor is East Germany. So far as Europe is concerned, the cold war is over and new configurations are about to begin.

What of the Future?

Let me turn, now, to the new configurations:

1. *The reunification of Europe.* The framework with which we have all been operating has been the idea of the European Economic Community, the twelve-nation "commonwealth" scheduled to come to fruition in 1992 and that, already, has taken distinct shape.

Now three new factors have to be taken into account. One is the possible—and probable—reunification of the two Germanys into a single entity of eighty million persons, which will make it the most powerful economic unit of Europe. The second is the inclusion of Eastern Europe in a European trade bloc. And the third is the relation of the Soviet Union to Europe.

Historically, the Soviet Union has feared the emergence of a new, unified Germany. Historically, the two have been antagonists, even though a different set of dreamers, the German geopolitical strategists, such as Karl Haushofer, envisioned a new Eurasia, spanning the heartland of Europe and Asia and becoming the center of world power.

Although history has always been important in understanding the destinies of nations, it can also be misleading. England and France were enemies at the beginning of the nineteenth century and allies at the beginning of the twentieth. History has been important when *land* and *territory* were the goals of national states. Today these are less important than *technology.* The overriding need of the Soviet Union is for technology. And here, Germany, even a reunified Germany, becomes a useful partner. Already a deal had been struck ten years ago for a new pipeline that would bring natural gas from Siberia to Germany.

Until now, the Soviet Union has depended upon Czechoslovakia and East Germany for much of its manufactured products and for steel and machine tools. But both economies have become increasingly outmoded and incapable of supplying the Soviet Union with the new modern technology that it needs, particularly computer technology and telecommunications. West Germany becomes the "natural" source of this technology.

In effect, the logic of the economic interdependencies and needs, the huge timber, oil and gas, and mineral resources of the Soviet Union and the technology of Western Europe, dovetail into a pattern. Eastern Europe itself, if its industries are modernized, can provide the light industry (shoes and textiles) as well as the older manufactured products, including steel, as well as cheaper labor, for Western Europe.

These closer bonds would mean the destruction of the older NATO and Warsaw Pact configurations. England and France are bound to be wary of such moves—unless the security issue is completely resolved. Here the key is the Soviet Union. If Gorbachev takes convincing steps to reduce the Soviet military posture, then the economic logic can begin to operate. From his point of view, there is a contradictory problem. Reducing the military sector means freeing resources for the consumer sector. At the same time, the military has been an important power base for him—especially as the Communist party itself has become weakened. The military remains the major organized base of power within the Soviet Union. How Gorbachev manages these tasks will be decisive for his own retention of power, as well as for the necessary economic moves he has to make vis-à-vis Europe.

2. *The end of "The American Century."* The American Century was a phrase fashioned by

Henry Luce—proprietor of *Time, Life* and *Fortune,* the most influential periodicals of their day—during World War II to herald a new and majestic role for the United States. Like all such ambitions, it had a mixture of idealism and economic self-interest. Luce, the son of Christian missionaries, whose early years had been spent in China, saw the American Century as fulfilling the Christian obligations of the United States to be "the good Samaritan," the helper of the poor and the needy. At its best, this was expressed politically by the Marshall Plan, which led to the economic reconstruction of Europe, and by substantial aid to Japan. As the cold war developed, the United States—which had begun to disarm after World War II—became the military protector of both Europe and Japan against the Soviet Union. Its economic role became intertwined with its military role, creating what President Eisenhower called "the military-industrial complex." While military expenditure has never been the *necessary* basis for America's continuing economic growth, it has been an important one.

Four elements conjoin to reduce the centrality and power of the United States as the twenty-first century emerges: One is the reduction of the great power confrontations, and therefore the decisive political role of the United States as the "leader" of the world. Second is the rise of Japanese economic power, especially in the central high-technology sectors. Third are the low investment and productivity features of the American economy, which begin to sap its strength. And fourth comes the increasing difficulty of coping with domestic social problems such as crime and drugs, the aging infrastructures, and the declining quality of life in the central cities.

However, there has been a tendency, of late, to assume that the United States is almost "finished" as a major power. That would be misleading. The United States still maintains the general lead in technological *innovation*—if not always in development. (VCRs, facsimile, multivalve engines, and dozens of other products were created in the United States, though quickly developed elsewhere, as in Japan.) The United States maintains the foremost graduate education and scientific power of any country in the world. Japan, for example, has had strong universities but almost no graduate schools of any consequence. England and Europe, also with strong universities, do not have the scientific manpower and talent or the graduate schools of the United States. The United States remains the largest market for many export-led countries such as Korea to sell their products to. And in military and space technology, including aircraft, the United States maintains sizable leads.

The new free-trade pact with Canada and the growing integration of Mexican manufacture with U.S. industries provide a possible foundation for economic expansion. Nor should one ignore the political stability that provides a haven for jittery capital in other countries.

3. *The Pacific Rim.* What is evident here is the centrality of Japan as the major economic and financial power in the Pacific. And events in the last year have given Japan two "reprieves." One is the reduction of the Soviet military threat. In recent years, Japan has been under pressure from the United States to spend more on defense and military security. It has been yielding to that pressure. Now there is much less of that need. And the Soviet Union has even been making noises about returning some of the islands near Hokkaido to Japan, as a gesture of goodwill, and is seeking financial credits and technology from Japan. With the reduction of the Soviet threat, Japan is in a better position to resist American political and economic pressure on trade.

The second "reprieve" is China. The events in Tiananmen Square have, for the while, cut China off from the rest of the world. Historically, the United States, going back to the American Secretary of State John Hay, has always been *pro-China* in its policy. One of the "cards" open to the United States in recent years vis-à-vis Japan has been to develop political and economic relations with China. This was, particularly, the grand design of Henry Kissinger. And it would have led to a counterweight of U.S.-China relations to Japan and to the Soviet Union.

But as for Japan—and other East Asian countries—what is also evident is the recreation, with the cooperation of Australia and the Asian countries, of the old East Asia Co-Prosperity scheme. The industrialization of East Asia is proceeding rapidly, with Japan supplying most of the capital. A recent report of the Japan Center for Economic Research (October 1989) points out that in fiscal 1985 Japanese investments in manufacturing in Asian firms totaled $460 million. This increased 80 percent in the next year, and doubled the following one, and rose again by 40 percent in fiscal 1988. The total investments by electrical-machinery makers rose more than five times from 1985 to 1986 and have been increasing by 80 percent a year since then.

Given these emerging frameworks, what can one say, in summary, regarding the configuration of the twenty-first century as it is now appearing? I leave aside, as I said previously, the difficult questions of the increasing poverty and the widening gaps between the developed and the developing worlds, particularly in Africa. I leave aside the intractable passions of the Middle East. And there is the difficult question of the stability of the Soviet Union, given its economic and empire tensions.

North and South remain as an axis of division, which will likely become increasingly threatening after the first quarter of the twenty-first century. East vs. East is, for the while, in stasis, and much will depend upon the successors of Deng and even Gorbachev (who is likely to last, if he can surmount his difficulties, to the end of the century). And as for East vs. West, the United States and the Soviet Union may enter a period of détente.

The major new alignments that are coming into place are the regional blocs. These are economic-political units of a larger viability for nations to manage their problems of economic transition. A united Europe, a Continental North American economy, and a Japan-dominated Pacific region become the great land-mass units for economic, and even political, power. It would mean, if economic logic also followed, the replacement of the dollar by a managed basket of the ECU (European currency unit), the dollar, and the yen as the mechanisms of exchange and trade balance.

One major caution: one cannot "predict" events and their outcomes, crucial as they may be; for example, the direction of China with the passing of Deng Xiaoping and his generation. One can only, as I have tried to do here, define "structural arrangements" to provide a grid for analysis.

If one looks ahead to the end of the century, there are two "structural" problems that loom quite large. One is demographic. In the United States, Western Europe, and Japan, we have aging populations. In most of the Third World countries—Algeria and Mexico are the prime examples—the youth cohort under seventeen years of age is between 40 to 50 percent of the population. Logically there are only three things one can do; take their people, buy their goods, or give them capital. All three pose difficulties that are not easy to resolve.

The second "structural" problem is the rising tension between the contrary pulls of the global economy and the national polities. Capital can flow easily; people cannot. No nation today controls its own currency and capital flows to take advantage of differential interest rates, cheaper labor, and better investment opportunities. But people, unless destitute or highly skilled, cannot move as readily; nor are many countries prepared to take them. More than that, as jobs slip away, the question before a regime is does it protect capital or people. In the United States we have seen this in the textile and automobile business and now in semiconductors. A large economy such as ours may be able to manage such transitions, but many cannot, and the fragmentation of many polities around the world because of economic difficulties, multiplied subsequently by ethnic clashes, increases the chances for what is called in the jargon of the Pentagon planner, "low-intensity conflicts."

These are the undertows and riptides in the world society. The interplay of demography, global economy, and national polity becomes the framework for trying to understand the problems of the twenty-first century.

Discussion Questions

1. Bell views the collapse of the Soviet empire in terms of failed economics, failed ideology, and internal ethnic conflict. Did each play an equal role in bringing about change in the Soviet system?
2. How has Europe changed since World War II? How will the end of socialist rule in eastern Europe affect western Europe, both politically and economically?
3. Can the United States hope to compete economically with Pacific Rim countries in the next century? What arguments can you give for and against that possibility?

READING

Future Work

Joseph F. Coates, Jennifer Jarratt, and John B. Mahaffie

What kind of jobs can we expect from the future of the American economy and who is going to be competing for them? Coates, Jarratt, and Mahaffie attempt to answer such questions by comparing changes in the U.S. population with changes in the economy. In particular, they note the impact on the economy of increasing numbers of older, female, and nonwhite workers. These workers have different needs and skills, so the work force will have to change accordingly. The authors also view the impact of employment on family life and vice-versa, suggesting that women may choose different childbearing alternatives and businesses may move to new locations and alter worker scheduling. Finally, the cost of health care in the United States is examined with a close eye on the interrelations between those costs and economic growth.

The North American work force faces wrenching changes in its structure and composition that will radically alter how employers recruit, hire, manage, and hold on to good people.

Some of these changes are demographic. More women, minorities, and immigrants are entering the work force; the work force is aging, as is society in North America; and the number of younger, entry-level workers available is shrinking. Other changes are economic: For example, North American corporations confront growing competition at home and abroad from companies with lower labor costs and faster product-to-market rates. This means employers must contain labor costs and produce higher-quality goods and services with a smaller work force.

What an individual worker can bring to the workplace—in terms of education, skills, self-reliance, and attitude—is becoming ever more important in reaching an organization's business goals. Businesses are recognizing that a worker is a resource and an asset, rather than merely a fixed cost.

The North American work force has earned its reputation as one of the most vital and hard-working labor forces in the world. Other countries envy its education, mobility, and creativity, as they also admire the U.S. economy's capacity for generating new jobs. Maintaining this reputation and competing effectively in turbulent times will require flexibility and the ability to embrace and incorporate change. The ability of business planners and managers to anticipate changes and their effects on people in an organization thus becomes more critical, and competitive survival may depend on how well planners and managers can think about the future.

More than ever before, people are the dominant factor in both service and production. People plan, invent, design, operate, manage, and service the large corporation. People are its suppliers and its customers.

This increased attention being given to the demand for more-productive and more-effective workers is stimulating new ideas. When one thinks of innovation, one tends to think of science and high technology, such as robots and new ceramics. But now one also thinks of quality circles, innovative rewards, and new work arrangements.

One of the most positive developments is the growing interest on the part of business organizations in identifying and analyzing trends shaping the future work force. This interest in the future is a first step toward planning for work-force

Reprinted by permission of *The Futurist* and of the authors.

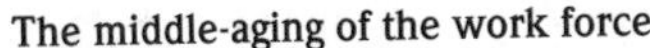

The middle-aging of the work force

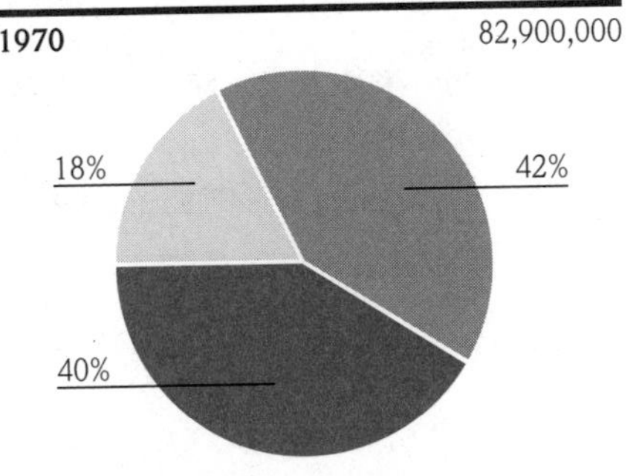

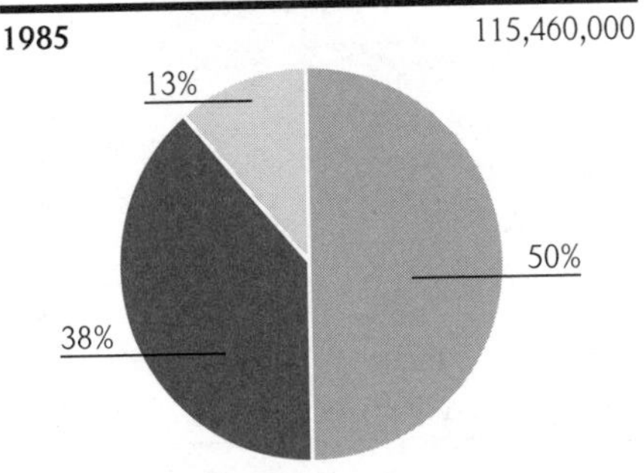

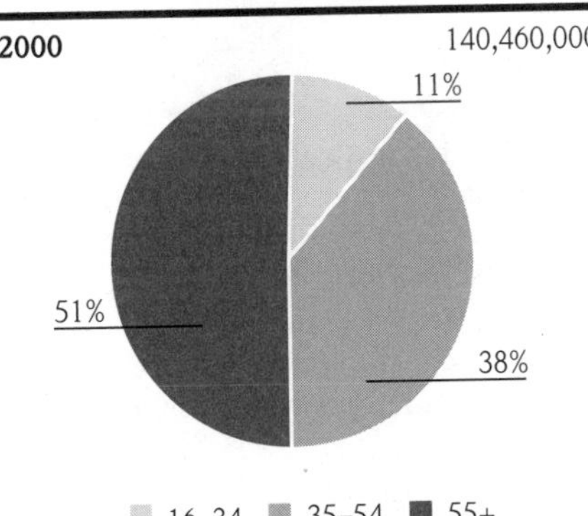

Source: Hudson Institute, *Workforce 2000*, 1987.

needs over the next 10 to 15 years. Actions taken now that are based on an informed look toward the future can prepare a company for changes and shifts in its available work force over time.

We have identified a number of trends that are likely to influence the North American work force in the next 15 years. The potential effect of these trends signals the need for action and response. Actions can range from merely continuing to monitor the trend to reviewing policies and creating major shifts in business strategy.

Increasing Diversity in the Work Force

• **The continuing aging of the work force will create problems and opportunities.** The aging of the baby-boom generation is raising the median age of the U.S. population. The median age, about 33 in 1990, will be 36 by the year 2000. By 2010, one-quarter of the U.S. population will be at least 55, and one in seven Americans will be at least 65. The rapid growth of the U.S. labor force has been pushed by the baby boomers who have now matured into working-age adults. Between 1990 and 2000, the number of people between 35 and 44 will jump by 16%, and those between the ages of 45 and 54 will increase by 46%, compared with an overall expected population growth of 7.1%.

In addition to the baby boomers (people born between 1946 and 1964), three age groups are influencing the shifting structure and composition of the work force: 1930s Depression babies (1929-1940); the baby-bust cohort (1965-1978); and the baby-boom echo (1979+).

• **Older Americans will increase in number and grow in influence.** Older people are becoming a larger segment of the population, enjoying better health and longer life, and wielding economic and political power. More than 31 million Americans—12.4% of the nation's population—are estimated to be 65 or older. By 2020, when baby boomers reach 65, old people will be 20% of the U.S. population. At that time, there will be at least 7 million Americans over age 85.

This aging of the U.S. society will have several significant effects. First, there will be changes in buying habits and consumer preferences. Second, there will be effects of the work force, such as aging workers and their productivity, health-care needs, retirement plans, rehired retirees as a part of the work force, and so on. Third, society will change with the rise of the four-generation family in which the older generation is active and economically independent.

PROJECTIONS OF THE U.S. LABOR FORCE—1988-2000 (ALL POPULATION NUMBERS IN THOUSANDS)

	U.S. Labor Force			Net Change		% Change/Yr	
	1976	1988	2000	'76-'88	'88-2000	'76-'88	'88-2000
Total, age							
16 & over	96,158	121,669	141,134	25,511	19,465	2.0%	1.2%
Men, age							
16 & over	57,174	66,927	74,324	9,753	7,397	1.3%	0.9%
16-24	12,572	11,753	11,352	-999	-401	-0.7%	-0.3%
25-54	35,576	46,383	53,155	10,807	6,772	2.2%	1.1%
55+	8,846	8,791	9,817	-55	1,026	-0.1%	0.9%
Women, age							
16 & over	38,984	54,742	66,810	15,758	12,068	2.9%	1.7%
16-24	10,588	10,782	11,104	194	322	0.2%	0.2%
25-54	22,925	37,659	48,112	14,734	10,453	4.2%	2.1%
55+	5,471	6,301	7,594	830	1,293	1.2%	1.6%
White	84,767	104,755	118,981	19,988	14,226	1.8%	1.1%
Black	9,565	13,205	16,465	3,640	3,260	2.7%	1.9%
Asian/other	1,826	3,709	5,688	1,883	1,979	6.1%	3.6%
Hispanics*	4,289	8,982	14,321	4,693	5,339	6.4%	4.0%

*Persons of Hispanic origin may be of any race.
Source: U.S. Department of Labor.

• **Hispanics will be the largest fast-growing minority population in the United States.** Hispanics are changing the face of America. The Bureau of the Census estimates that the Hispanic population grew from 14.6 million in 1980 to 21.9 million in 1990, about 50% in 10 years. Hispanic growth is five times that of non-Hispanics. By 2010, there will be 39.5 million U.S. Hispanics. Most U.S. Hispanics live in nine states. Mexican Americans are mostly in California, Arizona, New Mexico, Colorado, and Texas. Puerto Ricans are largely in New York, New Jersey, and Illinois. Cubans are mostly in Florida.

Despite similarity of language, Hispanics are not a homogeneous group. Several different cultures, drawing on different national bases, make up the so-called Hispanic culture. But although there may be cultural differences, most Hispanics in the United States share North American values, including a desire for upward mobility.

• **Most black Americans will advance—but not all.** In 1987, blacks accounted for 10.8% of the U.S. work force and about 12.2% of the population. They will grow to a projected 11.7% of the labor force by the year 2000. About 70% of black Americans are advancing in nearly every aspect of American life. In their transition to the mainstream, they have already moved from the rural South to cities throughout the country and advanced in large numbers from unskilled and blue-collar work to white-collar work. They are moving up in corporations and government, making great educational advances, moving toward closer income parity with whites, and gaining political and economic power. In a generation or two, they have risen into the middle class and are moving to the suburbs. They are part of the mainstream.

Nevertheless, 30% of blacks did not make these transitions after the great northward

SELECTED MARKET CHARACTERISTICS (WITH PERCENTAGES OF PARTICIPATION) OF SCIENTISTS AND ENGINEERS, 1986

	All scientists & engineers	Scientists	Engineers
Labor-force participation rate	94.5	95.3	93.8
Unemployment rate	1.5	1.9	1.2
Employment rate	84.7	76.7	91.9
Underemployment rate	2.6	4.3	1.0
Average annual salary	$38,400	$35,700	$40,800

Source: National Science Foundation, *Science Resources Studies Highlights,* 1987.

migration, which began in the 1920s and accelerated during and after World War II. They are stuck in a new American social situation—in urban ghettos, in multigenerational poverty, off the upward-mobility ladder—and locked into a goalless culture.

• **Women will move gradually into the executive suite.** By sheer force of their growing numbers in management ranks, women will force open the door to the executive suite over the next two decades. They will be counted among the 15 to 25 people in each of the largest corporations who run the show.

• **High-achieving Asians are outperforming North American whites in the classroom and the workplace.** For the most part, Asian Americans are affluent and well educated, but they are a diverse group differentiated by language, culture, and geography. Seven of the largest Asian groups in the United States are the Chinese, Filipinos, Japanese, Asian Indians, Koreans, Vietnamese, and Laotians. By the turn of the century, the number of Asian Americans will rise to more than 8 million.

Asian Americans are outstandingly successful in education. Japanese males between 25 and 39 have a 96% high-school-completion rate. For Koreans and Indians, the completion rate is 94%; for Chinese, 90%; and for Filipinos, 89%. These rates compare with a white rate of 87%. Young Asian Americans graduating at the top of their class will be well acculturated and will have high expectations of the workplace and their prospects in it.

• **A shrinking labor pool will create opportunities for traditionally underemployed workers.** A shortage of workers in the United States—especially entry-level workers and those with specialized talent—is making many underutilized workers more attractive. These workers fall into two categories: those of limited skill or ability and those who are only partially available for work. The first are underutilized because they lack particular abilities or skills; the second either are not available to work at preferred times and places or do not have the desired commitment. Both categories are a substantial part of the human resource pool. Labor shortages may make workers who are often considered unemployable or problematic—such as the disabled, emotionally impaired, or illiterate—more attractive.

• **The scientific and engineering work force is growing and becoming more diverse in national origin, gender, and race.** Nearly 5 million scientists and engineers were employed in the United States in 1986, double the number employed in 1976, demonstrating the increasing importance of science and technology to U.S. society. At the same time, the scientific and engineering work force is becoming more diverse by gaining more foreign-born workers, women, and minorities. Women and black scientists and engineers are still a relatively small part of this work force, although their numbers are increasing. Universities and employers who need Ph.D. qualifications find themselves increasingly dependent on foreign-born workers.

Home Life and Work Life

• **Corporations will adopt new programs to support employees' family responsibilities.** Although it is currently focused on day care, the issue of workplace support for employees' family obligations is indicative of a larger concern for better integration of home and work life. Employers, once able to assume that the demands of male workers' home lives were taken care of by wives and families, are now being pushed to pay attention to family issues such as day care, sick children, eldercare, and schooling. One reason why corporations may lag behind in this trend could be that their older senior managers have not experienced these pressures in their own lives.

Drivers of this trend include more families in which both husband and wife work, the dramatic increase in the number of women in the work force who are mothers, and the growing need for long-term care of the aging.

• **Work and education will influence women's childbearing choices and will shape national fertility patterns.** Of the 50.3 million employed women in 1987, 59.2% were married and most were in their prime childbearing and working years. Women are returning to work after childbearing sooner than ever.

For many women, especially those with more than average education and with career prospects, there is an economic and opportunity cost for bearing children that may be limiting their lifetime fertility, as well as encouraging them to postpone childbearing. Demographers now expect the average U.S. woman to bear fewer than two children, although she herself may anticipate having at least two. Many more women will be childless than had planned to be. While the consequences of these trends have yet to be fully estimated, one likely outcome is childbearing that is explicitly planned to coincide with career choices.

• **Work will move to unconventional sites and arrangements.** Employers are becoming willing to consider almost any work arrangement that will get work done at less cost. Businesses are seeking to contain costs, are responding to the need for flexibility to meet sudden demands or slowdown in work, and are finding workers with critical skills either too scarce or too expensive to hire full time. Workers, on the other hand, find flexible schedules appealing, particularly in terms of childcare, and are more concerned about such factors as long commutes. Temporary workers, part-time contractors, and independent workers constitute the fastest-growing employment category. These workers accounted for half of the growth in the U.S. work force between 1980 and 1987.

Companies are exploring options such as contingent workers and flexible scheduling. Contingent workers are paid only for working, may not qualify for benefits, and are less likely to join labor unions. At the same time, emerging computer and networking technologies are enabling work to be done anywhere, at any time, and at any distance from the office or factory.

• **The new focus on workers as an asset will make attitudes and values more central.** Pressed by demands for an adequate return on investment in the work force, managers are becoming increasingly concerned about factors shaping their employees' behavior. More is being invested in training. Expectations of the individual's productivity, skills, and capacity for responsibility are greater. Yet at the same time, the work force is increasingly diverse in its attitudes and lifestyles. It is better educated than ever before and more acquainted with psychology and sociology.

As a result, researchers are prodding workers and their families about their values and attitudes toward work, their bosses, and the workplace. Surveying is becoming a tool for assessing employees' loyalty and productivity.

• **Mobility continues to be a strength of the North American work force.** North Americans, more than others, are ready to pack up and go. The average American moves every six years—11 times in a lifetime. During 1986-1987, 18% of people living in the United States moved to a different home. Many of these movers moved more than once in a year. A steady stream of immigrants to North America adds mobility to the work force. Such mobility is a strength for the future work force: Workers can move to where the jobs are, acquiring

Countries most active in U.S. mergers and acquisitions, 1986

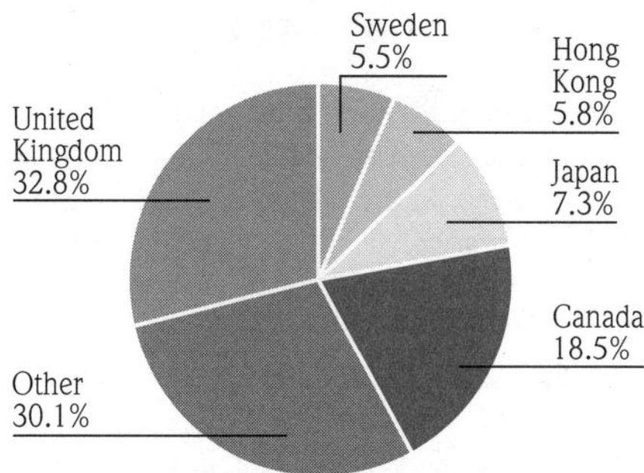

Source: U.S. General Accounting Office, *Foreign Investment,* 1987.

experience and skills in the process. And a mobile work force means that employers can attract skilled workers to new sites, making it easier for business to relocate closer to markets and resources.

Globalization: Competing in a World Economy

• **Mergers and acquisitions will continue —with more international actors involved.** Globalization encourages the flow of capital as barriers to the movement of capital fall. The increase in capital movement among countries results in mergers and acquisitions, with more foreign actors involved as nations look for more-productive investments. Over the long term, as a global economy emerges and structural and economic differences fade, there is the potential for large international shifts in corporate ownership and the development of new organizational structures for doing business internationally.

• **Work-force and market demographics in Europe and Asia will present new opportunities.** Birthrates are falling almost everywhere in the industrialized world. Between 2020 and 2025, the birthrates of Europe, Asia (including Japan, South Korea, Taiwan, Hong Kong, and Singapore), and North America are projected to have declined to about 12-14 births per 1,000 population. As the work forces of the industrially advanced nations of Europe and Asia grow in sophistication, those countries will grow economically and reap the benefits of world trade.

• **Sweeping changes will alter market basics.** New stresses on time, the increasing diversity of lifestyles, the opening up of overseas markets, and the restructuring of many corporations will shift the basics of marketing. At the same time, workers at all levels will become integral to marketing, sales, and customer relations. Broad change will affect when products and services are marketed (time), what is sold (quality, experience), how marketing and selling are done (technologies and new strategies), to whom products and services are marketed and sold (demographic change and segmentation), and by whom products are marketed and sold (worker as representative, customer as salesperson).

Several factors are also pushing new approaches to marketing and sales. These include overseas competition and competition for foreign markets; changing social values in the United States and other advanced nations, including new demands for quality and service; and the opening up of new avenues and new markets through electronic technology, such as television, fax copying, videotex, home computers, and satellite transmission. One of the most important of these factors, especially in the United States, is greater demands on time.

• **Worldwide technical and scientific competence will sharpen competition.** Although the United States is the center of scientific and technical education, has the world's largest technically educated work force, and holds a sizable share of world trade in high technology, other countries are catching up. Their efforts are being driven by several factors: the greater significance of technical education as a route to economic success; transborder data flows and technical and scientific exchanges between nations; and new scientific and technical developments occurring worldwide, including the growth in research and development. Scientists and the technically educated are becoming the first truly international, mobile work force.

Employees and Health

• **The United States is an increasingly sedentary society.** As the United States changes into a post-industrial society, the characteristics of work will change. A feature of this shift is more indoor working and living. About 60% of American adults live sedentary lives. Americans are spending 90% of their time indoors, whether at home, in the office or factory, or in closed spaces during travel. Work is far more sedentary than in the past. Aside from sleeping, eating, and dressing, the big consumer of indoor time is watching television—six hours and 59 minutes daily in U.S. households in 1988-1989.

The trend toward a sedentary society will lead to more exposure to the risks of an indoor environment, such as indoor air pollution; a sharp decline in muscular activity; new bad habits associated with a sedentary life, such as smoking, coffee and soda drinking, and candy nibbling; and even more social friction and interpersonal annoyances. Healthy workers lose less time and have fewer accidents. People in good physical shape live longer and healthier lives. Attention to health at the workplace also may be seen as an amenity and a factor in morale.

• **Strong long-term forces will work against cutting health costs.** The United States spends at least $500 billion a year on health care, more than 11% of its gross national product. As a percent of GNP, national health-care expenditures have almost tripled since 1940. Cost-containment attempts so far have only slightly slowed an inexorable rise. At the same time, there is no evidence that the quality of health care, of health maintenance, or of disease prevention is improving to match the increase in spending.

At least four strong long-term forces are boosting the soaring cost of health care in the United States—and are likely to keep those costs high. The United States has huge institutionalized health-care obligations, created by factors such as the aging U.S. population. Insurance and liability costs in an increasingly litigious society are enormous. New medical technologies, such as those used for heart and other organ transplants, have been tremendously expensive. And the public's expectation of universal entitlement to health care and health protection continues to grow.

• **The significance of the worker's contribution to occupational health and safety will increase.** In the changing workplace, the worker increasingly is responsible for his or her personal health and safety, as well as that of fellow workers. The worker can contribute through awareness of and concern for health and safety or may aggravate workplace risks by inappropriate behavior or attitudes.

New technologies and new workstyles have shifted occupational health and safety issues from the acute to the chronic and long term. There are also new issues (such as mental stress, eyestrain from computer use, and back fatigue) associated with the white-collar work force. In the blue-collar work force, averting injury is no longer strictly a matter of enforcing safety regulations. Greater use of automation requires more responsibility and cooperation from workers to ensure safety.

• **The AIDS epidemic is killing people in the prime of their working lives.** What makes AIDS uniquely important to business is that those who are infected and die at present are mostly young men in the prime of their working years. At the same time, the long incubation period of AIDS will cause greater distress for individuals and higher medical costs for employers than any other acute epidemic.

AIDS-related deaths are expected to rise to 68.63 per 100,000 U.S. population by the end of 1991. Evidence aside, most employers do not view AIDS as a problem. A Harris executive poll for *Business Week* showed little concern among the 1,000 companies surveyed; 89% of the executives reported that their companies did not have an AIDS policy.

Discussion Questions

1. Why is the American work force aging? How will that change affect other aspects of the economy?

2. Why should the American work force become increasingly nonwhite in coming years? What different kinds of experiences likely await Hispanics, African-Americans, and Asian-Americans?

3. How have changes in the American family affected American employers? How might the role of women change in both institutions?

PART Five
SOCIAL CHANGE

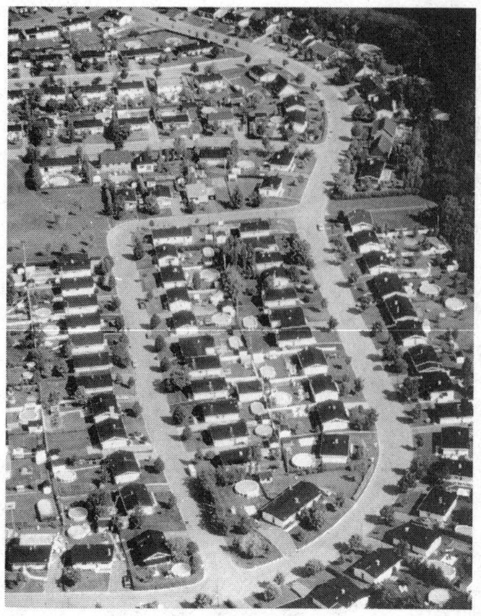

CHAPTER 12 HUMAN POPULATIONS AND DEMOGRAPHY

Unlike many of the areas that occupy the sociological outlook, human populations are very easy to measure—all that's required is a head count. If the head count changes from time to time, there are only a few possible explanations. If you count more people this year than last, you had either more births than deaths, some immigration (movement into a country), or both; if you count fewer heads, there must have been more deaths than births, some emigration (movement out of a country), or both. A very large population may make the logistics of this head count somewhat difficult, but in principle it's a pretty basic process.

After the heads are counted, new babies tallied, deaths recorded, and overall migration noted, the discipline of demography takes over. **Demography** is the study of human population. Demographers are particularly interested in the changes related to human populations, from two points of view.

First, demographers seek to explain the causes of population changes. Why did people have more babies this year than last? Why are fewer people dying now than in the past? Why do people move? Second, demographers attempt to trace the effects of population changes. What happens to the distribution of food when births go up and deaths go down? What happens to the social life of a country when large numbers of immigrants enter? Demography places human population in a pivotal position in relation to the other aspects of society.

This chapter will explore some of the theories offered by demographers in light of the many important recent and historical changes in the world's population. We will compare population changes in the industrial and nonindustrial world, paying particular attention to the population explosion of recent years and its effects on natural resources. At the other extreme, we will explore the possibility of zero population growth (a stable population) and look at the effects of a stable population on the rest of society. Finally, we will examine human migration, with a focus on why people move and what happens when they get where they're going. This look at migration will be coupled with a special section on the most important form that migration has taken over the last two centuries: the movement from farms to cities. The field of demography is an especially clear example of how the sociological outlook helps us understand our own lives in relation to society.

DEMOGRAPHY: CONCEPTS AND PERSPECTIVES

The concepts and perspectives of demography are largely shared with sociology. Demography represents an application of sociological ideas to questions of human population; its uniqueness comes from the object of its study rather than either its methods or its theories. Box 12.1 defines some of the special terms demographers use in their study of population changes. These terms describe numerical changes in the population but tell us little about the composition of the population. At the outset we will want to know at least something about the age range of the population and the sex of its members.

The age-sex pyramid is one of the demographer's most basic tools. For any given year it shows the percentage of the overall population to be found in any given age range and sex. Figure 12.1 depicts age-sex pyramids for three countries: Mexico, the United States, and West Germany. For example, in Mexico 16 percent of the population is under the age of 4, while only 5 percent of the West German population falls in that age range. You can also see from

BOX 12.1

A TRAVELER'S PHRASE BOOK FOR THE WORLD OF DEMOGRAPHY

Like members of any specialized occupation, demographers have their own vocabulary for the matters they deal with. Many of these specialized terms relate to the measures demographers use; aside from those measures a demographer sounds pretty much like any garden-variety sociologist. Although the measures of demography are essentially basic counting, some of the numbers are transformed into other kinds of statistics, which have specific names.

Birth rate: The number of births for every 1,000 people in the population. The statistic is created as follows:

$$\frac{\text{number of live births in a given year}}{\text{population}} \times 1{,}000 = \text{birth rate}$$

General fertility rate: The number of births for every 1,000 women of childbearing age. This statistic tells you more about individuals in the population. A society with a great many women of childbearing age would tend to have a high birth rate even if most of the women were not having that many children. Fertility rate is calculated like birth rate except for changing the "population" number to the number of "women of childbearing age."

Death rate: The number of deaths for every 1,000 people in the population. It is figured like the birth rate with the substitution of "number of deaths" for "number of live births."

Immigration rate: The number of immigrants for every 1,000 people in the population in a given year. It is figured like the birth rate with the substitution of "number of immigrants" for "number of live births."

Rate of natural increase (or decrease): The difference between the birth rate and the death rate. Because you are subtracting "rates," your answer will also be a "rate"; thus, the difference between the birth rate and the death rate will give you the natural (nonimmigrant) increase in the population for every 1,000 members of the population.

Growth rate: The rate of natural increase plus the immigration rate. Once again, you are adding rates and will end up with a rate. The growth rate tells you how many new people there are in a population for every 1,000 people already there. It tells you, in short, just how fast your population is growing no matter what the source. More births will make it grow, but so will fewer deaths, more immigrants, or fewer emigrants. The growth rate combines all this information.

Keep in mind that a phrase book is for tourists. The vocabulary of demography goes far beyond this short list. These few terms will get you started and give you a clue as to the kinds of concerns demographers have. Consider the growth rate. A population of 100 could grow to 150 over a year,

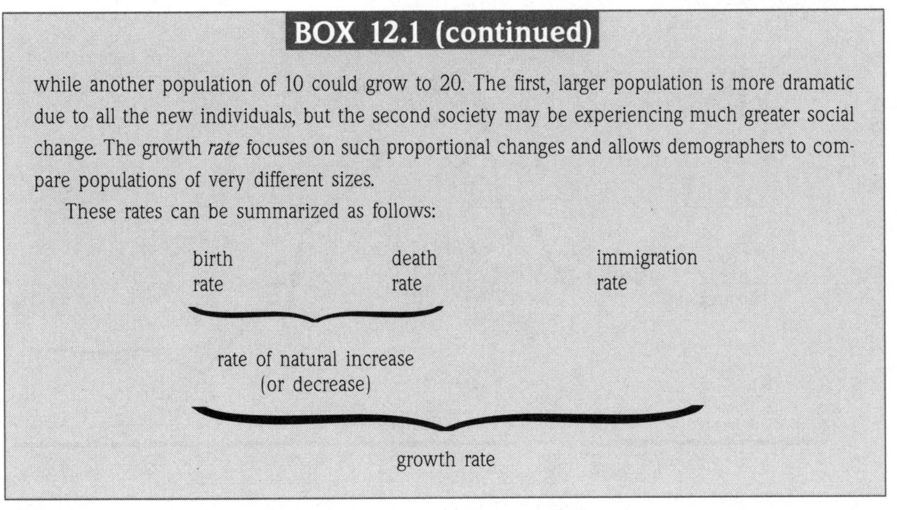

BOX 12.1 (continued)

while another population of 10 could grow to 20. The first, larger population is more dramatic due to all the new individuals, but the second society may be experiencing much greater social change. The growth *rate* focuses on such proportional changes and allows demographers to compare populations of very different sizes.

These rates can be summarized as follows:

these pyramids that, in most societies at most ages, the two sexes are roughly even. The major exception is among people over the age of 75, where women make up a larger share of the population than men. Such exceptions to balanced sexes can also be found in societies at the close of major wars, which usually remove sizable portions of the men in the younger age groups.

Turning our attention to the United States, we see, in Figure 12.1, that one prominent feature of the population in 1980 was a definite bulge between the ages of fifteen and thirty-five and a slight indentation between ages forty and fifty. The indentation is the result of lower birth rates during the Depression of the 1930s. The Depression created extreme hardships for many

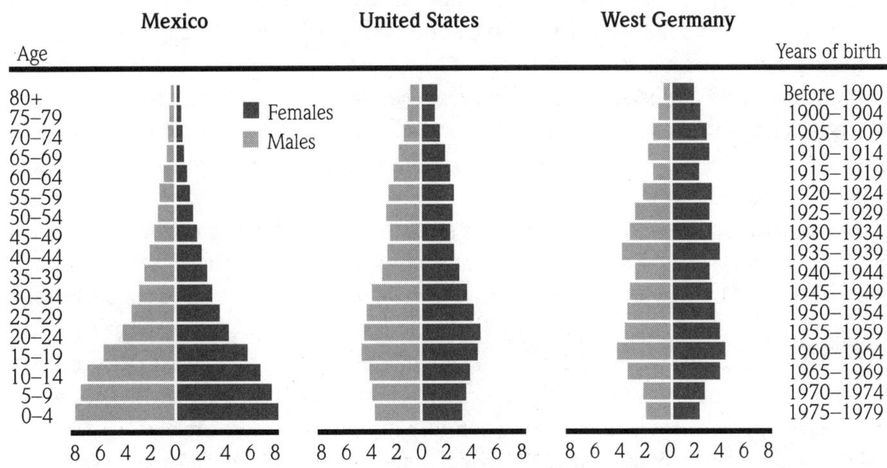

Figure 12.1 1980 population comparison by age and sex for Mexico, the United States, and West Germany. (Data from Population Reference Bureau, 1984.)

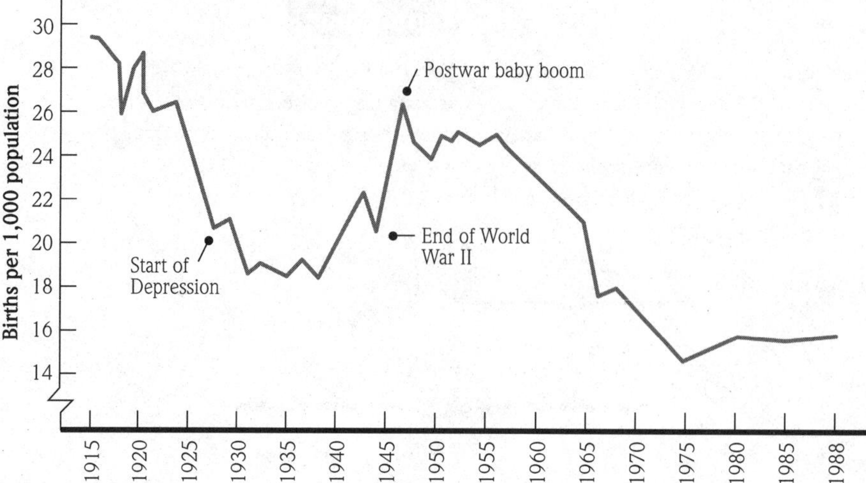

Figure 12.2 United States birth rates, 1915-1988.

American families, which they chose not to increase with added children. The bulge in the population is the result of the famous "baby boom" in the United States following World War II (see Figure 12.2). World War II, like all major wars, was highly disruptive of family life. Beginning in 1946, the children that families had put off for so long entered the United States population like water through a broken dam. This baby boom was then followed by lowered birth rates through the 1960s, reaching a very low point in the mid-1970s. In 1975 the baby boom babies were of childbearing age and should have created another bulge in the population just by the sheer number of women. However, many changes in U.S. society had created alternatives for those women, who apparently selected options other than motherhood. Some observers have suggested that these women have simply delayed having babies (because of occupational options, for example) and are now starting their families, as is evidenced by the higher birth rates since 1975 (see Sklar and Berkov, 1975). All of these statistics will receive a much closer inspection later in this chapter; for the time being they illustrate some of the social explanations offered by demographers for population changes.

The age-sex pyramids in Figure 12.1 illustrate some other population characteristics of extreme interest to demographers. Mexico is an example of an *expanding population.* The extreme pyramid shape of Mexico indicates that a relatively small number of women are having a relatively large number of babies. Most of the countries in the nonindustrial world today have age-sex pyramids similar to Mexico's. If the children currently under the age of ten in Mexico have the same fertility rates in the future that their parents have now, the pyramid will acquire an even more extreme shape and the population will expand even more rapidly.

The age-sex pyramid of the United States represents a *slow-growth population.* A key term here is **replacement level**, the number of babies necessary in a population for the parents to replace themselves, thus leading to a stable population, or **zero population growth**, as it is often called. Two parents having two babies (on average) provides for replacement, but the baby boom bulge in the U.S. population will still lead to later population bulges because of the large percentage of women of childbearing age. Population bulges exhaust themselves over time much like ripples in a pool of water, each ripple being smaller than the one before. A large number of women of childbearing years, each having two babies, will still produce a large number of children. And when all of those children reach childbearing age themselves, we will have another (although smaller) spurt in population growth. A population that simply replaces itself in each generation will ultimately lead to zero population growth when the ripples disappear. In the meantime, the United States is growing slowly. The age-sex pyramid for West Germany (shown for 1980, before reunification with East Germany) is fairly close to a *negative growth population.*

When age-sex pyramids are combined with the other measures of population demographers use, an overall picture of population change emerges. The ages, sexes, and other characteristics of the population come to be viewed through measures of births, deaths, and migration into and out of the population. All of these changes occur within the fabric of society, and, in turn, they all change the society in which they occur. That is where the sociologist/demographer takes over.

POPULATION IN THE INDUSTRIAL WORLD

The world currently has a population of over 5 billion people and is growing at a rate of between 1.5 and 2 percent a year. This means that by the year 2000 there should be well over 6 billion people who, along with their other needs, will want places to live and food to eat. The population of the United States in 1989 was over 248 million. This relatively small population in comparison to livable area is characteristic of industrialized societies, such as Canada, Australia, and most European countries, which make up a minority of the world's population and only a fraction of its growth rate. The differences between the industrialized and nonindustrialized nations are far from chance. Industrialization fundamentally altered the societies in which it occurred and, consequently, it altered the human populations of those societies. Demographers refer to this set of changes as the **demographic transition**.

The Demographic Transition

Before 1750 the world's population was under 800 million people. Perhaps more important, it was growing at no more than .1 percent a year. This low growth rate wasn't for lack of trying, but high death rates effectively counteracted high birth rates. This was *stage one* of the demographic transition. Infant and maternal mortality took a heavy toll, along with infectious disease; between 1346 and 1350 bubonic plague (the "black death") claimed 25 million lives (one-fourth of the world's population).

Starting around 1750, fundamental changes began to occur in the societies that now make up the industrialized nations. The most important change was in nutrition. New crops and agricultural techniques created an amount and a variety of foods that allowed more people to survive. For one example, the potato became the staple of the lower classes; it was nutritious, easy to grow, and easy to store. The population of Ireland increased 172 percent between 1780 and 1840, almost entirely as a result of the potato and the lowered death rates to which it led. The resistance to disease brought about by better nutrition was aided by improved sanitation techniques, which helped lower the incidence of the diseases themselves. These changes ushered in the next stage of the demographic transition.

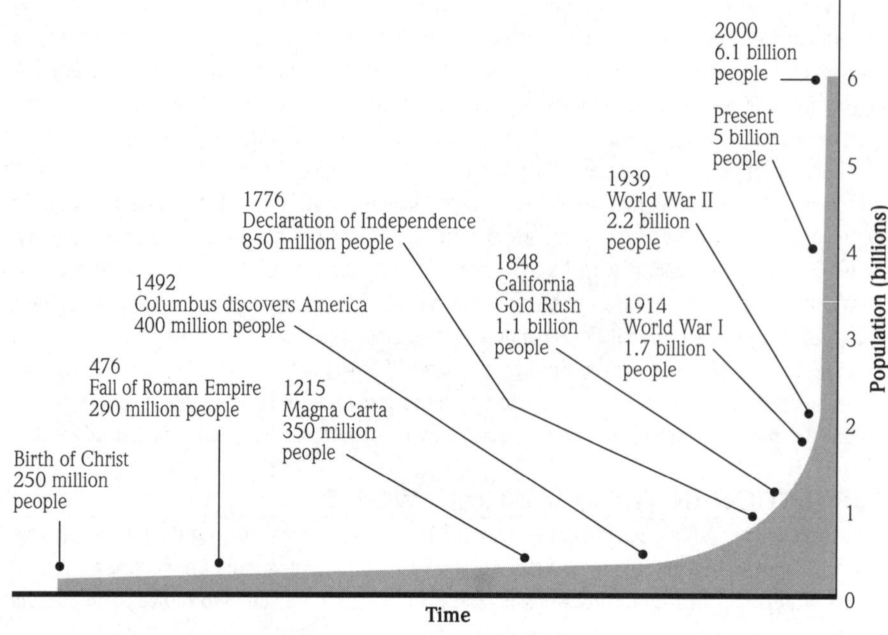

Figure 12.3 World population growth.

Stage two of the demographic transition was characterized by high birth rates coupled with rapidly declining death rates. The result, of course, was a population explosion. The case of Ireland was extreme but typical of many countries during this stage; as Figure 12.3 illustrates, the world's population began to grow at an unprecedented rate at this time.

The population continued to grow as death rates dropped still further over time, but finally fertility rates began to drop as well; this was the beginning of *stage three.* Throughout the nineteenth century and into the twentieth century women of childbearing years began having fewer and fewer babies. Various explanations have been offered for this drop in fertility rates, but all the explanations are related to industrialization. Industrialization led to urbanization as people left the farms and headed for the factories (see the section on urbanization at the end of this chapter). Large families were both useful and inexpensive on the farm, but in the city they were neither. In addition, the industrial lifestyle lessened the individual's economic dependence on the family (see Chapter 9) and led to major changes in family roles (particularly women's roles) and values. People no longer wanted as many children. In the realm of technology, contraceptives entered the picture in the 1870s. Although the death rate continued to drop throughout stage three (and is still dropping), the birth rate began to drop at the same rate until it finally caught up in many industrial countries (Brown, 1973). The relative balance of birth and death rates makes stage three of the demographic transition a stable stage.

The Modern Industrial World: Changes in Women's Roles and Family Values

Pronatalism is the societal value of having children and large families. Included within this view, by necessity, is the value of the motherhood role for women. In stage one of the demographic transition pronatalism was clearly a necessary value for the survival of society; the high death rates of that period required spending considerable energy having children. Motherhood was a full-time job that was both essential and dangerous; pronatalism encouraged women to accept it.

Industrialization ended all of that. Children were no longer needed either to support the current generation in their old age or to stock the next generation. Simultaneously (and clearly related to this change), new doors were opening for women outside the home. Many industrial occupations opened to women, and with those occupations came a previously unknown sense of independence. Women's roles in industrial society have changed steadily over the last century and are still changing today with the growth of the women's movement. Early women's leaders, such as Margaret Sanger (who fought for birth control) and Susan B. Anthony (who fought for the vote), were clearly important to this change, but the real source of change came from growing industrialization.

Modifications of pronatalism have been occurring in the United States for some years. In just the brief span from 1967 to 1973 the number of women in their early twenties who wanted three or more children dropped from 55 percent to 30 percent (Griffith, 1973). A more extreme illustration is the rise of the childless marriage. In direct opposition to pronatalism, younger Americans are carefully calculating the economic and social costs of children; those who have them are having fewer, and many are deciding against having any at all. It has become increasingly common for apartment complexes to bar children and to evict those residents who have them after moving in. While these changes horrify some Americans, other Americans are becoming more and more vocal about their right to remain childless.

POPULATION IN THE NONINDUSTRIAL WORLD

Until as recently as World War II the growth rate of the industrialized nations was still higher than that of the developing (then undeveloped) nations of the nonindustrial world. The industrialized world had not fully settled into stage three of the demographic transition, while the nonindustrialized world was still firmly locked into the high death rates of stage one. The story of the world's current population explosion is largely the story of how the industrialized nations dragged the nonindustrialized world (not always kicking and screaming) into stage two of the demographic transition.

The example of Sri Lanka (formerly Ceylon) provides a pointed illustration of this interference. Before World War II Ceylon had a very high death rate, due largely to the malaria-carrying mosquito. Between 1934 and 1935, for example, 100,000 people died of malaria. Following World War II DDT was sprayed in the swamps of Ceylon, killing the mosquitoes and producing a 34 percent drop in the death rate in a single year (Davis, 1956). Today, malaria is practically unknown in Sri Lanka, and the population is exploding.

The case of Sri Lanka is not unusual. Most of the developing nations are growing three times faster than the United States. In every case the populations are growing because of dropping death rates and stable (though still very high) birth rates. Insecticides provide an interesting example but, as with the history of the demographic transition in the industrial world, the dropping death rates are largely due to better nutrition and sanitation. This "interference" from the industrialized world appears very humane, but the resulting population explosions in the nonindustrialized world have made it very hard for the developing nations to develop. In some cases, such as Ethiopia, an expanding population makes people more vulnerable to environmental problems (such as drought) or even creates environmental problems through an overexpansion of agriculture to feed the growing population. And as we've seen in Ethiopia, the results of such population changes can be tragic.

Economic Development in the Nonindustrial World

Part of the problem faced by the developing nations is the ratio of dependent young and old to mature adults in their populations. Demographers generally separate populations into three general groups on the basis of their age. Both the very young and the very old are dependent groups that require assistance from those in the middle if they are to survive. An age-sex pyramid such as Mexico's does not have too many dependent elderly, but close to half its population is under the age of fourteen. This kind of ratio between the dependent and active sectors of the population makes economic development extremely difficult. The society has more than it can handle just in feeding the present dependent portion of the population without directing its energies into economic expansion and the formation of a strong industrial base. A high birth rate in itself does not ensure long-term poverty for a country, but it clearly acts as a hindrance for economic growth (Merrick, 1986).

The absence of economic expansion in the nonindustrial world results in poverty and hunger. Death rates remain relatively low, while high birth rates make the populations larger and more bottom heavy all the time. The already-begun process of industrialization in these countries has forced people from the rural areas into the cities, where there is too little economic activity to support them. Almost all of the major cities in the nonindustrialized world today contain massive numbers of very poor residents, many of whom have no shelter. Calcutta, India, is perhaps the best-known example, but similar poor populations can be found in Hong Kong, Mexico City, Cairo, and elsewhere. Meanwhile, the separation between the haves and the have nots in these countries stays extreme or grows as industrialization advances.

Responses to Poverty

The Marxist Position Modern-day Marxists (or socialists) see the solution to poverty in the developing nations as existing apart from the population explosion. In keeping with the theories of Karl Marx (see Chapter 7), modern socialists argue that poverty in the developing world is caused not by overpopulation but by the unequal distribution of wealth characteristic of capitalism. Some argue that the ruling classes in the industrialized nations have put off revolutions in their own countries by making the nonindustrialized nations poorer in order to support the middle classes at home. Others focus more on levels of exploitation within the developing nations. In either case the solution to poverty is seen as a revolution that will bring about a fundamental redistribution of wealth.

Marx predicted that revolutions would occur first in the most industrialized nations. As it has turned out, however, the socialist revolutions have occurred in the least industrialized nations, such as China, Cuba, Vietnam, Cambodia, and Angola. These countries may not be in the throes of capitalism, but they are certainly good illustrations of extreme poverty and gross inequalities in the distribution of wealth. While modern-day Marxists may argue that the population explosion is not the cause of poverty in these countries, it certainly doesn't help. It also, incidentally, provides large numbers of young people in the population, who are the most likely to become active revolutionaries.

The Green Revolution One way to feed more people is to produce more food. During the 1960s, a scientific effort (termed the *Green Revolution*) searched for new hybrid strains of wheat and rice in hopes of creating an easier to grow, faster to harvest, and more productive substitute for the crops in current use. Between 1965 and 1971 the amount of Asian land devoted to these new crops jumped from 200 acres to over 50 million (Brown, 1973).

Reviews of the Green Revolution are mixed. On the one hand, the new strains of rice and wheat have provided more food for the world; clearly, they do have a higher yield than the older varieties. On the other hand, it turns out that these new varieties are more easily used by larger and wealthier farmers than smaller and poorer farmers; that is, anyone can use them but the real advantage comes with access to credit, fertilizers, and irrigation. They also force farmers away from a subsistence form of living to producing a cash crop—a change that brings them into the twentieth century and places them at the mercy of international markets. Thus the income differentials in the developing nations tend to become even larger than they were before (Brown, 1973). Furthermore, more and better food lowers the death rate, raises the birth rate, and makes the population problem worse in the long run.

Reducing Fertility The general consensus among demographers is that the population explosion must be stopped before poverty can be reduced in the developing nations. This consensus, which is shared by many government officials in the nonindustrial world, has led to the formation of fertility-control programs around the world. Through these programs governments try to convince the members of the population not to have so many babies; in addition, they provide means of birth control. The techniques of convincing have varied considerably.

Probably the most extreme attempt at fertility control occurred in India, where some states required sterilization of either the husband or the wife after the birth of two children. This was not a popular law in India—nor would it be elsewhere. Childbearing is generally considered a personal activity that should be decided on without government interference. Also, typically, enforced sterilization programs affect only the poor, and, if the poor happen to differ ethnically from the rich, as they do in many countries, the sterilization programs raise questions of genocide. No one seems to like the population explosion, but it's always someone else's babies that should be limited.

China has approached the problem somewhat differently. Given a huge population of approximately 1 billion, extreme measures seemed called for. The government responded in a variety of ways, but the most effective and the most controversial measure was the one child per family rule (Tien, 1983). If every two married people produce one offspring, that should slowly halt the population growth. While it makes sense on paper, it goes against the value of pronatalism that exists in China as elsewhere. Probably the most striking response by the Chinese people to this law has been the rise of abortions and the infanticide of female babies; Chinese parents have a strong preference for sons and, if they can only have one child, seem prepared to go to extreme lengths to have their wishes fulfilled (Merrick, 1986; Yuan, 1983).

These Chinese women are taking a birth control class. China's population problem is not unique in the nonindustrial world, nor is its effort to control population growth through reducing fertility. The hope is that classes like this will provide both the means and the desire to have smaller families.

Most fertility-control programs direct their efforts toward changing values of pronatalism and providing information about birth control. Most American women use some form of contraception, but in other parts of the world such use may be rare, because of unavailability of birth control materials or values that prohibit them. When you combine the values of pronatalism (which are almost universal around the world) with feelings of nationalism and ethnocentrism ("We're the best so we should have more babies"), it's amazing that fertility ever goes down. On the more practical level, poorer families in the developing nations needed large numbers of children for survival. In India, for example, poor people are dependent on their children in old age. Furthermore, the traditional division of sex roles in most societies, with women locked into the wife and mother role, makes children almost essential if a woman is to have any social status in the community. (Sadik's article following this chapter explores high birth rates and fertility-control programs in more detail.)

Government programs aside, the most effective way to lower fertility is economic development. The same industrial development that lowered the death rate in the developing nations will, if it continues, also lower the birth rate. This, you'll note, is basically what happened in Europe and the United States. One explanation for this predicted change is that economic development will automatically alter values of pronatalism. Demographer David Heer (1966) argues that the key factor in industrialization is the level of education that accompanies economic development. As Heer points out, educational levels must rise if economic development is to occur, and those developing nations that have emphasized education seem to have the most rapidly declining birth rates. Whatever the case, there is something inherent in the process of industrialization that lowers birth rates. Merrick (1986) predicts that most less-developed countries will stabilize by the year 2025, but considerable problems can develop before then. Nigeria, for example, currently has a population of 100 million; by the time it stabilizes in the year 2025, it will have a population of 532 million somehow packed into its relatively small area.

THE EFFECTS OF ZERO POPULATION GROWTH

Let us return to the age-sex pyramids in Figure 12.1. If the demographers had to predict, their prediction would be that Mexico's 1980 pyramid would be more likely to look like that of West Germany someday than vice versa, given the effect of industrialization on birth rate. West Germany, on the other hand, was in a situation of negative growth before its reunification with East Germany. The United States appears to be approaching a situation of no growth.

But what are the effects on society of a stable population? We've already seen that an age-sex pyramid like Mexico's makes economic development difficult because of the large dependent portion of the population. What about the other extreme? Part of the answer to this question will consist of guesses as we project into the future. Before we get into the future, however, it might be useful to look at some of the past effects from different age-sex pyramids in the United States. Figure 12.4 illustrates some age-sex pyramids for the past and projected ones for the future in the United States, the latter presuming a relatively stable fertility rate. But what have been the effects of the 1960 and 1970 pyramids?

In 1960 the United States had an expanding population with high percentages of the population under the age of fourteen. Also note the indentation between the ages of twenty and thirty that reflects the low birth rates during the Depression of the 1930s (see Figure 12.2). Just to begin with, we might posit that 1960 was a good year to buy stock in baby food companies. It was also a good year to be an elementary school teacher: because of all the baby boom children entering schools, there was a shortage of teachers in the late 1950s and early 1960s. How about the Depression babies? The early 1960s was a good time to be twenty-two years old and out on the job market; the relatively small number of people in that age bracket reduced competition for available jobs in the economy.

As the 1960s progressed and the baby boom children grew older, a tremendous emphasis on youth developed in American society. Not only was this a large segment of the population, but, unlike young people of past generations, they had money and independence. Whole industries, such as segments of the clothing and record industries, grew up in response to this very large potential market. It was important during the 1960s for everyone to think, act, and look young. As this young age cohort organized politically, one slogan was "Don't trust anyone over thirty." The age-sex pyramids for this period suggest that it wasn't so easy to find someone over thirty.

The Vietnam War of the 1960s had a major impact on all of American society, but consider this impact with relation to the age characteristics of the American population. The potential warriors for that war were the baby boom males. There were certainly enough of them for the purpose, but there were also enough of them to hold some political clout in opposition to that war. The famous "generation gap" of the 1960s will probably never appear in American society in quite the same way as the numbers of young people shrink in proportion to a population growing steadily older.

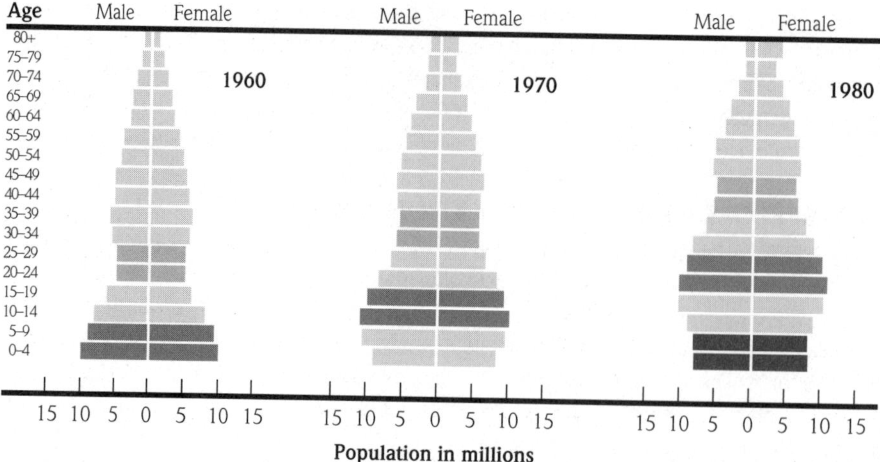

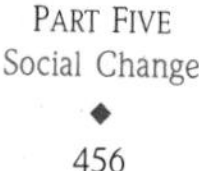

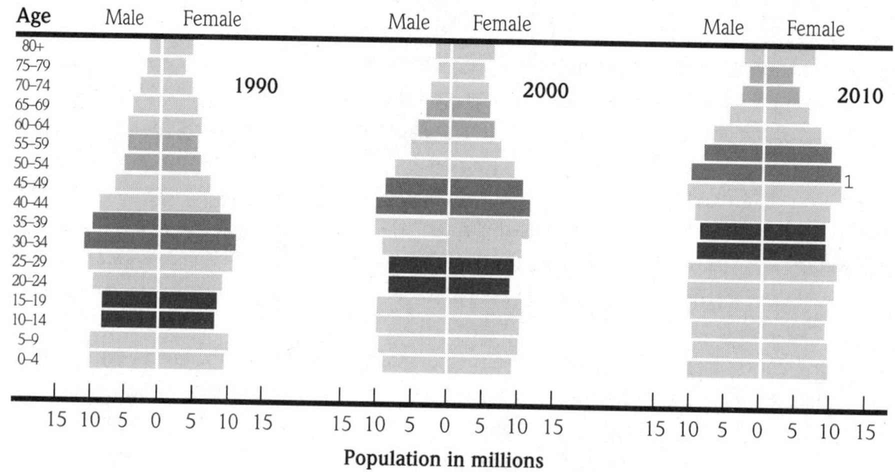

Figure 12.4 Population composition by age and sex, past and projected. (From Bouvier, 1980. Reprinted by permission.)

Moving ahead to 1980, we find a bad time to be out of college and on the job market. Everyone else was out there, too. It was also a bad time for elementary school teachers; fewer babies in the 1960s and 1970s meant school closings in the early 1980s. With the aging of the baby boomers, the actors and models we see on television commercials and in magazines seem to be getting a little older to reflect the changing age distribution of the population. Where magazines and newspapers used to emphasize the youth culture, they now seem to be swamping us with minute details of Yuppie life—the "thirtysomething" generation.

For a little speculation, what will it be like in the year 2000? The average age in the United States is getting older and older as the baby boomers move through the pyramid, and by their sheer numbers they will have to have an impact on society at each stage of their maturation. They will begin reaching retirement age in about 2010.

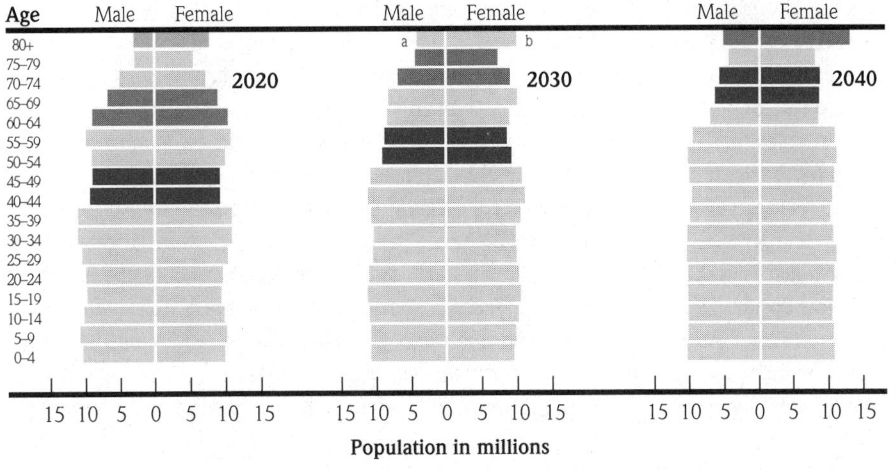

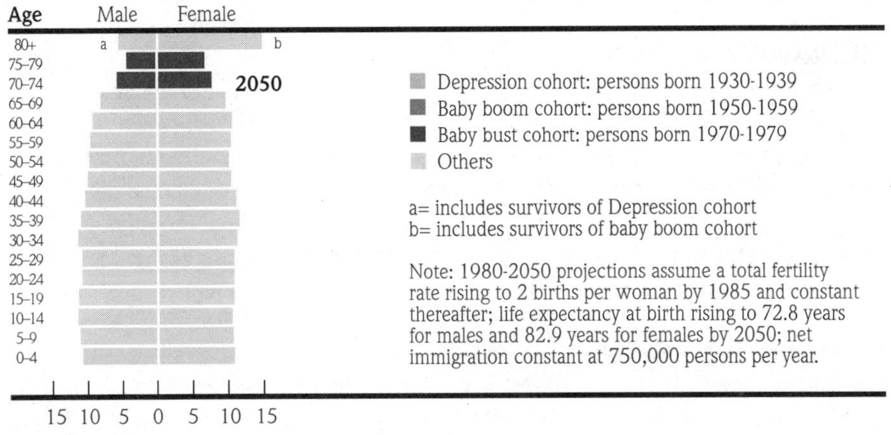

What will be the impact of this "graying" of America? How will the Social Security System survive? Currently, people working provide the funds for those retired, but a higher proportion of retired people could put an unmanageable strain on the system. This has already become a major economic and political question (Wynne, 1986). How about medical care? Now is the time to go into the medical professions, since the demand for medical care is bound to go up with the advancing age of the population. It also may be the time to get out of law enforcement. We've already seen that young people commit far more than their share of index crime. Who is going to commit those crimes when we run out of young people? Probably no one, which will put policemen out of work. On the other hand, the years ahead should see an increase in white-collar crime (which is more frequently committed by people of middle age), so if you do want to go into law enforcement, you probably should specialize in embezzlement, tax fraud, and price fixing.

The American family has already felt the effects of slower growth, and it will continue to feel those effects. Women are having fewer children and living longer after they have them. That leaves a lot of years for other things. The woman's role in the family is changing from an emphasis on motherhood to an emphasis on an economic role. Every year, more and more women enter the labor force; that trend should continue. Simultaneously, men in the future will have to take more of a role in child care to make up for this change. This also might be a good year to get into some aspect of child care. There may not be as many children out there, but larger and larger percentages of them are spending their early years in day-care centers.

The increasing age of the population has already had political and economic effects on American society. Older people have organized politically in order to have more clout in society. Just one of their successes has been the removal of many mandatory retirement rules. With more and more people older and healthier than ever before, it makes sense that people might want to work longer. What impact will this have on younger people coming along with hopes of promotions? There may be fewer occupational opportunities for younger people, and they may have to wait longer for those opportunities that do exist.

MIGRATION

Thus far we've been focusing on the comings and goings of warm bodies through birth and death. Humans are notorious movers, however, and populations can swell or shrink from the effects of **migration**, the physical movement of a population. Migration forms a particularly interesting aspect of population change; births and deaths bring (or take away) more of the same people, but migration brings cultural diversity into the population. For purposes of convenience, we can separate migration into *international migration* (movement that crosses national boundaries) and *internal migration* (movement within the same country).

International Migration

International migration is the most extreme form of migration in that it creates legal problems (such as changing citizenship) and generally involves greater cultural clashes between the immigrant and the host culture, as typically, cultures vary more across than within national boundaries. International migration is a particularly fascinating study, as it must take a lot before an individual is willing to leave home for unknown problems elsewhere. Furthermore, until relatively recently most international migration was permanent because of the time and the cost of travel; those who left knew there was no coming home. People can have a variety of reasons for taking such a big step, but most of them fall under the headings of economics or politics.

Economic Reasons for International Migration Historically, economic reasons have been the primary motivating force in all forms of migration. People leave home in hopes of enjoying a better standard of living elsewhere. This story is perhaps as old as human existence; wherever the first humans originated, they've done a lot of traveling since. In more recent history knowledge of other societies plus improved transportation technology has made possible migration on a scale not known before. This can be seen very clearly in the history of the United States.

The first immigrants to the United States are the ancestors of those people today known as American Indians. They were followed by the Spanish, French, and English and later by people from the rest of Europe and much of Asia. In almost every case an economic factor emerges as the primary motivation. In Europe, for example, populations were growing rapidly as a result of a declining death rate. In addition, economic arrangements were in the process of changing to large-scale industry and agriculture, making existence increasingly difficult for the poor (Jones, 1960). In Asia economic concerns were also in the front of the emigrants' minds. The rigid social structure of nineteenth-century China could be broken by poor individuals only if they earned money in a foreign country; the early Chinese immigrants to the United States came here fully expecting to return home with great wealth to buy land (Lyman, 1975). The early Japanese immigrants to the United States were interested in the system of private enterprise that prevailed here and became very successful at it (Kitano, 1976). Until 1924, when the United States government finally closed most of the doors to foreign immigrants, millions of immigrants pulled up stakes to come here. In the early 1900s, particularly, the numbers of European immigrants were large enough to change the cultural landscape of America as well as add considerably to the population.

Of all the economic motivations for international migration one of the most dramatic examples is the Irish potato famine. As we've seen, the potato improved nutrition throughout Europe and led to rapidly declining death rates and high growth rates. The population of Ireland, in particular, grew dramatically in the first part of the nineteenth century and Ireland had become the most densely populated country in Europe, almost entirely because of the potato. For most peasants in Ireland the potato was the *only* food. Starting in 1845, a blight attacked the Irish potato crop and continued for several years, leading to almost complete crop loss. As a consequence, 8 million Irish were literally without food, and starvation became a part of everyday life. Between 1846 and 1850, 870,000 Irish came to the United States to escape the famine, and by 1860 there were a total of 1,600,000 Irish in the United States (Duff, 1971). The histories of other immigrants are not always this extreme, but the story of the Irish suggests something of the economic reasons that lead people to take such chances.

Demographers generally look at all forms of migration in terms of push and pull (Bouvier and Gardner, 1986). On the one hand, there is often a "push" from the home region (such as the Irish potato famine) that encourages migration. On the other hand, there is also generally some kind of "pull" from the host region; after all, the Irish could have gone elsewhere, but in the nineteenth century America was viewed as the "land of opportunity" and attracted immigrants from all over. It is still attractive to many people around the world, as evidenced by the large numbers of Mexicans who enter the country illegally. The push and pull factors in migration make it impossible to characterize economically motivated immigrants as particular types of people, as some observers may want to do. A push from a home region generally has the greatest effect on the poorest and most unskilled members of the population since they are usually the most affected by bad times at home. On the other hand, the pull from the host region tends to select for the most enterprising immigrants who are interested in trying something new in hopes of bettering themselves. In looking at immigrants to the United States who came largely for economic reasons (which was most of them), it is often hard to separate the push factors from the pull factors. American society became home to many poor and unskilled foreigners but also gained a sturdy group of enterprising people who played a major role in the development of American society.

Political Reasons for International Migration Crossing national boundaries changes politics as well as economics. Political difficulties at home have always been a prime reason (or push) for people to submit to the upheaval and disruption of immigration. While political motivations are not as common as economic motivations (since they generally don't affect as large a percentage of the home population), they are nevertheless important motivations and certainly result in some colorful immigrants.

Political motivations for immigration to the United States have been more important because of the political and religious freedom that characterizes this society relative to others. The French Huguenots (Protestant French) came to the United States in the late 1600s to avoid persecution in their predominantly Catholic home country; in this sense they were much like the more famous Pilgrims who arrived here earlier. The first Jewish immigrants to the United States came in hopes of finding religious tolerance. European political upheavals and revolutions in the late 1840s brought a variety of Germans and Austrians to the United States. More recently, individuals fleeing from fascism in Europe in the 1930s and later from communist countries such as Hungary, Cuba, and Vietnam have come to the United States to avoid political problems at home.

Who are the political immigrants? There is no easy answer to this question. Those who were a problem to their home governments may be perceived the same way by the host government. Some radical European immigrants, for example, were important members of many of the early radical labor unions in the United States, and many were deported by the United States government. On the other hand, the scientists who created the atom bomb for the United States during World War II, Einstein and Fermi, for example, had fled their home countries to avoid fascism. Individuals who flee after communist revolutions tend to be the upper and professional classes, who have the most to lose under a socialist political regime. Push and pull are certainly both operative in political migration, but they yield no easy generalizations.

Internal Migration

People move around within their own countries far more freely than they cross national boundaries, but they move for many of the same reasons. Their primary reasons are economic (since politics wouldn't change significantly), and very definite pushes and pulls are in operation.

Roughly 20 percent of the American population move each year. Some move down the street, but many move from state to state or across the country. They move largely in response to occupational concerns and fluctuations in the economy. The increasing rate of occupational specialization in American society has increased the rate of internal migration as people must move to where the jobs are. American employers also have come to take migration for granted in their expectations that higher level employees should be open to relocating in the interests of the company. The more new occupations are created in the United States and the more individuals go through specialized training programs for those occupations, the more internal migration we should see.

As jobs vary from place to place, so does the economy. In the early days of the industrial revolution in the United States the movement was from the farms to the cities as jobs changed from agricultural to industrial. This process of urbanization, which will receive a closer look in the following section, required people to move if they wanted to survive. In the past few decades, some industry moved out of the cities, in particular to the West, South, and Southwest.

Americans are highly mobile, with some 20 percent of the American population changing addresses each year. Many move to new cities or states in search of better education or better jobs, responding to economic pushes and pulls.

Not surprisingly, employees once again moved to follow the employers; migration to the "Sunbelt" (as these areas are called) was the dominant goal for most internal migrants in the United States in recent years.

Who are the internal migrants? As with the economic pushes and pulls of international migration, they can be a mixed bunch. Scudder and Anderson (1954) found that the sons who left smaller communities in the United States for larger communities tended to be more upwardly mobile than those who stayed behind. They may have been a more enterprising group of people or, on the other hand, they may just have benefited from the increased opportunities to be found in larger communities in the 1950s. Biggar (1979) compared recent migrants to the South and West to the overall United States population and found that the migrants were apt to be younger, better educated, and better employed than the average American. Young people are perhaps less tied to an area than their elders. Their migration probably reflects both a need and a desire to follow specialized occupations. In short, economically motivated migrants are not typically motivated by poverty.

What is the social impact of internal migration? Part of the impact will be caused by differences in population size. The area deserted will have to get by with fewer people, which means a lower tax base, fewer workers, empty buildings, vacant desks in the schools, fewer voters, fewer representatives in Congress, and a whole range of other changes. The area moved to will have opposite problems: a lack of housing, insufficient public services, overcrowded classrooms, perhaps too many workers, not enough hospital beds, and so on. Migration can change population size much more quickly than changes in fertility.

There is more to the social impact of internal migration than just population size change, however. As we saw earlier, it is generally not a random sample of the population that moves but a specific part of it. The current move to the Sunbelt by younger and better-educated members of the population will change not only population size but the age-sex pyramids in each place as well. Moreover, higher education levels among migrants probably mean that not just workers but different kinds of workers are moving, which will drastically change the nature of the labor force in each area. If the migrants are of a particular racial or ethnic group, racial and ethnic group relations will change in both locations (see Box 12.2). The possibilities are endless and will be different in each case of internal migration. As Will Rogers (a native Oklahoman) once said about the 1930s migration from Oklahoma to California, it raised the level of intelligence in both states.

URBANIZATION

Urbanization, the concentration of people in urban areas, results from the large-scale migration of people from rural to urban areas. The term is generally reserved for societies in which that migration remains steady over time. Though urbanization is a form of migration, it was not included in that section because of its own historical importance. The movement of a society toward industrialization requires urbanization, a relationship we'll examine momentarily. As a result, urbanization is far more than a lot of individuals deciding to make a move. It is the outcome of particular social pressures that force people to move, and it comes to play a major role in the kinds of lifestyles characteristic of a society. This section will examine urbanization with an emphasis on cities in the United States. Particular attention will be paid to the causes of urbanization, its effects on the lives of individuals, and the current situation of American cities.

Why Urbanization?

The physical patterns of human settlements have always been related to the ways human beings earn their living. Hunting and gathering societies, for example, required their members to move constantly in search of new food supplies. Consequently, as we saw in Chapter 9, such societies had to remain small and without a good many of the creature comforts we take for granted today. The first horticultural societies allowed humans to sit and rest a little. Producing your own food allows you to produce more of it more efficiently and allows you to stay put while you do it. Horticulture led to some of the first permanent human communities. Typically small, those communities were geared to the farm life that permitted them to form.

Most of us in the United States have given up on hunting and gathering as a form of survival, but agriculture is still a basic necessity of life. We grow and raise more than ever before, in fact, but we do it differently. In 1920, over 30 percent of the American population (almost 32 million people) lived on farms; by 1988, only about 2 percent of the American population (a little less than 5 million people) remained on farms (U.S. Bureau of the Census, 1990g). Who is doing the farming? Fewer people working more acres. Agribusiness has largely replaced the family farm, making it almost impossible for smaller operations to be profitable. Between 1940 and the late 1970s the average-size American farm grew from 175 acres to 400 acres (U.S. Bureau of the Census, 1978). Changes in the industrial economy of the United States forced these changes on the American farmer; just as hunting and gathering societies could not compete with

BOX 12.2

THE INTERNAL MIGRATION OF BLACK AMERICANS

Black Americans have moved within the United States for some of the same reasons—primarily economic—that white Americans move. In addition, they have moved to escape discrimination, although many times such moves have taken them out of the frying pan and into the fire. Whatever their reasons for moving, the arrival of many black Americans in any section of the United States in any time of its history has been an event of considerable concern to the people already there.

Before the end of the Civil War approximately 90 percent of all black Americans were locked into the system of slavery in the American South. The other side of that statistic is that 10 percent of them were free, and many of them lived in the northern cities. During the 1800s blacks were commonly used as strikebreakers in northern cities—when the immigrant workers went on strike, management would hire blacks. Though the immigrants were angry at management, they were furious with blacks; this was the beginning of much of the prejudice these new immigrant groups came to feel toward blacks. The use of blacks as strikebreakers continued well into the twentieth century. Edna Bonacich (1976) counted twenty-five separate strikes between 1916 and 1934 where blacks were brought in to break the strike.

The end of slavery did not dramatically change the residence of most black Americans; 90 percent of them remained in the South as late as 1910. The big change was World War I, which ended immigration from Europe and created a labor shortage at home. Between 1914 and 1920 an estimated 400,000 to 1,000,000 blacks left the South for work in northern industry (Pinkney, 1975). Though many of the jobs didn't last beyond the war, the migration changed the patterns of black life tremendously. New York City developed a concentrated and highly talented black community with noted poets, composers, and historians, many of whom are being rediscovered today. New York was also the center of Marcus Garvey's "back to Africa" political movement in the 1920s (see Chapter 9), which preached racial separation and black power. By 1924 Garvey had 100,000 dues-paying members—made possible by the concentration of black Americans into cities (Vander Zanden, 1972).

World War II again brought blacks to northern cities for the same reasons that World War I did, but this time far more blacks made the move. They also moved to new locations, most notably the West Coast. The years following World War II provide a picture of social change through racial migration. Since World War I white northern Americans had been learning to discriminate against blacks; there were no official antiblack laws on the books as in the South, but the practice in the North was every bit as effective: Blacks lived in separate neighborhoods, attended separate schools, and worked at the dirtiest and most poorly paid jobs. Robert Blauner (1975) argues that their late arrival in northern industrial occupations has handicapped blacks greatly. The newly concentrated black population was in a position to organize politically more effectively than it ever had before. The civil rights movement grew during the 1950s, followed by the more radical black power movement of the 1960s. Just as black migration stimulated white northerners to acts of discrimination, those acts coupled with the new physical environment of the cities allowed blacks to make an effective political response to their situation.

(continues)

BOX 12.2 (continued)

In the 1970s (and for the first time since World War I) the direction of black migration turned around; blacks began moving from the northern cities back into the South along with the rest of the Sunbelt migrators. Many of the forms of discrimination in the South that encouraged northern migration are now gone. Perhaps most important, there are economic opportunities for blacks in the South today that were closed through discrimination yesterday. As the South and West respond to the influx of internal migrants in general, part of that response will no doubt include the changing black communities and work force brought about through the paths of migration.

agricultural societies, the family farm has not been able to compete with the new economic patterns in American society.

Those new economic patterns reflect the increasing dominance of industry and technology. The same economic and technological transformation that turned the family farm into agribusiness has turned the "mom and pop" grocery store into the supermarket and the small manufacturing plant into the conglomerate corporation. The United States has been an industrial society for over a century, but the change is gradual and is still continuing. As economic life becomes more centralized, it also becomes necessary for the population to become more centralized. The American population has become centralized in the cities, as Figure 12.5 suggests.

Urbanization drives people to cities because it drives employers to cities. Big businesses need large labor forces that live in close proximity to the office or factory. Just as important, big business needs to be near other big business. The division of labor that affects all aspects of American life is reflected in the business world as well. A steel mill needs to be near supplies of iron ore. Manufacturers who use steel must be near the steel mills. And all of these businesses must be near other businesses that supply paper, machinery, paper clips, transportation, work clothes, communication, and all of the many other items and services that must come together for an industrial economy to work. The concentration of business forces people to concentrate as they pursue the ends of their own survival in a society that offers progressively fewer options in rural areas and more in urban areas. And as people concentrate, so too will the services and other businesses that people need in their everyday lives. Urbanization is therefore far more than just a movement of people; it is a concentration of all aspects of society into one physical setting called a city. Like all human societies, it reflects the way people earn a living.

The Effects of Urbanization

In the early 1960s a New York City woman named Kitty Genovese was attacked and murdered on her street, the attack lasting over 30 minutes from start to finish. It was discovered later that thirty-eight different people had heard her screams, but not one had come to her aid; no one even called the police because they "didn't want to get involved" (Rosenthal, 1964). This story fits in with many of the stereotypes Americans hold about cities. Cities are jungles, large impersonal environments in which everyone looks out for number one. Cities are hotbeds of sin and crime in which traditional moral values are quickly forgotten. These stereotypes sit in contrast to a prevalent view of rural life in which we go over the river and through the woods to a nice wholesome dinner at Grandma's house. What, in fact, does city life do to us?

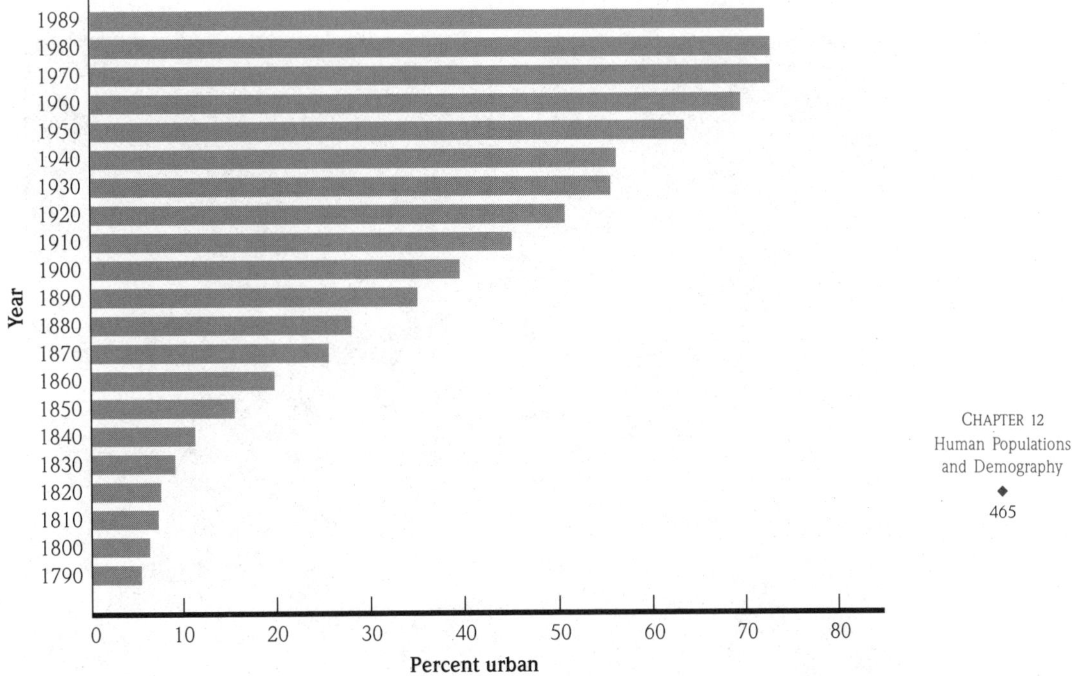

Figure 12.5 Percent of U.S. population living in urban areas, 1790-1989. (Data from U.S. Bureau of the Census, 1990.)

The negative stereotype of cities has been around as long as cities. An early sociological view of cities comes from German sociologist Georg Simmel in his article "The Metropolis and Mental Life," written in the early 1900s (Simmel, 1950). In this article Simmel offers two of the dominant ideas regarding the effects of urban life on the individual. On the one hand, says Simmel, the city is an environment of intense nervous stimulation that would "short circuit" the personality of a rural person. To counteract this, the city dweller learns to respond "with his head instead of heart." As a result of urban intensity, the city dweller becomes somewhat blase; other people and situations are viewed in terms of rational calculations much in the same way one would enter into a business relationship.

On the other hand, says Simmel, the city is the source of individual freedom. Small groups tend to be very restrictive of their members. They hold strongly to certain values and pay close attention to behavior to see that norms are adhered to. The anonymity cities provide for their residents allows individual personalities to develop without the shackles of continual surveillance. Our modern ideal of individuality and individual rights is a creature of the city. And what of Kitty Genovese? Simmel would argue that individual freedom to not become involved goes hand in hand with the intellectual (as opposed to the emotional) response of the city dweller.

Louis Wirth, an American sociologist, offered a more recent but in some ways similar view of the city in his famous 1938 article, "Urbanism as a Way of Life." Wirth emphasized the diversity of city life and the effect of that diversity on its members. We deal with many strangers in cities, and most of the people we encounter we see only in very specialized roles. This

Suburbia may offer space and quiet, but big-city life has its pluses, too. People spend more time out on the streets (weather permitting) and so have more social contacts. When there are hundreds of families on a block, there's rarely a problem in finding enough kids for a game.

is in contrast to small communities, where we know the "whole person." This difference understandably would alter the nature of human relationships. In addition, says Wirth, the diversity of city life can be very confusing and can produce a state of anomie in its members.

The diversity of urban life is certainly one of its most striking characteristics. People move to cities from all over and bring their cultures with them. They usually try to live with others from their home town (or state or country) when they get there. Herbert Gans (1962) emphasized this aspect of urban life, pointing out that cities may appear at first glance to be vast mixtures of people but are, in fact, joined-together communities in which people have many of the interpersonal contacts and emotions common to small towns. Meeting people from other cultures provides a new perspective on our own, perhaps calling attention to beliefs or behaviors to which we had never given a second thought. Thus, cities have the potential for reducing ethnocentrism as individuals can become more understanding of cultural differences. On the other hand, cities can also become a vast battleground in which people from different backgrounds discover just how much they hate each other.

Cities are fertile ground for politics. Urban life concentrates people and exposes them directly to outsiders and assorted other threats. If you have a gripe, there are probably a number of others around with the same gripe acquired in the same way. There is also probably a potential

political leader around who will find the physical concentration of potential followers to be convenient for purposes of organization; a speaker can draw a much bigger crowd in downtown New York City than in the grasslands of west Texas. It is not surprising, therefore, that most American political movements—from labor unions and political machines to a variety of revolutionary movements—have grown in cities.

One of the most important changes brought about by urbanization occurs with the family. Migration of any kind tends to break up extended families as the members become scattered and lose touch. Moreover, urban life accompanies industrialization, which tends to reduce family size. All in all, families change quite a bit as a result of the urban move. And as families change, so, too, do many of the norms, roles, and values that are associated with families. Urbanization affects childrearing practices, sex roles within the family, religion, education, leisure-time activities, and friendship patterns, to name just a few.

Generalizations about urban impact should be taken with a grain of salt. A massive overall change in our way of life, the growth of cities has been a many-faceted phenomenon. Our responses to the urban environment have been just as varied. The urban experience is clearly a factor of change in all aspects of life, but sociologists have yet to discover exactly how that factor operates.

Trends in Urbanization: Cities Today and Tomorrow

Since World War II American cities have become increasingly decentralized—largely in size and less dense in population. The popular term for this change is **suburbanization**—more and more people leaving the central cities for the dream house and lot in the suburbs. Once again, however, it is not only the people who are moving. Between 1954 and 1963, for example, the central areas in the forty largest American cities lost an average 25,798 manufacturing jobs; during that same period, almost an identical number of such jobs opened up in the suburbs (Kain, 1968). Since 1963, that trend has largely continued, as it has grown less and less necessary for businesses to locate in urban areas. The loss of people to the suburbs is hard enough on the city's tax base, but the loss of all those jobs can be backbreaking. A thriving city factory generates tax revenue in a whole variety of ways, while an empty shell of a building (especially one nobody wants) is worth very little. And, as money leaves, the cities have to cut back on services, either temporarily or permanently. Some of the central areas of American cities are beginning to look more like wastelands than the center of activity they once were. The South Bronx in New York City, for example, has been largely deserted and left to the arsonists.

The people who leave for the suburbs are specifically middle-class people. Many suburbs control this immigration by zoning regulations that force certain kinds of structures (expensive) to be added to certain size lots (large). When middle-class people leave the cities, lower-class people are left behind. To the extent that the urban poor are nonwhite, the process of suburbanization in American society is leading to racial segregation: Whites live out in suburbia while nonwhites struggle in the remains of the central cities. In addition, central cities are becoming the loci for increasing numbers of homeless Americans (Snow and Anderson, 1987; Rossi et al., 1987). Changes in the structure of the American family coupled with 1980s decreases in government spending on social programs have produced larger numbers of people who spend years without a permanent residence except a street corner or bus station. A study of homeless people in Chicago found that most tend to have the same education as the rest of the population (about twelve years) but are characterized by either mental or physical disabilities and by a lack of family ties; a full 50 percent of those in the sample had never married (Rossi et al., 1987).

Decentralization appears to be occurring in American society today even beyond the bounds of general metropolitan areas. The mass migration to the Sunbelt indicates a movement not only out of the central city but even away from the city altogether. Businesses are taking advantage of new advances in communication and transportation that permit them to enjoy the low tax rates and nonunion labor of smaller communities in the South and the West. Where businesses used to have to huddle together, usually near a major waterway, today they apparently feel they can spread out connected only by telephone lines and highways. And where business goes, people follow.

However, one of the questions for the future of cities concerns their relation to the growing energy shortages we face. Suburbs grew along with railroad commuter lines and, more importantly, the automobile. Living far from work was no problem as the transportation costs were negligible. Today, however, cities appear in a new light. Expensive transportation makes centralized living patterns appear once again attractive. Some Americans are looking at cities as if for the first time, thinking how convenient it would be to have people living and working in close proximity—add a church, a school, and a corner grocery store, and folks would have everything they needed. Some American cities have in fact experienced something of a rebirth as people and business have moved back, bringing restored buildings and new tax revenues with them. It is certainly too early to speak of a centralization trend (countering the decentralization we've experienced for several decades), but American cities are clearly far from dead.

SUMMARY

Demography is the study of human populations, focusing on the social factors that affect populations and the effects of changes in those populations on the rest of society. Populations increase or decrease through the interplay of three fundamental processes: birth, death, and migration.

In the eighteenth century advances in nutrition and sanitation caused the death rate in Europe to drop, which resulted in a population explosion. The population continued to rise well into the Industrial Revolution, after which the birth rate began to drop, causing population growth to level out. This historical occurrence, today called the demographic transition, is thought by some demographers to be a general pattern for population change.

The nonindustrial world today appears to be in stage two of the demographic transition as death rates have dropped but birth rates remain high. This situation creates a population explosion as well as a very high proportion of the population under the age of fourteen and in a state of dependency. Modern-day Marxists argue that poverty in the nonindustrial world is due to capitalism rather than to the population explosion. Some scientists have tried to aid the situation by creating more productive crops (the Green Revolution). Most demographers see fertility control as essential to ending poverty.

A stable population (zero population growth) has occurred in several industrial countries already, but its long-term effects are not known. One effect would be a change in the age distribution of the population—fewer young people and more older people. This change would certainly alter the economic structure of society.

Migration is the movement of people from one physical location to another. International migration crosses national political boundaries, whereas internal migration is movement within such boundaries. In both cases, the primary motivations for migration have been economic, although significant numbers of international migrants move for political reasons. Most demographers view migration from the dual perspective of the "push" the migrant feels from the home area and the "pull" from the host area.

Urbanization is the most extreme historical example of migration, but its importance goes beyond the mere movement of people. It refers to the ongoing concentration of people, things, and activities into relatively small geographical areas known as cities. This concentration has coincided with industrialization as the city has been a necessary physical setting for industrialization to occur. The physical concentration of people and their activities into cities, from the individual standpoint, tends to increase personal freedom while simultaneously loosening the individual's attachment to the social group. Recently, some trends toward decentralization have been noted in the United States and elsewhere through both the growth of suburbs and industrial movement to less urban settings.

GLOSSARY

Birth rate The number of births in a given year for every 1,000 people in the population.

Death rate The number of deaths in a given year for every 1,000 people in the population.

Demographic transition The set of population changes that occurs with industrialization, eventually resulting in a drop in both birth and death rates, leaving them in relative balance.

Demography The study of human populations, emphasizing the causes and effects of population changes.

General fertility rate The number of births in a given year for every 1,000 women of childbearing age.

Growth rate The rate of natural population increase plus the immigration rate.

Immigration rate The number of immigrants for every 1,000 people in the population in a given year.

Migration The physical movement of a population, either international (if it crosses national boundaries) or internal (if it does not).

Pronatalism The societal value of having children and large families.

Rate of natural increase (or decrease) The difference between the birth rate and the death rate in a given year.

Replacement level The number of babies necessary in a population for parents to replace themselves.

Suburbanization The movement of people to, and the growth of, residential housing surrounding a city.

Urbanization The physical concentration of people in urban areas resulting from the large-scale migration from rural areas.

Zero population growth A stable population in which each individual is replaced through a stable birth rate.

SUPPLEMENTARY READINGS

Bogue, Donald *The Population of the United States: Historical Trends and Future Projections.* New York: Free Press, 1985.
A view of how population specialists examine a single country, projecting the future from the past.

Ehrlich, Paul R., and Ann H. Ehrlich *Population, Resources, Environment.* San Francisco: W. H. Freeman, 1972.
A readable discussion of the relationship among population growth, diminishing resources, and environmental pollution.

Fischer, Claude S. *The Urban Experience* (2nd ed.). New York: Harcourt Brace Jovanovich, 1984.
An introduction to urban sociology that, along the way, counters many of the negative stereotypes about cities.

Haupt, Arthur, and Thomas T. Kane *Population Handbook.* Washington, D.C.: Population Reference Bureau, 1978.
A basic guide to demographic terms and measures, including a glossary. In general, the Population Reference Bureau is an excellent source of all kinds of demographic information.

Jacobs, Jane *The Death and Life of Great American Cities.* New York: Vintage, 1961.
An analysis of cities from the perspective of city planning. Jacobs criticizes many assumptions and offers policies designed to maintain current urban areas through maintaining multiuse neighborhoods.

Weeks, John R. *Population: An Introduction to Concepts and Issues.* 5th ed. Belmont, Calif.: Wadsworth, 1992.
A general and basic introduction to demography, tracing the role of population change in its impact on the remainder of society.

World Population Continues to Rise

NAFIS SADIK

World population growth is undoubtedly the most pressing social problem brought to center stage through the efforts of demographers. Nafis Sadik provides a clear picture of the world population crisis in the following article, calling our attention to the slow growth in the wealthiest countries as compared with the rapid growth in the poorest developing countries. This growth is coupled with a decline of food production in a majority of these developing countries, leading to the mass malnutrition and starvation we've seen in recent years, particularly in Africa. While different demographers offer many different approaches to this problem, Sadik, executive director of the United Nations Population Fund, focuses her attention on the role of women worldwide, emphasizing the need for better education in general for women and a greater emphasis on providing them with family planning information and more effective (and cheaper) contraceptives.

The 1990s will be a critical decade. The choices of the next 10 years will decide the speed of population growth for much of the next century; they will decide whether world population triples or merely doubles before it finally stops growing; they will decide whether the pace of damage to the environment speeds up or slows down.

The world's population, now 5.3 billion, is increasing by three people every second—about a quarter of a million every day. Between 90 and 100 million people—roughly equivalent to the population of Eastern Europe or Central America—will be added every year during the 1990s; a billion people—a whole extra China—over the decade.

No less than 95% of the global population growth over the next 35 years will be in the developing countries of Africa, Asia, and Latin America.

It has been more than 20 years since the population growth rate of developing countries reached its peak in 1965-70. But it will be during only the last five years of this century that the additions to total numbers in developing countries will reach their maximum. This 35-year lag is a powerful demonstration of the steamroller momentum of population growth.

Racing to provide services to fast-growing populations is like running up the down escalator: You have to run very fast indeed to maintain upward motion. So far, all the effort put into social programs has not been quite enough to move upward in numerical terms. The absolute total of human deprivation has actually increased, and unless there is a massive increase in family planning and other social spending, the future will be no better.

Population Trends

Southern Asia, with almost a quarter of the current total world population, will account for 31% of the total increase between now and the end of the century; Africa, with 12% of the world's population today, will account for 23% of the increase. By contrast, eastern Asia, which has another 25% of the current world population, will account for only 17% of the total increase. Similarly, the developed countries—Europe (including the Soviet Union), North America, and Japan, which represent 23% of the current world population—will account for only 6% of the increase. The remaining 15% of the world's

Reprinted with permission, from *The Futurist,* March-April, 1991.

population, living in developing countries, will produce 23% of the increase.

By and large, the increases will be in the poorest countries—those by definition least equipped to meet the needs of the new arrivals and invest in the future.

Because of the world's skewed growth patterns, the balance of numbers will shift radically. In 1950, Europe and North America constituted 22% of the world's population. In 2025, they will make up less than 9%. Africa, only 9% of the world population in 1950, will account for just under a fifth of the 2025 total. India will overtake China as the world's most populous country by the year 2030.

Toward the end of the twenty-first century, a number of countries seem set to face severe problems if populations grow as projected. Nigeria could have some 500 million citizens—as many as the whole African continent had around 1982. This would represent more than 10 people for every hectare of arable land. Modern France, with better soils and less erosion, has only three people per hectare. Bangladesh's 116 million inhabitants would grow to 324 million, with density on its arable land more than twice as high as in the Netherlands today. This does not take into account any land that may be lost to sea-level rises caused by global warming.

It should be emphasized that these are not the most-pessimistic projections. On the contrary, they assume steadily declining fertility during most of the next 100 years.

Food

Between 1979-81 and 1986-87, cereal production per person actually declined in 51 developing countries and rose in only 43. The total number of malnourished people increased from 460 million to 512 million and is projected to exceed 532 million by the end of the century.

Developing countries as a whole have suffered a serious decline in food self-sufficiency. Their cereal imports in 1969-71 were only 20 million tons. By 1983-85, they had risen to 69 million tons and are projected to total 112 million tons by the end of the century. These deficits have so far been met by corresponding surpluses in the industrialized countries—of which the overwhelming bulk comes from North America.

World food security now depends shakily on the performance of North American farmers. Following the drought-hit U.S. harvest of 1988, world cereal stocks dropped from 451 million tons in 1986-87 to only 290 million tons in 1989, down from a safe 24% of annual consumption to the danger level of 17%.

Poverty

The world produces enough food to feed everyone today—yet malnutrition affects as many as 500 million people. The problem is poverty and the ability to earn a livelihood. The total numbers of the poor have grown over the past two decades to around one billion now.

Absolute poverty has shown a dogged tendency to rise in numerical terms. The poorest fifth of the population still dispose of only 4% of the world's wealth, while the richest dispose of 58%. Economic recession, rising debt burdens, and mistaken priorities have reduced social spending in many countries.

But populaton growth at over 2% annually has also slowed social progress. So much additional investment has been required to increase the quantity of health, education, and other services to meet the needs of increased populations that the quality of service has suffered.

In many sectors, the proportion of deprived people has declined. But this is a reduced proportion of a higher total population swelled by rapid growth. As a result, the total numbers of deprived people have grown.

The growth of incomes may be affected by population growth. On a regional basis, there is an inverse relationship between population growth and growth of per capita income. There is a lag of 15-20 years between the peak of population growth and the peak growth in the labor force. Already there are severe problems in absorbing new entrants to the labor force in regions such as Africa or South Asia. Yet, in numerical terms, the highest rates of labor-force growth in developing countries lie ahead, in the years 2010-2020.

The labor force in developing countries will grow from around 1.76 billion today to more than

3.1 billion in 2025. Every year, 38 million new jobs will be needed, without counting jobs required to wipe out existing underemployment, estimated at 40% in many developing countries. Complicating the issue will be the spread of new, labor-saving technologies.

The land still provides the livelihood of almost 60% of the population of developing countries. But most of the best and most-accessible land is already in use, and what is left is either less fertile or harder to clear and work. The area available per person actually declined at the rate of 1.9% a year during the 1980s.

Urban and Education Issues

In recent decades, urban growth in developing countries has been even more rapid than overall population growth. Town populations are expanding at 3.6% a year—four and a half times faster than in industrialized countries and 60% faster than rural areas. Rural migrants swell the total, but an increasing share of this growth now comes from natural growth within the cities themselves.

The speed of growth has outpaced the ability of local and national government to provide adequate services. The number of urban households without safe water increased from 138 million in 1970 to 215 million in 1988. Over the same period, households without adequate sanitation ballooned from 98 million to 340 million.

The total number of children out of school grew from 284 million in 1970 to 293 million in 1985 and is projected to rise further to 315 million by the end of the century. Also between 1970 and 1985: The total number of illiterates rose from 742 million to 889 million, and the total number of people without safe sanitation increased from about a billion to 1.75 billion.

Eating Away at the Earth

These increasing numbers are eating away at the earth itself. The combination of fast population growth and poverty in developing countries has begun to make permanent changes to the environment. During the 1990s, these changes will reach critical levels. They include continued urban growth, degradation of land and water resources, massive deforestation, and buildup of greenhouse gases.

Many of these changes are now inevitable because they were not foreseen early enough, or because action was not taken to forestall them. Our options in the present generation are narrower because of the decisions of our predecessors. Our range of choice, as individuals or as nations, is narrower, and the choices are harder.

The 1990s will decide whether the choices for our children narrow yet further—or open up. We know more about population—and interactions among population, resources, and the environment—than any previous generation. We have the basis for action. Failure to use it decisively will ensure only that the problems become much more severe and much more intractable, the choices harder and their price higher.

At the start of the 1990s, the choice must be to act decisively to slow population growth, attack poverty, and protect the environment. The alternative is to hand on to our children a poisoned inheritance.

What Needs to Be Done?

Immediate action to widen options and improve the quality of life, especially for women, will do much to secure population goals. It will also widen the options and improve the quality of life of future generations.

Education is often the means to a new vision of options. It encourages a sense of control over personal destiny and the possibility of choices beyond accepted tradition. For women, it offers a view of sources of status beyond childbearing. Because of this, education—especially for girls—has a strong impact on the health of the family and on its chosen size.

Women assume the burden of childcare along with their other tasks. They are in charge of nutrition, hygiene, food, and water. As a result, the effect of women's education on child survival is very marked.

Education's impact on fertility and use of family planning is equally strong. Women with seven or more years of education tend to marry an average of almost four years later than those who have had none.

Yet, there remains a great deal to be done in women's education, even to bring it level with men's. Women make up almost two-thirds of the illiterate adults in developing countries. The importance of literacy programs for adult women goes far beyond reading and writing: It also allows access to practical information on such matters as preventive health care and family planning, which are often part of the programs themselves.

Sustained improvements in health care give people a sense of control over their lives. With adequate health care, parents develop the sense that they have some choice over their children's survival. Parents' feeling of control over their lives is extended by modern family planning; they can protect the health of both mother and child by preventing or postponing childbirth. Preventive measures that the family itself can apply assist the process.

Support for Family-Planning Efforts

Political support from the highest levels in the state is essential in making family planning both widely available and widely used. Political backing helps to legitimize family planning, to desensitize it, and to place it in the forum of public debate. It helps win over traditional leaders or counter their hostility. It also helps to ensure that funding and staffing for family planning are stable and protected against damaging budget cuts or the competing demands of rival departments.

Support must extend far beyond the national leadership before programs take off. It may be necessary to involve a wide range of religious and traditional leaders in discussions before introducing population policies and programs on a wide scale. If these leaders feel that they have been sidestepped, their opposition may become entrenched. If they are consulted and involved, on the other hand, they may often turn into allies. In Indonesia, for example, Muslim religious leaders were consulted at national and local levels; they not only withdrew their opposition, but have added their voices to the government's call for family planning.

Four main barriers block the way to easy access to family planning. The most obvious is geographical: How long do people have to travel to get supplies, and how long do they have to wait for service when they get there?

The second barrier is financial: While many surveys show that people are willing to pay moderate amounts for family-planning supplies, most poor people have a fairly low price threshold. Costs of more than 1% of income are likely to prove a deterrent.

Culture and communication are a third barrier: opposition from the peer group, husband, or mother-in-law; shyness about discussing contraception or undergoing gynecological examination; language difficulties; or unsympathetic clinic staff.

A fourth barrier is the methods available: There is no such thing as the perfect contraceptive. Most people who need one can find a method suited to their needs—if one is available. However, if high contraception use is to be achieved, suitable services must be not only available, but accessible to all who need them.

Suitable services mean high-quality services. In the long run, the quantity of continuing users will depend on the quality of the service.

Service providers do not need to be highly educated, but they should be sympathetic, well informed, and committed to their work. The service must be reliable, so that users can count on supplies when they need them. Good counseling is one of the most important aspects of quality. Family planning is loaded with emotional, social, and sometimes religious values. It is vulnerable to poor information, rumor, and outright superstition. Along with reliable supplies and a good system for referral in problem cases, good counseling can make a big difference to continuation rates.

Two other channels are useful in broadening the base and increasing the appeal of family planning: community-based distribution and social marketing.

Community-based distribution (CBD) programs use members of the community—housewives, leaders, or members of local groups—to distribute contraceptives. Older married mothers who are themselves contraceptive users have proved the best candidates. Maturity, tact, perseverance, and enthusiasm are essential requirements for the good distributor.

FRONTIERS OF TECHNOLOGY

Research must continue for the ideal method of contraception: cheap, totally effective, risk-free, reversible, without undesirable side effects, and simple enough for use without medical provision or supervision.

No such method is yet on the horizon. But research continues to push forward the frontiers, under conditions that have become more and more difficult.

The business of developing new contraceptives has changed radically. Tighter controls on testing and rising risks of costly lawsuits have made drug companies wary. The leading role has been assumed by the World Health Organization (WHO) and by nonprofit organizations such as the Population Council and Family Health International. But real spending on contraceptive research and development has not increased.

Some promising new candidates have been developed. Norplant, already approved for use in several countries, is probably closest to wide dissemination. It consists of six tiny rods containing the progestin hormone levonorgestrol. These are implanted under the skin of a woman's inside arm. Norplant, particularly suitable for women who have completed their families, prevents pregnancies for five years before it needs replacing. A two-rod version providing protection for three years is being developed. Norplant is highly effective, and unlike the injectable Depo-Provera, its contraceptive effect ends soon after it is removed. The drawback for some situations is that it requires a physician to insert and remove. The cost, at $2.80 per year of protection, is more than the pill at $1.95, but less than Depo-Provera at $4 per year.

Other long-acting hormonal methods may be introduced during the 1990s. They include biodegradable implants, providing 18 months of protection, and injectable microspheres lasting between one and six months. Vaginal rings containing levonorgestrol, which can be inserted and removed by the woman, are also being tested. And the Population Council is researching a male contraceptive vaccine.

—Nafis Sadik

After many years of relying only on clinic and health workers to deliver services, family-planning programs are discovering the uses of the marketplace. The private sector provides contraceptives to more than half the users in many developing countries.

Social-marketing programs reduce the cost to the user and increase sales by subsidizing supplies. These two aspects—the integration of suppliers with regular health services through training and the subsidization of supplies—are felt to combine the ease of access of the market with the sense of social responsibility of service programs.

The potential of community-based distribution and social marketing has not been exploited in most countries. Out of 93 countries studied for one survey, only 37 had a CBD or social-marketing project. There is clearly a considerable potential for expansion as an essential complement to integrated health services.

The technology of contraception is usually thought of in terms of safety and reliability. But it should also be seen as another important aspect of improving access and choice in family-planning programs.

Currently, the most popular method worldwide is sterilization, with around 119 million women and 45 million men in 1987. Next in popularity was the intrauterine device (IUD), with 84 million users, followed by the pill, with 67 million. The pattern of use differs considerably from one country to another and between developing countries and developed. Sterilization is by far the most common method in developing countries, with 45% of users, though only one-quarter of these were male. The IUD comes next in popularity, with 23%. In the North, sterilization accounts for only 14% of users and IUDs for 8%.

Users balance all the advantages and disadvantages they are aware of before deciding on a method—or no method. If they do not like the available alternatives, they will simply drop out and use no method at all, or revert to less reliable traditional methods. One recent study in East Java found that, among women who were not given the method they preferred, 85% had discontinued use within one year. Where women were given the method they wanted, the dropout rate was only 25%.

Diversity, then, is the key to providing options. Diverse channels of distribution create the widest possible access to contraception. Diverse technology offers the widest possible choice of methods. The combination maximizes use.

Developing Human Resources

Investment in human resources provides a firm base for rapid economic development and could have a significant impact on the environmental crisis. It is essential for global security. But in the past, it has often commanded a lower priority than industry, agriculture, or military expenditure.

It is time for a new scale of priorities: There is no other sphere of development where investment can make such a large contribution both to the options and to the qualitiy of life, both in the present and in the future. Whatever the future returns, investment is needed now.

About the Author

Nafis Sadik is executive director of the United Nations Population Fund, 220 East 42nd Street, New York, New York 10017. This article is adapted from the Fund's *The State of World Population 1990.*

Discussion Questions

1. What is the connection between population growth and poverty in developing countries? What connection is there between spurts in the population and increases in the labor force?
2. What problems, both economic and cultural, confront family planners in developing countries? How can such problems be overcome?
3. Do you agree with Sadik that family planning is the most effective response to the crisis in world population growth? What other responses, if any, would you think might be required?

CHAPTER 13 COLLECTIVE BEHAVIOR AND SOCIAL MOVEMENTS: SOURCES OF SOCIAL CHANGE

What do "mooners" (who bare their backsides in public) have in common with flood victims attempting to recover from their disaster? What do both mooners and flood victims have in common with urban rioters and early Christians? These examples may appear a strange collection, but they all have one important similarity within the sociological outlook: all of them are norm breakers. It's true they break (or broke) different norms, and flood victims do not choose to become refugees, but all of them replace standard patterns of behavior with something new. They also engage in these creative activities with collections of other people; neither mooners nor rioters can exist in the singular, and flood victims generally band together as the early Christians did. In the sociological outlook such collective norm-breaking activities come together to form the field of collective behavior. As we shall see in this chapter, the existence of collective behavior raises some important questions about the degree to which social coordination controls our lives.

Collective behavior is unpatterned (or not norm-governed) behavior that is typically transitory and spontaneous. The *collective* part of collective behavior is significant because this behavior emerges from the interactions of people. These interactions may occur in the same physical setting—as with a crowd—or they may cross both time and space—as with people who follow a fad because they know that others have done so. Breaking into a store is an individual crime, but looting is collective behavior. Believing that you are the son of God may win you a quick trip to a mental hospital, but a religious movement is collective behavior. Turning your hair orange or pink and fashioning it into spikes could be either the work of a berserk hairdresser or a statement by a "with-it" member of the punk community. In each case the size of the group changes the way we think about the behavior. Moreover, the group itself can cause behavior to happen. An individual who might never think to break into a store might join in with some looters. An individual who was never particularly religious might become so from associating with the members of a religious movement.

We have seen throughout this book that socialization results in people's becoming attached to their norms and values, and it usually takes something fairly forceful to push them out of their groove. It is easy to see how floods, tornadoes, and other disasters do this, but an economic depression or a political decision can also force people out of the norms of everyday life. In a strange twist of logic, social groups can keep people in line through social control measures while simultaneously creating conditions that drive people into spontaneous and often creative forms of collective behavior.

Beyond being important in its own right, collective behavior is an important source of social change. The norms we follow today were created by someone who broke the norms that prevailed yesterday. In its early days Christianity was collective behavior, although today it is commonly found in rigidly structured formal organizations; the government of the United States was generated through collective behavior 200 years ago. This chapter will explore the wide range of collective behaviors, focusing in particular on their causes and the way they develop once they get started. Of the many forms collective behavior may take, the particular form known as the social movement will be treated in a separate section because of its importance for social change.

COLLECTIVE BEHAVIOR

All collective behavior is spontaneous and collective; beyond these common characteristics it can comprise a wide range of human behaviors. It can be fairly trivial (such as doing "the wave" at football games) or extremely important (such as urban rioting). It can be looked upon as fine and exemplary behavior by societal authorities (such as altruism in the face of a natural disaster), or it can receive the full force of repression from those same authorities (as is often the experience of revolutionary social movements). It can occur in small groups (as in a work group's effort to get their superior fired) or can affect the whole society (such as a response to famine). The sociological outlook reveals a great variety of manifestations of collective behavior in everyday life.

Fads and Fashions

Fads and fashions make up a separate category of collective behavior primarily because of their triviality. **Fads** are new forms of behavior that catch on among certain groups of people for a limited time. Fads break norms but not important norms (which means they usually do not upset societal authorities to any great extent); they also tend to disappear almost as quickly as they arise. Within this category we would include such examples as streaking, goldfish swallowing, "Valley girl" talk, and the like. Fads generally develop within specific social groups, with one of their functions being boundary maintenance; the group that follows the fad reminds itself and others that it is different from groups that don't. Interestingly, behavior that catches on primarily in poor or powerless social groups—such as young people or the urban poor—tends to be labeled as a fad; punk standards of dress and hair are a good example. If the behavior catches on in more influential social groups, it becomes fashion.

Fashion is basically the same as fads except that it characterizes the behavior of more powerful social groups and it tends to last longer than fads (probably due to the influence of those social groups in "selling" their behavior as a model to the rest of society). Fashions include clothing styles (the most common use of the term), but they also include hair length, leisure activities (such as jogging or tennis), reading preferences, styles of verbal expression, taste in art, and a whole variety of behaviors that certain social groups look upon as correct for certain times and places. As noted, fads can become fashions if they spread to the right groups. Longer hair length for men, for example, first appeared as a fad with young people and then spread as a fashion to older people. Similarly, slang expressions can move from the ghetto to high society. Like fads, fashions also serve to maintain boundaries between groups. Wearing last year's clothes means either that you can't afford to change to this year's clothes or, even worse, that you're too "out of it" to know there has been a change. Part of the reason fashions change is to serve this boundary maintenance function (see Veblen, 1899).

Fads and fashions are collective behavior in that they introduce new forms of behavior and spread through the interactions of people. They are also somewhat trivial in terms of the norms they break—being "out of fashion" may result in your not being invited back but will seldom result in a call to the police. Nevertheless, these forms are interesting to the sociologist in that they illustrate the persistence of social change within social groups. Collective behavior is not limited to deviants; it is an ongoing part of everyday life.

Few of these women would likely consider themselves slaves to fashion, yet the photograph perfectly captures their collective behavior.

Publics and Public Opinion

One important kind of behavior generated within social groups and spread through interactions is people's attitudes and opinions about current issues. A **public** is a collection of people that forms because of their common concern about a current issue. Laws concerning abortion, for example, have led to the creation of publics as individuals have formed opinions through their interactions with others, ultimately finding themselves on one side or the other of the issue. These formed attitudes are referred to as **public opinion**.

Like ideas about clothing or hair styles, opinions move through already existing social groups. The idea of legal abortion, for example, formed a public from among American Catholics, who had already-existing religious objections to it. On the other side of the coin, people already dedicated to women's liberation and women's rights favored legalized abortion as consistent with other attitudes they had already formed. There are comparable occurrences in regard to almost every major issue.

Just as members of social groups attempt to influence others to adhere to their fads and fashions, similar techniques are used in the formation of publics. The most notable technique is **propaganda**—the conscious attempt to manipulate public opinion through control over the nature and flow of information. Societal authorities are in an excellent position to use propaganda to sway public opinion toward support of their interests. Perhaps the most famous example in recent history is the systematic efforts by Hitler's propaganda minister, Joseph Goebbels, to maintain loyalty to the Third Reich. Such extreme examples, however, should not prevent us from being aware of the use of propaganda in everyday life in all societies. The United States today, for example, is a vast sea of propaganda representing almost every conceivable viewpoint on every imaginable issue. Unlike Nazi Germany, however, more than one side is presented in most cases, which gives publics the right to choose which propaganda they wish to believe.

The measurement of public opinion is of interest to all members of society, not just sociologists. In the United States the Gallup Poll and the Roper Poll are just two examples of the many full-time organizations devoted to collecting public opinion on a variety of issues. These organizations use standard sampling techniques: A small portion of a population is questioned with fairly reliable assumptions that the range of opinions within the sample will be the same as opinions within the wider population. The programs we watch on television are determined in this manner as the selections made on a relatively few television sets are assumed to represent the viewing preferences of the whole society. Within certain bounds of sampling error such sampling techniques are amazingly efficient.

The best-known use of public opinion polls in the United States is probably in the realm of politics. Every election produces endless polls on public preferences regarding candidates and ballot issues. Political polling raises an interesting question with regard to public opinion: When we find out that a majority of the people feel a certain way about something, are we more likely to join in, thus adding to the majority? Polls give us remarkably accurate information, but they may also have an effect on the very information they hope to collect. This question becomes increasingly important when we notice newscasters confidently predicting results from voter polls before all the votes are cast.

Responses to Disaster

Within the study of collective responses *disaster* normally includes the human experience of such occurrences as earthquakes, hurricanes, floods, tornadoes, fires, and volcanic eruptions. With the exception of some fires and a very few floods, all these examples are natural and tend to strike quite rapidly. Some sociologists might also include some of the slower moving (and usually human-made) threats under this heading, such as overpopulation or famine. One reason they are not usually included is that their long-term impact gives people time to organize their behavior in response. Natural disasters, on the other hand, often strike an unprepared group of people who must be collectively creative at short notice. In such responses to disaster we find some of the classic examples of collective behavior.

Nevertheless, most disasters allow for some warning. Fires, earthquakes, and volcanic eruptions are currently exceptions, but scientific research improves constantly, bringing even those disasters somewhat under human control. At the other extreme hurricanes can be tracked over great distances, giving people considerable time to prepare. Somewhere between these extremes are tornadoes—we can be warned of tornado-producing conditions though not of tornadoes themselves. The ambiguity in disaster warning produces collective behavior among the individuals involved as they attempt to verify the warnings. Rumors (which will be examined later) often accompany disaster warnings as individuals search for information and enthusiastically pass it on when they find it, accurate or not. Disaster warnings are most effective when they come from societal authorities who have had a good record in the past without too many false alarms.

People's experience with a particular kind of disaster plays a major role in their response to it. Hurricanes, for example, typically hit the southern Gulf states, and people who live in those areas gain experience from past hurricanes that they can use in coping with future ones. The more experience a group of people has with a particular disaster in their immediate environment, the less their response will be an example of collective behavior. In fact, their disaster response may become routine, with particular members of the community taking on specific roles and following certain norms whenever the disaster hits. Consider, however, how people in Minnesota might respond to a hurricane, or how people in Florida might cope with a severe blizzard.

Responses to disaster most clearly take on the character of collective behavior when the people involved are unprepared for and inexperienced with the situation they face. Under these circumstances it is common for people who normally play insignificant roles to take on positions of authority. In a 1977 fire at the Beverly Hills Supper Club in northern Kentucky a busboy was instrumental in evacuating many people who otherwise would have died in the fire. This kind of role reversal is common in disaster response as those who had been in authority find their normal activities interrupted and useless in the new situation. It is also common to find ongoing social groups turning *as groups* to disaster recovery activities. A group of construction workers, for example, might work as a rescue unit during tornado recovery, leaving their old roles behind.

Disasters also have an effect on social groups after the initial impact. Generally, a disaster will create unity among those affected as it gives them a dramatic feeling of having shared an important common experience. The more they encounter outsiders who didn't share their experience, the more they may tend to have these feelings, which can last well into the future. The winter of 1977, a very difficult one for many people, was particularly so in Buffalo, New York. After the snow cleared, T-shirts appeared that identified the wearer as having been through the winter of 1977 in Buffalo, and "survivors" celebrated their common experience at annual anniversary parties. Groups who fought and survived the Yellowstone Park fires of 1988 may come to exhibit similar nostalgia about the time when they all worked together. Such occurrences are not unlike the veterans' organizations that form around common survival of the war experience.

The unity caused by disaster can turn to disunity as survivors may attempt to assign blame for failures in the disaster recovery. Police departments and fire departments may be held accountable if residents feel they didn't respond properly in their assigned duties. The fire at the Beverly Hills Supper Club led to years of legal disputes over the causes of the fire and legal responsibilities of those involved. The destruction of coal mining communities in West Virginia by the flood of the Buffalo Creek falls even more clearly into this heading. The Buffalo Creek had been held back by an earth dam that had previously been noted as unsafe; when the dam gave way, it seemed fairly clear that efforts by the coal company to save a few dollars on dam construction cost many their lives and property. Not surprisingly, the coal company found itself facing lawsuits (Erikson, 1976).

Panic and Mass Hysteria

Panic is a nonrational response to a threatening situation; specifically, it occurs when individuals perceive a danger, feel that escape is possible, and believe that the passing of time will make that escape less possible. The classic example of panic is probably the fire in the crowded theater,

Panic, which is an emotional response to a threatening situation, may not always be irrational. The crowd shown here is reacting with panic—trying to get out of town—after poisonous fumes from a chemical plant began filling the air. The town is Bhopal, in India, 1984. The poison killed 2,000 people.

where the audience flees in a group toward the exits and clogs them, with the result that no one gets out. This hypothetical example is not so hypothetical; it comes from the Iroquois Theater fire of December 1903. A curtain caught fire, someone shouted "Fire!" and everyone ran toward the exits. There were too many people, and many of the doors would not open. Approximately 600 people died in the crush; the fire itself was quickly put out and harmed no one.

Panic is believed to be a common response to disaster. There is a popular picture of people wildly fleeing the oncoming flood, hurricane, or tornado. Actually, a much more common response to disaster (although far less colorful) is that people diligently go to work to limit the damage to people and property. The violence of many disasters often makes this response active and emotionally charged, but it should not be confused with panic. Agitated behavior can be rational, as there are times when it is rational to move quickly.

Panic can have aftereffects similar to disasters. A number of people were killed in Cincinnati's Riverfront Coliseum in 1980 when a crowd waiting outside to attend a rock concert pushed through the doors, crushing people in the process. This case of panic was caused by the desire to be first to get the best seats. The deaths were followed by a community memorial parade and discussions as to the cause of the deaths and a new city ordinance prohibiting open seating at rock concerts (a law that other cities have not adopted).

Mass hysteria refers to the spread of some nonrational belief or behavior throughout a group of people. It is similar to panic in many ways. Seeing your neighbor rush to an exit in a crowded theater can convince you to join in for fear of being left behind in a fire; in that case, the form of escape spreads throughout the crowd as more and more people follow the modeled behavior. Mass hysteria also takes in other kinds of phenomena, however. In one incident investigated by Kerckhoff et al. (1965), sixty-two factory workers came to believe they were being bitten by bugs. The bugs didn't exist, but the workers' physical symptoms of rashes and nausea were very real. A similar study of mass hysteria in the workplace is described in Box 13.1.

Mass hysteria can take over in communities as well as in the smaller confines of the workplace. Medalia and Larsen (1958) studied a situation in Seattle in which people became convinced that some foreign substance was pitting the windshields of their cars. Conjecture was that meteors or perhaps radioactive fallout were responsible. The story appeared in newspapers and on the radio. People began covering their cars, and the mayor of Seattle ultimately appealed to President Eisenhower for help. As it turned out, Seattle had an average number of cars with pitted windshields. A similar case of community-wide hysteria occurred in Mattoon, Illinois, in September 1944 (Johnson, 1945). A woman reported that someone had opened her bedroom window and sprayed her with a gas that made her feel ill and partially paralyzed her legs. The story of the "phantom anesthetist" appeared in the newspapers. On the next day the police were notified of another attack, and two days later of two more. Over a space of about a week, the police received twenty-three reports of attacks by the phantom anesthetist. Scientists reported that no known gas could have produced the symptoms that people reported. The only other conclusion is that the residents of Mattoon were the victims of a mass hysteria in which their collective beliefs made them sick.

Probably the most famous case in this group of phenomena has been called both panic and mass hysteria, highlighting the similarity bttween these two kinds of behavior. On October 30, 1938, Orson Welles produced a radio program dramatizing H. G. Wells's novel *The War of the Worlds.* The novel described an invasion of earth by alien creatures. Welles gave the program a sense of reality (as a Halloween joke) by presenting the story in the form of news bulletins and changing the locale from England to New Jersey. Many people became highly agitated upon hearing the program, believing that a real invasion was occurring, and some of them even attempted to flee the areas described in the program as the site of the invasion (Cantril, 1966).

The causes of panic and mass hysteria in various cases have been linked to overwork, economic insecurity, boredom, and lack of intelligence. Their spread is also associated with group phenomena, however. Hysteria in the workplace follows preexisting friendship groups; people get sick by following models provided by their friends. In the case of panic the actions of the person next to you can influence your behavior. As with most forms of collective behavior, the *collective* part is a major factor. This brings us to probably the ultimate object of study within the field of collective behavior: the crowd.

Crowds: Mobs, Riots, Audiences, Gatherings, and Other Collections

The **crowd situation** is one in which a large number of people are in face-to-face contact with each other in a particular physical setting. As we've seen, collective behavior can occur even

BOX 13.1

TAKE THIS JOB AND SHOVE IT: JOB DISSATISFACTION AND MASS HYSTERIA

Mass hysteria can occur wherever people congregate and face some kind of stress. The world of work commonly supplies both. On-the-job hysteria provides a natural setting for the sociologist of collective behavior, as some jobs are more stressful than others and people respond differently to the work they are given to do. Sidney Stahl and Marty Lebedun (1974) set out to study the relationship between on-the-job stress and mass hysteria.

On one day in March 1972, thirty-five women who worked at a university data-processing center became ill, suffering from fainting, nausea, and dizziness; ten of them required medical treatment. The cause of this mass illness was believed to be a gas (of unknown origin) in the atmosphere of the work setting. The building was evacuated and the air inside tested. In addition, the blood and urine of the affected workers were tested. Nothing was found in any of the tests, and the building was opened again. The next day more women became ill, and the building was once again closed. Again, no physical reason for the illness was found. Enter the sociologists.

Comparing the symptoms of illness the workers exhibited with how much they liked their work, Stahl and Lebedun found an interesting correlation: The more dissatisfied a woman was with her job, the more severe her symptoms. Apparently a job can make you sick in more ways than is commonly thought. For these women the spreading illness was apparently an appealing alternative to work they would rather not do. Stahl and Lebedun do not suggest that the illness was a charade by the women but rather that mass hysteria spreads more quickly in ground made fertile by social stress.

A similar study by Kerckhoff and his colleagues (1965) found that hysteria on the job spread primarily among friends; if your friend got sick, you would be much more likely to follow suit. Stahl and Lebedun checked these findings with the women in the data-processing center and found similar results. The women with the most severe symptoms tended to be friendly with other women with severe symptoms; women less affected by the gas were friendly with other women less affected. These women did not sit together on the job, so location in the building was not a factor.

What can we learn from such studies of mass hysteria? First, collective behavior may be new and different, but it often follows old paths. In both of these studies the hysteria spread through the chains of friendship that existed prior to the outbreak. Second, the study by Stahl and Lebedun suggests that certain social circumstances "encourage" collective behavior to occur. In particular, the change brought about by collective behavior becomes more appealing when we wish to avoid stress in our everyday lives.

when people are not together—as in the case of publics, fads, or fashions. The crowd situation, however, is considered the ultimate form of collective behavior because of the immediacy with which communication occurs and because of the social pressure generated by the physical presence of others.

Types of Crowds Not all crowds are examples of collective behavior. Collective behavior is determined by the degree to which behavior follows norms. Some crowds, such as audiences, behave pretty much the same way from one situation to the next. Performers, who are most acutely aware of this, use their knowledge of audience norms to manipulate the experience people have in the audience. A political speaker wishing to generate enthusiasm will alter the content of a speech as well as the style of delivery to the audience at hand; out-of-work factory workers will be addressed differently than business leaders. Rock musicians want to produce certain audience experiences so that individuals will have a good time and subsequently buy their records. Musical material will be presented in such an order that excitement builds; if the performer has a very popular number everyone is waiting for, it may be saved for the supposedly spontaneous encore, giving the audience the illusion that they provoked their favorite number themselves through the enthusiasm of their ovation. Everyone leaves happy. Members of the audience have an enthusiastic, spontaneous experience that is carefully planned for them. Yelling and shouting does not necessarily make for collective behavior.

A similar example of planned spontaneity occurs in religious gatherings. Some fundamentalist religious services rely upon growing excitement and enthusiasm within the crowd. The leader may typically be a trained evangelist who travels from town to town for such services. Wimberly and his colleagues (1975) studied one gathering from the Billy Graham Crusade and discovered that much of the spontaneity is carefully planned. In particular, the experience of "coming forward" to be saved is encouraged by behavioral models provided by "counselors." The authors observed, however, that these models may not even have been necessary, as many people in the audience seemed to have made advance plans for being saved at a particular point in the ritual set aside for that event. In short, it is necessary to look closely at crowds to determine the degree to which people are breaking new ground or following old norms. (The reading by John Denton following this chapter describes the religious revival in more detail.)

Crowds can be active or expressive. **Acting crowds** are those with an apparent goal outside the crowd itself. Riots or lynch mobs would fall under this heading. **Expressive crowds** are those formed solely for the self-expression of the members. Some religious gatherings are expressive in that their members come together solely for the communal expression of religious faith.

When crowds are examples of collective behavior, the norms that are broken may be important or trivial from the point of view of societal authorities. Sports fans throwing trash onto the playing field during a game would be violating a relatively trivial norm, whereas rioters engaged in arson, personal violence, and looting would receive a much more violent response. But both are examples of collective behavior.

Finally, we should note a learning factor in crowd behavior. A certain crowd behavior may be novel and inventive today but governed by norms tomorrow. Sociologists who study collective behavior are particularly interested in the formation of novel behavior in the group setting and the way that behavior spreads. After it happens once, it can be planned the next time or at least more easily picked up on by crowd participants. At some time in the distant past, for example, a college football crowd decided to tear down the goal posts after a game; that was collective behavior. But how about the many instances of the same crowd behavior that have occurred since the first? Are they collective behavior, or do they fall closer to the heading of norm-governed behavior? At what point is repeated behavior norm-governed and no longer inventive? The type of crowd under study must be examined carefully in this light.

Theories of Crowd Behavior The first serious theorist of crowd behavior has influenced sociological theory ever since. Gustave LeBon presented his theory in his 1897 work *The Mind of Crowds.* To LeBon crowds were far more than the sum of their members; they had an existence in their own right. He pictured crowd members as having lost all sense of rational thought and being highly suggestible to whatever ideas dominated the crowd. LeBon spoke of the law of mental unity in crowds, in which individuals were "leveled" into the common denominator of a "group mind." This state was brought about by an effective leader who, according to LeBon, "hypnotized" the crowd members through rhetoric, flattery, and the repetition of important symbols. In this situation crowd members came to see themselves as anonymous parts of the whole, ignored the norms and values that had previously governed their lives, and developed an irrational sense of their own invincibility ("No one can stop us now," etc.). In short, LeBon pictured crowd members as a herd of sheep likely to do anything their leader directed.

LeBon's theory is the basis for most popular conceptions of crowd behavior, particularly those fostered by Hollywood. In movies, people in crowds are swayed by persuasive speakers, begin making noises like a bunch of animals, and march off to lynch some poor devil in the local jail. If the victim turns out to be innocent (which is usually the case), the mob participants individually search their consciences at the end of the movie, wondering how they could have done such a thing. The famous western novel (and subsequent film) *The Ox-Bow Incident* by Walter Van Tilburg Clark is a classic example of this perspective. The crowd is pictured as a totally uncontrolled and irrational creature capable of dangerous acts, and individuals within it are given no credit for thinking for themselves.

Modern theories of crowd behavior have been heavily influenced by LeBon, but many of them have moved away from this extreme position to some degree. American sociologist Herbert Blumer (1969) followed fairly close to LeBon with his idea of *circular reaction.* Ignoring LeBon's emphasis on the hypnotic leader, Blumer maintained that irrational crowd behavior is generated among the crowd members themselves as they react to each other in a circular manner. In panic, for example, my running for an exit would encourage you to do the same. When I see you begin to run, I become all the more convinced that my behavior was correct in the first place and begin to run faster, and so on. In this way, says Blumer, crowd behavior operates by **contagion**; as with a virus, its spread is apparently beyond the control of the individual members.

Neil Smelser is another American sociologist of crowd behavior and one of the most famous; his book *Theory of Collective Behavior* (1962) has generated considerable research in crowd behavior (see Box 13.2). Smelser maintains that a series of events must occur for crowd collective behavior to occur:

1. There must first be *structural conduciveness.* An urban race riot, for example, could not occur without the urban concentrations of two or more races; student draft protests could not occur without colleges that concentrate people of draft age.
2. There must be *structural strain,* described by Smelser as tensions or contradictions that are built into society. For example, Americans value equality, yet inequalities exist between the sexes and among different ethnic and racial groups.

BOX 13.2

A Study of a Riot: The Kent State Incident

The Vietnam War was the cause of considerable political activity on college campuses during the 1960s. President Nixon's announcement in the spring of 1970 that the United States had invaded Cambodia caused violent activity on campuses throughout the country, but the deaths that occurred on the campus of Kent State University are the most remembered today.

What happened at Kent State? That particular question raises many of the general problems faced by sociologists who study collective behavior. For many reasons riots are very difficult to study; some of the reasons for these difficulties will be apparent as we try to piece together what happened at Kent State, following the research of sociologist Jerry M. Lewis (1972).

After Nixon's announcement, political activities began to build at Kent State. On Friday, May 1, two peaceful rallies were held. That night, in downtown Kent, Ohio, people began gathering in the streets, shouting antiwar chants, and throwing bottles. They were joined by people from the downtown bars. This larger crowd was in turn joined by the local police in riot gear, who attempted to disperse the crowd. The crowd grew and became more violent. During this time the police closed the bars, which resulted in putting still more people into the street and forming a larger crowd.

On Saturday morning rumors began to fly. One persistent rumor was that members of a radical and sometimes violent left-wing organization, the Weathermen, were in town; the rumor was never substantiated. Saturday evening a crowd gathered on the University Commons, a central meeting point on the Kent State campus. The crowd grew to over 1,000 and began to take notice of the nearby ROTC building, an old barracks structure. Some rocks were thrown at the building, and it was finally set on fire. Firemen arrived and had their hoses cut. The riot police arrived with tear gas and dispersed the crowd. And while all of this was going on, the national guard was quietly moving onto the campus.

On Sunday morning Governor James Rhodes of Ohio arrived in Kent and announced, "I think we are up against the strongest, well-trained militant group that has ever assembled in America," repeating the rumor that moved throughout Kent the day before (Lewis, 1972:90). Sunday evening there was a brief sit-in, which was dispersed by the national guard.

Classes resumed on Monday morning, but people began to gather on the Commons around noon. The guard believed that rallies had been prohibited on campus, though there is some evidence that not all the students knew this (Taylor et al., 1971), and many students who did know of the prohibition felt the guard had no right to make or enforce rules on campus. The rally grew. In response to this apparent threat to their authority, the national guardsmen moved to disperse the crowd. The crowd broke up into several groups and took to throwing rocks and tear-gas cannisters, the latter in an attempt to return the cannisters to their source (the guardsmen). At one point the guard marched to the top of a hill and began firing on the crowd, leaving four dead and nine wounded. Five hours later, the campus was closed and most students had gone home. Shortly thereafter, most campuses around the country closed as well to prevent similar occurrences.

Once again, what happened at Kent State? All those involved have vested interests in presenting an account that reflects well on them. The guardsmen were young and untrained. Were they ordered to fire, or was firing on the crowd a mini-act of collective behavior within the overall scene?

(continues)

BOX 13.2 (continued)

The guardsmen aren't saying since no one wants the responsibility. Did the students really know about the rule prohibiting rallies on campus, or is ignorance of the rule a convenient excuse after the fact? The students believed (or later said they believed) the guardsmen would never shoot, but they did. The guardsmen believed the student rally was carefully orchestrated by a militant group, but it wasn't. The flow of information was not smooth.

Were the students a herd of sheep led by a hypnotic leader, or were they a mixed bag with a variety of motives for being there? According to Lewis, there were different kinds of crowd members—the active core, the cheerleaders, and the spectators; members of all three groups became victims of rifle fire. Furthermore, there was no single effective leader of the crowd; the events that occurred emerged from the collective situation and not through careful planning.

Lewis was particularly interested in Neil Smelser's (1962) theory of collective behavior and wanted to see whether it applied to Kent State. Much of it did, he discovered, with the major exception of Smelser's emphasis on a generalized belief. According to Smelser, the crowd situation thrives on ambiguity and anxiety; the generalized belief is a belief generated within the crowd that eliminates this ambiguity and anxiety by assigning blame to whichever societal authority happens to be handy. At Kent State the national guard was forced into the role of facing student hostility toward the government. Anger toward the Nixon administration had turned to anger toward the presence of the guard on campus. On the other hand, says Lewis, the predicted anxiety was missing. Students at Kent were not the subjects of some nameless confusion and worry; they were very angry and knew exactly what angered them. They were, in short, not a herd of sheep.

3. A *generalized belief* must develop. In many ways the central element of Smelser's theory, the generalized belief is a definition of the situation that develops among crowd members as to what they dislike and what should be done about it. According to Smelser, the generalized belief short-circuits reality, often producing an irrational picture and an unjustified victim for crowd violence.
4. A *precipitating event* must occur. In an urban race riot, for example, the arrest of a black person might set things off.
5. *Mobilization* comes next. The crowd must be able to assemble, spread the generalized belief, and act.
6. The *response by societal authorities* (such as police) may serve to end the crowd violence or to promote it, depending on how the authorities act. For example, police efforts to disperse crowds are an attempt to interrupt the assembly process; bluffing force and not carrying through encourage rioters.

According to Smelser, a break in the action at any point in this chain will end the episode of collective behavior. This can even be accomplished at the first stage of structural conduciveness. College campuses, for example, commonly have centralized meeting places (usually around the library or a student union building) where students gather and pass through between classes. Such a meeting place, says Smelser, invites collective behavior. If universities were built without

Box 13.2 tells about the events at Kent State University in 1970: an antiwar rally on campus ended in shocking violence as the National Guard, called out earlier by the governor, fired on unarmed students, killing four undergraduates. The soldiers feared a unified and dangerous mob, when actually the students challenging them were a diverse collection, not organized at all.

such areas (and some are), university authorities could save themselves a lot of trouble. At the other extreme, we've already noted that police interference in the assembly process can terminate the collective behavior episode. As simple a matter as cutting off the speaker's microphone or turning off lights at night during a political rally, for example, would prevent communication within the crowd and could break up the crowd behavior.

Smelser makes two important departures from LeBon and Blumer. First, his emphasis on structural strain suggests that crowd members may actually have some reason for their behavior, particularly in the case of violent outbursts such as riots. Interestingly, neither LeBon nor Blumer assumes that rioters have any justification whatsoever for their behavior. Second, through his idea of the generalized belief, Smelser focuses on the ideas that motivate crowd members. This concept takes away somewhat from his emphasis on strain since he assumes that the belief will probably have little to do with the actual source of the strain. He also assumes that all crowd members will adhere to this belief equally rather than thinking for themselves. Nevertheless, he does raise the issue of how crowd members *think*, which is at least a step away from LeBon's herd of sheep.

A differing view of the crowd is provided by Turner and Killian's *emergent norm* perspective (Turner and Killian, 1972). According to this theory, norm-governed behavior develops (or emerges) within the crowd situation as the crowd members interact; individuals look to each other for models of action and ultimately come to agreement and act in concert. They do *not,* however, necessarily do so with the same motives or for the same reasons. Crowd members may vary considerably in their commitment to the crowd and its emerging actions. Some may be little more than spectators, while others may have hopes of manipulating the crowd and exploiting it for their own purposes. A crowd viewed through the emergent norm perspective may appear unified in action, but not because it is a herd of sheep.

At the far extreme from LeBon we find the theories of Richard Berk (1974a, 1974b). Berk believes that crowd members are as rational as anyone else and enter the crowd situation with the same question we would have in entering a game: How can I win? Say you are in a crowd and interested in acquiring a little free merchandise from the nearby department store through looting. You know that if thousands of people begin looting, the chances of your getting caught will go down. If no one else joins in, however, you may very likely get caught. Therefore, you will be interested in estimating the number of other crowd members who might go along with such behavior, and they will be watching you with the same interests. According to Berk, all the crowd members are asking themselves these same questions, deciding what they want to achieve and trying to estimate the chances for their personal success or failure in reaching this end. The contagion described by LeBon and Blumer is not the result of irrational thinking, says Berk, but rather the product of a great many individual thinking processes coming to the same conclusion at the same time.

Berk differs from all other theorists in two major ways. First, he assumes that crowd members have concerns vital to them and that they use the crowd situation to satisfy those concerns. Reasons for crowd behavior will be found not in hypnotic leaders or animal instincts but in perceived injustices and inequalities in society. Second, Berk says that crowd members are rational in their thinking processes and they may not all think the same way (as opposed to Smelser's generalized belief). For instance, some may loot for the goods, while others may join in for the excitement. All this individual behavior becomes sociologically important in the ways individuals estimate support for various courses of action. My engaging in a given behavior may encourage you to join in, and, together, we may encourage a third party. Each new person joins in more readily, since a large number of people engaging in the same behavior lowers the potential costs to each new person. Crowds are contagious, says Berk, but not for the reasons normally assumed.

Another perspective on crowds is offered by the social behavioral/interactionist perspective of Clark McPhail and his students (see McPhail, 1991). The social behavioral/interactionist perspective also brings us some distance from LeBon in that it suggests that there is no real difference between crowd behavior and any other kind of human behavior. People enter into crowds (according to this perspective) as they enter into any social situation, depending upon their interests, their free time, their personal connections with other people involved, and their knowledge that the situation exists for them to join. Once in the crowd, people respond to forms of communication (either from other crowd members or from outsiders, such as police) about upcoming behaviors and subsequent movements (termed collective locomotion). McPhail's perspective is extremely sensitive to physical factors that affect these processes. For example, the presence of a wide open area (such as a square or campus central area) facilitates a crowd's assembling by providing open space and not interfering with communication processes necessary for crowd instructions. Narrow, closed-in areas make these processes difficult. If smoke is added to such closed-in areas, as in a burning building, communication is further hindered, collective locomotion (here, evacuation of the building) is difficult, and deaths occur. From McPhail's point of view, crowds are full of normal people engaging in normal interaction in sometimes unusual and unclear settings.

Theories of Crowd Formation Questions about why crowds form are related to questions about how they act. If you assume crowds behave as they do because of some herd instinct, your theory of crowd formation will look into why people become susceptible to joining the herd. If you assume that crowd members have valid complaints about their social situation, your theory of crowd formation will focus on how people in social groups come to develop those complaints. Though it may seem that theories of crowd formation should logically come before theories of crowd behavior, in practice most sociologists have studied the matter the other way around.

At the most basic level *crowds draw crowds.* You can test this proposition easily with a few friends. First, go to a busy pedestrian thoroughfare, stop, and fix your eyes on anything up high (a building if there is one). Have a confederate note how many people look where you are looking and how many people stop to look where you are looking. You probably won't attract too many. Then try the same experiment with six or eight friends all looking at the same thing. According to most sociological research, a much higher percentage of passersby should become interested in your behavior, perhaps stopping to ask a few questions. In other words, once a crowd gets started, there appears to be a momentum factor that helps keep it going. But what gets people there in the first place or keeps them there after they've stopped out of curiosity?

The *outside agitator* explanation ties in with the herd instinct theories. According to this perspective, outsiders trained in crowd-formation techniques may systematically get a local population worked up with untrue rumors and effective speaking techniques. This theory of crowd formation is adequate only if you believe that a few trained organizers can effectively control (or hypnotize) a group of basically unwilling crowd participants. Today this theory most commonly comes from societal authorities who have just had a riot on their hands and wish to make it clear that local problems were *not* the cause (for example, see Box 13.2 on explanations surrounding the Kent State killings).

The *riff-raff theory* of crowd formation blames the crowd members rather than the leaders. This theory assumes that crowd members are typically the malcontents and ne'er-do-wells of the community who have never accomplished anything and who generally look for trouble. This particular theory has been studied a little more than some of the others and has been found wanting in most cases. In the United States urban riots of the late 1960s, for example, it was found that rioters were more likely than nonrioters to be educated, long-term residents of the city and have high occupational aspirations; they tended to be roughly the same as nonrioters in income and community activities (see Perry and Pugh, 1978). In the student rebellions of the 1960s the students who took part tended to have higher grade-point averages and parents of higher occupational prestige than those who did not take part (Middleton and Putney, 1963). According to most research, those who are really down and out don't actively complain about it too much.

The *mass society theory* was first applied to crowd formation by LeBon. According to this theory, modern society tends to cut people adrift from their traditional moorings in small, stable social groups characteristic of smaller, less urban environments. As society has changed from a collection of many small groups to a collection of individuals, there have been two important results: First, individuals are no longer insulated from persuasive leaders by the confines of their small groups. Second, the social control function of the small group is gone, which makes individuals more likely to get carried away in the crowd situation, thinking little of the consequences of their actions. In short, modern society leaves individuals open to manipulation from outsiders. Mass society theory assumes that manipulation is the key to crowd behavior; not surprisingly, it fits in well with the theories of LeBon and Blumer.

Absolute deprivation theory is the first of the crowd-formation theories to focus on reasons for participants to join the crowd. This very simple theory states that people deprived of social rewards (jobs, money, respect, etc.) will be the most likely to join acting crowds. It also predicts the greater the deprivation, the more likely the participation. The theory makes sense—but it doesn't work well. As we've seen, people who are really down and out rarely take any action at all. In many societies researchers have noted a strange conservatism among those at the bottom when they are faced with the possibility of change. It would seem that, from their perspective, any change would have to be for the better, but they don't appear to see it that way.

Relative deprivation theory turns away from actual deprivation and focuses on perceived deprivation (Morrison, 1971). In other words, it's not so much a matter of how deprived you are but how deprived you think you are—which will probably be determined by which people you compare yourself to. Most Americans, for example, compare themselves not to the Rockefeller family (against whom we would all feel terribly deprived) but to the people down the block. If the neighbors get a new car and you can't afford one, you will feel deprived. The real question for relative deprivation theory is the reasons people select particular others for purposes of comparison. In the United States today the mass media have widened the scope for most of us in the kinds of comparisons we make. For example, we become aware of the hourly wages a certain union has achieved for its members. We also become aware of how much others in our own occupation make in other locations. If we're in a minority group, we become aware of the political gains made by other minorities elsewhere. The *relative* of relative deprivation is a rapidly changing social phenomenon.

The *J-curve theory* of rising expectations is one of the more sophisticated of the modern deprivation theories (Davies, 1969). According to the J-curve theory, what we want (or expect) is generally one step ahead of what we get. If our situation has been improving over time, our expectations will begin to rise at the same speed. Normally, this creates a gap we can tolerate. Collective behavior occurs when something happens to the satisfaction of our needs. For example, if our society experiences a severe depression, our economic situation will go down (thus creating the *J* of the J-curve), yet our expectations will continue to rise at the same rate they had been; most of us have expectations rising well into the future based on the current rate of improvement in our experience. If we have been enjoying increasing degrees of political freedom and are then faced with less, once again the gap will occur. Whatever the case, the source of our perceived deprivation has little to do with our objective situation; it is the product of our rising expectations. This theory has been used to explain the urban riots of the late

1960s, in which black inner-city residents took to the streets in many American cities just a few years after the passage of the 1964 Civil Rights Act. The new law caused expectations to rise but did little to elevate the satisfaction of needs in the black community.

These theories reflect some of the variety and some of the contradictions in the sociological explanations of crowd formation. (Many of them can also be applied to the formation of social movements, which sometimes emerge from crowd situations.) Nevertheless, there are still more unanswered than answered questions about crowd formation. For example, the economic situation of most black Americans has been little better in the 1970s and 1980s than in the 1960s, yet there has been very little crowd violence in the last two decades. The J-curve would have predicted it with the rising unemployment and high inflation that characterized this period. Relative deprivation theory would also have predicted crowd violence due to the increased knowledge we all have of each other and the tendency we have to take a more global perspective on our problems. No doubt sociologists will add new theories to our list, and those additions will be very welcome.

The Role of Rumor

We come finally to an aspect of collective behavior that colors all others—rumor. A **rumor** is a piece of information that spreads among members of a group. It is neither accurate nor inaccurate by necessity; it can be either, and is often partly both. Sociologists of collective behavior are interested in how rumors spread, why they spread, and how they affect other instances of collective behavior.

Rumors typically are unconfirmed pieces of information. *Unconfirmed* means that societal authorities have either not taken a stand on the information or are unable to convince people when they do. Rumors travel most readily in social situations that are ambiguous to the participants (Buckner, 1965). People who are unsure as to "what's going on" will be the most likely to turn to rumor for answers. Generally, people believe what they see on television or read in the papers, and through these media societal authorities can pass on information that may end a rumor by making the situation less ambiguous. It should be kept in mind, however, that people do not always believe such information. Societal authorities may also present inaccurate information intentionally if it serves their purposes; thus, an accurate rumor may be replaced by inaccurate "official information."

Just as important as situation ambiguity is the importance of the information (Buckner, 1965). People are unlikely to spend their time receiving or passing on information they don't care about. Generally speaking, the greater the importance of a particular piece of information, the more quickly the rumor will spread.

The third factor influencing the spread of rumor is called the *critical ability* of the individuals among whom the rumor is spreading—the ability of an individual (or a group of individuals) to determine the truth or falsity of a rumor from past experience (Buckner, 1965). Important information in a highly ambiguous social situation may be ignored if the participants have good reasons for not believing the rumor they receive. Different groups of people will have different critical abilities about different kinds of information. Nuclear scientists, for example, would probably respond to rumors of a meltdown at the local nuclear power plant differently than you or I would. Those same scientists, however, might have an uncritical ability in relation to rumors about local politics.

Rumors can be accurate, but they are more prone to inaccuracies. According to Gordon Allport and Leo Postman (1947), there are three different processes that help good information "go bad"—leveling, sharpening, and assimilation. *Leveling* eliminates detail from the rumor as it passes from person to person. *Sharpening,* working in concert with leveling, is the process by which elements of the rumor become emphasized in the telling. Finally, *assimilation* refers to the changes rumors go through to fit the prejudices of the teller. People commonly want to alter rumors somewhat to make them more interesting or to illustrate an important concern they have.

The accuracy of rumor is greatly affected by the social network within which it moves. A rumor can move from person to person with each person hearing it only once. In this instance the rumor can change meaning greatly as each person has a chance to alter it. On the other hand, a rumor can move within a social group in which all members interact with each other. The rumor bounces off all group members as A tells it to B, B tells it to C, and C tells it back to A. In such a situation group members will notice changes in the rumor's content.

Rumors can be a form of harmless recreation or can have devastating results for the individuals or groups involved. An example of the former would be the growing number of urban legends that have grown and spread throughout the United States. *Urban legends* are stories that are generally presented as having happened to a friend or a friend of a friend. The stories are typically harmless but have a punch line that helps them spread. One such famous rumor concerns a pet lover who comes across (or sometimes runs over) a cat, which soon expires. The pet lover places the dead cat in a brown paper sack (not wanting to leave it on the road) and the sack is subsequently stolen. The thief is located when she (or he) faints after looking in the sack some blocks away (Brunvard, 1981).

An example of rumors in less playful senses would be rumors about products or corporations. The McDonald's wormburger episode is one of the more famous. The rumor spread that McDonald's hamburgers contained worm meat—the Big Mac had become the Crawling Mac. Business at McDonald's fell rapidly until the rumor faded away. And lest you think the rumor might have been started by a competitor of McDonald's, the rumor actually began about Wendy's hamburgers and, for some reason, switched victims. Of the corporation rumors, the most famous is the rumor connecting Procter & Gamble to satan worship. This old rumor has been spread through church newsletters as well as word of mouth. There is always someone who claims to have seen some top executive from the company on a television talk show (the show varies) claiming that a portion of Procter & Gamble's profits is donated to satan worship every year. Even the corporate logo is interpreted as symbolizing this devotion. While these rumors may seem crazy or silly, they cost American business dearly in lost sales and extra advertising designed to combat the rumors (Koenig, 1985).

The process of rumor transmission is a form of collective behavior itself. In addition, rumors also play roles in disaster recovery, mobs, riots, mass hysteria, panic, and other forms of collective behavior. Disaster warnings typically are accompanied by rumors; the less accurate or dependable the official warnings, the more common the rumors. Mass hysteria and some kinds of panic depend on the spread of rumor for the spread of the collective behavior. The "phantom anesthetist," for example, was allowed to thrive through rumors of his existence. It is probably in mobs and riots, however, that rumors have one of the clearest and most important roles.

Almost all sociologists of collective behavior agree that riots form around some kind of precipitating event, or spark, that sets things off. As with checking a gas tank with a lighted match, the cause of the conflagration is more the gas than the match, but both are necessary. In the case of race riots, precipitating events typically have a heavy symbolic meaning, such as the arrest of a black person by a white police officer. Such precipitating events gain importance through their spread by rumor. For example, a riot that occurred in Harlem, New York, in 1935 began with the police arrest of a black youth for stealing a knife from a department store. The boy's hand was cut during the arrest, and he was taken to the basement of the store to wait for an ambulance. A rumor spread that the boy had been taken to the basement for the police to beat him up. This rumor was supported by the arrival of the ambulance (Perry and Pugh, 1978).

A similar event and rumor occurred at the beginning of the Newark, New Jersey, riot of 1967. A black cab driver was arrested for driving with a revoked license. Upon arriving at the police station, he either refused or was unable to walk and was dragged into the station in full view of a housing project across the street. Residents in the project started the rumor that the cab driver had been beaten by the police. In addition, the cab company was notified of the arrest, and the news spread to cab drivers all over town on their car radios. Complaints were received by local black leaders, but by the time they arrived at the police station to check on the cab driver, a crowd was already beginning to form on the grounds of the housing project. The riot began that night and escalated on following nights. The rumor escalated along with the riot, proclaiming by then that the cab driver had died of his beating (National Advisory Commission on Civil Disorders, 1968). There were long-standing divisions between the police department and the black community of Newark, and police brutality was not unknown. Thus the rumor fit in well with already existing prejudices held by the black community toward the police, was spread for that reason, and helped set off the riot that followed.

While rumors often accompany urban riots, a definite word or two of caution is in order here. First, not all riots contain rumors that have any impact on the riot's outcome. Second, and more important, riots often have very real causes in community tensions that can be overlooked or trivialized by a focus on rumors. By way of example, the Miami riot of 1980 began over the trial of several white policemen. Race relations had never been good between the black community of Miami and the largely white police force. Events came to a head when a black man on a motorcycle, Arthur McDuffie, was caught after attempting to elude police and was beaten to death by a group of policemen when caught. Enough were involved that some testified (under immunity) against the others. Medical evidence supported the testimony; the injuries could not have been caused by a motorcycle accident. Nevertheless, the officers were acquitted. On that day, a riot began in the Liberty City black area of Miami and lasted for several days, leaving a number of both whites and blacks dead (Porter and Dunn, 1984).

Rumor might best be described as the collective behavior of communication. The study of rumor focuses on one aspect of collective behavior—communication—and shows how communication processes affect other aspects of collective behavior. Information spreads in much the same way (and at the same time) as riot behavior, disaster responses, or mass hysteria.

Miami has been the site of many riots in the 1980s and 1990s. This 1981 riot in Overtown was sparked by the shooting of a black youth in a video arcade by a police officer who reported that he thought the teenager was going to attack him with a knife. Similar incidents—police using violence on young blacks who are reported to be innocent of wrongdoing, with no punishment of the police involved—have provoked riots as late as 1990.

SOCIAL MOVEMENTS

Social movements are organized efforts by groups of people to bring about social change, either in the members themselves or in members and society alike. Social movements are considered to be a type of collective behavior since they deviate from societal norms and values, yet their often high degree of social organization makes them look very much like the organized social life they seek to change. Unlike mobs, riots, or disaster responses, in which group behavior emerges on the spur of the moment, social movements develop leaders and followers, goals and tactics, and their own set of norms and values to govern all these roles and activities. Since they are highly coordinated forms of group life, social movements are easier for sociologists to study than other forms of collective behavior; some would even argue that they are not collective behavior at all since they lack spontaneity compared with crowds. Nevertheless, social movements often emerge from other forms of collective behavior and, perhaps more important, are responsible for a major portion of the social change that arises from collective behavior in general. Riots rarely bring about lasting change, but social movements can change the whole fabric of society when they are successful in attaining their goals.

Types of Social Movements

Though all social movements seek to bring about social change, they vary considerably in the kind and degree of change they seek. Those movements that seek change in the outside society (that is, outside the movement) can vary from revolutionary movements to reform movements. **Revolutionary movements** seek massive change in the society. The Communist Party in Czarist Russia, for example, brought about the end of the ruling family and the whole system of politics and economics governed by that family; rule by the aristocratic elite was replaced by rule from the Communist Party, and private ownership of property was largely replaced by state ownership. **Reform movements**, by contrast, seek far less radical change, preferring to work within the existing system. In the United States, for example, the civil rights movement sought equal rights and opportunities for black Americans within the democratic capitalistic system already in force. The goal was not to change the operation of the society but to include blacks within that operation. Reform movements typically want to change the way the pie is sliced rather than create a different pie.

Reform and revolutionary movements are ideal types in that few actual social movements fit perfectly into either category. Rather, they represent a range in terms of the amount of social change they seek. Any but the smallest reforms will have some lasting effect on the structure of society, while even the most vocal revolutionary movements retain some traces of the old order if they are successful. This range is an important one to keep in mind, however, for the way societal authorities perceive the social movement will determine the way they respond to it. Not surprisingly, revolutionary movements often receive violent repression from established authorities since their goal is the overthrow of those authorities; reform movements, on the other hand, can even lean toward respectability if their means and goals agree with established values and don't threaten authorities.

Social movements also vary in the *kind* of social change they seek. Specifically, some social movements seek to transform only their own members and have no desire for any social change outside the boundaries of their movement. This is particularly common with some religious movements that seek to change the spiritual life of individuals but care little about political power or the distribution of economic rewards in society. The Shakers, for example, were a religious movement that reached a peak in the last century in the United States. Their most notable attribute from the outsider's perspective was their ban on sexual intercourse; they formed Shaker communities in which men and women lived together yet sexually separate. Not surprisingly, they had a problem keeping up their membership after a time. But more interesting are the many peaceful economic relations they had with members of the outside society. The Shakers didn't approve of sex for themselves but were willing to tolerate it in others.

As we have noted, the 1970s saw the proliferation of religious cults in the United States. Krishna Consciousness, Scientology, the Unification Church, and Synanon all found their way into the news at one time or another, primarily as a result of parental complaints over the resocialization of their children (see Chapter 4). With the exception of the Unification Church (which has been accused of lobbying illegally for the Republic of South Korea), these cults appear to be interested primarily in increasing their membership and keeping their movements economically viable (which is a concern of all social movements). Social movements that seek to change only individuals who join the movement are generally tolerated more than those that seek to change the larger society, all else being equal. In terms of deviating from traditional American values, all of the religious cults are more extreme than Martin Luther King, Jr.'s civil rights activities of the 1950s and 1960s, yet none received the political oppression that King faced. Nevertheless, many new religious cults have provoked widespread opposition in the United States, particularly from parents who feel that their children have been "brainwashed" by charismatic movement leaders. Through a variety of controversial court decisions, parents have been allowed to legally kidnap their own adult children for the purposes of "deprogramming"—a technique designed to alter their values away from the cult and back to mainstream values of American culture (Shupe, 1980).

It should be kept in mind that *all* social movements must transform their individual members from "outsiders" to "movement followers" if they are to get anything accomplished. Movements that seek only to change their members can stop at that, but movements that seek to change elements of society must first acquire the loyalty and dedication of their members before they can turn their attention outward. Extreme revolutionary movements will even employ resocialization techniques since the dedication they require will be so much greater; a movement that seeks to change basic values in society will first have to change the basic values of its members. At the other extreme, a reform movement that seeks additional resources for the eradication of a specific disease conforms to basic American values and will have less difficulty converting members to the "rightness" of its cause. It will, however, have the same problems that all movements have in keeping members interested and working for the movement. Whatever type the social movement, loss of interest among the members is a far greater enemy than the armed might of any nation.

The Structure of Social Movements

Social movements are coordinated social groups, however strange or revolutionary their ideas may be. And like any such group, social movements have a social structure with different roles, activities, norms, and values. Unlike other groups, however, social movements emerge from a collective desire for change among the organizers and develop over time in relation to that desire. Studying the structure of social movements turns our attention to the way in which social coordination develops among groups that seek change.

Some mobs and riots produce leaders on the spot, but all social movements have specially created leadership roles and follower roles. One of the leader's jobs is to maintain group cohesion and efficiency of operation. The way in which this job is approached can vary considerably; there are, in short, different types of leadership roles.

The most colorful type of social movement leader is the charismatic leader. The **charismatic leader** rules by virtue of great personal charm, persuasiveness, and magnetism (which is about as near as sociologists can come to defining *charisma*). Charismatic leaders are typically moving speakers, exciting personalities, and talented at attracting new membership along with maintaining the loyalty of the old. Social movements are rarely lucky enough to find more than one charismatic leader over time, and if they do have one, it will almost always be the first (or founding) leader.

An extremely different kind of social movement leader is the administrative leader who, in social movements or elsewhere, sits at the head of a bureaucracy, overseeing the activities

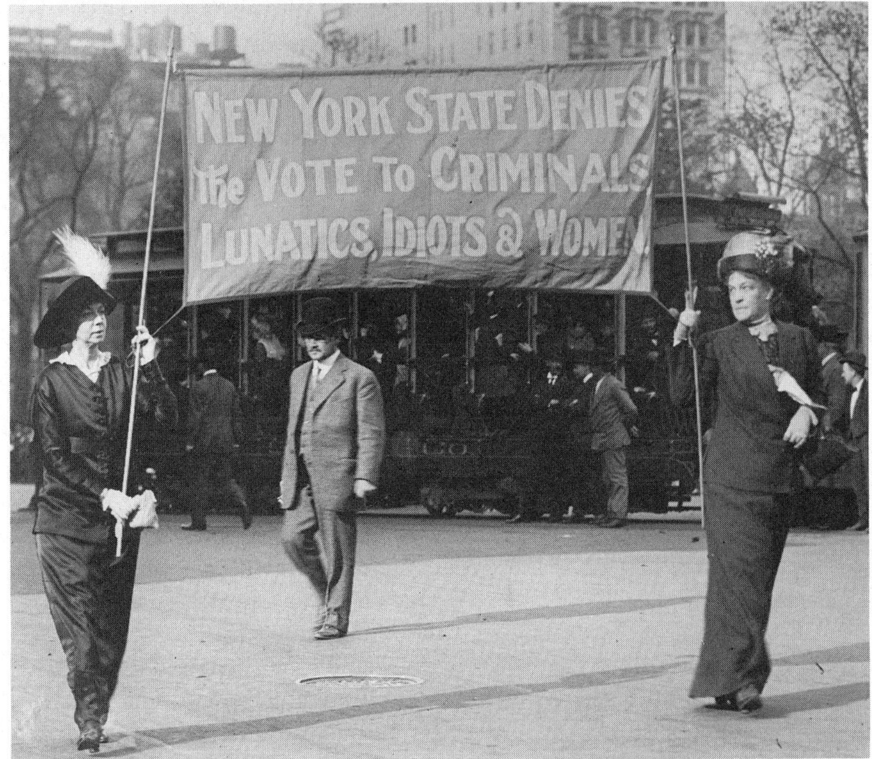
NEW YORK STATE DENIES
the VOTE To CRIMINALS
LUNATICS, IDIOTS & WOMEN

These women were pioneers in an important social movement that only began to gain its strength when women obtained the vote.

below. The **administrative leader** governs by virtue of bureaucratic position and legal authority within the movement's social organization. As we'll see shortly, social movements that survive long enough often become bureaucracies, making an administrative leader necessary; it is in fact a classic case for a charismatic leader to run a loose-knit, dedicated group for a generation and then be replaced by an administrative leader who heads a by then more formal organization. If a social movement has a formal organization, it must have an administrative leader. Remember, however, we are talking about roles and not people. An initial leader with charismatic qualities could learn administrative duties as the movement changed and become both kinds of leader simultaneously. A social movement could also have two different individuals in leadership roles simultaneously, one charismatic and the other administrative, each having very specific duties.

A third type of social movement leadership role is the **intellectual leader**, who takes charge of the movement's ideas: Why does the movement exist? Why is it necessary? How will the movement bring about change? What should those changes be? All these questions must have answers if the social movement is to survive, and it is the job of the intellectual leader to see that the answers are forthcoming. Again, remember that the intellectual leader is a *role* and that either a charismatic or an administrative leader could fulfill this function. One individual could, in fact, perform all three roles.

Thinking accomplished by the intellectual leader produces other important elements in the social movement's structure. At the most general level this thinking becomes the ideology and propaganda of the social movement. The movement's **ideology** is basically its world view; it includes a picture of what's wrong with the world (and why), who's responsible, and what the movement could (and should) do to make things right. Like all ideologies, the ideology of a social movement supports the interests of the movement. Propaganda is often a close relative of ideology; in many cases the movement's propaganda is a simplified version of the ideology (often including catch-phrases) used in, among other ventures, the recruitment of new members. There can be substantial differences between the two, however, if the movement's leaders feel the true ideology is too radical and might scare off potential recruits. Followers might not be let in on "what's really going on" until they prove themselves loyal; in extreme cases they might be viewed as only expendable tools for the movement's leadership and might never be told.

The ideology/propaganda will make up the public presentation of the social movement. It will generally include an interpretation of the past and a vision of the future with and without the benefits of the social movement. For example, the Ku Klux Klan believes that problems in the United States can be traced to a conspiracy of Jewish people who wish to take over the country and destroy Christianity. Since Jews are thought to be manipulating American blacks to achieve this end, the Klan doesn't think too highly of blacks either. These ideas are part of the Klan's interpretation of the past. Their vision of the future without the changes they propose is a black-white race war in which blacks will rape and murder a disarmed white population, leaving the way clear for Jews to take over. If the Klan becomes strong, say their leaflets, all this can be prevented. This tells you how the movement sees the world and why the movement is necessary for the future.

Within its vision of the future a movement's ideology/propaganda must specify tactics and goals. The *goals* are included within the vision of the future if the movement is successful; the *tactics* describe how the movement intends to bring that happy vision about. Both tactics and goals must be marketable if the movement is to be successful. The goals (or at least the stated goals contained in movement propaganda) must generally tie in with accepted values of the society. All religious movements, for example, claim to make people happy and content. Political movements generally claim they will produce equality, prosperity, freedom, and, again, happiness. Stated goals should be general enough to leave room for everyone but specific enough for prospective members to get their teeth into. They should also be somewhat flexible so that they can change with the times. Perhaps most important, they should also appear at least possible to achieve (see King, 1956).

If anything, tactics are even more important to the movement's success than goals. You can claim to support total revolution but never be bothered by authorities if you don't do anything. Like goals, tactics must appear acceptable in terms of dominant values, but they must also appear to be workable. This is a particularly difficult problem for most social movements, since almost by definition, they are relatively powerless; otherwise, they would be benefiting from the status quo and less interested in bringing about change. What kinds of tactics can a relatively powerless group employ to force changes on societal authorities? Box 13.3 presents the ideas of one noted social activist.

BOX 13.3

Rules for Radicals: The Social Movement Tactics of Saul Alinsky

Effective tactics are prime commodities in the world of social movements. Social movements are typically poor and powerless groups that, by definition, are limited in the kinds of pressure they can exert. Moreover, the wrong kinds of tactics might alienate prospective movement members or result in harsh repression from societal authorities. A good tactic is practical, effective, and tailored to the social environment within which it will be applied.

Saul Alinsky (1971) was one of the most creative tacticians ever to give advice to social movements. He describes his approach as "mass jujitsu"—you use the strength of your aggressive opponent to your advantage. The following describes Alinsky's approach to dealing with a Chicago department store that discriminated against blacks in hiring:

> There is a particular department store that happens to cater to the carriage trade. It attracts many customers on the basis of its labels as well as the quality of its merchandise. Because of this, economic boycotts had failed to deter even the black middle class from shopping there. At the time its employment policies were more restrictive than those of the other stores. Blacks were hired for only the most menial jobs.
>
> We made up a tactic. A busy Saturday shopping date was selected. Approximately 3,000 blacks all dressed up in their good churchgoing suits or dresses would be bused downtown. When you put 3,000 blacks on the main floor of a store, even one that covers a square block, suddenly the entire color of the store changes. Any white coming through the revolving doors would take one pop-eyed look and assume that somehow he had stepped into Africa. He would keep right on going out of the store. This would end the white trade for the day.
>
> For a low-income group, shopping is a time-consuming experience, for economy means everything. This would mean that every counter would be occupied by potential customers, carefully examining the quality of merchandise and asking, say, at the shirt counter, about the material, color, style, cuffs, collars, and price. As the group occupying the clerks' attention around the shirt counters moved to the underwear section, those at the underwear section would replace them at the shirt counter, and the personnel of the store would be constantly occupied.
>
> Now pause to examine the tactic. It is legal. There is no sit-in or unlawful occupation of premises. Some thousands of people are in the store "shopping." The police are powerless and you are operating within the law.
>
> This operation would go on until an hour before closing time, when the group would begin purchasing everything in sight to be delivered C.O.D.! This would tie up truck-delivery service for at least two days—with obvious further heavy financial costs, since all the merchandise would be refused at the time of delivery.

(continues)

BOX 13.3 (continued)

The threat was delivered to the authorities through a legitimate and "trustworthy" channel. Every organization must have two or three stool pigeons who are trusted by the establishment. The stool pigeons are invaluable as "trustworthy" lines of communication to the establishment. With all plans ready to go, we began formation of a series of committees: a transportation committee to get the buses, a mobilization committee to work with the ministers to get their people to their buses, and other committees with other specific functions. Two of the key committees deliberately included one of these stoolies each, so that there would be one to back up the other. We knew the plan would be quickly reported back to the department store. The next day we received a call from the department store for a meeting to discuss new personnel policies and an urgent request that the meeting take place within the next two or three days, certainly before Saturday!

The personnel policies of the store were drastically changed. Overnight, 186 new jobs were opened. For the first time, blacks were on the sales floor and in executive training.

This is the kind of tactic that can be used by the middle class too. Organized shopping, wholesale buying plus charging and returning everything on delivery, would add accounting costs to their attack on the retailer with the ominous threat of continued repetition. This is far more effective than canceling a charge account. Let's look at the score: (1) sales for one day are completely shot; (2) delivery service is tied up for two days or more; and (3) the accounting department is screwed up. The total cost is a nightmare for any retailer, and the sword remains hanging over his head. The middle class, too, must learn the nature of the enemy and be able to practice what I have described as mass jujitsu, utilizing the power of one part of the power structure against another part. (From *Rules for Radicals* by Saul Alinsky. Copyright © 1971 by Saul Alinsky. Reprinted by permission of Pantheon Books, a division of Random House, Inc.)

Ralph Turner (1970) points out that social movement tactics fall under three general headings. *Coercion* is possible only when the social movement controls something of value to the authorities. Labor unions coerce with the strike, removing their valuable labor from management. A boycott removes consumers from a particular product. The civil rights movement began in the 1950s when blacks in Montgomery, Alabama, refused to ride the city buses until the buses were desegregated. Since blacks in that city tended to be poorer and more likely than whites to be bus riders, the city transit system was hurt by the boycott.

Bargaining is the positive side of coercion; it also requires movement control over something of value but emphasizes rewards rather than penalties for societal authorities. An ethnic minority social movement, for example, can use votes to bargain with politicians for favors. And finally, perhaps the least effective tactic, *persuasion* occurs when the movement attempts to enlist support for its goals by presenting the goals as advantageous to all. A telethon to raise money to fight disease would fall under this heading; persuasion generally works only when movement goals are highly respectable in the minds of most people.

The Natural History of Social Movements

In looking at various leadership roles, we noted that different kinds of leaders are appropriate for different types of social movement organization; the more formal the organization, the more necessary it is for the movement to have an administrative leader. Movements tend to have different kinds of organizations as a result of their goals or their size. The hippie movement of the 1960s, for example, contained groups with goals of "doing your own thing" and "hanging loose"; these goals made formal organization impossible—which ultimately made the hippie movement impossible. Many of these same individuals, however, altered their lifestyles and goals when the war in Vietnam became a salient political issue, joining forces in both organized and effective protest groups (Kohn, 1986; Levitt, 1984). Size is another variable. Terrorist revolutionary movements generally have to remain small and emotionally tight-knit because of the danger in which their activities place them. At the other extreme, nationwide reform movements, such as a political party, require elaborate formal organizations to coordinate all the varied activities required to elect candidates. Beyond these requirements the internal structure of all social movements tends to change over time.

Social movements have a natural history of their own. Movements that survive tend to become increasingly formally organized over time. Many sociologists have attempted to depict this change in terms of stages, but the change is actually continuous. Before we look at this process more closely, one good example to keep in mind is the world history of the Christian religion. Based on a charismatic leader and a loose-knit group of twelve followers 2,000 years ago, Christianity developed from small persecuted groups into formalized international churches with tremendous power and influence. Those beliefs that were once on the outside looking in have now become societal authorities in their own right; like the Romans 2,000 years ago, Christian churches now have the right to pass judgment.

The earliest stage of most social movements is a premovement stage, sometimes termed the *incipient* or the *preliminary* stage of social excitement (see King, 1956; Hopper, 1950). This period is usually a classic case of collective behavior in which groups of people face a dilemma but don't quite know what to do about it. Americans have been shown in laboratory research to react in significant fashion when confronted by situations structured to include elements of injustice or illegality (Gamson, Fireman, and Rytina, 1982). Martin Luther King, Jr., described his initial entry into the civil rights movement as typical of this first stage. A black woman, Rosa Parks, had refused to give up her bus seat to a white man as the law required in Montgomery, Alabama. Her subsequent arrest antagonized the black community and led them to search for ideas and a leader in order to make some kind of response. King was a new Baptist minister in town and was asked to help. When he began, he had no idea that their efforts would have any impact beyond the city limits of Montgomery.

When leaders, goals, and tactics begin to appear, the budding social movement begins to take shape. People begin to congregate around the leader and the movement's new ideas, but behavior is far from set at this point. Jobs that need doing get done by whoever is around to do them; there are as yet no formal roles with assigned responsibilities. As in the case of the Montgomery bus boycott, goals may still be in their infancy and limited to immediate matters. As goals are still growing, so too is the movement's ideology, which is highly fluid. The boundaries of the movement are loose, with people coming and going from movement activities with no one having a sense of formal movement membership. The vast majority of social movements never make it past this point largely because of the organizational problems of keeping people working and getting the jobs done.

As the movement seeks to make its activities more efficient and effective, it moves into a stage of formal organization of some sort. This is the stage where an intellectual leader will emerge with an ideology, and some sort of administrative leader will emerge to handle the growing complexity of movement operations. It will become quite clear who is a member of the movement and who is not. Movement symbols begin to be used that identify members, and rituals develop among members as an aid in reminding them of their membership. One of the main problems the movement will face at this point is a question of priorities: Is it more important to spend time keeping the movement together or to continue forging ahead with original movement goals? Margaret Sanger, an early advocate of women's rights, organized the Birth Control League in the late 1800s to give women more control over pregnancy. This accepted position today was considered quite sinful in her time, and she had quite a sales job on her hands. She describes returning from a trip to Europe to discover that other members had their eyes fixed on the movement's bank balance and were spending little effort on anything else (Sanger, 1938).

As in the example of Christianity, a social movement can survive indefinitely into the institutionalized stage when it becomes established as a societal authority. This fourth and last stage sees the movement turn from attacker of the status quo to its defender. Before the Russian Revolution, the Communist Party was in favor of all types of revolutionary activity; once the Communists came into power themselves, the last thing they wanted was revolutionaries running around. One of their foremost agitators during the revolution, Leon Trotsky, ended his life in exile in Mexico because he had become unwelcome at home. Even in exile Trotsky was apparently still viewed as a threat, and he was assassinated. Similarly, the established Catholic Church rejected Martin Luther, which led to the Protestant Reformation.

Individual social movements may seem to come to an end at this point, but the cycle of social movement formation goes on as new ones continue to develop. The importance of social movements can also be seen clearly from this perspective: Many of the dominant ideas of almost any age were once the wild and crazy ideas proposed by a social movement sometime in the past. Margaret Sanger's plea for birth control is now taken for granted—as are Christianity, the United States Constitution, scientific research, the illegality of slavery, and organized labor (see Box 13.4).

One modern theory of social movements that attempts to integrate many of these observations is *resource mobilization theory* (McCarthy and Zald, 1973, 1977; Zald, 1979). In the terms of this perspective, a social movement is redefined as a collection of opinions and beliefs regarding social change; a social movement *organization,* on the other hand, refers to the actual organization of individuals (what has been referred to as a "social movement" in this chapter) that forms to fight for the goals of those opinions and beliefs. Often many organizations form with similar beliefs and goals and must then compete with one another for members who already occupy the same social movement. Such a collection of movement organizations is termed a *social movement industry.* They may operate within a subset of a society, as, for example, a labor union will be limited to organizing certain kinds of workers. They may also potentially have an entire society from which to draw members, as was the case with movement organizations fighting for nuclear arms limitations (see Katz, 1986; Price, 1982). McCarthy and Zald

BOX 13.4

SOCIAL MOVEMENTS BY OCCUPATION: THE NATURAL HISTORY OF THE LABOR MOVEMENT

Sociologists have noted the tendency of social movements to become increasingly formally organized over time. There is also a tendency, if the movement survives, for its goals to appear less and less radical to the rest of society. One of the best examples of this overall tendency can be found in the history of labor unionism.

The organization of industrial workers is about as old as the Industrial Revolution itself. In 1769 the British Parliament passed a law making the intentional destruction of an industrial machine a capital offense. The organization of workers for the purpose of raising wages also was against the law; such organization was viewed as a "conspiracy."

The United States had labor laws similar to England's. In 1806, for example, boot and shoemakers in Philadelphia were indicted for their attempts to secure higher wages. The first large-scale labor organizations were the Knights of Labor, formed in 1869, followed by the American Federation of Labor (AFL), formed in the 1880s. The latter, which has survived to this day, was formed around particular craft occupations. The unions were far from accepted, however, and often met with considerable violence. The Chicago Haymarket Square bombing and shooting of May 3, 1886, played a major role in the demise of the Knights of Labor. In 1894 Eugene Debs and his American Railway Union had a confrontation with federal troops; the meeting left thirty strikers dead.

In the 1930s the Congress of Industrial Organizations (CIO) gained strength. Unlike the AFL, the CIO focused on the organization of workers within particular industries rather than particular occupations, including many blue-collar workers who previously had no union open to them. The 1930s also brought the labor movement some of the strongest support it had ever received from the federal government. Under new legislation from the Roosevelt administration, workers were guaranteed the right to organize, strike, and bargain collectively. Not long after World War II, the AFL and the CIO merged and settled into a highly respectable and accepted corner of the American society. As this respectability grew, the more radical elements of the labor movement either drifted away or were expelled. The earlier, charismatic leaders, such as Eugene Debs or John L. Lewis of the United Mine Workers, gave way to the newer administrative leaders of today. Union leaders who used to go to jail for organizing workers now face prison terms for the mismanagement of union funds. Respectability and success have their price.

Some of the brand-new unions in the United States are in almost the same boat older unions occupied earlier this century. The most noted example is the United Farm Workers, led by Cesar Chavez (see Jenkins, 1986). Organizing a group of workers to whom unions had previously been closed, Chavez gained recognition for his union through a successful nationwide boycott of table grapes. It is curious, however, that not all established unions welcomed this addition to their ranks. The Teamsters Union was brought in by farm owners in an attempt to break the United Farm Workers by having workers switch to the Teamsters; the hope among farm owners was that the Teamsters would settle more easily than the United Farm Workers (U.S. News and World Report,

(continues)

BOX 13.4 (continued)

1975). As with all social movements, older versions at the stage of formal organization may resist newer models still in the early stages of organization.

The future of labor unions should prove interesting. Currently, more and more professional and white-collar occupations are turning from loose-knit and largely powerless "associations" to unions. One of the best-known cases is the American Federation of Teachers, which adopted a strike policy in the early 1960s and has since closed schools many times by calling strikes. Public employees such as police and fire fighters have become better organized and increasingly militant. At the same time, however, membership in American unions is today at an all time modern low, having fallen off considerably since its high point during the 1940s. Activism and enthusiasm in a few select unions can hardly suggest a growing social movement interest in the face of such widespread disinterest among most American workers.

Perhaps the most interesting trend comes from the Polish workers' strike that began in the summer of 1980. Beyond higher wages, their primary goal was to achieve the right to organize and strike outside the control of the government. After initial success, martial law was imposed and the union leaders were imprisoned, silenced, or forced to go underground. A new generation of workers brought the union back to life in 1988, however, leading ultimately to the overthrow of the Communist Party in Poland and the rise of union leaders—most notably Lech Walesa—to governmental positions. Organizations at the workplace can be generalized to other arenas.

emphasize that social movement organizations be viewed in terms of their abilities to control societal resources and mobilize those resources to bring about social change.

Social Movements as Agents of Social Change

All forms of collective behavior can leave their marks on society, but social movements tend to have the most far-reaching effects. A group of unorganized rioters may not last long against trained military personnel, but an organized social movement stands a chance. It is sometimes difficult, however, to know just how much social change can be attributed to social movements and how much would have occurred anyway. Social movements, after all, are the products of social change as well as creators of it. On the other hand, there are times when they appear to be clearly successful in reaching their goals with only minimal help from outside trends.

However much hard work may pay off, the most successful social movements are those that hop aboard ongoing social change. Consider the women's movement. Social movements supporting women's rights have been in existence for over a century, concentrating first on political freedom and more recently on ending economic discrimination. The last century has also been a period of great advances for women. At first glance, it would appear that these social movements have been phenomenally successful. At second glance, however, a question arises as to the role of industrialization in this change in women's status. Industrialization altered living areas, lifestyles, occupations, fertility rates, mortality rates, and political processes, to name just a few of the changes. Women were less needed in the family and as mothers while being both more useful and more needed as workers. They certainly didn't have to become *equal* workers with men; the growing equality of women workers with men obviously has been affected by the existence of women's movements. But the basic changes in women's roles were probably already in the cards before the first women's social movements were formed. Movements that capitalize on such trends will have advantages that others won't.

If a trend doesn't appear in the offing for your particular issue, another strategy for success is to align your social movement with a built-in societal contradiction. Martin Luther King, Jr., was a master of this technique. "All men are created equal" is a dominant American theme, and King found dramatic ways for illustrating how this value was limited in its application to black Americans. Americans want strong law enforcement but they also value equal rights. King's tactic of nonviolence made very public how law enforcement agencies used violence against unarmed demonstrators. Contradictions are inherent in all human societies, but people generally develop the ability to ignore them. A well-organized social movement removes these blinders and exploits the situation.

Finally, one of the most important roles played by social movements is changing habits of thought. Social movements create and publicize issues. Even the most radical issue tends to sound less radical after it has been expressed a few hundred times. Social movements keep questions alive and allow people to get used to them. So many of the important issues of as little as ten or twenty years ago are taken for granted today. The apparently ironclad structure of coordination in human society appears a little less solid viewed in light of history.

Social change brought about by social movements provides an appropriate moment to recall the introductory discussion in Chapter 1 on coordination in society. The sociological outlook on society presents a picture of norms, roles, social control, and authority, explaining much of the coordination we see in everyday life. As we've seen throughout this book, however, the sociological outlook also presents a picture of social strains, individual creativity, deviance, and collective efforts to produce social change. As noted at the outset of this book, the individual cannot be understood outside of society, but neither can a society be understood without coming to terms with individual creativity and the dynamic nature of social change.

SUMMARY

Collective behavior is unpatterned behavior that occurs within, or emerges from, collections of people. It is distinctive through its collective nature (as being the product of group interactions) and its norm-creating characteristics.

Collective behavior can take many forms. Fads and fashions are forms of behavior that develop within social groups for limited periods of time and serve to distinguish group members and separate them from others. Publics form around the existence of an issue. Public opinion refers to the opinions that develop through the interactions of publics. Natural and human-made disasters produce collective behavior by forcing people out of their normal routines and requiring that they attend to problems they have not encountered before. Collective behavior can also occur in any situation with a perceived threat as people panic to remove themselves from that threat. Rumor—the spread of information within ambiguous social situations—takes on the characteristics of collective behavior as uncertainties create new information and new social interactions as the rumors spread.

Face-to-face interaction of a crowd is probably the ultimate form of collective behavior. In this situation behavior develops through the simultaneous interactions of crowd members.

Theories of crowd behavior range from those that picture crowd members as suggestible sheep subject to the contagion of social behavior to those that portray crowd members as rationally calculating personal benefits from the crowd situation. Theories of crowd formation range from those that depict crowd members as confused or marginal members of society to those based on social deprivation. Of the latter much attention lately has been paid to the perceived deprivation of the crowd member and the relation of deprivation to other social factors.

Social movements are particular forms of collective behavior, occurring when that behavior becomes organized for the purpose of bringing about social change. Social movements can vary in the kinds and amounts of change they seek. Some movements seek change only in their memberships, whereas others seek change in the outside society. Of the latter, reform movements seek relatively minor change, whereas revolutionary movements hope to change the basic structure of society. Social movements are characterized by the emergence of specific norms and roles that define leaders and followers as well as organizing labor within the movement. Types of leadership roles include the charismatic leader, the administrative leader, and the intellectual leader. Movement ideologies describe the world view typical of the movement and, along vith propaganda, provide tools for the recruitment of new members.

Over time social movements change internally. The typical progression is from some form of collective behavior to a loosely knit group that, if it survives, develops some kind of formal organization. Over time social movements become institutionalized and commonly become part of society. Related to their varying degrees of success, social movements are important in bringing about social change.

GLOSSARY

Acting crowds Crowds with apparent goals outside the crowd gathering itself.

Administrative leader Social movement leadership role that governs by virtue of bureaucratic position and legal authority within the movement's social organization.

Charismatic leader Social movement leadership role that governs through great personal charm, persuasiveness, and personal magnetism.

Collective behavior Unpatterned (or not norm-governed) behavior, typically transitory and spontaneous.

Contagion The spread of an idea or behavior among the members of a crowd.

Crowd situation A social situation in which a large number of people are in face-to-face contact with each other in a particular physical setting.

Expressive crowds Crowds that are formed solely for the self-expression of the members.

Fads New forms of behavior that catch on among certain groups of people for a limited time.

Fashion Forms of behavior that are popular with certain groups of people (typically upper class) for a limited period of time, typically longer than a fad.

Ideology An idea or set of ideas that represents a particular interest of a particular social group. (As defined by Karl Marx, it refers specifically to the set of beliefs that supports the interests of a ruling class in society.) Within a social movement, an ideology represents the movement's world view, including their perception of the world along with a proposed role for the movement.

Intellectual leader Social movement leadership role that takes charge of the movement's ideas, specializing in the construction of movement ideology and propaganda.

Mass hysteria The spread of a nonrational belief or behavior throughout a group of people.

Panic A nonrational response to a threatening situation that can occur when inaction is perceived to be dangerous, escape is perceived to be possible, and escape seems less possible with the passage of time.

Propaganda (1) The conscious attempt to manipulate public opinion through control over the nature and flow of information. (2) In a social movement, typically a simplified version of the movement's ideology designed to attract new members and/or to further the movement's goals.

Public A collection of people that forms because of their common concern about a current issue.

Public opinion The attitudes common to the members of a public.

Reform movements Social movements that seek moderate amounts of social change and work within the existing system.

Revolutionary movements Social movements that seek massive changes in society.

Rumor Information, typically unconfirmed, that spreads among members of a group.

Social movement An organized effort by a group of people to bring about social change, either in the members themselves or in members and society alike.

SUPPLEMENTARY READINGS

Erikson, Kai *Everything in Its Path: Destruction of Community in the Buffalo Creek Flood.* New York: Simon & Schuster, 1976.
Erikson describes (in often painful detail) the West Virginia flood caused by a below-standard dam built by a coal company. He shows the results of disaster, both in terms of forced community changes and the legal aspects of assigning blame.

Goldstone, Jack A. (ed.) *Revolutions: Theoretical, Comparative and Historical Studies.* New York: Harcourt Brace Jovanovich, 1986.
A good overview of social revolutions, from the Mexican to the Iranian.

Lanternari, Vittorio *The Religions of the Oppressed: A Study of Modern Messianic Cults.* New York: Knopf, 1963.
An interesting and comprehensive account of religious social movements from all around the globe. All of the movements studied were messianic—that is, they were also somewhat political in response to felt deprivation.

McPhail, Clark *The Myth of the Madding Crowd.* New York: Aldine de Gruyter, 1991.
McPhail is the originator of the social behavioral/interactionist perspective discussed in this chapter. In this book, he not only presents his own point of view in a clear way but also takes the reader for a tour of other crowd theorists (most viewed less than enthusiastically by the author). McPhail offers an overview of the field from one point of view.

Malcolm X *Autobiography of Malcolm X.* New York: Grove, 1966.
While this book tells us a lot about Malcolm X, it also presents an interesting picture of a modern American social movement, the Black Muslims. Following Malcolm into the movement, the reader develops a sense of the ways followers in movements are acquired from the population and of the psychological changes that occur in an individual after joining a movement.

Miller, David L. *Introduction to Collective Behavior.* Pacific Heights, Ill: Waveland, 1989.
One of the better overviews to the entire field of collective behavior, running from panic to social movements. This is one of the more readable texts available.

Roberts, Ron E., and Robert Marsh Kloss *Social Movements: Between the Balcony and the Barricade* (2nd ed.). St. Louis: Mosby, 1979.
A lively introduction to political social movements around the world from a critical perspective. Roberts and Kloss introduce major sociological perspectives on social movements.

Smelser, Neil J. *Theory of Collective Behavior.* New York: Free Press, 1962.
An effort to provide a systematic theory for the field of collective behavior; an often-quoted though difficult-to-read book.

Turner, Ralph H., and Lewis M. Killian *Collective Behavior* (3rd ed.). Englewood Cliffs, N.J.: Prentice-Hall, 1987.
A basic, comprehensive introduction to the sociological study of collective behavior, covering rumor, crowd behavior, publics, and social movements.

Zald, Mayer N. (ed.) *The Dynamics of Social Movements: Resource Mobilization, Social Control and Tactics.* Englewood N.J.: Winthrop, 1977.
A good sourcebook for background on the resource mobilization perspective on social movements.

READING

The Traveling Salvation Salesman: Organizing the Religious Revival

JOHN DENTON

Before becoming a sociologist, author John Denton spent a number of years working with a traveling evangelist who moved from town to town organizing religious revivals. Religious revivals, typically highly emotional gatherings, give the impression of a spontaneous religious experience. As Denton describes them, however, revivals are carefully planned by professionals in ways that are not apparent to those who attend. There is an implicit warning in this description for the sociologist of collective behavior: Crowds are not always what they seem.

After reading the following description, you may get the impression that this evangelist and his assistants are charlatans who organize revivals solely for the money they receive. In actuality, these particular people are sincere in what they are doing. Their experience has led them to use many of the organizing tactics described in order to provide more effective revivals. Their goal is not to fool those who attend so much as to spread their message more effectively. As with most human endeavors, things look different from the inside than they do from the outside.

"Oh God!" and the roar of the words shook the walls of the frail wooden structure like the crack of the largest passing jet. The panes rattled before the sound, and the megaphone speakers suspended from the ceiling swayed as if they would fall from the force of the delivery. "Wait one more minute, Lord; have mercy for just one more minute! Oh God, don't let them refuse you and be forever damned. Oh God. . . ."

But the words were lost in a groan that began deep in the bowels of a hundred swaying believers, rose through their throats, and was forced from them by a fear of damnation, a fear of hellfire from which there could be no escape if they delayed for another minute. A staccato beat began to fill the room, a tapping that was out of synch with the driving rhythm of the electric guitars and piano and yet which added to it. A rapid beat that caught the feet of an old woman and propelled them into a dance in the aisle, where she pirouetted wildly to the rising tide of sound. A rapid beat from which there was no escape for those caught between it and the heavy rock beat of the band. Caught in the dual beat, their bodies contorted and their heads snapped as they attempted futilely to absorb a dualism between fast and slow, or good and bad, or heaven and hell. "Damnation . . . eternity . . . forever . . . no more chances. . . ." Tension showed in the sweat-soaked shirts. Upraised, pleading, begging, grasping arms ended in moist pools as believers begged for one more chance for their lost, damned, bound-for-hell loved ones. A scream was lost as the waves of sound transcended the shell of the building and crept outward to where a neighbor turned up his television to cover the unusually loud street sounds this Sunday night. A father, his face lined and wet with fear of death, sank to his knees, and his hands, grasping frantically for a life line to keep him from sinking directly into hell, found the back of the seat in front of him. His hands, taken over by fear, shook the bench, and the power of his conviction raised and

Essay © 1982 by John Denton. Used by permission of the author.

lowered it rapidly on the floor, adding to the staccato beat.

"God, Gooooood, has shown his mercy! He has allowed you to live to see this revival. You have refused his goodness. Tonight is the night. You, brother; you, sister; you, son; you, daughter: this is your last chance. Don't trifle with God! Don't cross the threshold! Don't leave this revival, for the unpardonable sin is yours! You have played with God, and his wrath is upon you!" The father broke, and a board on the roughly made bench snapped as his 220 pounds slumped sideways and then rolled onto the floor. His work boots drummed on the floor and his head rolled rapidly from side to side, his tongue protruding from his mouth as he begged, pleaded, cried for mercy. A dirge rolled out over the crowd from the band as the trumpets blasted through the noise with a death knell for the damned. The evangelist groaned loudly into the mike as the wife of the father danced out her joy and shook down her hair at seeing her man brought low.

"There is a young man . . . ," the voice of thunder again. "There is a young man in the back two rows who will not live a week if he does not seek God. Don't wait, young man! Tonight is the night." The groans sang out in agony for a lost soul. "Saints go to him. Bring him in. Don't let him leave lost. Mothers, go to him." A dam was loosed. Two dozen of the faithful descended on the hapless four men seated on the back row with their girlfriends. "Oh God! My boy, My boy." The floor at the back of the church was covered with the bodies of those agonizing for the lost. Hands grasped at the sleeves, at the backs of the lost. "Bobby, please come"; a sister was pulling frantically on the hand of a sinner. "This song is for you," the voice dictated, "it is your last. There is no more. Come now, NOW!"

And, with the NOW, the tide began to move. As if caught in a tremendous rip current over which the swimmer had no control, one of the young men was borne slowly into the aisle. Dozens of hands were now pushing and now pulling him, carrying him toward the dirge, toward the stern, sweating voice commanding his destiny, toward salvation or release or relief or freedom, but carrying him nevertheless. Suddenly he broke. He pushed, he shoved, and he was loose. The music rose, screams of joy, the voice always, and the panes shuddered as he ran, not for the door, but for salvation. He wanted it, and he screamed his desire. "Oh God, have mercy on me!" His body slapped the rough floor as, fifteen feet from the altar, he was overcome and slid head first under the altar, where he was smothered by weeping, pounding relatives, friends, neighbors—all praying at the top of their voices. God had to hear them over the noise.

Among the first to arrive were his friends and their girlfriends, walking, running, with tears streaming down faces horror stricken by their future. They added to the pile, and the tide of noise began to concentrate at the altar. Above the sinners pleading for their souls the voice directed the "saints" to the other lost, but there was a change in tone now. The victory had been won as the tide of sinners grew on its own. The "lost" ran so as not to lose this last chance. A few members of the band broke and stumbled down the steps from the pulpit. The music became ragged, the voice quieted, but the tide of noise continued as it began to turn to shouts of joy that the lost had been found, the damned had been saved. There would be no joy in hell tonight.

The last sounds of the rejoicing saints were still ringing out in the little building when the pastor of the church approached our car. We had packed the car Sunday afternoon, and now we only had to talk to him briefly before we could leave for another revival scheduled to begin Tuesday night in western New York State. It was always the same with these pastors, and sure enough it was with this one. He pushed through the driver's window a small cloth bag that clinked when he let it go. "I sure wish, brother, that it could be more. We've had a bad year around here, though, and my people are just not able to give as much as they usually do. . . ." The preacher ended in mid-sentence waiting for the customary response, and it came. "That's OK, brother pastor, we preach for the Lord and for the uplifting of his kingdom. We would have come even if we had known that there would be no offering." We didn't tell the pastor, as he began to recover from his embarrassment over having to discuss money, about the number of twenty dollar bills that had been slipped into our pockets before and after services, or about the elderly woman who had changed her will in order to leave her house and land to our evangelistic effort and the work of the Lord. The pastor had not yet discovered, as we had, that people do not want to give anonymously by putting their money into a collection plate and piling up riches in heaven. They want to get a little advance reward, words of thanks and praise from the evangelist or a member of his team.

These thoughts were not expressed aloud by any of us, however, because the pastor was still hanging in our window completing the ritual. "This was a wonderful revival, brother. We have never had so many people saved. Could you give us another meeting next fall?" Our response was predictable and well known by all in the car. "Well, when we get home, we will look at what we have to do next year, and we will let you know." We did not tell him that the revival schedule book was in the glove compartment of the car and that his question could have been answered immediately. The same way that pastors and evangelists do not like to talk about money in relation to saving souls, they also do not like to talk about schedules and availability of time for a revival, so we deferred such questions whenever possible. More importantly, if we brought out the schedule book, the pastor might see it and be able to put pressure on us to come during a time of his choosing. We didn't want that at all. We had not finished our present fall run of meetings and did not know which churches would be the best to return to. There would be others, we were sure, that would pay better, would provide a better setting for a revival, and would want us next year for a longer period of time. We had to be prepared for these opportunities. None of us was completely satisfied with this revival, and we were just not sure that we wanted to return at all. We knew, even as we indicated to the pastor otherwise, that the chances were we would never be back here. At the very best, this pastor might be able to get this evangelist and his team for a few days between our other major revivals. To have a full-length two-week meeting next year, he would probably have to get an evangelist of less repute.

As an evangelistic team, our entire success was based on our reputation for "being associated with successful revivals" (in our realistic moments we would say "for producing"). We were afraid of failures and worked hard not to have them or have our name associated with them. The word gets around in this business. Thus, it was with a sigh of relief from us all that we edged onto the highway and left behind what had appeared, until the very end, to be a failure. There had been very few saved (converted, redeemed, brought into the fold, sanctified, filled with the holy ghost) until the last night. The ones who had come had been kids. They always broke first, the kids. Some of them would come running to the altar with pants and legs wet where they had urinated on themselves in fear. Parents would gather in, and everyone would smile that little Johnnie or Janie had decided to "give themselves to the Lord." But that was not a way to create a revival. There had to be some "hardened" sinners, some symbolic successes in order to start things flowing, and it just had not happened here until almost too late.

We were all still mentally tense from the work of the last hours, and the noise in the small building still roared in our ears, so the conversation naturally drifted to the revival just ended and the one toward which we were headed. "That old lady who always wore the little hat with the flower sure liked to shout, didn't she? Start the music, and she was on her feet. And then the fat lady who sat by the second window on the right just couldn't stand it. She'd be up and bouncing all over."

"Yeah," from the front seat, "there's nothing like a shouter to ruin a good meeting. Just as you begin to get people into the proper spirit for a good service, the shouter will cut loose and ruin the entire thing. What they lack is 'discernment.' They can't discern how the spirit is moving the crowd."

"Well, you can call it lack of discernment if you want to, but I call it plain old pride. They just want to be seen. It looked to me as if the old lady and the fat lady were competing for attention. Did you notice how they would always shout in different parts of the church?"

"There's nothing wrong with a little competition now and then," came the reply. "As a matter of fact, competition between them would have been good if they had only broken down later in the revival and admitted their pride in trying to best each other. It would have worked well if they had humbled themselves before God and congregation. There's nothing that will bring a church around faster than old bosses on their knees begging God and each other for forgiveness. But not those two. From the pulpit you could see the looks on the faces of the congregation when the shouters would start. It was a look of 'Oh no, not again.' If they both had not gotten sick the last weekend, we wouldn't have had a meeting at all."

The evangelist and leader of the team was starting to get his voice back. Even with the microphone used in revivals, the effort of shouting over the crowd took its toll on his voice, and it got worse yearly. Now there was a gravelly rattle from the driver's seat. It started, coughed, started again on a slightly different theme. "You know, I think our problems in this meeting go back further than the shouters to the lack of preparation for this revival. A church has got to be ready for a revival, and the pastor is largely responsible for that. You have got to get people into an agonizing attitude. They have got to believe with all their hearts that the end is approaching, that their loved ones are damned and may never have another chance. The image of a real, hot, and very near hell has got to be painted for them. Now, I can create the image of hell, but the stage has got to be set by careful preparation.

"The pastor has got to get his congregation clearly divided into the saints and the sinners. There can be no wishy-washy people in the congregation. And he has got to get the saints to travailing for the lost. They have got to work at it—and hard. There's nothing that works better for this than a good old-fashioned prayer chain. Get people praying all night long for days in a continuous chain of prayer for their loved ones. Have these prayer meetings out in homes where the sinners can hear it. That way, they can't escape. They know that Mom, Dad, brothers, and sisters are agonizing—in love—for them. The tired, weary faces, and red-rimmed eyes of those who have been praying cannot be run from by the damned. Have the saints concentrate on some really hard cases that are really in need of God. Now be careful in this not to get those who are hopeless, mind you. Watch out for drunks. They'll be saved one day and drunk the next. Watch out for couples in love when one of the lovers is not part of the church or related to it. But get some sinner man whose wife is a saint and whose mother has just passed away, or who has just lost his job, or something like that. Concentrate on some cases that are just ready to break.

"You've got to have this atmosphere in order to get a revival, and you've got to keep it going. It's so easy to lose it if you're not careful. All those men and young girls standing around outside the church every night when we would pull up is a good way to ruin a service. There is too much frivolity out there, and the laughter can be heard in the church. The lightness is a letup on the sinners. Frivolity and revivals do not go together. The pastor had no idea how to, or that he even should, stop this. If he'd known how to organize a ring meeting it would have solved the problem. Goodness, I thought everyone knew that you just get everyone outside the church in a big circle and have saints testify about being saved. If the town had been a little larger, we could have had a street-corner meeting close to the church before the regular service.

"Prayer meetings before each service are really necessary to create a good atmosphere too. All the saints feel obligated to go to them or otherwise be questioned in their devotion. The loud praying in a Sunday school room or in the church basement filters through into the auditorium to create a mood for the entire service.

"In this revival the pastor also had not advertised or organized visitation teams of church members to visit in neighboring homes to extend invitations. Lord knows, we have to have sinners to have a revival, and the pastor has got to go after them. There is nothing worse than a congregation full of people who think they're saints. They'll pat their feet, shout, smile, nod, and 'amen' everything you say. There's nothing like good sinners to help out a revival."

"The music was good here, though," comes a defense from the back seat. "The song director was a gem. What success we had was partially due to him. He never missed a cue. He used songs everyone knew so they could put their books down and get their hands up. He sang fast, repetitious songs when we wanted joy, and he played the good, old, slow ones when he wanted solemnness. The music was great."

"By the way," the evangelist spoke up, "I appreciate the way you all got the band going. There were musicians in the church that the pastor never knew about, and it really added to the service to have them there. Your trumpets came through well, too. I really needed them when the old gentleman began to ramble on last Wednesday night. Remember that? The old fellow really liked the attention he was getting from testifying about how bad he had been. He was just killing the service. Remember how quiet it was getting? There's nothing like starting a song with the trumpets leading to stop somebody from talking. You should have seen his face as people turned from him and began to respond to the music. He wanted to get mad, but he'd just told everyone what a saint he was, so about all he could do after trying to talk over the music for a few minutes was to join in with a smile. The trumpets and music worked out well."

"You know," the oldest member of the evangelistic team finally spoke up, "I disagree with the pastor. I don't think they're having it bad there at all. Those people are too prosperous. They've got their fancy cars, TV sets, and clothes, and they come to church to show off, not to worship. Pride is the key. You can't have a revival with pride in the heart. People have got to be humbled. These people were too afraid they would get their clothes dirty kneeling on the floor. Nothing humbles more than to have nothing. Why, in the old days during the Depression, we had revivals wherever we went. People were hungry to hear about the Lord, and they welcomed us with open arms. They opened their doors for us, and even the hardest sinners would tell us with tears streaming down their face that they needed to be saved. You don't find people like that anymore. Our best meetings now are in the few places where you've still got good honest poor people. Think about it. Where do we travel? In the mountains from Georgia to New York. And when we go to states like Ohio, Indiana, or Michigan, who comes to our meetings? Why, the people who used to live in Tennessee, Kentucky, North Carolina. Poor people, that's who wants revivals. It's people with families. You've got to have families. You've got to love someone instead of things to want a revival. It's the poor we need. Why when I was a boy. . . ." and the voice trailed off into sleep.

After a silence someone finally brought up the event that had been in our minds all along. "It's sad that the high school kid was killed in the wreck Friday night."

"Yes," the evangelist noted, "But it sure helped us Sunday night. People were suddenly face-to-face with death, and you could see it as I preached. Sweat stood out on every face in the church, and even some of the saints seemed a little uncertain of their salvation. That's a great situation, though. Uncertain saints will work twice as hard to get people to the altar to beg forgiveness. I guess their success gives them some proof or security of being in the fold. Yes, we were fortunate, but the Lord works in mysterious ways his wonders to perform. He gave us that opportunity after everything else failed. We used it to the best of our ability.

"I doubt if the results will last long, though," the evangelist continued. "That church just has too many old bosses to allow any of those new converts in. I'm afraid the new sheep will become discouraged and will quit. The old need a good shaking up, and we weren't able to produce it. The best revival is one in which last night's scene occurs on Thursday or Friday night. Then on Saturday and Sunday you try to work the new converts into the church. You get them to teach on Sunday. You have them lead singing and testify to their change. You may have one of the more zealous preach at the jail on Sunday afternoon or lead ring meetings. You call on them to lead in prayer and to sing special songs. You suggest to them, the pastor, and the church new jobs that the converts can fill in the church. And you preach to the old members about humility, stepping aside, making way for the new. Without getting the converts involved the next revival will be like starting all over again. In fact, it will be even harder for whoever is holding it in this church next year.

"I think it won't be us here next year, not again. Maybe the Lord will move next year in such a way that the revival before this one will run over its scheduled time, and it will take up the two weeks left open by our not coming here. Yes, I believe that's what will happen. The Lord does work in mysterious ways. . . ."

Discussion Questions

1. How do the evangelists use ongoing social relationships in the communities they visit to gain converts? How do they use those relationships to build and maintain enthusiasm during their revivals?
2. How do the evangelists control the atmosphere during the revival?
3. What other kinds of apparently spontaneous crowd situations may be similarly controlled by professionals such as these?

Bibliography

Abrahamson, Mark, Ephraim Mizruchi, and C. Harnung. *Stratification and Mobility.* New York: Macmillan, 1976.

Adams, Bert N. *The Family: A Sociological Interpretation* (4th ed.). New York: Harcourt Brace Jovanovich, 1986.

Adams, Bert N. "Fifty Years of Family Research: What Does It Mean?" *Journal of Marriage and the Family* 50 (1988): 5-17.

Adorno, T. W., E. Frenkel-Brunswik, Daniel Levinson, and R. Nevitt Sanford. *The Authoritarian Personality.* New York: Harper & Row, 1950.

Albrecht, William P. *Economics* (3rd ed.). Englewood Cliffs, N.J.: Prentice Hall, 1983.

Alexander, Charles. "A Most Debated Issue." *Time,* July 8, 1985.

Alexander, Karl, Doris R. Entwisle, and Maxine S. Thompson. "School Performance, Status Relations, and the Structure of Sentiment: Bringing the Teachers Back In." *American Sociological Review* 52 (1987): 665-682.

Alinsky, Saul D. *Rules for Radicals.* New York: Random House, 1971.

Allen, Brandt. "Embezzler's Guide to the Computer." *Harvard Business Review* 53 (1975): 79-89.

Allen, James Paul, and Eugene James Turner. *We the People: An Atlas of America's Ethnic Diversity.* New York: Macmillan, 1988.

Allport, Gordon W. *The Nature of Prejudice.* Reading, Mass.: Addison-Wesley, 1954.

Allport, Gordon W., and Leo J. Postman. *The Psychology of Rumor.* New York: Holt, 1947.

Altman, Dennis. *AIDS in the Mind of America.* Garden City, N.Y.: Doubleday, 1986.

Andrews, L. "Family Violence in Florida's Panhandle." *Ms* 12 (1984): 23.

Apple, Michael. *Education and Power: Reproduction and Contradiction in Education.* London: Routledge & Kegan Paul, 1982.

Asch, Solomon E. "Effects of Group Pressures upon the Modification and Distortion of Judgments." In Eleanor Maccoby, Theodore Newcomb, and Eugene Hartley (eds.), *Readings in Social Psychology* (3rd ed.). New York: Holt, Rinehart and Winston, 1958.

Baker, James H. "Raises, Reform and Respect." *Newsweek* 110 (1987): 92.

Balkan, Sheila, Ronald J. Berger, and Janet Schmidt. *Crime and Deviance in America: A Critical Approach.* Belmont, Calif.: Wadsworth, 1980.

Barrera, Mario. *Race and Class in the Southwest: A Theory of Racial Inequality.* Notre Dame, Indiana: University of Notre Dame Press, 1979.

Barrow, Georgia M., and Patricia A. Smith. *Aging, Ageism and Society.* St. Paul, Minn.: West, 1979.

Basso, K. H. "To Give Up on Words: Silence in Western Apache Culture." *Southwestern Journal of Anthropology,* Autumn 1970.

Becker, Howard S. *Outsiders: Studies in the Sociology of Deviance.* New York: Free Press, 1963.

Bellah, Robert N. *Beyond Belief.* New York: Harper & Row, 1970.

Berger, Peter L. *The Noise of Solemn Assemblies.* Garden City, N.Y.: Doubleday, 1961.

Berger, Peter L. *The Capitalist Revolution: Five Propositions about Prosperity, Equality, and Liberty.* New York: Basic Books, 1986.

Berk, Richard A. *Collective Behavior.* Dubuque, Iowa: Wm. C. Brown, 1974a.

Berk, Richard A. "A Gaming Approach to Crowd Behavior." *American Sociological Review* 39 (1974b): 355-373.

Bernard, Jesse. *The Future of Marriage.* New Haven, CT: Yale University Press, 1982.

Best, Raphaela. *We've All Got Scars: What Boys and Girls Learn in Elementary School.* Bloomington: Indiana University Press, 1985.

Biggar, Jeanne C. "The Sunning of America: Migration to the Sunbelt." *Population Bulletin* 34. Washington, D.C.: Population Reference Bureau, 1979.

Blau, Peter, and Otis Dudley Duncan. *American Occupational Structure.* New York: Wiley, 1967.

Blau, Peter M., and W. Richard Scott. *Formal Organizations: A Comparative Approach.* San Francisco: Chandler, 1962.

Blauner, Robert. "Colonized and Immigrant Minorities." In N. Yetman and H. Steele (eds.), *Majority and Minority: The Dynamics of Racial and Ethnic Relations.* Boston: Allyn & Bacon, 1975.

Bluestone, Barry, and Bennett Harrison. *The Deindustrialization of America.* New York: Basic Books, 1982.

Blumer, Herbert. "Collective Behavior." In Alfred McClung Lee (ed.), *Principles of Sociology* (3rd ed.). New York: Barnes & Noble, 1969.

Blumstein, Philip, and Pepper Schwartz. *American Couples.* New York: William Morrow, 1983.

Bogue, Donald. *The Population of the United States: Historical Trends and Future Projections.* New York: Free Press, 1985.

Bonacich, Edna. "A Theory of Ethnic Antagonism: The Split Labor Market." *American Sociological Review* 37 (1972): 547-559.

Bonacich, Edna. "Advanced Capitalism and Black/White Relations." *American Sociological Review* 41 (1976): 34-51.

Boocock, Sarene Spence. "The Social Organization of the Classroom." In Ralph Turner, James Coleman, and Renee C. Fox (eds.), *Annual Review of Sociology,* pp. 1-28. Palo Alto, CA: Annual Reviews.

Bouvier, Leon F. "America's Baby Boom Generation: The Fateful Bulge." *Population Bulletin* 35. Washington, D.C.: Population Reference Bureau, 1980.

Bouvier, Leon F., and Robert W. Gardner. "Immigration to the U.S.: The Unfinished Story." *Population Bulletin* Vol. 41, no. 4 (November 1986).

Bowers, William J., Glenn Pierce, and John McDevitt. *Legal Homicide: Death as Punishment in America 1964-1982.* Boston: Northeastern University Press, 1984.

Bradburn, Norman M., and David Caplovitz. *Reports on Happiness: A Pilot Study of Behavior Related to Mental Health.* Chicago: Aldine, 1965.

Brand, David. "This Is the Selma of the Deaf." *Time,* March 21, 1988.

Brodeur, Paul. "Indian Land Claims." *The New Yorker,* October 11, 1982, pp. 76-155.

Brodeur, Paul. "Asbestos." *The New Yorker,* June 10, 1985/July 1, 1985.

Bromley, David G., and Anson D. Shupe, Jr. *New Christian Politics.* Macon, GA: Mercer University Press, 1984.

Bronfenbrenner, Urie. "Socialization and Social Class Through Space and Time." In Eleanor Maccoby, T. Newcomb, and E. L. Hartley (eds.), *Readings in Social Psychology.* New York: Holt, 1958.

Brown, Bernard. "Head Start: How Research Changed Public Policy." *Young Children* 40 (1985): 9-13.

Brown, Lester R. "Population and Affluence: Growing Pressures on World Food Resources." *Population Bulletin* 29. Washington, D.C.: Population Reference Bureau, 1973.

Brown, R., and A. Gilman. "The Pronouns of Power and Solidarity." In T. A. Sebeok (ed.), *Style in Language.* New York: Wiley, 1960.

Brunvand, Jan H. *The Vanishing Hitchhiker: American Urban Legends and Their Meanings.* New York: Norton, 1981.

Bucher, Rue, and Joan Stelling. "Characteristics of Professional Organizations." *Journal of Health and Social Behavior* 10 (1969): 3-15.

Buckner, H. Taylor. "A Theory of Rumor Transmission." *Public Opinion Quarterly* 29 (1965): 54-70.

Burgoon, Judee K., and Stephen B. Jones. "Toward a Theory of Personal Space Expectations and Their Violations." *Human Communication Research* 2 (1976): 131-146.

Cantril, Hadley. *The Invasion from Mars: A Study in the Psychology of Panic.* New York: Harper & Row, 1966.

Carlson, Bonnie E. "Dating Violence: A Research Review and Comparison with Spouse Abuse." *Social Casework* 68 (1987): 16-23.

Carrier, James G. *Social Class and the Construction of Inequality in American Education.* New York: Greenwood, 1986.

Centers, Richard. *The Psychology of Social Classes.* New York: Russell & Russell, 1949.

Centers for Disease Control. *HIV/AIDS Surveillance Report, November, 1990*: 1-18.

Chall, Jeanne S., Elizabeth Heron, and Ann Hilferty. "Adult Literacy: New and Enduring Problems." *Phi Delta Kappan.* 69 (1987): 190-196.

Chambliss, William J. "The Saints and Roughnecks." *Society* 11 (1973): 24-31.

Cherlin, Andrew. *Marriage, Divorce and Remarriage.* Cambridge, Mass.: Harvard University Press, 1983.

Chinoy, Ely. "The Tradition of Opportunity and the Aspirations of Automobile Workers." *American Journal of Sociology* 57 (1952): 453-459.

Clark, Ramsey. "When Punishment Is a Crime." *Playboy,* November 1970, pp. 100-201.

Clark, Walter Van Tilburg. *The Ox-Bow Incident.* New York: The Press of the Readers Club, 1942.

Clausen, John A. *The Life Course: A Sociological Perspective.* Englewood Cliffs, N.J.: Prentice-Hall, 1986.

Clinard, Marshall B., and Peter C. Yeager. *Corporate Crime.* New York: Free Press, 1980.

Cloward, R. A., and L. E. Ohlin. *Delinquency and Opportunity: A Theory of Delinquent Gangs.* New York: Free Press, 1960.

Cohen, Albert K. *Delinquent Boys: The Culture of the Gang.* Glencoe, Ill.: Free Press, 1955.

Cohen, Albert K., and Harold M. Hodges. "Characteristics of the Lower-Blue-Collar Class." *Social Problems* 10 (1963): 303-334.

Cohen, Marjorie. "Americanizing Services." In Ed Finn (ed.), *The Facts* 10(2) Spring 1988. Ottawa: Public Relations Department of The Canadian Union of Public Employees.

Cohen, Steven M. "Jews, More or Less." *Moment,* September 1984.

Colclough, Glenna, and E. M. Beck. "The American Educational Structure and the Reproduction of Social Class." *Sociological Inquiry* 56 (1986): 456-476.

Coleman, James S., et al. *Equality of Educational Opportunity,* Washington, D.C.: U.S. Office of Education, 1966.

Coleman, James S., and Thomas Hoffer. *Public and Private High Schools: The Impact of Communities.* New York: Basic Books, 1987.

Coleman, James S., Thomas Hoffer, and Sally Kilgore. *High school Achievement: Public, Catholic, and Other Private Schools Compared.* New York: Basic Books, 1982.

Collins, Randall. *The Credential Society: An Historical Sociology of Education and Stratification.* New York: Academic Press, 1979.

Collins, Randall. *Sociology of Marriage and the Family: Gender, Love and Property.* Chicago: Nelson-Hall, 1985.

Condry, John, and Sandra Condry. "Sex Differences: A Study of the Eye of the Beholder." *Child Development* 47 (1976): 812-819.

Congressional Research Service. *The Hispanic Population of the United States: An Overview.* Washington, D.C.: Subcommittee on Census and Population of the Committee on Post Office and Civil Service, U.S. House of Representatives, 1983.

Cooley, Charles Horton. *Human Nature and the Social Order.* New York: Scribner's, 1902.

Cooley, Charles Horton. *Social Organization.* New York: Scribner's, 1909.

Cox, Harvey. *The Secular City.* N.Y.: Macmillan, 1971.

Cox, Harvey. *Religion in the Secular City.* New York: Simon & Schuster, 1984.

Cuber, John F., and William Kenkel. *Social Stratification in the United States.* New York: Appleton, 1954.

Currie, Elliott. "Crime: The Pervasive American Syndrome." *These Times* 1 (1977).

Dadant & Sons (eds.). *The Hive and the Honey Bee.* Hamilton, Ill.: Dadant & Sons, 1975.

Dahl, Robert A. *Who Governs?* New Haven, Conn.: Yale University Press, 1961.

Dahl, Robert A. *Dilemmas of Pluralist Democracy.* New Haven, Conn.: Yale University Press, 1982.

Dahrendorf, Ralf. *Class and Class Conflict in Industrial Society.* Stanford, Calif.: Stanford University Press, 1959.

Daniel, Pete. *The Shadow of Slavery: Peonage in the South 1901-1969.* New York: Oxford University Press, 1972.

Danzger, M. Herbert. *Returning to Tradition: The Contemporary Revival of Orthodox Judaism.* New Haven, CT: Yale University Press, 1989.

Davies, James D. "The J-Curve of Rising and Declining Satisfactions as a Cause of Some Great Revolutions and Contained Rebellion." In Hugh Davis Graham and Ted Robert Gurr, *Violence in America* (vol. 2). Washington, D.C.: National Commission on the Causes and Prevention of Violence, 1969.

Davis, Cary, Carl Haub, and JoAnne Willette. "U.S. Hispanics: Changing the Face of America." *Population Bulletin* Vol. 38, no. 3 (June 1983).

Davis, Fred. "The Cabdriver and His Fare: Facets of a Fleeting Relationship." *American Journal of Sociology* 45 (1959): 158-165.

Davis, James, and Tom Smith. *General Social Survey Cumulative File, 1972-1982.* Ann Arbor, Mich.: Inter-University Consortium for Political and Social Research, 1984.

Davis, Kingsley. "The Amazing Decline of Mortality in Underdeveloped Areas." *American Economic Review* 46 (1956): 305-318.

Davis, Kingsley, and Wilbert E. Moore. "Some Principles of Stratification." *American Sociological Review* 10 (1945): 242-249.

Denton, John. "The Underground Economy and Social Stratification." *Sociological Spectrum* 5 (1985): 31-42.

Ditton, Jason. "Learning to 'Fiddle' Customers: An Essay on the Organized Production of Part-time Theft." *Sociology of Work and Occupations* 4 (1977): 427-451.

Domhoff, William G. *Who Rules America Now? A View for the 80s.* Englewood Cliffs, N.J.: Prentice-Hall, 1983.

Douglas, Jack D., and Frances C. Waksler. *The Sociology of Deviance: An Introduction.* Boston: Little, Brown, 1982.

Drover, Glenn (ed.). *Free Trade and Social Policy.* Ottawa: Canadian Council on Social Development, 1988.

Duff, John B. *The Irish in the United States.* Belmont, Calif.: Wadsworth, 1971.

Durkheim, Emile. *Suicide.* Trans. John A. Spaulding and George Simpson. New York: Free Press, 1951. (Originally published 1897.)

Durkheim, Emile. *The Elementary Forms of the Religious Life.* Trans. Joseph W. Swain. Glencoe, Ill.: Free Press. (Originally published 1915.)

Dusek, Jerome B. (ed.). *Teacher Expectancies.* Hillsdale, N.J.: Erlbaum, 1985.

Ehrenreich, Barbara, and John Ehrenreich. *The American Health Empire: Power, Profits, and Politics.* New York: Vintage, 1970.

Ellis, Dean S. "Speech and Social Status in America." *Social Forces* 45 (1967): 431-437.

Emery, Robert E., et al. "Divorce, Children and Social Policy." In Harold W. Stevenson and Alberta E. Siegel (eds.), *Child Development Research and Social Policy.* Chicago: University of Chicago Press, 1984.

Enloe, Cynthia. "The Growth of the State and Ethnic Mobilization: The American Experience." *Ethnic and Racial Studies* 4 (1981): 123-136.

Erikson, Kai. *Wayward Puritans: A Study in the Sociology of Deviance.* New York: Wiley, 1966.

Erikson, Kai. *Everything in Its Path: Destruction of Community in the Buffalo Creek Flood.* New York: Simon & Schuster, 1976.

Etzioni, Amitai. *A Comparative Analysis of Complex Organizations: On Power, Involvement and Their Correlates.* New York: Free Press, 1961.

Evans, William M. "The Organizational Set: Toward a Theory of Interorganizational Relations." In James D. Thompson (ed.), *Approaches to Organizational Design.* Pittsburgh: University of Pittsburgh Press, 1966.

Eyler, Janet, Valerie J. Cook, and Leslie E. Ward. "Resegregation: Segregation Within Desegregated Schools." In Christine H. Rossell and Willis D. Hawley (eds.), *The Consequences of School Desegregation,* pp. 126-162. Philadelphia: Temple University Press, 1983.

Fallows, James. "American Industry: What Ails It, How to Save It." *Atlantic Monthly,* September 1980, pp. 35-49.

Falsey, Barbara, and Barbara Heyns. "The College Channel: Private and Public Schools Reconsidered." *Sociology of Education* 57 (1984): 111-122.

Farkas, George, Robert P. Grobe, Daniel Sheehan, and Yuan Shuan. "Cultural Resources and School Success: Gender, Ethnicity, and Poverty Groups Within an Urban School District." *American Sociological Review* 55 (1990): 127-142.

Farley, Reynolds. *Blacks and Whites: Narrowing the Gap?* Cambridge, Mass: Harvard University Press, 1984.

Federal Bureau of Investigation. *Crime in the United States.* Washington, D.C.: United States Government Printing Office, August 5, 1990.

Feldberg, Roslyn. "Comparable Worth: Toward Theory and Practice in the United States." *Signs* 10 (1984): 311-328.

Finn, Ed (ed.). *The Facts.* 10(2) Spring 1988. Ottawa: Public Relations Department of The Canadian Union of Public Employees.

Fishman, Joshua A. *Advances in the Sociology of Language* (2 vols). The Hague: Mouton, 1971.

Flake, Carol. *Redemptorama: Culture, Politics and the New Evangelicalism.* Garden City, N.Y.: Anchor, 1984.

Foner, Nancy. *Ages in Conflict.* New York: Columbia University Press, 1984.

Fouts, Roger S. "Acquisition and Testing of Gestural Signs in Four Young Chimpanzees." *Science* 180 (1973): 978-980.

Fouts, Roger S., and Joseph B. Couch. "Cultural Evolution of Learned Language in Chimpanzees." In Martin Hahn and Edward Simmel (eds.), *Communicative Behavior and Evolution.* New York: Academic Press, 1976.

Fraker, S. "Why Women Aren't Getting to the Top." *Fortune,* pp. 40-45, 1984.

Frankel, Marvin E. *Criminal Sentences: Law Without Order.* New York: Hill and Wang, 1972.

Frankl, Razelle. *Televangelism: The Marketing of Popular Religion.* Carbondale, IL: Southern Illinois University Press, 1987.

Freud, Sigmund. *Civilization and Its Discontents.* New York: W. W. Norton, 1930.

Fuchs, Victo R. "Sex Differences in Economic Well-Being." *Science* 232 (April 25, 1986): 459-464.

Gabriel, Brother Angelus. *The Christian Brothers in the United States, 1848-1948: A Century of Catholic Education.* New York: Declan X. McMullen Co. 1948.

Gabrielli, William, and Sarnoff Mednick. "An Adoption Cohort Study of Genetics and Criminality." *Behavior Genetics* 13 (1983): 435.

Gallup, George, Jr. *The Gallup Report.* Report No. 285. Princeton, N.J.: The Gallup Poll, June 1989a.

Gallup, George, Jr. *The Gallup Report.* Report No. 289. Princeton, N.J.: The Gallup Poll, October 1989b.

Gamoran, Adam, and Robert D. Mare. "Secondary School Tracking and Educational Inequality: Compensation, Reinforcement, or Neutrality?" *American Journal of Sociology* 94 (1989): 1146-1183.

Gamson, William, Bruce Fireman, and Steven Rytina. *Encounters with Unjust Authority.* Homewood, Ill.: Dorsey Press, 1982.

Gans, Herbert J. *The Urban Villagers.* New York: Free Press, 1962.

Gardner, R. Allen, and Beatrice T. Gardner. "Teaching Sign Language to a Chimpanzee." *Science* 165 (1969): 664-672.

Gardner, Robert W., Bryant Robey, and Peter C. Smith. "Asian Americans: Growth, Change and Diversity." *Population Bulletin* Vol. 40, no. 4 (October 1985).

Garvey, Marcus. *Philosophy and Opinions of Marcus Garvey.* Amy Jacques-Garvey (ed.). New York: Arno, 1968. (Originally published 1923.)

Gaventa, John. *Power and Powerlessness: Quiescence and Rebellion in an Appalachian Valley.* Urbana: University of Illinois Press, 1980.

Gayle, Jacob A., Richard M. Selik, and Susan Y. Chu. "Surveillance for AIDS and HIV Infection Among Black and Hispanic Children and Women of Childbearing Age, 1981-1989." *Morbidity and Mortality Weekly Report,* Vol. 39 (No. SS-3): 23-30. July 1990.

Gelles, Richard J. "Family Violence." *Annual Review of Sociology* 11 (1985): 347-367.

Gelles, Richard J., and Claire Pedrick Cornell (eds.). *Intimate Violence in Families.* Beverly Hills, Calif.: Sage, 1985.

Gelles, Richard J., and Murray A. Straus. *Intimate Violence.* New York: Simon & Schuster, 1988.

Gerstel, Naomi. "Divorce and Stigma." *Social Problems* 43 (1987): 172-186.

Giddens, Anthony. *A Contemporary Critique of Historical Materialism, Vol. 2: The Nation-State and Violence.* Berkeley: University of California Press, 1985.

Glass, David, Peverill Squire, and Raymond Wolfinger. "Voter Turnout: An International Comparison." *Public Opinion* 6 (1984): 49-55.

Goffman, Erving. *Encounters.* New York: Bobbs-Merrill, 1961a.

Goffman, Erving. *Asylums.* Chicago: Aldine, 1961b.

Goffman, Erving. *Stigma: Notes on the Management of Spoiled Identity.* Englewood Cliffs, N.J.: Prentice-Hall, 1963.

Goldfield, Michael. *The Decline of Organized Labor in the United States.* New York: Basic Books, 1987.

Goldman, Ari L. "Mainstream Islam Rapidly Embraced by Black Americans." *The New York Times,* August 21, 1989, p. A1.

Goldscheider, Frances Kobrin, and Linda J. Waite. "Sex Differences in the Entry into Marriage." *American Journal of Sociology* 92 (1986): 91-109.

Gomez, Rudolph, Clement Cottingham, Russell Endo, and Kathleen Jackson (eds.). *The Social Reality of Ethnic America.* Lexington, Mass.: D.C. Heath, 1974.

Goode, William J. "A Theory of Role Strain." *American Sociological Review* 25 (1960): 483-496.

Goode, William J. *The Family* (2nd ed.). Englewood Cliffs, N.J.: Prentice-Hall, 1982.

Gordon, Milton. *Assimilation in American Life.* New York: Oxford University Press, 1964a.

Gordon, Milton. "Social Structure and Goals in Group Relations." In Morroe Berger, T. Abel, and C. Page (eds.), *Freedom and Control in Modern Society.* New York: Octagon Books, 1964b.

Gordon, Milton M. *Human Nature, Class and Ethnicity.* New York: Oxford University Press, 1978.

Gottfried, Adele Eskeles, and Allan W. Gottfried (eds.). *Maternal Employment and Children's Development: Longitudinal Research.* New York: Plenum, 1988.

Greeley, Andrew M. *Catholic High Schools and Minority Students.* New Brunswick, N.J.: Transaction Books, 1982.

Greeley, Andrew M. *Religious Change in America.* Cambridge: Harvard University Press, 1989.

Greer, Edward. "The 'Liberation' of Gary, Indiana." *Transaction,* January 1971, pp. 30-63.

Griffith, Janet. "Social Pressure on Family Size Intentions." *Family Planning Perspectives* 5 (1973): 237-242.

Guest, Dennis. "Canadian and American Income Security, Responses to Five Major Risks: A Comparison." In Glenn Drover (ed.), *Free Trade and Social Policy.* Ottawa: Canadian Council on Social Development, 1988.

Gumperz, John J. "The Speech Community." *International Encyclopedia of the Social Sciences.* London: Macmillan, 1968.

Guzzardi, Walter. "Can Big Still Be Beautiful?" *Fortune* 117 (1988): 50-64.

Gwartney-Gibbs, Patricia A., Jean Stockard, and Susanne Bohmer. "Learning Courtship Aggression: The Influence of Parents, Peers, and Personal Experiences." *Family Relations* 36 (1987): 276-282.

Hadden, Jeffrey K. "Religious Broadcasting and the Mobilization of the New Christian Right." *Journal for the Scientific Study of Religion* 26 (1987): 1-24.

Hall, Edward T. *The Silent Language.* Garden City, N.Y.: Doubleday, 1959.

Hall, Edward T., and Mildred Reed Hall. "The Sounds of Silence." *Playboy,* June 1971.

Hallinan, Maureen T., and Richard A. Williams. "Interracial Friendship Choices in Secondary Schools." *American Sociological Review* 54 (1989): 67-78.

Harkess, Shirley. "Women's Occupational Experiences in the 1970s: Sociology and Economics." *Signs* 10 (1985): 495-520.

Harlow, Harry F. "The Nature of Love." *American Psychologist* 13 (1958): 673-685.

Harlow, Harry F. *Learning to Love.* New York: Jason Aronson, 1974.

Harlow, Harry F., and R. Z. Zimmerman. "Affectional Responses in the Infant Monkey." *Science* 130 (1959): 421-432.

Harrington, Michael. *The New American Poverty.* New York: Penguin, 1984.

Harris, Lis. "Lubavitcher Hasidim." *The New Yorker,* September 16, 23, and 30, 1985.

Harrison, Bennett, and Barry Bluestone. *The Great U-Turn: Corporate Restructuring and the Polarizing of America.* New York: Basic Books, 1988.

Hartley, E. L. *Problems in Prejudice.* New York: Kings Crown, 1946.

Haub, Carl, and Mary Mederios Kent. *World Population Data Sheet.* Washington, D.C.: Population Reference Bureau, 1987.

Hauser, Robert M., and David L. Featherman. "Occupations and Social Mobility in the U.S." Data reprinted in *Social Indicators 1976.* Washington, D.C.: U.S. Department of Commerce, 1976.

Heer, David M. "Economic Development and Fertility." *Demography* 3 (1966): 423-444.

Hessel, Dieter. *Maggie Kuhn on Aging.* Philadelphia: Westminster Press, 1977.

Higley, John, and Michael G. Burton. "The Elite Variable in Democratic Transitions and Breakdowns." *American Sociological Review* 54 (1989): 17-32.

Hiller, Harry. *Canadian Society: A Macro Analysis.* Scarborough: Prentice-Hall, Canada, Inc., 1991.

Hirschi, T., and M. J. Hindelang. "Intelligence and Delinquency: A Revisionist Review." *American Sociological Review* 42 (1977): 571-587.

Hodges, Harold M., Jr. *Social Stratification: Class in America.* Cambridge, Mass.: Schenkman, 1964.

Hodgkinson, Harold L. "Reform? Higher Education? Don't Be Absurd." *Phi Delta Kappan* 68 (1986): 271-274.

Hollingshead, A. B. *Elmtown's Youth.* New York: Wiley, 1949.

Hollingshead, August, and Frederick Redlich. *Social Class and Mental Illness: A Community Study.* New York: Wiley, 1958.

Hopper, Rex D. "The Revolutionary Process: A Frame of Reference for the Study of Revolutionary Movements." *Social Forces* 28 (1950): 270-279.

Hout, Michael, and Andrew Greeley. "The Center Doesn't Hold: Church Attendance in the United States, 1940-1984." *American Sociological Review* 52 (1987): 325-345.

Hunter, James D. "Conservative Protestantism." In Phillip E. Hammond (ed.), *The Sacred in a Secular Age.* Berkeley: University of California Press, 1985, pp. 150-166.

Hymes, Dell H. *Foundations in Sociolinguistics: An Ethnographic Approach.* Philadelphia: University of Pennsylvania Press, 1974.

Jackson, Phillip W. *Life in Classrooms.* New York: Holt, Rinehart and Winston, 1968.

Jacquet, Constant H. *Yearbook of American and Canadian Churches, 1987.* Nashville, Tenn.: Abindgon Press, 1987.

Jacquet, Constant H. (ed.). *Yearbook of American and Canadian Churches, 1989.* Nashville, TN: Abindgon Press, 1989.

Jencks, Christopher, et al. *Inequality: A Reassessment of the Effect of Family and Schooling in America.* New York: Basic Books, 1972.

Jencks, Christopher, et al. *Who Gets Ahead? The Determinants of Economic Success in America.* New York: Basic Books, 1979.

Jenkins, J. Craig. *The Politics of Insurgency: The Farm Workers Movement in the 1960s.* New York: Columbia University Press, 1986.

Jennings, M. Kent, and Richard G. Niemi. *Generations and Politics.* Princeton, N.J.: Princeton University Press, 1981.

Jensen, Gary F. "Explaining Differences in Academic Behavior Between Public-School and Catholic-School Students: A Quantitative Case Study." *Sociology of Education* 59 (1986): 32-41.

Johnson, D. M. "The 'Phantom Anesthetist' of Mattoon: A Field Study of Mass Hysteria." *Journal of Abnormal and Social Psychology* 40 (1945): 175-186.

Johnstone, Ronald L. *Religion in Society: A Sociology of Religion* (3rd ed.). Englewood Cliffs, N.J.: Prentice Hall, 1988.

Jones, Maldwyn Allen. *American Immigration.* Chicago: University of Chicago Press, 1960.

Josephy, Alvin M. *Now That the Buffalo's Gone: A Study of Today's American Indians.* New York: Knopf, 1982.

Kagan, Jerome. *Emotions, Cognition and Behavior.* New York: Cambridge University Press, 1984.

Kain, John F. "The Distribution and Movement of Jobs and Industry." In James Q. Wilson (ed.), *The Metropolitan Enigma.* Cambridge, Mass.: Harvard University Press, 1968.

Katz, Milton S. *Ban the Bomb: A History of SANE—The Committee for a Sane Nuclear Policy, 1957-1985.* Westport, Conn.: Greenwood Press, 1986.

Kaufman, Michael. *Beyond Patriarchy: Essays by Men on Pleasure, Power and Change.* New York: Oxford University Press, 1987.

Keefe, Susan E., and Amado M. Padilla. *Chicano Ethnicity.* Albuquerque: University of New Mexico Press, 1987.

Kephart, William. *Extraordinary Groups:. The Sociology of Unconventional Life-Styles* (3rd ed.). New York: St. Martin's Press, 1987.

Kerbo, Harold R. *Social Stratification and Inequality: Class Conflict in the United States.* New York: McGraw-Hill, 1983.

Kerckhoff, Alan, Kurt Back, and Norman Miller. "Sociometric Patterns in Hysterical Contagion." *Sociometry* 28 (1965): 2-15.

Kessner, Thomas, and Betty Boyd Caroli. *Today's Immigrants: Their Stories.* New York: Oxford University Press, 1982.

King, C. Wendell. *Social Movements in the United States.* New York: Random House, 1956.

Kitano, Harry H. L. *Japanese Americans: The Evolution of a Subculture.* Englewood Cliffs, N.J.: Prentice-Hall, 1976.

Kitcher, Philip. *Vaulting Ambitions: Sociobiology and the Quest for Human Nature.* Cambridge, Mass.: MIT Press, 1985.

Knowlton, Clark. "Land-Grant Problems Among the State's Spanish-Americans." *New Mexico Business* 20 (1967): 1-13.

Koenig, Frederick W. *Rumor in the Marketplace.* Dover, Mass.: Auburn House, 1985.

Kohn, Melvin L., Atsushi Naoi, Carrie Schoenbach, Carmi Schooler, and Kazimierz M. Slomczynski. "Position in the Class Structure and Psychological Functioning in the United States, Japan and Poland." *American Journal of Sociology* 95 (1990): 964-1008.

Kohn, Melvin L., and Carmi Schooler. *Work and Personality: An Inquiry into the Impact of Social Stratification.* New York: Ablex Press, 1983.

Kohn, Stephen M. *Jailed for Peace: The History of American Draft Law Violators 1658-1985.* Westport, Conn.: Greenwood Press, 1986.

Kozol, Jonathan. *Illiterate America.* Garden City, N.Y.: Anchor Press, 1985.

Krauss, Irving. *Stratification, Class and Conflict.* New York: Free Press, 1976.

Kriesberg, Louis. *Social Inequality.* Englewood Cliffs, N.J.: Prentice-Hall, 1979.

Labov, William. "The Study of Language in Its Social Context." *Studium Generale* 23 (1970): 30-87.

Larson, Robert W. "The White Caps of New Mexico: A Study of Ethnic Militancy in the Southwest." *Pacific Historical Review* 22 (1975): 171-185.

Lazerwitz, Bernard, and Michael Harrison. "American Jewish Denomination: A Social and Religious Profile." *American Sociological Review* 44 (1979): 656-666.

LeBon, Gustave. *The Mind of Crowds.* London: Unwin, 1897.

Lee, Everett. "Migration in Relation to Education, Intellect, and Social Structure." *Population Index* 36 (1970).

Lee, Richard B. *The !Kung San: Men, Women, and Work in a Foraging Society.* New York: Cambridge University Press, 1979.

Lemert, Edwin. *Human Deviance, Social Problems and Social Control.* Englewood Cliffs, N.J.: Prentice-Hall, 1967.

Lenski, Gerhard E. "Social Participation and Status Crystallization." *American Sociological Review* 21 (1956): 458-464.

Lenski, Gerhard E. *Power and Privilege: A Theory of Social Stratification.* New York: McGraw-Hill, 1966.

Lenski, Gerhard E., and Jean Lenski. *Human Societies: An Introduction to Macro Sociology* (2nd ed.). New York: McGraw-Hill, 1974.

Levin, Jack. *The Functions of Prejudice.* New York: Harper & Row, 1975.

Levitt, Cyril. *Children of Privilege: Student Revolt in the Sixties.* Toronto: University of Toronto Press, 1984.

Lewis, Jerry M. "A Study of the Kent State Incident Using Smelser's Theory of Collective Behavior." *Sociological Inquiry* 42 (1972), 87-96.

Liebman, Robert C., John R. Sutton, and Robert Wuthnow. "Exploring the Social Sources of Denominationalism: Schisms in American Protestant Denominations." *American Sociological Review* 53 (1988): 343-352.

Lifton, Robert. "Thought Reform: Psychological Steps in Death and Rebirth." In Alfred Lindesmith and Anselm Strauss (eds.), *Readings in Social Psychology.* New York: Holt, Rinehart and Winston, 1969.

Lipset, Seymour M., and Earl Raab. "The Election and the Evangelicals." *Commentary* 71 (1981): 26-32.

Lipset, Seymour M., and William Schneider. "Political Sociology." In Neil J. Smelser (ed.), *Sociology: An Introduction* (2nd ed.). Pp. 399-491. New York: Wiley, 1973.

Lofland, John. *Doomsday Cult.* New York: Irvington, 1977.

Lorber, Judith. *Women Physicians: Careers, Status and Power.* New York: Tavistock, 1984.

Lord, Walter. *A Night to Remember.* New York: Holt, Rinehart and Winston, 1955.

Luhman, Reid. "Appalachian English Stereotypes: Language Attitudes in Kentucky." *Language in Society* 19 (1990): 331-348.

Luhman, Reid, and Stuart Gilman. *Race and Ethnic Relations: The Social and Political Experience of Minority Groups.* Belmont, Calif.: Wadsworth, 1980.

Lyman, Stanford M. "Contrasts in the Community Organization of Chinese and Japanese in North America." In N. Yetman and H. Steele (eds.), *Majority and Minority: The Dynamics of Racial and Ethnic Relations.* Boston: Allyn & Bacon, 1975.

McCarthy, John D., and Mayer N. Zald. *The Trend of Social Movements in America: Professionalization and Resource Mobilization.* Morristown, N.J.: General Learning Press, 1973.

McCarthy, John D., and Mayer N. Zald. "Resource Mobilization and Social Movements: A Partial Theory." *American Journal of Sociology* 82 (1977): 1212-1241.

MacKinnon, Carol E., and Donna King. "Day Care: A Review of Literature, Implications for Policy, and Critique of Resources," *Family Relations* 37 (1988): 229-236.

McNeill, William H. *Plagues and Peoples.* Garden City, N.Y.: Anchor Press/Doubleday, 1976.

McPhail, Clark. *The Myth of the Madding Crowd.* New York: Aldine de Gruyter, 1991.

McRae, Susan. *Cross-Class Families: A Study of Wives' Occupational Superiority.* New York: Oxford University Press, 1986.

Madsen, Axel. *Private Power: Multinational Corporations for the Survival of Our Planet.* New York: William Morrow, 1980.

Mahard, Rita E., and Robert L. Crain. "Research on Minority Achievement in Desegregated Schools." In Christine H. Rossell and Willis D. Hawley (eds.), *The Consequences of School Desegregation.* Pp. 103-125. Philadelphia: Temple University Press, 1983.

Makepeace, James M. "Gender Differences in Courtship Violence Victimization," *Family Relations* 35 (1986): 383-388.

Marmor, Judd. "'Normal' and 'Deviant' Sexual Behavior." *Journal of the American Medical Association* 217 (1971): 165-170.

Marx, Karl. *Selected Writings in Sociology and Social Philosophy.* Trans. T. B. Bottomore. New York: McGraw-Hill, 1956.

Marx, Karl. *Capital.* Trans. Eden Paul and Ceder Paul. (vol. 1). New York: Dutton, 1976. (Originally published 1897.)

Mead, George Herbert. *Mind, Self and Society: From the Standpoint of a Social Behaviorist.* Charles W. Morris (ed.). Chicago: University of Chicago Press, 1934.

Mechanic, David. "Sources of Power of Lower Participants in Complex Organizations." *Administrative Science Quarterly* 7 (1962): 349-364.

Medalia, Nahum Z., and Otto N. Larsen. "Diffusion and Belief in a Collective Delusion: The Seattle Windshield Pitting Epidemic." *American Sociological Review* 23 (1958): 221-232.

Meehl, P. "Schizotaxia, Schizotypy, Schizophrenia." *American Psychologist* 17 (1962): 211-221.

Mercer, Jane. *Labeling the Mentally Retarded.* Berkeley: University of California Press, 1973.

Merrick, Thomas W. "World Population in Transition." *Population Bulletin* Vol. 41, no. 2 (1986).

Merton, Robert. *Social Theory and Social Structure.* Glencoe, Ill.: Free Press, 1956.

Merton, Robert. "Manifest and Latent Functions." *Social Theory and Social Structure.* New York: Free Press, 1968.

Metz, Mary Haywood. *Different by Design: The Context and Character of Three Magnet Schools.* New York: Routledge & Kegan Paul, 1986.

Middleton, Russell, and Snell Putney. "Student Rebellion Against Parental Political Beliefs." *Social Forces* 41 (1963): 377-383.

Milgram, Stanley. *Obedience to Authority.* New York: Harper & Row, 1974.

Miller, David L. *Introduction to Collective Behavior.* Belmont, Calif.: Wadsworth, 1985.

Miller, W. B. "Lower Class Culture as a Generating Milieu of Gang Delinquency." *Journal of Social Issues* 14 (1958): 5-19.

Mills, C. Wright. *The Power Elite.* New York: Oxford University Press, 1956.

Mills, C. Wright. *The Sociological Imagination.* New York: Oxford University Press, 1959.

Mills, C. Wright. "The Sociology of Stratification." In Irving Horowitz (ed.), *Power, Politics and People: The Collected Essays of C. Wright Mills.* New York: Oxford University Press, 1963.

Mintz, Beth, and Michael Schwartz. "Interlocking Directorates and Interest Group Formation." *American Sociological Review* 46 (1981): 851-869.

Mintz, Beth, and Michael Schwartz. *The Power Structure of American Business.* Chicago: University of Chicago Press, 1985.

Moore, Joan W. *Mexican Americans.* Englewood Cliffs, N.J.: Prentice-Hall, 1976.

Morgan, S. Philip, Diane N. Lye, and Gretchen A. Condran. "Sons, Daughters, and the Risk of Marital Disruption." *American Sociological Review* 52 (1988): 278-285.

Morrison, Denton E. "Some Notes Toward Theory on Relative Deprivation, Social Movements, and Social Change." *American Behavioral Scientist* 14 (1971): 675-690.

Moynihan, Daniel P. *The Negro Family: The Case for National Action.* Washington, D.C.: U.S. Department of Labor, 1965.

Muehlenhard, C.L., and M.A. Linton. "Date Rape and Sexual Aggression in Dating Situations: Incidence and Risk Factors." *Journal of Counseling Psychology* 34 (1987): 186-196.

Muller, Edward N. "Democracy, Economic Development, and Income Inequality." *American Sociological Review* 53 (1988): 50-68.

Murdock, George P. *Ethnographic Atlas.* Pittsburgh: University of Pittsburgh Press, 1967.

Myers, Jerome K., and Lee L. Bean. *A Decade Later: A Follow-Up of Social Class and Mental Illness.* New York: Wiley, 1968.

Nagel, John S. "Mexico's Population Policy Turnaround." *Population Bulletin* 33. Washington, D.C.: Population Reference Bureau, Inc., 1978.

Naoi, Atsushi, and Carmi Schooler. "Occupational Conditions and Psychological Functioning in Japan." *American Journal of Sociology* 90 (1985): 729-752.

National Advisory Commission on Civil Disorders. *Report of the National Advisory Commission on Civil Disorders.* New York: Bantam, 1968.

National Center for Education Statistics. *Digest of Education Statistics—1989.* Washington, D.C.: United States Government Printing Office, 1989a.

National Center for Education Statistics. *1989 Education Indicators.* Washington, D.C.: United States Government Printing Office, 1989b.

National Center for Education Statistics. *The Condition of Education—1989: Volume One: Elementary and Secondary Education.* Washington, D.C.: United States Government Printing Office, 1989c.

National Center for Education Statistics. *The Condition of Education—1989: Volume Two: Postsecondary Education.* Washington, D.C.: United States Government Printing Office, 1989d.

National Center for Education Statistics. *The Condition of Education—1990: Volume One: Elementary and Secondary Education.* Washington, D.C.: United States Government Printing Office, 1990a.

National Center for Education Statistics. *The Condition of Education—1989: Volume Two: Postsecondary Education.* Washington, D.C.: United States Government Printing Office, 1990b.

National Commission on Excellence in Education. *A Nation at Risk: The Imperative for Educational Reform.* Washington, D.C.: U.S. Government Printing Office, 1983.

National Opinion Research Center. *General Social Surveys, 1972-1989.* Chicago: National Opinion Research Center, 1989.

National Opinion Research Center. *National Data Program for the Social Sciences, Code Book for the Spring 1976, General Social Survey.* Chicago: University of Chicago Press, 1976.

Newman, Dorothy, Nancy Amidei, Barbara Carter, Dawn Day, William Kruvant, and Jack Russell. *Protest, Politics, and Prosperity: Black Americans and White Institutions, 1940-75.* New York: Pantheon, 1978.

Newman, William M. *American Pluralism: A Study of Minority Groups and Social Theory.* New York: Harper & Row, 1973.

Newsweek. "The Next Minority." *Newsweek,* December 20, 1976, pp. 74-75.

Nichols, Eve K. *Mobilizing Against AIDS.* Cambridge, Mass: Harvard University Press, 1986.

Nielsen, Joyce McCarl. *Sex in Society: Perspectives on Stratification.* Belmont, Calif.: Wadsworth, 1978.

Noel, Donald L. "A Theory of the Origin of Ethnic Stratification." *Social Problems* 16 (1968): 157-172.

Oakes, Jeannie. "Classroom Social Relationships: Exploring the Bowles and Gintis Hypothesis." *Sociology of Education* 55 (1985): 197-212.

Ogburn, William Fielding. *Social Change.* Gloucester, Mass.: Peter Smith, 1964.

O'Hare, William P. "Poverty in America: Trends and New Patterns." *Population Bulletin* Vol. 40, no. 3 (June 1985).

O'Hare, William P., Kelvin M. Pollard, Taynia L. Mann, and Mary M. Kent. *African Americans in the 1990s.* Washington, D.C.: Population Reference Bureau, 1991.

Oppenheimer, Valerie Kincaide. "A Theory of Marriage Timing." *American Journal of Sociology* 94 (1988): 563-591.

Orum, Anthony M. *Introduction to Political Sociology: The Social Anatomy of the Body Politic.* Englewood Cliffs, N.J.: Prentice Hall, 1978.

Owen, David. *None of the Above: Behind the Myth of Scholastic Aptitude.* Boston: Houghton Mifflin, 1985.

Parkinson, C. Northcote. *Parkinson's Law and Other Studies in Administration.* Boston: Houghton Mifflin, 1957.

Pearce, Dana. "The Feminization of Ghetto Poverty." *Society* (November-December 1983), pp. 70-74.

Pederson, D. M. "Developmental Trends in Personal Space." *Journal of Psychology* 83 (1973): 3-9.

Perrow, Charles. *Complex Organization: A Critical Essay* (3rd ed.). New York: Random House, 1986.

Perry, Joseph B., Jr., and M. D. Pugh. *Collective Behavior: Response to Social Stress.* St. Paul, Minn.: West, 1978.

Peter, Laurence, and Raymond Hull. *The Peter Principle.* New York: Bantam, 1969.

Phillips, Bernard. *Sociological Research Methods: An Introduction.* Homewood, Ill.: Dorsey, 1985.

Piaget, Jean. *The Moral Judgement of the Child.* Trans. Marjorie Gabain. New York: Free Press, 1965.

Pincus, Fred L. "Vocational Education: More False Promises." In L. Stephen Zwerling (ed.), *The Community College and Its Critics,* pp. 41-52. San Francisco: Jossey-Bass, 1986.

Pinkney, Alphonso. *Black Americans.* Englewood Cliffs, N.J.: Prentice-Hall, 1975.

Pleck, Joseph H. *Working Wives/Working Husbands.* Beverly Hills: Sage, 1985.

Population Reference Bureau. *World Population: Fundamentals of Growth.* Washington, D.C.: Population Reference Bureau, 1984.

Porter, Bruce, and Marvin Dunn. *The Miami Riot of 1980: Crossing the Bounds.* Lexington, Mass.: D. C. Heath, 1984.

Premack, David. *Gavagai! The Future History of the Animal Language Controversy.* Cambridge, Mass.: MIT Press, 1986.

Price, Jerome B. *The Antinuclear Movement.* Boston: Twayne, 1982.

Princeton Religion Research Center. *Religion in America 1990.* Princeton, N.J.: Princeton Religion Research Center, 1990.

Projector, Dorothy S., and Gertrude S. Weiss. *Survey of Financial Characteristics of Consumers.* Washington, D.C.: Board of Governors of the Federal Reserve System, 1966.

Quinney, Richard. *Class, State and Crime: On the Theory and Practice of Criminal Justice* (2nd ed.). New York: Longman, 1980.

Raschke, Helen J. "Divorce." In Marvin B. Sussman and Suzanne K. Steinmetz (eds.), *Handbook of Marriage and the Family,* pp. 597-624. New York: Plenum, 1987.

Rawlings, Steve W. "Single Parents and Their Children." In *Studies in Marriage and the Family.* Current Population Reports, Series P-23, No. 162, pp. 13-26. Washington, D.C.: U.S. Government Printing Office, U.S. Bureau of the Census, June 1989.

Reckless, W. C. *The Crime Problem* (4th ed.). New York: Appleton-Century-Crofts, 1967.

Reiman, Jeffrey H. *The Rich Get Richer and the Poor Get Prison* (2nd ed.). New York: Wiley, 1984.

Reynolds, Paul D. *Ethnics and Social Science Research.* Englewood Cliffs, N.J.: Prentice-Hall, 1982.

Riesman, David, Nathan Glazer, and Reuel Denney. *The Lonely Crowd.* New Haven, Conn.: Yale University Press, 1950.

Roach, Jack L., and Orville R. Gursslin. "The Lower Class, Status Frustration and Social Disorganization." *Social Forces* 43 (1965): 501-507.

Roethlisberger, Fritz, and William Dickson. *Management and the Worker.* New York: Wiley, 1964.

Roiphe, Anne. "Confessions of a Female Chauvinist Sow." *New York Magazine,* October 1972.

Rolle, Andrew F. *The American Italians.* Belmont, Calif.: Wadsworth, 1972.

Roof, Wade Clark, and William McKinney. *American Mainline Religion: Its Changing Shape and Future.* New Brunswick: Rutgers University Press, 1987.

Rosenhan, D. L. "On Being Sane in Insane Places." *Science* 179 (1973): 250-258.

Rosenthal, Alvin S., Keith Baker, and Alan Ginsburg. "The Effect of Language Background on Achievement Level and Learning Among Elementary School Students." *Sociology of Education* 56 (1983): 157-169.

Rosenthal, D. "The Heredity-Environment Issues in Schizophrenia." In D. Rosenthal and S. S. Kety (eds.), *The Transmission of Schizophrenia.* Oxford, England: Pergamon, 1968.

Rosenthal, Robert, and Lenore Jacobson. *Pygmalion in the Classroom.* New York: Holt, Rinehart and Winston, 1968.

Ross, Catherine. "The Division of Labor at Home." *Social Forces* 65 (1987): 816-833.

Ross, Catherine E., John Mirowsky, and Joan Huber. "Dividing Work, Sharing Work, and In-Between: Marriage Patterns and Depression." *American Sociological Review* 48 (1983): 809-823.

Rossi, Peter, James Wright, Gene Fisher, and Georgianna Willis. "The Urban Homeless: Estimating Composition and Size." *Science* 235 (1987): 1336-1341.

Rossides, Daniel W. *The American Class System: An Introduction to Social Stratification.* Boston: Houghton Mifflin, 1976.

Rowe, David C., and Wayne D. Osgood. "Heredity and Sociological Theories of Delinquency: A Reconsideration." *American Sociological Review* 49 (1984): 526-540.

Roy, Donald. "Quota Restriction and Goldbricking in a Machine Shop." *American Journal of Sociology* 57 (1952): 427-442.

Roy, William G. "The Unfolding of the Interlocking Directorate Structure of the United States." *American Sociological Review* 48 (1983): 248-257.

Sagarin, Edward (ed.). *The Other Minorities.* Waltham, Mass.: Ginn, 1971.

Sanger, Margaret. *An Autobiography.* New York: W. W. Norton, 1938.

Schein, Edgar, Inge Schneier, and Curtis Barker. *Coercive Persuasion: A Sociopsychological Analysis of the "Brainwashing" of American Civilian Prisoners by the Chinese Communists.* New York: W. W. Norton, 1961.

Schur, Edwin. *Crimes Without Victims.* Englewood Cliffs, N.J.: Prentice-Hall, 1965.

Schutz, Alfred. *On Phenomenology and Social Relations.* Chicago: University of Chicago Press, 1970.

Science. "The Handicapped: HEW Moving on Civil Rights in Higher Education." *Science* 194 (1976): 1399-1402.

Scudder, Richard, and C. Arnold Anderson. "Migration and Vertical Occupational Mobility." *American Sociological Review* 19 (1954): 329-334.

See, Katherine O'Sullivan. *First World Nationalisms: Class and Ethnic Politics in Northern Ireland and Quebec.* Chicago: University of Chicago Press, 1986.

Seeman, Melvin. "The Signals of '68: Alienation in the Pre-Crisis France." *American Sociological Review* 37 (1972): 385-402.

Seltzer, Judith A., and Deborah Kalmuss. "Socialization and Stress Explanations for Spouse Abuse." *Social Forces* 67 (1988): 473-491.

Selznick, Philip. *TVA and the Grass Roots.* Berkeley: University of California Press, 1949.

Sewell, William H. "Inequality of Opportunity for Higher Education." *American Sociological Review* 36 (1971): 793-809.

Sheppard, Harold. "Work and Retirement." In R. Binstock and E. Shanas (eds.), *Handbook of Aging and the Social Sciences.* New York: Van Nostrand-Reinhold, 1976.

Sherif, Muzafer, and Carolyn W. Sherif. *An Outline of Social Psychology.* New York: Harper & Row, 1956.

Shoemaker, Donald J., and Donald R. South. "White-Collar Crime." In Clifton D. Bryant (ed.), *Deviant Behavior: Occupational and Organizational Bases.* Chicago: Rand McNally, 1974.

Shupe, Anson D. *The New Vigilantes: Deprogrammers, Anti-Cultists and the New Religions.* Beverly Hills, Calif.: Sage, 1980.

Shupe, Anson, William A. Stacey, and Lonnie R. Hazelwood. *Violent Men, Violent Couples: The Dynamics of Domestic Violence.* Lexington, MA: Lexington Books, 1987.

Simmel, Georg. *The Sociology of Georg Simmel.* Trans. and ed. Kurt H. Wolff. New York: Free Press, 1950.

Simmel, Georg. *Conflict and the Web of Group Affiliations.* Trans. Kurt H. Wolff and Reinhard Bendix. New York: Free Press, 1955.

Simon, David R., and D. Stanley Eitzen. *Elite Deviance* (2nd ed.). Boston: Allyn & Bacon, 1986.

Simpson, Richard L. "A Modification of the Functional Theory of Stratification." *Social Forces* 35 (1956): 130-139.

Sinclair, Ward. "For Miners the Contract Is the Ace in the Hole." *Los Angeles Times—Washington Post News Service,* 1978.

Sklar, June, and Beth Berkov. "The American Birth Rate: Evidences of a Coming Rise." *Science* 29 (1975): 693-700.

Slater, Courtenary. "Who's Hiring?" *American Demographics* 9 (1987): 4-6.

Smelser, Neil J. *Theory of Collective Behavior.* New York: Free Press, 1962.

Snow, David L., and Leon Anderson. "Identity Work Among the Homeless: The Verbal Construction Avowel of Personal Identities." *American Journal of Sociology* 82 (1987): 1336-1371.

Soltow, Lee, and Edward Stevens. *The Rise of Literacy and the Common School in the United States: A Socioeconomic Analysis to 1870.* Chicago: University of Chicago Press, 1981.

Sowell, Thomas. *The Economics and Politics of Race.* New York: Morrow, 1983.

Spragins, Ellyn E. "When Power Investors Call the Shots." *Business Week* 1988 (June 20): 126-130.

Stack, Carol B. *All Our Kin: Strategies for Survival in a Black Community.* New York: Harper & Row, 1975.

Stahl, Sidney, and Marty Lebedun. "Mystery Gas: An Analysis of Mass Hysteria." *Journal of Health and Social Behavior* 15 (1974): 44-50.

Stark, Rodney, and Williams Sims Bainbridge. *The Future of Religion: Secularization, Revival, and Cult Formation.* Berkeley: University of California Press, 1985.

Stark, Rodney, and Charles Y. Glock. *American Piety: The Nature of Religious Commitment.* Berkeley: University of California Press, 1968.

Stebbins, Robert A. "Role Distance, Role Distance Behavior and Jazz Musicians." *British Journal of Sociology* 21 (1969): 406-415.

Stedman, Lawrence C., and Carl F. Kaestle. "Literacy and Reading Performance in the United States from 1880 to the Present." In *Literacy in the United States,* Carl F. Kaestle, Helen Damon-Moore, Lawrence C. Stedman, Katherine Tinsley, and William Vance Trollinger, Jr. (eds.). New Haven, CT: Yale University Press, 1991.

Steinfels, Peter. "American Jews Stand Firmly to the Left." *The New York Times,* January 8, 1989.

Stern, Joyce D., and Mary F. Williams (eds.). "The Condition of Education." Statistical Report Center for Education Statistics. Washington, D.C.: U.S. Department of Education, 1986.

Stevens, William K. "Despite Defeats, Fundamentalists Vow to Press Efforts to Reshape Schools." *The New York Times,* August 29, 1987, p. 6.

Straus, Murray A., and R. J. Gelles. "Societal Change and Change in Family Violence From 1975 to 1985 as Revealed by Two National Surveys." *Journal of Marriage and the Family* 48 (1986): 465-479.

Strauss, Anselm, Leonard Schatzman, Rue Bucher, Danuta Ehrlich, and Melvin Sabshin. *Psychiatric Ideologies and Institutions.* New York: Free Press, 1964.

Sudnow, David. "Dead on Arrival." In A. Strauss (ed.), *Where Medicine Fails.* Chicago: Aldine, 1970.

Sumner, William Graham. *Folkways.* Boston: Ginn, 1906.

Sutherland, Edwin. *White Collar Crime.* New York: Dryden, 1949.

Sutherland, Edwin. "Differential Association." In Marvin Wolfgang, Leonard Savity, and Norman Johnston (eds.), *The Sociology of Crime and Delinquency.* New York: Wiley, 1962.

Swadesh, Frances Leon. *Los Primeros Pobladores: Hispanic Americans of the Ute Frontier.* Notre Dame, Indiana: University of Notre Dame Press, 1974.

Taylor, S., R. Shuntich, and R. Genthner. *Violence at Kent State: The Student's Perspective.* New York: College Notes and Texts, 1971.

Teachman, Jay D., and Paul T. Schollaert. "Economic Conditions, Marital Status, and the Timing of First Births: Results for Whites and Blacks." *Sociological Forum* 4 (1989): 27-46.

Teixeira, Ruy A. *Why Americans Don't Vote: Turnout Decline in the United States, 1960-1984.* Westport, CT: Greenwood, 1987.

Thernstrom, Stephen. *Poverty and Progress; Social Mobility in a Nineteenth Century City.* Cambridge, Mass.: Harvard University Press, 1964.

Thorton, Russell. *American Indian Holocaust and Survival: A Population History Since 1492.* Norman: University of Oklahoma Press, 1987.

Time. "More Seniority for the Victims." *Time,* April 5, 1976, p. 65.

Toffler, Alvin. *The New Wave.* New York: Morrow, 1980.

Tönnies, Ferdinand. *Community and Society.* Trans. Charles P. Loomis. East Lansing: Michigan State University Press, 1957.

Traub, Stuart H., and Craig B. Little. *Theories of Deviance* (3rd ed.). Itasca, Ill.: F. E. Peacock, 1985.

Travery, Andrew. "Ritual Power in Interaction." *Symbolic Interaction* 5 (1982): 277-286.

Trillin, Calvin. "Louisiana." *The New Yorker,* April 14, 1986.

Tumin, Melvin M. "Some Principles of Stratification: A Critical Analysis." *American Sociological Review* 18 (1953): 387-394.

Turner, Ralph. "Determinants of Social Movement Strategies." In Tamatsu Shibutani (ed.), *Human Nature and Collective Behavior.* Englewood Cliffs, N.J.: Prentice-Hall, 1970.

Turner, Ralph H., and Lewis M. Killian. *Collective Behavior* (2nd ed.). Englewood Cliffs, N.J.: Prentice-Hall, 1972.

U.S. Bureau of the Census. *International Migration and Naturalization.* Washington, D.C.: Government Printing Office, 1970.

U.S. Bureau of the Census. *Current Population Reports.* Washington, D.C.: Government Printing Office, 1976.

U.S. Bureau of the Census. *Statistical Abstract of the United States.* Washington, D.C.: Government Printing Office, 1978.

U.S. Bureau of the Census. *General Population Characteristics.* Washington, D.C.: Government Printing Office, 1980a.

U.S. Bureau of the Census. *Census of Population and Housing: Advance Reports.* Washington, D.C.: Government Printing Office, 1980b.

U.S. Bureau of the Census. *Current Population Reports.* Washington, D.C.: Government Printing Office, 1985.

U.S. Bureau of the Census. *Current Population Reports.* Washington, D.C.: Government Printing Office, 1986a.

U.S. Bureau of the Census, *Statistical Abstract of the United States.* Washington, D.C.: Government Printing Office, 1986b.

U.S. Bureau of the Census. *Statistical Abstract of the United States.* Washington, D.C.: Government Printing Office, 1987.

U.S. Bureau of the Census. Current Population Reports, Series P-20, No. 443. *School Enrollment—Social and Economic Characteristics of Students: October 1988 and 1987.* Washington, D.C.: U.S. Government Printing Office, 1990a.

U.S. Bureau of the Census. *Statistical Abstract of the United States: 1990.* Washington, D.C.: U.S. Government Printing Office, 1990b.

U.S. Bureau of the Census. Current Population Reports, Series P-20, No. 445. *Martial Status and Living Arrangements: March 1989.* Washington, D.C.: U.S. Government Printing Office, 1990c.

U.S. Bureau of the Census. Current Population Reports, Series P-70, No. 22. *Household Wealth and Asset Ownership: 1988.* U.S. Government Printing Office, Washington, D.C., 1990d.

U.S. Bureau of the Census. Current Population Reports, Series P-20, No. 444, *The Hispanic Population in the United States: March 1989.* U.S. Government Printing Office, Washington, D.C., 1990e.

U.S. Bureau of the Census. Current Population Reports, Series P-25, No. 1057. *U.S. Population Estimates, by Age, Sex, Race, and Hispanic Origin: 1989.* U.S. Government Printing Office, Washington, D.C., 1990f.

U.S. Bureau of the Census. Current Population Reports, Series P-20, No. 446. *Residents of Farms and Rural Areas: 1989.* Washington, D.C.: U.S. Government Printing Office, 1990g.

U.S. Bureau of Prisons. "Correlation of Unemployment and Federal Prison Population." Washington, D.C.: Government Printing Office, 1975.

U.S. Department of Health, Education and Welfare. *The Condition of Education, 1976.* Washington, D.C.: Government Printing Office, 1976.

U.S. Department of Justice. *Survey of Inmates of Local Jails: Advance Report.* U.S. Law Enforcement Assistance Administration, National Criminal Justice Information and Statistics Service. Washington, D.C.: Government Printing Office, 1974.

U.S. Department of Justice. *Report to the Nation on Crime and Justice.* Washington, D.C.: Bureau of Justice Statistics, October 1983.

U.S. Department of Justice. *The Prevalence of Imprisonment.* Washington, D.C.: Bureau of Justice Statistics, 1985.

U.S. Department of Justice. *Prison Admissions and Releases, 1983.* Washington, D.C.: Bureau of Justice Statistics, March 1986a.

U.S. Department of Justice. *Capital Punishment, 1985.* Washington, D.C.: Bureau of Justice Statistics, October 1986b.

U.S. Department of Justice. *Criminal Victimization, 1988.* Washington, D.C.: United States Government Printing Office, 1989.

U.S. Department of Justice. *Sourcebook of Criminal Justice Statistics, 1989.* Washington, D.C.: United States Government Printing Office, 1990.

U.S. News and World Report. "Chavez vs. the Teamsters: Farm Workers' Historic Vote." *U.S. News & World Report* 79 (1975): 82-83.

U.S. Supreme Court Reports. *"McCleskey* v. *Kemp." Supreme Court Reports,* 95L Ed 2d. Rochester, N.Y.: Lawyers Co-operative Publishing Co., 1987.

Updike, John. *Rabbit, Run.* New York: Knopf, 1960.

Useem, Michael. "Corporations and the Corporate Elite." In Alex Inkeles et al. (eds.), *Annual Review of Sociology.* Vol. 6. Palo Alto, CA: Annual Reviews, 1980: 41-77.

Usher, Sean. "Health Care Endangered." In Ed Finn (ed.), *The Facts.* 10(2) Spring 1988. Ottawa: Public Relations Department of The Canadian Union of Public Employees.

Van den Berge, Pierre L. "Bringing Beasts Back In: Toward a Bisocial Theory of Aggression." *American Sociological Review* 39 (1974): 777-788.

Vander Zanden, James W. *American Minority Relations* (3rd ed.). New York: Ronald Press, 1972.

Vanfossen, Beth E. *The Structure of Social Inequality.* Boston: Little, Brown, 1979.

Veblen, Thorstein. *The Theory of the Leisure Class.* New York: Macmillan, 1899.

Verba, Sidney, Garry Oren, and G. Donald Ferree. *Equality in America: The View from the Top.* Cambridge, Mass.: Harvard University Press, 1985.

Wallerstein, Immanuel. *Capitalist World Economy.* Cambridge: Cambridge University Press, 1979.

Wardhaugh, Ronald. *An Introduction to Sociolinguistics.* New York: Basil Blackwell, 1986.

Warner, W. Lloyd, and Paul S. Lunt. *The Social Life of a Modern Community.* New Haven, Conn.: Yale University Press, 1941.

Wax, Rosalie. *Doing Fieldwork.* Chicago: University of Chicago Press, 1978.

Weber, Max. *From Max Weber: Essays in Sociology.* Trans. and ed. H. H. Gerth and C. Wright Mills. New York: Oxford University Press, 1946.

Weed, James. "The Life of a Marriage." *American Demographics* February 1989, p. 12.

Weinberg, Martin S. "Sexual Modesty, Social Meanings, and the Nudist Camp." *Social Problems* 12 (1965): 311-318.

Weinberg, S. Kirson, and Henry Arond. "The Occupational Culture of the Boxer." *American Journal of Sociology* 58 (1952): 460-469.

Weinstein, Deena. *Bureaucratic Opposition: Challenging Abuses at the Workplace.* New York: Pergamon, 1979.

Weiss, Robert S. "The Impact of Marital Dissolution on Income and Consumption in Single-Parent Households." *Journal of Marriage and the Family* 46 (1984): 115-127.

Weitzman, Lenore. *Divorce Revolution: The Unexpected Social and Economic Consequences for Women and Children in America.* New York: Free Press, 1985.

Westphall, Victor. *The Public Domain in New Mexico, 1854-1891.* Albuquerque, N.M.: University of New Mexico Press, 1965.

White, Lynn K., and Alan Booth. "The Quality and Stability of Remarriages: The Role of Stepchildren." *American Sociological Review* 50 (1985): 689-698.

Whorf, Benjamin. *Language, Thought and Reality.* Cambridge, Mass.: MIT Press, 1956.

Wilson, Edward O. *Sociobiology: A New Synthesis.* Cambridge, Mass.: The Belknap Press of Harvard University Press, 1975.

Wilson, Edward O. *On Human Nature.* Cambridge, Mass.: Harvard University Press, 1978.

Wimberley, Ronald C., Thomas C. Hood, C. M. Lipsey, Donald Clelland, and Marguerite Hay. "Conversion in a Billy Graham Crusade: Spontaneous Event or Ritual Performance?" *Sociological Quarterly* 16 (1975): 162-170.

Wirth, Louis. "Urbanism as a Way of Life." *American Journal of Sociology* 44 (1938): 1-24.

Witkin, Herman A., et al. "Criminality in XYY and XXY Men." *Science* 193 (1976): 547-555.

Wonnacott, Paul. *The United States and Canada: The Quest For Free Trade.* Washington: Institute For International Economics, 1987.

Wright, Erik Olin. *The Politics of Punishment: A Critical Analysis of Prisons in America.* New York: Harper & Row, 1973.

Wuthnow, Robert, and Kevin Christiano. "The Effects of Residential Migration on Church Attendance in the United States." In Robert Wuthnow (ed.), *The Religious Dimension.* New York: Academic Press, 1979, pp. 257-276.

Wynne, Edward A. "Will the Young Support the Old?" In Alan Pifer and Lydia Bronte (eds.), *Our Aging Society: Paradox and Promise.* New York: W. W. Norton, 1986.

Young, Whitney. *To Be Equal.* New York: McGraw-Hill, 1964.

Yuan, Tien H. "China: Demographic Billionaire." *Population Bulletin* 38 (April 1983).

Zald, Mayer N. (ed.). *The Dynamics of Social Movements: Resource Mobilization, Social Control and Tactics.* Englewood, N.J.: Winthrop, 1979.

Zelizer, Viviana. *Pricing the Priceless Child: The Changing Social Value of Children.* New York: Basic Books, 1985.

Zimbardo, Philip G. "Pathology of Imprisonment." *Society* 9 (1972): 4-8.

Index

C

D

E

F

G

H

I

J

K

L

M

Q

R

S

T

U

V

W

X

Y

Z